MACROMEDIA®

Dreamweaver® 8

Comprehensive Concepts and Techniques

Ksmith

Gary B. Shelly
Thomas J. Cashman
Dolores J. Wells
Steven M. Freund

THOMSON
COURSE TECHNOLOGY

THOMSON COURSE TECHNOLOGY
25 THOMSON PLACE
BOSTON, MA 02210

SHELLY
CASHMAN
SERIES®

Australia • Canada • Denmark • Japan • Mexico • New Zealand • Philippines • Puerto Rico • Singapore
South Africa • Spain • United Kingdom • United States

THOMSON

COURSE TECHNOLOGY

Macromedia Dreamweaver 8:
Comprehensive Concepts and Techniques

Gary B. Shelly
Thomas J. Cashman
Dolores J. Wells
Steven M. Freund

Executive Editor:
Alexandra Arnold

Senior Marketing Manager:
Joy Stark

Developmental Editor:
Laurie Brown

Senior Product Manager:
Karen Stevens

Product Manager:
Reed Cotter

Associate Product Manager:
Heather Hawkins

Editorial Assistant:
Klenda Martinez

Print Buyer:
Justin Palmeiro

Production Editor:
Pamela Elizian, Marissa Falco

Copy Editor:
Gary Michael Spahl

Proofreader:
John Bosco

QA Manuscript Reviewers:
John Freitas, Burt LaFountain,
Jeff Schwartz, Ashlee Welz

Cover Artist:
John Still

Composition:
GEX Publishing Services

MACROMEDIA®

Dreamweaver 8

Comprehensive Concepts and Techniques

Contents

Project Four
Forms

Project Five
Templates and Style Sheets

Project Six
Layers, Image Maps, and Navigation Bars

Project Seven

Page Layout with Frames

Project Eight

Animation and Behaviors

Project Nine

Media Objects

Special Feature

Dreamweaver Web Photo Album

Appendix A

Dreamweaver Help

Appendix B

Dreamweaver and Accessibility

Appendix C

Publishing to a Web Server

Preface

The Shelly Cashman Series® offers the finest textbooks in computer education. We are proud of the fact that our textbook series has been the most widely used books in education. With each new edition of our Dreamweaver books, we have made significant improvements based on the software and comments made by the instructors, reviewers, and students. *Macromedia® Dreamweaver® 8: Comprehensive Concepts and Techniques* continues with the innovation, quality, and reliability that you have come to expect from the Shelly Cashman Series.

Macromedia Dreamweaver is known as the standard in visual authoring. Macromedia Dreamweaver 8 enhances the work experience for users in the following ways: simplified XML integration; unified CSS panel and new layout visualizer; style rendering toolbar and CSS rendering improvements; and an updated accessibility evaluation tool.

In this *Macromedia Dreamweaver 8* book, you will find an educationally sound and easy-to-follow pedagogy that combines a step-by-step approach with corresponding screens. All projects and exercises in this book are designed to take full advantage of the Dreamweaver 8 enhancements. The Other Ways and More About features offer in-depth knowledge of Dreamweaver 8. The popular Q&A feature provides answers to common questions students have about the Web design process. The Learn It Online page presents a wealth of additional exercises to ensure your students have all the reinforcement they need. The project material is developed carefully to ensure that students will see the importance of learning Dreamweaver for future coursework.

Objectives of This Textbook

Macromedia Dreamweaver 8: Comprehensive Concepts and Techniques is intended for a course that offers an introduction to Dreamweaver 8 and creation of Web sites. No experience with a computer is assumed, and no mathematics beyond the high school freshman level is required. The objectives of this book are:

- To teach students how to use Dreamweaver 8
- To expose students to proper Web site design and management techniques
- To acquaint students with the proper procedures to create Web sites suitable for coursework, professional purposes, and personal use
- To develop an exercise-oriented approach that allows learning by doing
- To introduce students to new input technologies
- To encourage independent study and help those who are working alone

The Shelly Cashman Approach

Features of the Shelly Cashman Series *Macromedia Dreamweaver 8* books include:

- **Project Orientation** Each project in the book presents a practical problem and complete solution using an easy-to-understand approach.
- **Step-by-Step, Screen-by-Screen Instructions** Each of the tasks required to complete a project is identified throughout the project. Full-color screens with callouts accompany the steps.

- **Thoroughly Tested Projects** Unparalleled quality is ensured because every screen in the book is produced by the author only after performing a step, and then each project must pass Thomson Course Technology's award-winning Quality Assurance program.

- **Other Ways Boxes and Quick Reference** The Other Ways boxes displayed at the end of many of the step-by-step sequences specify the other ways to do the task completed in the steps. Thus, the steps and the Other Ways box make a comprehensive reference unit. The Quick Reference at the back of the book provides a quick reference to common keyboard shortcuts.

- **More About and Q&A Features** These marginal annotations provide background information, tips, and answers to common questions that complement the topics covered, adding depth and perspective to the learning process.

- **Integration of the World Wide Web** The World Wide Web is integrated into the Dreamweaver 8 learning experience by (1) More About annotations that send students to Web sites for up-to-date information and alternative approaches to tasks; and (2) the Learn It Online page at the end of each project, which has project reinforcement exercises, learning games, and other types of student activities.

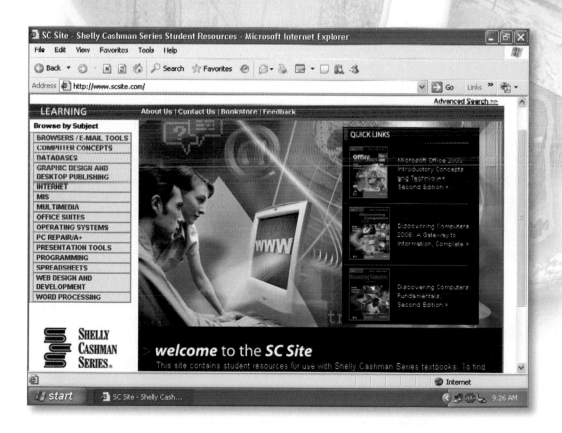

Organization of This Textbook

Macromedia Dreamweaver 8: Comprehensive Concepts and Techniques provides detailed instruction on how to use Dreamweaver 8. The material is divided into an introduction chapter, six projects, three appendices, and a quick reference summary.

Introduction – Web Site Development and Macromedia Dreamweaver 8 In the Introduction, students are presented with the basics of the Internet and World Wide Web and their associated terms. Topics include differentiating between Web pages and Web sites and types of Web pages; identifying Web browser features; an overview of planning, designing, developing, testing, publishing, and maintaining a Web site; a discussion of XHTML/HTML; and various methods and tools used in Web site creation.

Project 1 – Creating a Dreamweaver Web Page and Local Site In Project 1, students are introduced to the Dreamweaver environment. Students create a local site and the home page for the Web site that they develop throughout the projects in the book. Topics include starting and quitting Dreamweaver; an introduction to the Dreamweaver workspace and panel groups; creating a local site; creating a Web page, applying a background image, and formatting Web page properties; inserting line breaks and special characters; using the Check Spelling feature; previewing and printing a page in a Web browser; and an overview of Dreamweaver Help.

Project 2 – Adding Web Pages, Links, and Images In Project 2, students learn how to add new pages to an existing Web site and then how to add links and images. Topics include using Dreamweaver's file browser feature; understanding and modifying image file formats; adding page images to a Web page; creating relative, absolute, and e-mail links; changing the color of links and editing and deleting links; using the site map; displaying the page in Code view; using Code view to display HTML code; and an overview of Dreamweaver's accessibility features.

Project 3 – Tables and Page Layout In Project 3, students are introduced to techniques for using tables in Web site design. Topics include an introduction to page layout using tables in Standard view and Layout view to design a Web page; modifying a table structure; understanding HTML table tags; adding content to a table and formatting the content; formatting the table; and creating head content.

Project 4 – Forms In Project 4, students are introduced to the concept of forms and form processing. Topics include client-side versus server-side processing; designing and creating a form; the different form objects; adding text fields and text areas to a form; using a table to help with form layout; form accessibility options; and how to add behaviors to a form.

Project 5 – Templates and Style Sheets In Project 5, students learn how to use templates and style sheets. Topics include creating a template; understanding differences between HTML styles and cascading style sheets; creating a cascading style sheet; applying CSS attributes to a template; and creating a Web page from a template.

Project 6 – Layers, Image Maps, and Navigation Bars In Project 6, students learn how to add layers and create image maps and navigation bars. Topics include understanding the concept of a layer; resizing, positioning, and aligning layers; how an image map works; creating an image map; adding and editing behaviors; inserting the Date object; and creating a navigation bar.

Project 7 – Page Layout with Frames In Project 7, students learn how to use frames to design the presentation of a Web page. Topics include understanding the advantages and disadvantages of using frames; creating a frameset and frames; setting and modifying the properties for a frame and a frameset; adding static content to a frame; and adding Flash buttons as navigation elements.

Project 8 – Animation and Behaviors In Project 8, students learn the concept of animation using the timeline and how to create linear and nonlinear timelines. Topics include understanding the applications of a timeline; using the Timelines panel; adding a layer to a timeline; adding a behavior to a layer; showing and hiding layers; and adding a play button to a timeline.

Project 9 – Media Objects In Project 9, students learn about different media objects and how to add media objects to a Web site. Topics include inserting Flash text and Flash movies into a Web page; adding linked sound and embedded sound to a Web page; inserting video into a Web page; checking for plug-ins; and inserting Shockwave movies and Java applets into a Web page.

Special Feature – Web Photo Album In this new Special Feature, students learn how to plan, create, and view a Web Photo Album. Creating this photo album requires that Fireworks 8, image manipulation software that is part of Macromedia Studio, be installed on the students' computer, although students will not work directly with this software.

Appendices The book includes three appendices. Appendix A presents an introduction to the Macromedia Dreamweaver Help system. Appendix B discusses Dreamweaver and Accessibility features; and Appendix C illustrates how to define and publish a Web site to a remote server.

Quick Reference In Dreamweaver, you can accomplish a task in a number of ways, such as using the mouse, menu, context menu, and keyboard. The Quick Reference provides a quick reference to common keyboard shortcuts.

End-of-Project Student Activities

A notable strength of the Shelly Cashman Series *Macromedia Dreamweaver 8* books is the extensive student activities at the end of each project. Well-structured student activities can make the difference between students merely participating in a class and students retaining the information they learn. The activities in the Shelly Cashman Series *Macromedia Dreamweaver 8* books include the following:

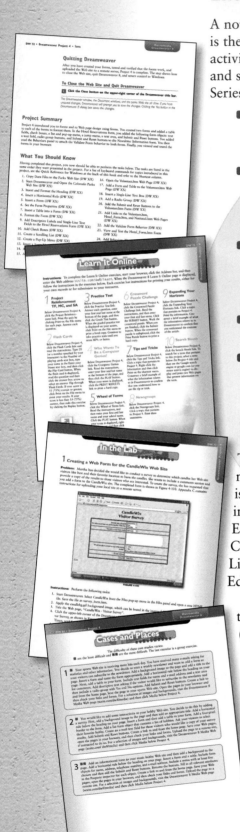

- **What You Should Know** A listing of the tasks completed within a project together with the pages on which the step-by-step, screen-by-screen explanations appear.

- **Learn It Online** Every project features a Learn It Online page comprising ten exercises. These exercises include Project Reinforcement quizzes, Flash Cards, Practice Test, two Learning Games, Crossword Puzzles, Tips and Tricks, Newsgroup usage, Expanding Your Horizons, and Search Sleuth.

- **Apply Your Knowledge** This exercise usually requires students to open and manipulate a file that is provided in the Data Files for Students. To obtain a copy of the Data Files for Students, follow the instructions on the inside back cover of this textbook.

- **In the Lab** Three in-depth assignments per project require students to utilize the project concepts and techniques to create additional Web sites.

- **Cases and Places** Five unique real-world case-study situations, including one small-group activity.

Shelly Cashman Series Instructor Resources

The Shelly Cashman Series is dedicated to providing you with all of the tools you need to make your class a success. Information on all supplementary materials is available through your Thomson Course Technology representative or by calling one of the following telephone numbers: Colleges, Universities, Continuing Education Departments, and Post-Secondary Vocational Schools: 800-648-7450; Career Colleges, Business, Industry, Government, Trade, Retailer, Wholesaler, Library, and Resellers: 800-477-3692; K-12, Secondary Vocational Schools, Adult Education, and School Districts: 800-824-5179.

The Instructor Resources for this textbook include both teaching and testing aids. The contents of each item on the Instructor Resources CD-ROM (ISBN 1-4239-1200-4) are described below.

INSTRUCTOR'S MANUAL The Instructor's Manual is made up of Microsoft Word files, which include detailed lesson plans with page number references, lecture notes, teaching tips, classroom activities, discussion topics, projects to assign, and transparency references. The transparencies are available through the Figure Files described below.

LECTURE SUCCESS SYSTEM   The Lecture Success System consists of intermediate files that correspond to certain figures in the book, allowing you to step through the creation of an application in a project during a lecture without entering large amounts of data.

SYLLABUS   Sample syllabi, which can be customized easily to a course, are included. The syllabi cover policies, class and lab assignments and exams, and procedural information.

FIGURE FILES   Illustrations for every figure in the textbook are available in electronic form. Use this ancillary to present a slide show in lecture or to print transparencies for use in lecture with an overhead projector. If you have a personal computer and LCD device, this ancillary can be an effective tool for presenting lectures.

POWERPOINT PRESENTATIONS   PowerPoint Presentations is a multimedia lecture presentation system that provides slides for each project. Presentations are based on project objectives. Use this presentation system to present well-organized lectures that are both interesting and knowledge based. PowerPoint Presentations provides consistent coverage at schools that use multiple lecturers.

SOLUTIONS TO EXERCISES   Solutions are included for the end-of-project exercises, as well as the Project Reinforcement exercises.

TEST BANK & TEST ENGINE   The ExamView test bank includes 110 questions for every project (25 multiple-choice, 50 true/false, and 35 completion) with page number references, and when appropriate, figure references. A version of the test bank you can print also is included. The test bank comes with a copy of the test engine, ExamView, the ultimate tool for your objective-based testing needs. Exam-View is a state-of-the-art test builder that is easy to use. ExamView enables you to create paper-, LAN-, or Web-based tests from test banks designed specifically for your Course Technology textbook. Utilize the ultra-efficient QuickTest Wizard to create tests in less than five minutes by taking advantage of Course Technology's question banks, or customize your own exams from scratch.

DATA FILES FOR STUDENTS   All the files that are required by students to complete the exercises are included. You can distribute the files on the Instructor Resources CD-ROM to your students over a network, or you can have them follow the instructions on the inside back cover of this book to obtain a copy of the Data Files for Students.

ADDITIONAL ACTIVITIES FOR STUDENTS   These additional activities consist of Project Reinforcement Exercises, which are true/false, multiple choice, and short answer questions that help students gain confidence in the material learned.

Online Content

Thomson Course Technology offers textbook-based content for Blackboard, WebCT, and MyCourse 2.1.

BLACKBOARD AND WEBCT As the leading provider of IT content for the Blackboard and WebCT platforms, Thomson Course Technology delivers rich content that enhances your textbook to give your students a unique learning experience. Thomson Course Technology has partnered with WebCT and Blackboard to deliver our market-leading content through these state-of-the-art online learning platforms.

MYCOURSE 2.1 MyCourse 2.1 is Thomson Course Technology's powerful online course management and content delivery system. Completely maintained and hosted by Thomson, MyCourse 2.1 delivers an online learning environment that is completely secure and provides superior performance. MyCourse 2.1 allows nontechnical users to create, customize, and deliver World Wide Web-based courses; post content and assignments; manage student enrollment; administer exams; track results in the online gradebook; and more.

Macromedia Dreamweaver 8 30-Day Trial Edition

A copy of the Dreamweaver 8 30-Day trial edition can be downloaded from the Macromedia Web site (www. macromedia.com). Point to Downloads in the top navigation bar, click Free Trials, and then follow the on-screen instructions. When you activate the software, you will receive a license that allows you to use the software for 30 days. Thomson Course Technology and Adobe (formerly Macromedia) provide no product support for this trial edition. When the trial period ends, you can purchase a copy of Macromedia Dreamweaver 8, or uninstall the trial edition and reinstall your previous version.

The minimum system requirements for the 30-day trial edition is a 800 MHz Intel Pentium III processor (or equivalent) and later; Windows 2000 or Windows XP; 256 MB RAM (1 GB recommended to run more than one Studio 8 product simultaneously); 1024 × 768, 16-bit display (32-bit recommended); and 650 MB available disk space.

To the Student... Getting the Most Out of Your Book

Welcome to *Macromedia Dreamweaver 8: Comprehensive Concepts and Techniques*. You can save yourself a lot of time and gain a better understanding of Dreamweaver 8 if you spend a few minutes reviewing the figures and callouts in this section.

1 Project Orientation

The project orientation lets you see firsthand how Web development problems are solved from start to finish using Dreamweaver 8. Each project begins by presenting a practical Web page development problem and then shows the Web pages that will be created to solve the problem. The remainder of the project steps through creating the Web pages.

2 Consistent Step-By-Step, Screen-By-Screen Presentation

Project solutions are built using a step-by-step, screen-by-screen approach. This pedagogy allows you to build the solution on a computer as you read through the project. Generally, each step is followed by an italic explanation that indicates the result of the step.

3 More Than Just Step-By-Step

More About and Q&A annotations in the margins of the book and substantive text in the paragraphs provide background information, Web design techniques, and tips that complement the topics covered, adding depth and perspective. When you finish with this book, you will be ready to use Dreamweaver 8 to create sophisticated Web pages on your own.

4 Dreamweaver Quick Reference

The Quick Reference provides a listing of keyboard shortcuts to use with Dreamweaver 8.

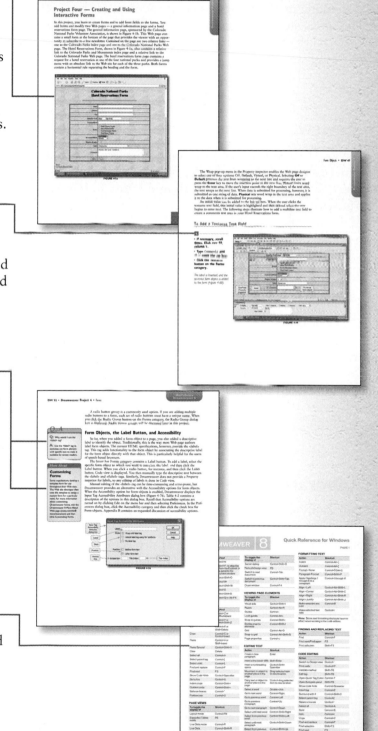

5 Refer to the Introduction for Guidelines on Planning and Designing a Web Site

In any Web site development project, including the exercises at the end of each project, you should use a systematic methodology to create Web pages to ensure consistency and completness. The Introduction project takes you from the planning stage to the publishing stage.

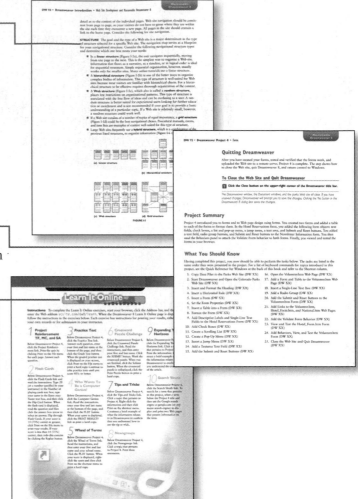

6 Review

After you successfully step through a project, a section Know summarizes the project tasks with which you should be familiar. Terms you should know for test purposes are bold in the text.

7 Reinforcement and Extension

The Learn It Online page at the end of each project offers reinforcement in the form of review questions, learning games, and practice tests. Also included are Web-based exercises that require you to extend your learning beyond the book.

8 Laboratory Exercises

If you really want to learn how to create Web pages using Dreamweaver, then you must design and implement solutions on your own. Every project concludes with several carefully developed laboratory assignments that increase in complexity. In addition, the Cases and Places exercises at the end of each project are unique real-world situations, including one small-group activity.

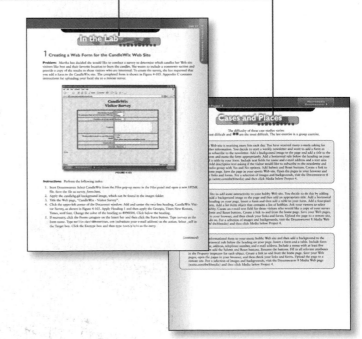

MACROMEDIA
Dreamweaver 8

Macromedia DREAMWEAVER 8

Web Site Development and Macromedia Dreamweaver 8

Objectives

You will have mastered the material in this project when you can:

- Describe the significance of the Internet and its associated terms
- Describe the World Wide Web and its associated terms
- Identify the difference between the Internet and the World Wide Web
- Specify the difference between a Web page and a Web site
- Define Web browsers and identify their main features

- Identify the nine types of Web sites
- Discuss how to plan, design, develop, test, publish, and maintain a Web site
- Identify the various methods and tools used to create a Web page and Web site
- Recognize the basic elements within XHTML
- Discuss the advantages of using Web page authoring programs such as Dreamweaver

The Internet

The **Internet**, sometimes simply called the **Net**, is a global network connecting millions of computers. Within this network, a user who has permission at any one computer can access and obtain information from any other computer within the network. A **network** is a group of computers and associated devices that are connected by communications facilities. A network can span a global area and involve permanent connections, such as cables, or temporary connections made through telephone or other communications links. Local, regional, national, and international networks constitute a global network. Each of these networks provides communications, services, and access to information.

No one person or organization is responsible for the birth of the Internet. The Internet origin, however, can be traced to the early 1960s when the Advanced Research Projects Agency (ARPA) working under the U. S. Department of Defense began a networking project. The purpose of the project was to create a network that would allow scientists at different locations to share military and scientific information. Today, the Internet is a public, cooperative, and self-sustaining facility that hundreds of millions of people worldwide access.

The World Wide Web and Web Browsers

The **World Wide Web** (**WWW**), also called the **Web**, is one of the more popular services on the Internet. The Web consists of a system of global **network servers**, also known as **Web servers**, that support specially formatted documents and provide a means for sharing these resources with many people at the same time. A network server is known as the **host computer**, and your computer, from which you access the information, is called the **client. Hypertext Transfer Protocol** (**HTTP**) enables the transfer of data from the host computer to the client.

Accessing the Web

Users access Web resources, such as text, graphics, sound, video, and multimedia, through a **Web page**. A unique address, or Uniform Resource Locator (URL), identifies every Web page. The URL provides the global address of the location of the Web page. URLs are discussed later in this Introduction. Viewing data contained on a Web page requires a **Web browser,** a software program that requests a Web page, interprets the code contained within the page, and then displays the contents of the Web page on your computer display device.

Web Browsers

Web browsers contain special buttons and other features to help you navigate through Web sites. The more popular Web browser software programs are **Microsoft Internet Explorer, Mozilla Firefox,** and **Netscape Navigator**. This book uses Internet Explorer as the primary browser. When you start Internet Explorer, it opens a Web page that has been set as the start, or home, page (Figure I-1) on the next page. Using the browser's Tools menu, the user can designate any page on the Web as the home page or start with a blank page. Important features of Internet Explorer are summarized in Table I-1 on the next page.

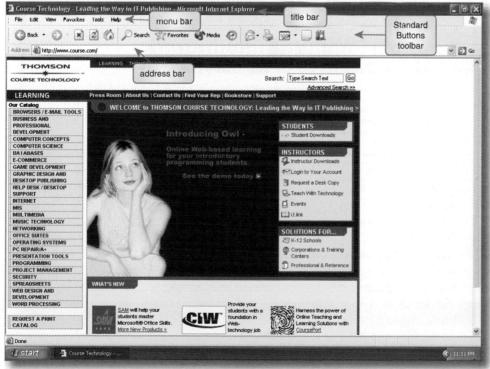

FIGURE I-1

Table I-1 Internet Explorer Features	
FEATURE	DEFINITION
Title bar	Displays the name of the Web page and the name of the program you are viewing
Menu bar	Displays the names of the menus; each menu contains a list of commands you can use to perform tasks such as printing, saving, and editing
Standard Buttons toolbar	Contains buttons, boxes, and menus that allow you to perform tasks more quickly than using the menu bar and related menus
Address bar	Displays the Web site address, or URL, of the Web page you are viewing
Document window	Contains the Web page content

Nearly all Web pages have unique characteristics, but almost every Web page contains the same basic elements. On most Web pages, you will find headings or titles, text, pictures or images, background enhancements, and hyperlinks. A **hyperlink**, or **link**, can connect to another place in the same Web page or site—or to an entirely different Web page on a server in another city or country. Normally, you click the hyperlink to follow the connected pathway. Figure I-2 contains a variety of link types. Clicking a link causes the Web page associated with the link to be displayed in a browser window. Linked pages can appear in the same browser window or in a separate browser window, depending on the HTML or XHTML code associated with the link. HTML and XHTML are discussed later in this Introduction.

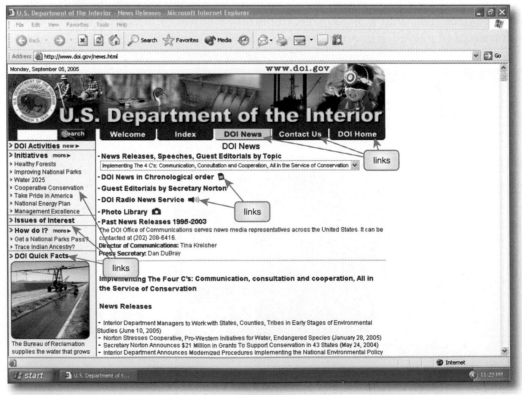

FIGURE I-2

Most Web pages are part of a **Web site,** a group of related Web pages that are linked together. Most Web sites contain a home page, which generally is the first Web page visitors see when they enter the site. A **home page** (also called an **index page**) typically provides information about the Web site's purpose and content. Most Web sites also contain additional content and pages. An individual, company, or organization owns and manages each Web site.

Accessing the Web requires a connection through a regional or national Internet service provider (ISP), an online service provider (OSP), or a wireless service provider (WSP). Figure I-3 illustrates ways to access the Internet using these service providers. An **Internet service provider** (**ISP**) provides temporary connections to individuals, companies, or other organizations through its permanent Internet connection. Similar to an ISP, an **online service provider** (**OSP**) provides additional member-only services such as financial data and travel information. America Online and CompuServe are examples of OSPs. A **wireless service provider** (**WSP**) provides Internet access to users with Web-enabled devices or wireless modems. Generally, all of these providers charge a fee for their services.

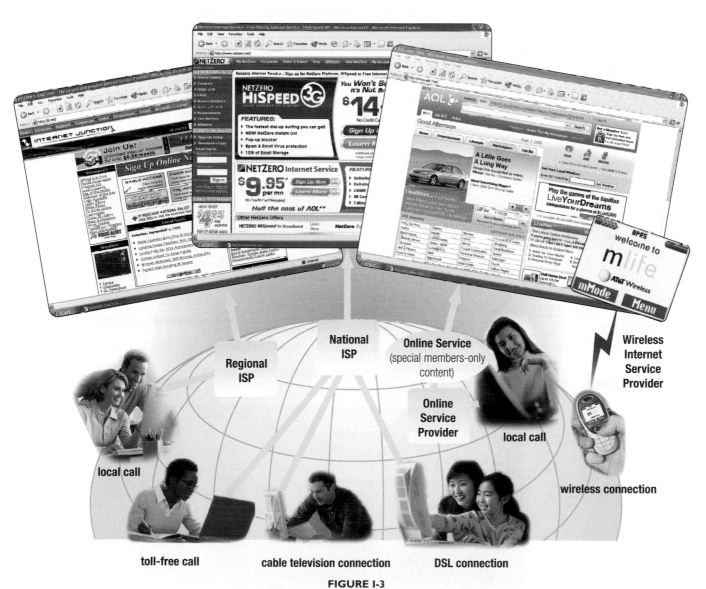

FIGURE I-3

Types of Web Sites

Web sites are classified as nine basic types: portal, news, informational, business/
marketing, educational, entertainment, advocacy, personal, and blog. A **portal Web
site** (Figure I-4a) provides a variety of Internet services from a single, convenient
location. Most portals offer free services such as search engines; local, national, and
worldwide news; sports; weather; reference tools; maps; stock quotes; newsgroups;
chat rooms; and calendars. A **news Web site** (Figure I-4b) contains news articles
relating to current events. An **informational Web site** (Figure I-4c) contains factual
information, such as research and statistics. Governmental agencies and nonprofit
organizations are the primary providers of informational Web pages. A **business/
marketing Web site** (Figure I-4d) contains content that promotes or sells products
or services. An **educational Web site** (Figure I-4e) provides exciting, challenging
avenues for formal and informal teaching and learning. An **entertainment Web site**
(Figure I-4f) offers an interactive and engaging environment and contains music,
video, sports, games, and other similar features. Within an **advocacy Web site**
(Figure I-4g), you will find content that describes a cause, opinion, question, or idea.
A **personal Web site** (Figure I-4h) is published by an individual or family and generally is not associated with any organization. A **blog** (Figure I-4i), which is short for
Web log, uses a regularly updated journal format to reflect the interests, opinions,
and personality of the author and sometimes of site visitors. As you progress through
this book, you will have an opportunity to learn more about different types of
Web pages.

FIGURE I-4a (portal)

FIGURE I-4b (news)

FIGURE I-4c (informational)

FIGURE I-4

FIGURE I-4d (business/marketing)

FIGURE I-4e (educational)

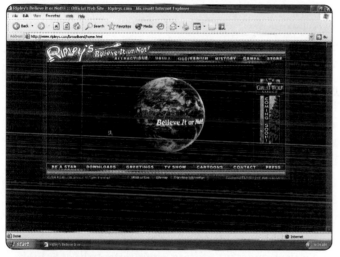

FIGURE I-4f (entertainment)

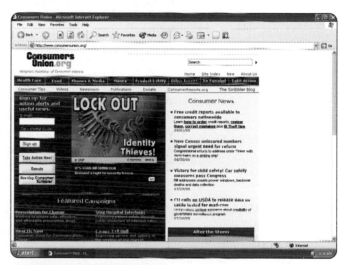

FIGURE I-4g (advocacy)

FIGURE I-4h (personal)

FIGURE I-4i (blog)

FIGURE I-4 (continued)

Planning a Web Site

Thousands of individuals create and publish Web pages every day, some using word-processing software or markup languages, such as XHTML, to create their pages. Others use professional design and management editors such as Dreamweaver. Although publishing a Web page and/or a Web site is easy, advanced planning is paramount in ensuring a successful Web site. Publishing a Web site, which makes it available on the Internet, is discussed later in this Introduction.

Planning Basics — Purpose

Those who rush into the publishing process without proper planning tend to design Web sites that are unorganized and difficult to navigate. Visitors to this type of Web site often lose interest quickly and do not return. As you begin planning your Web site, consider the following guidelines to ensure that you set and attain realistic goals.

PURPOSE AND GOAL Determine the purpose and goal of your Web site. Create a focus by developing a **purpose statement**, which communicates the intention of the Web site. Consider the nine basic types of Web sites mentioned previously. Will your Web site consist of just one basic type or a combination of two or more types?

TARGET AUDIENCE Identify your audience. The people who visit your Web site will determine the success of your site. Although you welcome all visitors, you need to know as much as possible about the primary group of people you wish to reach—your target audience. To learn more about the visitors to your Web site, determine whether you want to attract people with similar interests, and consider the gender, education, age range, income, profession/job field, and computer proficiency of your target audience.

NEW WEB TECHNOLOGIES Evaluate whether your potential visitors have access to high-speed broadband media or to baseband media, and use this information to determine what elements to include within your Web site. **Broadband** can transmit a large number of moving images or a vast quantity of data simultaneously at a high speed. Media and hardware such as **T1 lines, DSL (digital subscriber lines), ISDN (Integrated Services Digital Network), fiber optics**, and **cable modems** work with broadband. **Baseband** transmits one signal at a time over a telephone line and includes media and hardware such as 28K to 56K modems. Baseband works well with a Web site composed mostly of text and small images. Web sites that contain many images or multimedia, such as video and animations, generally require that visitors have a broadband connection.

WEB SITE COMPARISON Visit other Web sites that are similar to your proposed site. What do you like about these sites? What do you dislike? Look for inspirational ideas. How can you make your Web site better?

Planning Basics — Content

To ensure a successful Web experience for your visitors, consider the following guidelines to provide appropriate content and other valuable Web page elements.

VALUE-ADDED CONTENT Consider the different types of content you can include within your Web site. Use the following questions as guidelines:

- What topics do you want to cover?
- How much information will you present about each topic?
- What will attract your target audience to your Web site?
- What methods will you use to keep your audience returning to your site?
- What changes will you have to make to keep your site updated?

TEXT Text accounts for the bulk of all content on most Web pages, so be brief and incorporate lists whenever possible. Statistical studies indicate that most people tend to scan the page, picking out individual words and sentences. Use common words and simple language, and check your spelling and grammar. Create your textual content to accomplish your goals effectively by highlighting key words, using bulleted lists, maintaining one idea per paragraph, and including meaningful subheadings.

IMAGES After text, images constitute the next most commonly included content. Ask yourself these questions with respect to your use of images:

- Will you have a common logo and/or theme on all of your Web pages?
- Are these images readily available?
- What images will you have to locate?
- What images will you have to create?
- How many images per page will you have?

COLOR PALETTE The color palette you select for your Web site can enhance or detract from your message or goal. Do not think in terms of your favorite colors. Instead, consider how color can support your goal. Ask yourself the following questions:

- Do your selected colors work well with your goal?
- Are the colors part of the universal 216-color, browser-safe color palette?
- Did you limit the number of colors to a selected few?

MULTIMEDIA Multimedia adds interactivity and action to your Web pages. Animation, audio, and video are types of **multimedia**. If you plan to add multimedia, determine whether the visitor will require plug-ins. A **plug-in** extends the capability of a Web browser. Some of the more commonly used plug-ins are Shockwave Player, Macromedia Flash, and Windows Media Player. Most plug-ins are free and can be downloaded from the Web.

Web Site Navigation

Predicting how a visitor will access a Web site or at what point the visitor will enter within the Web site structure is not possible. Visitors can arrive at any page within a Web site by a variety of ways: a hyperlink, a search engine, a directory, typing a Web address directly, and so on. On every page of your Web site, you must provide clear answers to the three basic questions your visitors will ask: Where am I? Where do I go from here? How do I get to the home page? A well-organized Web site provides the answers to these questions. Once the visitor arrives at a Web site, **navigation**, the pathway through your site, must be obvious and intuitive. Individual Web pages cannot be isolated from the rest of the site if you want it to be successful. At all times and on all pages in your site, you must give the visitor a sense of place, of context within the site. Most Web designers use a navigation map to visualize the navigation pathway.

Design Basics — Navigation Map

Q: I want to develop a Web site. What should I do first?

A: Start with and organize your content. Then create your navigation map.

A **navigation map**, or **site map**, outlines the structure of the entire Web site, showing all pages within the site and the connections from one page to the others. The navigation map acts as a road map through the Web site, but does not provide detail of the content of the individual pages. Web site navigation should be consistent from page to page, so your visitors do not have to guess where they are within the site each time they encounter a new page. All pages in the site should contain a link to the home page. Consider the following for site navigation:

STRUCTURE The goal and the type of a Web site often determine the structure selected for a specific Web site. Create a navigation map to serve as a blueprint for your navigational structure. Consider the following navigational structures and determine which one best meets your needs:

- In a **linear structure** (Figure I-5a on the next page) the user navigates sequentially, moving from one page to the next. Information that flows as a narrative, as a timeline, or in logical order is ideal for sequential treatment. Simple sequential organization, however, usually works only for smaller sites. Many online tutorials use a linear structure.

- A **hierarchical structure** (Figure I-5b on the next page) is one of the better ways to organize complex bodies of information efficiently. Because many visitors are familiar with hierarchical charts, many Web sites employ this structure. Be aware that effective hierarchical structures require thorough organization of the content.

- A **Web structure** (Figure I-5c on the next page), which also is called a **random structure**, places few restrictions on organizational patterns. This type of structure is associated with the free flow of ideas and can be confusing to a user. A random structure is better suited for experienced users looking for further education or enrichment and is not recommended if your goal is to provide a basic understanding of a particular topic. If a Web site is relatively small, however, a random structure could work well.

- Use a **grid structure** if your Web site consists of a number of topics of equal importance (Figure I-5d on the next page). Procedural manuals, events, and item lists work well in a grid structure.

- Large Web sites frequently use a **hybrid structure**, a combination of the previous listed structures, to organize information (Figure I-6 on the next page).

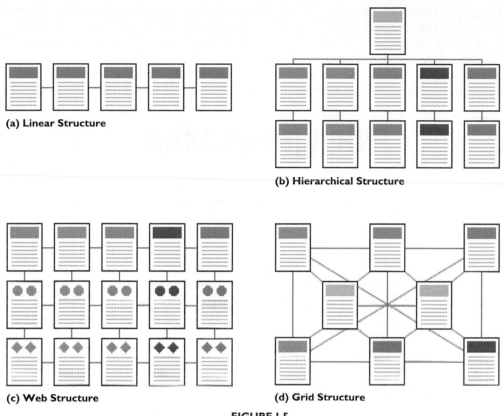

(a) Linear Structure

(b) Hierarchical Structure

(c) Web Structure

(d) Grid Structure

FIGURE I-5

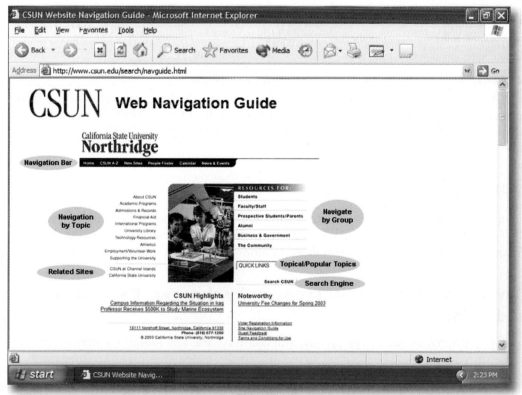

FIGURE I-6

TOOLS Determine the tool necessary to create the navigation map. For small Web sites, consider using the organizational chart included in the Microsoft PowerPoint application, as shown in Figure I-7. For larger, more diverse Web sites, you can chart and organize your content using Visio Professional, Flow Charting PDQ, FlowCharter Professional, and OrgPlus. Dreamweaver also provides a site map feature. An ideal tool for laying out and evaluating a site structure, the Dreamweaver site map shows the site structure two levels deep, starting from the home page.

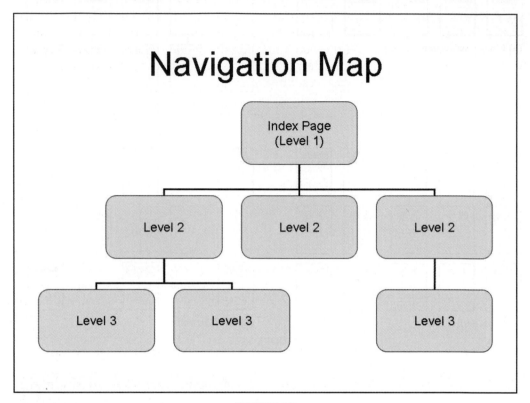

FIGURE I-7

NAVIGATION ELEMENTS The more common types of navigation elements include text, buttons, other images, image maps, a site index, a menu, a search feature, navigation bars, and frames. Depending on the complexity of your Web site, you may want to include some or all of these elements.

Developing a Web Site

Once you have established a structure for your Web site, you can begin developing the site. Make text and images the main focus because they are the more common elements. Then consider page layout and color.

Development Basics — Typography, Images, Page Layout, and Color

Typography, images, page layout, and color are the key design elements that will make up your finished Web site. Correct use of these elements plays an important part in the development process. Consider the following guidelines:

TYPOGRAPHY As in all media, good **typography**, the appearance and arrangement of the characters that make up your text, is vital to the success of your Web page. A **font** consists of all the characters available in a particular style and weight for a specific design. Text should always be easy to read, whether in a book, magazine, Web page, or billboard. Keep readability in mind as you select fonts, especially when you consider that some of your visitors may only be viewing them onscreen.

When selecting a font, determine its purpose on your Web page. Is it to be used for a title? For onscreen reading? Is it likely to be printed? Will the font fit in with the theme of the Web site? Is it a Web-safe font, such as Times New Roman, Courier, or Arial? **Web-safe fonts** are the more popular fonts and the ones that most visitors are likely to have installed on their computers. Also, while visitors to your Web page may never consciously notice the design of the text characters, or the **typeface**, it often subconsciously affects their reaction to the page.

IMAGES Images can enhance almost any Web page if used appropriately. Without the visual impact of shape, color, and contrast, Web pages can be visually uninteresting and will not motivate the visitor to investigate their contents. Consider the balance between the number of images and page performance as you develop your site. When adding images, consider your potential audience and the technology they have available. Remember that a background image or a graphical menu increases visitor download time. You may lose visitors who do not have broadband access if your Web page contains an excessive number of graphical items.

PAGE LAYOUT The importance of proper page layout cannot be overemphasized. A suitable design draws visitors to your Web site. Although no single design system is appropriate for all Web pages, establish a consistent, logical layout that allows you to add text and images easily. The Web page layouts shown in Figure I-8 on the next page illustrate two different layouts. The layout on the left (Figure I-8a) shows a plain page with a heading and text. The page layout on the right (Figure I-8b) presents strong visual contrast by using a variety of layout elements.

Maintaining consistency and updating changes throughout a site are two of the biggest challenges faced by Web designers. A **template,** a special type of document, can help with these challenges. Dreamweaver provides several page layout templates that can be modified easily. In laying out your Web pages, consider the following guidelines to ensure that visitors have the best viewing experience:

- Include only one topic per page.
- Control the vertical and horizontal size of the page.
- Start text on the left to accommodate the majority of individuals who read from left to right.
- Use concise statements and bulleted points to get your point across; studies indicate most people scan the text.

COLOR When creating a Web page, use color to add interest and vitality to your site. Include color in tables, as backgrounds, and with fonts. Use the right combination of colors to decorate the layout and tie the Web site pages together.

Q&A

Q: Many pages on the Web contain multiple elements and appear very "busy." Is this a good practice?

A: Not necessarily. Simple pages download faster and make an immediate impression on the reader.

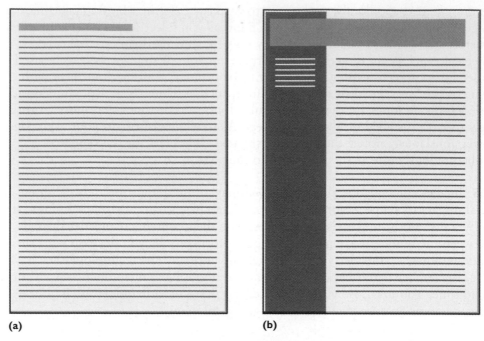

(a)   (b)

FIGURE I-8

Reviewing and Testing a Web Site

Some Web site developers argue that reviewing and testing should take place throughout the developmental process. While this may be true, it also is important to review and test the final product. This ongoing process ensures that you identify and correct any problems before publishing to the Web. When reviewing and testing your Web site, ask the following questions:

- Is the Web site free of spelling and/or grammatical errors?
- Is the page layout consistent, and does it generate a sense of balance and order?
- Are any links broken?
- Do multimedia interactivity and forms function correctly?
- Do the more widely used browsers display the Web site properly?
- Does the Web site function properly in different browsers, including older browser versions?
- Have you initiated a **group test**, in which you have asked other individuals to test your Web site and provide feedback?

Publishing a Web Site

After your Web site has been tested thoroughly, it can be published. **Publishing** a Web site, making it available to your visitors, involves the actual uploading of the Web site to a server. After you complete the uploading process, all pages within the Web site should be tested again.

Publishing Basics — Domain Name, Server Space, and Uploading

With your Web site thoroughly tested and any problems corrected, you must make the site available to your audience by obtaining a domain name, acquiring server space, and uploading the site. Consider the following to ensure site availability:

OBTAIN A DOMAIN NAME To allow visitors to access your Web site, you must obtain a domain name. Visitors access Web sites by an IP address or a domain name. An **IP address** (**Internet Protocol address**) is a number that uniquely identifies each computer or device connected to the Internet. A **domain name** is the text version of an IP address. The **Domain Name System** (**DNS**), an Internet service, translates domain names into their corresponding IP addresses. The **Uniform Resource Locator** (**URL**), also called a **Web address**, tells the browser on which server the Web page is located. A URL consists of a communications standard, such as **Hypertext Transfer Protocol** (**HTTP**), the domain name, and sometimes the path to a specific Web page (Figure I-9 on the next page).

Domain names are unique and must be registered. The **Accredited Registrar Directory** provides a listing of **Internet Corporation for Assigned Names and Numbers** (**ICANN**) accredited domain name registrars. Your most difficult task likely will be to find a name that is not already registered. You can locate a name by using a specialized search engine at one of the many accredited domain name registrars listed on the ICANN Web site (icann.org/registrars/accredited-list.html). In addition to registering your business name as a domain name, you may want to register the names of your products, services, and/or other related names. Expect to pay approximately $10 to $35 per year for a domain name.

Consider the following guidelines when selecting a domain name:

- Select a name that is easy to pronounce, spell, and remember.
- Select a name that relates to the Web site content and suggests the nature of your product or service.
- If the Web site is a business, use the business name whenever possible.
- Select a name that is free and clear of trademark issues.
- Purchase variations and the .org and .net versions of your domain name.
- Some ISPs will obtain a domain name for you if you use their service to host your Web site.

ACQUIRE SERVER SPACE Locate an ISP that will host your Web site. Recall that an ISP is a business that has a permanent Internet connection. ISPs offer temporary connections to individuals and companies free or for a fee.

If you select an ISP that provides free server space, most likely your visitors will be subjected to advertisements and pop-up windows. Other options to explore for free server space include the provider from which you obtain your Internet connection; online communities, such as Yahoo! GeoCities (geocities.yahoo.com), Tripod (tripod.lycos.com), and MSN Web Communities (communities.msn.com); and your educational institution's Web server. An **online community** is a group whose members are connected by means of information technologies, typically the Internet.

More About

Selecting a Domain Name

When selecting a domain name, keep it simple. If possible, avoid hyphens. To learn more about domain name selection, visit the Dreamweaver 8 More About Web page (scsite.com/dw8/more.htm) and then click Domain Name Selection.

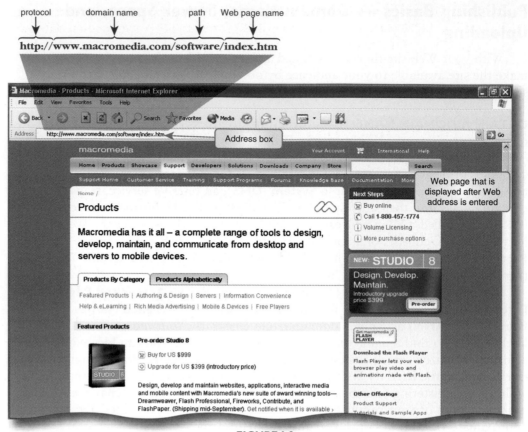

FIGURE I-9

If the purpose of your Web site is to sell a product or service or to promote a professional organization, you should consider a fee-based ISP. Use a search engine such as Google (google.com) and search for Web site hosting, or visit the WebSite Hosting Directory (www.websitehostdirectory.com), where you will find thousands of Web hosting plans, as well as reviews and ratings of Web hosting providers. Selecting a reliable provider requires investigation on your part. Many providers offer multiple hosting plans. When selecting an ISP, consider the following questions and how they apply to your particular situation and Web site:

1. What is the monthly fee? Is a discount available for a year-long subscription? Are setup fees charged?
2. How much server space is provided for the monthly fee? Can you purchase additional space? If so, how much does it cost?
3. What is the average server uptime on a monthly basis? What is the average server downtime?
4. What are the server specifications? Can the server handle many users? Does it have battery backup power?
5. Are **server logs**, which keep track of the number of accesses, available?
6. What is the ISP's form of connectivity — that is, how does it connect to the Internet: OC3, T1, T3, or some other way?
7. Is a money-back guarantee offered?
8. What technical support does the ISP provide, and when is it available? Does it have an online knowledge base?
9. Does the server on which the Web site will reside have CGI capabilities and Active Server Page (ASP) support?

10. Does the server on which the Web site will reside support e-commerce, multimedia, and **Secure Sockets Layer (SSL)** for encrypting confidential data such as credit card numbers? Are additional fees required for these capabilities?

11. Does the ISP support Dreamweaver and/or other Web site development software programs?

12. Are mailboxes included in the package? If so, how many?

PUBLISH THE WEB SITE You must publish, or upload, the files from your computer to a server where your Web site will then be accessible to anyone on the Internet. Publishing, or **uploading**, is the process of transmitting all the files that make up your Web site from your computer to the selected server or host computer. The files that make up your Web site can include Web pages, PDF documents, images, audio, video, animation, and others.

A variety of tools and methods exist to manage the upload task. Some of the more popular of these are FTP programs, Windows Web Publishing Wizard, Web Folders, and Web authoring programs such as Dreamweaver. These tools allow you to link to a remote server, enter a password, and then upload your files. Dreamweaver contains a built-in function similar to independent FTP programs. The Dreamweaver FTP function to upload your Web site is covered in Project 3 and in Appendix C.

Maintaining a Web Site

Most Web sites require maintenance and updating. Some types of ongoing Web maintenance include the following:

- Changing content, either by adding new text and images or by deleting obsolete material
- Checking for broken links and adding new links
- Documenting the last change date (even when no revisions have been made)

Use the information from the server logs provided by your ISP to determine what needs to be updated or changed. Statistics contained within these logs generally include the number of visitors trying to access your site at one time, what resources they request, how long they stay at the site, at what point they enter the site, what pages they view, and what errors they encounter. Learning to use and apply the information contained within the server log will help you to make your Web site successful.

After you make updates and/or changes to the site, notify your viewers with a What's New announcement.

Methods and Tools Used to Create Web Pages

Web developers have several options for creating Web pages: a text editor, an HTML or XHTML editor, software applications, or a WYSIWYG text editor (discussed in detail on page DW 21). Microsoft Notepad and WordPad are examples of a **text editor**. These simple, easy-to-use programs allow the user to enter, edit, save, and print text. An **HTML** or **XHTML editor** is a more sophisticated version of a text editor. In addition to basic text-editing functions, these programs include more advanced features such as syntax highlighting, color coding, and spell-checking. Software applications such as Microsoft Word, Excel, and Publisher provide a Save as Web Page command on the File menu. This feature converts the application document into a file Web browsers are able to display. Examples of a WYSIWYG text editor are programs such as Microsoft FrontPage and Macromedia Dreamweaver. These programs provide an integrated text editor with a graphical user interface that allows the user to view both the code and the document as you create it.

A Web developer can use any of these options to create Web pages. Regardless of the option selected, however, it still is important to understand the specifics of HTML and XHTML.

Web Site Languages

Web pages are written in plain text and saved in the **American Standard Code for Information Interchange**, or **ASCII** (pronounced ASK-ee), format — the most widely used coding system to represent data. Using the ASCII format makes Web pages universally readable by different Web browsers regardless of the computer platform on which they reside.

The language of the Web is not static; it evolves just like most other languages. HTML (Hypertext Markup Language) has been the primary language of the Web and most likely will continue to be so for at least the near future. HTML is useful for creating headings, paragraphs, lists, and so on, but is limited to these general types of formatting. XHTML is a rewritten version of HTML using XML (Extensible Markup Language).

Unlike HTML, **Extensible Hypertext Markup Language** (**XHTML**) is an authoring language which defines the structure and layout of a document so that it displays as a Web page and is compatible with Web browsers such as Microsoft Internet Explorer, Mozilla Firefox, or Netscape Navigator. Browser rules for interpreting HTML are flexible. XHTML, however, requires Web designers to adhere strictly to its markup language rules.

Two components constitute a Web page: source code and document content. The **source code**, which contains elements, acts as the program instructions. The **elements** within the source code control the appearance of the document content. Browsers display the **document content,** or the text and images. The browser interprets the elements contained within the code, and the code instructs the browser how to display the Web page. For instance, if you define a line of text on your Web page as a heading, the browser knows to display this line formatted as a heading.

All XHTML element formats and HTML tags start with a left angle bracket (< or less than symbol), are followed by the name of the element, and end with a right angle bracket (> or greater than symbol). Most elements have a start and an end element and are called **two-sided elements**. End elements are the same as start elements except they are preceded by a forward slash (/). Some XHTML elements, such as the one used to indicate a line break <br />, do not have an end element. Instead, the right angle bracket is preceded by a space and forward slash. These are known as **one-sided elements**, or **self-closing elements**. In some browsers, the end element can be omitted from certain elements, such as the end element for a new paragraph, </p>. However, unlike HTML, XHTML standards require you to include both the start and end elements for all two-sided elements.

Some elements can contain an **attribute**, or **property**, which is additional information placed within the angle brackets. Attributes are not repeated or contained in the end element. Some attributes are used individually, while other attributes can include a value modifier. A **value modifier** specifies conditions within the element, and should always be enclosed in double quotation marks. For example, you can use a value modifier to specify the font type or size or the placement of text on the page. To create and display a centered heading, for instance, you would use the following code:

```
<h1 style="text-align:center">This is the largest header element and the text will be
centered</h1>
```

In this example, h1 is the XHTML element, align is the attribute, and center is the value modifier. Notice that the attribute does not appear as part of the end element, </h1>.

You can use Microsoft Notepad or WordPad (text editors) to create XHTML documents. Place each element in a pair around the text or section that you want to define (**mark up**) with that element. Use lowercase characters when typing XHTML elements.

XHTML elements also format the hyperlinks that connect information on the World Wide Web. While XHTML elements number in the hundreds, some are used more than others. All documents, however, require four basic elements. Figure I-10 illustrates the basic elements required for all XHTML documents. Table I-2 summarizes the more commonly used XHTML elements.

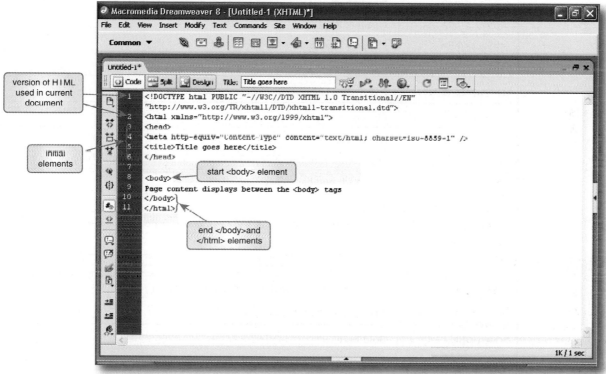

FIGURE I-10

Table I-2 Commonly Used XHTML Elements

ELEMENT (TAGS)	STRUCTURE
<html>...</html>	Encloses the entire XHTML document
<head>...</head>	Encloses the head of the XHTML document
<body>...</body>	Encloses the body of the XHTML document
ELEMENT (TAGS)	**TITLE AND HEADINGS**
<title>...</title>	Indicates the title of the document
<h1>...</h1>	Heading level 1
<h2>...</h2>	Heading level 2
<h3>...</h3>	Heading level 3
<h4>...</h4>	Heading level 4
<h5>...</h5>	Heading level 5
<h6>...</h6>	Heading level 6
ELEMENT (TAGS)	**PARAGRAPHS, BREAKS, AND SEPARATORS**
<p>...</p>	Plain paragraph
 	Line break
<hr />	Horizontal rule line
<ol>...</ol>	Ordered, numbered list
<ul>...</ul>	Unordered, bulleted list
<li>...</li>	List item, used with <ol>, <ul>, <menu>, and <dir>
<dl>...</dl>	Definition of glossary list
<dt>...</dt>	Definition term; part of a definition list
<dd>...</dd>	Definition corresponding to a definition term
ELEMENT (TAGS)	**CHARACTER FORMATTING**
...	Bold text
<u>...</u>	Underlined text
<i>...</i>	Italic text
ELEMENT (TAGS)	**LINKS**
<a>...</a>	Combined with the href attribute, creates a link to another document or anchor
<a>...</a>	Combined with the name attribute, creates an anchor which can be linked to
ELEMENT (TAGS)	**IMAGE**
<img />	Inserts an image into the document

Web Page Authoring Programs

Many of today's Web page authoring programs, including Dreamweaver, are What You See Is What You Get (WYSIWYG) text editors. As mentioned earlier, a **WYSIWYG text editor** allows a user to view a document as it will appear in the final product and to edit the text, images, or other elements directly within that view. Before programs such as Dreamweaver existed, Web page designers were required to type, or hand-code, Web pages. Educators and Web designers still debate the issue surrounding the necessity of knowing HTML and XHTML. Technically, you do not need to know either HTML or XHTML to create Web pages in Dreamweaver; however, an understanding of HTML and XHTML will help you if you need to alter Dreamweaver-generated code. If you know HTML and XHTML, then you can make changes to the code and Dreamweaver will accept the changes.

Macromedia Dreamweaver 8

The standard in visual authoring, Macromedia Dreamweaver 8 is part of the Macromedia Studio family, which includes Macromedia Flash, ColdFusion, and Fireworks. Dreamweaver provides features that access these separate products. Some of the new features of Dreamweaver 8 include the following:

- A drag-and-drop workflow
- Expanded Cascading Style Sheets (CSS) support
- A zoom tool which makes it easier to check graphics alignment, select small items, and work with small type
- Secure FTP
- Increased support for a platform-independent development environment
- Enhanced coding and editing tools, including two new toolbars: coding and style rendering
- A hand tool that lets you drag items
- Added support for Flash video

Dreamweaver makes it easy to get started and provides you with helpful tools to enhance your Web design and development experience. Working in a single environment, you create, build, and manage Web sites and Internet applications. In Dreamweaver, you can customize the workspace environment to fit your particular needs.

Dreamweaver contains coding tools and features that include references for HTML, XHTML, XML, CSS, and JavaScript as well as code editors that allow you to edit the code directly. Using **Macromedia Roundtrip technology**, Dreamweaver can import Microsoft Office or other software Web pages and delete the unused code. Downloadable extensions from the Macromedia Web site make it easy to add functionality to any Web site. Examples of these extensions include shopping carts and online payment features.

Instead of writing individual files for every page, you can use a database to store content and then retrieve the content dynamically in response to a user's request. Implementing and using this feature, you can update the information once, in one place, instead of manually editing many pages. Another key feature is **Cascading Style Sheets styles** (**CSS styles**). CSS styles are collections of formatting definitions that affect the appearance of Web page elements. You can use CSS styles to format text, images, headings, tables, and so forth. Implementing and applying this feature, you can update the formatting one time across many Web pages.

Dreamweaver provides the tools that help you author accessible content. These accessible pages comply with government guidelines and Section 508 of the Federal Rehabilitation Act. Accessibility is discussed in more detail as you progress through the book.

Dreamweaver allows you to publish Web sites with relative ease to a local area network, which connects computers in a limited geographical area, or to the Web, so that anyone with Internet access can see them. The concepts and techniques presented in this book provide the tools you need to plan, develop, and publish professional Web sites, such as those shown in Figures I-11 and I-12.

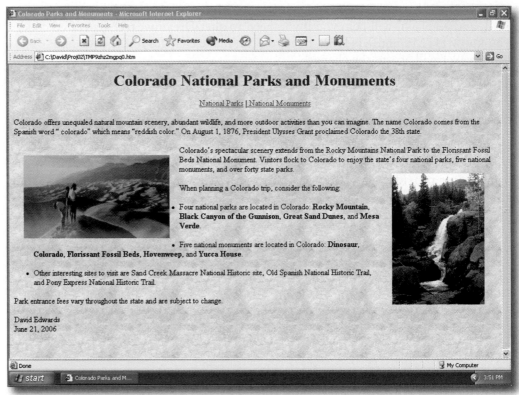

FIGURE I-11

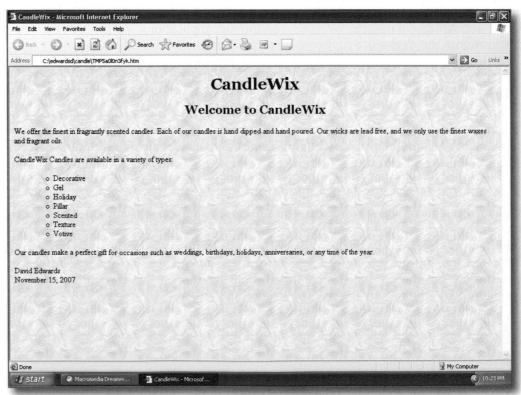

FIGURE I-12

Summary

The Introduction to Web Site Development and Macromedia Dreamweaver 8 provided an overview of the Internet and the World Wide Web and the key terms associated with those technologies. An overview of the nine basic types of Web pages was also presented. The Introduction furnished information on developing a Web site, including planning basics. The process of designing a Web site and each phase within this process were discussed. Information about testing, publishing, and maintaining a Web site was also presented, including an overview of obtaining a domain name, acquiring server space, and uploading a Web site. Methods and tools used to create Web pages were introduced. A short overview of HTML and XHTML and some of the more commonly used HTML tags and XHTML elements were presented. Finally, the advantages of using Dreamweaver in Web development were discussed. These advantages include a WYSIWYG text editor; a visual, customizable development environment; accessibility compliance; downloadable extensions; database access capabilities; and Cascading Style Sheets.

Learn It Online

For an updated list of links, visit the Dreamweaver companion site at http://scsite.com/dw8.
Instructions: To complete the Learn It Online exercises, start your browser, click the Address bar, and then enter the Web address `scsite.com/dw8/learn`. When the Dreamweaver 8 Learn It Online page is displayed, follow the instructions in the exercises below. Each exercise has instructions for printing your results, either for your own records or for submission to your instructor.

1 Project Reinforcement TF, MC, and SA

Below Dreamweaver Introduction Project, click the Project Reinforcement link. Print the quiz by clicking Print on the File menu for each page. Answer each question.

2 Flash Cards

Below Dreamweaver Introduction Project, click the Flash Cards link and read the instructions. Type 20 (or a number specified by your instructor) in the Number of playing cards text box, type your name in the Enter your Name text box, and then click the Flip Card button. When the flash card is displayed, read the question and then click the ANSWER box arrow to select an answer. Flip through Flash Cards. If your score is 15 (75%) correct or greater, click Print on the File menu to print your results. If your score is less than 15 (75%) correct, then redo this exercise by clicking the Replay button.

3 Practice Test

Below Dreamweaver Introduction Project, click the Practice Test link. Answer each question, enter your first and last name at the bottom of the page, and then click the Grade Test button. When the graded practice test is displayed on your screen, click Print on the File menu to print a hard copy. Continue to take practice tests until you score 80% or better.

4 Who Wants To Be a Computer Genius?

Below Dreamweaver Introduction Project, click the Computer Genius link. Read the instructions, enter your first and last name at the bottom of the page, and then click the PLAY button. When your score is displayed, click the PRINT RESULTS link to print a hard copy.

5 Wheel of Terms

Below Dreamweaver Introduction Project, click the Wheel of Terms link. Read the instructions, and then enter your first and last name and your school name. Click the PLAY button. When your score is displayed, right-click the score and then click Print on the shortcut menu to print a hard copy.

6 Crossword Puzzle Challenge

Below Dreamweaver Introduction Project, click the Crossword Puzzle Challenge link. Read the instructions, and then enter your first and last name. Click the SUBMIT button. Work the crossword puzzle. When you are finished, click the Submit button. When the crossword puzzle is redisplayed, click the Print Puzzle button to print a hard copy.

7 Tips and Tricks

Below Dreamweaver Introduction Project, click the Tips and Tricks link. Click a topic that pertains to the Introduction Project. Right-click the information and then click Print on the shortcut menu. Construct a brief example of what the information relates to in Dreamweaver to confirm you understand how to use the tip or trick.

8 Newsgroups

Below Dreamweaver Introduction Project, click the Newsgroups link. Click a topic that pertains to the Introduction Project. Print three comments.

9 Expanding Your Horizons

Below Dreamweaver Introduction Project, click the Expanding Your Horizons link. Click a topic that pertains to the Introduction Project. Print the information. Construct a brief example of what the information relates to in Dreamweaver to confirm you understand the contents of the article.

10 Search Sleuth

Below Dreamweaver Introduction Project, click the Search Sleuth link. To search for a term that pertains to this project, select a term below the Introduction Project title and then use the Google search engine at google.com (or any major search engine) to display and print two Web pages that present information on the term.

Apply Your Knowledge

1 Web Site Creation

Instructions: As discussed in this Introduction, creating a Web site involves planning, designing, developing, reviewing and testing, publishing, and maintaining the site. Open the Apply I-1 Web Site Creation file on the Dreamweaver Data Disk. See the inside back cover of this book for instructions for downloading the Data Disk or see your instructor for information on accessing the files required for this book. As shown in Table I-3, the Apply I-1 Web Site Creation file contains information about the Web site creation process. Use the information contained in this table to develop a plan for creating a Web site.

Table I-3 Creating a Web Site	
PLANNING	
Web site name	What is your Web site name?
Web site type	What is the Web site type: portal, news, informational, business/marketing, educational, entertainment, advocacy, personal, or blog?
Web site purpose	What is the purpose of your Web site?
Target audience	How can you identify your target audience?
Web technologies to be used	Will you design for broadband or baseband? Explain your selection.
Content	What topics will you cover? How much information will you present on each topic? How will you attract your audience? What will you do to entice your audience to return to your Web site? How will you keep the Web site updated?
Text, images, and multimedia	Will your site contain text only? What type of images will you include? Where will you obtain your images? Will you have a common logo? Will plug-ins be required?
DESIGNING	
Navigation map	What type of structure will you use? What tools will you use to design your navigation map?
Navigational elements	What navigational elements will you include?
DEVELOPING	
Typography	What font will you use? How many different fonts will you use on your site?
Images	How will you use images to enhance your site? Will you use a background image?
Page layout	What type of layout will you use? How many topics per page? How will text be presented: bulleted or paragraph style? Will the audience need to scroll the page?
Color	What color combinations will you use for your site? To what elements will you apply the color(s) — fonts, background, tables, other elements?

(continued)

Apply Your Knowledge

Web Site Creation *(continued)*

Table I-3 Creating a Web Site *(continued)*	
REVIEWING AND TESTING	
Review	What elements will you review? Will you use a group review?
Testing	What elements will you test? Will you use self-testing? Will you use group testing?
PUBLISHING	
Domain name	What is your domain name? Have you registered your domain name? What ISP will host your Web site? What criteria did you use to select the ISP?
MAINTAINING	
Ongoing maintenance	How often will you update your Web site? What elements will you update? Will you add additional features? Does your ISP provide server logs? Will you use the server logs for maintenance purposes?

Perform the following steps using your word-processing program and browser.

1. With the Apply I-1 Web Site Creation file open in your word-processing program, select a name for your Web site.
2. Use a specialized search engine at one of the many accredited domain name registrars to verify that your selected Web site name is available.
3. Answer each question in the table. Use complete sentences to answer the questions. Type your answers in column 3.
4. Save the document with the file name Apply I-1 My Web Site Creation.doc. Submit a copy to your instructor.

In the Lab

1 Using Internet Explorer

Problem: Microsoft's Internet Explorer (IE) has many new features that can make your work on the Internet more efficient. Using the Media feature, for example, you can play music, video, or multimedia files; listen to your favorite Internet radio station; and enhance your browsing experience. You can customize the image tool-bar that displays when you point to an image on a Web page. IE also includes other enhancements. Visit the Microsoft Internet Explorer How-to-Articles Web page (Figure I-13) and select three articles concerning topics with which you are not familiar. Read the articles and then create a word-processing document detailing what you learned.

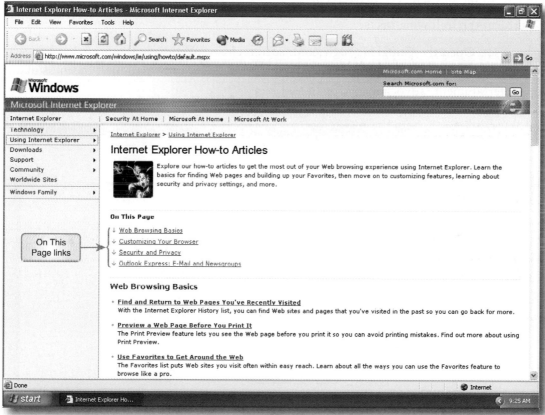

FIGURE I-13

Instructions: Perform the following tasks:

1. Start your browser. Open the Microsoft Internet Explorer How-to Articles Web page (microsoft.com/windows/ie/using/howto/default.mspx).
2. Click one of the On This Page links.
3. Select three articles that contain information with which you are not familiar.
4. Click the link for each article and read the article.
5. Start your word-processing program.
6. List three important points that you learned from this Web site.
7. Write a summary of what you learned from each article. Include within your summary your opinion of the article and if you will apply what you learned or use it with your Web browser.

(continued)

In the Lab

Using Internet Explorer *(continued)*

8. Save the document with the file name Lab I-1 How-to.doc. Print a copy of the document if instructed to do so and submit the assignment to your instructor.

2 Types of Web Pages

Problem: A Web designer should be familiar with different types of Web pages and the sort of information displayed on these types of Web pages. The Introduction describes nine types of Web pages. Search the Internet and locate at least one example of each type of Web page.

Instructions: Perform the following tasks:

1. Start your browser. Open the Google (google.com) search engine Web page (Figure I-14) and search for an example of each of the following types of Web pages: portal, news, informational, business/marketing, educational, entertainment, advocacy, personal, and blog.

FIGURE I-14

2. Start your word-processing program.
3. Copy and paste the link for each of these Web page types into your word-processing document.
4. Identify the type of Web page for each link.
5. Explain why you selected this Web page and how it fits the definition of the specific type.

6. Save the document with the file name Lab I-2 Web Page types.doc. Print a copy of the document if instructed to do so.

7. Submit the assignment to your instructor.

3 Web Site Hosting

Problem: Selecting the correct host or ISP for your Web site can be a confusing process. Many Web sites offer this service, but determining the best one for your particular needs can be somewhat complicated. Assume your Web site will sell a product. Compare several ISPs and select the one that will best meet your needs.

Instructions: Perform the following tasks:

1. Review the information and questions on pages DW 16–18 discussing the guidelines for acquiring active server space to host your Web site.

2. Start your browser. Open the Web Site Hosting Directory Web page shown in Figure I-15 (www. websitehostdirectory.com).

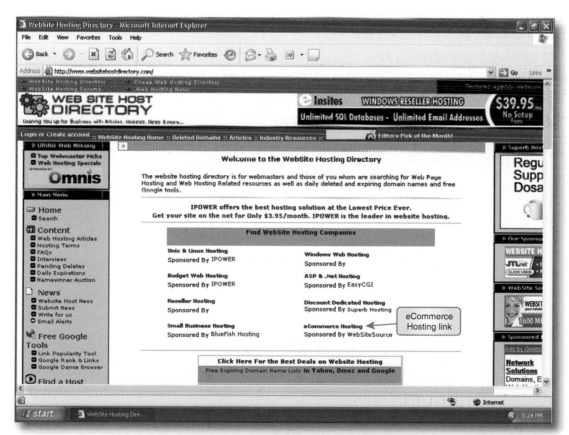

FIGURE I-15

3. Click the eCommerce Hosting link.

(continued)

In the Lab

Web Site Hosting *(continued)*

4. Click one of the host server links and review the information relating to the services offered by your selected ISP.

5. Start your word-processing program.

6. Read and answer the questions on pages DW 17–18. Use the information provided in the list of services offered by your selected ISP.

7. Write a short summary explaining why you would or would not select this ISP to host your Web site.

8. Save the document with the file name Lab I-3 Web Site Hosting.doc. If instructed to do so, print a copy of the document and submit it to your instructor.

Cases and Places

The difficulty of these case studies varies:
■ are the least difficult and ■■ are more difficult. The last exercise is a group exercise.

1 ■ Use a search engine such as Google (google.com) and research information about planning a Web site. Use your word-processing program and write a two-page summary of what you learned. Save the document as caseI-1.doc. Print a copy and hand it in or e-mail a copy to your instructor.

2 ■ Your goal is to create a personal Web site navigation map that contains three pages — the home page, a page about your favorite hobbies, and a page about places you like to visit. On a piece of paper, draw a navigation map for your proposed Web site. Write a sentence or two describing the type of structure you used and why you selected that structure.

3 ■■ Plug-ins are used on many Web sites. Start your browser and search the Web for plug-ins. Prepare a list of the plug-ins you found. Create a summary statement describing how and why you could use each plug-in in a Web site. Include the link where you can download each of the plug-ins.

4 ■■ Typography within a Web page is one of its more important elements. Start your browser and search for examples of Web sites that include what you consider appropriate typography and Web sites with inappropriate typography. Write a short summary of why you consider these to be appropriate and inappropriate. Copy and paste the Web site addresses into your document. Save the document as caseI-4.doc.

5 ■■ **Working Together** Each team member is to search the Internet for Web sites illustrating each of the Web site structures on page DW 12. Each team member will then use word-processing software to write a minimum of 100 words describing the Web sites and explaining why he or she thinks the structure used is appropriate or inappropriate for that particular Web site.

MACROMEDIA
Dreamweaver 8

Creating a Dreamweaver Web Page and Local Site

CASE PERSPECTIVE

Colorado native David Edwards worked with you last summer at a state environmental agency. Your job at the agency included Internet communications. Because you both love the outdoors, particularly Colorado's national parks and monuments, you became good friends. David visits several parks every year. During each visit, he discovers something new and exciting. David wants to share his knowledge and to provide a way to make Colorado residents and visitors aware of the uniqueness, beauty, and wildlife of the parks.

David knows the far-reaching capabilities of the Internet. He wants to use the Web to communicate to the public about Colorado's parks, but he has limited knowledge about Web design and development. David knows that your interest and experience with the Internet could assist him in this endeavor, and he asks for your help. You like the idea and tell him that you can create a Web site using Dreamweaver. You get together to define the Web site and to plan the index page. When you are finished creating the Colorado National Parks and Monuments Web page, you will show it to David for his feedback.

As you read through this project, you will learn how to use Dreamweaver 8 to define a local site, create a Web page, and display the Web page in a browser.

Creating a Dreamweaver Web Page and Local Site

Objectives

You will have mastered the material in this project when you can:

- Describe Dreamweaver and identify its key features
- Start Dreamweaver
- Describe the Dreamweaver window and workspace
- Define a local site
- Create and save a Web page
- Add a background image
- Open and close panels
- Display and describe the Property inspector
- Format and modify text elements on a Web page

- Define and insert a line break
- Change a Web page title
- Check spelling
- Preview a Web page in a Web browser
- Print a Web page
- Define Dreamweaver Help
- Quit Dreamweaver
- Open a new Web page

What Is Macromedia Dreamweaver 8?

Macromedia Dreamweaver 8 is a powerful Web page authoring and Web site management software program with an HTML editor that is used to design, code, and create professional-looking Web pages, Web sites, and Web applications. The visual-editing features of Dreamweaver allow you to create pages without writing a line of code. Dreamweaver provides many tools and features, including the following:

- **Automatic Web Page Creation** — Dreamweaver provides tools you can use to develop Web pages without having to spend hours writing HTML code. Dreamweaver automatically generates the HTML code necessary to publish your Web pages.
- **Web Site Management** — Dreamweaver enables you to view a site, including all local and remote files associated with the selected site. You can perform standard maintenance operations such as viewing, opening, and moving files; transferring files between local and remote sites; and designing your site navigation with the Site Map.

Standard Macromedia Web Authoring Tools — Dreamweaver includes a user interface that is consistent across all Macromedia authoring tools. This consistency enables easy integration with other Macromedia Web-related programs such as Macromedia Flash, Director, Shockwave, and ColdFusion.

Other key features include the integrated user interface, the integrated file explorer, panel management, database integration, and standards and accessibility support. Dreamweaver 8 is customizable and runs on many operating systems including Windows XP, Windows 2000, Windows NT, Mac OS X, and others.

Project One — Colorado Parks

To create documents similar to those you will encounter on the Web and in academic, business, and personal environments, you can use Dreamweaver to produce Web pages such as the Colorado National Parks and Monuments Web page shown in Figure 1-1. This Web page is the index page for the Colorado Parks Web site. This informational page provides interesting facts about Colorado's national parks and monuments. The page begins with a centered main heading, followed by two short informational paragraphs, then an introductory sentence for a bulleted list. The list contains three bulleted items. A concluding sentence, the author's name, and current date end the page. A background image is applied to the page.

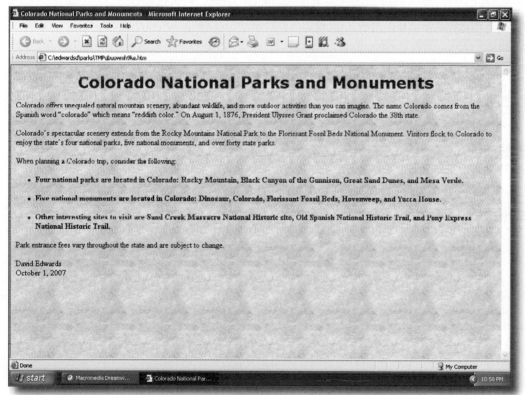

FIGURE 1-1

Starting Dreamweaver

Your **screen resolution** is the number of pixels in the width and height of your screen (width × height). A higher resolution results in a sharper image, but items appear smaller. Having a high screen resolution (1024 × 768) gives you more space — your computer can display more of a program or a Web page or more icons on your desktop.

If you are stepping through this project on a computer and you want your screen to agree with the Dreamweaver figures in this book, you should change your screen's resolution to 1024 × 768. The browser used to display the Web page figures is Internet Explorer. The browser text size is set to Medium.

Getting started in Dreamweaver is as easy as opening an existing HTML document or creating a new document. The Dreamweaver environment consists of toolbars, windows, objects, panels, inspectors, and tools you use to create your Web pages and to manage your Web site, which is a collection of Web pages. It is important to learn the basic concepts behind the Dreamweaver workspace and to understand how to choose options, use inspectors and panels, and set preferences that best fit your work style.

The first time you launch Dreamweaver 8 after the initial installation, a Workspace Setup dialog box is displayed with two options: Designer or Coder. This Workspace Setup choice is a one-time event. Programmers who work primarily with HTML and other languages generally select the Coder workspace. The Designer workspace contains a visual integrated workspace and is ideal for beginners and non-programmers. For the exercises in this book, select the Designer workspace.

Following the Workspace Setup choice, the Dreamweaver 8 program starts. The settings on your computer determine what is displayed. By default, the Start page is displayed each time you start Dreamweaver. The Start page's visual representation is a good tool for beginners, but more proficient Dreamweaver users generally disable this feature. You will disable the Start page at the end of this project. If you are opening Dreamweaver from a computer at your school, most likely the program is set up and ready to use.

To start Dreamweaver, Windows must be running. The following steps show how to start Dreamweaver, or you can ask your instructor how to start the program.

More About

Dreamweaver Features

For more information about Dreamweaver 8 features, visit the Dreamweaver 8 More About Web page (scsite.com/dw8/more.htm) and then click Dreamweaver 8 Features.

To Start Dreamweaver

1

• Click the Start button on the Windows taskbar, point to All Programs on the Start menu, point to Macromedia on the All Programs submenu, and then point to Macromedia Dreamweaver 8 on the Macromedia submenu.

The Start menu, All Programs submenu, and Macromedia submenu are displayed (Figure 1-2). Your Start menu will display different programs than those in Figure 1-2.

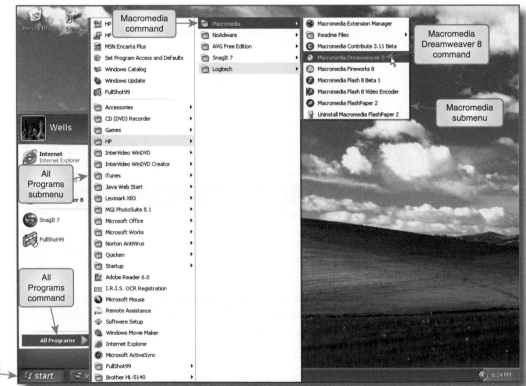

FIGURE 1-2

2
_____

• **Click Macromedia Dreamweaver 8.**

The Start page appears (Figure 1-3). You disable the Start page at the end of this project.

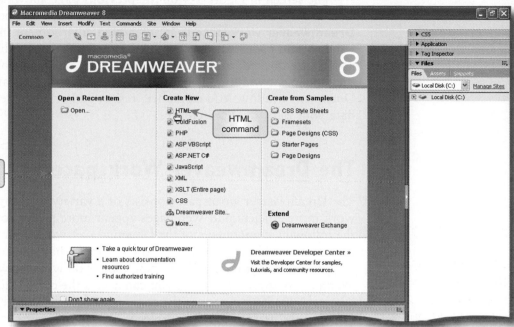

FIGURE 1-3

3
_____

• **Click HTML in the Create New column. If necessary, maximize the Dreamweaver window and the Document window by clicking the Maximize button in the upper-right corner of the windows.**

• **If the Insert bar does not display, click Window on the menu bar and then click Insert.**

The Start page closes, and the Dreamweaver workspace is displayed (Figure 1-4). The Dreamweaver workspace contains menu names, toolbars, and panel groups. The Windows taskbar displays the Macromedia Dreamweaver 8 button, indicating that Dreamweaver is running.

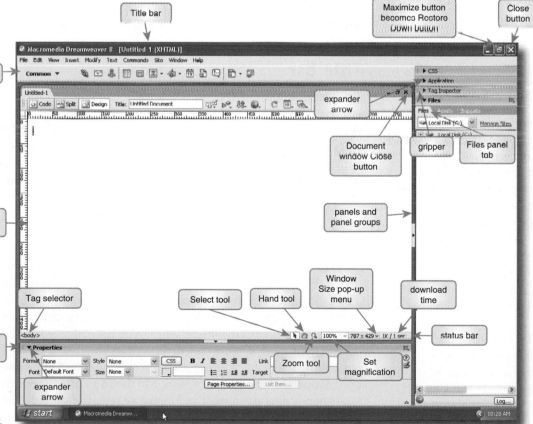

FIGURE 1-4

Other Ways

1. Double-click Dreamweaver icon on desktop

The screen in Figure 1-4 on the previous page shows a typical Dreamweaver workspace, with some of the more commonly used components displayed. The **Dreamweaver workspace** is an integrated environment in which the Document window and panels are incorporated into one larger application window. The panel groups are docked, or attached, on the right. The Insert bar is located at the top of the Document window, and the Property inspector is located at the bottom of the Document window. You can move, resize, and/or collapse the panels to accommodate your individual preferences.

The Dreamweaver Workspace

The Dreamweaver workspace consists of a variety of components to make your work more efficient and Web pages appear more professional. This section discusses the following components of the Dreamweaver workspace: title bar, Document window, panels and panel groups, status bar, menu bar, and toolbars.

As you learn to use each of these tools, you will discover some redundancy. For example, to apply a Font tag, you can access the command through the Property inspector, the Text menu, or the context menu. The different options accommodate various user preferences. The projects in this book present the more commonly used methods. The Other Ways boxes at the end of many of this book's step-by-step sequences describe additional methods to accomplish a task when they are available. As you become proficient working in the Dreamweaver environment, you will develop techniques for using the tools that best suit your personal preferences.

Title Bar

The **title bar** displays the application name, Macromedia Dreamweaver 8; in brackets, the Web page title; and, in parentheses, the file path and file name of the displayed Web page. In Figure 1-4, the title bar displays [Untitled-1 XHMTL]. Untitled-1 represents the file path and file name, and XHTML represents the coding. Following the file name, Dreamweaver displays an asterisk if you have made changes that have not yet been saved. After you give a Web page a title and save the document, the title bar reflects the changes by displaying the document path and title and removing the asterisk.

Document Window

The **Document window** displays the current document, or Web page, including text, tables, graphics, and other items. In Figure 1-4, the Document window is blank. The Document window is similar in appearance to the Internet Explorer or Netscape browser window. You work in the Document window in one of three views: **Design view**, the design environment where you assemble your Web page elements and design your page (Figure 1-4 displays Design view); **Code view**, which is a hand-coding environment for writing and editing code; or **Split view**, which allows you to see both Code view and Design view for the same document in a single window. When you open a new document in Dreamweaver, the default view is Design view. These views are discussed in detail in Project 2.

Panels and Panel Groups

Panel groups are sets of related panels docked together below one heading. Panels provide control over a wide range of Dreamweaver commands and functions. Each panel group can be expanded or collapsed, and can be docked or undocked with other panel groups. Panel groups also can be docked to the integrated Document window. This makes it easy to access the panels you need without cluttering your workspace. Panels within a panel group are displayed as tabs. Each panel is explained in detail as it is used in the projects throughout the book.

Some panels, such as the Property inspector and the Insert bar, are stand-alone panels. The **Insert bar** allows quick access for frequently used commands. It contains buttons for creating and inserting various types of objects—images, tables, layers, frames, and tags—into a document. As you insert each object, a piece of source code allows you to set and manipulate various attributes. The buttons on the Insert bar are organized into several categories, which you can switch through a pop-up menu on the left side of the Insert bar. Some categories also have buttons with pop-up menus. When you select an option from a pop-up menu, it becomes the default action for the button. Clicking the Insert bar's pop-up menu and selecting Forms, for example, provides quick access to the form tool and form objects. The default position for the Insert bar is at the top of the Document window (Figure 1-4 on page DW 37). When you start Dreamweaver, the category in which you were last working is displayed.

The **Property inspector** (Figure 1-4) displays settings for the selected object's properties or attributes. This panel is context sensitive, meaning it changes based on the selected object, which can include text, tables, images, and other objects. When Dreamweaver starts, the Property inspector is positioned at the bottom of the Document window and displays text properties if a Document window is open. Otherwise, the Property inspector is blank.

To expand or collapse a panel group, click the expander arrow to the left of the group's name; to undock and move a panel group, drag the gripper at the left edge of the group's title bar (Figure 1-4). To open panels, use the Window menu.

Status Bar

The **status bar** at the bottom of the Document window (Figure 1-4) provides additional information about the document you are creating. The status bar presents the following options:

- **Select tool**: Use the Select tool to return to default editing after using the Zoom or Hand tool.
- **Hand tool**: To pan a page after zooming, use the Hand tool to drag the page.
- **Zoom tool**: Available only in Design view. Use the Zoom tool to zoom in and out from a document to check the pixel accuracy of graphics or to better view the page.
- **Set magnification**: Use the Set magnification pop-up menu to change the view from 6% to 6400%; default is 100%.
- **Tag selector**: Displays the hierarchy of tags surrounding the current selection. Click any tag in the hierarchy to select that tag and all its contents.
- **Window Size**: Displays the Window size, which includes the window's current dimensions (in pixels) and the Window size pop-up menu.
- **Estimated document size and download time**: Displays the size and estimated download time of the current page. Dreamweaver 8 calculates the size based on the entire contents of the page, including all linked objects such as images and plug-ins.

Vertical Bar

A vertical bar separates the panel groups, and a horizontal bar separates the Property inspector from the Document window. Both bars contain an expander

More About

Panel Groups

To drag a floating (undocked) panel group without docking it, drag the panel group by the bar above its title bar. The panel group does not dock as long as it is not dragged by its gripper.

arrow. Clicking this arrow hides/displays the panel groups and the Property inspector (Figure 1-5). If your screen resolution is set to 800 × 600, a portion of the Property inspector does not display when the panel groups are expanded.

Menu Bar

The **menu bar** displays the Dreamweaver menu names (Figure 1-5). Each menu contains a list of commands you can use to perform tasks such as opening, saving, modifying, previewing, and inserting data into your Web page. When you point to a menu name on the menu bar, the area of the menu bar containing the name is highlighted.

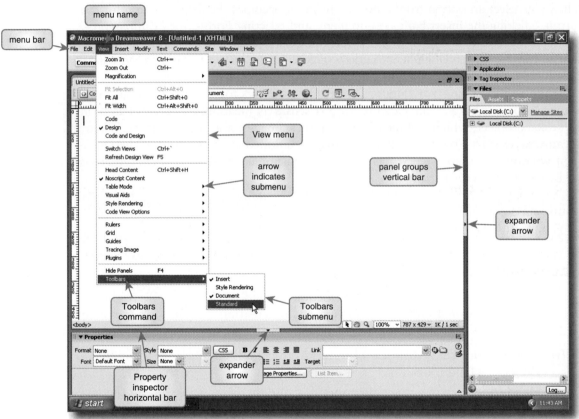

FIGURE 1-5

To display a menu, such as the View menu (Figure 1-5), click the menu name on the menu bar. If you point to a menu command that has an arrow at its right edge, a submenu displays another list of commands. Many menus display some commands that appear gray, or dimmed, instead of black, which indicates they are not available for the current selection.

Toolbars

Dreamweaver contains five toolbars: Document, Standard, Coding, Style Rendering, and Insert. You can choose to display or hide the toolbars by clicking View on the menu bar and then clicking Toolbars. If a toolbar name has a check mark next to it, it is displayed in the window. To hide the toolbar, click the name of the toolbar with the check mark, and it no longer displays. The Insert toolbar, more commonly referred to as the Insert bar, was discussed previously in this Project. The Coding toolbar displays in Code view only and is not available as an option on the Toolbars submenu when in Design view. Programmers and coders use this toolbar to modify and tweak source code.

The **Document toolbar** (Figure 1-6) is the default toolbar that displays in the Document window. It contains buttons that provide different views of the Document window (e.g., Code, Split, and Design) and some common operations, such as No Browser Check Errors, Validate Markup, File Management, Preview/Debug in Browser, Document Title, Refresh Design View, View Options, and Visual Aids. All View option commands also are available through the View menu.

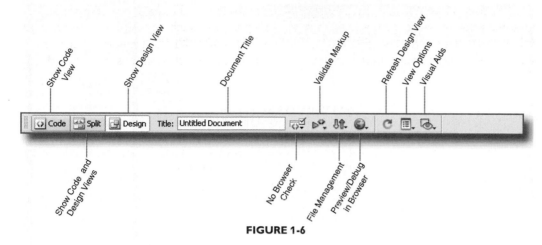

FIGURE 1-6

The **Standard toolbar** (Figure 1-7) contains buttons for common operations from the File and Edit menus: New, Open, Save, Save All, Print Code, Cut, Copy, Paste, Undo, and Redo. The Standard toolbar does not display by default in the Dreamweaver Document window when you first start Dreamweaver. You can display the Standard toolbar through the Toolbars command on the View menu, or by right-clicking a blank area on a toolbar and then clicking Standard on the context menu. Similar to other toolbars and panels, you can dock/undock and move the Standard toolbar, so it may be displayed in a different location on your screen.

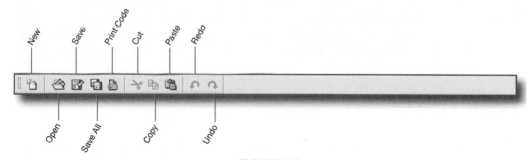

FIGURE 1-7

A new feature in Dreamweaver 8, the **Style Rendering toolbar**, provides options for designing for different media types, such as screen, print, handheld, projection, TTY (teletype), and television. The CSS (Cascading Style Sheets) Styles button works independently of the other six buttons and provides the option to disable/enable the displaying of CSS styles.

Opening and Closing Panels

The Dreamweaver workspace accommodates different work styles and levels of expertise. Through the workspace, you can open and close the panel groups and display/hide other Dreamweaver features as needed. To open a panel group, select and then click the name of a panel on the Window menu. Closing unused panels provides uncluttered workspace in the Document window. To close an individual panel group, click Close panel group on the Options pop-up menu accessed through the panel group's title bar (Figure 1-8). To expand/collapse a panel, click the panel's expander arrow at the left of the group's name.

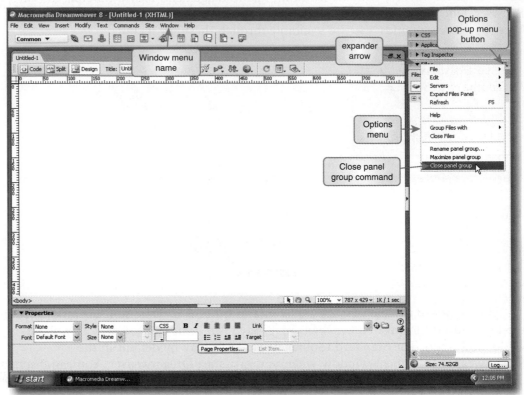

FIGURE 1-8

Opening and closing each panel individually is a time-consuming task. Dreamweaver provides a shortcut to accomplish this job quickly. The F4 key is a toggle key that opens and/or closes all panels and inspectors at one time. The following steps illustrate how to display the Standard toolbar and close and open the panels.

To Display the Standard Toolbar and To Close and Open Panels

1

• **Click View on the menu bar, point to Toolbars, and then point to Standard on the Toolbars submenu.**

The View menu is displayed and Standard is highlighted (Figure 1-9).

2

• **Click Standard.**

The Standard toolbar is displayed. Previous settings determine the location of the Standard toolbar. The Standard toolbar on your computer may be displayed below the Document toolbar or in another location.

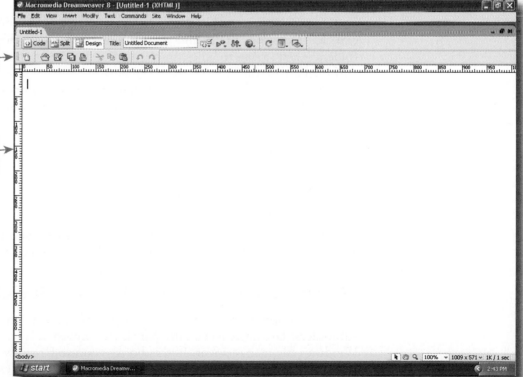

FIGURE 1-9

3

• **Press the F4 key.**

All the open panels and inspectors close, and the maximum workspace is available in the Document window (Figure 1-10).

4

• **Press the F4 key again to redisplay the panels.**

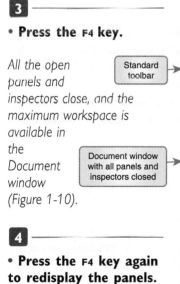

FIGURE 1-10

Defining a Local Site

Web design and Web site management are two important skills that a builder of Web sites must understand and apply. Dreamweaver 8 is a site creation and management tool. To use Dreamweaver efficiently, you first must define the local site. After defining the local site, you then publish to a remote site. Publishing to a remote site is discussed in Project 3 and Appendix C.

The general definition of a **site**, or Web site, is a set of linked documents with shared attributes, such as related topics, a similar design, or a shared purpose. In Dreamweaver, however, the term site can refer to any of the following:

- **Web site**: A set of pages on a server that are viewed through a Web browser by a visitor to the site.
- **Remote site**: Files on the server that make up a Web site, from the author's point of view rather than a visitor's point of view.
- **Local site**: Files on your local disk that correspond to the files on the remote site. You edit the files on your local disk, and then upload them to the remote site.
- **Dreamweaver site definition**: Set of defining characteristics for a local site, plus information on how the local site corresponds to a remote site.

All Dreamweaver Web sites begin with a local root folder. As you become familiar with Dreamweaver and complete the projects in this book, you will find references to a **local root folder**, a **root folder**, and **root**. These terms are interchangeable. This folder is no different from any other folder on your computer's hard drive or other storage media, except for the way in which Dreamweaver views it. When Dreamweaver looks for Web pages, links, images, and other files, the program defaults to the designated root folder. Any media within the Web site that are outside of the root folder will not display when the Web site is previewed in a Web browser. Within the root folder, you can create additional folders or subfolders to organize images and other objects. A **subfolder** (also called a **nested folder**) is a folder inside another folder.

Dreamweaver provides two options to define a site and create the hierarchy: You can create the root folder and any subfolders, or create the pages and then create the folders when saving the files. In this book, you create the root folder and subfolders and then create the Web pages.

One of Dreamweaver's more prominent organizational tools is the Files panel. Use the **Files panel** for standard file maintenance operations, such as the following:

- Creating files
- Viewing, opening, and moving files
- Creating folders
- Deleting items
- Managing a site

The Files panel enables you to view a site, including local, remote, and testing server files associated with a selected site. In this project, you view only the local site.

Creating the Local Root Folder and Subfolders

Several options are available to create and manage your local root folder and subfolders: Dreamweaver's Files panel, Dreamweaver's Site Definition feature, or Windows file management. In this book, you use Dreamweaver's Site Definition feature to create the local root folder and subfolders, the Files panel to manage and edit your files and folders, and Windows file management to download the data files.

To organize and create a Web site and understand how you access Web documents, you need to understand paths and folders. The term, path, sometimes is confusing for new users of the Web. It is, however, a simple concept: A **path** is the succession of folders that must be navigated to get from one folder to another. In the DOS world, folders are referred to as **directories**. These two terms often are used interchangeably.

A typical path structure has a **master folder**, usually called the root and designated by the symbol "\". This root folder contains within it all of the other subfolders or nested folders. Further, each subfolder may contain additional subfolders or nested folders. These folders contain the Web site files. One of the more commonly used subfolders contains the site's images.

Because many files are required for a Dreamweaver Web site, it is advisable to create the projects using another type of media rather than the floppy drive (A:). Steps in this project instruct you to create the local site on the C:\ drive, the computer's hard drive. It is suggested, however, that you check with your instructor to verify the location and path you will use to create and save your local Web site. Other options may include a Zip drive, USB drive, or a network drive.

For this book, you first create a local root folder using your last name and first initial. Examples in this book use David Edwards as the Web site author. Thus, David's local root folder is edwardsd. Next, for this project, you create a subfolder and name it parks. Finally, you create another subfolder within parks and name it images. All Colorado Parks related files and subfolders are stored within the parks folder. When you navigate through this folder hierarchy, you are navigating along the path. The path and folder within the Colorado Parks Web site are C:\edwardsd\parks\. The path to the images folder is C:\edwardsd\parks\images\. In all references to edwardsd, substitute your last name and first initial.

Using Site Definition to Create a Local Site

You create a site definition using Dreamweaver's Site Definition dialog box. Two options are available: Basic or Advanced. The Basic method, or **Site Definition Wizard**, guides you through site setup step by step and takes you through a series of six screens. In the Advanced method, all options are contained on one screen. The Advanced method is more efficient. Using this view, you set all the same basic information that the Site Wizard collects, plus additional options such as the following:

- **Refresh local file list:** Updates the site list whenever a new file is added to the site folder; checked by default
- **Enable cache:** Allocates memory to store frequently used site data; checked by default
- **Default images folder:** An optional feature to specify the location of images in the site
- **HTTP address:** Used to define the URL of a Web site and to verify absolute links

The two main categories in a site definition are **Local Info** (Local Information) and **Remote Info** (Remote Information). In this project, you create the local site definition using the Advanced method. The site definition is stored in the Windows registry and is not part of the site. If you use removable media to store your files and move to another computer, you must recreate the site definition on that computer. Remote site definition is discussed in Project 3.

After you have completed the Site definition, the hierarchy structure displays in Dreamweaver's Files panel. This hierarchy structure is similar to the Windows XP file organization. The Files panel provides a view of the devices and folders on your computer and shows how these devices and folders are organized. A small device icon or folder icon is displayed next to each object in the list. The device icon represents a device such as the Desktop or a disk drive, and the folder icon represents a folder. Many of these icons have a plus or minus sign next to them, which indicates whether the device or folder contains additional folders. The plus and minus signs are controls that you can click to expand or collapse the view of the file hierarchy. In the Files panel, the site folders and files appear in a different color than non-site folders and files so that you easily can distinguish between the two.

You define a local site by telling Dreamweaver where you plan to store local files. Use the Site Definition Advanced approach and the following steps to create a local Web site. The C:\ drive is used in the following exercise. If you are saving your sites at another location or on removable media, substitute that location for Local Disk C:\.

To Use Site Definition to Create a Local Web Site

1

• **Click Site on the menu bar and then point to New Site.**

The Site menu is displayed, and New Site is selected (Figure 1-11).

FIGURE 1-11

2

• **Click New Site.**

• **If necessary, click the Advanced tab. Verify that Local Info is selected in the Category column.**

The Site Definition dialog window is displayed, and the Advanced tab is selected. Unnamed Site 1 is highlighted in the Site name text box (Figure 1-12). A default path is displayed in the Local root folder. A different path may be displayed on your computer.

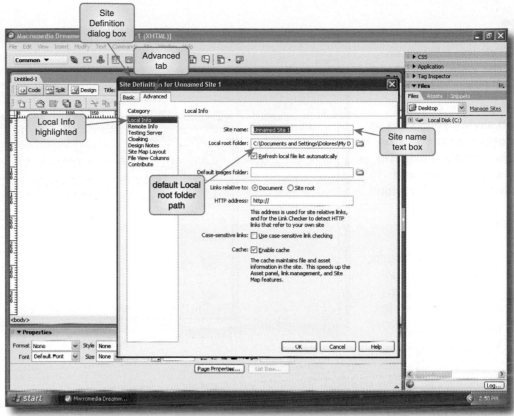

FIGURE 1-12

3

• **Type** Colorado Parks **as the site name.**

This name is for your reference only. It is not part of the path and is not visible to viewers of your site (Figure 1-13).

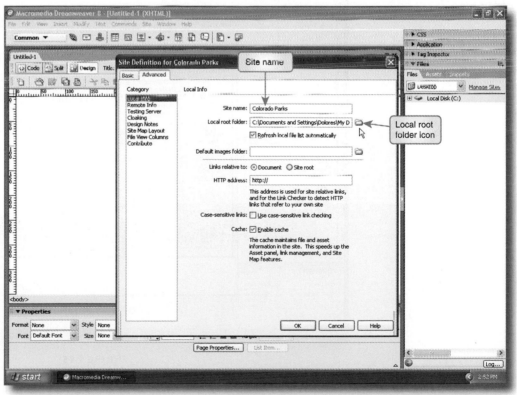

FIGURE 1-13

4

• **Click the folder icon to the right of the Local root folder text box.**

• **If you are creating and saving your sites at another location or on other media, navigate to that location and substitute the location for Local Disk (C): default path.**

The Choose local root folder for site dialog box is displayed. Local Disk (C): default path appears in the Select text box (Figure 1-14). Folders displayed in the Choose Local root folder for site dialog box will be different on your computer.

FIGURE 1-14

5

• **Click the Create New Folder icon.**

The New Folder text box is displayed (Figure 1-15). New Folder is selected.

FIGURE 1-15

6

• **Type your last name and first initial (with no spaces between your last name and initial) in the folder text box.**

• **Press the ENTER key to select the folder.**

In Figure 1-16, the author's name, edwardsd, is displayed in the folder's text box. On your computer, you are the author. Your last name and first initial will be displayed in the folder's text box (Figure 1-16).

FIGURE 1-16

7

• **Double-click the your name folder.**

The author's folder name is displayed in the Select text box (Figure 1-17). In Figure 1-17, edwardsd is displayed as the folder name. Your last name and first initial will be displayed on your computer screen.

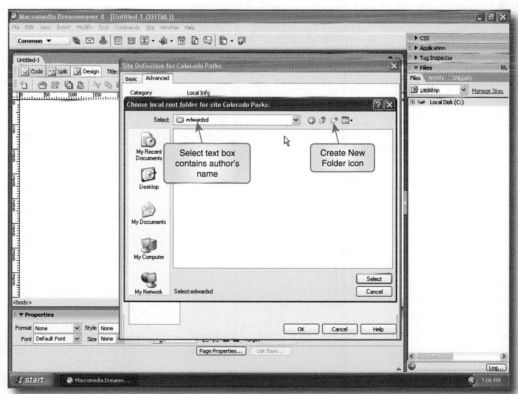

FIGURE 1-17

8

• **Click the Create New Folder icon.**

• **Type** parks **as the name of the new folder and then press the ENTER key.**

• **Double-click the parks folder name.**

The parks subfolder is created, and the folder name is displayed in the Select text box (Figure 1-18).

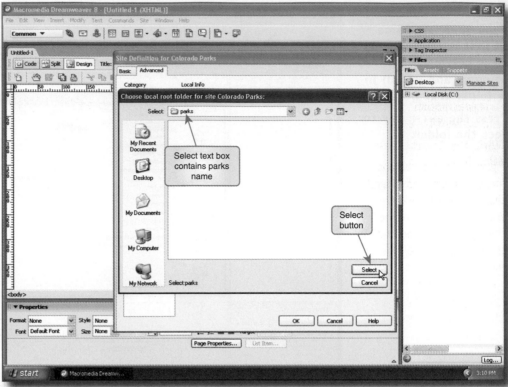

FIGURE 1-18

9

• **Click the Select button.**

The Site Definition dialog box is displayed, the Advanced tab is selected, and the Local root folder text box contains the C:\edwardsd\parks\ path (Figure 1-19). Your name will display instead of edwardsd on your computer screen.

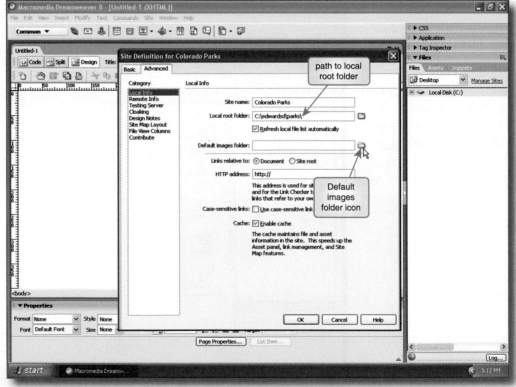

FIGURE 1-19

10

• Click the folder icon to the right of the Default images folder text box.

• Navigate to the your name\parks folder.

• Click the Create New Folder icon.

• Type images as the name of the new folder and then press the ENTER key. Double-click the images folder.

An images subfolder is created, and the folder name is displayed in the Select text box (Figure 1-20).

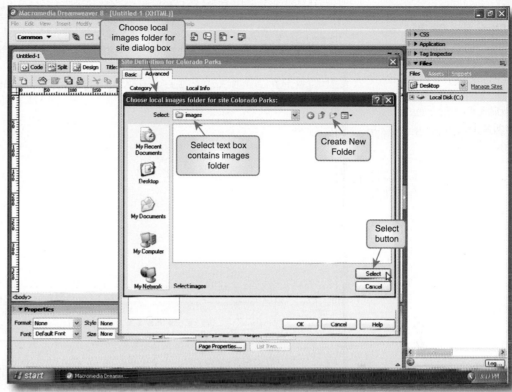

FIGURE 1-20

11

• Click the Select button.

• Verify that the Refresh local file list automatically and the Enable cache check boxes are selected in the Site Definition dialog box.

• Point to the OK button.

The Site Definition dialog box is displayed, and the path for the default images folder is displayed in the Default images folder text box (Figure 1-21).

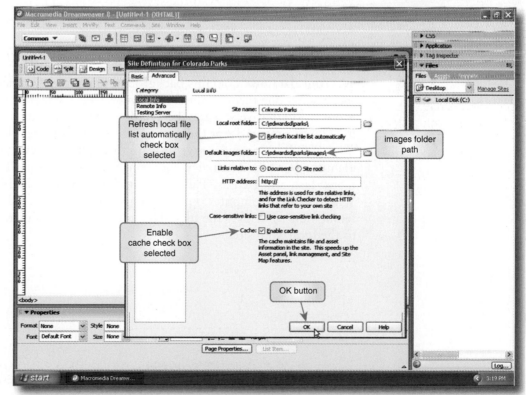

FIGURE 1-21

12

• **Click the OK button.**

The Dreamweaver workspace is displayed. The Colorado Parks Web site hierarchy is displayed in the Files panel (Figure 1-22).

FIGURE 1-22

Copying Data Files to the Colorado Parks Folder

Your data disk contains background images for Project 1. You can copy data files one by one through the Dreamweaver Files panel as you progress through this project. Alternatively, using the Windows My Computer option, you can establish the basic framework for the parks Web site by copying all the files and images at one time. Windows provides several ways through the View menu for you to arrange and identify your files when viewing them: Show in Groups, Thumbnails, Tiles, Filmstrip, Icons, List, and Details. The figures in this book use the List view when using the Windows My Computer option to copy the data files. Your computer may use a different view to display the files. The following steps illustrate how to copy data files to the local Web site.

To Copy Data Files to the Local Web Site

1

• **Click the Start button on the Windows taskbar and then click My Computer.**

The My Computer window is displayed (Figure 1-23).

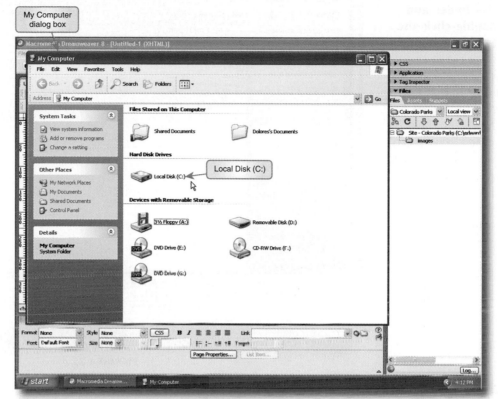

FIGURE 1-23

2

• **Double-click Local Disk (C:) and then navigate to the location of the data files for Project 1. If necessary, click View on the menu bar and then click List.**

If necessary, check with your instructor to verify the location of the data files. In Figure 1-24, the data files are located on Drive C:\. Your computer will display different folders than those in Figure 1-24.

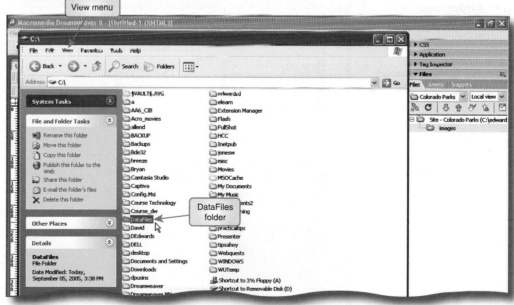

FIGURE 1-24

3

• **Double-click the DataFiles folder and then double-click the Proj01 folder.**

The Proj01 folder is selected, and the path to Proj01 is displayed in the Address text box (Figure 1-25). Figure 1-25 shows four additional folders. These folders are for the end-of-project exercises. You will have an opportunity to create these sites when you complete the exercises at the end of this project.

FIGURE 1-25

4

• **Double-click the parks folder and then double-click the images folder.**

The images folder is opened, and the path to the images folder is displayed in the Address text box (Figure 1-26).

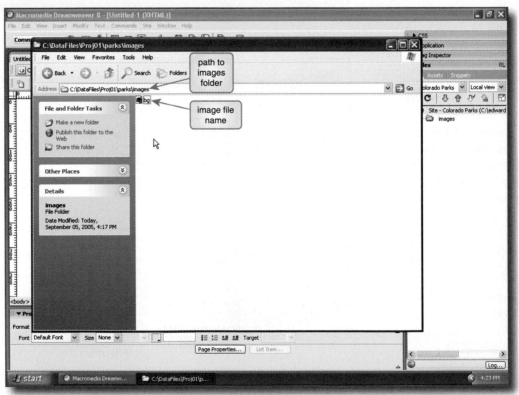

FIGURE 1-26

5

• **Right-click the bg image file.**

• **Point to the Copy command.**

The context menu is displayed (Figure 1-27). Your context menu most likely will display different commands.

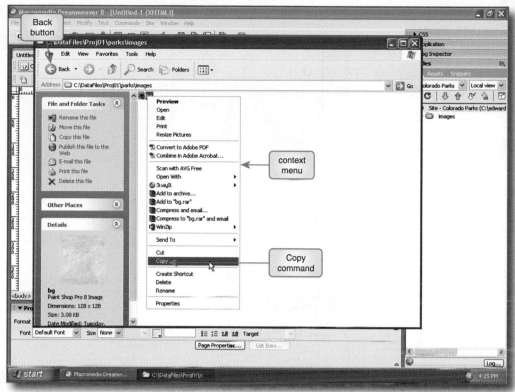

FIGURE 1-27

6

• **Click Copy and then click the My Computer Back button the number of times necessary to navigate to the your name folder.**

• **Double-click the your name folder, double-click the parks folder, and then double-click the images folder.**

• **Right-click anywhere in the open window to display the context menu.**

• **Point to the Paste command.**

The context menu is displayed and Paste is highlighted (Figure 1-28).

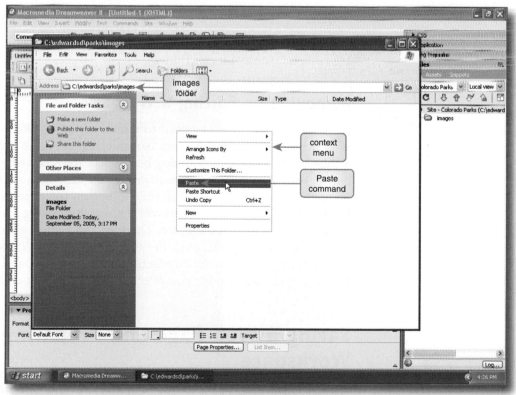

FIGURE 1-28

• Click the Paste command.

The bg image is pasted into the Colorado Parks Web site images folder (Figure 1-29).

• Click the images window Close button.

• Double-click the images folder.

The images window closes and Dreamweaver is displayed. The images folder is opened, and the bg file name is displayed in Dreamweaver's Files panel.

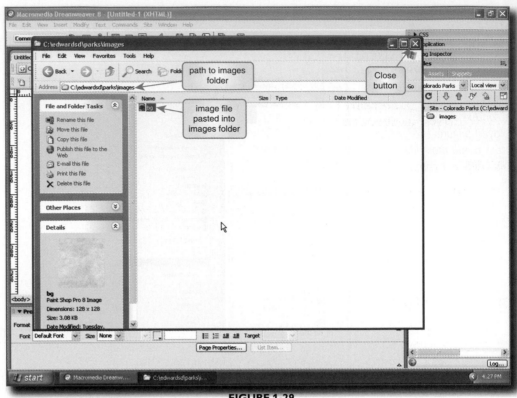

FIGURE 1-29

Your site definition and file hierarchy structure is complete, and your data files are copied into the images folder.

Removing or Editing a Web Site

On occasion, you may need to remove or edit a Web site. To remove or edit a Web site, click Site on the menu bar and then click the Manage Sites command. This displays the Manage Sites dialog box. Select the site name and then click the Remove button to remove the site. Dreamweaver displays a caution box providing you with an opportunity to cancel. Click the No button to cancel. Otherwise, click the Yes button, and Dreamweaver removes the site. Removing a site in Dreamweaver removes the settings for the site. The files and folders remain and must be deleted separately. To edit a site, click the site name and then click the Edit button. Dreamweaver displays the Site Definition dialog box, and from there, you can change any of the options you selected when you first created the site.

Saving a Web Page and Preparing Your Workspace

With the Colorado Parks site defined and the data file copied to the site, the next step is to save the untitled Dreamweaver document. When you defined the site, you designated C:\edwardsd\parks\ as the local root folder. You can copy and paste files into this folder using Windows XP, or use Dreamweaver's file management tools to copy and paste. You also can save a Dreamweaver document into this folder. Dreamweaver treats any item placed in the folder as part of the site.

When a document is saved as a Web page, the Web page also remains in the computer's memory and is displayed in the Document window. It is a good practice to save when you first open the document and then save regularly while you are working in Dreamweaver. By doing so, you protect yourself from losing all the work you have done since the last time you saved.

Rulers

Rulers help you measure, organize, and plan your layout. By default, they appear on the left and top borders of the page, marked in pixels, inches, or centimeters. They especially are helpful when working with tables or layers. Rulers, however, sometimes can be distracting when first learning how to use Dreamweaver. They easily are turned on and off through the View menu.

The Index Page

The **home page** is the starting point for the rest of your Web site. For most Web sites, the home page is named index. This name has special significance because most Web servers recognize index.htm (or index.html) as the default home page.

Dreamweaver comes with a number of default commands. These defaults are stored in 20 different categories in Dreamweaver's Preferences dialog box. Dreamweaver's default extension for new documents is .html. Although there is some debate about which extension to use — .htm or .html — most Web sites use .htm. You change the default through the Preferences dialog box. Therefore, when you save your document, Dreamweaver automatically appends the extension .htm to the file name. Documents with the .htm extension display in Web browsers.

The home page for your Colorado Parks Web site is named index.htm. The following steps show how to prepare your workspace by turning off the Rulers and changing the .html default extension to .htm. You then save the untitled document as index.htm in the parks local root folder. If the Rulers do not display in your Document window, omit Steps 1 and 2 on the next page.

To Hide the Rulers, Change the .htm Default, and Save a Document as a Web Page

1

• **Click View on the menu bar, point to Rulers, and then point to Show on the Rulers submenu.**

Dreamweaver displays the View menu and the Rulers submenu (Figure 1-30).

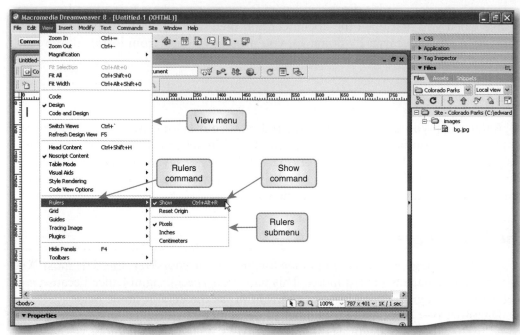

FIGURE 1-30

2

• **Click Show.**

The Rulers no longer display in the Dreamweaver workspace (Figure 1-31).

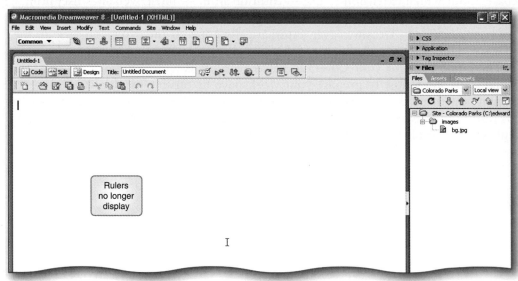

FIGURE 1-31

3

• **Click Edit on the menu bar and then click Preferences.**

The Preferences dialog box is displayed (Figure 1-32).

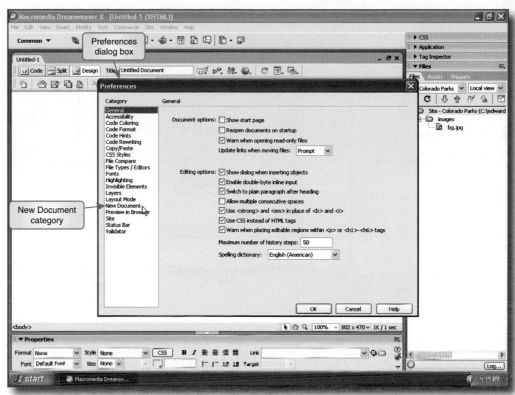

FIGURE 1-32

4

• **Click the New Document category, delete .html as the default extension, and then type** .htm **as the default.**

The default is changed to .htm (Figure 1-33).

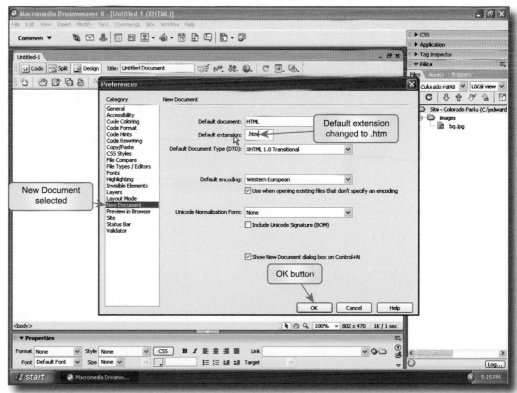

FIGURE 1-33

5

• **Click the OK button.**

The default is changed to .htm and the Document window is displayed.

6

• **Click the Save button on the Standard toolbar.**

The Save As dialog box is displayed (Figure 1-34). The parks folder name is displayed in the Save in text box. The default file name, Untitled-1, is selected in the File name text box.

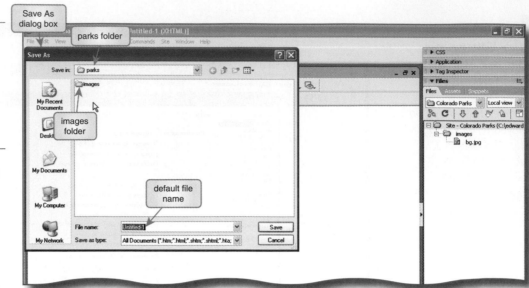

FIGURE 1-34

7

• **Type** index **as the file name.**

The index file name is displayed in the File name text box (Figure 1-35).

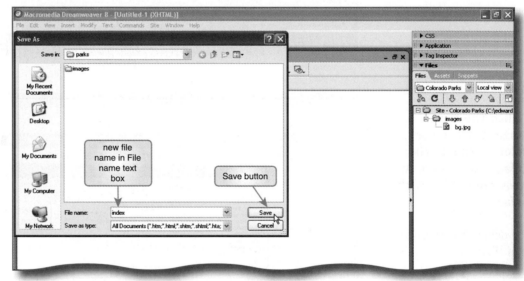

FIGURE 1-35

8

• **Click the Save button.**

The parks index page is saved in the parks local folder and is displayed in the Files panel (Figure 1-36). The path and file name (parks\index.htm) are displayed on the Dreamweaver title bar.

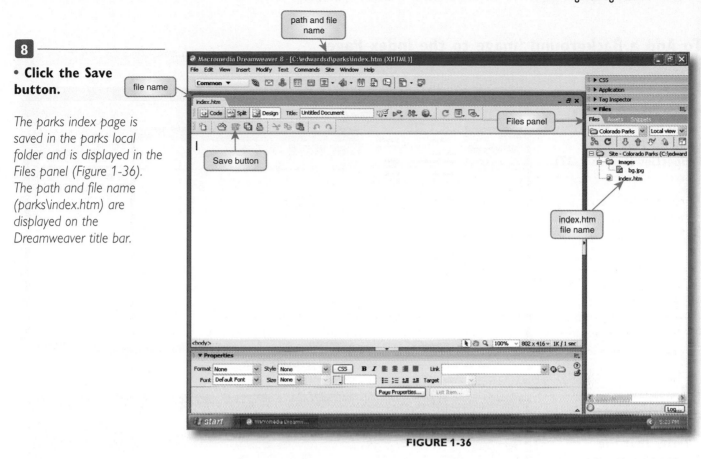

FIGURE 1-36

Web Page Backgrounds

Each new Web page you create displays with a default white or gray background and other default properties. You can modify these default properties using the **Page Properties** dialog box. The Page Properties dialog box lets you specify appearance, links, and many other aspects of page design. You can assign new page properties for each new page you create, and modify properties for existing pages. The page properties you select apply only to the active document.

You can change the default background and enhance your Web page, for example, by adding a background image and/or background color. If you use both a background image and a background color, the color appears while the image downloads, and then the image covers the color. Additionally, Dreamweaver provides a series of Web-safe color schemes, accessed through the Commands menu. In this project, you add a background image to the Web page.

Adding a Background Image

When you copied the data files earlier in this project, you copied an image file that will be the background for the Colorado Parks Web site pages. You use a background image to add texture and interesting color to a Web page. Use background images cautiously, however. Web page images displayed on top of a busy background image may not mix well, and text may be difficult to read. Images and image formats are discussed in more detail in Project 2.

The following steps illustrate how to use the Page Properties dialog box to add a background image to the home page.

To Add a Background Image to the Index Page

1

• **Click Modify on the menu bar and then point to Page Properties (Figure 1-37).**

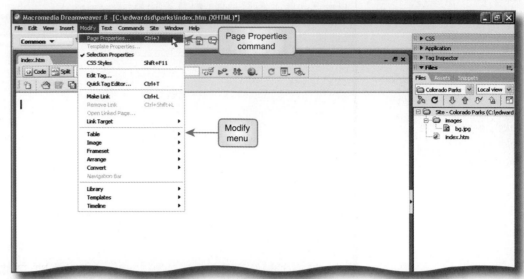

FIGURE 1-37

2

• **Click Page Properties.**

• **Verify that the Appearance category is selected.**

The Page Properties dialog box is displayed, and the Appearance category is selected (Figure 1-38).

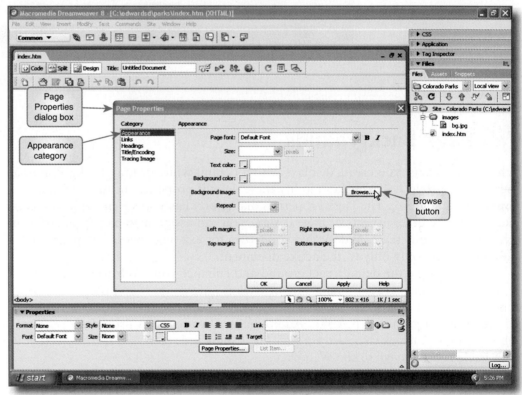

FIGURE 1-38

3

• **Click the Browse button and then click the images folder.**

Dreamweaver displays the Select Image Source dialog box (Figure 1-39). The parks folder name is displayed in the Look in text box, and the images folder is selected.

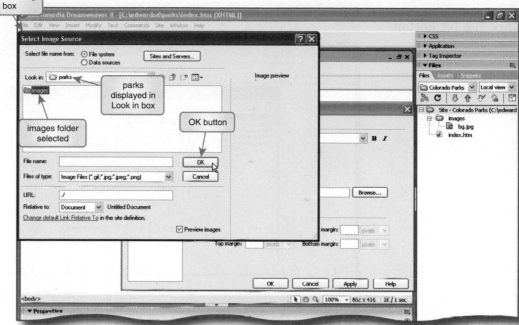

FIGURE 1-39

4

• **Click the OK button.**

• **Click the bg file.**

• **If necessary, click the Preview images check box to select it.**

The images folder is opened and displayed in the Look in text box. The file name, bg, is displayed in the File name text box. A preview of the image is displayed in the Image preview area. The dimensions of the image, type of image, file size, and download time are listed below the image (Figure 1-40).

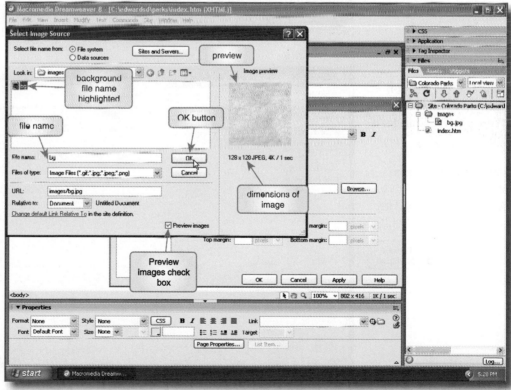

FIGURE 1-40

5

• **Click the OK button in the Select Image Source dialog box and then point to the OK button in the Page Properties dialog box.**

The Page Properties dialog box is displayed with the folder and file name in the Background image text box (Figure 1-41).

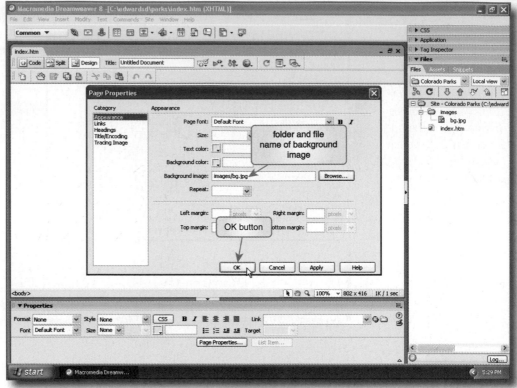

FIGURE 1-41

6

• **Click the OK button and then click the Save button on the Standard toolbar.**

The background image is applied to the Colorado Parks page, and the updated page is saved (Figure 1-42).

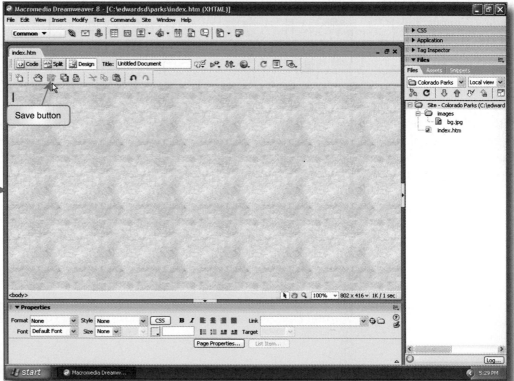

FIGURE 1-42

Other Ways

1. Right-click Document window, click Page Properties on shortcut menu
2. Click Page Properties button on Property inspector

Adding Text to a Web Page

In Dreamweaver, you can create a Web page in several ways: (1) you can type a new document; (2) you can open an existing HTML document, even if it was not created in Dreamweaver; (3) you can copy and paste text; and (4) you can import a Word document.

In this project, you create the index page for the Colorado Parks Web page by typing the text in the Document window. Entering text into a Dreamweaver document is similar to typing text in a word-processing document. You can position the insertion point at the top left of the Document window or within another object, such as a table cell. Pressing the ENTER key creates a new paragraph and inserts a blank line. Web browsers automatically insert a blank line of space between paragraphs. To start a new single line without a blank line between lines of text requires a **line break**. You can insert a line break by holding down the SHIFT key and then pressing the ENTER key or by clicking the Line Break command on the Insert HTML Special Characters submenu.

If you type a wrong letter and notice the error before pressing the ENTER key, press the BACKSPACE key to erase all the characters back to and including the one that is incorrect. If you mistakenly press the ENTER key and then discover the error, simply press the BACKSPACE key to return the insertion point to the previous line. Clicking the **Undo** button on the Standard toolbar reverses the most recent actions. The **Redo** button reverses the last undo action. The Undo and Redo commands also are accessible on the Edit menu.

Organizing Your Workspace

To organize your workspace, you hide the panel groups and collapse the lower portion of the Property inspector. This gives you additional workspace in the Dreamweaver Document window. The following steps show how to organize your workspace by hiding the panel groups.

To Hide the Panel Groups

1

• **Click the expander arrow on the panel groups vertical bar.**

• **Click the Property inspector expander arrow.**

The panel group is hidden, and the Property inspector is collapsed (Figure 1-43).

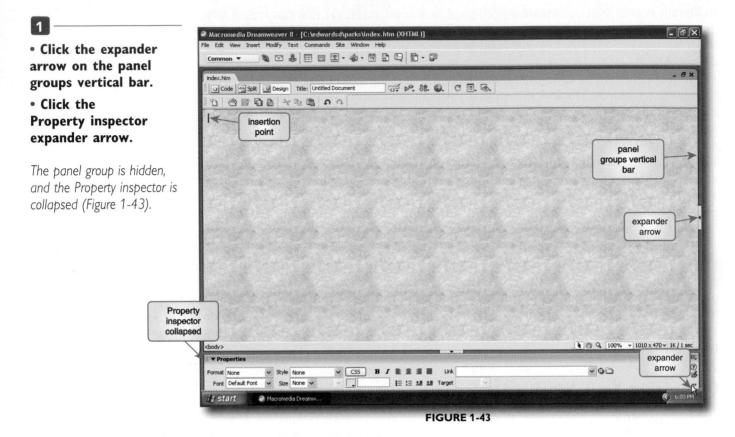

FIGURE 1-43

Adding Text

Table 1-1 includes the text for the Colorado Parks Web page. After typing the sections of the document, you will press the ENTER key to insert a blank line.

Table 1-1 Discovering Scenic Colorado Web Page Text

SECTION	HEADING, PART 1, AND PART 2	SECTION	PART 3, ITEMS FOR BULLETED LIST, AND CLOSING
Heading	Colorado National Parks and Monuments	Part 3	When planning a Colorado trip, consider the following:
Part 1	Colorado offers unequaled natural mountain scenery, abundant wildlife, and more outdoor activities than you can imagine. The name Colorado comes from the Spanish word "colorado" which means "reddish color." On August 1, 1876, President Ulysses Grant proclaimed Colorado the 38th state.	Items list	Four national parks are located in Colorado: Rocky Mountain, Black Canyon of the Gunnison, Great Sand Dunes, and Mesa Verde. \<enter\> Five national monuments are located in Colorado: Dinosaur, Colorado, Florissant Fossil Beds, Hovenweep, and Yucca House. \<enter\> Other interesting sites to visit are Sand Creek Massacre National Historic site, Old Spanish National Historic Trail, and Pony Express National Historic Trail. \<enter\>
Part 2	Colorado's spectacular scenery extends from the Rocky Mountains National Park to the Florissant Fossil Beds National Monument. Visitors flock to Colorado to enjoy the state's four national parks, five national monuments, and over forty state parks.	Closing	Park entrance fees vary throughout the state and are subject to change

The following steps show how to add text to the Document window and insert blank lines between sections of text.

To Add Text

1

• **Type the heading** Colorado National Parks and Monuments **as shown in Table 1-1, and then press the ENTER key.**

The heading is entered in the Document window (Figure 1-44). Pressing the ENTER key creates a new paragraph.

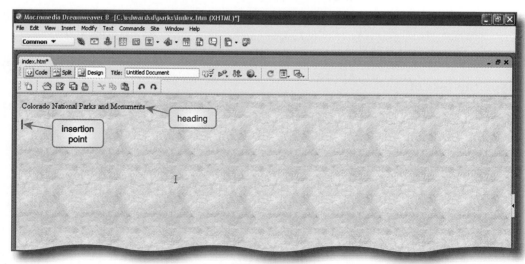

FIGURE 1-44

2

• **Type the text of Part 1 as shown in Table 1-1 on page DW 67, and then press the ENTER key.**

The introductory paragraph is entered (Figure 1-45). Pressing the ENTER key creates a new paragraph.

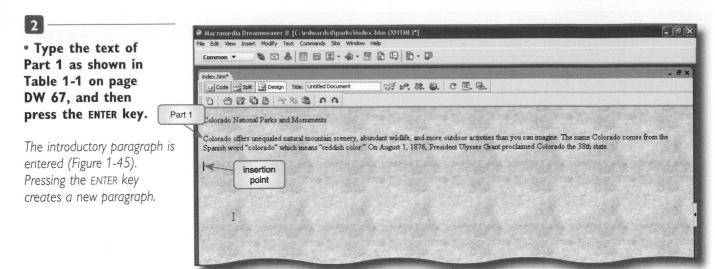

FIGURE 1-45

3

• **Type the text of Part 2 as shown in Table 1-1, and then press the ENTER key.**

The second paragraph is entered (Figure 1-46).

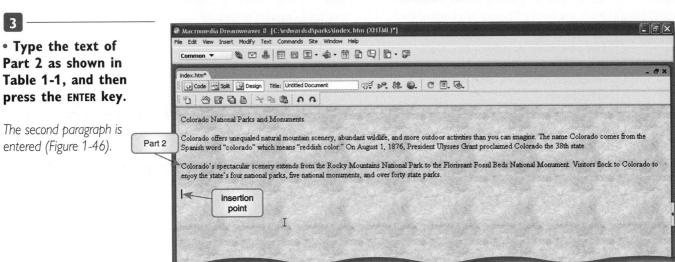

FIGURE 1-46

4

• **Type the text of Part 3 as shown in Table 1-1, and then press the ENTER key.**

The third paragraph is entered (Figure 1-47).

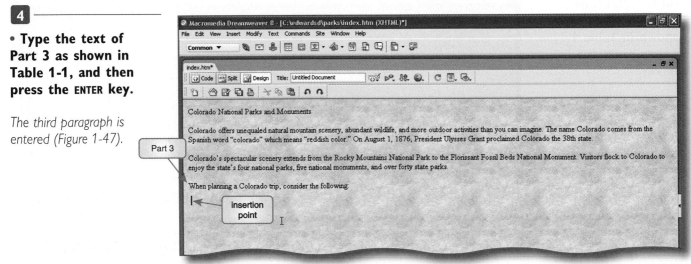

FIGURE 1-47

5

• **Type the three items for the bulleted list as shown in Table 1-1 on page DW 67. Press the ENTER key after each entry.**

The items for the bulleted list are entered (Figure 1-48). Later in this project, you will format the list so it becomes a bulleted list.

Items list

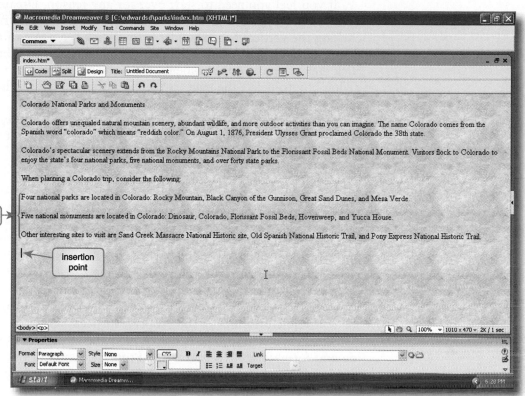

insertion point

FIGURE 1-48

6

• **Type the closing paragraph shown in Table 1-1, and then press the ENTER key.**

• **Click the Save button on the Standard toolbar.**

The paragraph is entered (Figure 1-49).

Closing

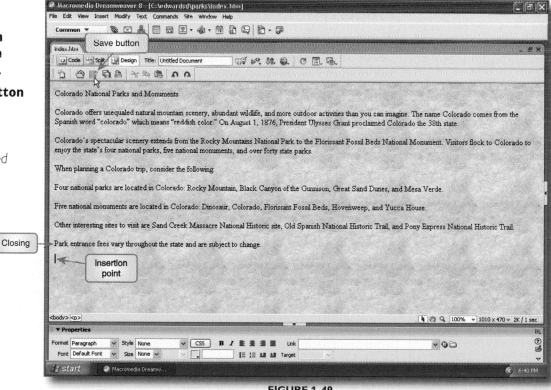

Save button

insertion point

FIGURE 1-49

If you feel you need to start over for any reason, Dreamweaver makes it easy to delete a Web page or other file. Save and close the page, display the panel groups by clicking the vertical bar expander arrow, click the name of the page you want to delete, right-click to display the context menu, point to Edit, and then point to and click Delete on the Edit submenu. Click the Yes button in the Dreamweaver caution dialog box to delete the page or the No button to cancel the action. You also can select a file and press the DELETE key.

Dreamweaver will display a warning dialog box. If files are linked to other files, information will be displayed indicating how to update the links. To delete the file, click Yes in the dialog warning box or click NO to cancel.

Formatting Text

The next step is to format the text on your Web page. **Formatting** means to apply different fonts, change heading styles, insert special characters, and insert other such elements that enhance the appearance of the Web page. Dreamweaver provides three options for formatting text: the Text menu, the Insert bar Text category, and the Property inspector. To format the text for the Colorado Parks index page, you use the text-related features of the Property inspector.

The Property inspector is one of the panels you will use most often when creating and formatting Web pages. The Property inspector initially displays the more commonly used attributes, or properties, of the selected object. The object can be a table, text, an image, or some other item. The Property inspector is context sensitive, so options within the Property inspector change relative to the selected object.

Property Inspector Features

Divided into two sections, the Property inspector lets you see the current properties of an object and allows you to alter or edit them. You can click the expander arrow in the lower-right corner of the Property inspector to collapse the Property inspector to show only the more commonly used properties for the selected element or to expand the Property inspector to show more options. Some objects, such as text, do not contain additional properties within the expanded panel (Figure 1-50 on DW 71). The question mark icon opens the Help window.

Collapsing/Hiding the Property Inspector

Having panels such as the Property inspector display in the Dreamweaver window requires considerable window space. If you are finished working with a panel, it generally is better to collapse it, hide it, or close it. **Collapsing** it leaves the title bar in the window, which allows you to expand it easily by clicking the expander arrow instead of using the Properties command on the Window menu. Pressing CTRL+F3 also collapses/expands the Property inspector. **Hiding** it hides the panel and the title bar. To hide the Property inspector and the Property inspector title bar, click the expander arrow on the horizontal bar. **Closing** it removes the Property inspector from the Document window. To close the Property inspector, display the context menu by right-clicking on the Properties title bar, and then selecting the Close panel group command—or click the Options menu button and select the Close panel group command from the pop-up menu.

By default, the Property inspector displays the properties for text on a blank document. Most changes you make to properties are applied immediately in the Document window. For some properties, however, changes are not applied until you

Q: When a change is made in the Property inspector, when is the change applied?

A: Most changes are applied immediately. You can confirm that changes are applied, however, by clicking the TAB or ENTER key.

click outside the property-editing text fields, press the ENTER key, or press the TAB key to switch to another property. The following section describes the text-related features of the Property inspector (Figure 1-50 and Figure 1-51).

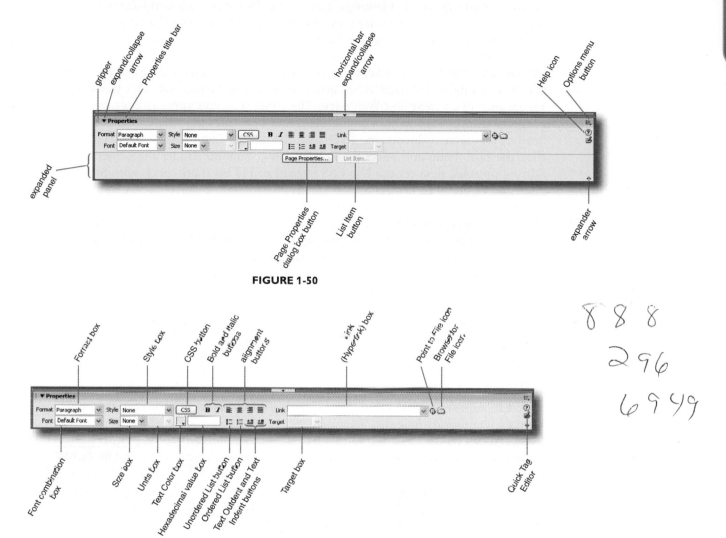

FIGURE 1-50

FIGURE 1-51

FORMAT The **Format box** allows you to apply a Paragraph, Heading, or Preformatted style to the text. Clicking the Format box arrow displays a pop-up menu from which you can select a style.

The **Paragraph style** is the normal default style for text on a Web page. **Paragraph formatting** is the process of changing the appearance of text. **Heading styles** are used to create divisions and separate one segment of text from another. These formats are displayed based on how different browsers interpret the tags, offering little consistency and control over layout and appearance. When you apply a heading tag to a paragraph, Dreamweaver automatically adds the next line of text as a standard paragraph. You can use the **Preformatted style** when you do not want a Web browser to change the line of text in any way.

FONT The **Font combination** box applies the selected font combination to the text and determines how a browser displays text on your Web page. The browser uses the first font in the combination that is installed on the user's system. If none of the fonts in the combination are installed, the browser displays the text as specified by the user's browser preferences. Most font faces in common usage on the Web are serif, sans-serif, or monospace fonts. The default font used on most Web pages is Times (also called Times New Roman or New Times), which is a serif font. The most commonly used sans-serif fonts are Arial, Helvetica, Geneva, and Verdana, while the most commonly used monospace font is Courier (also called Courier New). Use the Font combination pop-up menu to apply a font combination.

STYLE By default, Dreamweaver uses Cascading Style Sheets (CSS) styles to format text. Cascading Style Sheets (CSS) are a collection of formatting rules that control the appearance of content in a Web page. The styles that you apply to text using the Property inspector or menu commands create CSS rules that are embedded in the head of the current document. To change the default from CSS tags to HTML tags, click the Edit menu and select the Preferences command. Under the General category, Editing options, deselect the Use CSS instead of HTML tags check box. Styles are discussed in detail in Project 5.

SIZE The **Text Size box** provides options that allow you to apply a font size to a single character or to an entire page of text. Font sizes in HTML and XHTML range from 1 through 7, with size 7 being the largest. The default font size, or **BASEFONT**, is 3, which equates to 12 points in a word-processing document. The **UNITS** box is activated when a specific size is selected.

TEXT COLOR When you create a new document in Dreamweaver, the default text color is black. The **Text Color** box contains palettes of colors available on the color picker that you can apply to emphasize, differentiate, and highlight topics. To display the text in a selected Web-safe color, click the Text Color box to access the different methods of selecting preset colors or creating custom ones. Colors also are represented by a hexadecimal value (for example, #FF0000) in the adjacent text field.

BOLD AND ITALIC The **Bold button** and the **Italic button** allow you to format text using these two font styles in the Property inspector. These are the two more commonly used styles. Dreamweaver also supports a variety of other font styles, which are available through the Text menu. To view these other styles, click Text on the menu bar and then point to Style. The Style submenu contains a list of additional styles, such as Underline, Strikethrough, and Teletype.

ALIGN LEFT, ALIGN CENTER, ALIGN RIGHT, AND JUSTIFY In Dreamweaver, the default alignment for text is left alignment. To change the default alignment, select the text you want to align or simply position the mouse pointer at the beginning of the text. Click an alignment button: Align Center, Align Right, or Justify. You can align and center complete blocks of text, but you cannot align or center part of a heading or part of a paragraph.

LINK The **Link (Hyperlink) box** allows you to make selected text or other objects a hyperlink to a specified URL or Web page. To select the URL or Web page, you can (a) click the Point to File or Browse for File icon to the right of the Link box to browse to a page in your Web site and select the file name, (b) type the URL, or (c) drag a file from the Files panel into the Link box. Links are covered in detail in Project 2.

TARGET In the **Target pop-up menu box**, you specify the frame or window in which the linked page should load. If you are using frames, the names of all the frames in the current document are displayed in the list. If the specified frame does not exist when the current document is opened in a browser, the linked page loads in a new window with the name you specified. Once this window exists, other files can be targeted to it.

UNORDERED LIST Web developers often use a list to structure a page. An unordered list turns the selected paragraph or heading into an item in a bulleted list. If no text is selected before the **Unordered List button** is clicked, a new bulleted list is started.

ORDERED LIST An ordered list is similar to an unordered list. This type of list, however, turns the selected paragraph or heading into an item in a numbered list. If no text is selected before the **Ordered List button** is clicked, a new numbered list is started.

INDENT AND OUTDENT To set off a block quote, you can use the Indent feature. The **Text Indent button** will indent a line or a paragraph from both margins. In XHTML and HTML, this is the blockquote tag. The **Text Outdent button** removes the indentation from the selected text by removing the blockquote tag. In a list, indenting creates a nested list, and removing the indentation unnests the list. A **nested list** is one list inside another list and is not the same as the block quote created by the Indent feature.

PAGE PROPERTIES Clicking the Page Properties button opens the Page Properties dialog box.

LIST ITEM Clicking the List Items button opens the List Properties dialog box. This button appears dimmed until an existing list is created and the insertion point is contained within the list.

Applying Property Inspector Text-Related Features

The text for your Web page displays in the Document window. The next step in creating your Web page is to format this text. You use commands from the Property inspector to format the text.

Within Dreamweaver, you can format text before you type, or you can apply new formats after you type. If you have used word-processing software, you will find many of the Dreamweaver formatting commands similar to the commands within a word-processing program. At this point, your Web page contains only text, so the Property inspector displays attributes related to text.

To set block formatting, such as formatting a heading or an unordered list, position the insertion point in the line or paragraph and then format the text. To set character formatting, such as choosing a font or font size, however, you must first select the character, word, or words.

Text Headings

Just as in a word-processing document, designers use the heading structure in a Web page to set apart document or section titles. The six levels of HTML headings are Heading 1 through Heading 6. **Heading 1 <h1>** produces the largest text and **Heading 6 <h6>** the smallest. By default, browsers will display the six heading levels in the same font, with the point size decreasing as the importance of the heading decreases. The following steps show how to format the heading.

More About

The Property Inspector

The Property inspector initially displays the most commonly used properties of the selected object. Click the expander arrow in the lower-right corner of the Property inspector to see more of the object's properties.

More About

Text Size

You can set the size of the text in your Web page, but viewers of your Web page also can change the size through their browser. When creating a page, use the font size that looks right for the page you are creating.

To Format Text with Heading 1

1

• If necessary, scroll up and then position the insertion point anywhere in the heading text, Colorado National Parks and Monuments (Figure 1-52).

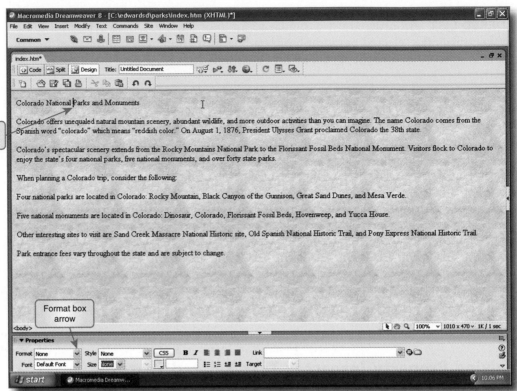

FIGURE 1-52

2

• Click the Format box arrow in the Property inspector and then point to Heading 1.

The Format pop-up menu is displayed with a list of formatting styles. Heading 1 is selected in the list (Figure 1-53).

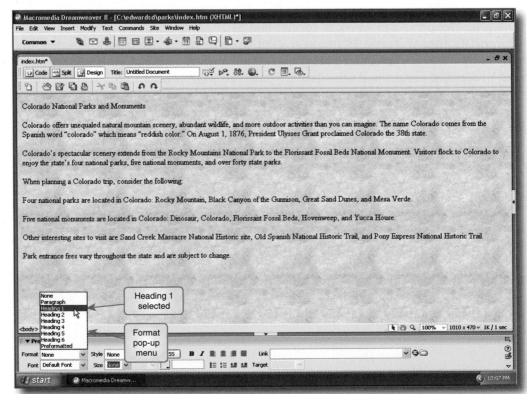

FIGURE 1-53

3

• **Click Heading 1.**

The Heading 1 style is applied to the Colorado National Parks and Monuments heading (Figure 1-54). The <h1> HTML tag is displayed in the Tag selector.

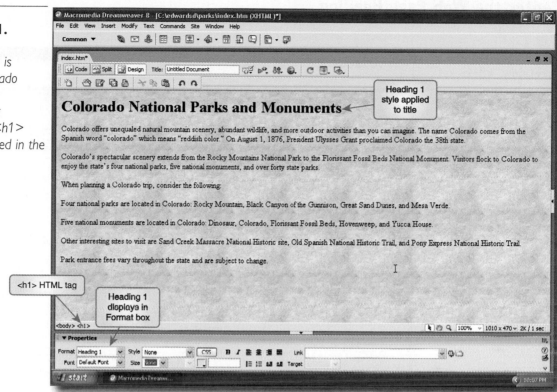

FIGURE 1-54

Centering Text

Using the **Align Center button** in the Property inspector allows you to center text. This button is very similar to the Center button in a word-processing program. To center a single line or a paragraph, position the mouse pointer anywhere in the line or paragraph, and then click the button to center the text. You do not need to select a single line or single paragraph to center it. To center more than one paragraph at a time, however, you must select all paragraphs. The following step illustrates how to center the heading.

Other Ways

1. On Text menu point to Paragraph Format, click Heading 1 on Paragraph Format submenu
2. Right click selected text, point to Paragraph Format on context menu, click Heading 1 on Paragraph Format submenu

To Center the Web Page Heading

1

• **If necessary, click anywhere in the heading, Colorado National Parks and Monuments. Click the Align Center button in the Property inspector.**

The heading, Colorado National Parks and Monuments, is centered (Figure 1-55).

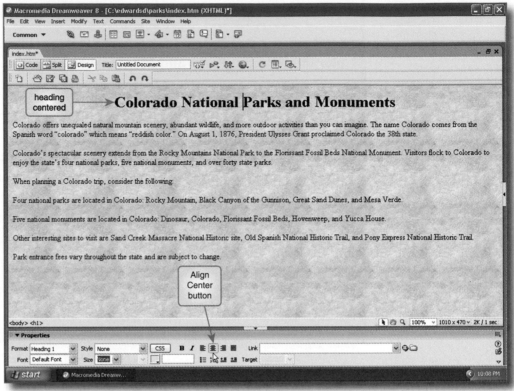

FIGURE 1-55

Text is one of the more important elements of most Web pages. How the text displays on a Web page can impact the overall appearance of the page. Using the appropriate font type can enhance and entice viewers to browse your Web site.

Specifying Font Types

Type is important because it attracts attention, sets the style and tone of a Web page, influences how readers interpret the words, and defines the feeling of the page. The **font type** refers to the basic design of the lettering. Several methods are used to classify fonts. The most common way is to place them in different families based on shared characteristics. The five basic font type families are:

1. Serif, such as Times or Times New Roman
2. Sans-serif, such as Helvetica and Arial
3. Monospace, such as Courier
4. Cursive, such as Brush Script
5. Decorative and fantasy

Two general categories of typefaces are serif and sans-serif. **Sans-serif** typefaces are composed of simple lines, whereas **serif** typefaces use small decorative marks to embellish characters and make them easier to read. Helvetica and Arial are sans-serif types, and Times New Roman is a serif type. A **monospace** font, such as Courier, is one in which every character takes up the same amount of horizontal space. **Cursive**

Q: Can I add a font to the Font list in the Property inspector?

A: Yes—Click Edit Font List in the Font pop-up menu. In the Edit Font List dialog box, select the font(s) from the Available fonts list, and add them to the Chosen fonts box.

font styles emulate handwritten letterforms. **Decorative and fantasy** is a family for fonts that do not fit any of the other families.

Most Web pages use only the first three families. Dreamweaver provides a font combination feature available in the Property inspector. **Font combinations** determine how a browser displays your Web page's text. In the Property inspector, you can select one of six font combinations. A browser looks for the first font in the combination on the user's computer, then the second, and then the third. If none of the fonts in the combination is installed on the user's computer, the browser displays the text as specified by the user's browser preferences.

As discussed earlier in this lesson, Dreamweaver uses Cascading Style Sheets (CSS) styles to format text. The commands that you apply to text using the Property inspector or menu options create CSS rules which are embedded in the head of the current document. CSS styles provide you with greater flexibility and control over the appearance of your page, from the precise positioning of layout to specific fonts and text styles. When you change the font type in the following steps, Dreamweaver automatically creates a style and names it Style 1. The next style is named Style 2 and so on. If you want to apply the same attributes to other text, select the text and then select the style from the Style pop-up menu.

The following steps show how to change the font type.

More About

Formatting Text

Research shows that people read on-screen text differently than they read the printed word. They are more apt to scan and look for the important concepts. Many changes in formatting could make a site confusing.

To Change the Font Type

1

• **Click to the left of the heading, Colorado National Parks and Monuments, and then drag through the entire heading.**

The heading is selected (Figure 1-56).

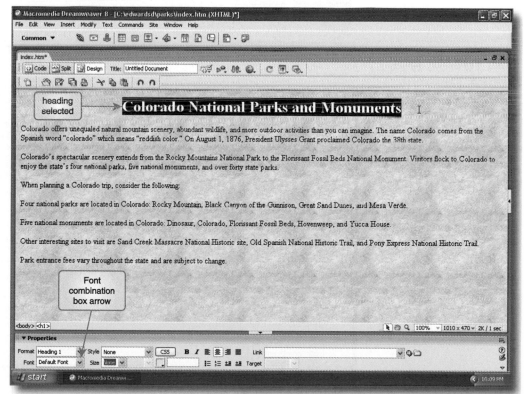

FIGURE 1-56

2

• **Click the Font combination box arrow and then point to Verdana, Arial, Helvetica, sans-serif.**

The Font combination pop-up menu is displayed, and the Verdana, Arial, Helvetica, sans-serif combination is highlighted (Figure 1-57). The menu includes six different font combinations and the default font.

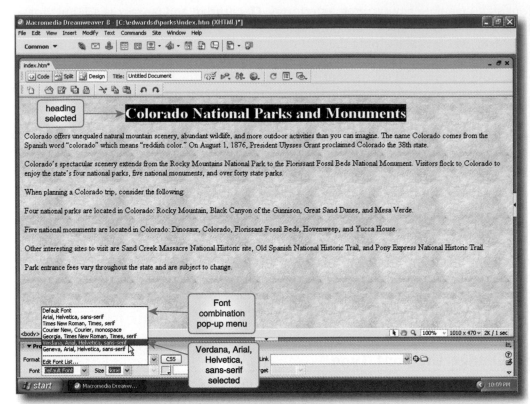

FIGURE 1-57

3

• **Click Verdana, Arial, Helvetica, sans-serif.**

The new font type is applied to the selected heading, and style1 is displayed in the Style text box (Figure 1-58).

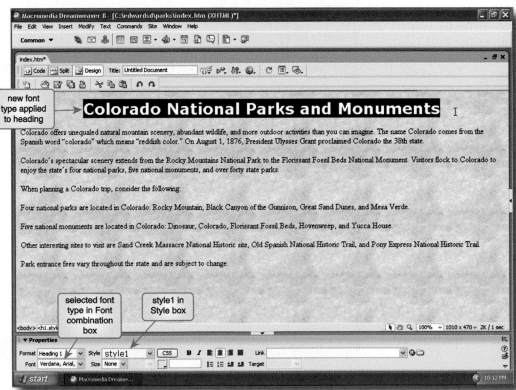

FIGURE 1-58

Other Ways

1. On the Text menu point to Font, click Verdana, Arial, Helvetica, sans-serif.
2. Right-click selected text, point to Font on context menu, click Verdana, Arial, Helvetica, sans-serif.

In addition to headings and font type attributes, other text design options are available. Presenting information in small chunks, such as bulleted or numbered lists, is a design element used by many Web page authors. Dreamweaver makes it easy to add lists such as these to your Web page.

Types of Lists

One way to group and organize information is by using lists. Web pages can have three types of lists: ordered (numbered), unordered (bulleted), and definition. **Ordered lists** contain text preceded by numbered steps. **Unordered lists** contain text preceded by bullets (dots or other symbols) or image bullets. You use an unordered list if the items need not be listed in any particular order. **Definition lists** do not use leading characters such as bullet points or numbers. Glossaries and descriptions often use this type of list.

The Unordered List and Ordered List buttons are available in the Property inspector. You can access the Definition List command through the Text menu List command submenu. Through the List Properties dialog box, you can set the number style, reset the count, or set the bullet style options for individual list items or for the entire list. To access the List Properties dialog box, click anywhere in the list, and then click the List Item button in the Property inspector.

You can create a new list or you can create a list using existing text. When you select existing text and add bullets, the blank lines between the list items are deleted. Later in this project, you add line breaks to reinsert a blank line between each list item. The following steps show how to create an unordered list using existing text.

To Create an Unordered List

1

• Click to the left of the line, Four national parks are located in Colorado: Rocky Mountain, Black Canyon of the Gunnison, Great Sand Dunes, and Mesa Verde. (Figure 1-59).

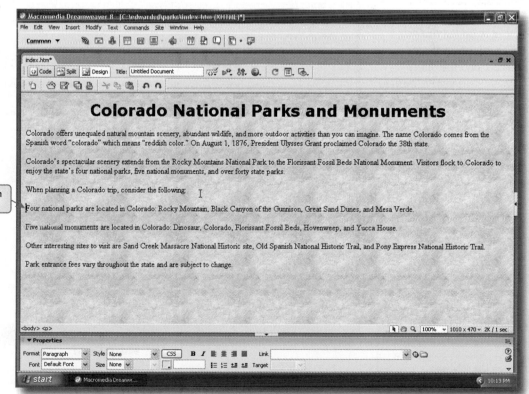

FIGURE 1-59

2

• **Drag to select the text, Four national parks are located in Colorado: Rocky Mountain, Black Canyon of the Gunnison, Great Sand Dunes, and Mesa Verde, and the next two lines.**

• **Point to the Unordered List button in the Property inspector.**

The text is selected (Figure 1-60).

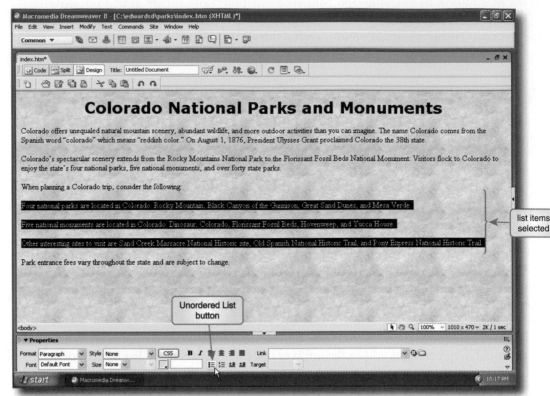

FIGURE 1-60

3

• **Click the Unordered List button.**

A bullet is added to each line, the three lines are indented, and the space between each item is deleted (Figure 1-61).

FIGURE 1-61

Other Ways

1. On Text menu point to List, click Unordered List on List submenu
2. Right-click, point to List, click Unordered List on List submenu

Other text formatting options are applying bold or italic styles to text. **Bold** characters display somewhat thicker and darker than those that are not bold. **Italic** characters slant to the right. The Property inspector contains buttons for both bold and italic font styles.

Bold Formatting

To bold text within Dreamweaver is a simple procedure. If you have used word-processing software, you are familiar with this process. The next step illustrates how to emphasize the bulleted items by applying bold formatting.

To Bold Text

1

• If necessary, drag through the bulleted points to select all three lines.

2

• Click the Bold button and then click anywhere in the Document window to deselect the text (Figure 1-62).

Bold formatting is applied to the unordered list items.

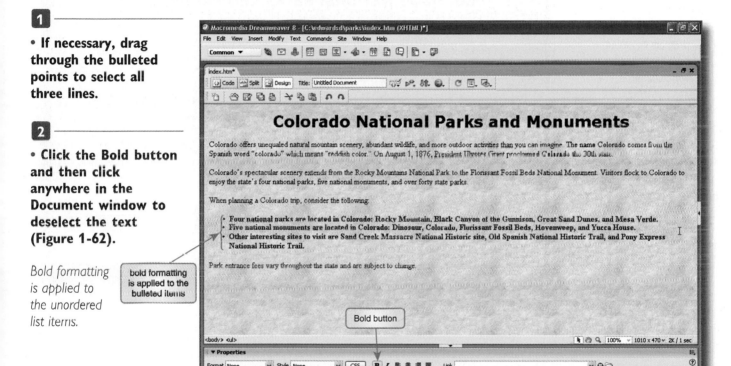

bold formatting is applied to the bulleted items

Bold button

FIGURE 1-62

Understanding Line Breaks

When you added bullets to the items list earlier in this project, the blank line between each item was removed. Removing the blank line between items is a result of how Dreamweaver interprets the HTML code. A blank line between the bulleted items, however, will provide better spacing and readability when viewing the Web page in a browser. You can add blank lines in several ways. You might assume that pressing the ENTER key at the end of each line would be the quickest way to accomplish this. Pressing the ENTER key, however, adds another bullet. The easiest way to accomplish the task of adding blank lines is to insert line breaks. Recall that the line break starts a new single line without inserting a blank line between lines of text. Inserting two line breaks, however, adds a single blank line.

More About

HTML

For more information about HTML, visit the Dreamweaver 8 More About Web page (scsite.com/dw8/more.htm) and then click HTML.

Dreamweaver provides a Line Break command through the Insert HTML Special Characters submenu. It is easier, however, to use the SHIFT+ENTER keyboard shortcut. The following steps show how to add a blank line between each of the bulleted items.

To Add a Line Break

1

• **Click at the end of the first bulleted item.**

• **Press SHIFT+ENTER two times.**

Two line breaks are inserted (Figure 1-63). When the Web page is viewed in Dreamweaver, it appears that two blank lines are inserted. When viewed in a browser, however, only one blank line is displayed between each item. You will view your Web page in a browser later in this project.

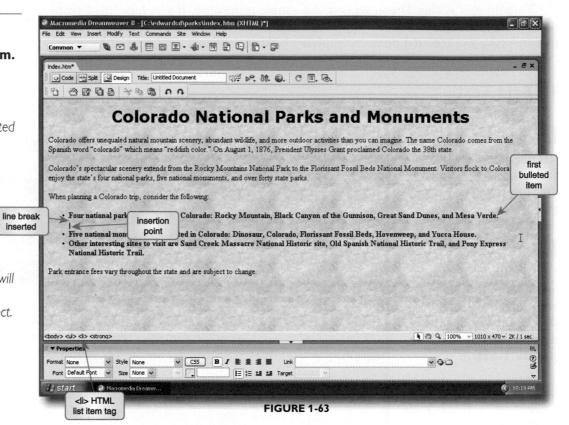

FIGURE 1-63

2

• **Press SHIFT+ENTER two times at the end of the second bulleted item to insert blank lines between the second and third bulleted list items.**

• **Press SHIFT+ENTER two times at the end of the third bulleted list item.**

Dreamweaver displays the bulleted items with blank lines between them and a blank line between the third bulleted item and the last sentence in the Document window (Figure 1-64).

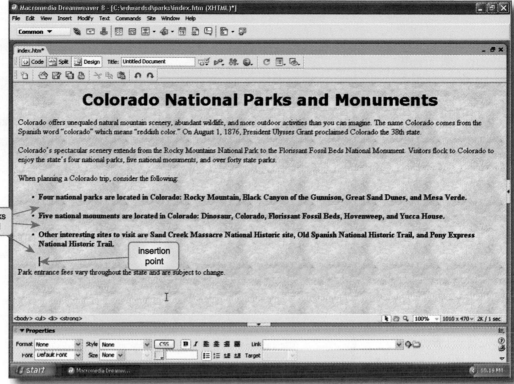

FIGURE 1-64

When creating a Web document, it is a good idea to add your name and date to the document. Insert a single line break between your name and the date. The following steps show how to add this information.

To Add Your Name and Date

1

• **If necessary, scroll down to display the closing paragraph. Click at the end of the closing paragraph.**

• **Press the ENTER key.**

The insertion point moves to the next paragraph (Figure 1-65).

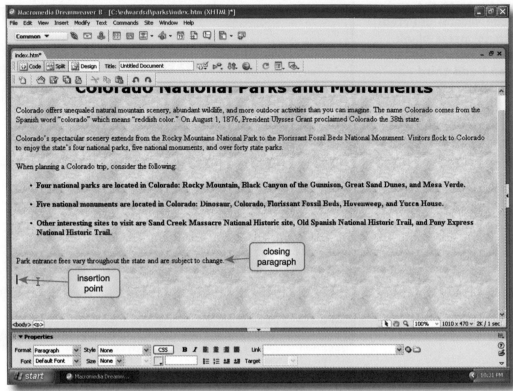

FIGURE 1-65

2

• **Type your name and then press SHIFT+ENTER.**

The insertion point moves to the next line (Figure 1-66). No line space is displayed between the name and the insertion point.

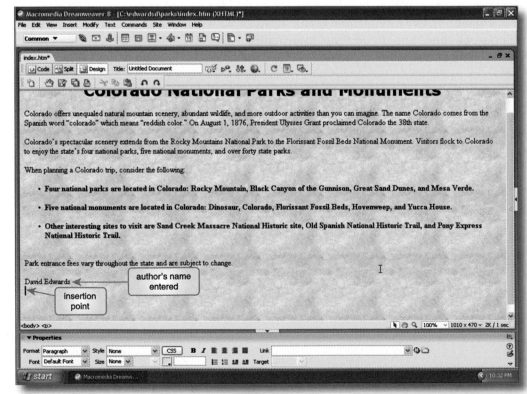

FIGURE 1-66

3

• **Type the current date and then press the ENTER key (Figure 1-67).**

Your name and date are added to the Web page.

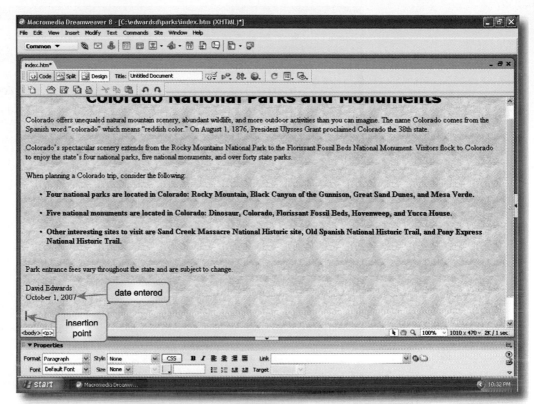

FIGURE 1-67

Web-Safe Colors

Adding color to text can attract attention to important information and emphasize different aspects of a Web page. You easily can change the color of an individual character, a word, a line, a paragraph, or the text of an entire document. In HTML, colors are expressed either as hexadecimal values (for example, #FF0000) or as color names (such as red).

Use the **color picker** to select the colors for page elements or text. Through the Property inspector, Dreamweaver provides access to five different color palettes: Color Cubes, Continuous Tone, Windows OS, Mac OS, and Grayscale. Color Cubes is the default color palette. Figure 1-68 on the next page shows the Color Cubes color palette available on the color palette pop-up menu.

More About

The Color Picker

To open the system color picker, click the Color Wheel button or click Color on the Text menu.

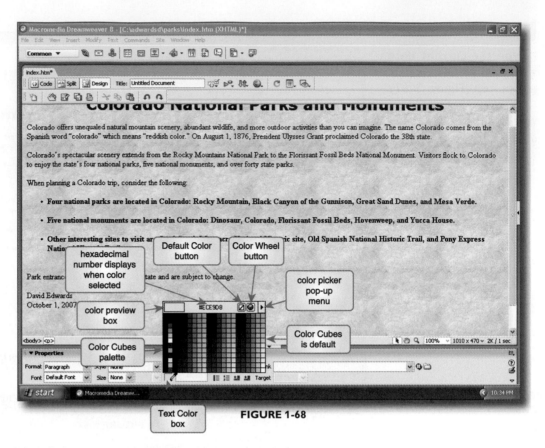

FIGURE 1-68

Q&A

Q: Are there other reasons why I would use Web-safe colors?

A: If you will be developing for alternative Web devices such as PDA and cell phone displays, you should use the Web-safe color palette. Many of these devices offer only black-and-white (1-bit) or 256 color (8-bit) displays.

Two of the color palettes, Color Cubes and Continuous Tone, display Web-safe colors. Web-safe colors are colors that display correctly on the screen when someone is viewing your Web page in a browser. A Web-safe color appears the same in Netscape Navigator, Microsoft Internet Explorer, and other browsers, on both Windows and Macintosh systems. Most experts agree that approximately 212 to 216 Web-safe colors exist. Testing by experts, however, suggests that Internet Explorer renders only 212 Web-safe colors. Table 1-2 contains a list of the color picker options.

Table 1-2 Color Picker Options	
OPTION	FUNCTION
Color preview box	Provides a preview of the currently selected color or the color picked up by the eyedropper
Hex value area	Displays the hexadecimal value of the current color or the color picked up by the eyedropper
Strikethrough button	Clears the current color and retains the default color
Color Wheel button	Opens the system color pickers via the operating system Color dialog box
Option button	Displays a pop-up menu from which you can select one of five color pickers or the Snap to Web Safe command
Snap to Web Safe command	Automatically changes non-Web-safe colors to the nearest Web-safe values

Dreamweaver has an **eyedropper** feature that lets you select colors and make perfect color matches. When you are working with color palettes, you can use the eyedropper to choose a color from anywhere on the screen, including outside of Dreamweaver, and apply the color to a selected object in the Document window. You place the eyedropper over the color you want to select and then click the mouse button. As soon as you click the mouse button, the color automatically is applied to the selected object. If you move the eyedropper to an object outside of Dreamweaver, the eyedropper changes to the block arrow mouse pointer shape until you move it back into the Dreamweaver window. Clicking the color picker pop-up menu button and then selecting the Snap to Web Safe command will ensure the selected color is a Web-safe color.

Changing Text Color

The default color for Dreamweaver text is black. The following steps show how to change the text color of the heading to a shade of brown.

To Change the Text Color

1

• **Select the heading and then click the Text Color box in the Property inspector.**

The Color Cubes palette is displayed (Figure 1-69). The color palette includes Web-safe colors, the color preview box, and the six-digit hexadecimal number that represents the selected color.

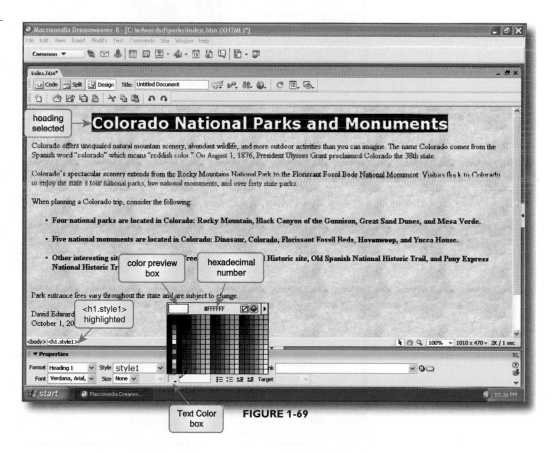

FIGURE 1-69

2

• **Position the eyedropper on the shade of brown represented by hexadecimal number #993300 (row 7 and column 5 from the left).**

The selected color is displayed in the color preview box, and the hexadecimal value area displays the number for the color (Figure 1-70).

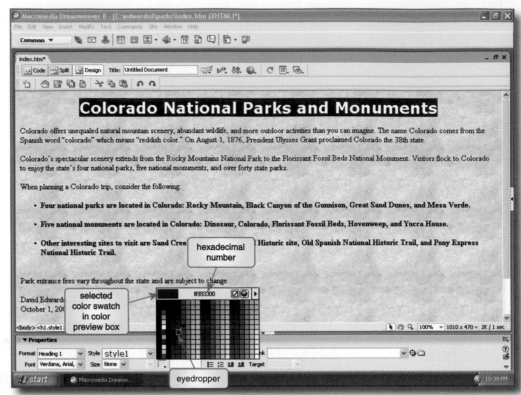

FIGURE 1-70

3

• **Click the eyedropper to apply the color to the selected text, and then deselect the heading.**

The color is applied to the text. The heading is displayed in the selected color (Figure 1-71). Occasionally you may have to press the ESC key to close the picker. Note in the Property inspector that Style 1 changed to display the text color.

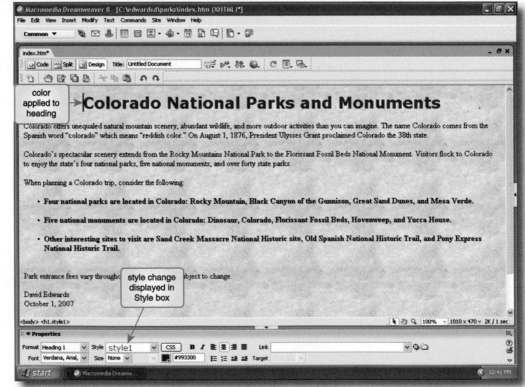

FIGURE 1-71

Web Page Titles

A **Web page title** helps Web site visitors keep track of what they are viewing as they browse. It is important to give your Web page an appropriate title. When visitors to your Web page create bookmarks or add the Web page to their Favorites lists, the title is used for the reference. If you do not title a page, the page will be displayed in the browser window, Favorites lists, and history lists as Untitled Document. Because many search engines use the Web page title, it is important to use a creative and meaningful name. Giving the document a file name by saving it is not the same as giving the page a title.

Changing a Web Page Title

The current title of your Web page is Untitled Document. Unless you change the title of the Web page, this name will be displayed on the browser title bar when the page is opened in a browser window. The following steps show how to change the name of the Web page to Colorado National Parks and Monuments.

To Change the Web Page Title

1

• **Drag through the text, Untitled Document, in the Title text box on the Document toolbar.**

The text is highlighted to indicate that it is selected (Figure 1-72).

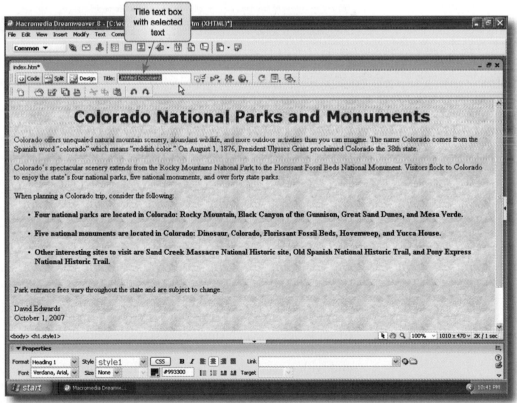

FIGURE 1-72

• **Type** Colorado
National Parks and
Monuments **in the Title
text box and then
press the ENTER key.**

*The new name, Colorado
National Parks and
Monuments, is displayed
in the Title text box
(Figure 1-73).*

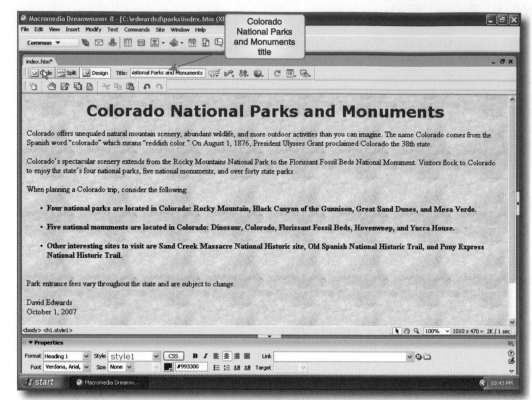

FIGURE 1-73

• **Click the Save button
on the Standard
toolbar.**

*The document changes are
saved. When displayed in a
browser, the title will display
on the title bar.*

Other Web Page Enhancements

Dreamweaver includes many other features that you can use to enhance your Web page. One of the more commonly used enhancements which you may want to apply to a Web page is special characters.

Special Characters

Sometimes it is necessary to enter non-alphanumeric characters such as quotation marks and ampersands as well as non-keyboard symbols like trademarks and registrations into a Web page. To have the browser display these special characters requires a character code. **Character entities,** another name for character codes, allow a browser to show special characters. HTML represents these codes by a name (named entity) or a number (numbered entity). Both types of entities begin with an ampersand (&) and end with a semicolon (;). HTML includes entity names for characters such as the copyright symbol (©), the ampersand (&), and the registered trademark symbol (®). Some entities, such as the left and right quotation marks, include a number sign (#) and a numeric equivalent (such as —). Table 1-3 contains a list of HTML entities supported by Dreamweaver. To add an entity to your Web page, you click Insert on the menu bar, point to HTML, point to Special Characters on the HTML submenu, and then click the entity name on the Special Characters submenu.

Table 1-3 Character Entities

NAME	DESCRIPTION	HTML TAGS AND CHARACTER ENTITIES
Non-breaking Space	Places a non-breaking space at the insertion point	
Left Quote	Places opening, curved double quotation mark at the insertion point	&#147;
Right Quote	Places closing, curved double quotation mark at the insertion point	&#148;
Em Dash	Places an em dash at the insertion point	&#151;
Pound	Places a pound (currency) symbol at the insertion point	&pound;
Euro	Places a euro (currency) symbol at the insertion point	&euro;
Yen	Places a yen (currency) symbol at the insertion point	&yen;
Copyright	Places a copyright symbol at the insertion point	&copy;
Registered Trademark	Places a registered trademark symbol at the insertion poin	&reg;
Trademark	Places a trademark symbol at the insertion point	&#153;
Other Characters	Provides a set of special characters from which to select	Other ASCII characters select

Check Spelling

After you create a Web page, you should check it visually for spelling errors. In addition, you can use Dreamweaver's Check Spelling command to identify possible misspellings. The Check Spelling command ignores HTML tags and attributes. Recall from the Introduction that attributes are additional information contained within an HTML tag.

The following steps show how to start the Check Spelling command and check your entire document. Your Web page may contain different misspelled words depending on the accuracy of your typing.

Q: Does Dreamweaver contain a dictionary with American British spelling options?

A: Yes—Dreamweaver contains 14 different spelling option dictionaries, including English (British) and English (Canadian). Access the dictionaries by clicking the Preferences command on the Edit menu, selecting the General category, and then clicking the Spelling dictionary pop-up menu arrow.

To Check Spelling

- **Click at the beginning of the document.**
- **Click Text on the menu bar and then point to Check Spelling.**

Dreamweaver displays the Text menu (Figure 1-74).

FIGURE 1-74

- **Click Check Spelling.**

The Check Spelling dialog box is displayed. The Dreamweaver spelling checker displays the word, Gunnison, in the Word not found in dictionary text box. Suggestions for the correct spelling are displayed in the Suggestions list (Figure 1-75).

- **Click the Ignore button.**

The spelling checker ignores the word, Gunnison, and continues searching for additional misspelled words. If the spelling checker identifies a word that is spelled correctly, clicking the Ignore button skips the word.

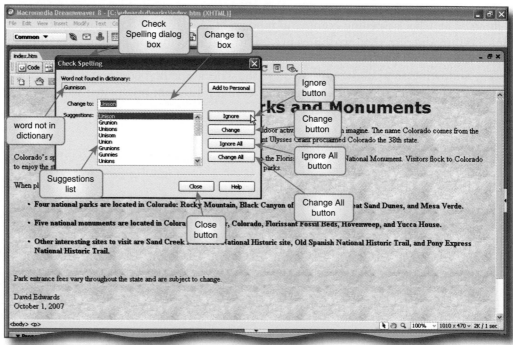

FIGURE 1-75

• **Continue to check the spelling and, as necessary, correct any misspelled word by accepting the suggested replacement, by clicking the Change or Change All buttons, or by typing the correct word in the Change to text box.**

When Dreamweaver has checked all text for misspellings, it displays a Macromedia Dreamweaver dialog box informing you that the spelling check is complete (Figure 1-76).

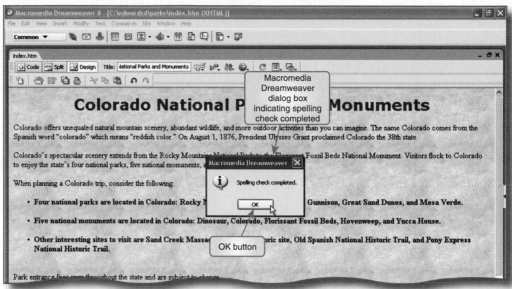

FIGURE 1-76

• **Click the OK button and then press CTRL+S to save any changes.**

Dreamweaver closes the Check Spelling dialog box and displays the Document window. The document is saved.

Before you can share your Web page with the world, you must select browsers to ensure your visitors can view the page properly. The two more popular browsers are Internet Explorer and Netscape.

Previewing a Web Page in a Browser

After you have created a Web page, it is a good practice to test your Web page by previewing it in Web browsers to ensure that it displays correctly. Using this strategy helps you catch errors so you will not copy or repeat them.

As you create your Web page, you should be aware of the variety of available Web browsers. More than 25 different Web browsers are in use, most of which have been released in more than one version. Most Web developers target recent versions of FireFox, Netscape Navigator, and Microsoft Internet Explorer, which the majority of Web visitors use. You also should know that visitors viewing your Web page might have earlier versions of these browsers. You can define up to 20 browsers for previewing. In this book, browsers are defined for Internet Explorer and Netscape.

Selecting a Browser

The browser preferences are selected in the Preferences dialog box. This dialog box provides options to select and define the settings for a primary and a secondary browser. Additionally, a Preview using temporary file option is available. When the check box for this option is checked, you can preview a page without first having to

---

More About

Web Page Design

Web pages reach a global audience. Therefore, to limit access to certain kinds of information, avoid including any confidential data. In particular, do not include your home address, telephone number, or other personal information.

save the page. Although it is a good practice to save before previewing in a browser, occasions will arise when you want to view a page before saving it.

The following steps show how to select your target browsers—Microsoft Internet Explorer and Netscape Navigator. To complete these steps requires that you have both Internet Explorer and Netscape Navigator installed on your computer.

To Select Primary and Secondary Target Browsers

1

• **Click Edit on the menu bar and then point to Preferences.**

Dreamweaver displays the Edit menu and Preferences is selected (Figure 1-77).

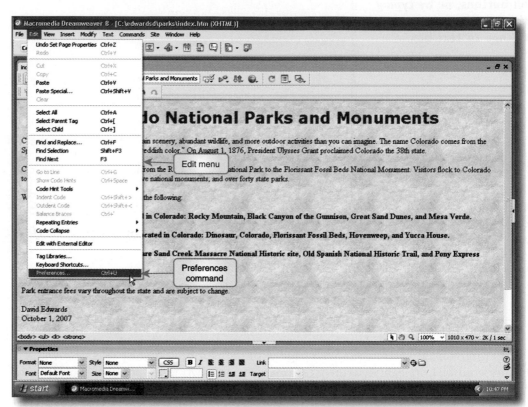

FIGURE 1-77

More About

Browsers

Just as you can specify a primary and secondary browser, you also can remove a browser from your list. Click Edit on the menu bar, click Preferences, and then click the Preview in Browser category. Select the name of the browser you want to remove and then click the minus (–) button.

2

• **Click Preferences and then, if necessary, click the Preview in Browser category.**

The Preferences dialog box is displayed, and the Preview in Browser category is selected (Figure 1-78). The primary browser was selected when Dreamweaver was installed on your computer. In this book, the primary browser is Internet Explorer. The browser name, iexplore, was selected automatically during the Dreamweaver installation. The browser name on your computer may be different. If you are using a different browser or the name is spelled differently, select the option appropriate for your computer and your preference.

FIGURE 1-78

3

• **Click the plus (+) button in the Preview in Browser area.**

Dreamweaver displays the Add Browser dialog box (Figure 1-79).

FIGURE 1-79

4

• **Click the Browse button and then locate the Netscp.exe file. Most likely this file is located on Local Drive (C:). Use the following path to locate the file: C:\Program Files\ Netscape\Netscape\ Netscp.exe, and then click the file name. The path and file name on your computer may be different.**

• **Click the Open button.**

The browser name and application path are added to the Add Browser dialog box (Figure 1-80).

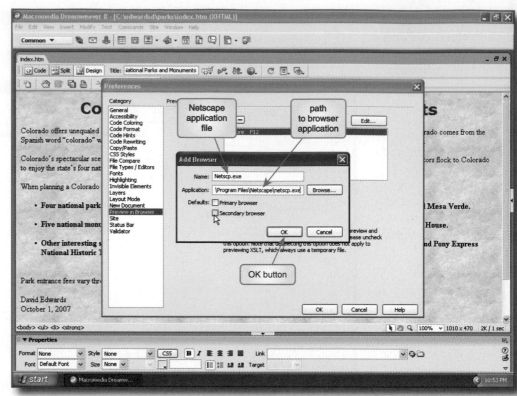

FIGURE 1-80

5

• **If necessary, click the Secondary browser check box to select it.**

The Name text box displays Netscp.exe. The Application text box displays the path and file name (Figure 1-81). The path and spelling of Netscape on your computer may be different than those shown.

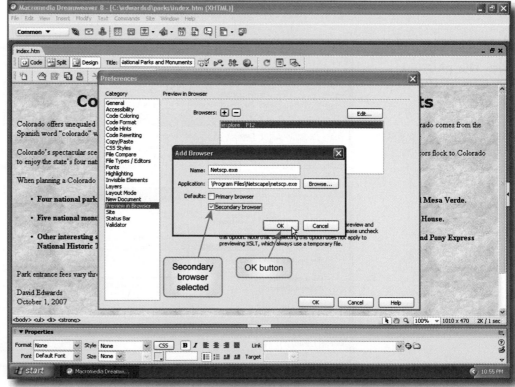

FIGURE 1-81

6

• **Click the OK button.**

Netscape is added as the secondary browser (Figure 1-82).

7

• **If necessary, click the Preview using temporary file check box to select it.**

• **Click the OK button. If a Dreamweaver 8 dialog box appears, click the OK button.**

The target browsers are selected, and Dreamweaver displays the Document window. If the Preview using temporary file check box is unselected, Dreamweaver requires you to save the file before previewing it in a browser.

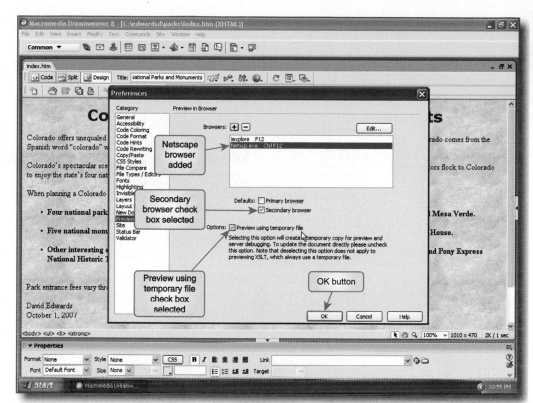

FIGURE 1-82

Previewing a Web Page

With the target browsers set up, you can preview your Web pages in the browsers at any time. You do not have to save the document first. The steps on the next page illustrate how to preview a Web page.

To Preview the Web Page

1

• Click File on the menu bar, point to Preview in Browser, and then point to iexplore or your selected browser name.

The File menu and Preview in Browser submenu are displayed (Figure 1-83). The Preview in Browser submenu includes the names of both your primary and secondary browsers and the Edit Browser List command. Clicking the Edit Browser List command displays the Preferences dialog box. The browser names on your computer may be different.

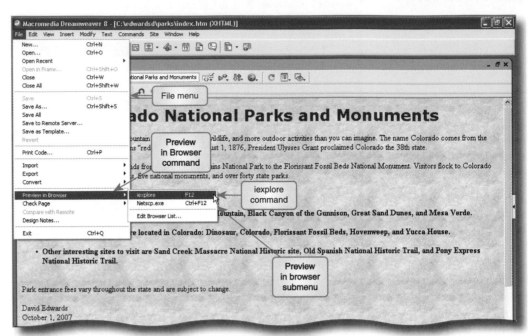

FIGURE 1-83

2

• Click iexplore or your selected browser name.

• If necessary, maximize your browser window.

Internet Explorer starts and displays the Web page in a browser window (Figure 1-84). Your browser name may be different. The file name displayed in the Address bar is a temporary name.

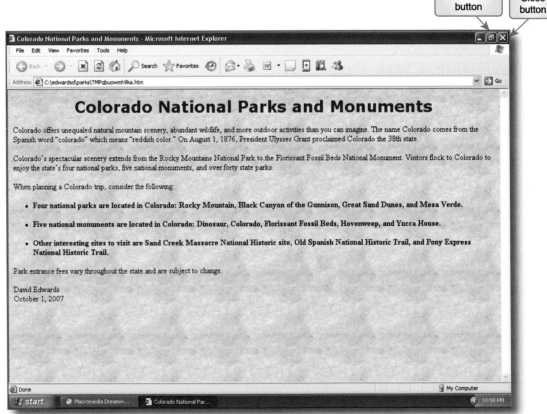

FIGURE 1-84

3

- **Click Internet Explorer's Close button.**
- **Click File on the menu bar and then point to Preview in Browser.**
- **Click Netscp.exe on the Preview in Browser submenu.**

Netscape opens and displays the Web page in a browser window. Your browser name may be different. Consider how the files display in the two browsers.

4

- **Click Netscape's Close button.**

Other Ways

1. Press F12 to display primary browser
2. Press CTRL + F12 to display secondary browser

Your instructor may require that you print a copy of your Web page. The next step illustrates how to print a page.

Printing a Web Page

You may want to print a Web page for a variety of reasons. Interestingly, Dreamweaver provides an option to print code, but does not provide an option to print the Design view. To print a Web page, you first must preview it in a browser. Printing a page from your browser is similar to printing a word-processing document. The following steps illustrate how to print the Web page in a browser.

To Print a Web Page

1

- **Press F12.**

The Web page is displayed in Internet Explorer.

2

- **Click File on the menu bar of the Internet Explorer window and point to Print (Figure 1-85).**

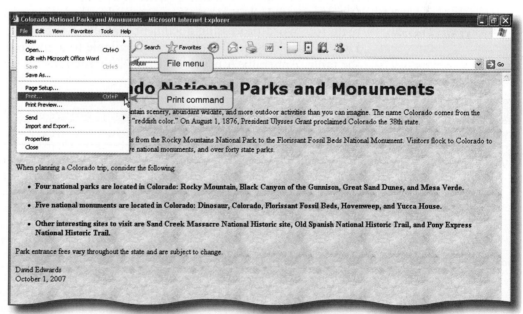

FIGURE 1-85

3

• **Click Print. If necessary, select an appropriate printer.**

Internet Explorer displays the Print dialog box (Figure 1-86). Your selected printer is likely to be different from the one shown in Figure 1-86.

4

• **Click the Print button.**

The Print dialog box closes, and your Web page is sent to the printer.

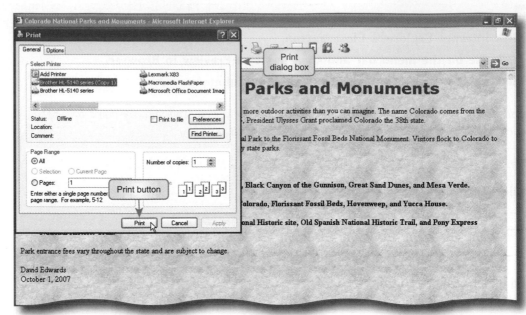

FIGURE 1-86

5

• **Retrieve the printout and then click Internet Explorer's Close button.**

The browser closes, and Dreamweaver displays the Document window.

Dreamweaver Help System

Reference materials and other forms of assistance are available using the Dreamweaver Help system. You can display these documents, print them, or copy them to a word-processing document. Table 1-4 summarizes the categories of online Help available. Several methods are available to activate the first four types listed in the table. Appendix A provides detailed instructions on using Dreamweaver Help.

Table 1-4 Dreamweaver Help System		
TYPE	**DESCRIPTION**	**HOW TO ACTIVATE**
Contents sheet	Use the Contents sheet to view information organized by topic and then by subtopic, as you would in the table of contents of a book.	• Press the F1 key. Click the Contents tab. • Click Help on the menu bar and then click Getting Started with Dreamweaver. Click the Contents tab. • Click the options button on the title bar of a panel group and then click Help on the Options pop-up menu. Click the Contents tab.
Index sheet	Use the Index sheet to look up specific terms or concepts, as you would in the index of a book.	• Press the F1 key. Click the Index tab. • Click Help on the menu bar and then click Getting Started with Dreamweaver. Click the Index tab. • Click the Options menu button on the title bar of a panel group and then click Help on the Options pop-up menu. Click the Index tab.

TYPE	DESCRIPTION	HOW TO ACTIVATE
Table 1-4 Dreamweaver Help System (*continued*)		
Search sheet	Use the Search sheet to find any character string, anywhere in the text of the Help system.	• Press the F1 key. Click the Search tab. • Click Help on the menu bar and then click Getting Started with Dreamweaver. Click the Search tab. • Click the options button on the title bar of a panel group and then click Help on the Options pop-up menu. Click the Search tab.
Question Mark button or Help icon	Click the Question Mark button to find context-sensitive help in dialog boxes and panels.	• Click a Help button or Question Mark button in a dialog box. • Click the Help icon in an inspector or other kind of window.
Tutorials	Offer step-by-step lessons that focus on a specific Web design feature or topic.	• Click Help on the menu bar and then click Getting Started with Dreamweaver and Tutorials.
Dreamweaver online tutorials	Use step-by-step online tutorials.	• Access the Dreamweaver tutorial Web site at http://www.macromedia.com/devnet/dreamweaver/video_tutorials.html

Disabling the Start Page and Quitting Dreamweaver

After you create, save, preview, and print the Colorado Parks Web page and review how to use Help, Project 1 is complete. The following step shows how to disable the Start page, close the Web page, quit Dreamweaver 8, and return control to Windows.

To Disable the Start Page, Close the Web Site, and Quit Dreamweaver

1 Click Edit on the menu bar and then click Preferences.

2 If necessary, click General in the Category column.

3 Click the Show start page check box under Document options to deselect it, and then click the OK button.

4 Click the Close button in the right corner of the Dreamweaver title bar.

The Document window, the Dreamweaver window, and the Colorado Parks Web site all close. If you have unsaved changes, Dreamweaver will prompt you to save the changes. Clicking the Yes button in the Dreamweaver 8 dialog box saves the changes. The next time you start Dreamweaver, the Start page will not be displayed.

Other Ways

1. On File menu, click Exit
2. Press CTRL+Q

Starting Dreamweaver and Opening a Web Page

Opening an existing Web page in Dreamweaver is much the same as opening an existing document in most other software applications: that is, you use the File menu and Open command. In addition to this common method to open a Web page, Dreamweaver provides other options. The Dreamweaver File menu also contains the Open Recent command. Pointing to this command displays the Open Recent submenu, which contains a list of the 10 most recently opened files. Additionally, if you want the page on which you currently are working to display when you next open Dreamweaver, you can select the Reopen Documents on startup command from the Open Recent submenu.

If the page you want to open is part of a Dreamweaver Web site, you can open the file from the Files panel. To open a Web page from the Files panel, you first must select the appropriate Web site. The Files pop-up menu in the Files panel lists sites you have defined. When you open the site, a list of the pages and subfolders within the site displays. To open the page you want, double-click the file name. After opening the page, you can modify text, images, tables, and any other elements.

Earlier in this project, you disabled the Start page. The next time you open Dreamweaver, therefore, the Start page will not display. Instead, a blank window is displayed, requiring that you open an existing document or open a new document. Dreamweaver provides four options to open a new Document window:

- Click File on the menu bar and then click the New command
- Press CTRL+N
- Select the site's root folder, right-click, and then click New File on the context menu
- Click the Files panel Options menu, click File on the pop-up menu, and then click the New File command

The first two options display the New Document dialog box. From this dialog box, you select the Basic page category and HTML Basic page and then click the Create button. When you select option three or four, a new untitled document is created and is displayed in the Files panel. You then name the document and double-click the name to open the document from the Files panel.

Project Summary

Project 1 introduced you to starting Dreamweaver, defining a Web site, and creating a Web page. You added an image background and used Dreamweaver's Property inspector to format text, change font color, and center text. You also learned how to apply color to text and use an unordered list to organize information. You added line breaks and learned about special characters. Once your Web page was completed, you learned how to save the Web page and preview it in a browser. You also learned how to print using the browser. To enhance your knowledge of Dreamweaver further, you learned basics about the Dreamweaver Help system.

What You Should Know

Having completed this project, you should now be able to perform the tasks below. The tasks are listed in the same order they were presented in the project. For a list of keyboard commands for topics introduced in this project, see the Quick Reference for Windows at the back of this book and refer to the Shortcut column.

1. Start Dreamweaver (DW 36)
2. Display the Standard Toolbar and Close and Open Panels (DW 43)
3. Use Site Definition to Create a Local Web Site (DW 47)
4. Copy Data Files to the Local Web Site (DW 53)
5. Hide the Rulers, Change the .htm Default, and Save a Document as a Web Page (DW 58)
6. Add a Background Image to the Index Page (DW 62)
7. Hide the Panel Groups (DW 66)
8. Add Text (DW 67)
9. Format Text with Heading 1 (DW 74)
10. Center the Web Page Heading (DW 75)
11. Change the Font Type (DW 77)
12. Create an Unordered List (DW 79)

13. Bold Text (DW 81)

14. Add a Line Break (DW 82)

15. Add Your Name and Date (DW 84)

16. Change the Text Color (DW 87)

17. Change the Web Page Title (DW 89)

18. Check Spelling (DW 92)

19. Select Primary and Secondary Target Browsers (DW 94)

20. Preview the Web Page (DW 98)

21. Print a Web Page (DW 99)

22. Disable the Start Page, Close the Web Site, and Quit Dreamweaver (DW 101)

Learn It Online

Instructions: To complete the Learn It Online exercises, start your browser, click the Address bar, and then enter the Web address scsite.com/dw8/learn. When the Dreamweaver 8 Learn It Online page is displayed, follow the instructions in the exercises below. Each exercise has instructions for printing your results, either for your own records or for submission to your instructor.

1 Project Reinforcement TF, MC, and SA

Below Dreamweaver Project 1, click the Project Reinforcement link. Print the quiz by clicking Print on the File menu for each page. Answer each question.

2 Flash Cards

Below Dreamweaver Project 1, click the Flash Cards link and read the instructions. Type 20 (or a number specified by your instructor) in the Number of playing cards text box, type your name in the Enter your Name text box, and then click the Flip Card button. When the flash card is displayed, read the question and then click the ANSWER box arrow to select an answer. Flip through the Flash Cards. If your score is 15 (75%) correct or greater, click Print on the File menu to print your results. If your score is less than 15 (75%) correct, then redo this exercise by clicking the Replay button.

3 Practice Test

Below Dreamweaver Project 1, click the Practice Test link. Answer each question, enter your first and last name at the bottom of the page, and then click the Grade Test button. When the graded practice test is displayed on your screen, click Print on the File menu to print a hard copy. Continue to take practice tests until you score 80% or better.

4 Who Wants To Be a Computer Genius?

Below Dreamweaver Project 1, click the Computer Genius link. Read the instructions, enter your first and last name at the bottom of the page, and then click the PLAY button. When your score is displayed, click the PRINT RESULTS link to print a hard copy.

5 Wheel of Terms

Below Dreamweaver Project 1, click the Wheel of Terms link. Read the instructions, and then enter your first and last name and your school name. Click the PLAY button. When your score is displayed, right-click the score and then click Print on the shortcut menu to print a hard copy.

6 Crossword Puzzle Challenge

Below Dreamweaver Project 1, click the Crossword Puzzle Challenge link. Read the instructions, and then enter your first and last name. Click the SUBMIT button. Solve the crossword puzzle. When you are finished, click the Submit button. When the crossword puzzle is redisplayed, click the Print Puzzle button to print a hard copy.

7 Tips and Tricks

Below Dreamweaver Project 1, click the Tips and Tricks link. Click a topic that pertains to Project 1. Right-click the information and then click Print on the shortcut menu. Construct a brief example of what the information relates to in Dreamweaver to confirm you understand how to use the tip or trick.

8 Newsgroups

Below Dreamweaver Project 1, click the Newsgroups link. Click a topic that pertains to Project 1. Print three comments.

9 Expanding Your Horizons

Below Dreamweaver Project 1, click the Expanding Your Horizons link. Click a topic that pertains to Project 1. Print the information. Construct a brief example of what the information relates to in Dreamweaver to confirm you understand the contents of the article.

10 Search Sleuth

Below Dreamweaver Project 1, click the Search Sleuth link. To search for a term that pertains to this project, select a term below the Project 1 title and then use the Google search engine at google.com (or any major search engine) to display and print two Web pages that present information on the term.

Apply Your Knowledge

1 Andy's Lawn Service Web Site

Instructions: Start Dreamweaver. Perform the following tasks to define a Web site and create and format a Web page for Andy's Lawn Service. The Web page as it displays in a browser is shown in Figure 1-87. The text for the Web site is shown in Table 1-5.

Software and hardware settings determine how a Web page is displayed in a browser. Your Web pages may display differently in your browser than the pages shown in the figures.

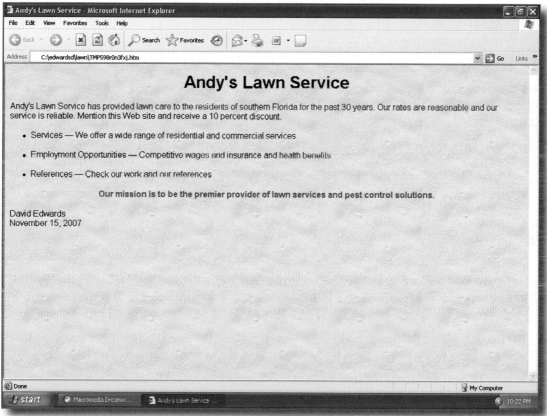

FIGURE 1-87

Table 1-5 Andy's Lawn Service Web Page	
SECTION	**WEB PAGE TEXT**
Heading	Andy's Lawn Service
Introductory Paragraph	Andy's Lawn Service has provided lawn care to the residents of southern Florida for the past 30 years. Our rates are reasonable and our service is reliable. Mention this Web site and receive a 10 percent discount.
List Item 1	Services — We offer a wide range of residential and commercial services
List Item 2	Employment Opportunities — Competitive wages and insurance and health benefits
List Item 3	References — Check our work and our references
Closing	Our mission is to be the premier provider of lawn services and pest control solutions.

(continued)

Apply Your Knowledge

Andy's Lawn Service Web Site *(continued)*

1. Click Site on the menu bar and then click Manage Sites. Create a new site. Use the Site Definition Advanced tab window to create a local Web site under the your name folder. In the Site Definition Site name text box, name the site Lawn Service. In the Local root folder text box, create a new subfolder under the your name folder, and name the new subfolder lawn. The path will be C:\yourname\lawn (substitute your name). In the Default images folder text box, create a new subfolder and name the folder images.

2. Click File on the menu bar and then click New. Click Basic Page in the Category column and HTML in the Basic page column in the New Document dialog box, and then click Create. If necessary, display the Standard toolbar. Use the Save As command on the File menu to save the page with the name index.htm.

3. Use the Windows My Computer option to copy the data file image (lawnbg.jpg) to your lawn images folder.

4. Click the Modify menu and then click Page Properties. Apply the background image (located in the images folder) to the index page.

5. Type the Web page text shown in Table 1-5 on the previous page. Press the ENTER key after typing the text in each section and after each one of the list items in the table. The em dash, used in the three list items, is an HTML object. To insert the em dash, click the Insert menu, point to HTML, point to Special Characters, and then click Em-Dash.

6. Select the heading text and then apply the Heading 1 format. Click the Align Center button in the Property inspector to center the heading.

7. Select the three list items. Click the Unordered List button in the Property inspector to create a bulleted list with these three items.

8. Select the closing paragraph. Click the Align Center button and then click the Bold button in the Property inspector. When this is complete, do not deselect the sentence.

9. Click the Text Color box in the Property inspector and select hexadecimal color #006600. This color swatch is located in the first row and sixth column from the left.

10. Click at the end of the first bulleted item. Insert one line break between the first and second bulleted items and then insert one line break between the second and third bulleted items.

11. Title the Web page Andy's Lawn Service, using the Title text box on the Document toolbar.

12. Click at the end of the closing paragraph and then press the ENTER key. Click the Align Left button. Type your name, insert a line break, and then type the current date.

13. Select your name and the current date, and use the Text Color box in the Property inspector to change the text color to #000000. If necessary, click the Bold button in the Property inspector to deselect it and remove the bold formatting.

14. Select the heading, introductory paragraph, list items, closing paragraph, your name, and the current date. Use the Font combination box to change the font type to Arial, Helvetica, sans-serif.

15. Click Text on the menu bar and then click Check Spelling. Spell check your document and correct any errors.

16. Click File on the menu bar and then click Save.

17. Press the F12 key to view the Web page in the primary browser. Print a copy if required and hand it in to your instructor. Click the browser's Close button to close the browser.

18. Click the Dreamweaver Close button to quit Dreamweaver.

1 CandleWix Web Site

Problem: A friend of yours, Martha Morgan, is starting her own business selling candles. She has asked you to assist her in preparing a Web page to help her advertise her candles (Figure 1-88).

Software and hardware settings determine how a Web page is displayed in a browser. Your Web pages may display differently in your browser than those shown in the figures.

Instructions: Start Dreamweaver. Perform the tasks on the following pages to define a Web site and create and format a Web page for CandleWix. The text for the Web page is shown in Table 1-6.

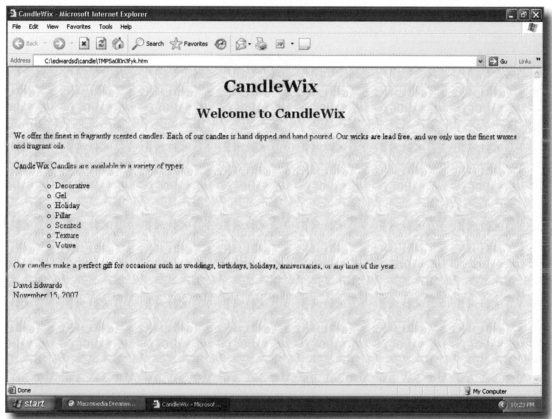

FIGURE 1-88

Table 1-6 CandleWix Web Page

SECTION	WEB PAGE TEXT
Heading	CandleWix
Subheading	Welcome to CandleWix
Introductory Paragraph	We offer the finest in fragrantly scented candles. Each of our candles is hand dipped and hand poured. Our wicks are lead free, and we use only the finest waxes and fragrant oils.
Second Paragraph	CandleWix candles are available in a variety of types:
List Item 1	Decorative

(continued)

CandleWix Web Site *(continued)*

SECTION	WEB PAGE TEXT
Table 1-6 CandleWix Web Page *(continued)*	
List Item 2	Gel
List Item 3	Holiday
List Item 4	Pillar
List Item 5	Scented
List Item 6	Texture
List Item 7	Votive
Closing	Our candles make a perfect gift for occasions such as weddings, birthdays, holidays, anniversaries, or any time of the year.

1. Click Site on the menu bar and then click Manage Sites. Create a new site. Use the Site Definition Advanced window option to create a local Web site under the your name folder. In the Site Definition Site name text box, name the site CandleWix. In the Local root folder text box, create a new subfolder under the your name folder, and name the new subfolder candle. The path will be C:\yourname\candle. In the Default images folder text box, create a new subfolder and name the folder images.

2. Click File on the menu bar and then click New. Click Basic Page in the Category column and HTML in the Basic page column in the New Document dialog box, and then click Create. Use the Save As command on the File menu to save the page with the name index.htm. If necessary, display the Standard toolbar.

3. Use the Windows My Computer option to copy the data file image (candlebg.gif) to your candle images folder.

4. Click the Modify menu and then click Page Properties. Apply the background image to the index page.

5. Click in the Document window and then type the Web page text shown in Table 1-6. Press the ENTER key after typing each section and after each list item in the table.

6. Apply the Heading 1 format to the heading and apply the Heading 2 format to the subheading text. Center both headings. Select the heading and subheading text. Change the font type to Georgia, Times New Roman, Times, serif.

7. Change the text color of the heading and subheading to #990000 (fourth column from the left, sixth row from the bottom).

8. Create an unordered list for the list items. With these items still selected, click the Text Indent button in the Property inspector.

9. Title the Web page CandleWix.

10. Click at the end of the closing line and then press the ENTER key. Type your name. Insert a line break and then type the current date.

11. Check the spelling of your document and correct any errors.

12. Save the file.

13. View the Web page in the primary browser. Print a copy, if required, and hand it in to your instructor. Close the browser.

14. Quit Dreamweaver.

In the Lab

2 Credit Protection Web Site

Problem: Monica Jacobs is an intern in a local bank. She recently lost her wallet, which contained all of her credit cards. She called the credit card companies and canceled her cards. One of the employees at the bank suggested she also call the three credit bureaus to make them aware of this problem. Because searching for the names, telephone numbers, and addresses of the credit bureaus was time-consuming, Monica decided she wants to have this information readily available for herself if she ever needs it again, and for others who might find themselves in a similar situation. Monica also feels this Web site will serve as a valuable resource for the bank's customers. She has asked you to prepare the Web page shown in Figure 1-89.

Software and hardware settings determine how a Web page is displayed in a browser. Your Web pages may display differently in your browser than those shown in the figures.

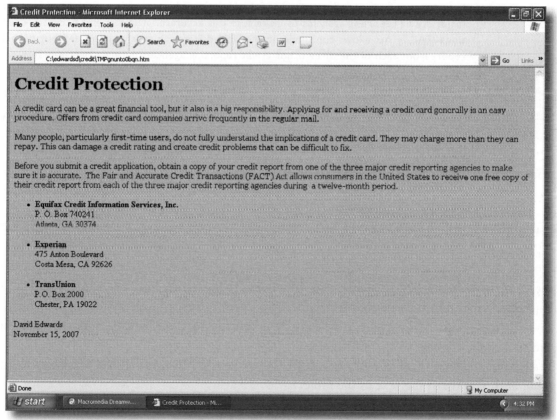

FIGURE 1-89

Instructions: Start Dreamweaver. Perform the following tasks to define a Web site and create and format an informational Web page on credit protection. The text for the Web page is shown in Table 1-7 on the next page.

(continued)

Credit Protection Web Site *(continued)*

Table 1-7 Credit Protection Web Page	
SECTION	**WEB PAGE TEXT**
Heading	Credit Protection
Introductory Paragraph	A credit card can be a great financial tool, but it also is a big responsibility. Applying for and receiving a credit card generally is an easy procedure. Offers from credit card companies arrive frequently in the regular mail.
Second Paragraph	Many people, particularly first-time users, do not fully understand the implications of a credit card. They may charge more than they can repay. This can damage a credit rating and create credit problems that can be difficult to fix.
Third Paragraph	Before you submit a credit application, obtain a copy of your credit report from one of the three major credit reporting agencies to make sure it is accurate. The Fair and Accurate Credit Transactions (FACT) Act allows consumers in the United States to receive one free copy of their credit report from each of the three major credit reporting agencies during a twelve-month period.
List Item 1	Equifax Credit Information Services, Inc. P. O. Box 740241 Atlanta, GA 30374
List Item 2	Experian 475 Anton Boulevard Costa Mesa, CA 92626
List Item 3	TransUnion P.O. Box 2000 Chester, PA 19022

1. Define a local Web site under the your name folder. Name the site Credit Protection. Create a new subfolder under the your name folder and name the new subfolder credit. Create an images folder and copy the image data file (creditbg.jpg) into the images folder.
2. Open a new Document window and use the Save As command to save the page with the name index.htm. Apply the background image to the index page.
3. Type the heading and first three paragraphs of the Web page text shown in Table 1-7. Press the ENTER key after typing each section of the text in the table.
4. Type list item 1. Insert a line break after the company name and after the address. Press the ENTER key after the city, state, and zip code. Type list items 2 and 3 in the same fashion.
5. Apply the Heading 1 format to the heading text. Align to the left (to ensure the heading is displayed properly in the browser).
6. Change the font type to Georgia, Times New Roman, Times, serif for all the text on the Web page.
7. Select the three list items (companies and addresses) and create an unordered list. Insert two line breaks between item 1 and item 2, and between item 2 and item 3.
8. Bold the company name of the first item in the bulleted list (Equifax Credit Information Services, Inc.). Apply the bold attribute to the names of the other two companies.
9. Title the Web page Credit Protection.

Line Break = Shift+enter

10. Click at the end of the last line of text and then press the ENTER key. If a bullet displays, click the Unordered List button in the Property inspector to remove the bullet. Type your name, add a line break, and then type the current date.

11. Check the spelling of your document, correct any errors, and then save the page.

12. View the Web page in your browser. Print a copy, if required, and hand it in to your instructor. Close the browser and then quit Dreamweaver.

3 Lexington, NC Web Site

Problem: John Davis recently moved to Lexington, North Carolina. He discovered that Lexington has a color-ful history and that many consider the city to be the Barbeque Capital of the World. He has asked you to help prepare a Web page (Figure 1-90) so he can share information with friends, relatives, and visitors to North Car-olina about the city's facts.

Software and hardware settings determine how a Web page is displayed in a browser. Your Web pages may display differently in your browser than those shown in the figures.

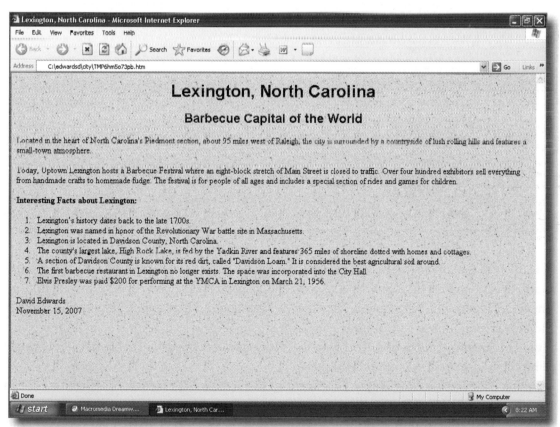

FIGURE 1-90

(continued)

In the Lab

Lexington, NC Web Site *(continued)*

Instructions: Start Dreamweaver. Perform the tasks on the next page to define a Web site and create and format an informational Web page on Lexington, North Carolina. The text of the Web page is shown in Table 1-8.

Table 1-8 Lexington, North Carolina Web Site	
SECTION	**WEB PAGE TEXT**
Heading	Lexington, North Carolina
Subheading	Barbeque Capital of the World
Introductory Paragraph	Located in the heart of North Carolina's Piedmont section, about 95 miles west of Raleigh, the city is surrounded by a countryside of lush rolling hills and features a small-town atmosphere.
Second Paragraph	Today, Uptown Lexington hosts a Barbeque Festival where an eight-block stretch of Main Street is closed to traffic. Over four hundred exhibitors sell everything from handmade crafts to home-made fudge. The festival is for people of all ages and includes a special section of rides and games for children.
Third Paragraph	Interesting Facts about Lexington:
List Item 1	Lexington's history dates back to the late 1700s.
List Item 2	Lexington was named in honor of the Revolutionary War battle site in Massachusetts.
List Item 3	Lexington is located in Davidson County, North Carolina.
List Item 4	The county's largest lake, High Rock Lake, is fed by the Yadkin River and features 365 miles of shoreline dotted with homes and cottages.
List Item 5	A section of Davidson County is known for its red dirt, called "Davidson Loam." It is considered the best agricultural soil around.
List Item 6	The first barbeque restaurant in Lexington no longer exists. The space was incorporated into the City Hall.
List Item 7	Elvis Presley was paid $200 for performing at the YMCA in Lexington on March 21, 1956.

1. Define a local Web site under the your name folder. Name the site Lexington, NC. Create a subfolder and name it city. Create an images subfolder and copy the image data file (citybg.gif) into the folder.
2. Open a new Document window and use the Save As command to save the page with the name index.htm. Apply the background image to the index page.
3. Click in the Document window and then type the Web page text shown in Table 1-8. Press the ENTER key after typing the text in each section in the table.
4. Apply Heading 1 to the heading. Apply Heading 2 to the subheading. Center both headings. Change the heading font type to Arial, Helvetica, sans-serif.
5. Select the third paragraph, Interesting Facts about Lexington:, and then apply bold formatting to the text.
6. Select list items 1 through 7 and apply an ordered list format.
7. Change the Web page title to Lexington, North Carolina.
8. Insert your name and the current date at the bottom of the Web page.
9. Check the spelling of your document and correct any errors. Save the Web page.
10. View the Web page in the browser. Print a copy, if required, and hand it in to your instructor. Close the browser. Quit Dreamweaver.

Cases and Places

The difficulty of these case studies varies:
■ are the least difficult and ■■ are the most difficult. The last exercise is a group exercise.

1 ■ Define a Web site named Favorite Sports with a subfolder named sports. Prepare a Web page listing your favorite sports and favorite teams. Include a title for your Web page. Bold and center the title, and then apply the Heading 1 style. Include a sentence or two explaining why you like the sport and why you like the teams. Bold and italicize the names of the teams and the sports. Give the Web page a meaningful title. Apply a background image to your Web page. Check the spelling in the document. Use the concepts and techniques presented in the project to format the text. Save the file in the sports folder. For a selection of images and backgrounds, visit the Dreamweaver 8 Media Web page (scsite.com/dw8/media).

2 ■ Your instructor has asked you to create a Web page about one of your hobbies. Define the Web site using Hobbies for the site name and hobby for the subfolder name. Italicize and center the title, and then apply the Heading 2 style. Type a paragraph of three or four sentences explaining why you selected the subject. Select and center the paragraph. Add a list of three items and create an ordered list from the three items. Include line breaks between each numbered item. Title the Web page the name of the hobby you selected. Check the spelling in your document. Use the concepts and techniques presented in the project to format the text. For a selection of images and backgrounds, visit the Dreamweaver 8 Media Web page (scsite.com/dw8/media).

3 ■■ Define a Web site and create a Web page that gives a description and information about your favorite type of music. Name the Web site Favorite Music and the subfolder music. Apply a background image to the Web page. Include a left-aligned heading formatted with the Heading 1 style. Include a subheading formatted with Heading 2. List four facts about why you selected this type of music. Include the names of three of your favorite songs and the names of the artists. Bold and italicize the name of the songs and artists and apply a font color of your choice. Create an ordered list from the four facts. Title the Web page Favorite Music. Save the file as index in the music folder. Use the concepts and techniques presented in the project to format the text. For a selection of images and backgrounds, visit the Dreamweaver 8 Media Web page (scsite.com/dw8/media).

Cases and Places

4 ■■ Assume you are running for office in your city's local government. Define a Web site using the name of the city in which you live and a subfolder named government. Include the following information in your Web page: your name, centered, with Heading 1 and a font color of your choice; the name of the office for which you are running, bold and italicized; and a paragraph about the duties of the office in Courier font. Create a bulleted list within your Web page. Change the title of the Web page from Untitled Document to your name. Use the concepts and techniques presented in the project to format the text. For a selection of images and backgrounds, visit the Dreamweaver 8 Media Web page (scsite.com/dw8/media).

5 ■■ **Working Together** Your school has a budget for student trips. Your assignment and that of your teammates is to put together a Web site and Web page that list locations and trips that students can select. Apply an appropriate background image. Include a title, formatted with Heading 1, and a subtitle, formatted with Heading 2. List three locations. Bold and apply a font color to each location name. Add a bullet to each location name. Include information about each location. Title the page Student Government. Use the concepts and techniques presented in the project to format the text. For a selection of images and backgrounds, visit the Dreamweaver 8 Media Web page (scsite.com/dw8/media).

MACROMEDIA
Dreamweaver 8

Adding Web Pages, Links, and Images

CASE PERSPECTIVE

Tracy Coady, a coworker at the state environmental agency, is interested in Colorado's parks and viewed the Web page that you and David created. She has offered some suggestions and asked to help with the design. Both you and David agreed, and the three of you have become a team.

Tracy suggests adding images to the home page. David proposes that the Web site include a page for Colorado's four national parks and another page with information about Colorado's five national monuments. You explain to David and Tracy that the addition of each new page will require hyperlinks from the home page and links from each page back to the home page. You assure them that Dreamweaver includes all the tools they need to add these and other types of links, including e-mail links, to related Web sites. You create a navigation map to illustrate how the links will work among the three pages. All team members agree that these two new pages should be added and that the pages will include images and links. With the addition of these two pages, the Web page you created in Project 1 will become a Web site.

As you read through this project, you will learn how to add pages to a Web site, how to add images to a Web page, and how to insert absolute, relative, and e-mail links.

Adding Web Pages, Links, and Images

P R O J E C T

Objectives

You will have mastered the material in this project when you can:

- Define and set a home page
- Add pages to a Web site
- Describe Dreamweaver's image accessibility features
- Describe image file formats
- Insert, resize, and align images within a Web page
- Describe the different types of links

- Create relative, absolute, and e-mail links
- Describe how to change the color of links
- Edit and delete links
- Describe and display the Site Map
- Describe Code view, Split view, and Design view
- View Code view

Introduction

Project 2 introduces the addition of Web pages to the local site created in Project 1 and the integration of links and graphics into the Web pages that make up the site. Recall from Project 1 that a site or a Web site is a set of linked documents with shared attributes, such as related topics, a similar design, or a shared purpose.

The Dreamweaver site structure feature provides a way to maintain and organize your files. A Web page essentially is a text document and a collection of HTML and XHTML code. The code defines the structure and layout of a Web document and is generated automatically by Dreamweaver. Images and other media content are separate files. For example, a page that displays text and three images consists of four separate files — one for the text document and one for each of the three images.

Most Web site builders include images on their Web pages. It is important that you take the time to learn about images, image properties, and the types of images best suited for a particular situation. Image properties, such as alignment, size adjustment, and alternative text for accessibility issues, help you to understand the effects of using images on Web pages.

When a file or image is referenced within the source code, a link (or hyperlink) exists within the source code to the external file or image. A link (hyperlink) is also a Web page element that, when clicked, accesses another Web page, or a different place within the existing Web page. A Web page can contain different types of links: internal, or relative; absolute; e-mail; and named anchors. A named anchor is a link to a specific place within a document and is discussed in Project 3. This project discusses how to create relative, absolute, and e-mail links.

Project Two — Two New Pages, Links, and Images

In this project, you continue with the creation of the Colorado Parks Web site. You add two additional Web pages, add image backgrounds to the two new pages, add images to the two new pages and to the index page, add links to and from the index page, and add absolute links to the five national Monuments (Figures 2-1a, 2-1b, and 2-1c).

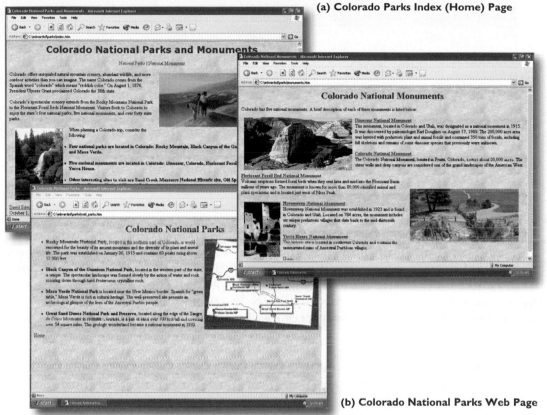

(a) Colorado Parks Index (Home) Page

(c) Colorado National Monuments Page

(b) Colorado National Parks Web Page

FIGURE 2-1

In the Introduction project, four types of Web structures were illustrated: linear, hierarchical, web (or random), and grid. This project uses a hierarchical structure (Figure 2-2 on the next page). The index page is the home page, or entrance to the Web site. From this page, the visitor to this site can link to a page about Colorado National Parks or to a page about Colorado National Monuments.

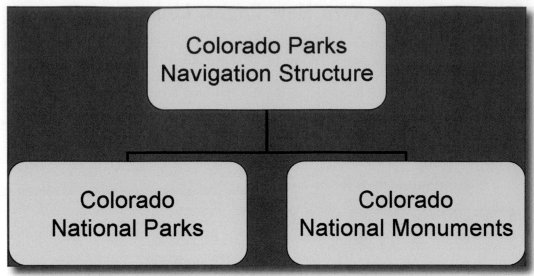

FIGURE 2-2

Managing a Web Site

Organization is a key element of Web design. Dreamweaver works best with entire sites rather than individual Web pages and has many built-in tools, such as checking links and organizing files, to make site creation easy. You defined the parks Web site in Project 1 and created the index page. You can add pages to your site by creating a new page and saving it as part of the site, or by opening an existing page from another source and saving it as part of the site. In this project, you will create two new pages.

Almost all Web sites have a home page. Compare the home page to your front door. Generally, the front door is the first thing guests see when they visit you. The same applies to a Web site's home page. When someone visits a Web site, he or she usually enters through the home page.

The home page normally is named **index.htm** or **index.html**. This file name has special significance. Most Web servers recognize index.htm (or index.html) as the default home page and automatically display this page without requiring that the user type the full Uniform Resource Locator (URL), or Web address. For example, if you type http://www.symantec.com into a Web browser address box to access the Web site, what you see is http://www.symantec.com/index.htm — the actual file name of the site's home page — even though you did not type it that way.

Organizing your Web site and using Dreamweaver's site management features can assure you that the media within your Web page will display correctly. Bringing all of these elements together will start you on your way to becoming a successful Web site developer.

Before you start enhancing your Web site, you need to copy the data files into the site's folder hierarchy.

Copying Data Files to the Local Web Site

Your Data Disk contains images for Project 2. These images are in an images folder. You use the Windows My Computer option to copy the Project 2 images to your parks images folder. See the inside back cover of this book for instructions for downloading the Data Disk, or see your instructor for information about accessing the files required for this book.

The Data Files folder for this project is stored on Local Disk (C:). The location on your computer may be different. If necessary, verify the location of the Data Files folder with your instructor. The following steps show how to copy the files to the parks local root folder.

To Copy Data Files to the Parks Web Site

1 Click the Start button on the Windows taskbar and then click My Computer.

2 Double-click Local Disk (C:) and then navigate to the location of the data files for Project 2.

3 Double-click the DataFiles folder and then double-click the Proj02 folder.

4 Double-click the parks folder and then double-click the images folder.

5 Click the dinosaur image file or the first file in the list.

6 Hold down the Shift key and then click the waterfall01 image file, or the last file in the list.

7 Right-click the selected files to display the context menu.

8 Click the Copy command and then click the My Computer Back button the number of times necessary to navigate to the your name folder.

9 Double-click the your name folder, double-click the parks folder, and then double-click the images folder.

10 Right-click anywhere in the open window to display the context menu.

11 Click the Paste command (Figure 2-3).

12 Click the images window Close button.

The six images are pasted into the Colorado Parks Web site images folder, and the folder now contains seven images, including the bg image file (Figure 2-3).

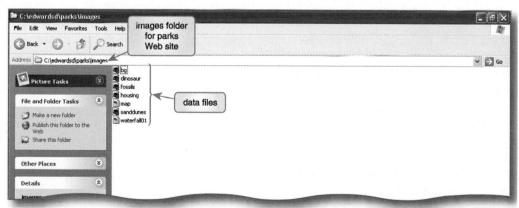

FIGURE 2-3

The data files are copied to the parks Web site file hierarchy. The next step is to start Dreamweaver.

Starting Dreamweaver and Opening a Web Site

Each time you start Dreamweaver, it opens to the last site displayed when you closed the program. It therefore may be necessary for you to open the parks Web site. Clicking the **Files pop-up menu** in the Files panel lists the sites you have defined. When you open the site, a list of pages and subfolders within the site is displayed. The following steps illustrate how to start Dreamweaver and open the Colorado Parks Web site.

To Start Dreamweaver and Open the Parks Web Site

1

• **Click the Start button on the Windows taskbar. Point to All Programs on the Start menu, point to Macromedia on the All Programs submenu, and then click Macromedia Dreamweaver 8 on the Macromedia submenu. If necessary, display the panel groups.**

Dreamweaver opens and displays panel groups and an empty Document window. If the Start page displays, click Open in the Open a Recent Item column and then select the parks index.htm file.

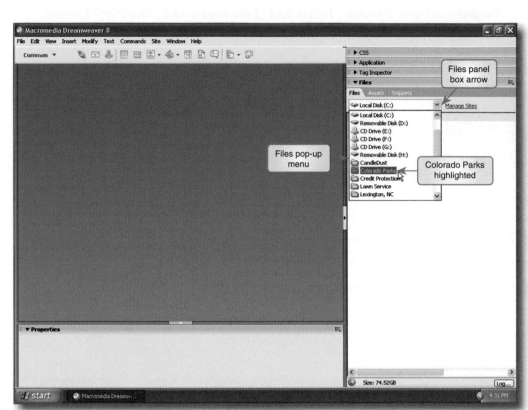

FIGURE 2-4

2

• **If the Colorado Parks hierarchy is not displayed, click the Files panel box arrow and point to Colorado Parks on the Files pop-up menu (Figure 2-4).**

3

• **Click Colorado Parks.**

The Colorado Parks Web site hierarchy displays in the Files panel (Figure 2-5).

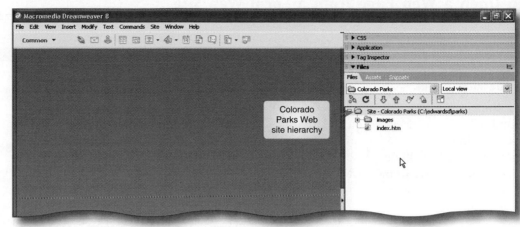

Colorado Parks Web site hierarchy

FIGURE 2-5

Opening a Web Page

Once you have created and saved a Web page or copied a Web page to a Web site, you often will have reason to retrieve it from disk. Opening an existing Web page in Dreamweaver is much the same as opening an existing document in most other software applications; that is, you use the File menu and Open command or you can use Dreamweaver's unique File and Open Recent command. If, however, the page is part of a Web site created with Dreamweaver, you also can open the file from the Files panel.

After opening the page, you can modify text, images, tables, and any other elements. The following step illustrates how to open a Web page from a local site in the Files panel.

To Open a Web Page from a Local Web Site

1

• **Double-click index.htm in the Files panel.**

• **If the Standard toolbar does not display, click View on the menu bar, point to Toolbars, and then click Standard.**

The Colorado Parks index page opens in the Document window, and the name of the page is displayed on the tab at the top of the window. The Standard toolbar is displayed (Figure 2-6).

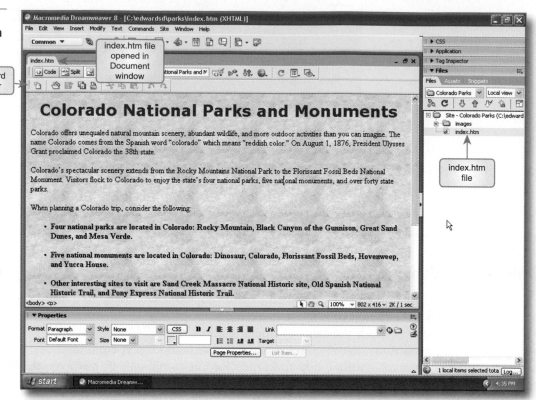

FIGURE 2-6

Other Ways

1. On File menu, click Open, select file

The Files Panel

Organization is one of the keys to a successful Web site. Creating documents without considering where in the folder hierarchy they should go generally creates a difficult-to-manage Web site. The Dreamweaver **Files panel** provides a view of the devices and folders on your computer and shows how these devices and folders are organized. You can create new folders and files for your site through the Files panel, which is similar to the Windows XP file organization method. You also can use the Files panel to drag or copy and paste files from one folder to another or from one Web site to another. You cannot, however, copy a file from a Windows folder and paste it into a site in the Dreamweaver Files panel.

In Windows, the main directory of a disk is called the **root directory** or the **top-level directory**. A small device icon or folder icon is displayed next to each object in the list. The **device icon** represents a device such as the Desktop or a disk drive, and the **folder icon** represents a folder. Many of these icons have a plus or minus sign next to them, which indicates whether the device or folder contains additional folders or files. Windows XP arranges all of these objects — root directory, folders, sub-folders, and files — in a hierarchy. The plus and minus signs are controls that you can click to expand or collapse the view of the file hierarchy. In the Files panel, Dreamweaver uses the same hierarchy arrangement, but site folders and other file icons appear in a different color than non-site folders and files so that you easily can distinguish between the two.

The Home Page and the Site Map

Most Web sites have a starting point, called a home page. In a personal home page within a Web site, for example, you probably would list your name, your e-mail address, some personal information, and links to other information on your Web site. The index page you created in Project 1 is the home page for the parks Web site.

Although you cannot tell which page in a Web site is the home page by viewing the site files, Dreamweaver provides a graphical option to view the home page — the Site Map. You access the Site Map through the Files panel. To create a Site Map requires that you designate one page in the Web site as a home page. You will use the Site Map to view the Web site later in this project. The next section sets the home page.

Setting a Home Page

Each Web site you create within Dreamweaver should have a home page. A **home page** is similar to a table of contents or an index in a book. The home page generally contains links to all the other pages within the Web site. Most home pages are named index.htm or index.html. The following steps show how to define the home page through Dreamweaver's Files panel.

More About

Refreshing the Files Panel

To update the Files panel, click the Refresh button on the Files panel toolbar or press the F5 key.

To Set a Home Page

1

• **Right-click the index.htm file name in the Files panel.**

• **Point to Set as Home Page.**

The context menu is displayed (Figure 2-7).

• **Click Set as Home Page on the context menu.**

The index.htm file is set as the home page for the parks Web site. In the files list, however, no changes are evident.

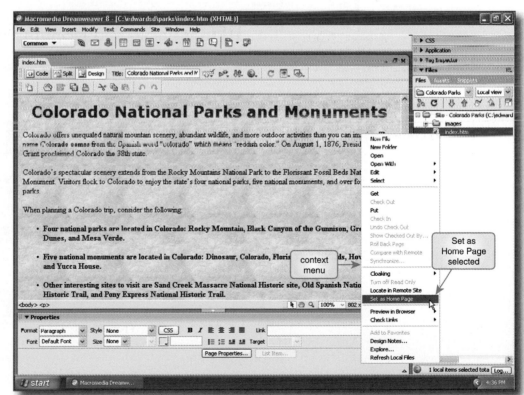

FIGURE 2-7

Other Ways

1. Click Files panel Option button, point to Site, click Set as Home Page

Q&A

Q: Is it necessary to create a folder for images within the Web site?

A: Critical to Web development is the hierarchy of folders and files in a Web site. Even for the very simplest of sites, you should create a separate folder for the images. The folder name can be any name you choose, but it is best to use a descriptive, meaningful name.

Adding Pages to a Web Site

You copied the files necessary to begin creating your Web site to the parks local root folder in the Files panel, and you set the home page. It is time to start building and enhancing your site. You will add two additional pages to the Web site: Colorado National Parks and Colorado National Monuments. You will add links and Web page images to the index or home page and add links, a background image, and Web page images to the two new pages.

Opening a New Document Window

The next step is to open a new Document window. This will become the Colorado National Parks page. The following steps illustrate how to open a new document window and save the page as natl_parks.htm.

To Open a New Document Window

1

• **Click File on the menu bar and then point to New.**

The File menu is displayed (Figure 2-8).

FIGURE 2-8

2

• **Click New. If necessary, click the General tab and then click Basic page in the Category list.**

• **If necessary, click HTML in the Basic page list. Verify that XHTML 1.0 Transitional is selected in the Document Type (DTD) pop-up menu.**

The New Document dialog box is displayed. Basic page is selected in the Category list. HTML is the default in the Basic page list (Figure 2-9).

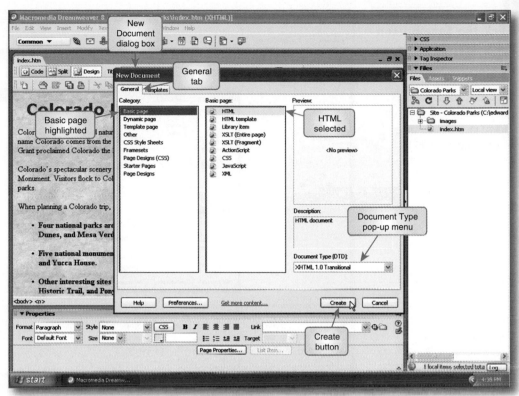

FIGURE 2-9

3

• **Click the Create button.**

A new Untitled-2 Document window opens (Figure 2-10). The number following Untitled increases each time you open a new Document window. Your computer may display a different number.

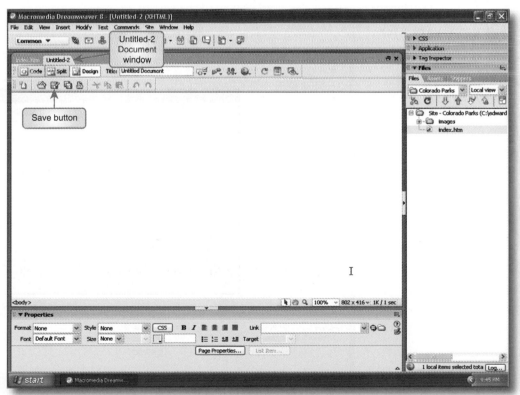

FIGURE 2-10

4

• **Click the Save button on the Standard toolbar.**

The Save As dialog box is displayed and Untitled-2 is selected in the File name text box (Figure 2-11).

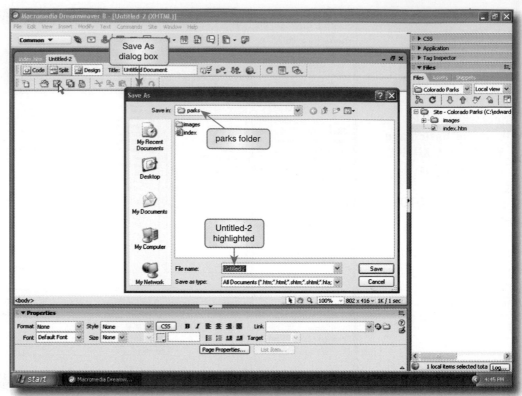

FIGURE 2-11

5

• **Type** natl_parks **for the file name.**

The natl_parks file name is displayed in the File name text box (Figure 2-12).

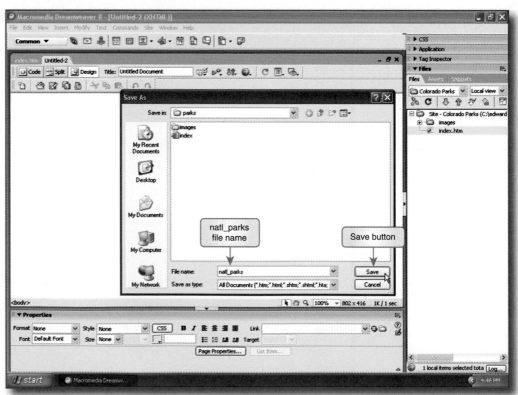

FIGURE 2-12

6

• **Click the Save button.**

The natl_parks.htm page is saved in the parks local folder and is displayed in Dreamweaver's Files panel. The .htm extension is added automatically by Dreamweaver. The path and file name (parks\natl_parks.htm) appear on the Dreamweaver title bar (Figure 2-13).

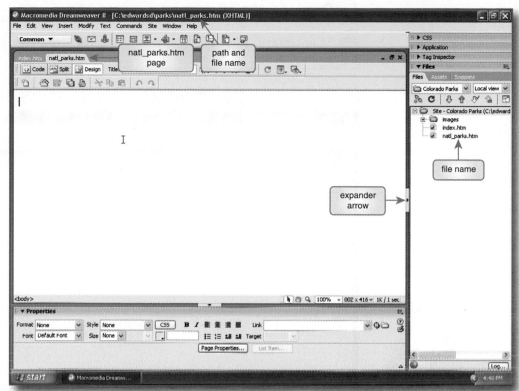

FIGURE 2-13

To organize your workspace, you collapse the lower portion of the Property inspector. This gives you additional window space in the Dreamweaver Document window. The following steps show how to organize your workspace by collapsing the lower portion of the Property inspector.

To Prepare the Workspace

1 If necessary, click the Property inspector expander arrow.

The natl_parks.htm Document window is open, and the Property inspector is collapsed (Figure 2-14).

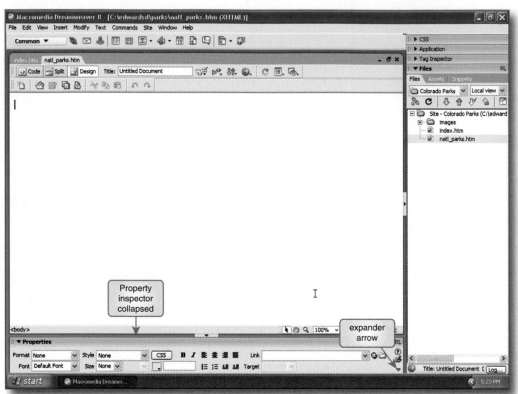

FIGURE 2-14

More About

**Using the
Keyboard
Shortcut Editor**

For more information about
using keyboard shortcuts, visit
the Dreamweaver 8 More
About Web page
(scsite.com/dw8/more) and
then click Dreamweaver 8
Shortcut Editor.

With the workspace prepared and the Document window displayed, you can begin creating the Web page for Colorado National Parks.

Creating the National Parks Web Page

To create the page for Colorado National Parks, you type the text in the Document window. Table 2-1 includes the text for the Colorado National Parks Web page. Press the ENTER key after typing each section as indicated in Table 2-1.

Table 2-1 Colorado National Parks Web Page Text

SECTION	WEB PAGE TEXT
Heading	Colorado National Parks<ENTER>
Part 1	Rocky Mountain National Park, located in the northern part of Colorado, is world renowned for the beauty of its ancient mountains and the diversity of its plant and animal life. The park was established on January 26, 1915 and contains 60 peaks rising above 12,000 feet.<ENTER>
Part 2	Black Canyon of the Gunnison National Park, located in the western part of the state, is unique. The spectacular landscape was formed slowly by the action of water and rock scouring down through hard Proterozoic crystalline rock.<ENTER>
Part 3	Mesa Verde National Park is located near the New Mexico border. Spanish for "green table," Mesa Verde is rich in cultural heritage. The well-preserved site presents an archeological glimpse of the lives of the Ancestral Pueblo people.<ENTER>
Part 4	Great Sand Dunes National Park and Preserve, located along the edge of the Sangre de Cristo Mountains in southern Colorado, is a pile of sand over 700 feet tall and covering over 54 square miles. This geologic wonder-land became a national monument in 1932.<ENTER>
Closing	Home<ENTER>

The following steps show how to create the Web page.

To Create the National Parks Web Page

1

• **Type the heading** Colorado National Parks **as shown in Table 2-1. Press the ENTER key.**

The heading is entered in the Document window (Figure 2-15). Pressing the ENTER key creates a new paragraph.

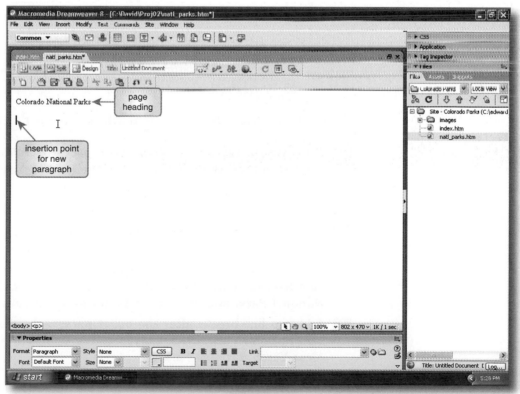

FIGURE 2-15

2

• **Type the rest of the text as shown in Table 2-1 on the previous page. Press the ENTER key as indicated in the table.**

The text for the Colorado National Parks is entered (Figure 2-16).

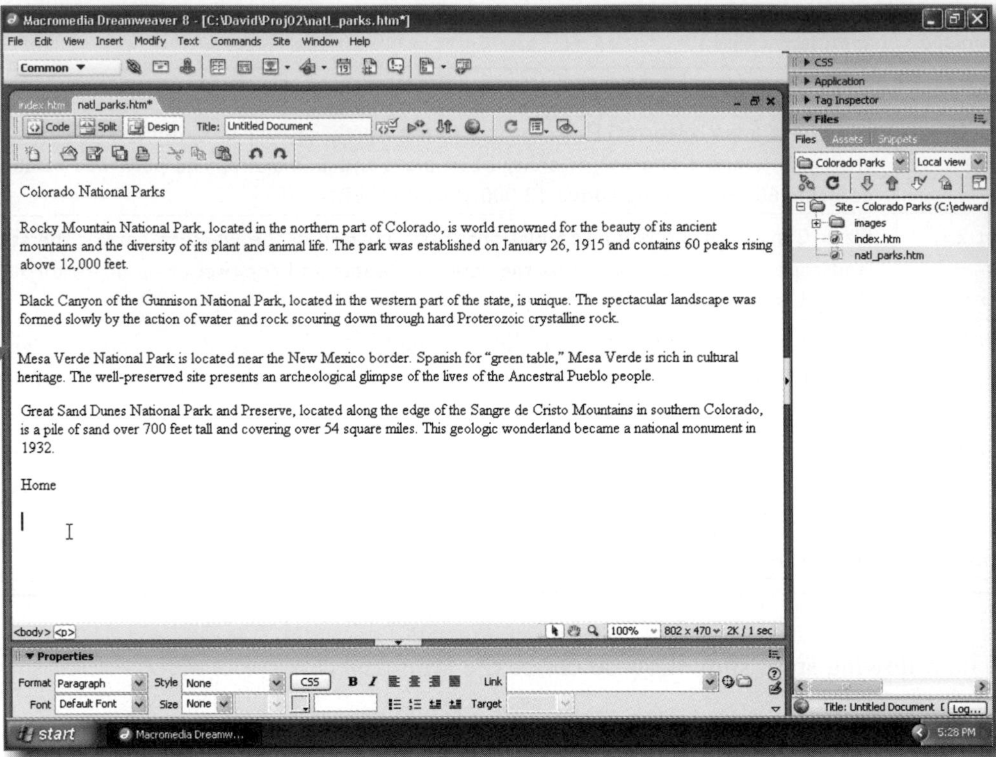

text for Web page entered

FIGURE 2-16

In Project 1, you formatted the index page by adding headings and bullets and by centering and bolding text. The following steps show how to apply similar formatting to the Colorado National Parks page.

To Format the Colorado National Parks Page

1 If necessary, expand the Property inspector, scroll up to the top of the Web page, and then apply Heading 1 to the heading text.

2 Center the heading.

3 Add bullets to the following four lines that begin: Rocky Mountain National Park, Black Canyon of the Gunnison National Park, Mesa Verde National Park, and Great Sand Dunes National Park and Preserve.

4 Bold the park names at the beginning of each of the four lines: Rocky Mountain National Park, Black Canyon of the Gunnison National Park, Mesa Verde National Park, and Great Sand Dunes National Park and Preserve.

5 Add two line breaks after the bullet paragraphs describing the Rocky Mountain National Park, Black Canyon of the Gunnison National Park, and the Mesa Verde National Park.

6 Type Colorado National Parks as the Web page title.

7 Save the natl_parks.htm Web page.

8 Press F12 to view the page in the browser and to verify that the line spacing is correct, as shown in Figure 2-17 on the next page.

9 Close the browser.

The Colorado National Parks Web page text is entered, formatted, and saved.

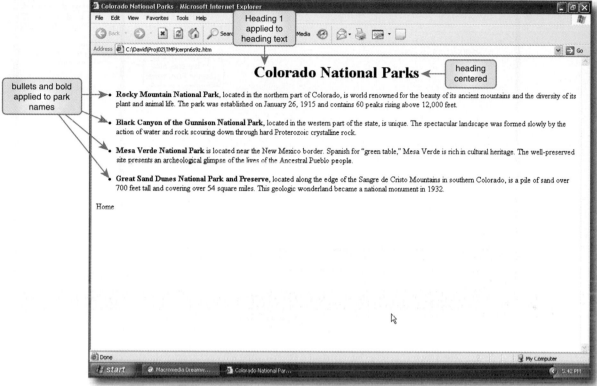

FIGURE 2-17

Creating the National Monuments Web Page

You will enter the text for the Colorado National Monuments page the same way you entered the text for the Colorado National Parks page. Table 2-2 on the next page includes all the text for the Colorado National Monuments Web page.

To Open a New Document Window

1 Click File on the menu bar and then point to New.

2 Click New. If necessary, click the General tab and then click Basic page in the Category list.

3 If necessary, click HTML in the Basic page list.

4 Click the Create button.

5 Save the Web page as monuments.htm in the parks folder.

A new Document window opens, and the name of the saved page is displayed on the title bar (Figure 2-18 on the next page).

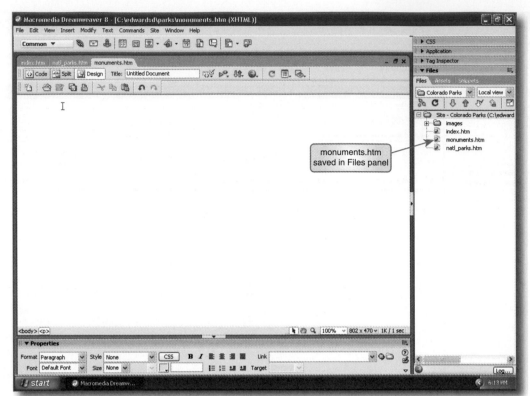

FIGURE 2-18

Type the text for the National Monuments Web page using Table 2-2 and the following steps. Press the ENTER key or insert a line break, or <br>, as indicated in the table.

Table 2-2 Colorado National Monuments Web Page Text	
SECTION	**WEB PAGE TEXT**
Heading	Colorado National Monuments<ENTER>
Part 1	Colorado has five national monuments located throughout the state. Each monument is unique and provides a different view of historic Colorado. <ENTER>
Part 2	Dinosaur National Monument This monument, located in Colorado and Utah, was designated as a national monument in 1915. It was discovered by paleontologist Earl Douglass on August 17, 1909. The 200,000 acre area was layered with prehistoric plant and animal fossils and contained 350 tons of fossils, including full skeletons and remains of some dinosaur species that previously were unknown.<ENTER>
Part 3	Colorado National Monument The Colorado National Monument, located in Fruita, Colorado, covers about 20,000 acres. The sheer walls and deep canyons are considered one of the grand landscapes of the American West. <ENTER>
Part 4	Florissant Fossil Bed National Monument Volcanic eruptions formed fossil beds when they sent lava and mud into the Florissant Basin millions of years ago. The monument is known for more than 80,000 identified animal and plant specimens and is located just west of Pikes Peak. <ENTER>
Part 5	Hovenweep National Monument Hovenweep National Monument was established in 1923 and is found in Colorado and Utah. Located on 784 acres, the monument includes six unique prehistoric villages that date back to the mid-thirteenth century. <ENTER>

Table 2-2 Colorado National Monuments Web Page Text (continued)	
SECTION	WEB PAGE TEXT
Part 6	Yucca House National Monument
	This historic site is located in southwest Colorado and contains the unexcavated ruins of Ancestral Puebloan villages. <ENTER>
Closing	Home<ENTER>

To Create the National Monuments Web Page

1 Type the text of the Web page as shown in Table 2-2.

The text for the Colorado National Monuments Web page is entered (Figure 2-19).

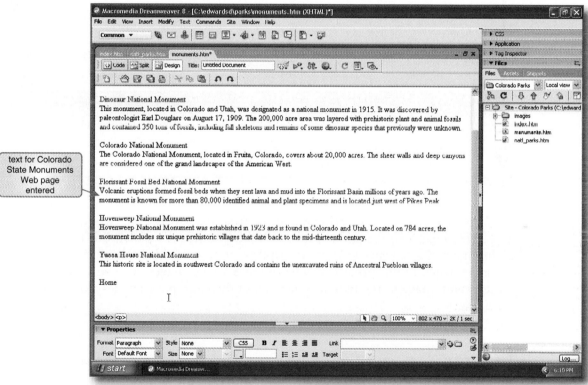

text for Colorado State Monuments Web page entered

FIGURE 2-19

To Format the Colorado National Monuments Page

1 If necessary, scroll to the top of the Web page and then apply Heading 1 to the heading.

2 Center the heading.

3 Bold the names of each of the five monuments where they are used as subtitles.

4 Type Colorado National Monuments as the Web page title (Figure 2-20 on the next page).

5 Click the Save button on the Standard toolbar.

6 Press F12 to view the page in the browser and to verify that the line spacing is correct.

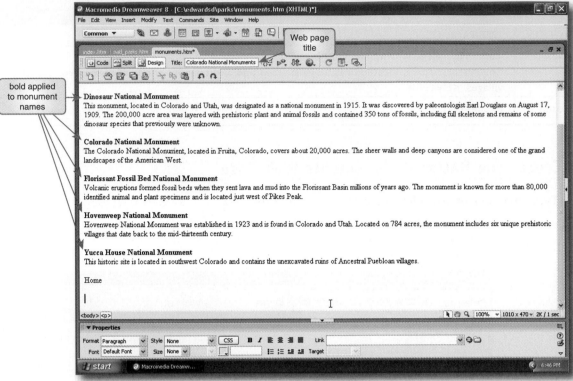

FIGURE 2-20

7 **Close the browser.**

The text for the Colorado National Monuments page is entered, formatted, and saved.

You have completed entering and formatting the text for the two new pages and copied the images to the parks local root folder in the Files panel. It is time to add additional enhancements to your site. In Project 1, you added a background image to the index page. In this project, you learn more about images. You will add the same background image to the two new pages, and then add page images and links to all three pages.

Images

If used correctly and with an understanding of the Web site audience, images add excitement and interest to a Web page. When you are selecting images for a Web site, it is important to understand that the size and type of image or images used within a Web page affect how fast the Web page downloads and displays in the viewer's Web browser. A Web page that downloads too slowly will turn away visitors.

Image File Formats

Graphical images used on the Web are in one of two broad categories: vector and bitmap. **Vector** images are composed of key points and paths, which define shapes and coloring instructions, such as line and fill colors. The vector file contains a description of the image expressed mathematically. The file describes the image to the computer, and the computer draws it. This type of image generally is associated with Macromedia's Flash or Adobe's LiveMotion animation programs. One of the benefits of vector images is the small file size, particularly relative to the larger file size of bitmap images.

Bitmap images are the more common type of image file. A bitmap file maps out or plots an image on a pixel-by-pixel basis. A **pixel**, or **picture element**, is the smallest point in a graphical image. Graphic monitors display images by dividing the display screen into thousands (or millions) of pixels, arranged in a **grid** of rows and columns. The pixels appear connected because they are so close together. This grid of pixels is a **bitmap**. The **bit-resolution** of an image is described by the number of bits used to represent each pixel. There are 8-bit images as well as 24- or 32-bit images, where each bit represents a pixel. An 8-bit image supports up to 256 colors, and a 24- or 32-bit image supports up to 16.7 million colors.

Web browsers currently support three bitmap image file types: GIF, JPEG, and PNG.

GIF (.gif) is an acronym for **Graphics Interchange Format**. The GIF format uses 8-bit resolution, supports up to a maximum of 256 colors, and uses combinations of these 256 colors to simulate colors beyond that range. The GIF format is best for displaying images such as logos, icons, buttons, and other images with even colors and tones. GIF images come in two different versions: GIF87 format and GIF89a format. The GIF89a format contains three features not available in the GIF87 or JPEG formats: transparency, interlacing, and animation. The **transparency** feature allows you to specify a transparency color, which allows the background color or image to display. The **interlacing** feature lets the browser begin to build a low-resolution version of the full-sized GIF picture on the screen while the file is still downloading, so there is something visible to the visitor as the Web page downloads. The **animation** feature allows you to include moving images. Animated GIF images are simply a number of GIF images saved into a single file and looped, or repeated, over and over. A number of shareware GIF editors are available to create animated GIFs. If you do not want to create your own animations, you can find thousands of free animated GIFs on the Internet available for downloading.

JPEG (.jpg) is an acronym for **Joint Photographic Experts Group**. JPEG files are the best format for photographic images because JPEG files can contain up to 16.7 million colors. **Progressive JPEG** is a new variation of the JPEG image format. This image format supports a gradually-built display similar to the interlaced GIFs. Older browsers do not support progressive JPEG files.

PNG (.png) stands for **Portable Network Graphics**. PNG, which is the native file format of Macromedia Fireworks, is a GIF competitor normally used for images. Many browsers do not support this format without a special plug-in. Generally, it is better to use GIF or JPEG images in your Web pages.

When developing a Web site that consists of many pages, you should maintain a consistent, professional layout and design throughout all of the pages. The pages in a single site, for example, should use similar features such as background colors or images, margins, and headings.

Background Colors and Background Images

Most Web pages are displayed with a default white or gray background. Generally, the browser used to display the Web page determines the default background. You can enhance your Web page by adding a background image and/or background color or adding one of Dreamweaver's Web-safe color schemes.

If you use a background color, the same cautions apply to background color as they do to text color. You want to use Web-safe colors, such as those in the Dreamweaver color schemes. This means the colors will display correctly on the computer screen when someone is viewing your Web page. To insert an image or color for the page background, you use the Page Properties dialog box.

Background images add texture and interesting color to a Web page and set the overall appearance of the document. Most browsers support background images. A background image can be a large image, but more frequently it is a smaller image.

Q: Is it necessary to add a background image to a Web page?

A: No, you do not need to add a background image. If you do add a background image to your Web page, however, select an image that does not clash with the text and other content. The background image should not overwhelm the Web page.

The image tiles to fill the screen in the Dreamweaver Document window and in the browser window. In Project 1, you added a background image to the index page. Now you add the same image to the National Parks Web page and the National Monuments page. The following steps illustrate how to add a background image to these two pages.

To Add a Background Image to the Colorado National Parks Web Page

1 Click the natl_parks.htm tab.

2 Click Modify on the menu bar and then click Page Properties.

3 Click the Browse button to the right of the Background image box.

4 If necessary, navigate to the images folder.

5 Click bg.jpg and then click the OK button in the Select Image Source dialog box.

6 Click the OK button in the Page Properties dialog box.

7 Click the Save button on the Standard toolbar.

The background image is applied to the Colorado National Parks page (Figure 2-21).

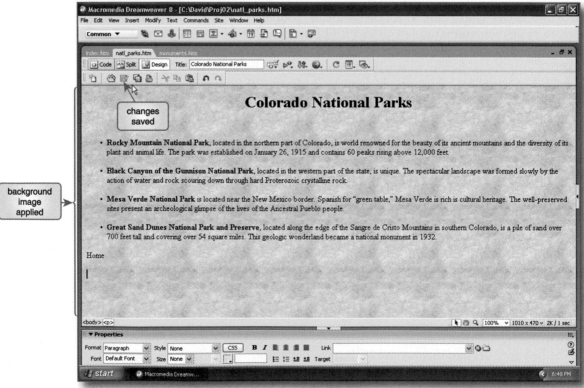

FIGURE 2-21

To Add a Background Image to the Colorado National Monuments Web Page

1 Click the monuments.htm tab.

2 Click Modify on the menu bar and then click Page Properties.

3 Click the Browse button to the right of the Background image box.

4 Click bg.jpg and then click the OK button in the Select Image Source dialog box.

5 Click the OK button in the Page Properties dialog box.

6 Click the Save button on the Standard toolbar.

Other Ways

1. Right-click Document window, click Page Properties on context menu
2. Expand the Property inspector, click Page Properties button

The background image is applied to the Colorado National Monuments page (Figure 2-22).

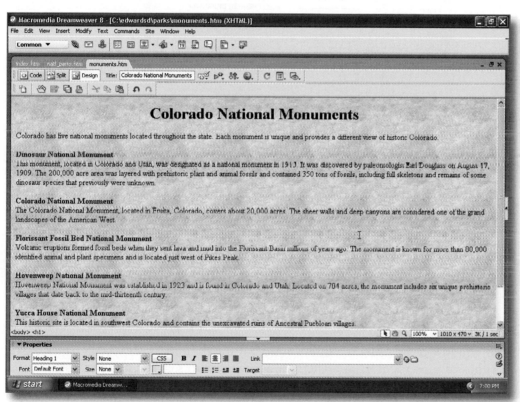

FIGURE 2-22

In addition to adding background images, you also can add images to your Web pages. To enhance your index.htm Web page further, you will add two images. One of the images will display at the top left of the document, and the second image will display to the right of the bulleted list. Dreamweaver has features to assist with placement and enhancement of images. The Assets panel provides visual cues for your images, the invisible element feature provides placement control for the images, and the accessibility feature provides information for individuals with disabilities.

Assets Panel

Assets are elements, such as images or Flash files, that you use in building a page or a site. The **Assets panel,** which is grouped with the Files panel, helps you manage and organize your Web site's assets (Figure 2-23 on the next page). This panel contains a list of all the asset types (images, colors, URLs, Flash and Shockwave files, movies, scripts, templates, and library items) within the selected local root folder. The Site option shows the assets in your site. The Favorites list shows only the assets you have selected and added to the list. To add an asset to the Favorites list, select the item in the Site list and then click the Add to Favorites button. Remove an item from the list by selecting the Favorites option button, selecting the item, and then clicking the Remove from Favorites button. The Assets panel in Figure 2-23 is resized to show all options. You resize the panels by moving the mouse pointer over the vertical bar until it displays as a two-headed arrow. Then you hold down the mouse button and drag.

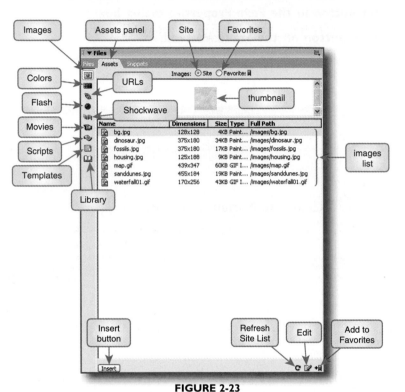

FIGURE 2-23

You can insert most asset types into a document by dragging them into the Document window or by using the Insert button at the bottom of the Assets panel. Also, you either can insert colors and URLs or apply them to selected text in Design view. Additionally, you can apply URLs to other elements in Design view, such as images. When an image file name is selected, a thumbnail of the image displays at the top of the Assets panel. You will use the Assets panel to insert the images into the Colorado Parks Web pages.

Accessibility

When developing a Web page, the Web page developer needs to consider the full spectrum of visitors who may access the site. Dreamweaver provides accessibility tools that allow the Web site developer to create pages to meet the needs of all visitors, including those with disabilities. The four accessibility object tools included in Dreamwaver are for forms, frames, media, and images. This project includes accessibility information relative to images. The three other objects are covered in later projects.

When you insert an image, the Image Tag Accessibility Attributes dialog box is displayed (Figure 2-24 on the next page). This dialog box contains two text boxes — one for Alternate text and one for Long description. Screen readers translate and read the information you enter in both text boxes. The information you enter for Alternate text displays when a Web site visitor moves the mouse pointer over the image. You should limit your alternate text entry to 50 characters or less. For a more detailed description of the image, create and save a text file and then add it as a link to the file. When the link is activated, the screen reader recites the text for visually impaired visitors. It is not required that you enter text in either text box. For images in this project and other projects, however, instructions are included to add alternate text. Clicking Cancel removes the dialog box and inserts the image. Appendix B contains a full overview of Dreamweaver's accessibility features.

FIGURE 2-24

Invisible Elements

Dreamweaver's Document window displays basically what you see in a Web browser window. It sometimes is helpful, however, when designing a Web page to see the placement of certain code elements. For example, viewing the Line Break code <br> provides a visual cue regarding the layout. Dreamweaver enables you to control the visibility of 13 different codes, including those for image placement, through the Preferences dialog box.

When you insert and align an image into a Document window, Dreamweaver can display an **invisible element marker** that shows the location of the inserted image within the HTML code. This visual aid displays as a small yellow icon. When you select the icon, it turns blue, and you can use it to cut and paste or drag and drop the image. When using invisible elements with images, however, the invisible element marker does not display if the image is aligned to the left. Other aligned elements include tables, ActiveX objects, plug-ins, and applets. To hide all invisible elements temporarily, select Hide All on the View menu Visual Aids submenu.

The following steps illustrate how to display the invisible element marker for aligned elements such as images and how to turn on Invisible Elements through the Visual Aids submenu command.

To Set Invisible Element Preferences and Turn on Visual Aids

1

• **Click Edit on the menu bar and then click Preferences.**

• **Click Invisible Elements in the Category list.**

The Preferences dialog box is displayed, and Invisible Elements is selected in the Category list (Figure 2-25).

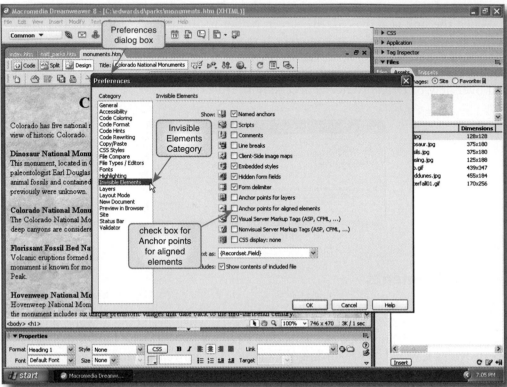

FIGURE 2-25

2

• **Click the Anchor points for aligned elements check box (Figure 2-26).**

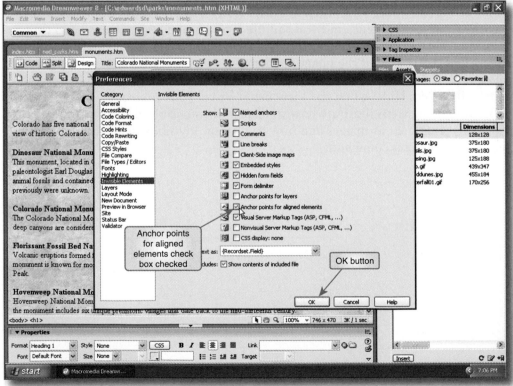

FIGURE 2-26

3

• **Click the OK button.**

The Document window is displayed with no visible change.

4

• **Click View on the menu bar, point to Visual Aids, and then point to Invisible Elements.**

The View menu and the Visual Aids submenu are displayed. Invisible Elements is selected (Figure 2-27). Note: If a check mark already appears to the left of the Invisible Elements command, do not complete the next step.

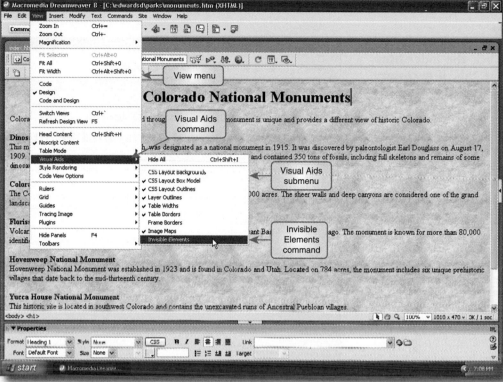

FIGURE 2-27

5

• **Click Invisible Elements.**

A check mark is added to the Invisible Elements command, and the Document window displays with no visible changes.

Inserting an Image into a Web Page

Inserting images into your Web page is easy and quick with Dreamweaver — just drag and drop the image from the Files panel or the Assets panel. Image placement, however, can be more complex. When you view the Web page in a browser, the image may display somewhat differently than in the Document window. If the images do not display correctly, you can select and modify the placement of the images in the Document window by dragging the invisible element marker to move the image.

To Insert an Image into the Index Page

• **Click the index.htm page tab. If necessary, scroll to the top of the page.**

• **Click the vertical bar expander arrow to display the panel groups.**

• **If necessary, click the Assets panel tab. Verify that the Images icon is selected.**

• **Click sanddunes.jpg in the Assets panel.**

The index page is displayed and the Assets panel is available. The file, sanddunes.jpg is selected (Figure 2-28).

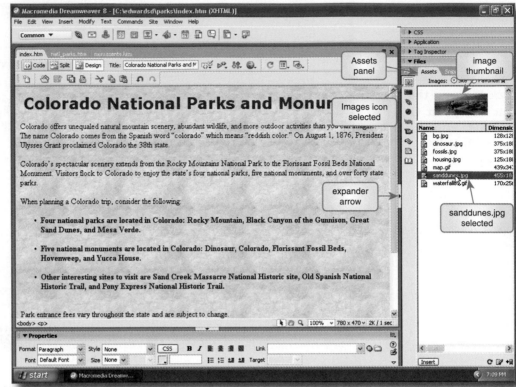

FIGURE 2-28

2

• **Drag sanddunes.jpg from the Assets panel to the left of the first line of the first paragraph.**

• **Expand the Property inspector.**

The Image Tag Accessibility Attributes dialog box is displayed (Figure 2-29).

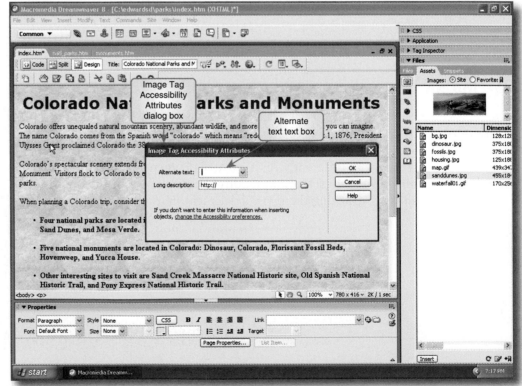

FIGURE 2-29

3

• **Type Sand Dunes National Park in the Alternate text text box.**

The alternate text is entered for the image (Figure 2-30).

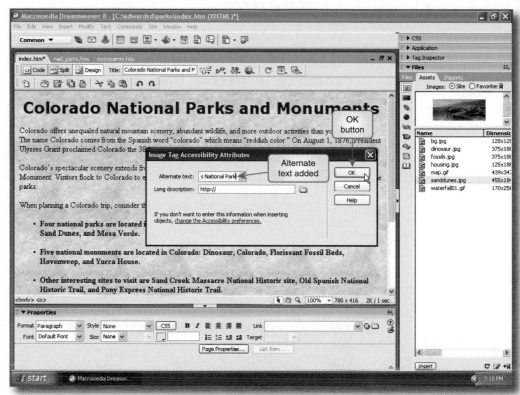

FIGURE 2-30

4

• **Click the OK button.**

The image appears in the Document window. The border and handles around the image indicate that it is selected. The attributes change in the Property inspector to reflect the selected object (Figure 2-31). The alternate text you entered in the Alternate text text box displays in the Alt box in the Property inspector.

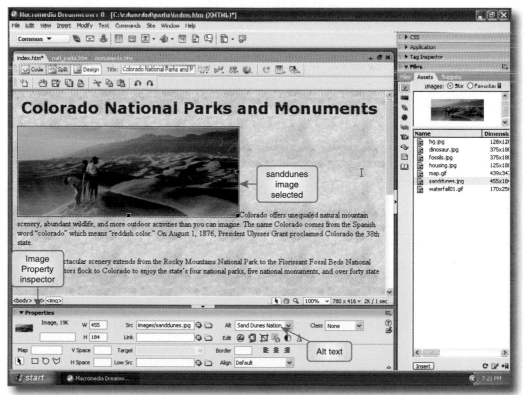

FIGURE 2-31

In addition to the visual aid feature, you use the Property inspector to help with image placement and to add other attributes. When you select an image within the Document window, the Property inspector displays properties specific to that image.

Property Inspector Image Features

The Property inspector lets you see the current properties of the selected element. The Property inspector is divided into two sections. Clicking the expander arrow in the lower-right corner of the Property inspector expands/collapses the Property inspector. When it is in collapsed mode, it shows only the more commonly used properties for the selected element. Expanded mode shows more advanced options. The Property inspector for images contains several image-related features in the top and lower sections.

The following section describes the image-related features of the Property inspector (Figure 2-32).

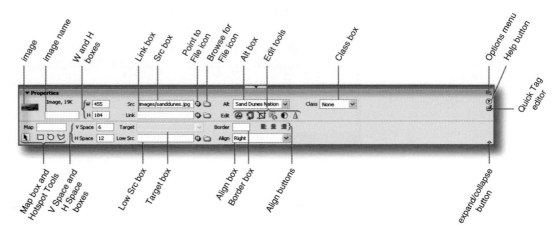

FIGURE 2-32

W AND H The **W** and **H** boxes indicate the width and height of the image, in pixels. Dreamweaver automatically displays the dimensions when an image is inserted into a page. You can specify the image size in the following units: pc (picas), pt (points), in (inches), mm (millimeters), cm (centimeters), and combinations, such as 2in+5mm. Dreamweaver converts the values to pixels in the source code.

LINK The **Link** box allows you to make the selected image a hyperlink to a specified URL or Web page. To create a relative link, you can click the Point to File or Browse for File icons to the right of the Link box to browse to a page in your Web site, or you can drag a file from the Files panel into the Link box. For an external link, you can type the URL directly into the Link box or use copy and paste.

ALIGN Set the alignment of an image in relation to other elements in the same paragraph, table, or line with **Align**. This property option is discussed in more detail later in this project.

ALT Use Alt to specify alternative text that appears in place of the image for text-only browsers or for browsers that have been set to download images manually. For visually impaired users who utilize speech synthesizers with text-only browsers, the text is spoken aloud. In some browsers, this text also appears when the mouse pointer is over the image.

MAP AND HOTSPOT TOOLS Use the **Map** box and the **Hotspot tools** to label and create an image map.

V SPACE AND H SPACE Use V Space and H Space to add space, in pixels, along the sides of the image. **V Space** adds space along the top and bottom of an image. **H Space** adds space along the left and right of an image.

TARGET Use **Target** to specify the frame or window in which the linked page should load. This option is not available when the image is linked to another file.

LOW SRC Use **Low Src** to specify the image that should load before the main image. Many designers use a small black-and-white version of the main image because it loads quickly and gives visitors an idea of what they will see when the page has fully loaded.

BORDER The **Border** is the width, in pixels, of the image's border. The default is no border.

EDIT Use **Edit** to select from six different editing option tools: (a) Edit, which opens the computer's default image editor; (b) **Optimize in Fireworks**, which opens the Macromedia Fireworks image-editing application; (c) **Crop**, which lets you edit images by reducing the area of the image; (d) **Image resampling**, which adds or subtracts pixels from a resized JPEG or GIF image file to match the appearance of the original image as closely as possible; (e) **Brightness/Contrast**, which modifies the contrast or brightness of pixels in an image; and (f) **Sharpening**, which adjusts the focus of an image by increasing the contrast of edges found within the image. Editing tools (c) through (f) do not require an external image-editing application. These editing functions are discussed in more detail later in this project.

RESET SIZE If you change an image size, use **Reset Size** to reset the W and H values to the original size of the image.

LEFT, CENTER, AND RIGHT In Dreamweaver, the default alignment for an image is left alignment. To change the default alignment, select the image you want to align. Click an alignment button: Align Left, Align Center, or Align Right.

SRC Use **Src** to specify the source file for the image.

After you insert the image into the Web page and then select it, the Property inspector displays features specific to the image. As discussed earlier, alignment is one of these features. **Alignment** determines where on the page the image displays and if and how text wraps around the image.

Aligning an Image

When you insert an image into a Web page, by default, the text around the image aligns to the bottom of the image. The image alignment options on the Align pop-up menu in the Property inspector let you set the alignment for the image in relation to other page content. Dreamweaver provides 10 alignment options for images. Table 2-3 on the next page describes these image alignment options.

Table 2-3 Image Alignment Options

ALIGNMENT OPTION	DESCRIPTION
Default	Aligns the image with the baseline of the text in most browser default settings
Baseline	Aligns the image with the baseline of the text regardless of the browser setting
Top	Aligns the image with the top of the item; an item can be text or another object
Middle	Aligns the image with the baseline of the text or object at the vertical middle of the image
Bottom	Aligns the image with the baseline of the text or the bottom of another image regardless of the browser setting
Text Top	Aligns the image with the top of the tallest character in a line of text
Absolute Middle	Aligns the image with the middle of the current line of text
Absolute Bottom	Aligns the image with the bottom of the current line of text or another object
Left	Aligns the image at the left margin
Right	Aligns the image at the right margin

The more widely used options are left and right. The following steps show how to align the sanddunes image to the right and create text wrapping to the left of the image. To have a better overview of how the page will display in a browser, you will collapse the panel groups.

To Align an Image

1

• Click the panel groups expander arrow to collapse the panel groups.

• If necessary, click the sanddunes image to select it and then click the Align box arrow in the Property inspector. Point to Right on the pop-up menu.

The Align pop-up menu is displayed, and Right is selected (Figure 2-33).

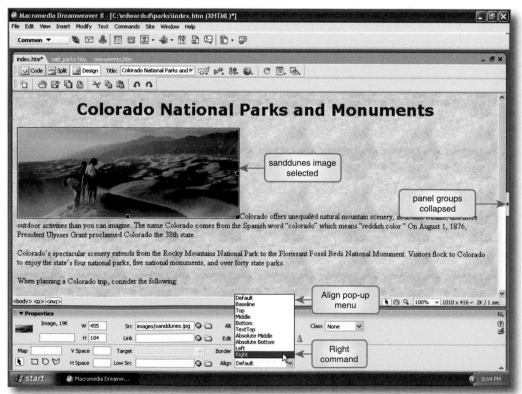

FIGURE 2-33

2

• Click Right.

The image moves to the right side of the window and is selected (Figure 2-34). An element marker is displayed to indicate the location of the insertion point.

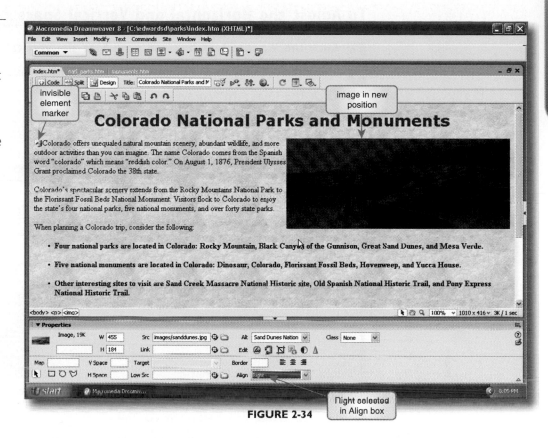

FIGURE 2-34

Adjusting Space around Images

When aligning an image, by default, only about three pixels of space are inserted between the image and adjacent text. You can adjust the amount of vertical and horizontal space between the image and text by using the V Space and H Space settings in the Property inspector. The V Space setting controls the vertical space above or below an image. The H Space setting controls the horizontal space to the left or right side of the image. The following step shows how to add vertical and horizontal spacing.

To Adjust the Horizontal and Vertical Space

1 Click the **V Space** text box and type 6 as the vertical space.

2 Press the TAB key and type 12 as the horizontal space. Press the TAB key.

3 Click the image to remove the highlighting.

Dreamweaver adds additional horizontal and vertical space between the image and the text (Figure 2-35).

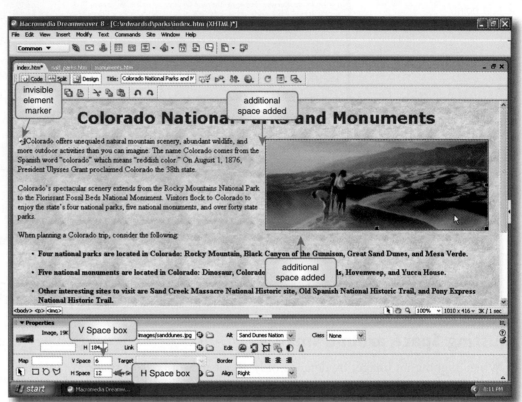

FIGURE 2-35

More About

Accessibility Issues

For more information about authoring for accessibility, visit the Dreamweaver 8 More About Web page (scsite.com/dw8/more) and then click Dreamweaver 8 Accessibility Issues.

To enhance your Web page further, you will add a waterfall image. This image will display on the left side of the page, to the left of the bulleted items. The following steps show how to insert an image of a waterfall in the Web page.

To Insert the Waterfall Image

1

• Scroll down and position the insertion point so it is to the left of the sentence introducing the bulleted list (Figure 2-36).

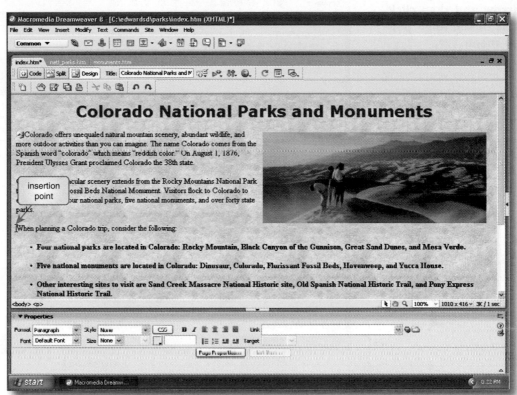

FIGURE 2-36

2

• Display the Assets panel and click waterfall01.gif

• Drag the image to the insertion point. Type Rocky Mountain waterfall in the Alternate text textbox, and then click the OK button.

• Collapse the panel groups.

The waterfall image is displayed (Figure 2-37). The border and handles around the image indicate that it is selected. The panel groups are collapsed.

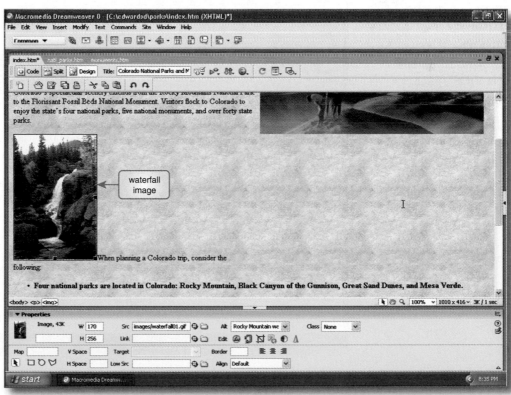

FIGURE 2-37

3

• **Click the Align box arrow and then click Left in the Align pop-up menu.**

The image moves to the left side of the window, and the text adjusts to the right (Figure 2-38). The bullets and some of the text is hidden by the image. Adjusting the spacing will make the bullets and text visible.

FIGURE 2-38

4

• **Click the V Space box and type** 6 **as the vertical space.**

• **Click the H Space box and type** 20 **as the horizontal space.**

• **Press the TAB key.**

• **Click anywhere in the Document window to deselect the image.**

Additional horizontal and vertical space is added between the image and the text, and the bullets are now visible (Figure 2-39).

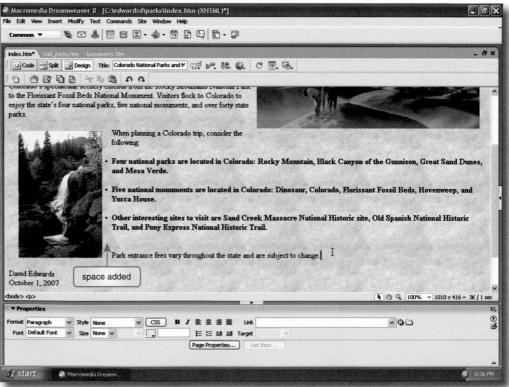

FIGURE 2-39

- **Click the Save button on the Standard toolbar.**
- **Press the F12 key.**
- **Move the mouse point over the sanddunes and waterfall images to display the Alt text.**

The index page is displayed in your browser and all changes to the index page are saved (Figure 2-40). Web pages may display differently in your browser. The browser and selected text size affect how a Web page is displayed. In Figure 2-40, the text size is set to Medium.

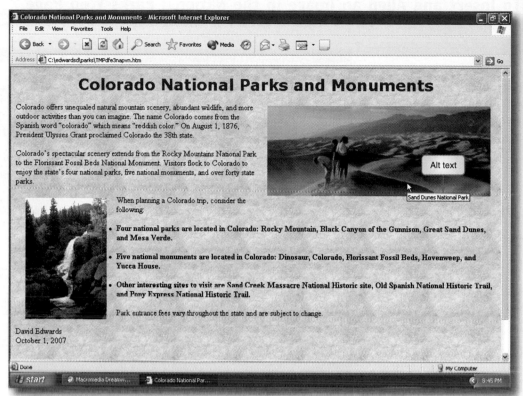

FIGURE 2-40

- **Close the browser to return to Dreamweaver.**

The second page in your Web site is the National Parks page. To develop the National Parks page further and add information showing the locations of the four Colorado national parks, you will add a Colorado map. References to each park are contained on the map. The following steps show how to add the Colorado map image to the National Parks Web page.

To Insert and Align an Image in the National Parks Web Page

1

• Click the natl_parks.htm Web page tab. Display the panel groups.

• Position the insertion point to the left of the first bulleted text item (Rocky Mountain National Park).

The insertion point is positioned to the left of Rocky Mountain National Park (Figure 2-41).

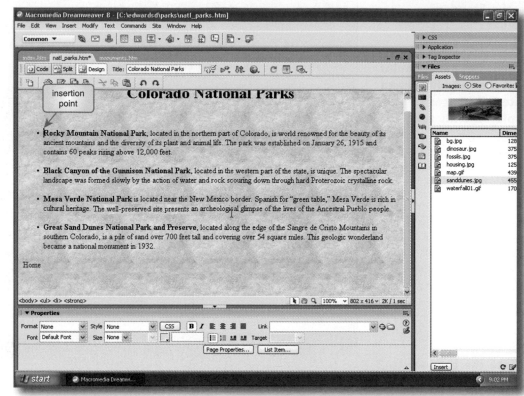

FIGURE 2-41

2

• Drag the map.gif file from the Assets panel to the insertion point.

• Type Colorado National Parks in the Alternate text text box and then click the OK button.

• Collapse the panel groups.

The image is selected (Figure 2-42). The attributes change in the Property inspector to reflect the selected object.

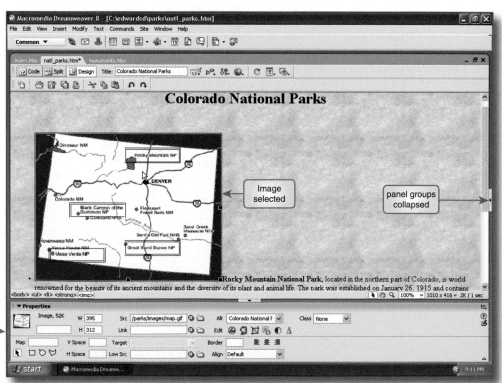

FIGURE 2-42

3

• **Click the Align box arrow and then click Right.**

The selected image is aligned to the right in the Document window (Figure 2-43).

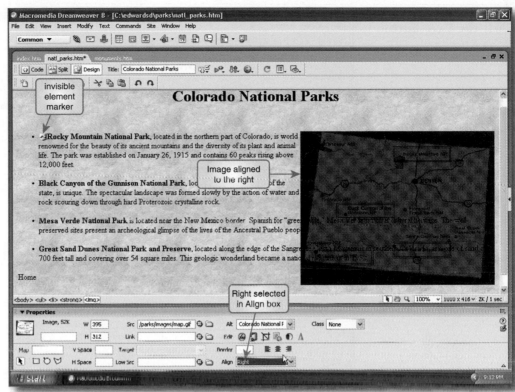

FIGURE 2-43

4

• **Click the V Space box and type 8 as the vertical space.**

• **Click the H Space box and type 10 as the horizontal space.**

• **Press the ENTER key.**

• **Click anywhere in the Document window to deselect the image (Figure 2-44).**

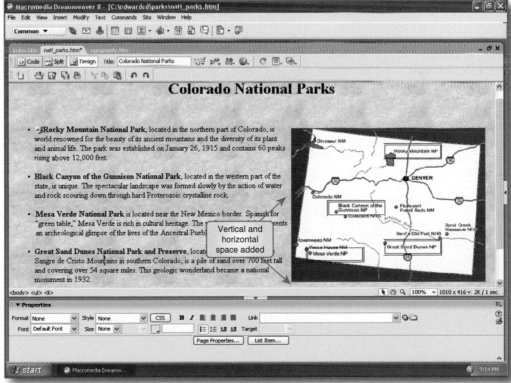

FIGURE 2-44

5

• **Click the Save button on the Standard toolbar.**

The Colorado National Parks Web page is saved.

• **Press the F12 key.**

The Colorado National Parks Web page is displayed in the browser (Figure 2-45).

• **Close the browser to return to Dreamweaver.**

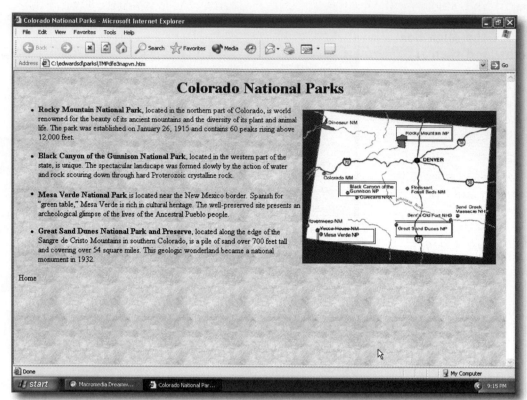

FIGURE 2-45

The third page in your Web site is the Colorado National Monuments page. To add interest to this page, you will add three images. You will align two of the images to the left and one to the right. When you added images to the index.htm and natl_parks.htm pages, you expanded and collapsed the panel groups. In the following steps, you leave the panel groups expanded. This enables you to experience both methods and determine the one which works best for you. The following steps illustrate how to add the images to the Colorado National Monuments Web page.

To Insert and Align Images in the National Monuments Web Page

1

• **Click the monuments.htm Web page tab. Display the panel groups and click the Assets tab, if necessary.**

• **Position the insertion point to the left of the paragraph following the Dinosaur National Monument subhead.**

The insertion point is to the left of the first sentence in the first paragraph (Figure 2-46).

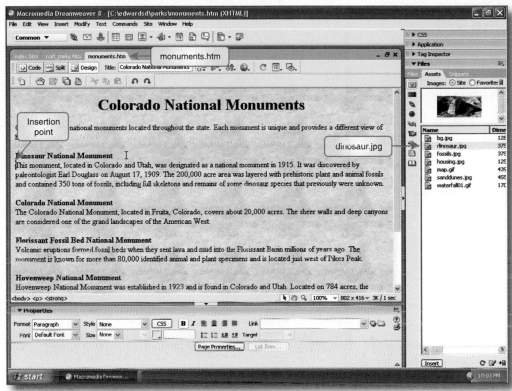

FIGURE 2-46

2

• **Drag the dinosaur.jpg file from the Assets panel to the insertion point.**

• **Type** Dinosaur National Park **in the Alternate text text box and then click the OK button.**

• **Click the Align box arrow in the Property inspector and then click Left on the Align pop-up menu.**

The image aligns to the left (Figure 2-47).

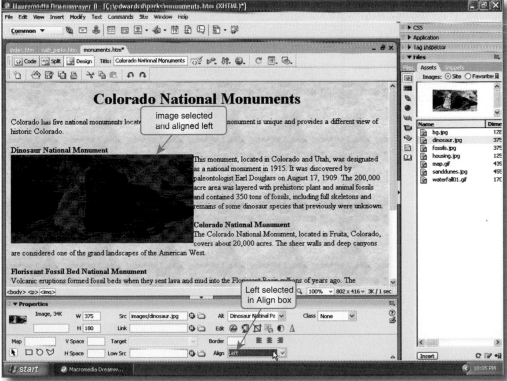

FIGURE 2-47

3

• Click the **V Space box** and then type 8 as the vertical space.

• Click the **H Space box**, type 10 as the horizontal space, and then press the ENTER key.

The image is highlighted. The V Space and H Space attributes are added for the Dinosaur image (Figure 2-48).

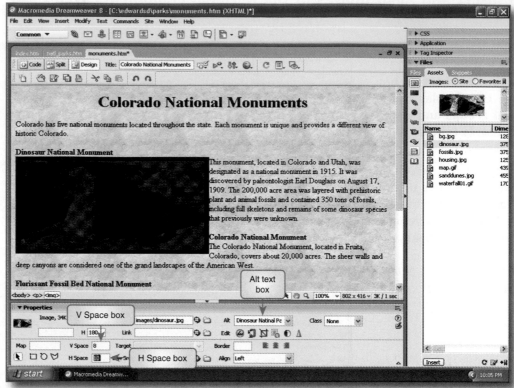

FIGURE 2-48

4

• If necessary, scroll down and then position the insertion point to the left of the word, Volcanic, in the first line in the Florissant Fossil Bed National Monument paragraph.

The insertion point is to the left of the first sentence in the fourth paragraph (Figure 2-49).

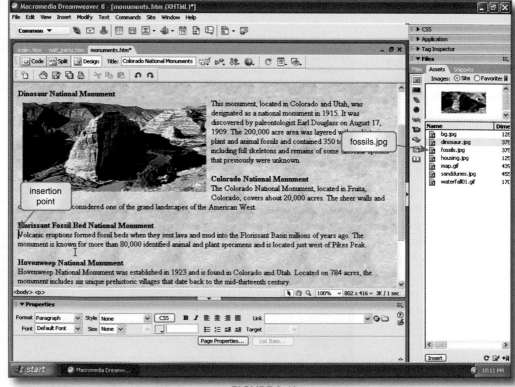

FIGURE 2-49

5

• **Drag the fossils.jpg image to the insertion point.**

• **Type** Florissant Basin **in the Alternate text text box and then click the OK button.**

The image is inserted into the Document window and is selected (Figure 2-50).

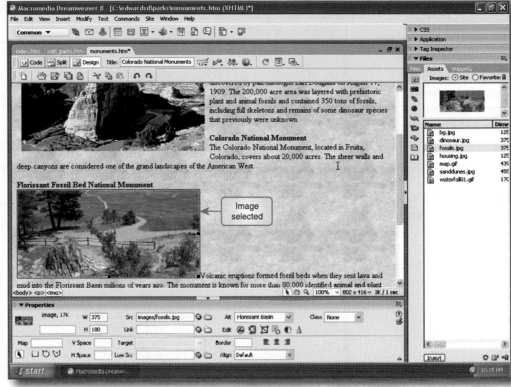

FIGURE 2-50

6

• **Click the Align box arrow and then click Right on the Align pop-up menu.**

• **Click the V Space box and then type** 35 **as the vertical space.**

• **Click the H Space box and then type** 20 **as the horizontal space. Press the ENTER key.**

The image is positioned on the page (Figure 2-51).

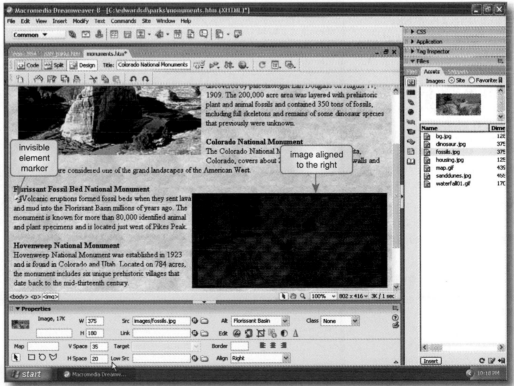

FIGURE 2-51

7

• **Position the insertion point to the left of the Hovenweep National Monument subhead.**

• **Drag the housing.jpg image from the Assets panel to the insertion point.**

• **Type** Yucca House prehistoric village **in the Alternate text text box and then press the ENTER key.**

The housing image is inserted on the page (Figure 2-52).

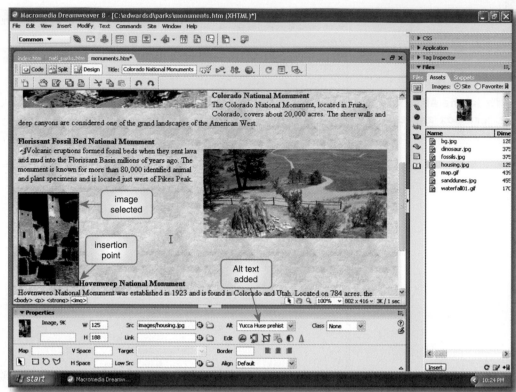

FIGURE 2-52

8

• **Click the Align box arrow and then click Left on the Align pop-up menu.**

• **Click the V Space box and then type** 5 **as the vertical space.**

• **Click the H Space box and then type** 10 **as the horizontal space. Press the ENTER key.**

• **Click anywhere on the page to deselect the image.**

• **Click the Save button on the Standard toolbar.**

The image is positioned on the page and the Web page is saved (Figure 2-53).

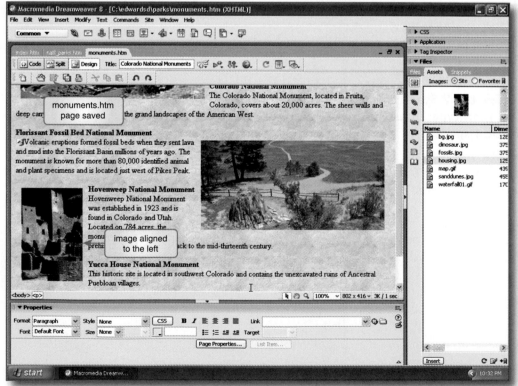

FIGURE 2-53

9

• **Press the F12 key.**

The National Monuments page is displayed in the browser (Figure 2-54).

• **Close the browser.**

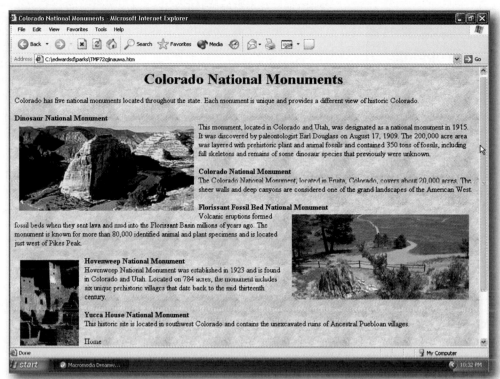

FIGURE 2-54

Image Editing Tools

Dreamweaver makes available several basic image editing tools to modify and enhance an image. You access these functions through the Property inspector.

- Use an external image editor: Macromedia's Fireworks is the default image editor, but you can specify which external editor should start for a specified file type. To select an external editor, click Edit on the menu bar and display the Preferences dialog box. Select File Types/Editors from the Category list to display the Preferences File Types/Editors dialog box. Select the image extension and then browse for the External Code Editor executable file.

- Crop an image: **Cropping** lets you edit an image by reducing the area of the image and allows you to eliminate unwanted or distracting portions of the image. Cropping can be very effective for improving the appearance of a photo by highlighting the main point of interest in an image. When you crop an image and then save the page, the source image file is changed on the disk. To return the image to its original size, click the Undo button on the Standard toolbar. Prior to saving, you may want to keep a backup copy of the image file in the event you need to revert to the original image.

- Brightness/Contrast: The **Brightness/Contrast** tool modifies the contrast or brightness of the pixels in an image. Recall that a pixel is the smallest point in a graphical image. Brightness makes the pixels in the image lighter or darker overall, while Contrast either emphasizes or de-emphasizes the difference between lighter and darker regions. This affects the highlights, shadows, and midtones of an image. The values for the brightness and contrast settings range from –100 to 100.

More About

Undo Cropping

You can undo the effect of
the Crop command and
revert to the original image
file up until the time that you
quit Dreamweaver or edit the
file in an external image-
editing application. To undo
the effects, click Edit on the
menu bar and then click the
Undo Crop command.

• Resampling: The process of **resampling** adds or subtracts pixels from a resized JPEG or GIF image file to match the appearance of the original image as closely as possible. Resampling an image also reduces an image's file size, resulting in improved download performance. When you resize an image in Dreamweaver, you can resample it to accommodate its new dimensions. To resample a resized image, resize the image as previously described and then click the Resample button in the Property inspector.

• Sharpening: **Sharpening** adjusts the focus of an image by increasing the contrast of edges found within the image.

The fossils image in the Colorado National Monuments page extends somewhat below the last line of the text. Cropping the image and emphasizing the fossil bed in the image will enhance the page. The following steps show how to crop the image, and then modify the brightness/contrast.

To Crop and Modify Brightness/Contrast of an Image

1

• **Select the fossils.jpg image.**

• **Click the Crop Tool icon in the Property inspector. If a Dreamweaver 8 caution dialog box is displayed, click the OK button.**

A bounding box with crop handles appears around the selected image (Figure 2-55).

FIGURE 2-55

2

• **Click the crop handle in the lower-right corner and adjust the handles until the bounding box surrounds the area of the image similar to that shown in Figure 2-56.**

The area of the image to retain is selected (Figure 2-56).

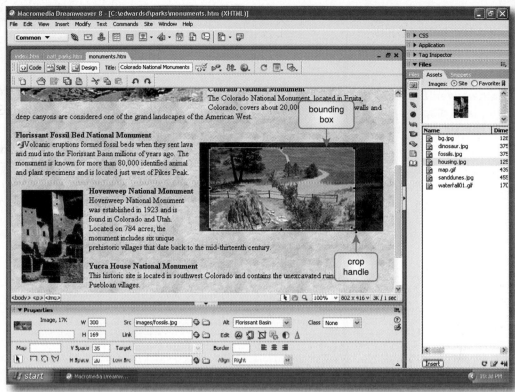

FIGURE 2-56

3

• **Double-click inside the bounding box.**

• **Click the image.**

The image is cropped and selected (Figure 2-57). If you need to make changes, click the Undo button on the Standard toolbar and repeat steps 1 and 2.

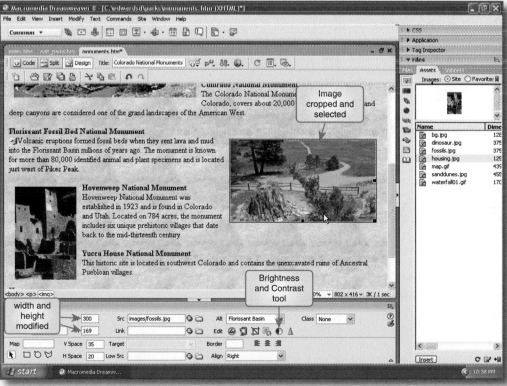

FIGURE 2-57

4

• **Click the housing.jpg image to select it. Click the Brightness and Contrast tool. If a Dreamweaver 8 caution dialog box displays, click the OK button.**

The Brightness/Contrast dialog box is displayed (Figure 2-58).

FIGURE 2-58

5

• **Drag the Brightness slider to the right and adjust the setting to -10.**

• **Drag the Contrast slider to the right and adjust the setting to 35.**

The brightness and contrast are changed in the image (Figure 2-59).

6

• **Click the OK button.**

• **Click the Save button on the Standard toolbar.**

The two images are adjusted and the National Monuments page is saved.

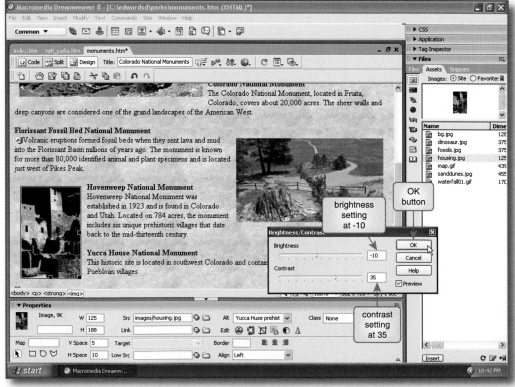

FIGURE 2-59

7

- **Press the F12 key to view the Monuments page in your browser.**

The Colorado National Monuments page is displayed in your browser (Figure 2-60).

8

- **Close the browser to return to the Dreamweaver window.**

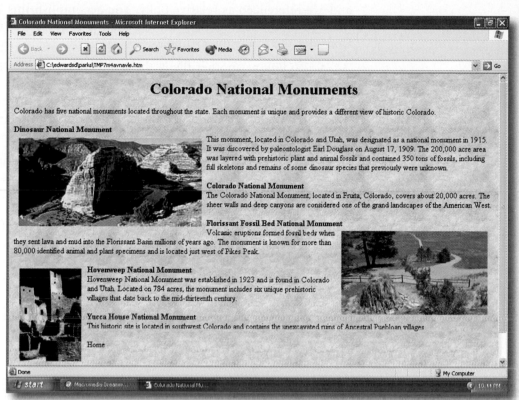

FIGURE 2-60

To connect the pages within the Web site and to display the navigation structure of the pages in the Site Map, you create links. The next section discusses the different types of links.

Understanding Different Types of Links

Links are the distinguishing feature of the World Wide Web. A link, also referred to as a hyperlink, is the path to another document, to another part of the same document, or to other media such as an image or a movie. Most links display as colored and/or underlined text, although you also can link from an image or other object. Clicking a link accesses the corresponding document, other media, or another place within the same document. If you place the mouse pointer over the link, the Web address of the link, or path, usually appears at the bottom of the window, on the status bar.

Three types of link paths are available: absolute, relative, and root-relative. An **absolute link** provides the complete URL of the document. This type of link also is referred to as an **external link**. Absolute links generally contain a protocol (such as http://) and primarily are used to link to documents on other servers.

You use **relative links** for local links. This type of link also is referred to as a **document-relative link**, or an **internal link**. If the linked documents are in the same folder, such as those in your parks folder, this is the best type of link to use. You also can use a relative link to link to a document in another folder, such as the images folder. All the files you see in the Files panel Local View are internal files and are referenced as relative links. You accomplish this by specifying the path through the folder hierarchy from the current document to the linked document. Consider the following examples.

- To link to another file in the same folder, specify the file name. Example: monuments.htm.
- To link to a file in a subfolder of the current Web site folder (such as the images folder), the link path would consist of the name of the subfolder, a forward slash (/), and then the file name. Example: images/sanddunes.jpg.

You use the **root-relative link** primarily when working with a large Web site that requires several servers. Web developers generally use this type of link when they must move HTML files from one folder or server to another folder or server. Root-relative links are beyond the scope of this book.

Two other types of links are named anchor and e-mail. A **named anchor** lets the user link to a specific location within a document. To create a named anchor, click the Named Anchor command on the Insert menu. An **e-mail link** creates a blank e-mail message containing the recipient's address. Another type of link is a **null**, or **script, link**. This type of link provides for attaching behaviors to an object or executes JavaScript code.

Named Anchor

To create a named anchor, place the insertion point where you want the named anchor. Then click the Named Anchor command on the Insert menu. Type a name for the anchor in the Named Anchor text box.

Relative Links

Dreamweaver offers a variety of ways in which to create a relative link. Three of the more commonly used methods are point to file, drag-and-drop, and browse for file. The point to file and drag-and-drop methods require that the Property inspector and the Files or Assets panels be open. To use the **point to file method**, you drag the Point to File icon to the file or image in the Files or Assets panel. In the **drag-and-drop method**, you drag the file from the Files or Assets panel to the Link text box in the Property inspector. The **browse for file method** is accomplished through the Select File dialog box. A fourth method is to use the context menu. To do this, you select the text for the link, right-click to display the context menu, and then select the Make Link command.

The next step is to add the text to create the relative links from the home page to the National Parks and National Monuments pages. You will use the drag-and-drop method to create a relative link from the text to a specific Web page.

Adding Text for the Relative Links

To create relative links from the index page, you add text to the index page and use the text to create the links to the other two Web pages in your Web site. You will center the text directly below the Colorado National Parks and Monuments heading. The following steps show how to add the text for the links.

To Add Text for Relative Links

 1

• **Click the Files panel tab.**

• **Click the index.htm tab in the Document window. If necessary, scroll to the top of the page and then position the insertion point at the end of the title, Colorado National Parks and Monuments.**

• **Press the ENTER key.**

• **If style1 displays in the Style text box in the Property inspector, click the Style pop-up menu and select None**

The insertion point is centered below the title, and the text color is returned to the default. The Files panel is displayed (Figure 2-61).

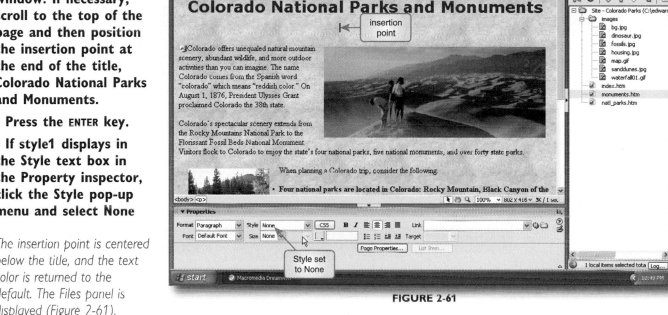

FIGURE 2-61

2

• **Type** National Parks **and then press the SPACEBAR.**

The text for the first link, National Parks, is displayed in the Document window (Figure 2-62).

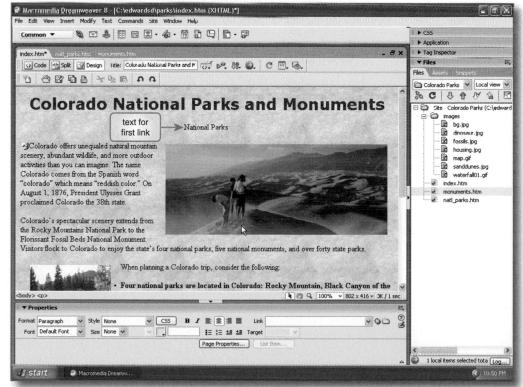

FIGURE 2-62

3

• Hold down the **SHIFT** key and then press the vertical line key (|). Press the **SPACEBAR** and then type National Monuments.

The text for both links is displayed in the Document window (Figure 2-63).

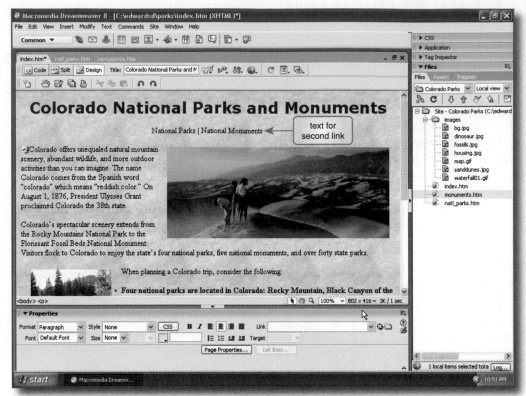

FIGURE 2-63

You will use the text, National Parks, to create a link to the National Parks Web page and the text, National Monuments, to create a link to the National Monuments page.

Creating a Relative Link Using Drag-and-Drop

A relative link is used to create links between local files or files within one Web site. The drag-and-drop method requires that the Property inspector be displayed and that the site files display in the Files or Assets panel. The following steps illustrate how to use the drag-and-drop method to create a relative link from the Colorado Parks home page to the National Parks Web page.

To Create a Relative Link Using Drag-and-Drop

1

• **Drag to select the text, National Parks.**

The National Parks text is selected (Figure 2-64).

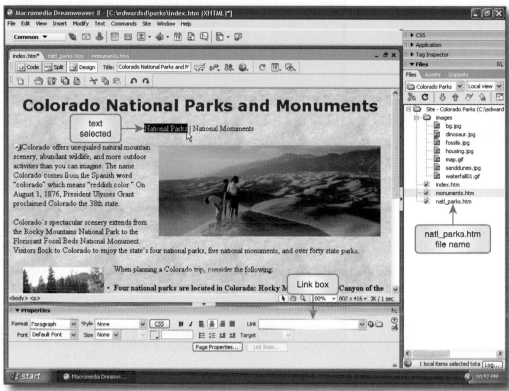

FIGURE 2-64

2

• **Drag the natl_parks.htm file from the Files panel to the Link box in the Property inspector. Do not release the mouse button.**

When you start to drag, a circle icon with a diagonal line through it appears next to the mouse pointer (Figure 2-65).

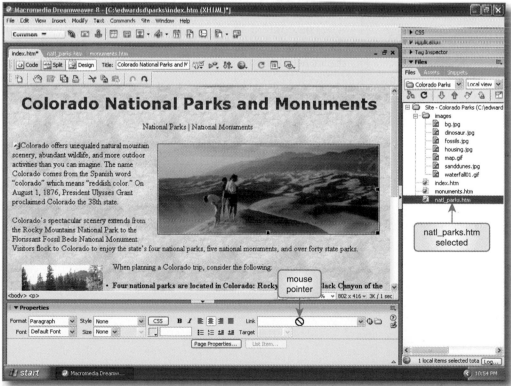

FIGURE 2-65

3

• **Release the mouse button.**

The linked text is displayed underlined and in a different color in the Document window, and the link text is displayed in the Link box (Figure 2-66). If you click anywhere else in the document, the linked document name does not display in the Link box.

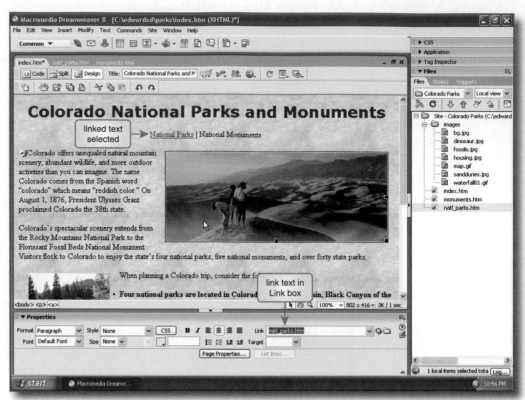

FIGURE 2-66

More About

Images as Links

It is easy to create a link from an image. Just select the image and then type or drag the file name into the Property inspector Link box.

Creating a Relative Link Using the Context Menu

The context menu is a second way to create a link. Using this method, you select the file name in the Select File dialog box. The following steps illustrate how to use the context menu to create a link to the National Monuments page.

To Create a Relative Link Using the Context Menu

1

• **Drag to select the text, National Monuments, and right-click to display the context menu. Point to Make Link.**

The text, National Monuments, is selected, and the context menu is displayed. The Make Link command is selected (Figure 2-67).

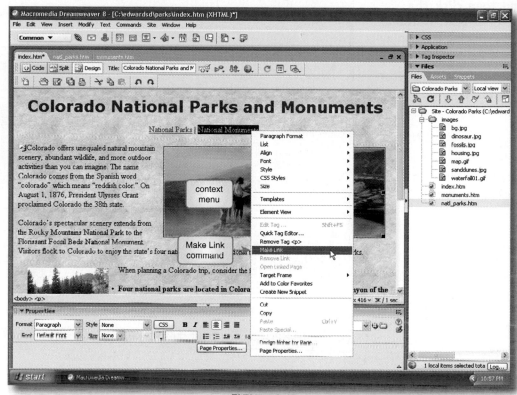

FIGURE 2-67

2

• **Click the Make Link command and click monuments.**

The Select File dialog box is displayed and monuments is selected (Figure 2-68).

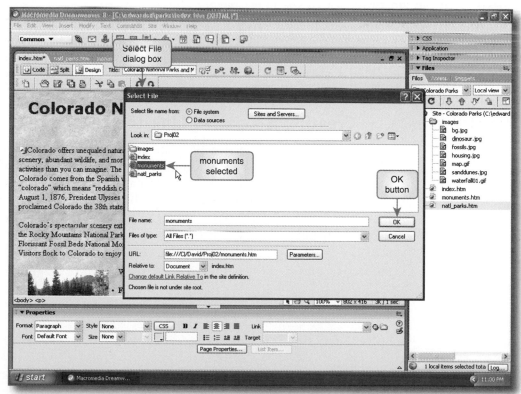

FIGURE 2-68

3

- **Click the OK button and then click the selected text, National Monuments, to display the link.**
- **Click the Save button on the Standard toolbar.**

The linked text is displayed underlined and in a different color in the Document window, and the link text is displayed in the Link box (Figure 2-69). If you click anywhere else in the document, the linked document name does not display in the Link box.

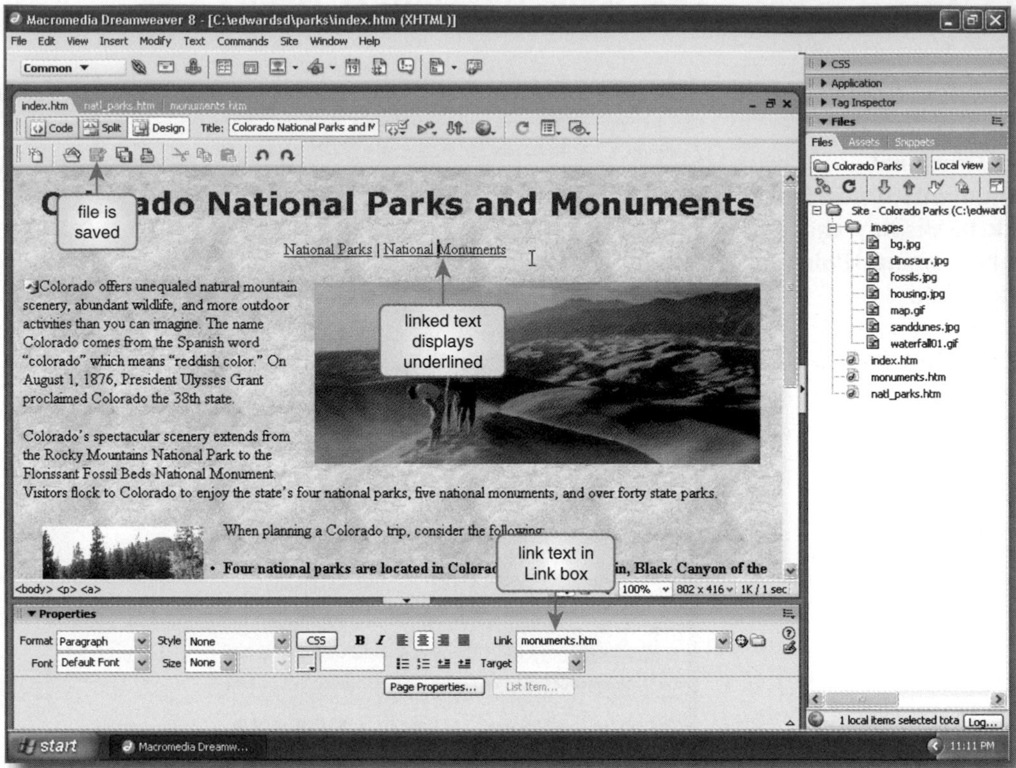

4

- **Press the F12 key to view the index page in your browser.**
- **Click the National Parks link to verify that the link works and then click the browser Back button to return to the index page.**
- **Click the National Monuments link to verify that the link works.**
- **Close the browser.**

FIGURE 2-69

Other Ways

1. Click Link box, type file name
2. Click Point to File icon in Property inspector, drag to file name

Creating a Relative Link to the Home Page

Visitors can enter a Web site at any point, so it is important always to include a link from each page within the site back to the home page. You must therefore create a relative link to the home page from the National Parks page and from the National Monuments page. The following steps show how to create a link from the National Parks page and a link from the National Monuments page to the home page.

To Create a Relative Link to the Home Page

1

• **Click the natl_parks.htm tab and then scroll to the bottom of the page. Drag to select Home.**

The text, Home, is selected (Figure 2-70). This text will become a link.

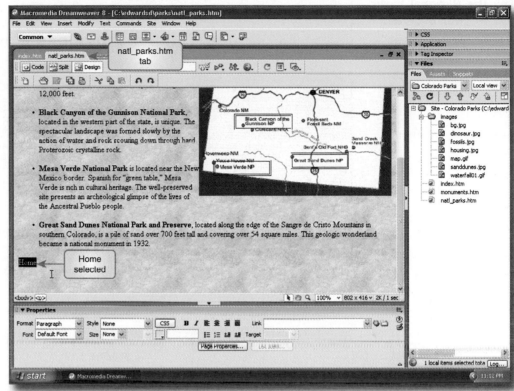

FIGURE 2-70

2

• **Drag the index.htm file name from the Files panel to the Link box.**

• **Click the Save button on the Standard toolbar.**

The link is created (Figure 2-71). The National Parks page is saved.

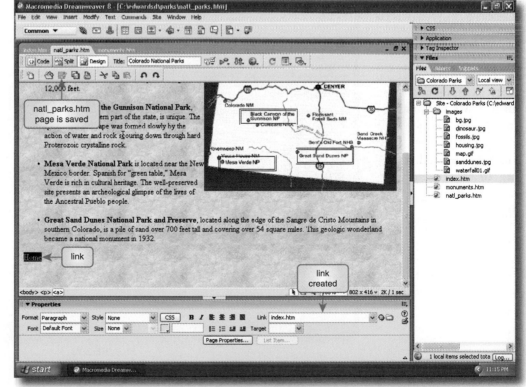

FIGURE 2-71

3

• Press the **F12** key to view the **National Parks** page in your browser.

• Click the **Home** link.

The index page is displayed in the browser (Figure 2-72)

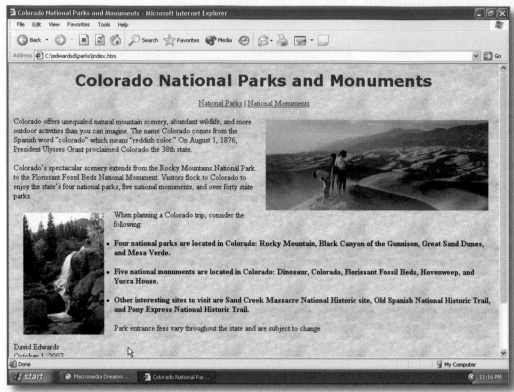

FIGURE 2-72

4

• Close the browser.

The browser is closed, and Dreamweaver is displayed.

5

• Click the **monuments.htm** tab. If necessary, scroll to the end of the document and then drag to select the text, **Home** (Figure 2-73).

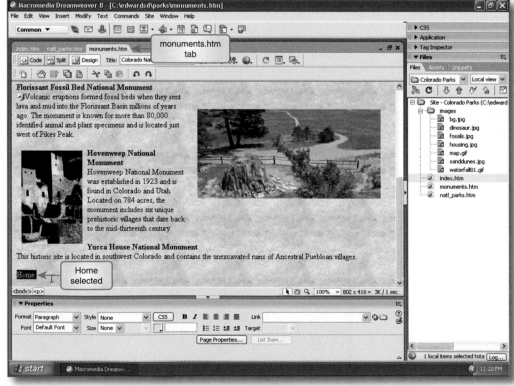

FIGURE 2-73

6

• **Collapse the Property inspector.**

• **Drag the index.htm file name from the Files panel to the Link box.**

• **Click the Save button on the Standard toolbar.**

The link is created, and index.htm is displayed in the Link box. The Property inspector is collapsed to provide a better view of the page (Figure 2-74). The National Monuments page is saved.

7

• **Press the F12 key to view the National Monuments page in your browser.**

• **Click the Home link to verify that it works.**

• **Close the browser.**

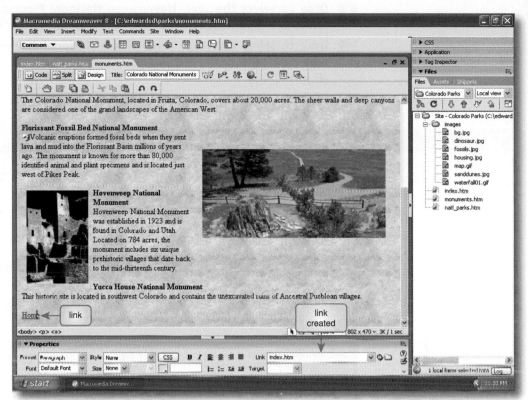

FIGURE 2-74

Creating an Absolute Link

Recall that an absolute link (also called an external link) contains the complete Web site address of a document. You create absolute links the same way you create relative links — select the text and paste or type the Web site address. You now will create five absolute links in the National Monuments page. These links are from the name of each of the five monuments to a Web page about the selected monument. The following steps show how to create the five absolute links. Keep in mind that Web site addresses change. If the absolute links do not work, check the Dreamweaver 8 companion site at http://www.scsite.com/dw8/ for updates.

To Create an Absolute Link

1 If necessary, scroll to the top of the page. Drag to select the text, Dinosaur National Monument.

2 Click the Link box and then type http://www.nps.gov/dino/ as the link. Press the ENTER key.

3 Drag to select the text, Colorado National Monument. Click the Link box and then type http://www.nps.gov/colm/ as the link. Press the ENTER key.

4 If necessary, scroll down and then drag to select the text, Florissant Fossil Bed National Monument. Click the Link box and then type http://www.nps.gov/flfo/ as the link. Press the ENTER key.

5 Drag to select the text, Hovenweep National Monument. Click the Link box and then type `http://www.nps.gov/hove/` as the link. Press the ENTER key.

6 Drag to select the text, Yucca House National Monument. Click the Link box and then type `http://www.nps.gov/yuho/` as the link. Press the ENTER key (Figure 2-75).

7 Click the Save button on the Standard toolbar.

8 Press the F12 key and then click each link to verify that they work.

9 Click the browser Back button after clicking each link.

10 Close the browser.

Other Ways

1. Start browser, open Web page, select URL, copy URL, close browser, paste in Link box

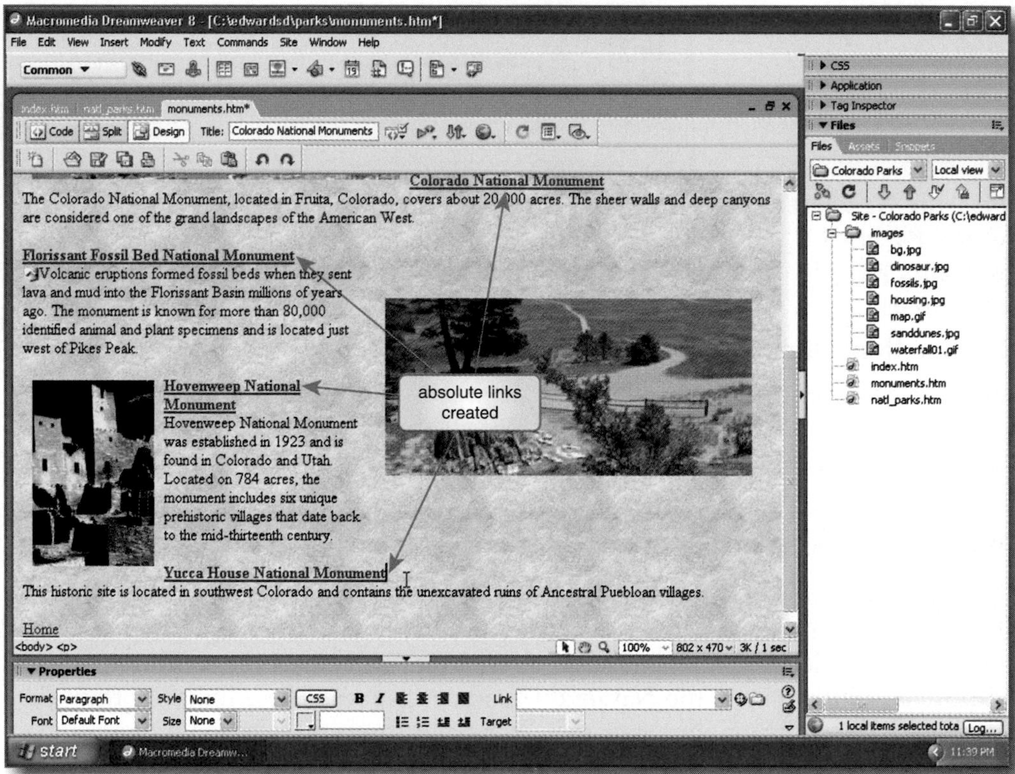

The five absolute links to the respective national monuments pages are added (Figure 2-75), and the Web page is saved.

FIGURE 2-75

E-Mail Links

An **e-mail link** is one of the foundation elements of any successful Web site. It is important for visitors to be able to contact you for additional information or to comment on the Web page or Web site. When visitors click an e-mail link, their default e-mail program opens a new e-mail message. The e-mail address you specify is inserted automatically in the To box of the e-mail message header.

Creating an E-Mail Link

The following steps show how to create an e-mail link for your home page using your name as the linked text. You do this through the Insert menu.

To Add an E-Mail Link

1

• **Click the index.htm tab, scroll down, and then drag to select your name. Click Insert on the menu bar and then point to Email Link.**

In this figure, David Edwards is selected, and the Insert menu is displayed (Figure 2-76). Your name should be selected on your screen.

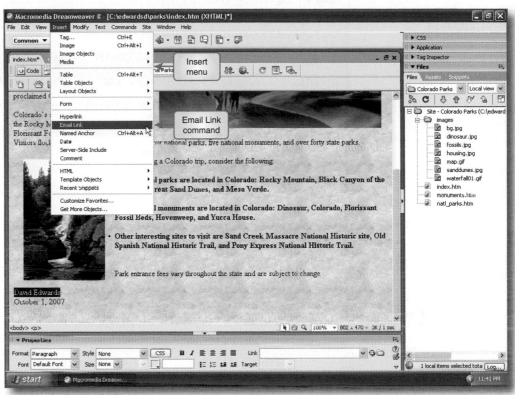

FIGURE 2-76

2

• **Click Email Link.**

The Email Link dialog box is displayed. In this figure, David Edwards is selected in the Text text box (Figure 2-77). On your computer, your name is displayed in the Text text box.

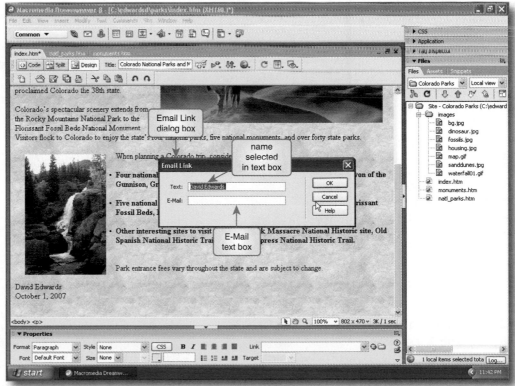

FIGURE 2-77

• **Click the E-Mail text box and then type your e-mail address.**

In this figure, the e-mail address for David Edwards is displayed in the E-Mail text box (Figure 2-78). On your computer, Dreamweaver displays your e-mail address.

• **Click the OK button.**

• **Click the expander arrow on the vertical bar to hide the panel groups.**

• **Click anywhere in the selected text of your name.**

• **Click the Save button on the Standard toolbar.**

The selected text for the e-mail link, David Edwards, is displayed as linked text and the index page is saved. The Link box displays the e-mail address (Figure 2-79). On your computer, Dreamweaver displays your name as the linked text.

• **Press the F12 key to view the page in your browser. Click your name.**

Your e-mail program opens with your e-mail address in the To text box.

• **Close your e-mail program and then close the browser.**

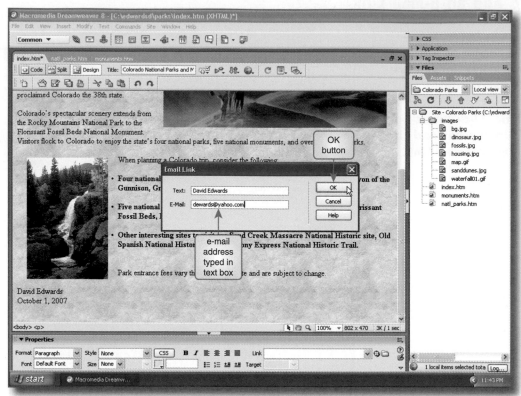

FIGURE 2-78

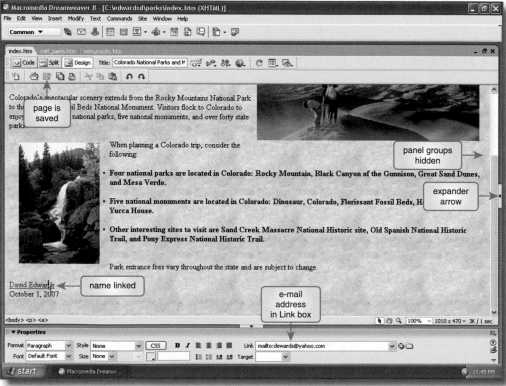

FIGURE 2-79

Changing the Color of Links

The Page Properties dialog box provides three options for link colors: Link (the link has not been clicked), Active Link (the link changes color when the user clicks it), and Visited Link (the link has been visited). The default color for the three options is black. You easily can make changes to these default settings and select colors that complement the background and other colors you are using on your Web pages. This is accomplished through the Page Properties dialog box. You display the Page Properties dialog box by clicking Modify on the menu bar. You then can click the box that corresponds to one of the three types of links and select a color to match your color scheme.

Editing and Deleting Links

Web development is a never-ending process. At some point, it will be necessary to edit or delete a link. For instance, an e-mail address may change, a URL to an external link may change, or an existing link may contain an error.

Dreamweaver makes it easy to edit or delete a link. First, select the link or click the link you want to change. The linked document name displays in the Link box in the Property inspector. To delete the link without deleting the text on the Web page, delete the text from the Link box in the Property inspector. To edit the link, make the change in the Link box.

A second method to edit or delete a link is to use the context menu. Right-click the link you want to change, and then click Remove Link on the context menu to eliminate the link or click Change Link on the context menu to edit the link. Clicking the URLs icon in the Assets panel displays a list of all absolute and e-mail links within the Web site.

The Site Map

Earlier in this project, you set the index page as the home page. Dreamweaver provides a visual site map for viewing the relationships among files. The **Site Map** is a graphical representation of the structure of a Web site. You visually can design and modify the Web site structure through the Site Map. The home page displays at the top level of the map, and linked pages display at the lower levels. The Site Map view allows you to create, change, display, save, and print a Web site's structure and navigation. As previously discussed, a Web site's structure is the relationship among the pages in the Web site.

Viewing the Site Map

The home page now contains links to other pages in the site, and each page in the site contains links back to the home page. The National Monuments page contains a link to five external Web sites, which are outside of the local site and located on a different server. You can use the Site Map to view a graphical image of these links. In addition to allowing you to view the Site Map, another Dreamweaver option lets you view your file list and Site Map simultaneously.

Displaying the Site Map and Local Files

The Site Map shows the pages as icons and displays links in the order in which they are encountered in the HTML source code. Starting from the home page, the Site Map default displays the site structure two levels deep. The relative links have a

More About

Targeting Links

By default, when you click a link, the linked Web page will open in the current browser window. You can specify, however, that a linked Web page open in a new browser window. To do this, first select the item and create the link. Then, in the Property inspector, click the Target box arrow and click _blank on the Target pop-up menu. When you view the page in a browser and click the link, it will display in a new window.

plus sign to their left. If you click the plus (+) sign, pages below the second level display. Some pages have a minus sign to their left. If you click the minus (-) sign, pages linked below the second level are hidden. Text displayed in blue and marked with a globe icon indicates a file on another site or a special link such as an e-mail link. Text displayed in red indicates a broken link. You access the Site Map through the Files panel. The following steps show how to display the site map with the newly created links among the pages in the Colorado Parks Web site.

To Display the Site Map and Local Files List

1

• **If necessary, click the index.htm tab.**

• **Click the expander arrow on the panel groups vertical bar to display the Files panel.**

• **Click the View box arrow and then point to Map view in the View pop-up menu (Figure 2-80).**

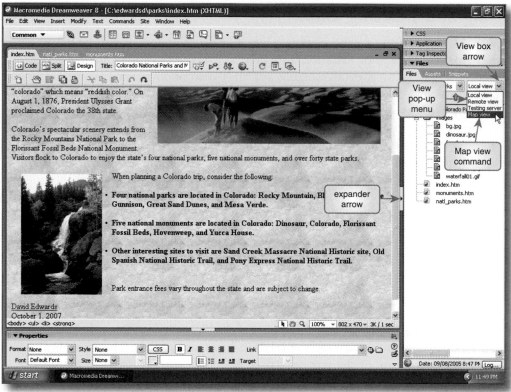

FIGURE 2-80

2

• **Click Map view.**

Dreamweaver displays a graphical view of the Web site in the Files panel, including all links from the index page (Figure 2-81).

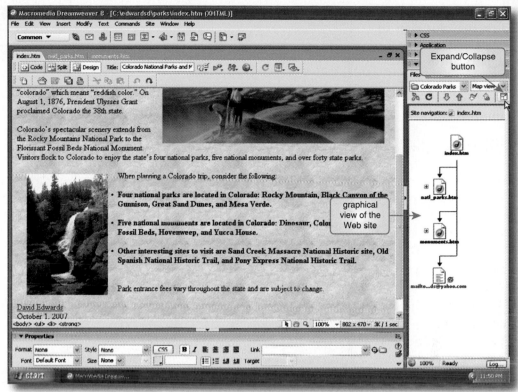

FIGURE 2-81

3

• **Click the Expand/Collapse button.**

The Site Map expands and displays a graphical structure of the links between the index page and the other two pages and external links (Figure 2-82). The plus signs to the left of the natl_parks.htm and monuments.htm pages indicate that additional files or links are below these pages.

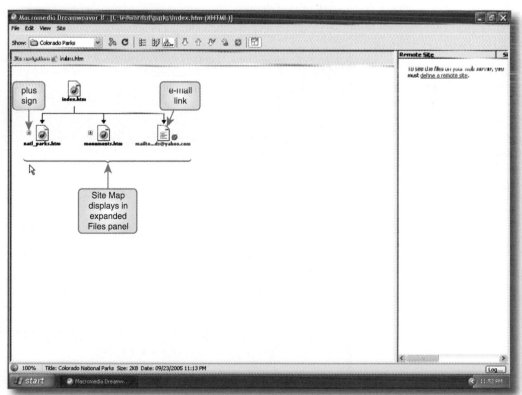

FIGURE 2-82

4

• **Click the plus sign to the left of the natl_parks.htm icon.**

• **Click the plus sign to the left of monuments.htm**

The structure expands and displays the relative link to the index page from the national parks page and from the national monuments page. The five external links are displayed under the mouments icon (Figure 2-83).

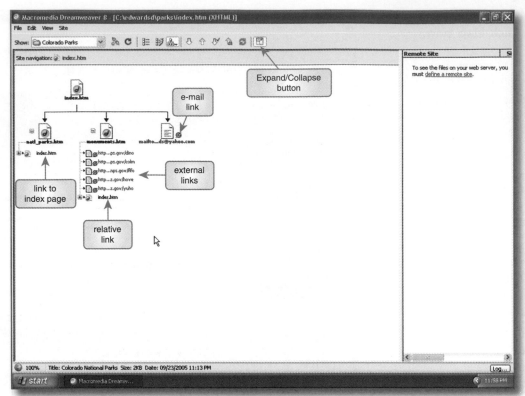

FIGURE 2-83

5

• **Click the Expand/Collapse button to hide the Site Map.**

• **Click the View box arrow and then point to Local view in the View pop-up menu (Figure 2-84).**

6

• **Click Local view.**

The local site is displayed.

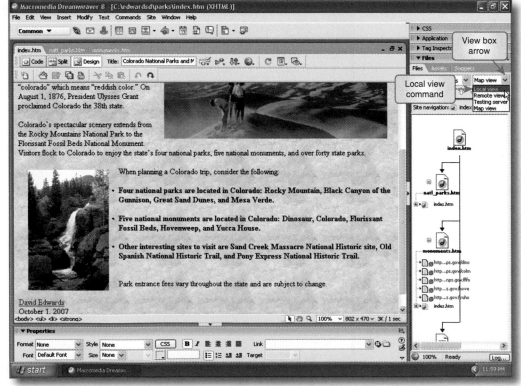

FIGURE 2-84

Source Code View

Dreamweaver provides two views, or ways, to look at a document: **Design view** and **Code view**. Thus far, you have been working in Design view. As you create and work with documents, Dreamweaver automatically generates the underlying source code. Recall that the source code defines the structure and layout of a Web document by using a variety of tags and attributes. Even though Dreamweaver generates the code, occasions occur that necessitate the tweaking or modifying of code.

Dreamweaver provides several options for viewing and working with source code. You can split the Document window so that it displays both the Code view and the Design view. You can display only the Code view in the Document window, or you can open the Code inspector. The **Code Inspector** opens in a separate window, so you can keep the whole Document window reserved for Design view.

Using Code View and Design View

In Split view, you work in a split-screen environment. You can see the design and the code at the same time. Splitting the Document window to view the code makes it easier to view the visual design while you make changes in the source code. When you make a change in Design view, the HTML code also is changed but is not visible in the Document window. You can set word wrapping, display line numbers for the code, highlight invalid HTML code, set syntax coloring for code elements, and set indenting through the View menu's Code View Options submenu. Viewing the code at this early stage may not seem important, but the more code you learn, the more productive you will become.

Within HTML source code, tags can be entered in uppercase, lowercase, or a combination of upper- and lowercase. The case of the tags has no effect on how the browser displays the output. When you view the code in Code view in Dreamweaver, some HTML tags display in lowercase letters and some attributes in uppercase letters. This is the Dreamweaver default.

If the code is XHTML compliant, however, all tags are lowercase. In this book, if you use the instructions provided in Project 1 to create a new Web page, then your page is XHTML compliant. XHTML was discussed in the Introduction project. Therefore, in this book, when describing source code tags, we use lowercase letters for tags and attributes to make it easier to differentiate them from the other text and to coordinate with the XHTML standard.

The following steps show how to use the Code View and Design View option to look at the code for the
 (line break) and <p> (paragraph) tags. The paragraph tag has an opening tag, <p>, and a closing tag, </p>. The
 (line break) tag does not have a closing tag.

More About

Using the Quick Tag Editor

For more information about using the Quick Tag Editor to review and edit HTML tags, visit the Dreamweaver 8 More About Web page (scsite.com/dw8/more) and then click Dreamweaver 8 Quick Tag Editor.

To View Design View and Code View Simultaneously

1

• Click the natl_parks.htm tab.

• Hide the Files panel and collapse the Property inspector.

• Position the insertion point to the left of the heading, Colorado National Parks. (Figure 2-85).

2

• Click the Split button. If the line numbers are not showing in the code, click the View menu, point to Code View Options, and then click Line Numbers.

The window splits. The upper window displays Code view and the lower window displays Design view (Figure 2-86). The insertion point is displayed in Code view in the same location as in Design view (to the left of the heading). The lines are numbered in Code view. The source code is displayed in color and in lowercase surrounded by < (less than) and > (greater than) symbols. Your window may display Design view in the upper window and Code view in the lower window.

3

• Click the Design button.

The Design view is displayed.

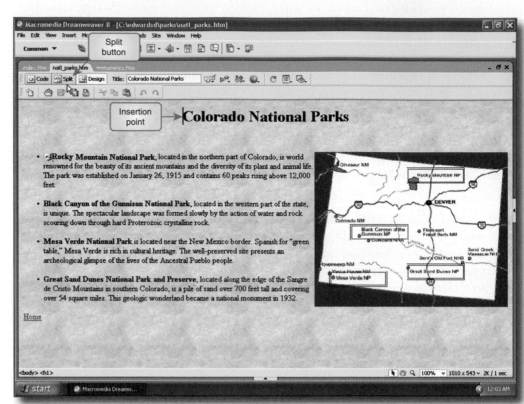

FIGURE 2-85

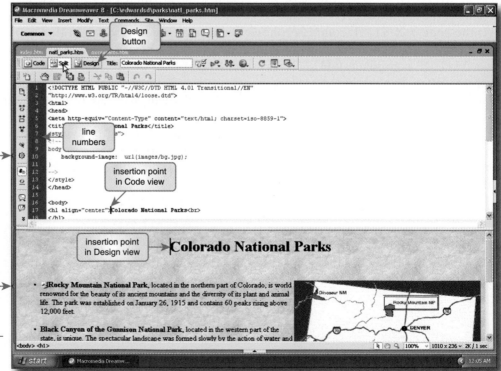

FIGURE 2-86

Modifying Source Code

One of the more common problems within Dreamweaver and the source code relates to line breaks and paragraphs. Occasionally, you inadvertently press the ENTER key or insert a line break and need to remove the tag. Or, you may copy and paste or open a text file that contains unneeded paragraphs or line breaks.

Pressing the backspace key or delete key may return you to the previous line, but does not always delete the line break or paragraph tag within the source code. The deletion of these tags is determined by the position of the insertion point when you press the backspace or delete keys. If the insertion point is still inside the source code, pressing the backspace key will not delete these tags and your page will not display correctly. When this occurs, the best solution is to delete the tag through Code view.

Formatting Titles for Consistency

To further create consistency among the Web pages, the titles of the two new pages (monuments and natl_parks) need to be formatted with the same style as that of the index page.

To Format the National Parks and National Monuments Titles

1 If necessary, display the Property inspector. Select the text, Colorado National Parks. Click the color hexadecimal text box and type #993300. Press the ENTER key.

2 Click the monuments.htm tab. Select the text, Colorado National Monuments. Click the color hexadecimal text box and type #993300. Press the ENTER key.

Quitting Dreamweaver

After you add pages to your Web site, including images and links, and then verify links using the Site Map, Project 2 is complete. The next step shows how to close the Web site, quit Dreamweaver 8, and return control to Windows.

To Close the Web Site and Quit Dreamweaver

1 Click the Close button on the right corner of the Dreamweaver title bar.

The Dreamweaver window, the Document window, and the Colorado Parks Web site all close. If you have unsaved changes, Dreamweaver will prompt you to save the changes. Clicking the Yes button in the Dreamweaver 8 dialog box saves the changes.

Project Summary

Project 2 introduced you to images, links, the Site Map, and how to view source code. You began the project by using the Windows My Computer option to copy data files to the local site. You added two new pages, one for Colorado National Parks and one for Colorado National Monuments, to the Web site you created in Project 1. Next, you added page images to the index page. Following that, you added a background image and page images to the National Park and National Monuments pages. Then, you added relative links to all three pages. You added an e-mail link to the index page and absolute links to the National Monuments page. You also learned to use the Site Map. Finally, you learned how to view source code.

What You Should Know

Having completed this project, you should be able to perform the tasks below. The tasks are listed in the same order they were presented in this project. For a list of keyboard commands for topics introduced in this project, see the Quick Reference for Windows at the back of this book and refer to the Shortcut column.

1. Copy Data Files to the Parks Web Site (DW 119)
2. Start Dreamweaver and Open the Parks Web Site (DW 120)
3. Open a Web Page from a Local Web Site (DW 122)
4. Set a Home Page (DW 123)
5. Open a New Document Window (DW 124)
6. Prepare the Workspace (DW 128)
7. Create the National Parks Web Page (DW 129)
8. Format the Colorado National Parks Page (DW 130)
9. Open a New Document Window (DW 131)
10. Create the National Monuments Web Page (DW 133)
11. Format the Colorado National Monuments Page (DW 133)
12. Add a Background Image to the Colorado National Parks Web Page (DW 136)
13. Add a Background Image to the Colorado National Monuments Web Page (DW 137)
14. Set Invisible Element Preferences and Turn on Visual Aids (DW 140)
15. Insert an Image into the Index Page (DW 142)
16. Align an Image (DW 146)
17. Adjust the Horizontal and Vertical Space (DW 148)
18. Insert the Waterfall Image (DW 149)
19. Insert and Align an Image in the National Parks Web Page (DW 152)
20. Insert and Align Images in the National Monuments Web Page (DW 155)
21. Crop and Modify Brightness/Contrast of an Image (DW 160)
22. Add Text for Relative Links (DW 165)
23. Create a Relative Link Using Drag-and-Drop (DW 167)
24. Create a Relative Link Using the Context Menu (DW 169)
25. Create a Relative Link to the Home Page (DW 171)
26. Create an Absolute Link (DW 173)
27. Add an E-Mail Link (DW 175)
28. Display the Site Map and Local Files List (DW 178)
29. View Design View and Code View Simultaneously (DW 182)
30. Format the National Parks and National Monuments Titles (DW 183)
31. Close the Web Site and Quit Dreamweaver (DW 183)

Learn It Online

Instructions: To complete the Learn It Online exercises, start your browser, click the Address bar, and then enter the Web address scsite.com/dw8/learnWhen the Dreamweaver 8 Learn It Online page is displayed, follow the instructions in the exercises below. Each exercise has instructions for printing your results, either for your own records or for submission to your instructor.

1 Project Reinforcement TF, MC, and SA

Below Dreamweaver Project 2, click the Project Reinforcement link. Print the quiz by clicking Print on the File menu for each page. Answer each question.

2 Flash Cards

Below Dreamweaver Project 2, click the Flash Cards link and read the instructions. Type 20 (or a number specified by your instructor) in the Number of playing cards text box, type your name in the Enter your Name text box, and then click the Flip Card button. When the flash card is displayed, read the question and then click the ANSWER box arrow to select an answer. Flip through the Flash Cards. If your score is 15 (75%) correct or greater, click Print on the File menu to print your results. If your score is less than 15 (75%) correct, then redo this exercise by clicking the Replay button.

3 Practice Test

Below Dreamweaver Project 2, click the Practice Test link. Answer each question, enter your first and last name at the bottom of the page, and then click the Grade Test button. When the graded practice test is displayed on your screen, click Print on the File menu to print a hard copy. Continue to take practice tests until you score 80% or better.

4 Who Wants To Be a Computer Genius?

Below Dreamweaver Project 2, click the Computer Genius link. Read the instructions, enter your first and last name at the bottom of the page, and then click the PLAY button. When your score is displayed, click the PRINT RESULTS link to print a hard copy.

5 Wheel of Terms

Below Dreamweaver Project 2, click the Wheel of Terms link. Read the instructions, and then enter your first and last name and your school name. Click the PLAY button. When your score is displayed, right-click the score and then click Print on the shortcut menu to print a hard copy.

6 Crossword Puzzle Challenge

Below Dreamweaver Project 2, click the Crossword Puzzle Challenge link. Read the instructions, and then enter your first and last name. Click the SUBMIT button. Work the crossword puzzle. When you are finished, click the Submit button. When the crossword puzzle is redisplayed, click the Print Puzzle button to print a hard copy.

7 Tips and Tricks

Below Dreamweaver Project 2, click the Tips and Tricks link. Click a topic that pertains to Project 2. Right-click the information and then click Print on the shortcut menu. Construct a brief example of what the information relates to in Dreamweaver to confirm that you understand how to use the tip or trick.

8 Newsgroups

Below Dreamweaver Project 2, click the Newsgroups link. Click a topic that pertains to Project 2. Print three comments.

9 Expanding Your Horizons

Below Dreamweaver Project 2, click the Expanding Your Horizons link. Click a topic that pertains to Project 2. Print the information. Construct a brief example of what the information relates to in Dreamweaver to confirm that you understand the contents of the article.

10 Search Sleuth

Below Dreamweaver Project 2, click the Search Sleuth link. To search for a term that pertains to this project, select a term below the Project 2 title and then use the Google search engine at google.com (or any major search engine) to display and print two Web pages that present information on the term.

Apply Your Knowledge

1 Modifying the Andy's Lawn Service Web Site

Instructions: Start Dreamweaver. Data and image files for the Andy's Lawn Service Web site are included on the Data Disk. See the inside back cover of this book for instructions for downloading the Data Disk or see your instructor for information on accessing the files in this book.

You need to add three new pages to the Andy's Lawn Service Web site: a services page, an employment page, and a references page. In this exercise, you will add relative and absolute links to each page. You also will add a background image to the new pages. Next, you will insert images on all pages and use the settings in Table 2-4 on page DW 188 to align the images and enter the Alt text. You then will add an e-mail link to the home page and relative links from the three new pages to the home page. The pages for the Web site are shown in Figures 2-87a through 2-87d on pages DW 186 through DW 188.

Software and hardware settings determine how a Web page is displayed in a browser. Your Web pages may display differently in your browser than those in the figures do.

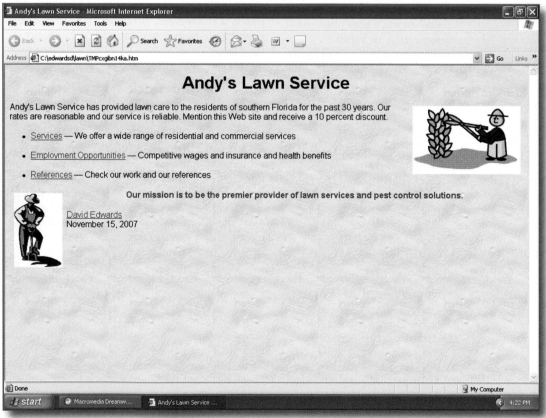

FIGURE 2-87 (a) Lawn Services Index (Home) Page

Apply Your Knowledge

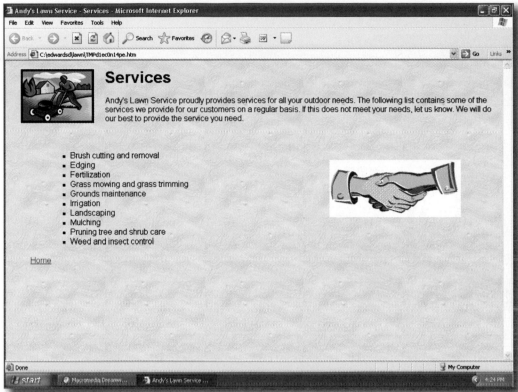

(b) Lawn Services - Services Pages

(c) Lawn Services - Employment Opportunities Pages

FIGURE 2-87

(continued)

Apply Your Knowledge

Modifying the Andy's Lawn Service Web Site *(continued)*

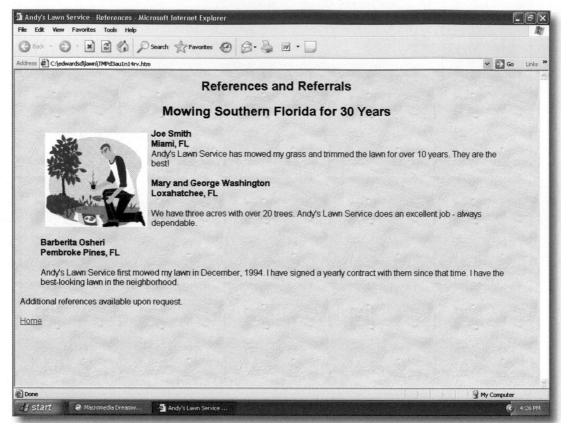

FIGURE 2-87 (d) References and Referrals Page

Table 2-4 Image Property Settings for the Andy's Lawn Service Web Site

IMAGE NAME	W	H	V SPACE	H SPACE	ALIGN	ALT
trimming.gif	206	130	6	6	Right	Tree trimming
shovel.gif	93	141	6	8	Left	Shovel
mowing.gif	150	112	None	20	Left	Grass mowing
shakehands.gif	264	114	None	75	Right	Shaking hands
planting.gif	150	112	6	None	Right	Tree planting
planting2.gif	197	177	8	8	Left	Tree planting

Perform the following tasks:

1. Use the Windows My Computer option to copy the data files and images to your lawn folder.
2. If necessary, display the panel groups. Select Lawn Service on the Files pop-up menu in the Files panel. Double-click the index.htm file in the Files panel. If necessary, click the expander arrow to expand the Property inspector. If necessary, display the Standard toolbar.
3. Click index.htm in the Files panel to select it. Right-click index.htm and then click Set as Home Page on the context menu.

Apply Your Knowledge

4. If necessary, click the expand/collapse button to the left of the images folder in the Files panel to display the contents of the images folder. Position the insertion point to the left of the first line of the first paragraph. Drag the trimming.gif image to the insertion point, add the alternate text as indicated in Table 2-4, and then select the image. Apply the settings shown in Table 2-4 to align the image. If necessary, scroll down. Position the insertion point to the left of the last sentence on the Web page. Drag the shovel.gif image to the insertion point and then apply the settings shown in Table 2-4.

5. If necessary, scroll up. Select Services (the first bulleted item heading). Use the drag-and-drop file method to create a link to the Services page. Repeat this process to add links from Employment Opportunities and References (the second and third bulleted item headings) to their respective Web pages. Select your name. Use the Insert menu to create an e-mail link using your name. Save the index page (Figure 2-87a on page DW 186).

6. Open services.htm. Click Modify on the menu bar and click Page Properties. Click the Background image Browse button to add the background image (lawnbg.jpg) to the services.htm page.

7. Position the insertion point to the left of the page heading, drag the mowing.gif image to the insertion point, and then apply the settings shown in Table 2-4. Position the insertion point to the right of the first bulleted item and then drag the shakehands.gif image to the insertion point. Apply the settings shown in Table 2-4.

8. If necessary, scroll down. Select Home and then create a relative link to the index page. Title the page Andy's Lawn Service - Services. Save the Services page (Figure 2-87b on page DW 187).

9. Open employment.htm. Add the background image to the employment.htm page, as you did in Step 6 to the services.htm page.

10. Position the insertion point to the right of the heading and then drag the planting.gif image to the insertion point. Apply the settings shown in Table 2-4.

11. Scroll to the bottom of the page. Select the words, To contact us, click here!. Use the Insert menu to create an e-mail link using your e-mail address. Select Home at the bottom of the page and then drag index.htm to the Link box in the Property inspector to create a relative link to the index.htm file. Title the page Andy's Lawn Service - Employment. Save the Employment page (Figure 2-87c on page DW 187).

12. Open references.htm and apply the lawnbg.jpg background image.

13. Create a link from Home to the index page.

14. Position the insertion point to the left of the text, Joe Smith. Drag the planting2.gif image to the insertion point. Select the image. Apply the settings in Table 2-4. Title the page Andy's Lawn Service - References. Save the References page (Figure 2-87d).

15. View the Web site in your browser. Check each link to verify that it works. Print a copy of each page if required and hand the copies in to your instructor. Close the browser. Quit Dreamweaver.

1 Modifying the CandleWix Web Site

Problem: Martha Morgan, for whom you created the CandleWix Web site and Web page, is very pleased with the response she has received. She has asked you to create a second page with links and images added to the index page. Martha wants the new page to include information about her company's history. The revised Web site is shown in Figures 2-88a and 2-88b. Table 2-5 includes the settings and Alt text for the images. Software and hardware settings determine how a Web page displays in a browser. Your Web pages may display differently in your browser than those in the figures do.

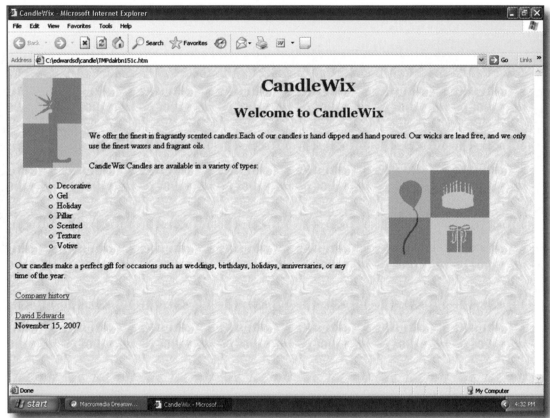

FIGURE 2-88 (a) CandleWix Index (Home) Page

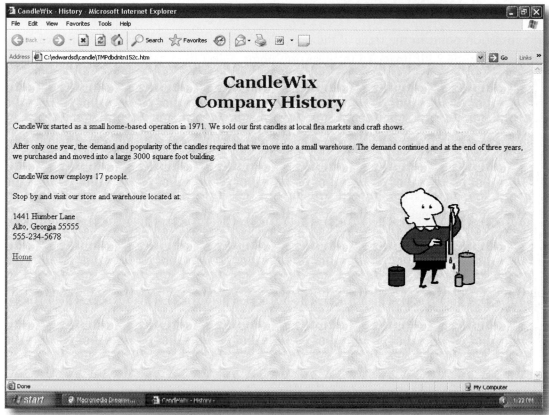

FIGURE 2-88 (b) CandleWix - History Web Page

Table 2-5 Image Property Settings for the CandleWix Web Site						
IMAGE NAME	W	H	V SPACE	H SPACE	ALIGN	ALT
candle1.gif	112	170	6	15	Left	Logo
candle2.gif	192	178	None	75	Right	Candles
candle_dip.gif	164	191	10	100	Right	Candle dipping

Instructions: Perform the following tasks:

1. Use the Windows My Computer option to copy the data files and images to your candle folder.
2. Start Dreamweaver. Display the panel groups. Select CandleWix on the Files pop-up menu in the Files panel. Open the index.htm file. If necessary, click the expander arrow to expand the Property inspector and display the Standard toolbar.
3. Click index.htm in the Files panel to select it. Right-click index.htm and then click Set as Home Page on the context menu.
4. Position the insertion point to the left of the heading and then drag the candle1.gif image to the insertion point. Select the image, enter the Alt text, and then apply the settings shown in Table 2-5 to align the image.

(continued)

In the Lab

Modifying the CandleWix Web Site *(continued)*

5. Position the insertion point to the right of the text, CandleWix candles are available in a variety of types:, and then drag the candle2.gif image to the insertion point. Select the image and then apply the settings shown in Table 2-5 on the previous page.

6. Position the insertion point to the right of the text, Our candles make a perfect gift for occasions such as weddings, birthdays, holidays, anniversaries, or any time of the year, and then press the ENTER key. Type `Company history`. Select the Company history text and use the drag-and-drop method to create a link to the history.htm page. Select your name. Use the Insert menu to create an e-mail link using your e-mail address. Save the index page (Figure 2-88a on page DW 190).

7. Open history.htm. Open the Page Properties dialog box. Click the Background image Browse button, and then add the background image (candlebg.gif) to the history.htm page.

8. Position the insertion point at the end of the sentence, CandleWix now employs 17 people, and then drag the candle_dip.gif image to the insertion point. Select the image and then apply the settings shown in Table 2-5. Title the page CandleWix - History.

9. Select Home and then create a relative link to the index page. Save the History page (Figure 2-88b on the previous page).

10. View your pages in your browser and verify that your links work. Print a copy of each page if required and hand the copies in to your instructor. Close your browser. Quit Dreamweaver.

2 Modifying the Credit Protection Web Site

Problem: Monica Jacobs has received favorable comments about the Web page and site you created on credit information. Her bank wants to utilize the Web site to provide additional information to its customers. Monica has asked you and another intern at the bank to work with her to create two more Web pages to add to the site. They want one of the pages to discuss credit protection and the other page to contain information about identity theft. The revised pages for the Web site are shown in Figures 2-89a, 2-89b, and 2-89c on pages DW 192 through DW 194. Table 2-6 on page DW 194 includes the settings and Alt text for the images. Software and hardware settings determine how a Web page displays in a browser. Your Web pages may display differently in your browser than those in the figures do.

In the Lab

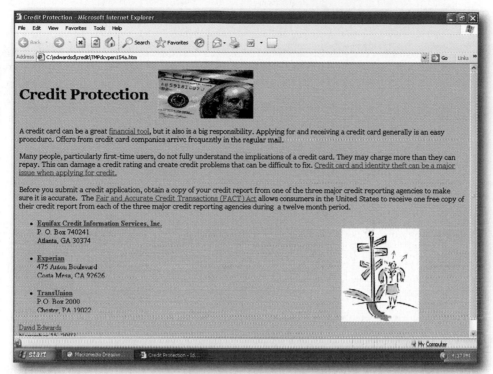

(a) Credit Protection Index (Home) Page

(b) Credit Protection - Identity Theft Web Page

FIGURE 2-89

(continued)

In the Lab

Modifying the Credit Protection Web Site *(continued)*

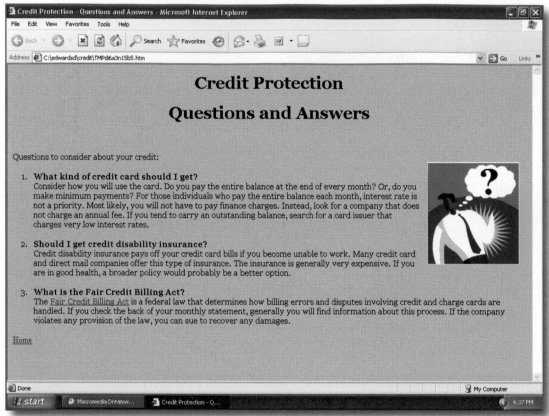

FIGURE 2-89 (c) Credit Protection - Questions and Answers Web Page

Table 2-6	Image Property Settings for the Credit Protection Web Site					
IMAGE NAME	W	H	V SPACE	H SPACE	ALIGN	ALT
money.gif	211	107	None	20	Absolute Middle	Money
answer.gif	172	204	None	100	Right	Reporting options
protection.gif	240	170	14	20	Left	Identity theft
theft.gif	179	183	20	None	Right	Protect personal information
question.gif	175	193	None	15	Right	Questions?

Instructions: Perform the following tasks:

1. Use the Windows My Computer option to copy the data files to your credit folder. The data files consist of five image files and two data files, questions.htm and theft.htm.
2. Start Dreamweaver. Display the panel groups. Select Credit Protection on the Files pop-up menu in the Files panel. Open index.htm.
3. If necessary, display the Property inspector and the Standard toolbar. Expand the Property inspector.
4. Right-click the index.htm file and set the page as the home page.

In the Lab

5. Position the insertion point to the right of the heading and then drag the money.gif image to the insertion point. Apply the settings shown in Table 2-6. Position the insertion point to the right of the text, Equifax Credit Information Services, Inc. Drag the answer.gif image to the insertion point. Apply the settings shown in Table 2-6.

6. Select the text, financial tool, located in the first sentence of the first paragraph. Create a relative link from the selected text to questions.htm. Select the text, Fair and Accurate Credit Transactions (FACT) Act, located in the second sentence of the third paragraph. Create an absolute link to http://www.annualcreditre-port.com. Select the name of the company in the first bulleted list item (Equifax Credit Information Ser-vices, Inc.) and create an absolute link using http://www.equifax.com. Create absolute links from the other two company names, using http://www.experian.com and http://www.transunion.com, respectively.

[handwritten annotations: 164, 173 or external link]

7. Position the insertion point at the end of the second paragraph. Press the SPACEBAR. Type Credit card and identity theft can be a major issue when applying for credit. Select the text you just typed and then create a relative link to the theft.htm file. Add an e-mail link to your name. Save the index page (Figure 2-89a on page DW 193).

8. Open theft.htm and apply the background image (creditbg.jpg) to the theft.htm page.

9. Position the insertion point to the left of the second line and then drag the protection.gif image to the insertion point. Apply the settings shown in Table 2-6. Position the insertion point after the first sentence in the second bulleted point and then drag the theft.gif image to the insertion point. Apply the settings shown in Table 2-6.

10. Drag to select the text, Identity theft, at the beginning of the first sentence and then create an absolute link using http://www.consumer.gov/idtheft/ as the URL. Create an absolute link from the protection.gif image using the same URL. Select the image and then type the URL in the Link box. Select Home and then create a relative link to the index.htm page. Title the page Credit Protection - Identity Theft. Save the Theft page (Figure 2-89b on page DW 193).

11. Open questions.htm. Apply the background image that you added to the theft.htm page in Step 8. Use the text, Home, at the bottom of the page to create a relative link to the index page.

12. Position the insertion point to the right of the first line of text, Questions to consider about your credit:, and then drag the question.gif image to the insertion point. Select the image. Apply the settings in Table 2-6.

13. Create an absolute link from the Fair Credit Billing Act text in question 3. Use http://www.ftc.gov/bcp/con-line/pubs/credit/fcb.htm as the URL. Title the page Credit Protection - Questions and Answers. Save the Questions page (Figure 2-89c).

14. View the site in the Site Map. Then view the Web site in your browser and verify that your external and rel-ative links work. *Hint:* Remember to check the link for the image on the theft.htm page. Print a copy of each page, if required, and hand the copies in to your instructor. Close your browser and quit Dreamweaver.

3 Modifying the Lexington, NC Web Page

Problem: John Davis recently became a member of a marketing group promoting Lexington's annual Barbecue Festival. He wants to expand the Web site you created for him by adding two new Web pages that will highlight other features of Lexington, North Carolina. You inform John that you can create the new pages. The revised

(continued)

Modifying the Lexington, NC Web Page *(continued)*

pages for the Web site are displayed in Figures 2-90a, 2-90b, and 2-90c. Table 2-7 on page DW 198 includes the settings and alternative text for the images. Software and hardware settings determine how a Web page displays in a browser. Your Web pages may display differently in your browser than those in the figures do.

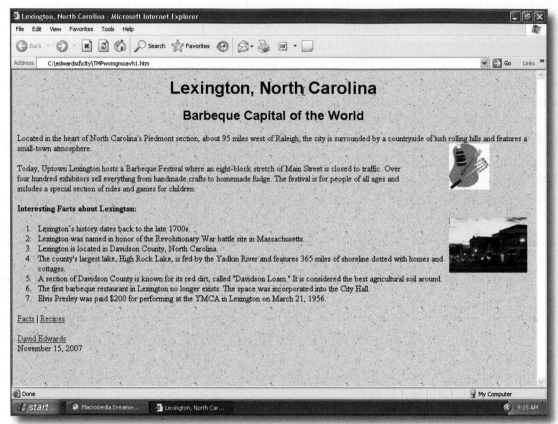

FIGURE 2-90   (a) Lexington, NC Index (Home) Page

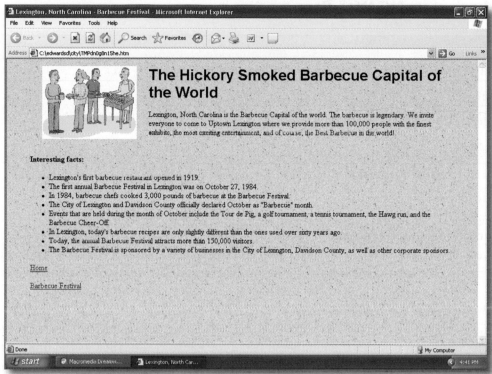

(b) Lexington, NC - Barbecue Festival Facts Web Page

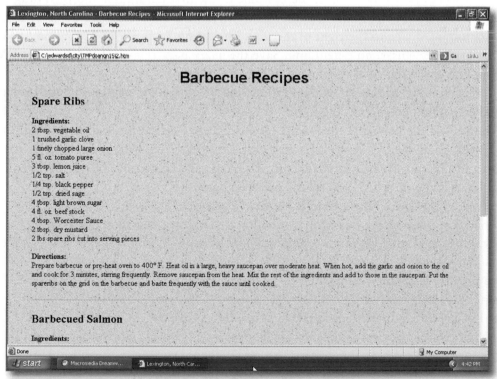

(c) Lexington, NC - Barbecue Recipes Web Page

FIGURE 2-90

(continued)

In the Lab

Modifying the Lexington, NC Web Page *(continued)*

Table 2-7 Image Property Settings for the Lexington, NC Web Site						
IMAGE NAME	W	H	V SPACE	H SPACE	ALIGN	ALT
bbq1.gif	77	87	None	80	Right	Barbecue
lexington.jpg	149	106	6	8	Right	Lexington
bbq2.gif	200	155	None	25	Left	Barbecue

Instructions: Perform the following tasks:

1. Use the Windows My Computer option to copy the data files. The data files consist of three images and two Web pages, facts.htm and recipes.htm.
2. Start Dreamweaver. Display the panel groups. Select Lexington, NC on the Files pop-up menu.
3. Open index.htm. If necessary, display the Property inspector and the Standard toolbar. Expand the Property inspector.
4. Set the index.htm page as the home page.
5. Position the insertion point after the last numbered item (7) on the page and then press the ENTER key. Click the Ordered List button to deselect the numbered list. Type Facts | Recipes as the link text.
6. Create a relative link from the text, Facts, to the facts.htm page and then create a relative link from the text, Recipes, to the recipes.htm page.
7. Position the insertion point to the right of the first line of the first paragraph and then drag the bbq1.gif image to the insertion point. Apply the settings shown in Table 2-7.
8. Insert the lexington.jpg image to the right of the text, Interesting Facts about Lexington:, and apply the settings shown in Table 2-7. Insert an e-mail link. Save the index page (Figure 2-90a on page DW 196).
9. Open facts.htm and apply the citybg.gif image to the background.
10. Position the insertion point to the left of the heading and then drag the bbq2.gif image to the insertion point. Apply the settings shown in Table 2-7.
11. Scroll to the bottom of the page and then select Home. Create a relative link to the index.htm page. Click to the right of Home. Press the ENTER key and then type Barbecue Festival. Select the text and create an absolute link to http://www.barbecuefestival.com. Title the page Lexington, North Carolina - Barbecue Festival. Save the Facts page (Figure 2-90b on the previous page).
12. Open recipes.htm. Apply the citybg.gif image to the background.
13. Position the insertion point at the end of the second horizontal line and then press the ENTER key. Type the following text. Press the ENTER key after typing each line of text:
    BBQ Sausage and Peppers
    Spinach-Stuffed Veal Chops
    Grilled Pineapple Slices
    Add absolute links to these three items in respective order as follows:
    http://barbeque.allrecipes.com/az/BBQSsgndPpprs.asp; http://www.barbecue-online.co.uk/barbecue-recipes/beef/bbq_spinach-stuffed_veal_chops_recipe.htm, and http://barbeque.allrecipes.com/az/71315.asp.
14. Create a relative link to the index page. Title the page Lexington, North Carolina - Barbecue Recipes. Save the Recipes page (Figure 2-90c on the previous page).
15. View the Web site in your browser and verify the links. Print a copy of each page if required and hand in the copies to your instructor. Close your browser and quit Dreamweaver.

Cases and Places

The difficulty of these case studies varies:
■ are the least difficult and ■■ are the most difficult. The last exercise is a group exercise.

1 ■ In Project 1, you created a Web site and a Web page listing your favorite sport. Now, you want to add another page to the site. Create and format the page. The page should include general information about your selected sport. Create a relative link from the home page to the new page and from the new page to the home page. Add a background image to the new page and insert an image on one of the pages. Include an appropriate title for the page. Save the page in the sports subfolder. For a selection of images and backgrounds, visit the Dreamweaver 8 Media Web page (scsite.com/dw8/media) and then click Media below Project 2.

2 ■ Several of your friends were impressed with the Web page and Web site you created about your favorite hobby in Project 1. They have given you some topics they think you should include on the site. You decide to create an additional page that will consist of details about your hobby and the topics your friends suggested. Format the page. Add an absolute link to a related Web site and a relative link from the home page to the new page and from the new page to the home page. Add a background image to the new page. Create an e-mail link on the index page. Title the page with the name of the selected hobby. Save the page in the hobby subfolder. For a selection of images and backgrounds, visit the Dreamweaver 8 Media Web page (scsite.com/dw8/media) and then click Media below Project 2.

3 ■■ Modify the favorite type of music Web site you created in Project 1 by creating a new page. Format the page. Discuss your favorite artist or band on the new page. Add a background image to the new page. On the index page, align the image to the right, and on the new page, align the image to the left. Add appropriate alternative text for each image. Position each image appropriately on the page by using the H Space and V Space property features. Add an e-mail link on the index page, and add text and a relative link from the new page to the index page. View your Web pages in your browser. Give the page a meaningful title and then save the page in your music subfolder. For a selection of images and backgrounds, visit the Dreamweaver 8 Media Web page (scsite.com/dw8/media) and then click Media below Project 2.

Cases and Places

4 ■■ In Project 1, you created a Web site and a Web page to publicize your campaign for public office. Develop two additional pages to add to the site. Apply a background image to the new pages. Apply appropriate formatting to the two new pages. Scan a picture of yourself or take a picture with a digital camera and include the picture on the index page. Add a second image illustrating one of your campaign promises. Include at least two images on one of the new pages and one image on the other new page. Add alternative text for all images, and then add appropriate H Space and V Space property features to position the images. Create e-mail links on all three pages and create relative links from the home page to both pages and from each of the pages to the home page. Create an absolute link to a related site on one of the pages. Set the index page as the home page. Give each page a meaningful title and then save the pages in the office subfolder. For a selection of images and backgrounds, visit the Dreamweaver 8 Media Web page (scsite.com/dw8/media) and then click Media below Project 2.

5 ■■ **Working Together** The student trips Web site you and your classmates created in Project 1 is a success. Everyone loves it. The dean is so impressed that she asks the group to continue with the project. Your team creates and formats three additional Web pages, one for each of three possible locations for the trip. Add a background image to all new pages. Add two images to each of the pages, including the index page, and set the index page as the home page. Resize one of the images. Add the Alt text for each image, and then position each image appropriately using the H Space and V Space property features. Create a link from the index page to each of the three new pages and a link from each page to the index page. Create an absolute link to a related informational Web site on each of the three new pages. Add an appropriate title to each page. Preview in a browser to verify the links. Save the pages in your trips subfolder. For a selection of images and backgrounds, visit the Dreamweaver 8 Media Web page (scsite.com/dw8/media) and then click Media below Project 2.

MACROMEDIA
Dreamweaver 8

Tables and Page Layout

PROJECT

3

CASE PERSPECTIVE

The Colorado Parks Web site has been very successful thus far. David has received several e-mail messages asking for additional information about the four national parks. Tracy suggests a separate page for Rocky Mountains and Mesa Verde and a combination page for the two smaller parks — Black Canyon and Great Sand Dunes parks. Both David and you agree this is a good idea and would be a good addition to the Web site. The two of you volunteer to research various sources and to create the content for the three new pages.

Tracy further suggests that, in addition to adding the same background to these pages as that on the rest of the site, the three new pages also should have some consistency in the displayed information. The team decides that each page should include a heading with the name of the park, that the information contained in the body content should describe the location and contain some interesting facts, and that each page should list the park's address, including an e-mail link. The footer will contain links to the home page and to all four national parks. You all are eager to get started on this new addition to the Colorado Parks Web site.

As you read through this project, you will learn how to plan and design Web pages and how to create pages using tables. You also will learn how to modify and delete tables.

Tables and Page Layout

PROJECT

3

You will have mastered the material in this project when you can:

- Understand and plan page layout
- Describe Standard mode and Layout mode
- Design a Web page using tables in Standard mode
- Design a Web page using tables in Layout mode
- Describe visual guides
- Modify a table structure

- Describe HTML table tags
- Add content to a table
- Format table content
- Format a table
- Create head content

Introduction

Project 3 introduces the use of tables for page layout and the addition of head content elements. Page layout is an important part of Web design because it determines the way your page will display in the browser, which is one of the major challenges for any Web designer.

Dreamweaver's table feature is a great tool for designing a Web page. The table feature is very similar to the table feature in word processing programs such as Microsoft Word. A table allows you to add vertical and horizontal structure to a Web page. Using a table, you can put just about anything on your page and have it display in a specific location. You can lay out tabular data. Using the many table features, you can create columns of text or navigation bars. You can delete, split, and merge rows and columns; modify table, row, or cell properties to add color and alignment; and copy and paste cells in the table structure.

Dreamweaver provides three views, or ways, to use the table feature: Standard mode, Layout mode, and Expanded mode. Standard mode uses the Insert Table dialog box, and Layout mode is a freeform process in which you draw the table and the individual cells. Expanded mode allows you to edit table elements. In Expanded mode, Dreamweaver adds cell padding and spacing to the tables, thus temporarily increasing the tables' borders. This provides easy access to items that are difficult to select and allows for precise insertion point placement. This project discusses the three views and the advantages and disadvantages of each.

The second part of this project discusses the addition and value of head content. When you create a Web page, the underlying source code is made up of two main sections: the head section and the body section. The body section contains the page content that displays in the browser. In Projects 1 and 2, you created your Web pages in the body section. The head section contains a variety of information. With the exception of the page title, all head content is invisible when viewed in the Dreamweaver Document window or in a browser. Some head content is accessed by other programs, such as search engines, and some content is accessed by the browser. This project discusses the head content options and the importance of this content.

Project Three — Colorado Parks Page Layout

In this project, you continue with the creation of the Colorado Parks Web site. You use tables to create three new Web pages focusing on Colorado's four national parks — a separate page for Rocky Mountains and Mesa Verde and a combination page for Black Canyon and Great Sand Dunes. You then add these new pages to the parks Web site and link to them from the natl_parks.htm Web page (Figures 3-1a, 3-1b, and 3-1c on pages DW 203 through 205). When you complete your Web page additions, you will add keywords and a description as the head content.

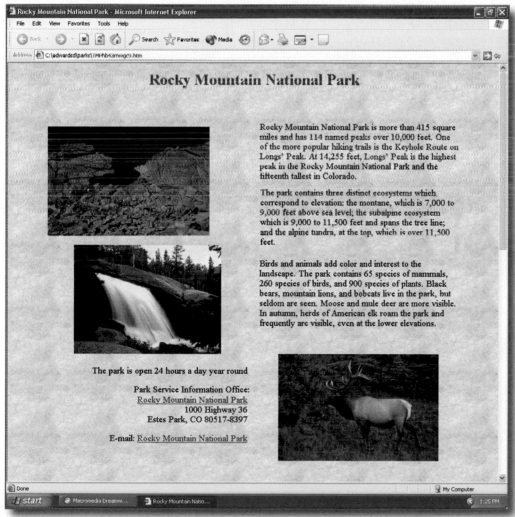

(a) Rocky Mountain National Park Page

FIGURE 3-1 *(continued)*

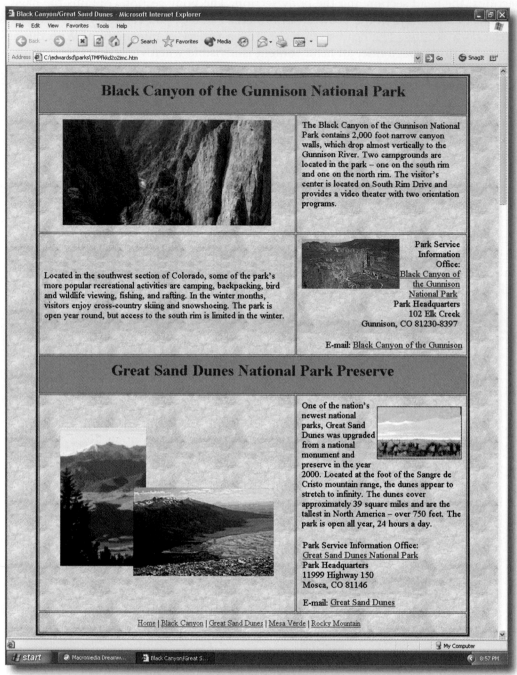

(b) Black Canyon and Great Sand Dunes National Park Page

FIGURE 3-1 (*continued*)

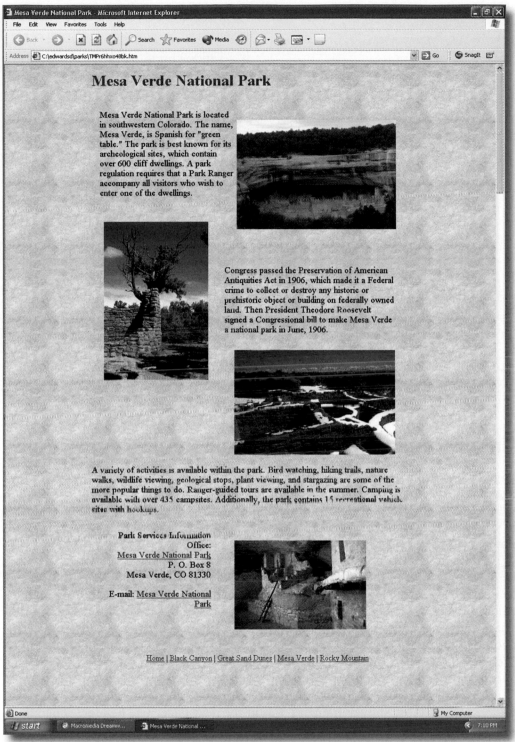

(c) Mesa Verde National Park Page

FIGURE 3-1 (*continued*)

This project uses a hierarchical structure. The structure now is expanded to include the three new pages (Figure 3-2 on the next page).

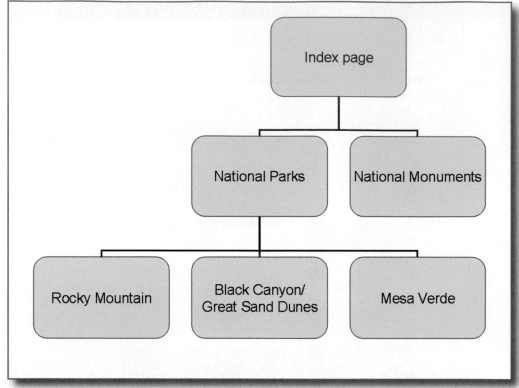

FIGURE 3-2

Understanding and Planning Page Layout

Page layout is the process of arranging the text, images, and other elements on the page. The basic rules of page layout are that your site should be easy to navigate, easy to read, and quick to download. Studies indicate that visitors will lose interest quickly in your Web site if the majority of a page does not download within 15 seconds. One popular design element that downloads quickly is tables.

Tables download very fast because they are created with HTML code. They can be used anywhere — for the home page, menus, images, navigation bars, frames, and so on. Tables originally were intended for presenting data arranged by rows and columns, such as tabular data within a spreadsheet. Web designers, however, quickly seized upon the use of tables to produce specific layout effects. You can produce good designs by using tables creatively. Tables allow you to position elements on a Web page with much greater accuracy. Using tables for layout provides the Web page author with endless design possibilities.

A typical Web page is composed of three sections: the header, the body, and the footer, such as those shown in Figure 3-3 on the next page. The **header**, generally located at the top of the page, can contain logos, images, or text that identifies the Web site. The header also may contain hyperlinks to other pages within the Web site.

The **body** of the Web page contains informational content about your site. This content may be in the form of text, graphics, animation, video, and audio, or a combination of any of these elements.

The **footer** provides hyperlinks for contact information and navigational controls. This may be in addition to the navigation controls in the header. Other common items contained within a footer are the name and e-mail address of the author or of the Webmaster. Sometimes, hyperlinks to other resources or to Help information are part of the footer.

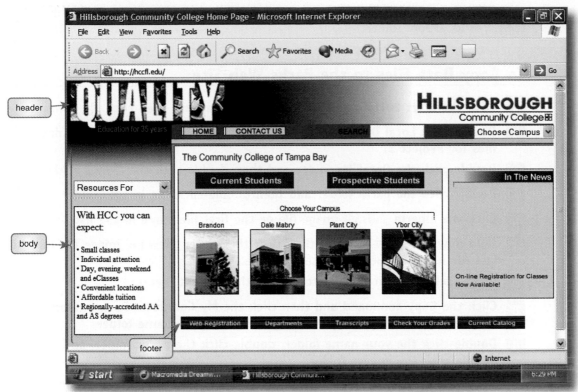

FIGURE 3-3

With tables, it is easy to create this header/body/footer structure or to create any other layout structure applicable to your specific Web page needs. The entire structure can be contained within one table or a combination of multiple and nested tables. A nested table is a table inside another table. You will use a structure similar to that shown in Figure 3-3 to create the three new pages for the Colorado Parks Web site.

Standard Mode and Layout Mode

Dreamweaver provides two options for creating tables: Standard mode and Layout mode. In **Standard mode**, a table is presented as a grid of rows and columns. This view is similar to a Microsoft Excel spreadsheet or a table created in a word processing program such as Microsoft Word. In **Layout mode**, you can draw, resize, and move boxes on the page while Dreamweaver still uses tables for the underlying structure. If you have used a desktop publishing program such as Microsoft Publisher or Adobe InDesign, then you are familiar with the format in which tables are created in Layout mode. Using Layout mode, you can place content at any location in the Document window.

Copying Data Files to the Local Web Site

Your Data Disk contains images for Project 3. These images are in an images folder. You use the Windows My Computer option to copy the Project 3 images to your parks images folder. See the inside back cover for instructions for downloading the Data Disk or see your instructor for information about accessing the files required for this book.

The Data Files folder for this project is stored on Local Disk (C:). The location on your computer may be different. If necessary, verify with your instructor the location of the Data Files folder. The following steps illustrate how to copy the files to the parks local root folder.

To Copy Data Files to the Parks Web Site

1 Click the Start button on the Windows taskbar and then click My Computer.

2 Double-click Local Disk (C:) and then navigate to the location of the data files for Project 3.

3 Double-click the DataFiles folder and then double-click the Proj03 folder.

4 Double-click the parks folder and then double-click the images folder.

5 Click the alberta_falls.gif image file or the first file name in the list.

6 Hold down the SHIFT key and then click the winter_view.jpg image file (or the last file name in the list) to select the eleven image files.

7 Right-click the selected files to display the context menu.

8 Click the Copy command and then click the My Computer Back button the number of times necessary to navigate to the your name folder.

9 Double-click the your name folder, double-click the parks folder, and then double-click the images folder.

10 Right-click anywhere in the open window to display the context menu, and then click Paste (Figure 3-4).

11 Click the images window Close button.

The 11 new image files are pasted into the Colorado Parks Web site images folder (Figure 3-4).

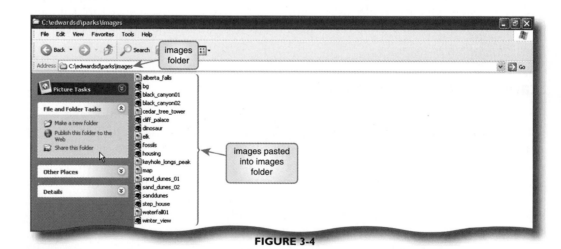

FIGURE 3-4

Starting Dreamweaver and Opening a Web Site

Each time you start Dreamweaver, it opens to the last site displayed when you closed the program. It, therefore, may be necessary for you to open the parks Web site. The Files pop-up menu in the Files panel lists sites you have defined. When you open the site, a list of pages and subfolders within the site are displayed. The following steps show how to start Dreamweaver and open the Colorado Parks Web site.

To Start Dreamweaver and Open the Colorado Parks Web Site

1 Click the Start button on the Windows taskbar.

2 Point to All Programs on the Start menu, point to Macromedia on the All Programs submenu, and then click Macromedia Dreamweaver 8 on the Macromedia submenu.

3 Click the Files panel box arrow and point to Colorado Parks on the Files panel pop-up menu.

4 Click Colorado Parks.

The Colorado Parks Web site hierarchy is displayed in the Files panel (Figure 3-5).

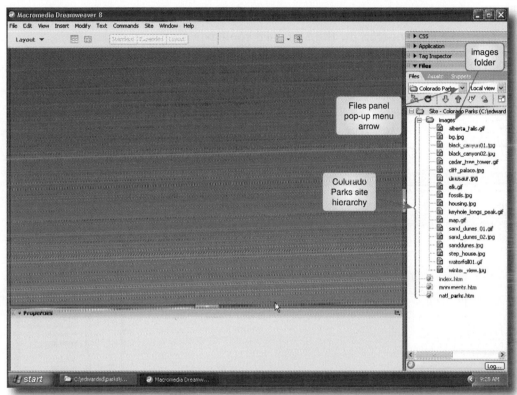

FIGURE 3-5

Adding Pages to a Web Site

You copied the images necessary to begin creating your new Web pages to the parks local root folder in the Files panel. You will add three additional pages to the Web site: separate pages for Rocky Mountains and Mesa Verde and a combination page for the two smaller parks — Black Canyon and Great Sand Dunes. You first create the Rocky Mountain National Park Web page. You then add the background image and a heading to the new page. Next, you use Dreamweaver's Standard mode to insert tables and add text, images, and links into the cells within the table.

Opening a New Document Window

The next step is to open a new Document window. This will become the Rocky Mountain National Park page. The following steps illustrate how to open a new Document window and save the page as rocky_mt.htm.

To Open a New Document Window

1 Click File on the menu bar and then point to New.

2 Click New. If necessary, click the General tab and then click Basic page in the Category list.

3 If necessary, click HTML in the Basic page list.

4 Click the Create button.

5 Click the Save button on the Standard toolbar.

6 Type rocky_mt as the file name. If necessary, select the parks folder, and then click the Save button.

The rocky_mt.htm page is saved in the parks local folder and is displayed in Dreamweaver's Files panel. The path and file name (edwards\parks\rocky_mt.htm) appear on the Dreamweaver title bar (Figure 3-6).

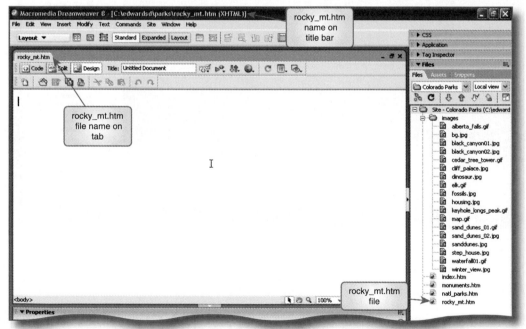

FIGURE 3-6

Creating the Rocky Mountain National Park Web Page

You start creating the Rocky Mountain National Park page by applying a background image. This is the same background image you used for the Colorado Parks Web site pages in Projects 1 and 2. To provide additional space in the Document window and to create a better overview of the layout, you hide the panel groups. You expand the Property inspector to display the additional table options. The following steps illustrate how to apply the background image.

To Add a Background Image to the Rocky Mountain National Park Web Page

1 Click the panel groups expander arrow to hide the panel groups.

2 If necessary, click the Property inspector expander arrow to display both the upper and lower sections.

3 Click Modify on the menu bar and then click Page Properties.

4 Click the Browse button to the right of the Background image box.

5 If necessary, navigate to the parks\images folder.

6 Click bg.jpg and then click the OK button in the Select Image Source dialog box.

7 Click the OK button in the Page Properties dialog box. If necessary, click the Document window.

The background image is applied to the Rocky Mountain National Park page. The panel groups are hidden, and the Property inspector is expanded. The insertion point is aligned at the left (Figure 3-7).

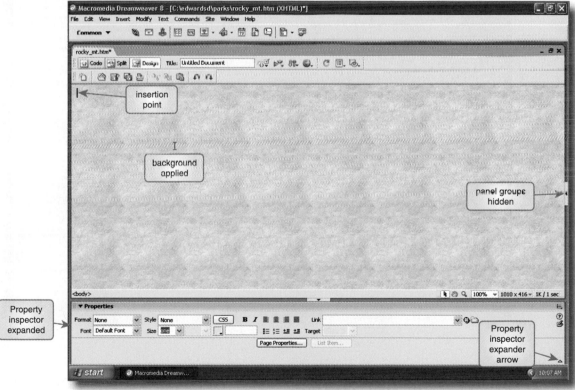

FIGURE 3-7

Next, you add, format, and change the color of the heading. You apply the same heading style and color you applied to the heading in the index page. Recall that Dreamweaver designated this as style1. The following steps show how to add the heading, apply the Heading 1 format, and change the text color.

To Insert and Format the Heading

1 **Click the Document window. Type** Rocky Mountain National Park **as the heading.**

2 **Apply Heading 1, click the Align Center button in the Property inspector.**

3 **Drag to select the title. Type** #993300 **in the color hexadecimal value box in the Property inspector. Press the ENTER key.**

4 **Click the Style pop-up menu in the Property inspector and select None.**

5 **Title the page Rocky Mountain National Park.**

6 **Click the Save button on the Standard toolbar.**

The heading is centered and formatted, and the title is added (Figure 3-8). The style is turned off.

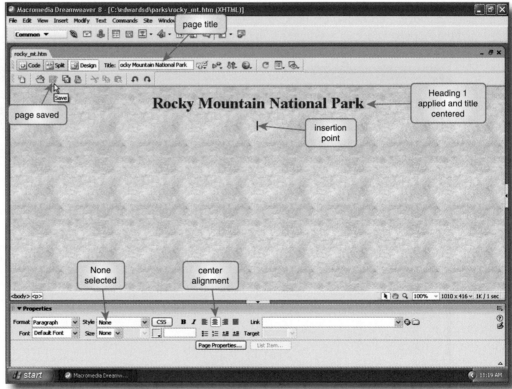

FIGURE 3-8

Understanding Tables

Tables have many uses in HTML design. The most obvious is a table of data, but, as already mentioned, tables also are used for page layout, such as placing text and graphics on a page at just the right location. **Tables** provide Web designers with a method to add vertical and horizontal structure to a page. A table consists of three basic components: rows, columns, and cells. A **row** is a horizontal collection of cells, and a **column** is a vertical collection of cells. A **cell** is the container created when the row and column intersect. Each cell within the table can contain any standard element you use on a Web page. This includes text, images, and other objects.

Inserting a Table into the Rocky Mountain National Park Page

You will add two tables to the Rocky Mountain National Park page and then add text and images to the cells within the tables. The first table will consist of three rows and two columns, with a cell padding of 2 and cell spacing of 20. **Cell padding** is the amount of space between the edge of a cell and its contents, whereas **cell spacing** is the amount of space between cells. The border will be set to 0. When the table displays in Dreamweaver, a border outline is displayed around the table. When the table's border is set to 0 and the table is viewed in a browser, however, this outline does not display.

The table width is 90 percent. When specifying the width, you can select percent or pixels. A table with the width specified as a **percent** expands with the width of the window and the monitor size in which it is being viewed. A table with the width specified as **pixels** will remain the same size regardless of the window and monitor size. If you select percent and an image is larger than the selected percent, the cell and table will expand to accommodate the image. Likewise, if the **No Wrap** property is enabled and the text will not fit within the cell, the cell and table will expand to accommodate the text. It is not necessary to declare a table width. When no value is specified, the table is displayed as small as possible and then expands as content is added. If modifications are necessary to the original specified table values, these values can be changed in the Property inspector.

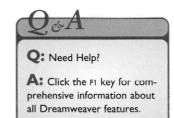

Q: Need Help?

A: Click the F1 key for comprehensive information about all Dreamweaver features.

The second table is a one-cell table, consisting of one row and one column. This table will contain links to the Home page and to the four national parks pages. You use the Insert bar with the Layout category and the Property inspector to control and format the tables.

The Insert Bar

The Insert bar displays at the top of the window below the menu bar. This toolbar contains buttons for creating and inserting objects such as tables, layers, and images. The Insert bar contains eight separate categories, and is fully customizable through the Favorites category. When the current document contains server-side code (such as that related to a database), additional categories display. Server-side code is an advanced topic and is not discussed in this book.

Some categories have buttons with pop-up menus. When you select an option from a pop-up menu, it becomes the default action for the button. Any time you select a new option from the pop-up menu, the default action for the button changes. The Insert bar displays when you start Dreamweaver. You can, however, hide or display the Insert bar as necessary. All selections within the categories also are available through the menu bar.

Category Types

The default Insert bar contains the following categories:

COMMON CATEGORY The **Common category** contains buttons for the most frequently used Web publishing tasks.

LAYOUT CATEGORY The **Layout category** contains buttons pertaining to the design modes for Web publishing and enables you to insert tables, div tags, layers, and frames. You also can choose from among three table modes: Standard (default), Expanded Tables, and Layout. When you select Layout mode, you can use the Dreamweaver layout tools: Draw Layout Cell and Layout Table.

FORMS CATEGORY The **Forms category** contains buttons for creating forms and inserting form elements.

TEXT CATEGORY The **Text category** contains buttons for text formatting.

HTML CATEGORY The **HTML category** contains buttons related to HTML code for head content, horizontal rules, tables, scripts, and frames.

APPLICATION CATEGORY The **Application category** contains buttons relating to records, dynamic data, and other database elements.

FLASH ELEMENTS CATEGORY The **Flash elements** category contains a button allowing you to insert Flash elements.

FAVORITES CATEGORY The **Favorites category** enables you to group and organize the Insert bar buttons you use the most in one common place.

You use the Layout category to assist with the page design and insert tables. The following steps illustrate how to display the Insert bar if necessary and select the Layout category. If the Insert bar already is displayed on your computer, skip Step 1.

To Display the Insert Bar and Select the Layout Category

1

• **If necessary, click Window on the menu bar. If the Insert command is not checked, click Insert.**

The category last displayed becomes the default category, so your screen may display a different category.

2

• **Click the arrow to the right of the Common category (or the displayed category), and then point to Layout on the category pop-up menu.**

The Common category pop-up menu is displayed (Figure 3-9).

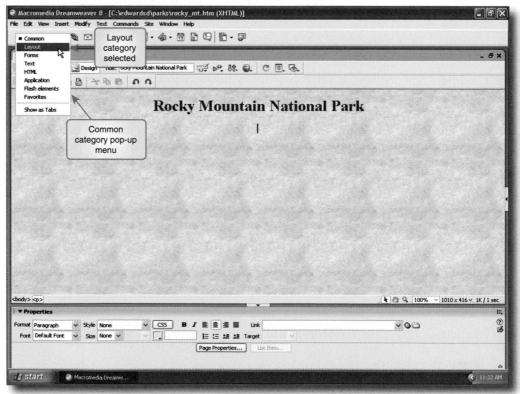

FIGURE 3-9

3

• **Click the Layout command.**

The Insert bar for the Layout category is displayed (Figure 3-10).

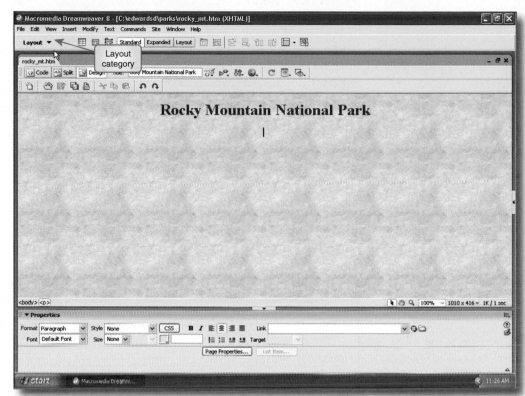

FIGURE 3-10

Layout Category

The Layout category (Figure 3-11 on the next page) enables you to work with tables and other features. Dreamweaver provides two ways to create tables — Standard mode and Layout mode. In Standard mode, a table displays as a grid and expands as you add text and images. You define the structure of the table using the Insert Table dialog box. In Layout mode, you create tables and cells by drawing them. You will work with Layout mode later in this project.

The Layout category also contains a button for Expanded Tables mode. This mode temporarily expands the cells, enabling you to select items in tables and to place the insertion point precisely. Use this mode as a temporary visual aid for insertion point placement. After placing the insertion point, return to Standard mode to make your edits and to provide a better visualization of your changes.

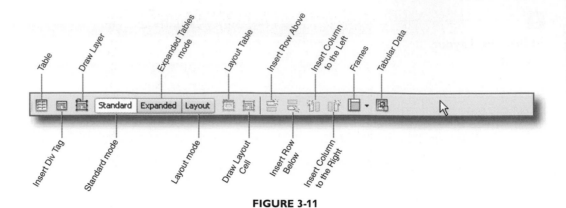

FIGURE 3-11

Table 3-1 lists the button names and descriptions available in the Insert bar Layout category.

Table 3-1 Buttons on the Layout Insert Bar

BUTTON NAME	DESCRIPTION
Table	Places a table at the insertion point
Insert Div Tag	Inserts a <div> tag
Draw Layer	Creates a layer
Standard mode	Displays a table as a grid of lines
Expanded Tables mode	Temporarily adds cell padding and spacing
Layout mode	Displays a table as boxes that can be drawn, dragged, and resized
Layout Table	Used to draw a layout table in the Design view of the Document window
Draw Layout Cell	Used to draw individual table cells in the Design view of the Document window
Insert Row Above	Used to insert a row above the selected row
Insert Row Below	Used to insert a row below the selected row
Insert Column to the Left	Used to insert a column to the left of the selected column
Insert Column to the Right	Used to insert a column to the right of the selected column
Frames	Displays Frames pop-up menu
Tabular Data	Imports tabular data

More About

Dreamweaver Table Views

For more information about Dreamweaver 8 table views, visit the Dreamweaver 8 More About Web page (scsite.com/ dw8/more.htm) and then click Dreamweaver 8 Tables.

Table Defaults and Accessibility

When you insert a table, the Table dialog box displays and contains default settings for each of the table attributes. The Table dialog box in Figure 3-12 on the next page contains the values shown in Table 3-2 on the next page. After you have created a table and made changes to these defaults, the settings that display for the next table you create are the settings from the last table created.

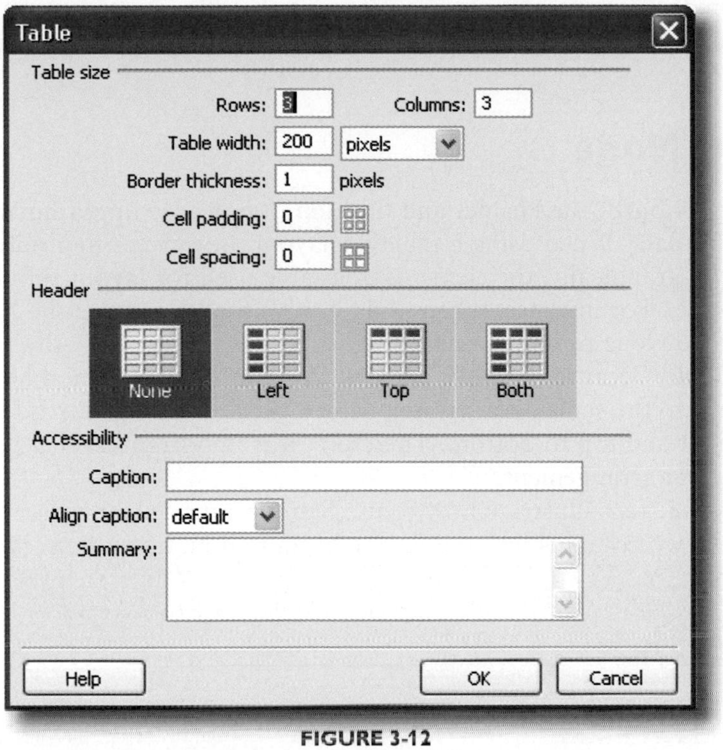

FIGURE 3-12

Table 3-2 Table Dialog Box Default Values

ATTRIBUTE	DEFAULT	DESCRIPTION
Rows	3	Determines the number of rows in the table
Columns	3	Determines the number of columns in the table
Table width	200 pixels	Specifies the width of the table in pixels or as a percentage of the browser window's width
Border thickness	1 pixel	Specifies the border width in pixels
Cell padding	0	Specifies the number of pixels between a cell's border and its contents
Cell spacing	0	Specifies the number of pixels between adjacent table cells
Header	None	Specifies if the top row and/or column is designated as a header cell
Caption	None	Provides a brief description of the table
Align caption	default	Specifies where the table caption appears in relation to the table
Summary	None	Provides a table description; used by screen readers

It is advisable to use headers for tables when the table presents tabular information. Screen readers read table headings and help screen-reader users keep track of table information. Additionally, the Caption option provides a table title that displays outside of the table, the Align caption option specifies where the table caption appears in relation to the table, and the Summary option provides a table description. Screen readers read the summary text, but the text does not appear in the user's browser. Summary text is similar to the Alt text you added for images in Project 2. You add Summary text to the tables you create in this project.

Standard Mode

Q&A

Q: What is the Web site address for Macromedia online support?

A: You can find Macromedia online support at www.macromedia.com/support/dreamweaver/.

As indicated previously, the Header and Caption options are important when a table displays tabular data. When using a table for layout, however, other options apply. Structurally and graphically, the elements in a table used for layout should be invisible in the browser. For instance, when using a table for layout, use the None option for Headers. The None option prevents the header tags <th> and </th> from being added to the table. Because the table does not contain tabular data, a header would be of no benefit to the screen-reader user. Screen readers, however, read table content from left to right and top to bottom. Therefore, it is important to structure the table content in a linear arrangement.

The following steps illustrate how to use Standard mode to insert a table with three rows and two columns into the Rocky Mountain National Park Web page.

To Insert a Table Using Standard Mode

1

• **If necessary, click the Standard button on the Insert bar and then click the Table button.**

The Table dialog box is displayed (Figure 3-13). The settings displayed are the default settings from the last table created, so your dialog box most likely will contain different values.

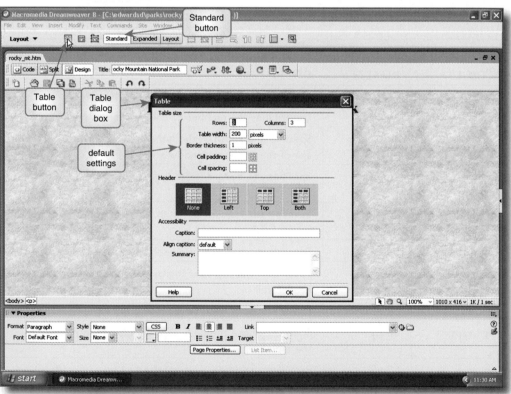

FIGURE 3-13

2

- **If necessary, type** 3 **and then press the TAB key to move to the Columns box.**

- **Type** 2 **as the new value in the Columns box and then press the TAB key.**

- **Type** 90 **as the new value in the Table width box and then click the Table width arrow.**

- **Click percent and then press the TAB key.**

- **Type** 0 **in the Border thickness box and then press the TAB key.**

- **Type** 2 **in the Cell padding box and then press the TAB key.**

- **Type** 20 **in the Cell spacing box and then press the TAB key.**

- **If necessary, select None for the Header.**

- **Click the Summary text box and type** Table layout for Rocky Mountain National Park Web page. The table contains three rows and two columns with images and text in the table cells.

The Table dialog box is displayed with the new settings, as shown in Figure 3-14.

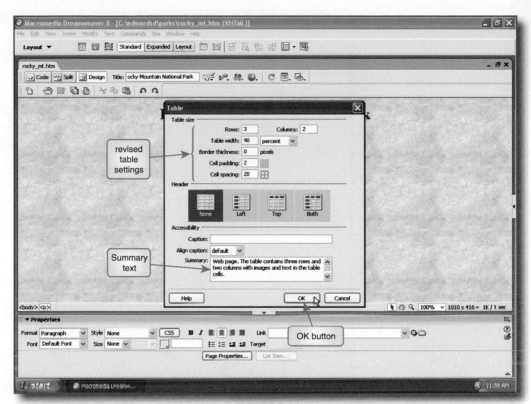

FIGURE 3-14

3

• **Click the OK button.**

The table is inserted into the Document window (Figure 3-15). The dark border around the table and the three handles on the lower and right borders indicate that the table is selected. The <table> tag displays as selected in the tag selector, also indicating that the table is selected. The cell spacing between each cell is 20 pixels. The default alignment for the table is left. The border is set to 0 and displays as an outline when the table is viewed in Dreamweaver. When the table is viewed in a browser, however, no border is displayed.

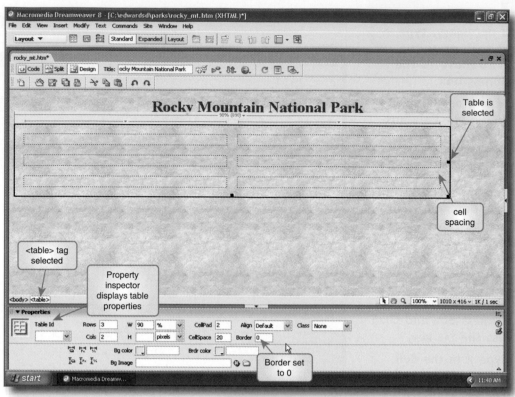

FIGURE 3-15

Other Ways

1. On Insert menu, click Table, select table properties, click OK button
2. Press CTRL+ALT+T

Property Inspector Table Features

As you have seen, the Property inspector options change depending on the selected object. You use the Property inspector to modify and add table attributes. When a table is selected, the Property inspector displays table properties in both panels. When another table element — a row, column, or cell — is selected, the displayed properties change and are determined by the selected element. The following section describes the table-related features of the Property inspector shown in Figure 3-16 on the next page.

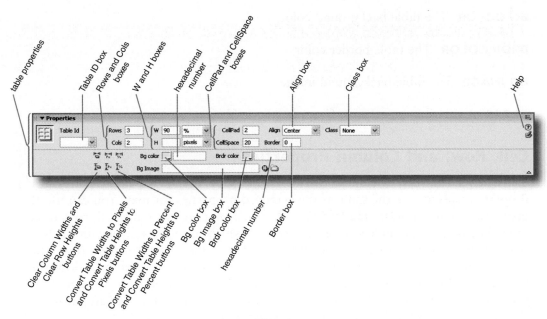

FIGURE 3-16

TABLE ID An identifier used for Cascading Style Sheets, scripting, and accessibility. A table ID is not required; however, it is a good idea to always add this identifier.

ROWS AND COLS The number of rows and columns in the table.

W Used to specify the minimum width of the table in either pixels or percent. If a size is not specified, the size can vary depending on the monitor and browser settings. A table width specified in pixels is displayed at the same size in all browsers. A table width specified in percent is altered in appearance based on the user's monitor resolution and browser window size.

H Used to specify the height of the table in either pixels or percent. Generally, the height of a table consists of the height of the collective rows and is not specified.

CELLPAD The number of pixels between the cell border and the cell content.

CELLSPACE The number of pixels between adjacent table cells.

ALIGN Determines where the table appears, relative to other elements in the same paragraph such as text or images. The default alignment is to the left.

BORDER Specifies the border width in pixels.

CLEAR COLUMN WIDTHS AND CLEAR ROW HEIGHTS Deletes all specified row height or column width values from the table.

CONVERT TABLE WIDTHS TO PIXELS AND CONVERT TABLE HEIGHTS TO PIXELS Sets the width or height of each column in the table to its current width expressed as pixels.

CONVERT TABLE WIDTHS TO PERCENT AND CONVERT TABLE HEIGHTS TO PERCENT Sets the width or height of each column in the table to its current width expressed as a percentage of the Document window's width and also sets the width of the whole table to its current width as a percentage of the Document window's width.

BG COLOR The table background color.

BRDR COLOR The table border color.

BG IMAGE The table background image.

CLASS An attribute used with Cascading Style Sheets.

Cell, Row, and Column Properties

When a cell, row, or column is selected, the properties in the upper pane of the Property inspector are the same as the standard properties for text. You can use these properties to incorporate standard HTML formatting tags within a cell, row, or column. The part of the table selected determines which properties display in the lower pane of the Property inspector. The properties for all three features (cell, row, and column) are the same, except for one element — the icon displayed in the lower-left pane of the Property inspector. The following section describes the row-related features (Figure 3-17), cell-related features (Figure 3-18), and column-related features (Figure 3-19 on page 223) of the Property inspector.

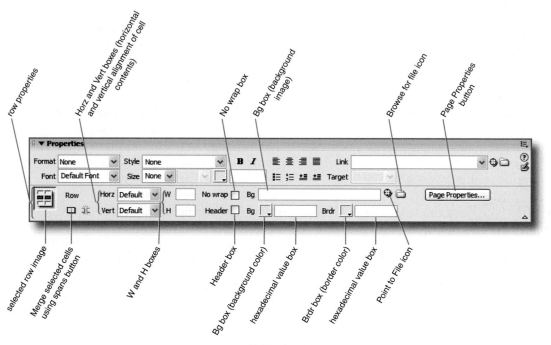

FIGURE 3-17

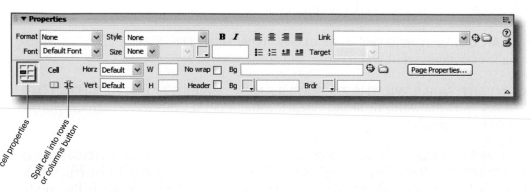

FIGURE 3-18

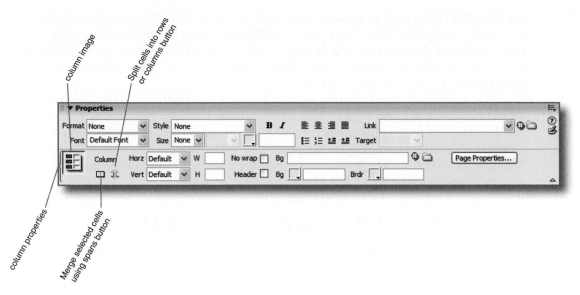

column image

Split cells into rows
or columns button

column properties

Merge selected cells
using spans button

FIGURE 3-19

HORZ Specifies the horizontal alignment of the contents of a cell, row, or column. The contents can be aligned to the left, right, or center of the cells.

VERT Specifies the vertical alignment of the contents of a cell, row, or column. The contents can be aligned to the top, middle, bottom, or baseline of the cells.

W AND H Specifies the width and height of selected cells in pixels or as a percentage of the entire table's width or height.

BG (UPPER TEXT FIELD) The file name of the background image for a cell, column, or row.

BG (LOWER COLOR BOX AND TEXT FIELD) The background color of a cell, column, or row, using the color picker.

BRDR The border color for the cells.

NO WRAP Prevents line wrapping, keeping all text in a given cell on a single line. If No Wrap is enabled, cells widen to accommodate all data as it is typed or pasted into a cell.

HEADER Formats the selected cells as table header cells. The contents of table header cells are bold and centered by default.

MERGE CELLS Combines selected cells, rows, or columns into one cell (available when rows or columns are selected).

SPLIT CELLS Divides a cell, creating two or more cells (available when a single cell is selected).

Table Formatting Conflicts

When formatting tables in Standard mode, you can set properties for the entire table or for selected rows, columns, or cells in the table. When you are applying these properties, however, a potential for conflict exists. To resolve this potential conflict,

HTML assigns levels of precedence. The order of precedence for table formatting is cells, rows, and table. When a property, such as background color or alignment, is set to one value for the whole table and another value for individual cells, cell formatting takes precedence over row formatting, which in turn takes precedence over table formatting.

For example, if you set the background color for a single cell to green, and then set the background color of the entire table to red, the green cell does not change to red, because cell formatting takes precedence over table formatting. Dreamweaver, however, does not always follow the precedence. The program will override the settings for a cell if you change the settings for the row that contains the cell. To eliminate this problem, you should change the cell settings last.

Understanding HTML Structure within a Table

As you work with and become more familiar with tables, it is helpful to have an understanding of the HTML structure within a table. Suppose, for example, you have a table with two rows and two columns, displaying a total of four cells, such as the following:

First cell	Second cell
Third cell	Fourth cell

The general syntax of the table is:

```
<table>
<tr>
    <td> First cell </td>
    <td> Second cell </td>
</tr>
<tr>
    <td> Third cell </td>
    <td> Fourth cell </td>
</tr>
</table>
```

More About

Table Formatting Conflicts

For more information about Dreamweaver 8 table formatting conflicts, visit the Dreamweaver 8 More About Web page (scsite.com/dw8/more.htm) and then click Dreamweaver 8 Tables.

When you view your table in Dreamweaver, the tag selector displays the <table>, <td>, and <tr> tags. The <table> tag indicates the whole table. Clicking the <table> tag in the tag selector selects the whole table. The <td> tag indicates table data. Clicking the <td> tag in the tag selector selects the cell containing the insertion point. The <tr> tag indicates table row. Clicking the <tr> tag in the tag selector selects the row containing the insertion point.

Selecting the Table and Selecting Cells

The Property inspector displays table attributes only if the entire table is selected. To select the entire table, click the upper-left corner of the table, anywhere on the top or bottom edge of the table, or on a row or column's border. When you move the pointer over the border, the pointer changes to a table grid icon, indicating that when the mouse button is clicked, the table is selected (Figure 3-20 on the next page).

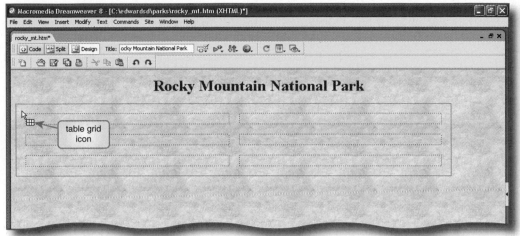

FIGURE 3-20

As discussed previously, another method for selecting a table is to click anywhere in the table and then click the <table> tag in the tag selector. When selected, the table will display with a dark border and selection handles on the table's lower and right edges (Figure 3-21).

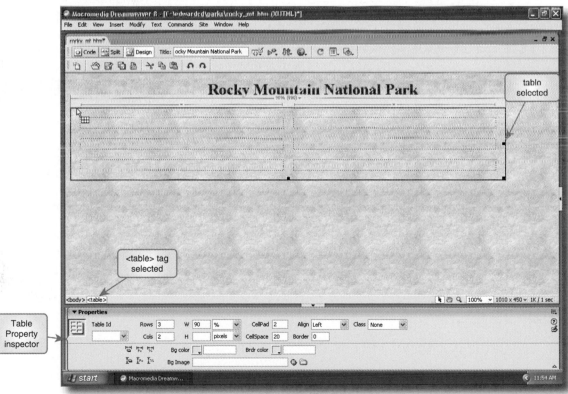

FIGURE 3-21

Selecting a row, column, or cell is easier than selecting the entire table. When a cell, row, or column is selected, the selected item has a dark border. To select a cell, click inside the cell. When you click inside the cell, the <td> tag displays as selected on the status bar. To select a row or column, click inside one of the cells in the row or column and drag to select the other cells. When you select a row, the <tr> tag displays in the status bar. A second method for selecting a row or column is to point to the left edge of a row or the top edge of a column. When the pointer changes to a selection arrow, click to select the row or column. In Figure 3-22, the selection arrow is pointing to a row and the row is selected.

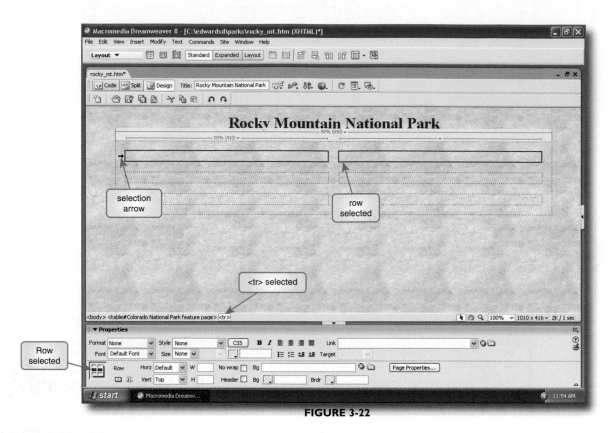

FIGURE 3-22

Centering a Table

When a table is inserted into the Document window with a specified width, it defaults to the left. Using the Property inspector, you can center the table by selecting it and then applying the Center command. The following steps illustrate how to select and center the table.

To Select and Center a Table

1

• **Click row 1, column 1.**

The insertion point is in the first cell of the first row and the first column (Figure 3-23).

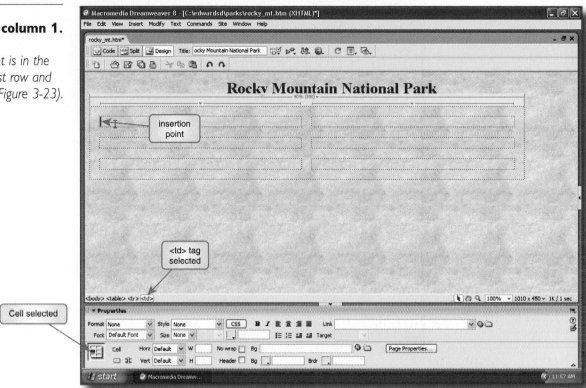

FIGURE 3-23

2

• **Click <table> in the tag selector.**

• **Click the Align box arrow in the Property inspector and then point to Center.**

The table is selected, and handles are displayed on the lower and right borders of the table. The <table> tag is selected. Center is selected in the Align pop-up menu (Figure 3-24).

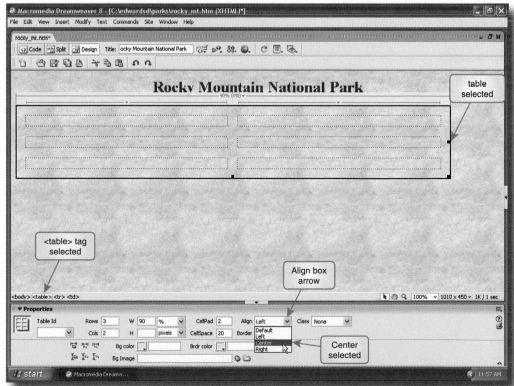

FIGURE 3-24

3

• **Click Center.**

The table is centered in the Document window (Figure 3-25).

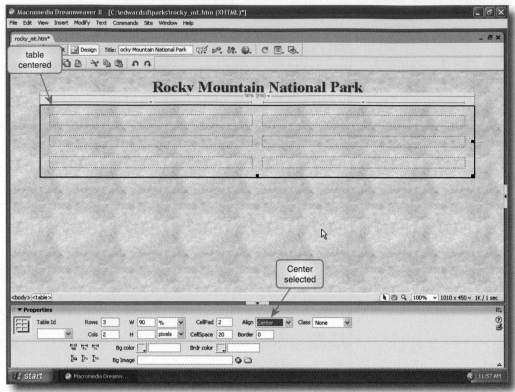

FIGURE 3-25

Changing the Default Cell Alignment

The default horizontal cell alignment is left. When you enter text or add an image to a cell, it defaults to the left margin of the cell. You can change the left alignment through the Property inspector by clicking the cell and then changing the default to Center or Right. The default vertical cell alignment is Middle, which aligns the cell content in the middle of the cell. Other vertical alignment options include the following:

Top — aligns the cell content at the top of the cell
Bottom — aligns the cell content at the bottom of the cell
Baseline — aligns the cell content at the bottom of the cell (same as Bottom)

You can change the vertical alignment through the Property inspector by clicking the cell and then selecting another vertical alignment option.

The following steps show how to select all of the cells and change the default vertical alignment from middle to top.

To Change Vertical Alignment from Middle to Top

1

• **Click in row 1, column 1 and then drag to the right and down to select the three rows and two columns in the table.**

• **Click the Vert box arrow and then point to Top in the Vert pop-up menu.**

The three rows in the table are selected. The Property inspector changes to reflect the properties for a row. The Vert pop-up menu is displayed, and Top is selected (Figure 3-26).

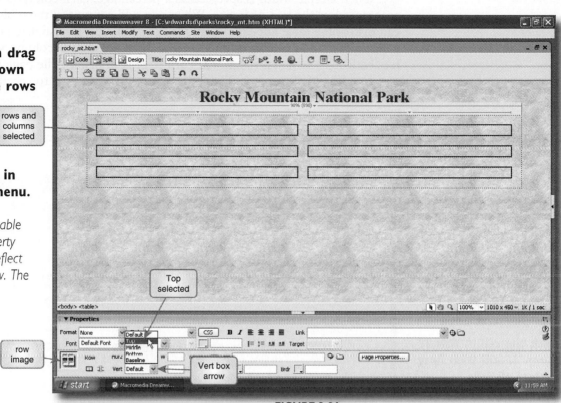

FIGURE 3-26

2

• **Click Top.**

The vertical alignment is changed to top (Figure 3-27). This change does not display in the Document window.

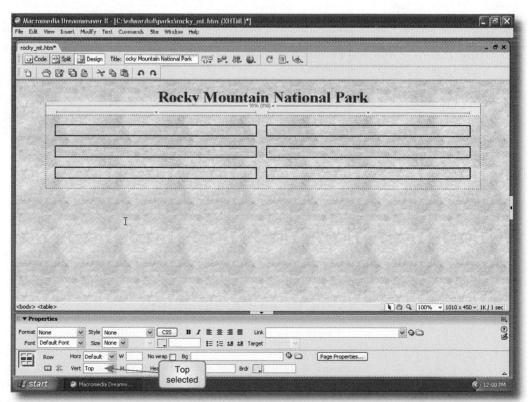

FIGURE 3-27

Specifying Column Width

When a table width is specified as a percentage, each column's width expands to accommodate the text or image. When you add content to the table, this expansion can distort the table appearance and make it difficult to visualize how the final page will display. You can control this expansion by setting the column width. The objective for the Rocky Mountain National Park page is to display the page in two columns of equal widths of 50 percent. The following step shows how to specify column width.

To Specify Column Width

1

• **Click the cell in row 1, column 1 and then drag to select all cells in column 1.**

• **Click the W box in the Property inspector. Type** 50% **and then press the** ENTER **key.**

• **Click the cell in row 1, column 2, and then drag to select all cells in column 2.**

• **Click the W box in the Property inspector. Type** 50% **and then press the** ENTER **key.**

The width for column 1 and column 2 is specified as 50% at the top of the table (Figure 3-28). The percentage bar located at the top of the table

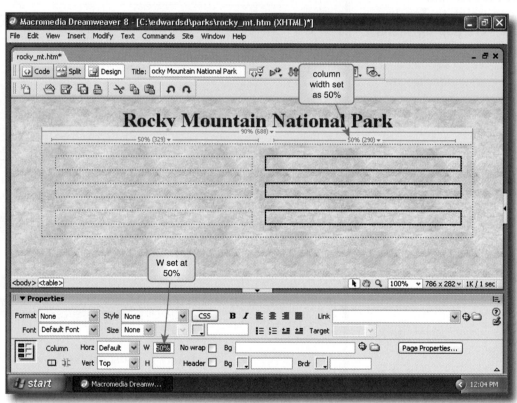

FIGURE 3-28

sometimes displays below the table, depending on available screen space and screen location.

2

• **Click anywhere in the table to deselect the column.**

Table ID and Accessibility

Earlier in this project, the accessibility options available through the Table dialog box were discussed. The Property inspector for tables contains another accessibility option — table ID. For accessibility purposes, it is recommended that you add a table ID. This provides a name for the table within the HTML code. The table ID is similar to the alternate text for an image, identifying the object to devices that read browser screens. You must select the table to display the Table ID text box. The following step illustrates how to select the table and add a table ID to the Rocky Mountain National Park feature table.

To Add a Table ID to the Rocky Mountain National Park Feature Table

1

• **Click <table> in the status bar to select the table.**

• **Click the Table ID text box and then type** Rocky Mountain National Park feature page **as the Table ID text.**

• **Press the ENTER key.**

The Table ID is added to the Table ID text box and appears on the status bar (Figure 3-29).

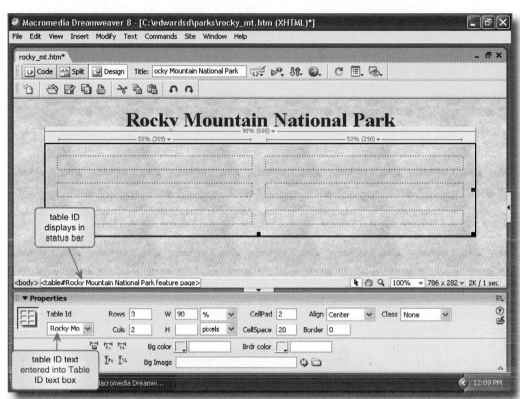

FIGURE 3-29

Adding Text to the Rocky Mountain National Park Web Page

Next, you will enter and format the text for the Rocky Mountain National Park Web page. Table 3-3 on the next page includes the text for the first table. The text is entered into the table cells. If you have not set the width and height of a cell, when you begin to enter text into a table cell, the cell expands to accommodate the text. The other cells may appear to shrink, but they also will expand when you type in the cells or add an image to the cells.

The following steps show how to add text to the Rocky Mountain National Park page. Press the ENTER key or insert a line break, <br>, as indicated in Table 3-3. Press SHIFT+ENTER to insert a line break. Press the TAB key to move from cell to cell.

Table 3-3 Rocky Mountain National Park Web Page Text	
SECTION	TEXT FOR ROCKY MOUNTAIN NATIONAL PARK WEB PAGE
Part 1	Rocky Mountain National Park is more than 415 square miles and has 114 named peaks over 10,000 feet. One of the more popular hiking trails is the Keyhole Route on Longs' Peak. At 14,255 feet, Longs' Peak is the highest peak in the Rocky Mountain National Park and the fifteenth tallest in Colorado. <ENTER>
	The park contains three distinct ecosystems which correspond to elevation: the montane, which is 7,000 to 9,000 feet above sea level; the subalpine ecosystem which is 9,000 to 11,500 feet and spans the tree line; and the alpine tundra, at the top, which is over 11,500 feet. <ENTER>
	Birds and animals add color and interest to the landscape. The park contains 65 species of mammals, 260 species of birds, and 900 species of plants. Black bears, mountain lions, and bobcats live in the park, but seldom are seen. Moose and mule deer are more visible. In autumn, herds of American elk roam the park and frequently are visible, even at the lower elevations.
Part 2	The park is open 24 hours a day year round.<ENTER>
	Park Service Information Office:
	Rocky Mountain National Park
	1000 Highway 36
	Estes Park, CO 80517-8397<ENTER>
	E-mail: Rocky Mountain National Park

More About

Table Data

If you have a table that contains data that requires sorting, you can perform a simple table sort based on the contents of a single column, or you can perform a more complicated sort based on the contents of two columns. Click Commands on the menu bar and then click Sort Table.

To Add Rocky Mountain National Park Text

1

• **Type the three paragraphs of Part 1 in Table 3-3 in row 1, column 2 of the table in the Document window. Press the ENTER key as indicated in the table.**

The three paragraphs are entered into row 1, column 2 (Figure 3-30).

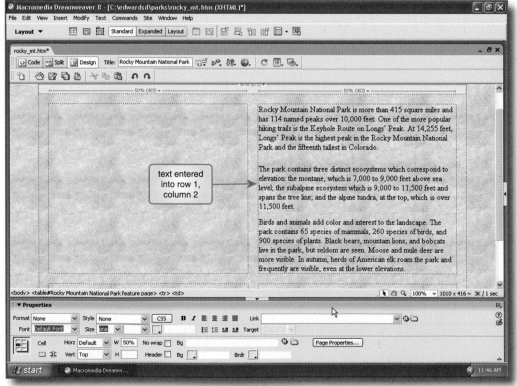

FIGURE 3-30

2

• **If necessary, scroll down to display the rest of the table. Type the text of Part 2, as shown in Table 3-3, into row 3, column 1 of the Document window. Use SHIFT+ENTER to insert the line breaks.**

The text is entered (Figure 3-31). The insertion point still is within the cell below the last line and may not display because a line break was added. A line break moves the insertion point to the next line, but does not create a blank space within a table cell such as when the ENTER key is pressed.

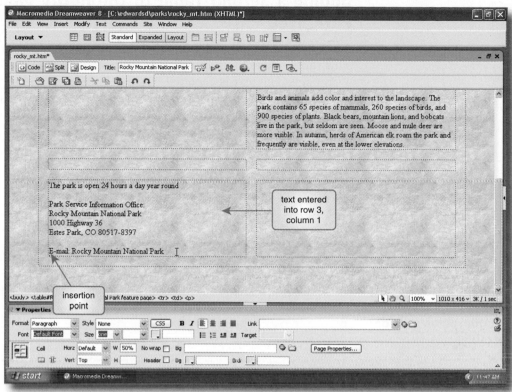

FIGURE 3-31

3

• **Select the text in row 3, column 1.**

• **Click the Align Right button in the Property inspector.**

The text is aligned to the right in the cell (Figure 3-32).

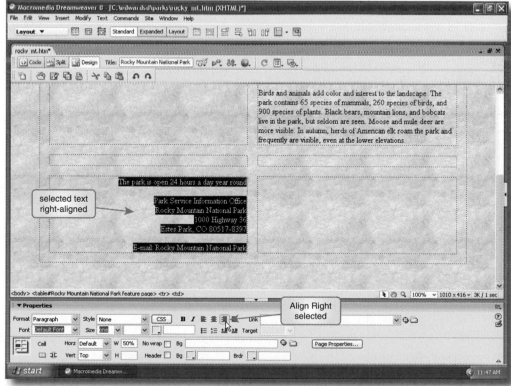

FIGURE 3-32

Other Ways

1. Right-click selected text, point to Align on context menu, click Right on Align submenu

Adding a Second Table to the Rocky Mountain National Park Web Page

Next, you add a second table to the Rocky Mountain National Park Web page. This table will contain one row and one column and will serve as the footer for your Web page. The text is centered in the cell and will contain links to the home page and to the other three national parks Web pages. When you create the pages for the other parks, you will be able to copy and paste these links into those pages. The following steps show how to add the second table and text.

To Add a Second Table to the Rocky Mountain National Park Web Page

1

• **Click outside the right border of the existing table to position the insertion point outside the table.**

The insertion point, a long dark line, is located and blinking to the right of the table border (Figure 3-33).

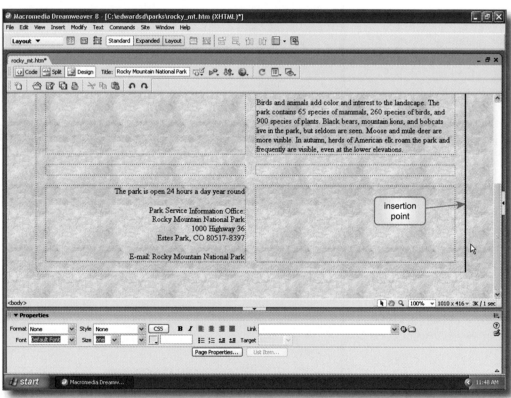

FIGURE 3-33

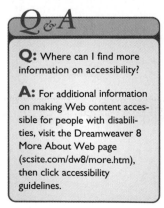

Q: Where can I find more information on accessibility?

A: For additional information on making Web content accessible for people with disabilities, visit the Dreamweaver 8 More About Web page (scsite.com/dw8/more.htm), then click accessibility guidelines.

2

• Press the **ENTER** key.

• Click the **Table button** on the Layout Insert bar.

The Table dialog box is displayed (Figure 3-34). The dialog box retains the settings from the first table. The dialog box on your computer may show different settings.

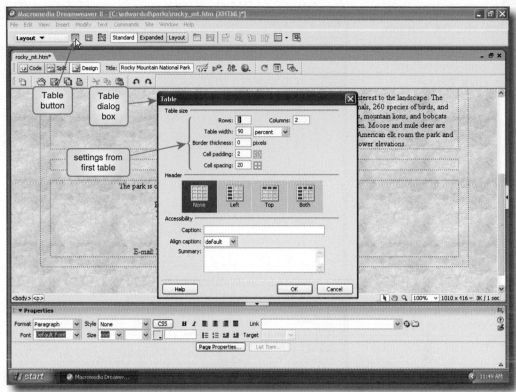

FIGURE 3-34

3

• Change the number of rows to 1, the number of columns to 1, the width to 75, the cell padding to 0, and the cell spacing to 10.

• Type **Links table** in the Summary text box.

• If necessary, change other settings to match the settings shown in Figure 3-35.

The Table dialog box displays the new table settings, as shown in Figure 3-35.

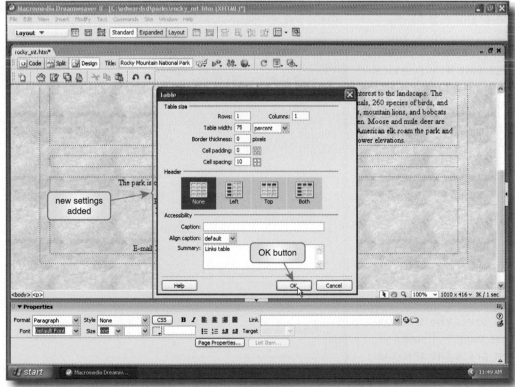

FIGURE 3-35

4

• **Click the OK button.**

• **If necessary, click the Align box arrow and then click Center.**

The table is inserted into the Document window (Figure 3-36). The dark border and handles indicate that the table is selected. The table contains one cell and is centered.

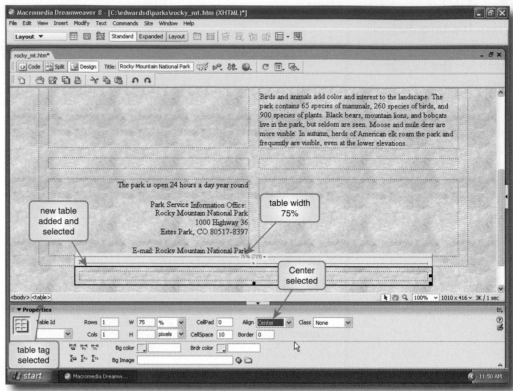

FIGURE 3-36

5

• **Click the cell in the table. Type** Home **and then press the SPACEBAR. Press SHIFT + | (vertical bar) and then press the SPACEBAR.**

• **Type** Black Canyon **and then press the SPACEBAR. Press SHIFT + | and then press the SPACEBAR.**

• **Type** Great Sand Dunes **and then press the SPACEBAR. Press SHIFT + | and then press the SPACEBAR.**

• **Type** Mesa Verde **and then press the SPACEBAR. Press SHIFT + | and then press the SPACEBAR.**

Type Rocky Mountain **as the last link text.**

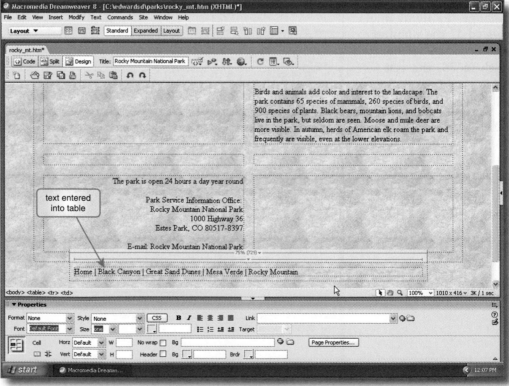

FIGURE 3-37

The text is entered into the table (Figure 3-37).

Adjusting the Table Width

Determining table width is a matter of judgment. You may overestimate or underestimate the table width when first inserting it into the Document window. When this happens, it is easy to make adjustments to the table width through the Property inspector. The table with the names that will contain links is too wide for the text it contains and needs to be adjusted. You adjust the table width by selecting the table and then changing the width in the Property inspector. The following steps illustrate how to adjust the width and add the table ID.

To Adjust the Table Width, Center the Text, and Add the Table ID

1

• **If necessary, click the cell in table 2. Click <table> in the tag selector to select the table.**

• **Double-click the W box in the Property inspector.**

• **Type** 60 **and then press the ENTER key.**

The dark border around the table indicates that the table is selected. The Property inspector displays table properties. The table width is decreased (Figure 3-38).

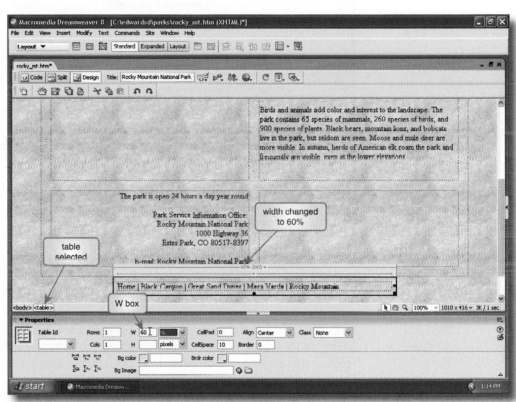

FIGURE 3-38

2

• **Click anywhere in the cell in the table.**

• **Click the Align box arrow and then click Center.**

• **Click <table> in the tag selector to select the table.**

• **Click the Table ID text box, type**

Colorado Parks links table, **and then press the ENTER key.**

The text is centered in the cell, and the table is named (Figure 3-39).

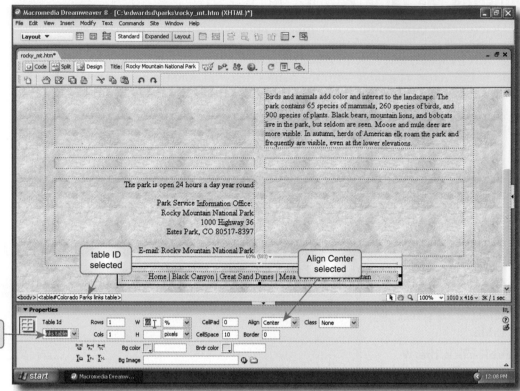

FIGURE 3-39

3

• **Click anywhere in the Document window to deselect the table.**

Next, you add absolute, e-mail, and relative links to the Rocky Mountain National Park page. The following steps show how to add the links. The relative links you add for the other three parks — Black Canyon, Great Sand Dunes, and Mesa Verde — are not active at this point. You will add pages for these three parks later in this project. As discussed previously, the Black Canyon and Great Sand Dunes parks are contained on one Web page. When you add the relative link for the Great Sand Dunes park, you also will add a link and a named anchor. When the Great Sand Dunes link is clicked, the portion of the Web page containing the Great Sand Dunes section is displayed. As discussed in Project 2, a **named anchor** is a link to a specific place within a document.

To Add Links to the Rocky Mountain National Park Page

1 Select the first instance of Rocky Mountain National Park located in the first table in row 3, column 1.

2 Type http://www.nps.gov/romo/ in the Link box. Press ENTER to create an absolute link.

3 Select the second instance of Rocky Mountain National Park, located in the first table in row 3, column 1.

4 Click Insert on the menu bar and then click Email Link. When the Email Link dialog box is displayed, type romo@parks.gov as the e-mail address. Click the OK button.

5 Select Home in the second table. Type index.htm in the Link box and press ENTER to create the relative link.

6 Select Black Canyon in the second table. Type blca.htm in the Link box and press ENTER to create the relative link.

7 Select Great Sand Dunes in the second table. Type blca.htm#sand_dunes in the Link box and press ENTER to create the relative link to the named anchor.

8 Select Mesa Verde in the second table. Type meve.htm in the Link box and press ENTER to create the relative link.

9 Select Rocky Mountain in the second table. Type rocky_mt.htm in the Link box and press ENTER to create the relative link.

10 Click the Save button on the Standard toolbar.

11 Press the F12 key to view the Web page. Scroll down to view the links, as shown in Figure 3-40.

12 Click the Home link to display the index.htm page and then click the Browser back button.

13 Close the browser and return to the Dreamweaver window.

The links are added to the Web page (Figure 3-40). The links for Black Canyon, Great Sand Dunes, and Mesa Verde National Parks are not active at this point. You will add these pages later in this project.

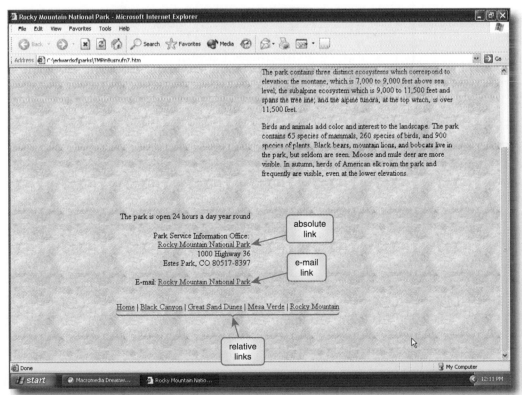

FIGURE 3-40

Editing and Modifying Table Structure

Thus far, you have created two tables and made adjustments in Dreamweaver for the Rocky Mountain National Park Web page. For various reasons, as you create and develop Web sites, you will need to edit and modify a table, change the dimensions of a table, add rows and columns, or delete the table and start over. The following section describes how to accomplish editing, modifying, and deleting table elements within the structure.

DELETE A ROW OR COLUMN Select a row or column and then press the delete key. You also can delete a row or column by clicking a cell within the row or column, right-clicking to display the context menu, pointing to Table, and then clicking Delete Row or Delete Column on the Table submenu.

INSERT A ROW OR COLUMN To insert a row or column, click in a cell. Right-click to display the context menu, point to Table, and then click Insert Row or Insert Column on the Table submenu. To insert more than one row or column and to control the row or column insertion point, click in a cell, right-click to display the context menu, point to Table, and then click Insert Rows or Columns on the Table submenu to display the Insert Rows or Columns dialog box (Figure 3-41). Make your selections and then click the OK button. To add a row automatically, press the tab key in the last cell of a table.

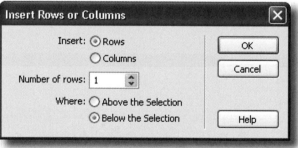

FIGURE 3-41

MERGE AND SPLIT CELLS By merging and splitting cells, you can set alignments that are more complex than straight rows and columns. To merge two or more cells, select the cells and then click Merge Cells in the Property inspector. The selected cells must be contiguous and in the shape of a line or a rectangle. You can merge any number of adjacent cells as long as the entire selection is a line or a rectangle. To split a cell, click the cell and then click Split Cells in the Property inspector to display the Split Cell dialog box (Figure 3-42 on the next page). In the Split Cell dialog box, specify how to split the cell and then click the OK button. You can split a cell into any number of rows or columns, regardless of whether it was merged previously. When you split a cell into two rows, the other cells in the same row as the split cell are not split. The same is true if a cell is split into two or more columns — the other cells in the same column are not split. To select a cell quickly, click in the cell and then click the <td> tag on the tag selector.

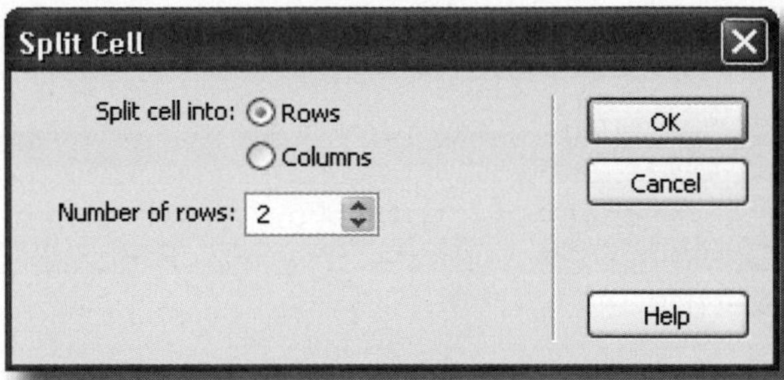

Split Cell

Split cell into: ⦿ Rows
⦾ Columns

Number of rows: 2

OK
Cancel
Help

FIGURE 3-42

More About

Deleting Cells

If you delete a cell, the content also is deleted. Dreamweaver does not caution you that this will occur. If you accidentally remove content, click the Undo button on the Standard toolbar or, on the Edit menu, click the Undo command.

RESIZE A TABLE, COLUMNS, AND ROWS   You can resize an entire table or resize individual rows and columns. To resize the table, select the table and change the W (width) in the Property inspector. A second method is to select the table and then drag one of the table selection handles. When you resize an entire table, all of the cells in the table change size proportionately. If you have assigned explicit widths or heights to a cell or cells within the table, resizing the table changes the visual size of the cells in the Document window but does not change the specified widths and heights of the cells. To resize a column or row, select the column or row and change the properties in the Property inspector. A second method to resize a column is to select the column and then drag the right border of the column. To resize a row, select the row and then drag the lower border of the row.

DELETE A TABLE   You easily can delete a table. Select the table tag in the tag selector and then press the DELETE key. All table content is deleted along with the table.

Merging Cells and Adding Images

The concept of merging cells probably is familiar to you if you have worked with spreadsheets or word processing tables. In HTML, however, merging cells is a complicated process. Dreamweaver makes this easy by hiding some complex HTML table restructuring code behind an easy-to-use interface in the Property inspector. Dreamweaver also makes it easy to add images to a table. When you add and then select an image in a table cell, the Property inspector displays the same properties as were displayed when you added and selected an image in the Document window in Project 2. When the image in the cell is not selected, the Property inspector displays the same properties as it does for any cell. These properties were described earlier in this project.

You will merge two cells (rows 1 and 2, column 1) and add three images to the Rocky Mountain National Park page. The first and second images go into the merged cells, and the third image goes in row 3, column 2. The following steps show how to merge two cells.

More About

Splitting and Merging Cells

An alternative approach to merging and splitting cells is to increase or decrease the number of rows or columns spanned by a cell.

To Merge Two Cells

1

• **If necessary, scroll up and then click row 1, column 1 in the first table.**

• **Drag to select the cells in rows 1 and 2 in column 1.**

The two cells are selected (Figure 3-43).

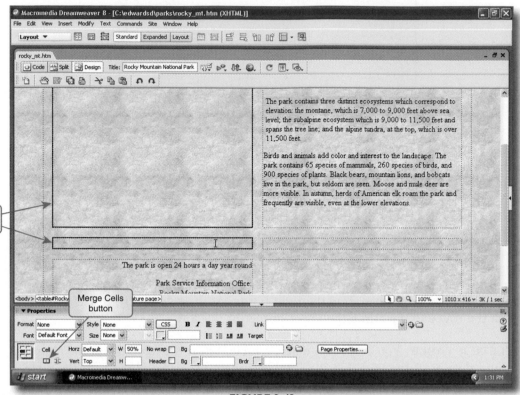

FIGURE 3-43

2

• **Click the Merge Cells button.**

The two cells are merged (Figure 3-44).

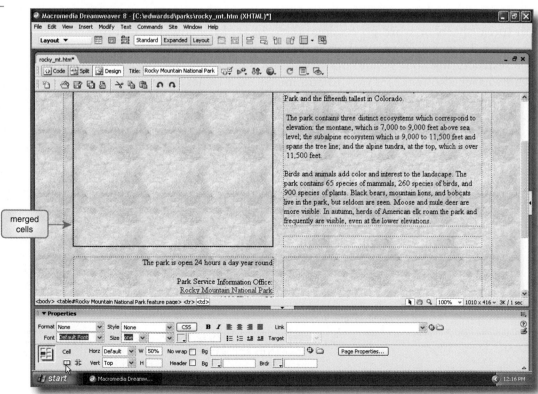

FIGURE 3-44

Recall from Project 2 that when you inserted an image, the default Image Tag Accessibility Attributes dialog box was displayed. In this box, you can add Alternate text or create a link to a text file with a long description. For images in this project and the other projects in this book, instructions are to add alternate text. The Property inspector for images contains an Alternate text option. Therefore, you will disable the Image Tag Accessibility Attributes dialog box and add the Alternate text through the Property inspector.

To Disable the Image Tag Accessibility Attributes Dialog Box

1 **Click Edit on the menu bar and then click Preferences.**

2 **Click Accessibility in the Category list.**

3 **Click the checkboxes to deselect Form objects, Frames, Media, and Images and then click the OK button.**

Next, you add three images to the table. You then align the three images and modify the size of one of the images. The following steps illustrate how to display the images in the Assets panel and then add, align, and modify images in a table displayed in Standard and Expanded modes.

To Add Images to a Standard Mode Table

1

• **Click the panel groups expander arrow and then click the Assets tab in the panel groups.**

• **If necessary, click the Images button and the Site option button.**

• **Scroll to the top of the table and then click the cell in row 1, column 1.**

• **Press the ENTER key.**

• **Drag the keyhole_longs_peak.gif image from the Assets panel to the insertion point in the merged cell. If necessary, click the Refresh Site List button to view the images.**

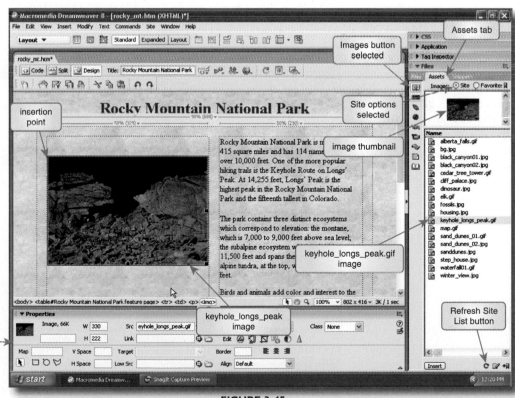

FIGURE 3-45

The keyhole_longs_peak.gif image is inserted in the cell and selected (Figure 3-45). The Property inspector for images is displayed.

2

• **Click the Expanded
Tables mode button
and then click to the
right of the
keyhole_longs_peak.gif
image. If a Getting
Started in Expanded
Tables Mode dialog box
is displayed, read the
information and click
the OK button. The
dialog box may not
display if the Don't
show me this message
again check box was
checked previously.**

• **Press the ENTER key.**

*The table expands and
the insertion point is
displayed below the
keyhole_longs_peak.gif
image (Figure 3-46). The
alberta_falls.gif image will
be inserted at the location
of the insertion point.*

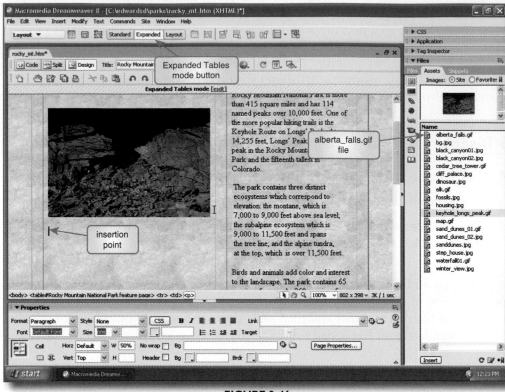

FIGURE 3-46

3

• **Drag the
alberta_falls.gif image
to the insertion point.**

*The alberta_falls.gif image is
displayed below the
keyhole_longs_peak.gif image
and is selected (Figure 3-47).*

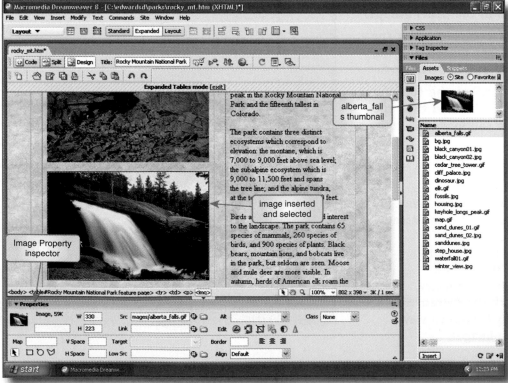

FIGURE 3-47

4

- **Scroll up and click the keyhole_longs_ peak.gif image to select it.**

The keyhole_longs_ peak.gif image is selected (Figure 3-48). The Property inspector displays image properties.

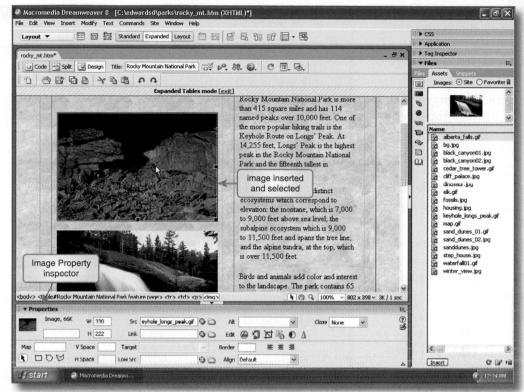

FIGURE 3-48

5

- **Click the Image text box in the Property inspector and type** Keyhole_Longs_Peak **as the Image ID.**

- **Click the Alt box, type** Keyhole Longs Peak **as the Alt text, and then press the ENTER key.**

The specified properties are applied to the keyhole_longs_peak.gif image (Figure 3-49).

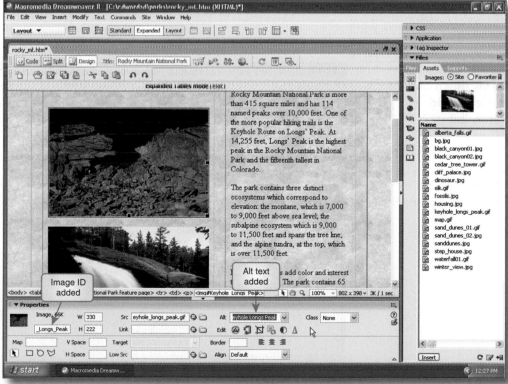

FIGURE 3-49

6

• **Scroll down and then click the alberta_falls.gif image to select it.**

• **Click the Image text box in the Property inspector and then type** Alberta_Falls **as the image ID.**

• **Press the TAB key and then type** 300 **in the W box.**

• **Press the TAB key to move to the H box and then type** 220 **as the new value.**

• **Click the Alt box, type** Alberta Falls **as the Alt text, and then press the ENTER key.**

• **Click the Align Center button.**

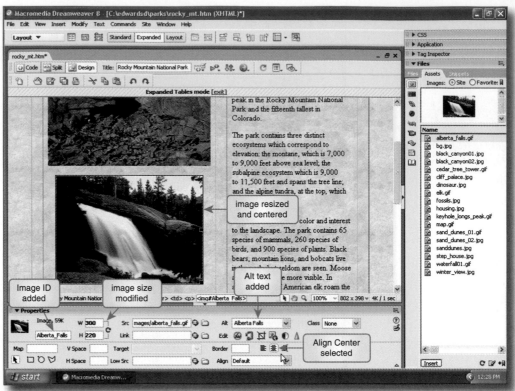

FIGURE 3-50

The specified properties are applied to the alberta_falls.gif image and the image is resized and centered in the cell (Figure 3-50).

7

• **Scroll down and to the right. Click row 3, column 2.**

The insertion point is displayed in the cell (Figure 3-51). The elk.gif image will be inserted at the location of the insertion point.

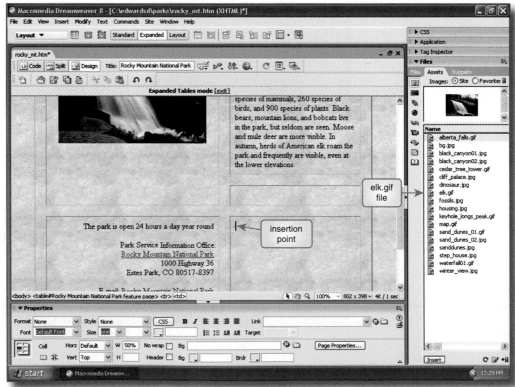

FIGURE 3-51

8

• **Drag the elk.gif image from the Assets panel to the insertion point in row 3, column 2.**

• **Verify that the elk.gif image is selected, click the Image text box, and type** Elk. **Click the Alt box, type** Rocky Mountain Elk **as the Alt text, and then press the ENTER key.**

• **Click the Align box arrow and select Top.**

• **Click the Align Center button.**

The elk.gif image is centered in the cell and is selected (Figure 3-52). The Alt text is entered and Top is selected in the Align box.

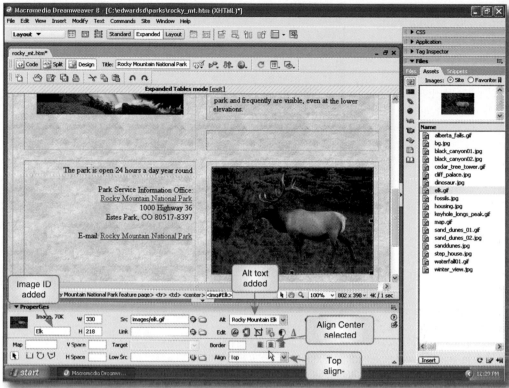

FIGURE 3-52

9

• **Scroll up. Click the cell in row 2, column 2 and then drag to select this cell and the cell in row 3, column 2.**

The two cells are selected (Figure 3-53).

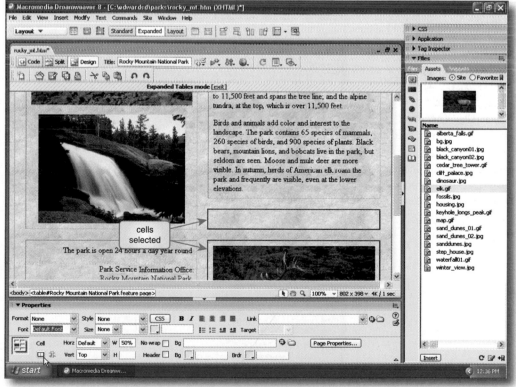

FIGURE 3-53

Macromedia
Dreamweaver 8

10

• **Click the Merge Cells button.**

The two cells are merged and the image moves up (Figure 3-54).

FIGURE 3-54

11

• **Scroll up and select all of the text in row 1, column 2.**

• **Click the Size arrow and select 18.**

• **Click the Vert box arrow and select Middle.**

The size is applied to the text and style2 is created. The text is centered vertically in the cell (Figure 3-55).

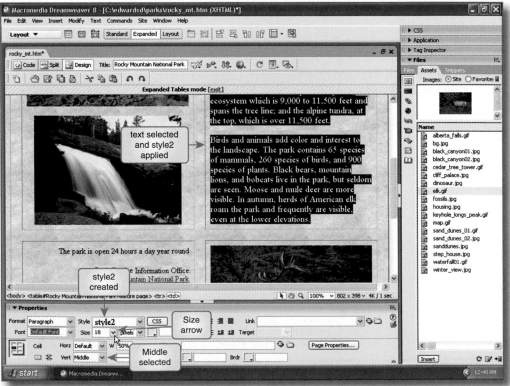

FIGURE 3-55

12

• **Scroll down and select the text in row 2, column 1.**

• **Click the Style arrow and select style2.**

• **Click anywhere in the document to deselect the text.**

Style2 is applied to the text (Figure 3-56).

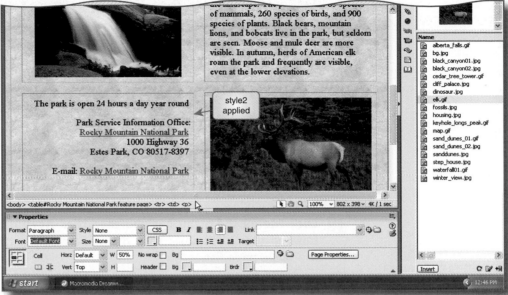

style2 applied

FIGURE 3-56

13

• **Click the Standard button.**

• **Click the Save button.**

• **Press the F12 key to view the page in your browser.**

• **The Rocky Mountain National Park page displays in the browser (Figure 3-57).**

14

• **Close the browser window.**

Dreamweaver is displayed.

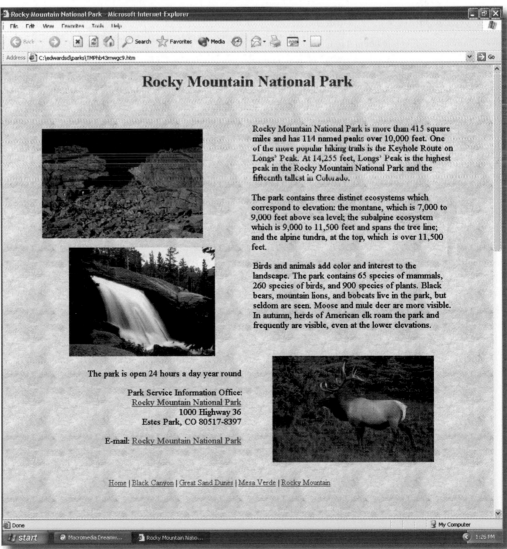

FIGURE 3-57

Creating the Black Canyon/Great Sand Dunes National Park Web Page

To create the Black Canyon/Great Sand Dunes Web page, you open a new Document window. You start by applying the background image. This is the same background image you used for the Colorado Parks Web site in Projects 1 and 2. The following steps illustrate how to open a new Document window and apply a background image.

To Open a New Document Window and Add a Background Image to the Black Canyon/Great Sand Dunes Web Page

1 Click File on the menu bar and then click New. If necessary, click the General tab and then click Basic page in the Category list. If necessary, click HTML in the Basic page list.

2 Click the Create button.

3 Click the Save button on the Standard toolbar and then type blca as the file name. Save the Web page in the parks folder.

4 Click Modify on the menu bar and then click Page Properties.

5 Click the Browse button to the right of the Background image box.

6 If necessary, navigate to the parks\images folder.

7 Click bg.jpg and then click the OK button in the Select Image Source dialog box.

8 Click the OK button in the Page Properties dialog box. If a warning dialog box displays, click OK.

The background is added. The path and file name (\edwardsd\parks\blca.htm) appear on the Dreamweaver title bar (Figure 3-58 on the next page). Your name will display instead of edwardsd.

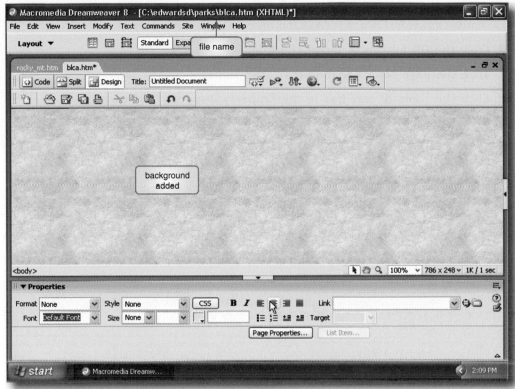

FIGURE 3-58

Next, you insert and center a six-row, two-column table. You create the Black Canyon section by adding text and two images. Next, you create the Great Sand Dunes section by adding text and two images and adding a named anchor. You modify image placement and create a text style. You also add absolute links and e-mail addresses for the two parks. Then you copy and paste the links table from the Rocky Mountain Park page to the Black Canyon/Great Sand Dunes page.

The next step is to insert and center a table and to add a title to the table, as shown in the following steps.

To Insert and Center a Table

1 Click the Table button on the Layout Insert bar.

2 In the Table dialog box, change the settings as follows: Rows 6, Columns 2, Table width 90 Percent, Border thickness 4, Cell padding 10, and Cell spacing 2.

3 Click the **Summary** text box and then type Black Canyon/Great Sand Dunes National Parks feature page **as the Summary text.**

4 Click the **OK** button to insert the table.

5 Title the page **Black Canyon/Great Sand Dunes.**

6 Click the **Table ID** text box in the **Property inspector** and then type Black Canyon/Great Sand Dunes National Parks feature page **as the table ID.**

7 Click the **Align** box arrow and then click **Center.**

8 Click the **Save** button on the **Standard toolbar.**

The centered table is added to the Web page (Figure 3-59). The Web page is saved in the parks folder.

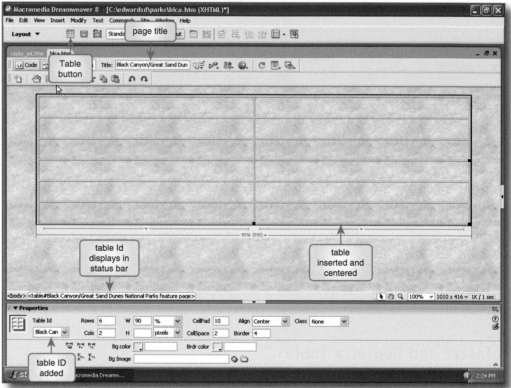

FIGURE 3-59

An understanding of HTML and how it relates to a table and to parts of a table provides you with the ability to use code to select a table and table components and to modify a table. Merging and varying the span of columns (as you did in the Rocky Mountain National Park page) and merging and varying the span of rows is helpful for grouping information, adding emphasis, or deleting empty cells. When you merge two cells in a row, you are spanning a column. Continuing with the <table> example on page DW 224 and spanning the two cells in row 1, the HTML tags would be <td colspan="2">First cellSecond cell</td>. When you merge two cells in a column, you are spanning a row. The attribute ROWSPAN would replace COLSPAN in the above example. Understanding COLSPAN and ROWSPAN will help you determine when and if two columns or two rows have been merged.

For the Rocky Mountain National Park page, you entered a heading outside the table and links to the other pages in a second table. For the Black Canyon/Great Sand Dunes page, you merge the cells in row 1 and then merge the cells in row 4. You enter a heading in row 1 and row 4. The following steps illustrate how to merge the cells in rows 1 and 4.

To Merge Cells in Row 1 and Row 4

1 Click row 1, column 1 and then drag to select all of row 1.

2 Click the Merge Cells button in the Property inspector.

3 Click row 4, column 1 and then drag to select all of row 4.

4 Click the Merge Cells button in the Property inspector.

The cells in row 1 are merged into one column, and the cells in row 4 also are merged into one column (Figure 3-60).

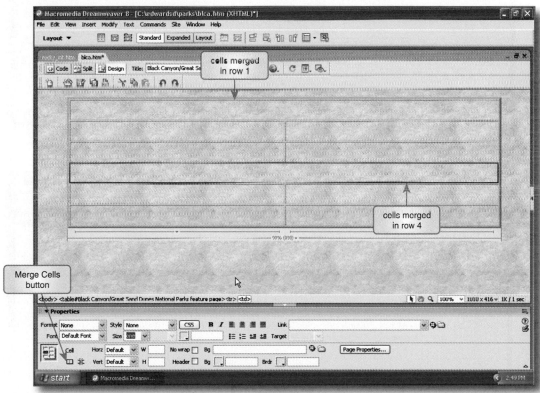

FIGURE 3-60

Next, you add and center a heading in row 1 of the table. The steps on the next page show how to add and center the heading in row 1.

To Add a Heading to Row 1

1

• **Click row 1 and then click the Align Center button in the Property inspector.**

The insertion point is aligned in the middle of the row (Figure 3-61).

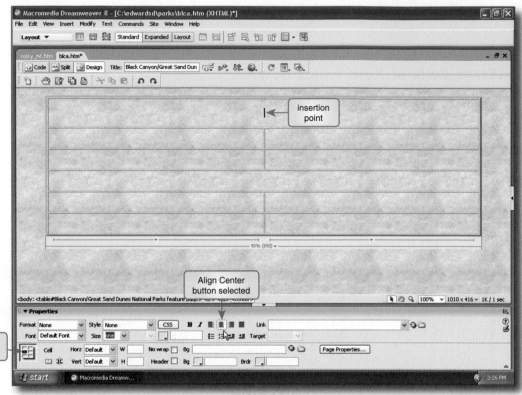

FIGURE 3-61

2

• **Type** Black Canyon of the Gunnison National Park **and then use the Format pop-up menu to apply Heading 1.**

• **Select the heading.**

• **Click the Color Hexadecimal box and type** #993300**.**

• **Click to the right of the heading.**

The text is centered in row 1, and Heading 1 and color are applied to the text. In the Style box, style1 is created (Figure 3-62).

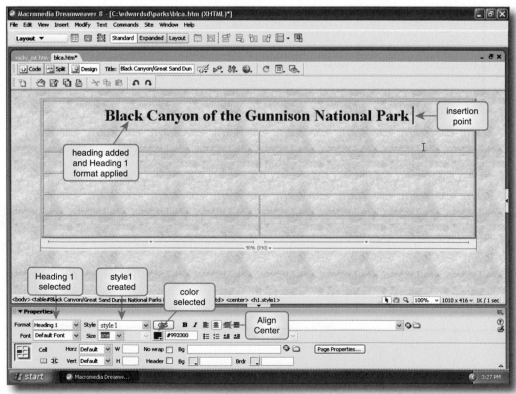

FIGURE 3-62

3

- **Click row 4 and then click the Align Center button in the Property inspector.**

- **Type** Great Sand Dunes National Park Preserve.

- **Apply Heading 1 and style1 to the text in row 4.**

The text is centered in row 4, and Heading 1 and color are applied to the text. (Figure 3-63).

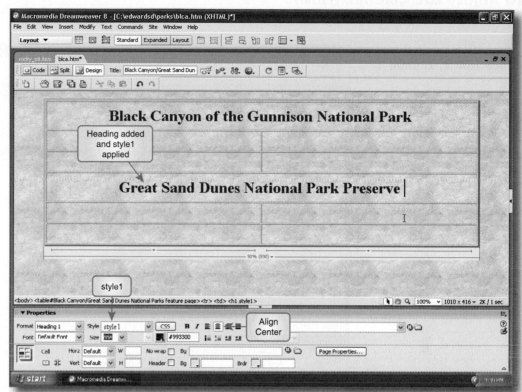

FIGURE 3-63

Splitting and Merging Cells

Tables in a traditional sense generally are thought of as having an internal **symmetry**; that is, cells of the same size form neatly arranged columns and rows. On a Web page, however, by varying the size of a cell, you can use tables to create an asymmetrical arrangement. This design option allows for more visual variation on a Web page. In a three-column table, for example, you could specify the width of the first column as 20 percent and that of the second and third columns as 40 percent each. Depending on the number of columns, hundreds of percentage variations can be applied. In the Black Canyon/Great Sand Dunes page, you adjust the width for columns 1 and 2 and then change the vertical alignment to Top within both columns. The following steps show how to adjust the width and change the vertical spacing.

More About

Column Width

In addition to using the Property inspector to change the width or height of a column, you also can change cell widths and heights directly in the HTML code.

To Adjust the Column Width

• **Click row 2, column 1.**

The insertion point is located in row 2, column 1 (Figure 3-64).

FIGURE 3-64

• **Click the W box in the Property inspector.**
• **Type** 60% **and then press the ENTER key.**
• **Click row 2, column 2.**
• **Click the W box in the Property inspector.**
• **Type** 40% **and then press the ENTER key.**

Column 1 is increased in size to reflect the new percentage. and column 2 is decreased in size to reflect the new percentage (Figure 3-65).

FIGURE 3-65

3 ─────────

• **Select row 2, columns 1 and 2.**

• **Click the Vert box arrow in the Property inspector and then select Top from the Vert pop-up menu.**

Top is selected in the Vert box (Figure 3-66). No noticeable differences display in the table. Any image or text in these cells, however, will align to the top.

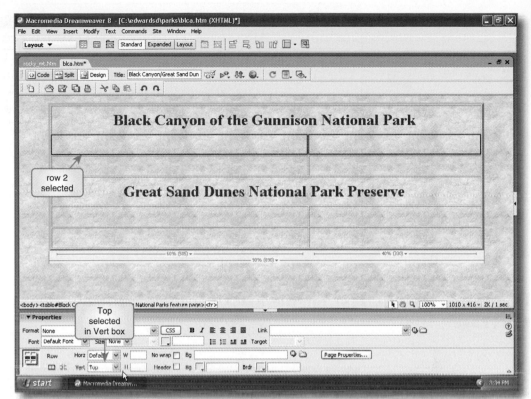

FIGURE 3-66

Now you add text to the table. Table 3-4 contains the text for the Black Canyon/Great Sand Dunes Web page. After you type the text, you format it using style2. When applying a style to text, it is not necessary to select the paragraph. Just click anywhere within the paragraph and then apply the style.

Table 3-4 Black Canyon/Great Sand Dunes Web Page Text	
SECTION	**TEXT FOR BLACK CANYON/GREAT SAND DUNES WEB PAGE**
Part 1	The Black Canyon of the Gunnison National Park contains 2,000 foot narrow canyon walls, which drop almost vertically to the Gunnison River. Two campgrounds are located in the park – one on the south rim and one on the north rim. The visitor's center is located on South Rim Drive and provides a video theater with two orientation programs.
Part 2	Located in the southwest section of Colorado, some of the park's more popular recreational activities are camping, backpacking, bird and wildlife viewing, fishing, and rafting. In the winter months, visitors enjoy cross-country skiing and snowshoeing. The park is open year round, but access to the south rim is limited in the winter.
Part 3	Park Service Information Office:\<br\> Black Canyon of the Gunnison National Park\<br\> Park Headquarters\<br\> 102 Elk Creek\<br\> Gunnison, CO 81230-8397\<ENTER\> E-mail: Black Canyon of the Gunnison

Table 3-4 Black Canyon/Great Sand Dunes Web Page Text (*continued*)	
SECTION	TEXT FOR BLACK CANYON/GREAT SAND DUNES WEB PAGE
Part 4	One of the nation's newest national parks, Great Sand Dunes was upgraded from a national monument and preserve in the year 2000. Located at the foot of the Sangre de Cristo mountain range, the dunes appear to stretch to infinity. The dunes cover approximately 39 square miles and are the tallest in North America – over 750 feet. The park is open all year, 24 hours a day.<ENTER> Park Service Information Office: Great Sand Dunes National Park Park Headquarters 11999 Highway 150 Mosca, CO 81146<ENTER> E-mail: Great Sand Dunes

More About

Inserting Images into a Table

In Macromedia Dreamweaver 8, you can work in Design view or Code view to insert images in a document.

To Add and Format Text for the Black Canyon/Great Sand Dunes Web Page

1

• **Click row 2, column 2.**

• **Type the text of Part 1 as shown in Table 3-4 on DW 259.**

The text is entered as shown in Figure 3-67.

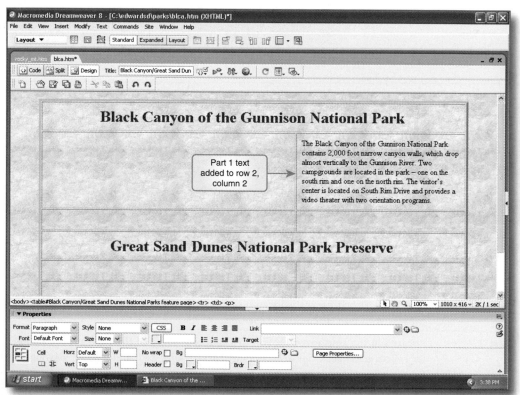

FIGURE 3-67

2

• **Click row 3, column 1.**

• **Type the text of Part 2 as shown in Table 3-4 on DW 257.**

The text is entered as shown in Figure 3-68.

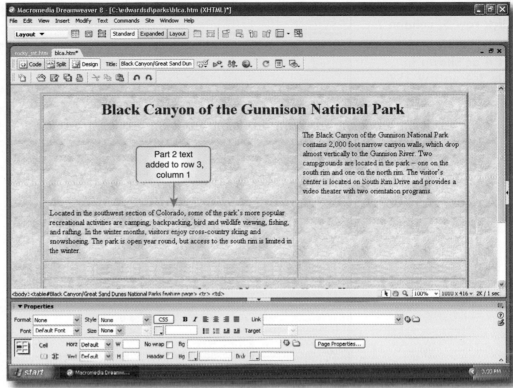

FIGURE 3-68

3

• **Click row 3, column 2.**

• **Type the text of Part 3 as shown in Table 3-4.**

• **Press the ENTER key and insert line breaks as indicated in Table 3-4.**

The text is entered as shown in Figure 3-69.

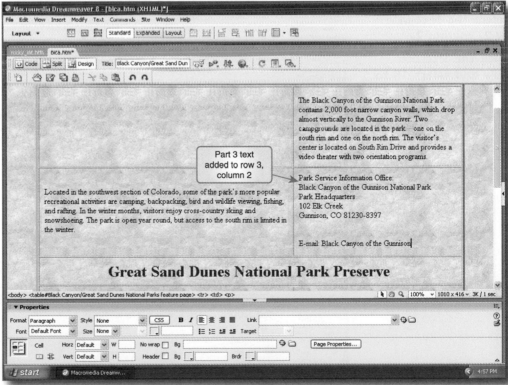

FIGURE 3-69

4

• **Click row 5, column 2.**

• **Type the text of Part 4 as shown in Table 3-4 on DW 258.**

• **Press the ENTER key and insert line breaks as indicated in Table 3-4.**

The text is entered as shown in Figure 3-70.

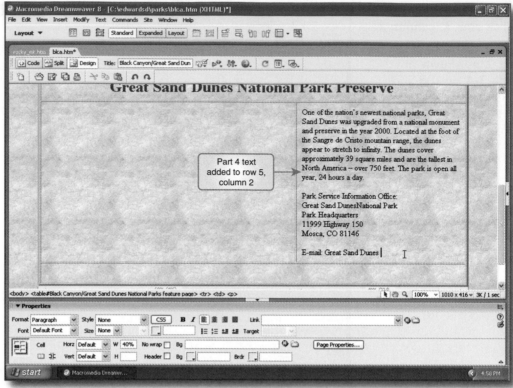

FIGURE 3-70

5

• **Select the text in row 2, column 2.**

• **Click the Size box arrow and select 18 to create style2**

• **Click anywhere in the row to deselect the text.**

Style2 is applied to the text (Figure 3-71).

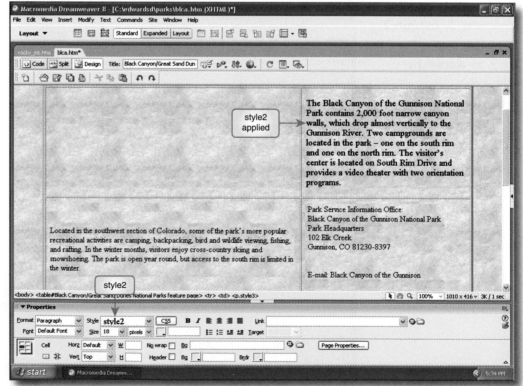

FIGURE 3-71

6

• **Apply style2 to the rest of the text in the table.**

• **Select the text in row 3, column 2 and right align.**

Style2 is applied to the rest of the text and the text in row 3, column 2 is aligned to the right (Figure 3-72).

FIGURE 3-72

The next step is to add the images to the Web page. You add and align four images and resize two of the images.

To Add Images to the Black Canyon/Great Sand Dunes Web Page

1

• **Click the panel groups expander arrow to display the panel groups. If necessary, click the Assets tab.**

• **Click row 2, column 1.**

• **Drag the black_ canyon01.jpg image to the insertion point in row 2, column 1.**

• **Click the Image text box and then type** canyon01 **as the image ID.**

• **Change the width in the W box to 425 and the height in the H box to 215.**

• **Click the Alt box and then type** Black Canyon view **as the Alt text. Press the ENTER key.**

• **Click the Align Center button.**

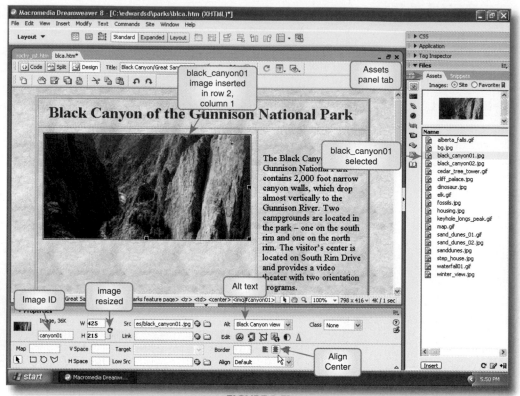

FIGURE 3-73

The black_canyon01.jpg image is displayed in row 2, column 1, and the selected image is resized and centered (Figure 3-73).

2

• **If necessary, scroll down and click to the left of Park Service in row 3, column 2.**

• **Drag the black_canyon02 image to the insertion point.**

• **Click the Image text box and then type** canyon02 **as the image ID.**

• **Change the W to 200.**

• **Click the Align Right button.**

• **Click the Align box arrow and select Left.**

• **Click the Alt text box and then type** Black Canyon view 2 **as the Alt text.**

• **Press the ENTER key.**

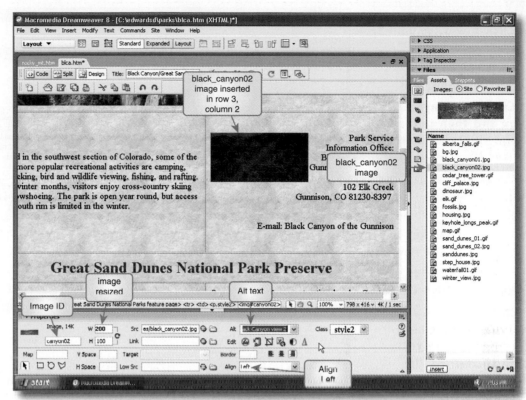

FIGURE 3-74

The black_canyon02 image is displayed in row 3, column 2. The selected image is resized and aligned to the left (Figure 3-74).

3

• **Click row 5, column 1.**

• **Drag the sand_dunes_ 01 image to the insertion point.**

• **Click the image text box and then type** sand_dunes01 **as the image ID.**

• **Press the TAB key and type** 435 **as the new value in the W box.**

• **Press the TAB key and type** 300 **as the new value in the H box**

• **Click the Align Center button.**

• **Type** Sand Dunes view **as the Alt text and then press the ENTER key.**

FIGURE 3-75

The image is inserted into the cell, resized, and centered (Figure 3-75).

4

- **Click to the left of the first word in the first paragraph in row 5, column 2 (to the left of the word "One").**

- **Drag the sand_dunes_02 image to the insertion point.**

- **Click the Files panel expander arrow to collapse the panel groups.**

- **Click the image text box and then type** sand_dunes02 **as the image ID.**

- **Press the TAB key and type** 170 **as the new value in the W box.**

- **Press the TAB key and type** 105 **as the new value in the H box.**

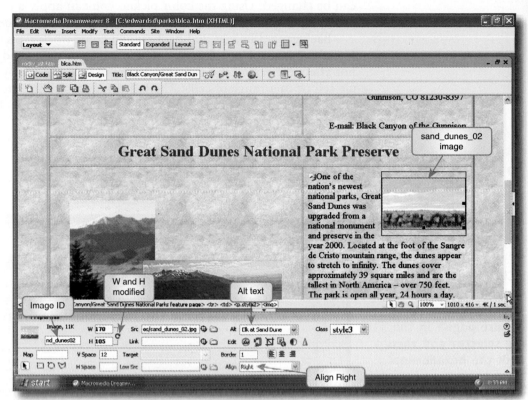

FIGURE 3-76

- **Click the V Space box and type** 12.

- **Click the Align box arrow and then click Right.**

- **Type** Elk at Sand Dune **as the Alt text and then press the ENTER key.**

- **Click the Border box and type** 1.

- **Click the Save button.**

The image is inserted into the cell, resized, and aligned right. A one-pixel border frames the image (Figure 3-76). When the Web page displays in the browser, the extra space around the border will not display.

Adding a Table Border and a Table Border Color

The purpose of most tables in a Web page is to provide a structure for the positioning of text and images. When a table is created within Dreamweaver, therefore, the default border is 0 (zero), or no visible border. The **Border** command specifies the width, in pixels, of the line that frames the table and its various parts. Adding a border to a table transforms the table into a graphical element itself. Depending on the content, a border can become a visual cue for the reader by separating content. For the Black Canyon/Great Sand Dunes page, a border is applied to the full table. You cannot apply a border to an individual cell unless the table consists of only one cell.

When you created the table for the Black Canyon/Great Sand Dunes Web page, you specified a border size of 4. By default, borders are gray, but the border color can be changed. Using the color picker, you can apply a color of your choice. You can apply a border color to a single cell or to a range of cells.

Background images and background color work the same for a table as they do for a Web page. The image or color, however, is contained within the table and does not affect the rest of the page. Background color and images can be applied to a single cell or to a range of cells. The following steps illustrate how to add color to the table border and a background color to the merged cells. The border color is the same color you applied to the titles of the two parks.

To Add Border Color and Cell Background Color

1

• **Scroll to the top of the page.**

• **Click <table#Black Canyon/Great Sand Dunes National Parks feature page> in the tag selector and then click the hexadecimal color box.**

• **Type** #993300 **and then press the ENTER key.**

The border color is applied to the table (Figure 3-77).

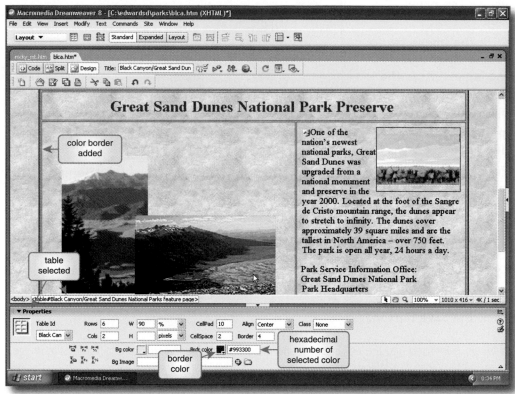

FIGURE 3-77

2 ──────────────

• **If necessary, scroll up. Click anywhere in row 1.**

• **Click the Bg hexadecimal color box, type #FF9966, and then press the ENTER key.**

• **Scroll down and click anywhere in row 4**

• **Click the Bg hexadecimal color box, type #FF9966, and then press the ENTER key.**

The background color is applied to rows 1 and 4 (Figure 3-78).

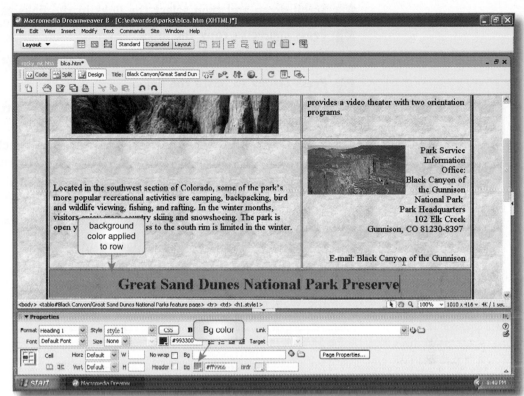

FIGURE 3-78

Your last tasks for the Black Canyon/Great Sand Dunes page are to add links, check spelling, copy the relative links you created in the rocky_mt page, and then save the page. The following steps illustrate how to spell check; add the absolute, relative, and e-mail links to the Black Canyon/Great Sand Dunes page; and then save the Web page.

To Add a Named Anchor and Links to and Spell Check the Black Canyon/Great Sand Dunes Page

1 **Scroll down and select the first instance of Black Canyon of the Gunnison National Park in the address in row 3, column 2. Type** http://www.nps.gov/blca/ **in the Link box and then press the ENTER key.**

2 **Select the second instance of Black Canyon of the Gunnison National Park. Click Insert on the menu bar and then click Email Link. Type** blca@parks.gov **in the E-mail text box. Click the OK button in the Email Link dialog box.**

3 **Scroll down and select the first instance of Great Sand Dunes National Park in the address in row 5, column 2. Type** http://www.nps.gov/grsa/ **in the Link box and then press the ENTER key.**

4 **Select Great Sand Dunes. Click Insert on the menu bar and then click Email Link. Type** grsa@parks.gov **in the Email text box. Click the OK button in the Email Link dialog box.**

5 **Click the rocky_mt.htm tab.**

6 Scroll down and then select the links in the links table.

7 Press CTRL+C to copy the links.

8 Click the blca.htm tab, click row 6, and then merge the cells.

9 Press CTRL+V to paste the links.

10 Select the links and then click the Align Center button. Click anywhere in the document to deselect the links.

11 Click Text on the menu bar and then click the Check Spelling command. Check the spelling and make any necessary corrections.

12 Click to the right of the Great Sand Dunes National Park Preserve heading. Click Insert on the menu bar and then click Named Anchor.

13 Type sand_dunes in the Named Anchor dialog box and then click the OK button.

14 Click the Save button on the Document toolbar.

15 Press the F12 key to view the Web page in your browser, as shown in Figure 3-79. If necessary, save any changes. Close the browser and then close the Web page.

In the browser, the Black Canyon/Great Sand Dunes page is displayed (Figure 3-79 on the next page).

FIGURE 3-79

Layout Mode

Tables created in Standard mode are useful for creating Web pages that are simple in format or contain tabular data. A second option for creating tables in Dreamweaver is the Layout mode. If you have used a desktop publishing program such as Microsoft Publisher, you will find that Dreamweaver's layout mode operates under a similar process. You can draw and place boxes anywhere on the page.

Layout mode provides more flexibility than Standard mode. Comparable to a desktop publishing program, you draw your own tables and cells in Layout mode. When using **Layout mode**, you are creating the framework for the entire table. The layout can be as simple or as complex as you want.

Layout mode is a tool unique to Dreamweaver. Terms such as Layout mode and layout cell do not exist in HTML. When you draw a **layout table**, Dreamweaver creates an HTML table. When you draw a **layout cell**, Dreamweaver creates a tag (<td>) in the table. The <td> tag is a container for the content rendered inside one cell of a table element. When a cell is drawn in a layout table, it stays within the row-and-column grid as it does in Standard mode. Cells cannot overlap, but they can span rows and columns. When you draw cells of different widths and different heights, Dreamweaver creates additional cells in the HTML table to fill in the empty spots.

You can use Layout mode to modify the structure of an existing page created in Standard mode. Layout mode, however, provides the greatest advantage when you are designing the page from the start. As you draw the table and/or cells in Layout mode, Dreamweaver creates the code. If you draw a layout cell first, a layout table is inserted automatically to serve as a container for the layout cell. A layout cell cannot exist outside of a layout table. You can create your page using one layout table with several layout cells contained within the table or you can have multiple layout tables. For uncomplicated pages, use one layout table. For a more complicated layout, use multiple tables. Using multiple layout tables isolates parts of your layout so one section does not affect another. For example, the cell size within a table can affect the other cells in the same row and column. Multiple tables eliminate this problem, especially for pages with numerous elements.

When you draw a table in Layout mode, Dreamweaver outlines the table in green and cells in blue. A tab labeled Layout Table displays at the top of each table. Clicking the tab selects the table. When you complete your page design for the Mesa Verde National Park, it will look similar to the page shown in Figure 3-80 on the next page. However, because this a freeform type of activity, most likely your page will have some variations.

The steps beginning on the next page show how to add a new page, add a background image, and prepare the work area of the page. This page contains one layout table and 10 layout cells.

Q: Can I change the color of the table outline when in layout mode?

A: Yes — click Edit, select Preferences, and then select the Layout Mode category. Click the Table Outline Color box and then select a color of your choice.

Q: Does Dreamweaver support nested layout tables?

A: Yes — you can draw a layout table inside another layout table.

FIGURE 3-80

To Add a New Page and Add a Background Image to the Mesa Verde National Park Web Page

1 Click File on the menu bar and then click New. If necessary, click the General tab and then click Basic page in the Category list. If necessary, click HTML in the Basic page list.

2 Click the Create button.

3 Click the Save button on the Standard toolbar and save the Web page in the parks folder. Type meve as the file name.

More About

The Grid Feature

Dreamweaver's grid feature is a visual guide that allows for precise positioning. Options include changing the grid square size and specifying that table and cell edges snap to the grid edges. To turn on the grid, click View on the menu bar, point to Grid, and then click Show Grid on the Grid submenu.

4 Click Modify on the menu bar and then click Page Properties.

5 Click the Browse button to the right of the Background image box.

6 If necessary, navigate to the parks\images folder.

7 Click bg.jpg and then click the OK button in the Select Image Source dialog box.

8 Click the OK button in the Page Properties dialog box. If a Macromedia alert dialog box appears, click OK.

9 Type Mesa Verde National Park as the title.

10 If necessary, click the expander button in the panel groups to hide the panels.

11 Click the Save button.

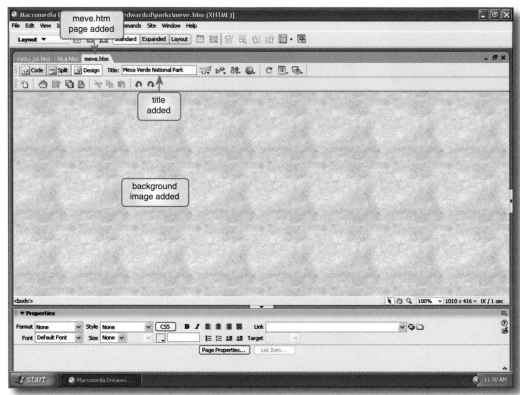

FIGURE 3-81

Using Visual Guides

Dreamweaver provides three types of visual guides — rulers, tracing image, and grid — to help you design documents and to project how the page will appear in a browser.

RULERS Provide a visual cue for positioning and resizing layers or tables

TRACING IMAGE Are used as the page background to duplicate a design

GRID Provides precise positioning and resizing of layer

You can use the rulers to help approximate cell width and height and cell location within a table, or you can use the pixel measurements that display in the right corner of the status bar. For this project, you use the rulers as a visual guide. Then, if necessary, you can make final adjustments to the cells and table using the settings in the Property inspector. The following steps illustrate how to display the rulers in the Document window.

To Display the Rulers

1

• **Click View on the menu bar, point to Rulers, and then click Show on the Rulers submenu.**

• **If necessary, select the Layout category in the Insert bar.**

• **Click the Property inspector expander arrow.**

The Layout category is selected, and the rulers are displayed at the top and left margins of the Document window (Figure 3-82). The rulers' measurements are in pixels. The lower pane of the Property inspector collapses.

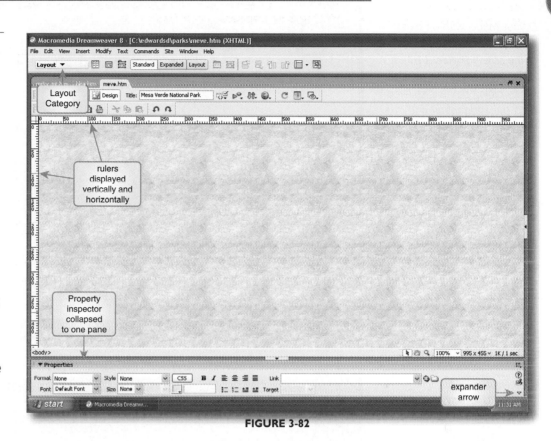

FIGURE 3-82

Creating a Layout Table for the Mesa Verde National Park Web Page

You begin creating the Mesa Verde National Park page by drawing a table. In the table, you create ten cells: one cell to hold the heading, four cells to hold text content, four cells to hold images, and one cell to contain links to the home page and the national park pages.

Your next task is to draw the layout table. This table has an approximate width of 650 pixels and an approximate height of 1100 pixels. The following steps illustrate how to create the layout table. Figure 3-80 on page DW 271 provides a visual guide for cell locations. Most likely, however, since this a freeform type of table, your cell locations will contain some variations.

To Create the Layout Table

1

• **Click the Layout Mode button.**

Layout mode, with an exit option, is displayed at the top of the screen (Figure 3-83). If a Getting Started in Layout Mode dialog box is displayed, read the information and click OK. The dialog box may not be displayed if the Don't show me this message again check box was checked previously.

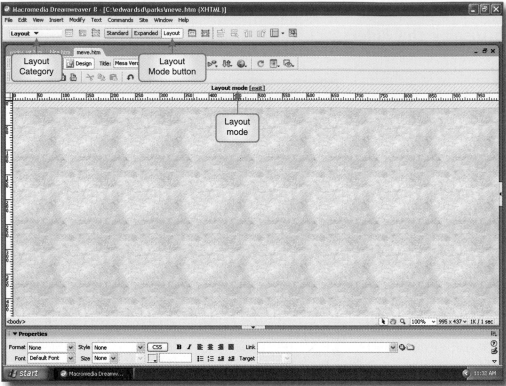

FIGURE 3-83

2

• **Click the Layout Table button.**

• **Position the mouse pointer at the upper-left corner of the Document window.**

The mouse pointer changes to a cross hair or plus sign (+), which indicates that you can draw a table (Figure 3-84).

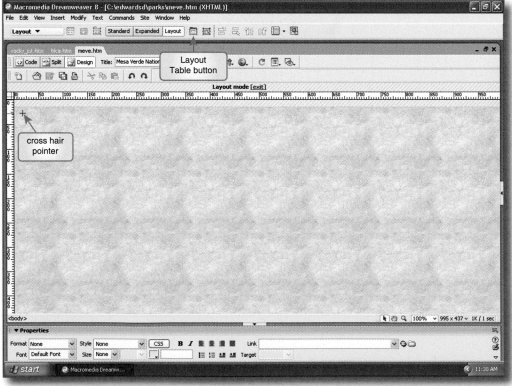

FIGURE 3-84

3

• **Use the rulers and pixel measurements in the right corner of the status bar as a guide and drag to draw a table with a width of approximately 650 pixels and a height of approximately 1100 pixels. Use the Rulers to help guide you with the width and height.**

• **If necessary, make any adjustments in the Property inspector Width and Height boxes.**

The table is added to the Document window and is outlined in green. The Property inspector changes to reflect the table in Layout mode (Figure 3-85). The Layout Table tab is displayed at the top of the table. If you are one or two pixels from the left margin, that is acceptable. You will center the table later.

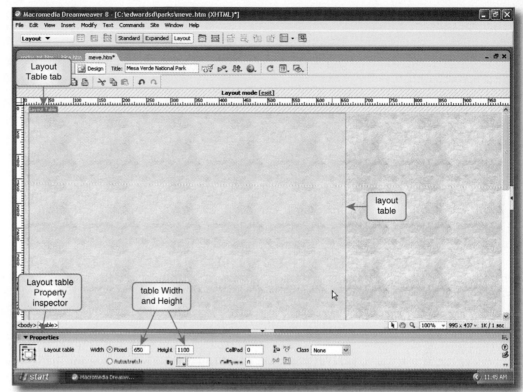

FIGURE 3-85

Layout Table and Layout Cell Properties

When a layout table is selected, the Property inspector displays properties related to the layout table. Some properties, such as width and height, background color, cell padding, and cell spacing, are the same as those for a table in Standard mode. The following describes the properties unique to the table in Layout mode (Figure 3-86 on the next page).

FIXED Sets the table to a fixed width

AUTOSTRETCH The rightmost column of the table stretches to fill the browser window width. The column header area for an autostretch column displays a wavy line instead of a number. If the layout includes an autostretch column, the layout always fills the entire width of the browser window.

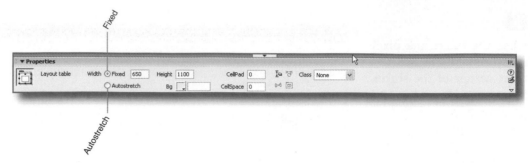

FIGURE 3-86

If the table is not the correct width or height or needs other modifications, adjustments can be made through the Width, Height, and other properties of the Property inspector.

For maximum flexibility, you should draw each cell as you are ready to add content to the cell. This method leaves blank space in the table, making it easier to move or resize cells. Occasionally, the value you enter will cause a cell to overlap another cell or cells. If this happens, a Dreamweaver alert dialog box displays. Read the information and then click OK. Dreamweaver will adjust the cell size to a valid value. The following steps show how to add five cells.

The first step is to add a cell that will contain the table heading. Once the cell is added, you type and format the heading within the layout cell. The heading is aligned to the left at the top of the table. The following steps illustrate how to add a layout cell and to enter and format a left-aligned heading.

To Add a Layout Cell and Heading

1

• **Click the Draw Layout Cell button on the Layout Insert bar.**

The status bar indicates the function of the button (Figure 3-87).

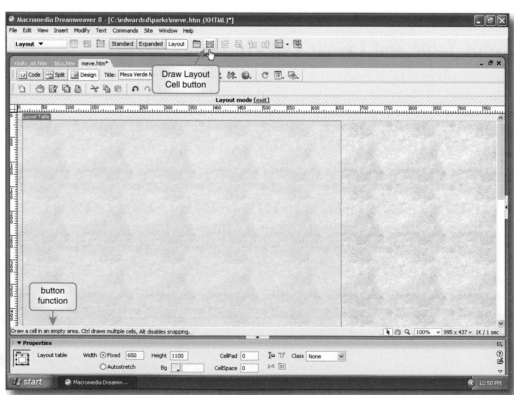

FIGURE 3-87

2

• **Click the upper-left corner of the layout table and drag to draw a cell with an approximate width of 425 and an approximate height of 50.**

• **Click the cell outline or the <td> in the tag selector to select the cell and make any necessary width and height adjustments in the Property inspector Width and Height boxes.**

A layout cell is created in the upper-left corner of the layout table. The cell is displayed in the table with a blue outline (Figure 3-88). The handles on the borders indicate that the cell is selected. This is the first cell.

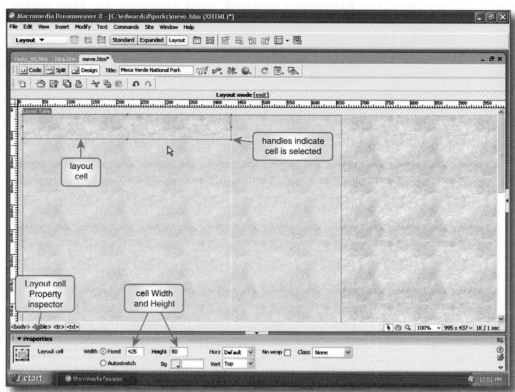

FIGURE 3-88

3

• **Click the cell and type** Mesa Verde National Park **as the heading.**

• **Apply Heading 1 to the text.**

• **If necessary, select the text. Click the hexadecimal color text box, type** #993300, **and then press the ENTER key.**

The heading is inserted into the cell, and Heading 1 and style1 are applied to the text (Figure 3-89). Text properties are displayed in the Property inspector.

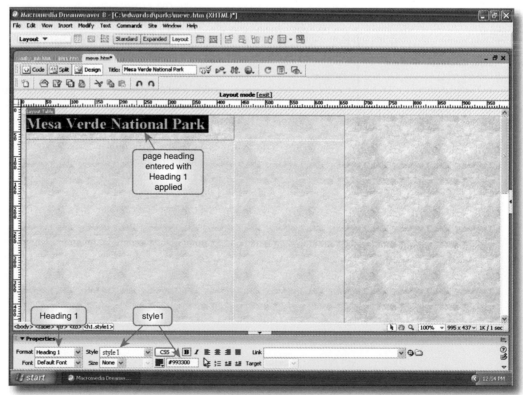

FIGURE 3-89

Adding Content and Images to the Cells

In the previous steps, you added content to a layout cell. Adding text content and images to layout cells is similar to adding content and images to cells in a Standard mode table. The only place content can be inserted in a layout table is in a layout cell. When Dreamweaver creates a layout cell, it automatically assigns a vertical alignment of Top. You have the same options as you did in Standard mode to change the alignment to Middle, Bottom, or Baseline. When you insert an image into a layout cell, all the properties in the Property inspector that were available for images in Standard mode also are available in Layout mode. If you need to move a layout cell, click the outline of the cell to select it. Hold down the mouse button and drag the cell to a new location. To move the cell in small increments, select the cell and then press the Up, Down, Left, or Right Arrow keys.

Next, you draw a layout cell directly below the heading cell. This cell will hold text. You enter the text into the layout cells just as you entered it in the cells in the Standard mode table. Table 3-5 contains the text for the Mesa Verde National Park Web page. If necessary, refer to Figure 3-80 on page DW 271 for a visual guide on the layout cell's placement.

Table 3-5 Mesa Verde National Park Web Page Text	
SECTION	**TEXT FOR MESA VERDE NATIONAL PARK WEB PAGE**
Part 1	Mesa Verde National Park is located in southwestern Colorado. The name, Mesa Verde, is Spanish for "green table." The park is best known for its archeological sites, which contain over 600 cliff dwellings. A park regulation requires that a Park Ranger accompany all visitors who wish to enter one of the dwellings.
Part 2	Congress passed the Preservation of American Antiquities Act in 1906, which made it a Federal crime to collect or destroy any historic or prehistoric object or building on federally owned land. Then President Theodore Roosevelt signed a Congressional bill to make Mesa Verde a national park in June, 1906.
Part 3	A variety of activities is available within the park. Bird watching, hiking trails, nature walks, wildlife viewing, geological stops, plant viewing, and stargazing are some of the more popular things to do. Ranger-guided tours are available in the summer. Camping is available with over 435 campsites. Additionally, the park contains 15 recreational vehicle sites with hookups.
Part 4	Park Service Information Office:\ Mesa Verde National Park\ P. O. Box 6208\ Mesa Verde, CO 81330\<ENTER> E-mail: Mesa Verde National Park\<ENTER>

To Create and Add Text to a Layout Cell for the Mesa Verde National Park Web Page

1

• **Click the Draw Layout Cell button.**

• **Click about 50 pixels to the right of and below the first cell, and then draw a cell with an approximate width of 250 and an approximate height of 150, as shown in Figure 3-90.**

• **Click the cell to select it and make any necessary width and height adjustments in the Property inspector Width and Height boxes.**

• **If necessary, select and drag the cell or use the keyboard arrow keys for placement.**

The second cell is added to the table and is selected (Figure 3-90). This cell will contain text.

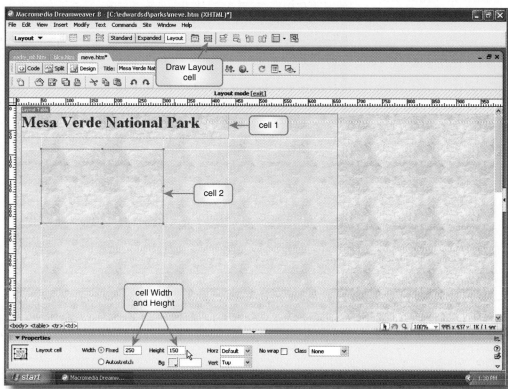

FIGURE 3-90

2

• **Click the cell and type the text of Part 1 as shown in Table 3-5 on page DW 278.**

The text is entered into the second cell (Figure 3-91).

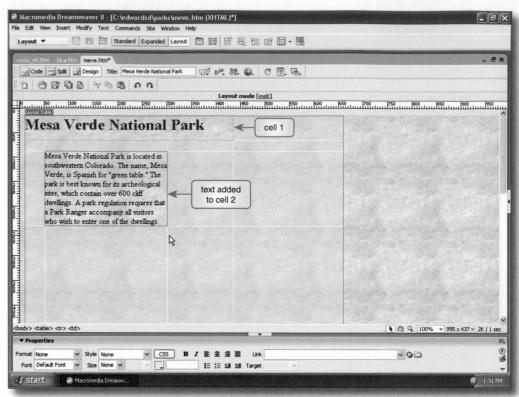

FIGURE 3-91

The third cell you draw will contain an image. You draw this cell to the right of the second cell. You add images to the layout cells just as you added images to the cells in the Standard mode table — by dragging the image from the Assets panel to the cell. The following steps show how to draw the third cell and insert an image into the cell.

To Add an Image to a Layout Cell

1

• **Click the Draw Layout Cell button and then draw a cell to the right of the second cell and about 25 pixels below the first cell, with an approximate width of 310 and an approximate height of 225, as shown in Figure 3-92.**

• **Click the cell outline to select it and make any necessary width and height adjustments in the Property inspector Width and Height boxes.**

• **If necessary, scroll to view the entire cell.**

• **Click the panel groups expander button and then, if necessary, click the Assets tab.**

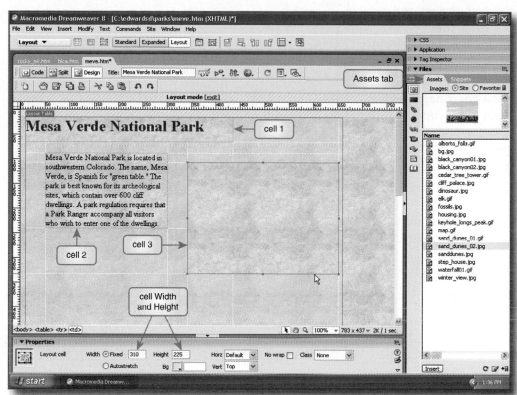

FIGURE 3-92

The third cell is added to the table and is selected, and the Assets panel is displayed (Figure 3-92). This third cell will contain an image.

2

• **Click the cell you have just drawn and then drag the cliff_palace.jpg file from the Assets panel to the insertion point.**

• **Click the Image text box in the Property inspector and then type** cliff_palace **as the image ID.**

• **Click the Alt text box and type** Cliff palace **as the alt text. Press the ENTER key.**

The image is selected and displayed in the third cell, and the Alt text and image ID are displayed in the Property inspector (Figure 3-93).

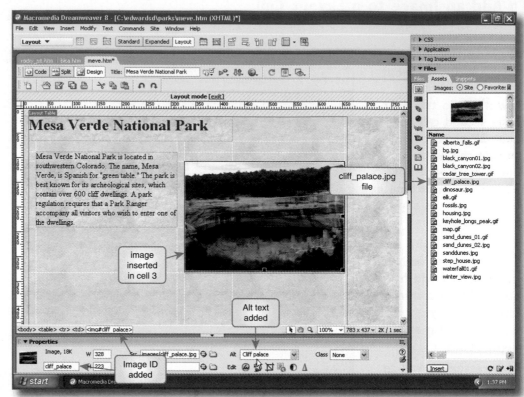

FIGURE 3-93

3

• **If necessary, scroll down and to the left, and then click the Draw Layout Cell button.**

• **Click approximately 50 pixels below the second cell and about 20 pixels to the right of the table border.**

• **Draw a cell with a width of approximately 220 and a height of approximately 320, as shown in Figure 3-94.**

• **Click the outline of the cell to select it and make any necessary width and height adjustments in the Property inspector Width and Height boxes.**

The fourth cell is added to the table and is selected (Figure 3-94). The cell will contain an image.

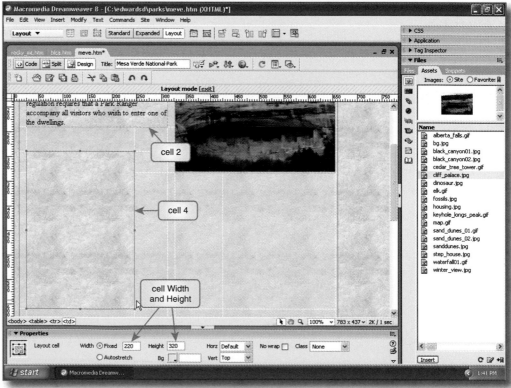

FIGURE 3-94

4

• **Click the cell and then drag the cedar_tree_tower.gif image from the Assets panel to the cell.**

• **Click the Image text box and type** `tree_tower` **as the image ID. Press the ENTER key.**

• **Click the Alt text box in the Property inspector and type** `Cedar tree tower` **as the Alt text. Press the ENTER key.**

The image is selected and displayed in the fourth cell, and the Alt text and image ID are displayed in the Property inspector (Figure 3-95).

• **Click anywhere on the page to deselect the image.**

FIGURE 3-95

So far, you have added four cells to the layout table — one containing the heading, one containing text, and two containing images. Now you add five more cells. Two of the cells will contain images and three will contain text.

To Add Five Additional Cells to the Mesa Verde National Park Web Page

1

• Click the Draw Layout Cell button.

• Click approximately 20 pixels below the third cell and 25 pixels to the left, and draw a cell with a width of approximately 340 and a height of approximately 120.

• Click the outline of the cell to select it and make any necessary width and height adjustments in the Property inspector Width and Height boxes.

• Click the cell and type the text of Part 2 as shown in Table 3-5 on page DW 278.

FIGURE 3-96

The fifth cell is added to the table. The cell contains text (Figure 3-96).

2

• **Scroll down. Click the Draw Layout Cell button.**

• **Click about 20 pixels below and about 10 pixels to the left of the fifth cell, and draw a cell with a width of approximately 330 and a height of approximately 215.**

• **Click the cell outline to select it and then make any necessary width and height adjustments in the Property inspector Width and Height boxes.**

• **Click the sixth cell and then drag the winter_view.jpg image to the insertion point.**

• **Click the Image text box and type** `winter_view` **as the image ID. Click the Alt text box in the Property inspector and then type** `Mesa Verde winter view` **as the Alt text.**

• **Click anywhere on the page to deselect the image.**

• **Click the Save button on the Standard toolbar.**

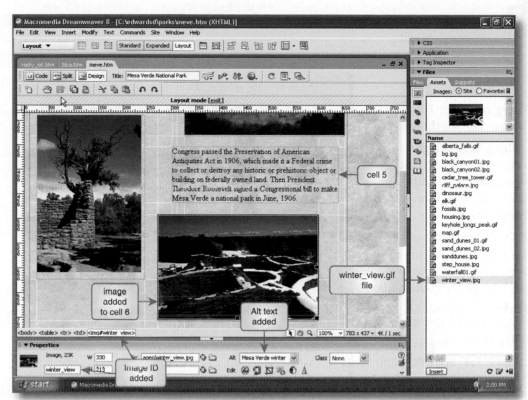

FIGURE 3-97

The sixth cell is added to the table and contains the winter_view.jpg image (Figure 3-97).

3

• **If necessary, scroll down. Click the Draw Layout Cell button.**

• **Click at the left margin about 20 pixels below the sixth cell.**

• **Drag to the right to create a cell with an approximate width of 650 and an approximate height of 85.**

• **Click the cell outline to select it and make any necessary width and height adjustments in the Property inspector Width and Height boxes.**

• **Click the cell and then type the text of Part 3 as shown in Table 3-5 on page DW 278.**

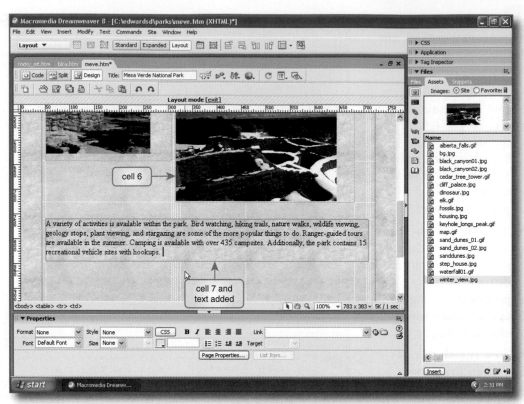

FIGURE 3-98

The seventh cell is inserted, and the text is displayed (Figure 3-98).

4

• **Click the Draw Layout Cell button and draw the eighth cell about 20 pixels below the seventh cell, with an approximate width of 210 and an approximate height of 145.**

• **Select the cell and make any necessary adjustments to the width and height in the Property inspector.**

• **Click cell 8 and type the text of Part 4 as shown in Table 3-5 into the cell.**

• **Align the text to the right.**

• **Click anywhere in the document to deselect the text.**

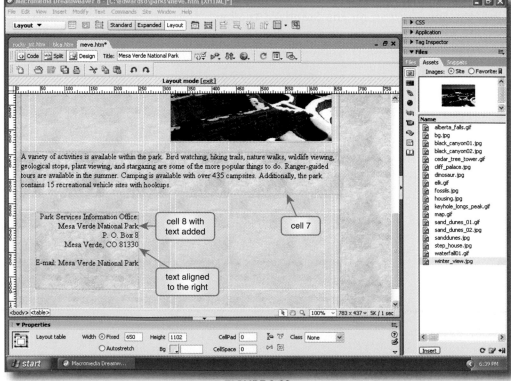

FIGURE 3-99

The eighth cell is inserted, and the text is displayed right-aligned in the cell (Figure 3-99).

5

• **Click the Draw Layout Cell button and draw the ninth cell to the right of the eighth cell and about 10 pixels lower than cell 8, with an approximate width of 270 and an approximate height of 180.**

• **Select the cell and make any necessary adjustments to the width and height in the Property inspector.**

• **Click cell 9 and then drag the step_house.jpg image to the ninth cell.**

• **Type** step_house **as the image ID and** Mesa Verde step house **as the Alt text. Press the ENTER key.**

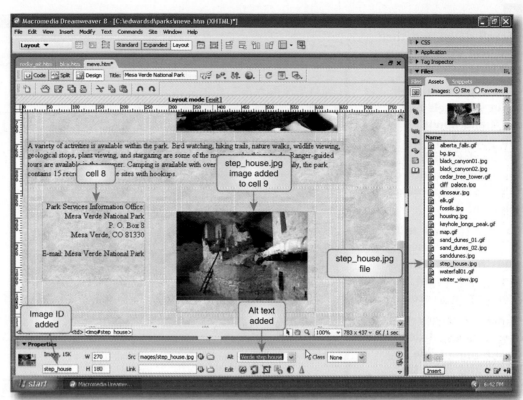

FIGURE 3-100

The ninth cell is inserted, and the step_house.jpg image is displayed (Figure 3-100).

6

• **Scroll down and then click the Draw Layout Cell button.**

• **Draw the tenth cell about 20 pixels below cell 9 and about 100 pixels from the left border, with an approximate width of 525 and an approximate height of 35.**

• **Select the cell and make any necessary adjustments to the width and height in the Property inspector.**

• **Click the rocky_mt. htm tab, scroll down to the links table. Select and copy the links text.**

• **Click the meve. htm tab.**

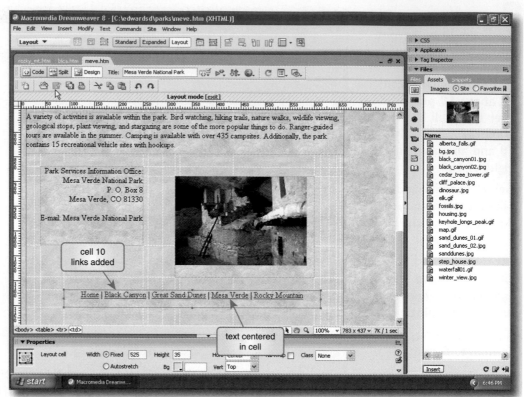

FIGURE 3-101

• **Click cell 10 and then paste the links text into the cell.**

• **Click the Align Center button.**

• **Select the cell, click the Horz box arrow, and then click Center.**

• **Click the Save button.**

The text for the links is displayed centered in cell 10, and the page is saved (Figure 3-101).

Next, you format the text, adding the same style that you did for the previous two National Park pages.

1

- **Scroll up and select the text in cell 2.**
- **Click the Size box arrow and select 18 to create style2.**
- **Select the text in cells 4, 7, and 8 one at a time and apply style2.**

The text is formatted with style2 (Figure 3-102).

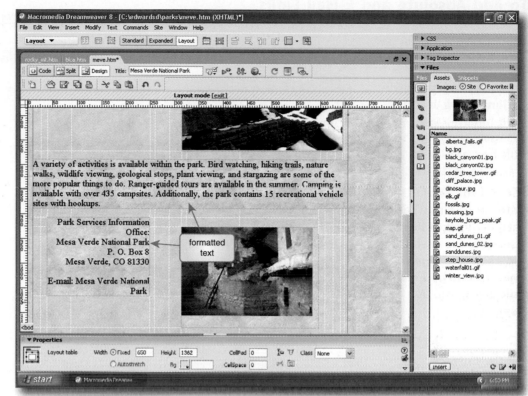

FIGURE 3-102

Next, you add absolute and e-mail links to the Mesa Verde National Park page. The steps on the next page show how to add the links.

To Add Absolute and E-Mail Links

1

• **Select the first instance of Mesa Verde National Park in cell 8. Type** http://www.nps.gov/meve/ **in the Link box and then press the ENTER key.**

• **Select the second instance of Mesa Verde National Park. Click Insert on the menu bar and then click Email Link. When the Email Link dialog box is displayed, type** mese@parks.gov **as the e-mail address. Click the OK button.**

The links are added, as shown in Figure 3-103.

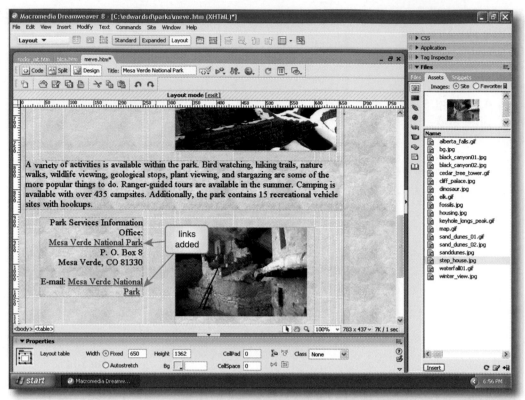

FIGURE 3-103

Centering the Table in Standard Mode

Layout mode does not provide all the features that are provided for a table in Standard mode. For example, you cannot select a number of rows or select a number of columns when creating Web pages in Layout mode, and you cannot center a table when in Layout mode. To access these features requires that the table be displayed in Standard mode. Your next task is to center the table. The steps on the next page illustrate how to display the Web page in Standard mode, center the table, and turn off the rulers.

To Center a Table Created in Layout Mode

1

• **Click the Standard Mode button on the Layout Insert bar. Click any cell in the table and then click the <table> tag in the tag selector.**

The table is displayed in Standard mode and is selected (Figure 3-104).

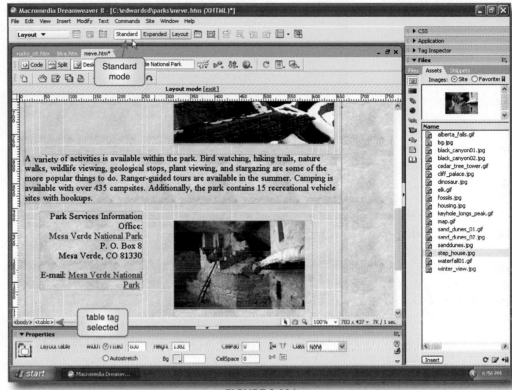

FIGURE 3-104

2

• **Click the Table ID text box and type** mesa_verde **for the ID.**

• **Click the Align box arrow in the Property inspector and then click Center.**

• **Click the Save button on the Standard toolbar.**

The table is selected and centered in the Document window (Figure 3-105).

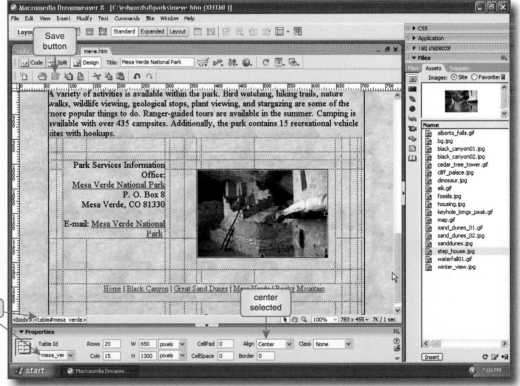

FIGURE 3-105

• Press the F12 key to view the page in your browser.

The Web page is displayed centered in the browser (Figure 3-106). If the table has excessive extra space at the end of the page, adjust the H number in the Property inspector.

• Close the browser.

• Click View on the menu bar, point to Rulers, and then click the Show command to deselect it.

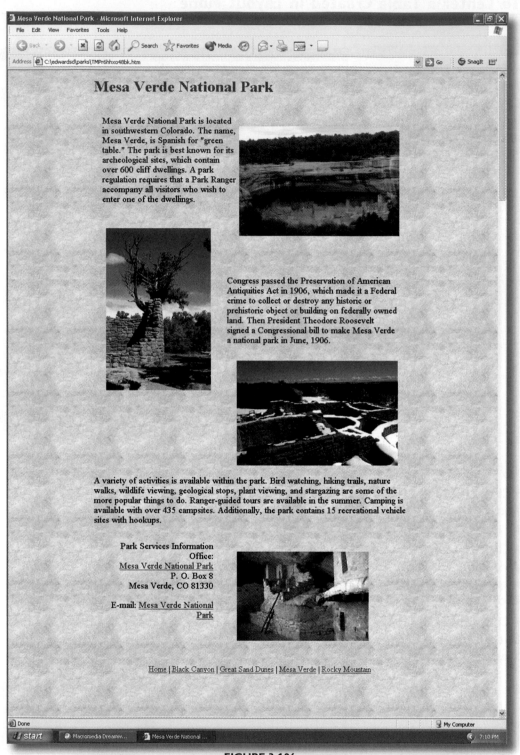

FIGURE 3-106

More About

Layout Tables

For more information about Dreamweaver 8 layout tables, visit the Dreamweaver 8 More About Web page (scsite.com/dw8/more.htm) and then click Dreamweaver 8 Layout Tables.

The Web site has expanded to include pages with information on the four National Parks located in Colorado. To integrate the pages within the Web site, you add links from the natl_parks.htm page. The steps on the next page show how to add the links.

To Add Links to the National Parks Web Page

1

• **Click File on the menu bar, select Open, and then open the natl_parks.htm page in the parks folder.**

• **If necessary, expand the panel groups and then select the Files tab.**

The natl_parks.htm page is displayed (Figure 3-107).

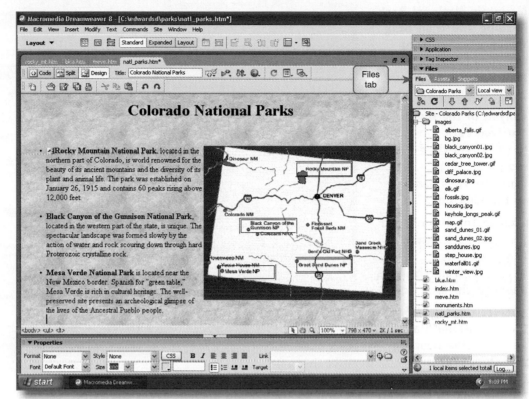

FIGURE 3-107

2

• Select the Rocky Mountain National Park heading and then drag rocky_mt.htm from the Files panel to the Link box.

• Select the Black Canyon of the Gunnison National Park heading and then drag blca.htm from the Files panel to the Link box.

• Select the Mesa Verde National Park heading and then drag meve.htm from the Files panel to the Link box.

• Select the Great Sand Dunes National Park and Preserve heading and then type blca.htm#sand_dunes for the link to the Web page and to the named anchor. Press the ENTER key.

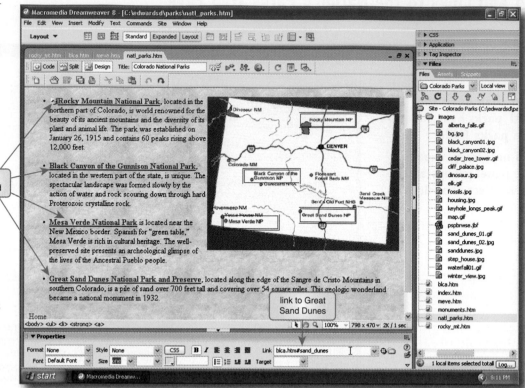

FIGURE 3-108

The links are added to the four parks (Figure 3-108).

3

• **Press the F12 key to view the page in your browser. Test each link and then close the browser.**

• **Save the natl_parks.htm page and then close the page.**

• **Close the other three pages — rocky_mt.htm, blca.htm, and meve.htm. Save these pages if necessary.**

Head Content

HTML files consist of two main sections: the head section and the body section. The head section is one of the more important sections of a Web page. A standard HTML page contains a <head> tag and a <body> tag. Contained within the head section is site and page information. With the exception of the title, the information contained in the head does not display in the browser. Some of the information contained in the head is accessed by the browser, and other information is accessed by other programs such as search engines and server software.

Head Content Elements

Dreamweaver makes it easy to add content to the head section by providing a pop-up menu in the Insert bar HTML category. The Head pop-up menu contains the following elements that can be added to your Web page.

META A <meta> tag contains information about the current document. This information is used by servers, browsers, and search engines. HTML documents can have as many <meta> tags as needed. Each item uses a different set of tags.

KEYWORDS Keywords are a list of words that someone would type into a search engine search field.

DESCRIPTION The description contains a sentence or two that can be used in a search engine's results page.

REFRESH The <refresh> tag is processed by the browser to reload the page or load a new page after a specified amount of time has elapsed.

BASE The base tag sets the base URL to provide an absolute link and/or a link target that the browser can use to resolve link conflicts.

LINK The link element defines a relationship between the current document and another file. This is not the same as a link in the Document window.

Keywords, descriptions, and refresh settings are special-use cases of the meta tag. The following steps show how to add keywords and a description to the index.htm page.

More About

Head Content

Meta tags are information inserted into the head content area of Web pages. The meta description tag allows you to influence the description of a page in the search engines that support the tag. For more information about meta tags, visit the Dreamweaver 8 More About Web page (scsite.com/dw8/more.htm) and then click Dreamweaver 8 Meta Tags.

To Add Keywords and a Description

• **Open the index. htm file.**

• **Click Insert on the menu bar, point to HTML, point to Head Tags on the HTML submenu, and then point to Keywords on the Head Tags submenu. (Figure 3-109).**

The Head Tags submenu is displayed (Figure 3-109).

FIGURE 3-109

2

• **Click the Keywords command.**

• **Type** parks, Colorado, national parks, state parks **in the Keywords text box:.**

The Keywords dialog box is displayed. Keywords are added to the Keywords dialog box (Figure 3-110). When a search engine begins a search for any of the keywords, the Web site address will be displayed in the browser search results.

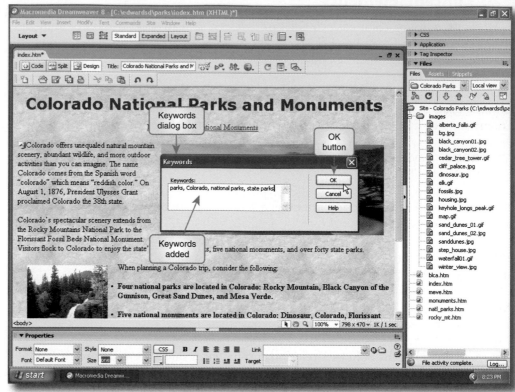

FIGURE 3-110

3

• **Click the OK button.**

• **Click Insert on the menu bar, point to HTML, point to Head Tags on the HTML submenu, and then click Description on the Head Tags submenu. Type** A Web site featuring Colorado state and national parks **in the Description text box.**

The Description dialog box is displayed as shown in Figure 3-111, with a description added.

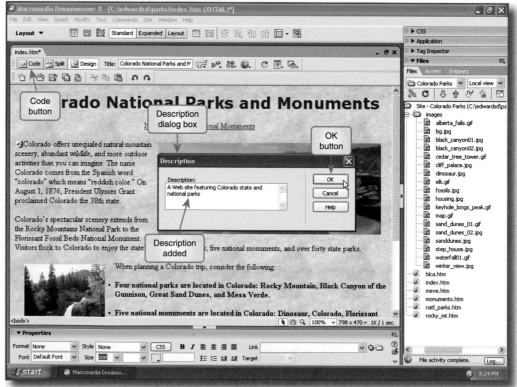

FIGURE 3-111

4

• **Click the OK button and then click the Code button on the Document toolbar.**

The keywords and description that you entered are displayed in Code view (Figure 3-112)

5

• **Click the Design button on the Document toolbar and then click the Save button on the Standard toolbar.**

The Web page is saved.

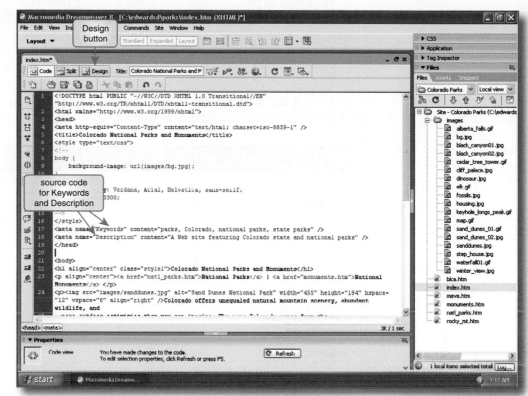

FIGURE 3-112

Other Ways

1. Click Code button on Document toolbar, type keywords code in code window
2. Change the Insert bar category to HTML, click the Head drop-down arrow, and then click Description or Keywords in the Head menu

Publishing a Web Site

In Project 1 you defined a local site, and in Projects 1, 2, and 3 you added Web pages to the local site. This local site resides on your computer's hard disk, a network drive, or possibly a USB drive or a Zip disk. You can view the organization of all files and folders in your site through the Files panel.

To prepare a Web site and make it available for others to view requires that you publish your site by putting it on a Web server for public access. A Web server is an Internet- or intranet-connected computer that delivers, or *serves up*, Web pages. You upload files to a folder on a server and download files to a folder in the Files panel on your computer. Generally, when Web site designers publish to a folder on a Web site, they do so by using a file transfer (FTP) program such as WS_FTP or Cute FTP, or Windows XP Web Folders. Dreamweaver, however, includes built-in support that enables you to connect and transfer your local site to a Web server without requiring an additional program. To publish to a Web server requires that you have access to a Web server.

Publishing and maintaining your site using Dreamweaver involves the following steps:

1. Using the Site Definition Wizard to enter the FTP information
2. Specifying the Web server to which you want to publish your Web site
3. Connecting to the Web server and uploading the files
4. Synchronizing the local and remote sites

Your school or company may have a server that you can use to upload your Web site. Free Web hosting services such as those provided by Angelfire, Tripod, or Geo-Cities are other options. These services, as well as many other hosting services, also offer low-cost Web hosting from approximately $3.95 to $9.95 a month. The FreeSite.com Web site contains a list of free and inexpensive hosting services, and FreeWebspace.net provides a PowerSearch form for free and low-cost hosting.

Table 3-6 contains a list of Web hosting services. Appendix C contains step-by-step instructions on publishing a Web site to a remote folder.

Table 3-6 Web Site Hosting Services		
NAME	**WEB SITE**	**COST**
Angelfire®	angelfire.lycos.com	Free (ad-supported); starting at $4.95 monthly ad-free
Yahoo! GeoCities	geocities.yahoo.com	Free (ad-supported); starting at $4.95 monthly ad-free
Tripod®	tripod.lycos.com/	Free (ad-supported); starting at $4.95 monthly ad-free
The FreeSite.com	thefreesite.com/Free_Web_Space	A list of free and inexpensive hosting sites
FreeWebspace.net	freewebspace.net	A searchable guide for free Web space

For an updated list of Web site hosting services, visit the Macromedia Dreamweaver 8 Web page (scsite.com/dw8) and then click Web Hosting. If required by your instructor, publish the Colorado Parks Web site to a remote server by following the steps in Appendix C.

With your work completed, you are ready to quit Dreamweaver.

Quitting Dreamweaver

After you add pages to your Web site and add the head content, Project 3 is complete. The following step illustrates how to close the Web site, quit Dreamweaver 8, and return control to Windows.

More About

Publishing Your Colorado Parks Web Site

Appendix C contains step-by-step instructions on publishing the Colorado Parks Web site.

To Close the Web Site and Quit Dreamweaver

1 Click the Close button on the right corner of the Dreamweaver title bar.

The Dreamweaver window, the Document window, and the Colorado Parks Web site all close. If you have unsaved changes, Dreamweaver will prompt you to save the changes. Clicking the Yes button in the Dreamweaver 8 dialog box saves the changes.

Project Summary

Project 3 introduced you to tables and to Web page design using tables. You created three Web pages, using the Standard mode for two pages and the Layout mode for the third page. You merged and split cells and learned how to add text and images to the tables. Next, you added a border color and cell background color. Finally, you added head content to one of the Web pages.

What You Should Know

Having completed this project, you should be able to perform the tasks below. The tasks are listed in the same order they were presented in the project. For a list of the buttons, menus, toolbars, and commands introduced in this project, see the Quick Reference Summary at the back of this book and refer to the Page Number column.

1. Copy Data Files to the Parks Web Site (DW 208)
2. Start Dreamweaver and Open the Colorado Parks Web Site (DW 209)
3. Open a New Document Window (DW 210)
4. Add a Background Image to the Rocky Mountain National Park Web Page (DW 211)
5. Insert and Format the Heading (DW 212)
6. Display the Insert Bar and Select the Layout Category (DW 214)
7. Insert a Table Using Standard Mode (DW 218)
8. Select and Center a Table (DW 227)
9. Change Vertical Alignment from Middle to Top (DW 229)
10. Specify Column Width (DW 230)
11. Add a Table ID to the Rocky Mountain National Park Feature Table (DW 231)
12. Add Rocky Mountain National Park Text (DW 232)
13. Add a Second Table to the Rocky Mountain National Park Web Page (DW 234)
14. Adjust the Table Width, Center the Text, and Add the Table ID (DW 237)
15. Add Links to the Rocky Mountain National Parks Page (DW 238)
16. Merge Two Cells (DW 242)
17. Disable the Image Tag Accessibility Attributes Dialog Box (DW 243)
18. Add Images to a Standard Mode Table (DW 243)
19. Open a New Document Window and Add a Background Image to the Black Canyon/Great Sand Dunes Web Page (DW 250)
20. Insert and Center a Table (DW 252)
21. Merge Cells in Row 1 and in Row 4 (DW 253)
22. Add a Heading to Row 1 (DW 254)
23. Adjust the Column Width (DW 256)
24. Add and Format Text for the Black Canyon/Great Sand Dunes Web Page (DW 258)
25. Add Images to the Black Canyon/Great Sand Dunes Web Page (DW 262)
26. Add Border Color and Cell Background Color (DW 266)
27. Adding an Anchor and Links to and Spell Check the Black Canyon/Great Sand Dunes Page (DW 267)
28. Add a New Page and Add a Background Image to the Mesa Verde National Park Web Page (DW 271)
29. Display the Rulers (DW 273)
30. Create the Layout Table (DW 274)
31. Add a Layout Cell and Heading (DW 276)
32. Create and Add Text to a Layout Cell for the Mesa Verde National Park Web Page (DW 279)
33. Add an Image to a Layout Cell (DW 281)
34. Add Five Additional Cells to the Mesa Verde National Park Web Page (DW 284)
35. Add and E-Mail Links (DW 290)
36. Center a Table Created in Layout Mode (DW 291)
37. Add Links to the National Parks Web Page (DW 293)
38. Add Keywords and a Description (DW 295)
39. Close the Web Site and Quit Dreamweaver (DW 298)

Learn It Online

Instructions: To complete the Learn It Online exercises, start your browser, click the Address bar, and then enter the Web address scsite.com/dw8/learn. When the Dreamweaver 8 Learn It Online page is displayed, follow the instructions in the exercises below. Each exercise has instructions for printing your results, either for your own records or for submission to your instructor.

1 Project Reinforcement TF, MC, and SA

Below Dreamweaver Project 3, click the Project Reinforcement link. Print the quiz by clicking Print on the File menu for each page. Answer each question.

2 Flash Cards

Below Dreamweaver Project 3, click the Flash Cards link and read the instructions. Type 20 (or a number specified by your instructor) in the Number of playing cards text box, type your name in the Enter your Name text box, and then click the Flip Card button. When the flash card is displayed, read the question and then click the ANSWER box arrow to select an answer. Flip through Flash Cards. If your score is 15 (75%) correct or greater, click Print on the File menu to print your results. If your score is less than 15 (75%) correct, then redo this exercise by clicking the Replay button.

3 Practice Test

Below Dreamweaver Project 3, click the Practice Test link. Answer each question, enter your first and last name at the bottom of the page, and then click the Grade Test button. When the graded practice test is displayed on your screen, click Print on the File menu to print a hard copy. Continue to take practice tests until you score 80% or better.

4 Who Wants To Be a Computer Genius?

Below Dreamweaver Project 3, click the Computer Genius link. Read the instructions, enter your first and last name at the bottom of the page, and then click the PLAY button. When your score is displayed, click the PRINT RESULTS link to print a hard copy.

5 Wheel of Terms

Below Dreamweaver Project 3, click the Wheel of Terms link. Read the instructions, and then enter your first and last name and your school name. Click the PLAY button. When your score is displayed, right-click the score and then click Print on the shortcut menu to print a hard copy.

6 Crossword Puzzle Challenge

Below Dreamweaver Project 3, click the Crossword Puzzle Challenge link. Read the instructions, and then enter your first and last name. Click the SUBMIT button. Work the crossword puzzle. When you are finished, click the Submit button. When the crossword puzzle is redisplayed, click the Print Puzzle button to print a hard copy.

7 Tips and Tricks

Below Dreamweaver Project 3, click the Tips and Tricks link. Click a topic that pertains to Project 3. Right-click the information and then click Print on the shortcut menu. Construct a brief example of what the information relates to in Dreamweaver to confirm that you understand how to use the tip or trick.

8 Newsgroups

Below Dreamweaver Project 3, click the Newsgroups link. Click a topic that pertains to Project 3. Print three comments.

9 Expanding Your Horizons

Below Dreamweaver Project 3, click the Expanding Your Horizons link. Click a topic that pertains to Project 3. Print the information. Construct a brief example of what the information relates to in Dreamweaver to confirm that you understand the contents of the article.

10 Search Sleuth

Below Dreamweaver Project 3, click the Search Sleuth link. To search for a term that pertains to this project, select a term below the Project 3 title and then use the Google search engine at google.com (or any major search engine) to display and print two Web pages that present information on the term.

Apply Your Knowledge

1 Modifying the Andy's Lawn Service Web Site

Instructions: Start Dreamweaver. See the inside back cover of this book for instructions for downloading the Data Disk or see your instructor for information on accessing the files in this book.

The Andy's Lawn Service Web site currently contains four pages. You will add a fifth page with a table created using Standard mode. The new Web page will include a seven-row, three-column centered table with a list of services, how often the services are scheduled, and the price of each service. You merge one of the rows and then add and center an image in the row. A border color is applied to the entire table, and the first row has a background color applied. Keywords and a description are added. You then add a link to the home page, save the page, and upload the Web site to a Web server. The new page added to the Web site is shown in Figure 3-113. Software and hardware settings determine how a Web page is displayed in a browser. Your Web page may display differently than the one shown in Figure 3-113.

Appendix C contains instructions for uploading your local site to a remote site.

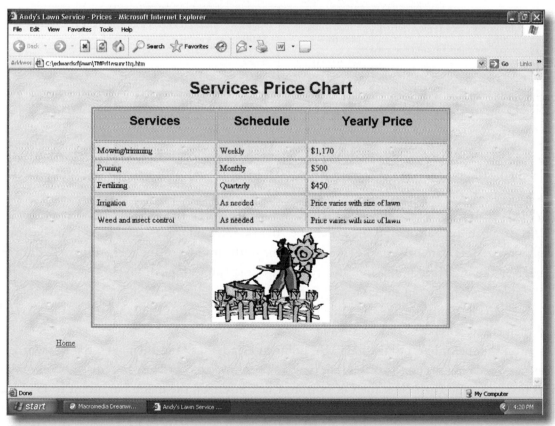

FIGURE 3-113

1. Use the Windows My Computer option to copy the fertilizing.gif image from the DataFiles folder to your /lawn/images folder.
2. Select Lawn Service from the Site pop-up menu in the Files panel. Click File on the menu bar and then click New. If necessary, click the General tab and then click Basic page in the Category list. Click the Create button. Save the page as prices.htm.
3. Use the Page Properties dialog box to apply the lawnbg.jpg image to the new page.

(continued)

Modifying the Andy's Lawn Service Web Site *(continued)*

4. If necessary, display the Insert bar. Click the upper-left corner of the Document window. Type Services Price Chart and then apply Heading 1 to the text. Center the text. Change the Font to Arial, Helvetica, sans-serif. If necessary, deselect the title, press the ENTER key, and then click the Layout category on the Insert bar. If necessary, click the Standard Mode button and then click the Table button in the Layout category. Type the following data in the Table dialog box: 7 for Rows, 3 for Columns, 70 for Table width, 3 for Border thickness, 5 for Cell padding, and 2 for Cell spacing. If necessary, select percent in the dropdown box to the right of the Table width text box.

5. Type the text as shown in Table 3-7. Press the TAB key to move from cell to cell.

Table 3-7 Andy's Lawn Services Price Chart		
SERVICES	SCHEDULE	YEARLY PRICE
Mowing/trimming	Weekly	$1,170
Pruning	Monthly	$500
Fertilizing	Quarterly	$450
Irrigation	As needed	Price varies with size of lawn
Weed and insect control	As needed	Price varies with size of lawn

6. Click anywhere in row 1 and then click the <tr> tag in the tag selector to select row 1. Apply Heading 2 and center the heading. Change the font to Arial, Helvetica, sans-serif. Click the Backgound Color box in the Property inspector and apply background color #FFCC66 .

7. Click anywhere in row 7 in the table and then click the <tr> tag in the tag selector to select row 7. Click the Merge Cells using spans button and then click the Align Center button in the Property inspector. If necessary, display the Assets panel. With the insertion point in the middle of the merged row 7, drag the fertilizing.gif image to the insertion point and then type Fertilizing as the Alt text.

8. Click the <table> tag in the tag selector and then apply border color #FF9900. Center the table.

9. Position the insertion point outside the table by clicking to the right of the table. Press the ENTER key. Type Home and then create a relative link to the index.htm file.

10. Click Insert on the menu bar, point to HTML, point to Head Tags, and then click the Keywords command. When the Keywords dialog box is displayed, type lawn service, price schedule, your name in the Keywords text box, and then click the OK button. Click Insert on the menu bar, point to HTML, point to Head Tags, and then click the Description command. When the Description dialog box is displayed, type Andy's Lawn Service price schedule in the Description text box and then click the OK button.

11. Title the page Andy's Lawn Service - Prices. Check spelling. Save the Web page.

12. Open the index.htm page and then scroll to the end of the page. Click at the end of the sentence that reads, "Our mission is to be the premier..." and then press the ENTER key. Type Check our Prices. If necessary, click the Bold button in the Property inspector to remove the bold formatting. Create a link from the words Check our Prices to the prices.htm page. Save the index.htm Web page.

13. If required, print a copy of the page for your instructor. If required by your instructor, publish the Lawn Service Web site to a remote server by following the steps in Appendix C. Close the Lawn Service Web site. Close Dreamweaver.

In the Lab

1 Adding a Page with a Table to the CandleWix Web Site

Problem: Publicity from the Web site has generated several requests for examples of Martha Morgan's candles. Martha has asked you to add a page to the site that shows some of her creations and the price of each candle. The Web page will have a link to the home page and will be named products. The new page is shown in Figure 3-114. Appendix C contains instructions for uploading your local site to a remote site.

FIGURE 3-114

Instructions: Perform the following tasks:

1. Use the Windows My Computer option to copy the six images (candle3.gif through candle8.gif) from the DataFiles folder to your /candle/images folder.
2. Start Dreamweaver. Select CandleWix from the Files pop-up menu in the Files panel. Click File on the menu bar and then click New. If necessary, click the General tab and then click Basic page in the Category list. Click the Create button. Save the page as products.htm.
3. Use the Page Properties dialog box to add the candlebg.gif image. Title the page CandleWix Specialty Candles.
4. Click the upper-left corner of the page and then press the ENTER key.
5. If necessary, click the Insert bar's Layout category, click the Standard Mode button, and then click the Table button. Type the following data in the Table dialog box: 6 for Rows, 3 for Columns, 80 for Table width, 3 for Border thickness, 3 for Cell padding, and 3 for Cell spacing. Select percent in the dropdown box to the right of the Table width text box.

(continued)

In the Lab

Adding a Page with a Table to the CandleWix Web Site *(continued)*

6. Merge the three cells in row 1 into one cell. Click the Align Center button in the Property inspector and then type `CandleWix Specialty Candles` as the heading. Apply Heading 1 to the text heading. Change the Font to Georgia, Times New Roman, Times, serif. Change the Text Color to #990000.

7. Click row 2, column 1 and then drag to select all cells in rows 2 through 6. Click the Align Center button, click the Vert box arrow, and then select Middle. Set the width to 33%. Repeat this step for rows 2 through 6 in both column 2 and column 3.

8. Display the Assets panel. Click row 2, column 1 and drag candle3.gif to the insertion point. If the Image Tag Accessibility Attributes dialog box displays, click the Cancel button. Repeat this step, dragging candle4.gif to row 2, column 2, and candle5.gif to row 2, column 3.

9. Type the following information in row 3: `$7.25` in column 1, `$7.25` in column 2, and `$4.50` in column 3.

10. Merge the three cells in row 4.

11. Click column 1, row 5 and drag candle6.gif to the insertion point. Repeat this step, dragging candle7.gif to column 2, row 5, and candle8.gif to column 3, row 5.

12. Type the following information in row 6: `$7.00` in column 1, `$4.50` in column 2, and `$3.75` in column 3.

13. Select the table by clicking <table> in the tag inspector. Use the Property inspector to center-align the table.

14. Click outside of the table to the right and then press the ENTER key. Type `Home` and create a link from the products.htm page to the index.htm page. Save the products.htm page.

15. Open the index.htm page and click to the right of the Company History link. Press the ENTER key. Type `Products` and then create a link to the products.htm page. Save the index.htm page.

16. View your page in your browser. Verify that your link works. Print a copy of the Web page if required and hand it in to your instructor. If required by your instructor, publish the CandleWix Web site to a remote server by following the steps in Appendix C. Close your browser. Close Dreamweaver.

2 Adding a Table Page to the Credit Web Site

Problem: The Credit Protection Web site has become very popular. Marcy receives numerous e-mail messages requesting that the Web site be expanded. Several messages have included a request to provide some hints and tips about how to save money. Monica asks you to create a new page for the Web site so she can share some of this information. Figure 3-115a shows the table layout, and Figure 3-115b shows the Web page. Appendix C contains instructions for uploading your local site to a remote site.

In the Lab

Tips and Hints
Saving Money

Automobiles

1. Select a model that combines a low purchase price with low financing, maintenance, and repair costs.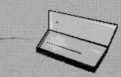
2. Comparison shop -- call at least five dealerships.

Checking

1. Select a checking account with a low or no minimum balance requirement.
2. Request a list of all fees.
3. Use direct deposit.

Credit Cards
1. Pay off the entire bill each month.
2. Switch to a credit card with a low Annual Percentage Rate (APR).
3. Get rid of all credit cards except one or two.

Home | Questions | Theft

(a) Table Layout

FIGURE 3-115

(continued)

Adding a Table Page to the Credit Web Site *(continued)*

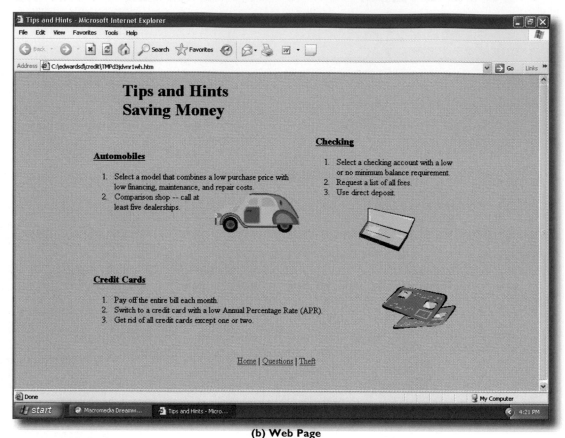

(b) Web Page

FIGURE 3-115

Instructions: Perform the following tasks:

1. Use the Windows My Computer option to copy the three images (car.gif, check.gif, and credit_card.gif) from the DataFiles folder to your /credit/images folder. Start Dreamweaver. Select Credit Protection from the Site pop-up menu in the Files panel.

2. Add a new Web page and name it saving.htm. Add the creditbg.jpg background image. Title the page Tips and Hints.

3. If necessary, display the rulers. Click the Insert bar's Layout category and then click the Layout button. If the Getting Started in Layout Mode dialog box displays, click the OK button.

4. Click the Draw Layout Table button on the Layout tab and then create a table with a fixed width of approximately 700 pixels and a height of approximately 550 pixels.

5. Use Figure 3-115a on the previous page as a guide and draw the five layout cells. Use the information in Table 3-8 for the widths and heights.

In the Lab

NUMBER	CELL NAME	W	H	IMAGE ALT TEXT	IMAGE NAME	CELL TEXT
	Table 3-8 Credit Protection Cell Layout Guide					
1	Heading	340	75	None	None	Tips and Hints Saving Money
2	Automobiles	365	185	Car	car.gif	1. Select a model that combines a low purchase price with low financing, maintenance, and repair costs. 2. Comparison shop — call at least five dealerships.
3	Checking	306	232	Checking Account	check.gif	1. Select a checking account with a low or no minimum balance requirement. 2. Request a list of all fees. 3. Use direct deposit.
4	Credit Cards	700	115	Credit Cards	credit_card.gif	1. Pay off the entire bill each month. 2. Switch to a credit card with a low Annual Percentage Rate (APR). 3. Get rid of all credit cards except one or two.
5	Links	700	40	None	None	Home | Questions | Theft

6. Use Table 3-8 as a reference and type the text into each of the layout cells. Apply Heading 1 to the text in the first cell. Apply Heading 3 to the headings in cells 2 through 4 and then underline the headings.
7. Insert the images into the cells. Refer to the invisible element marker in Figure 3-115a as the insertion point for the images in cells 2 and 4. For cell 3, press the ENTER key twice after item 3 and then click the Align Center button in the Property inspector. Drag the check.gif image to the insertion point. Use the Property inspector to select Right from the Align dropdown menu for the car.gif and credit_card.gif images.
8. Add the appropriate relative links to cell 5, using Table 3-9 as a guide.

TEXT	LINK
Table 3-9 Links for Cell 5	
Home	index.htm
Questions	questions.htm
Theft	theft.htm

9. Click the Standard mode button on the Layout tab, select the table, and then center the table.

(continued)

In the Lab

Adding a Table Page to the Credit Web Site *(continued)*

10. Click the Head button in the HTML category of the Insert bar. Click the Keywords button in the pop-up menu and then type credit, money, tips, checking, saving, your name in the Keywords dialog box. Open the Description dialog box and then type Tips and hints on how to save money. Save the Web page.

11. Open the index.htm page and click to the right of the last bulleted item. Press the ENTER key twice. Type Tips and Hints on Saving and create a link from this text to the saving.htm page. Save the index.htm page.

12. View the Web site in your browser and verify that your links work. Close the browser. If required, print a copy for your instructor. If required by your instructor, publish the Credit Protection Web site to a remote server by following the steps in Appendix C.

3 Adding a Table Page to the Lexington, NC Web Site

Problem: In his job as a member of the Lexington marketing group, John Davis has been exploring the city's services. On a recent tour, John discovered that the city contains an outstanding police department. He would like to feature the Lexington Police Department on the Web site and has requested that you add a new page to the Lexington, NC Web site. You elect to use a layout table to create this page. The Web page is displayed in Figure 3-116. Appendix C contains instructions for uploading your local site to a remote site.

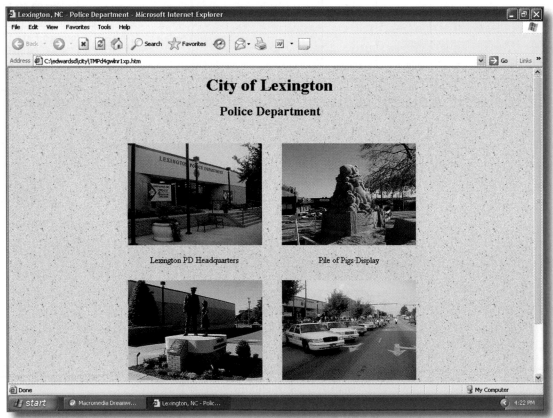

FIGURE 3-116

Instructions: Perform the following tasks:

1. Use the Windows My Computer option to copy the four images (police1.jpg through police4.jpg) from the DataFiles folder to your /city/images folder. Start Dreamweaver. Select Lexington, NC from the Site pop-up menu in the Files panel.
2. Add a new page and then save the page with the file name police.htm. Add the background image you added in Project 1. Add the citybg.gif background image. Title the page Lexington, NC - Police Department.
3. If necessary, display the rulers. Click the Insert bar's Layout category and then click the Layout button.
4. Create a layout table with a fixed width of approximately 650 pixels and a height of approximately 675 pixels.
5. Use Figure 3-116 as a guide and draw the 10 layout cells. Use the information in Table 3-10 for the widths, heights, and file names.

Table 3-10 Lexington, NC Cell Layout Guide

NUMBER	CELL TYPE	W	H	IMAGE ALT TEXT	FILE NAME	CELL TEXT
1	Heading	650	85	None	None	City of Lexington Police Department
2	Image	256	192	Police Department	police1.jpg	None
3	Text	256	30	None	None	Lexington PD Headquarters
4	Image	256	192	Tribute Statue	police2.jpg	None
5	Text	256	30	None	None	Tribute Statue
6	Image	256	192	Pile of Pigs	police3.jpg	None
7	Text	256	30	None	None	Pile of Pigs Display
8	Image	256	192	Cruisers	police4.jpg	None
9	Text	256	30	None	None	Lexington Police Department Cruisers
10	Text	650	30	None	None	Home

6. Type the text into each of the layout cells as indicated in Table 3-10. Apply Heading 1 to the first line of text in the first cell and Heading 2 to the second line of text.
7. Insert the images into the cells. Refer to Table 3-10 for the image file names.
8. Click the Standard mode button on the Layout category, select the table, and then center the table. Create a relative link to the index.htm Web page using the text in cell 10.
9. Add Lexington, North Carolina, police, safety, and your name as keywords. Add A tribute to the Lexington Police Department as the description. Save the police.htm page.
10. Open the index.htm page. Click to the right of the Recipes link. Add a vertical line, press the SPACEBAR, and then type Police Department. Create a link from the Police Department text to the police.htm page.
11. View the Web site in your browser. Close the browser. If required by your instructor, publish the Lexington, NC Web site to a remote server by following the steps in Appendix C. If required, print a copy for your instructor.

Cases and Places

The difficulty of these case studies varies:
■ are the least difficult and ■■ are the most difficult. The last exercise is a group exercise.

1 ■ The sports Web site has become very popular. Several of your friends have suggested that you add a statistics page. You agree that this is a good idea. Create the new page. Using the Internet or other resources, find statistics about your selected sport. Add a background image to the page and use Standard mode to insert a table that contains your statistical information. Add an appropriate heading to the table and an appropriate title for the page. Create a link to the home page. Save the page in your sports Web site. For a selection of images and backgrounds, visit the Dreamweaver 8 Media Web page (scsite.com/dw8/media) and then click Media below Project 3.

2 ■ Modify your hobby Web site. Expand the topic and add an additional page that includes a table created in Standard mode. The table should contain a minimum of three rows and three columns, and a 2-pixel border. Include information in the table about your hobby. Include a minimum of two images in the table. Merge one of the rows or one of the columns and add a border color. Add a background image to the page and give your page a title. Create a link to the home page. Save the page in your hobby Web site. For a selection of images and backgrounds, visit the Dreamweaver 8 Media Web page (scsite.com/dw8/media) and then click Media below Project 3.

3 ■■ Modify your favorite type of music Web site by adding a new page. The new page should contain a table with four rows and three columns created in Standard mode. Merge one of the rows and add a background color to the row. Add at least two images to your table. Center the images in the cell. View your Web pages in your browser. Give your page a title and save the page in your music sub-folder. Appendix C contains instructions for uploading your local site to a remote site. For a selection of images and backgrounds, visit the Dreamweaver 8 Media Web page (scsite.com/dw8/media) and then click Media below Project 3.

Cases and Places

4 ■■ Your campaign for office is going well. You want to add a new page to the Web site to include pictures and text listing some of your outstanding achievements. Apply a color scheme and a background image to the page. Draw a layout table with a minimum of four layout cells. Include your picture in one of the cells. Add an appropriate title, keywords, and a description to the page. Center the table. Save the page in the office subfolder and then view the page in your browser. Appendix C contains instructions for uploading your local site to a remote site. For a selection of images and backgrounds, visit the Dreamweaver 8 Media Web page (scsite.com/dw8/media) and then click Media below Project 3.

5 ■■ **Working Together** The students at your school are requesting more information about the student trips. To accommodate the request, the members of your team decide to add another page to the Web site. Each team member is responsible for researching possible destinations and developing content for the selected destination. Add a heading to the new page and format it appropriately. Draw a layout table with a minimum of six layout cells. Each member adds at least one image and text content to a cell. One member formats the page — including the text and images. Add a title, keywords, meta tags, and a description. Save the page and view it in your browser. Appendix C contains instructions for uploading your local site to a remote site. For a selection of images and backgrounds, visit the Dreamweaver 8 Media Web page (scsite.com/dw8/media) and then click Media below Project 3.

MACROMEDIA
Dreamweaver 8

Forms

PROJECT

4

CASE PERSPECTIVE

Each day, the Colorado Parks Web site receives increasingly more hits. Even though the Web site has been expanded, David is receiving numerous e-mail messages asking questions about the parks. Many of the messages request information about hotel accommodations, especially for the national parks. David meets with you and Tracy and asks for suggestions. Tracy is involved with a group of friends who coordinate the Colorado National Parks Volunteer Association. The members suggest to Tracy that adding a form to the Web site could provide access to hotel information for the four national parks. The volunteer group also distributes daily, weekly, and monthly newsletters. They suggest that the form contain an option for requesting one of the newsletters. David and Tracy like this idea and further suggest that both forms contain a link to the Colorado National Parks page and to the Home page.

The team agrees that this is a good idea and that interactive forms with links to the Colorado National Parks page and the Home page will enhance and add significantly to their effort to share their affection for Colorado's great outdoors.

As you read through this project, you will learn about form processing and how to design and create a form, add behaviors to a form, and review form accessibility options.

MACROMEDIA

Dreamweaver 8

Forms

Objectives

You will have mastered the material in this project when you can:

- Discuss form processing
- Describe the difference between client-side and server-side form processing
- Add a horizontal rule to a Web page
- Create a form
- Discuss form design
- Insert a table into a form
- Describe form objects
- Describe and add text fields and text areas to a form

- Describe and add check boxes and radio buttons to a form
- Describe and add lists and menus to a form
- Describe and add form buttons to a form
- Describe form accessibility options
- Apply behaviors to a form
- View and test a form

Introduction

Forms enable the Web page designer to provide visitors with dynamic information and to obtain and process information and feedback from the people viewing the Web page. Web forms are a highly versatile tool that can be used for surveys, guest books, order forms, tests, automated responses, user questions, and reservations. As you complete the activities in this project, you will find that forms are one of the more important sources of interactivity on the Web and are one of the standard tools for the Web page designer.

Project Four — Creating and Using Interactive Forms

In this project, you learn to create forms and to add form fields to the forms. You add forms and modify two Web pages — a general information page and a hotel reservations form page. The general information page, sponsored by the Colorado National Parks Volunteer Association, is shown in Figure 4-1b on the next page. This Web page contains a small form at the bottom of the page that provides the viewer with an opportunity to subscribe to a free newsletter. Contained on the page are two relative links — one to the Colorado Parks index page and one to the Colorado National Parks Web page. The Hotel Reservations Form, shown in Figure 4-1a, also contains a relative link to the Colorado Parks and Monuments index page and a relative link to the Colorado National Parks Web page. The hotel reservations form page contains a request for a hotel reservation at one of the four national parks and provides a jump menu with an absolute link to the Web site for each of the three parks. Both forms contain a horizontal rule separating the heading and the form.

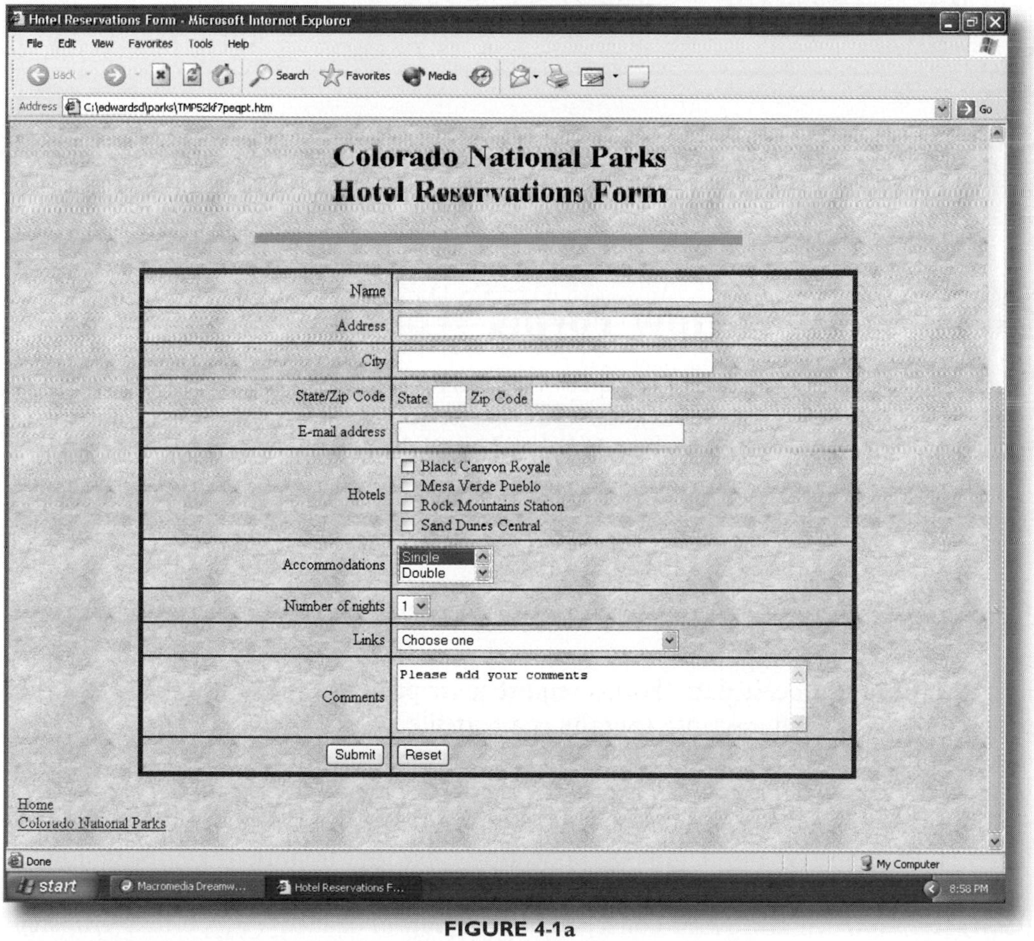

FIGURE 4-1a

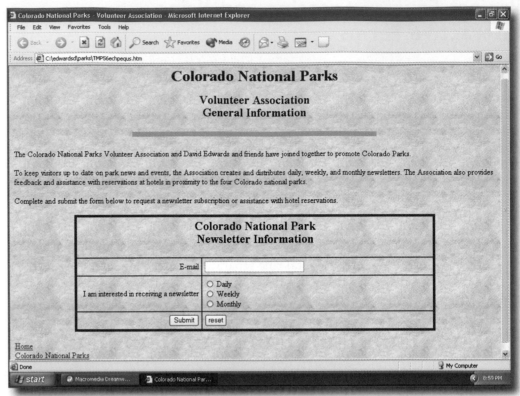

FIGURE 4-1b

Understanding How Forms Work

Forms are interactive elements that provide a way for the Web site visitor to interact with the site. A form provides a method for a user to give feedback, submit an order for merchandise or services, request information, and so on. Forms are created using HTML tags. Each form must have a beginning <form> tag and an ending </form> tag. You cannot nest forms. Each HTML document, however, may contain multiple forms.

Form Processing

A form provides a popular way to collect data from a Web site visitor. Forms, however, do not process data. Forms require a script in order for the form input data to be processed. Such a script generally is a text file that is executed within an application and usually is written in Perl, VBScript, JavaScript, Java, or C++. These scripts reside on a server. Therefore, they are called **server-side scripts**. Other server-side technologies include Macromedia ColdFusion, ASP, ASP.NET, PHP, and JavaServer Pages (JSP). Some type of database application typically supports these technologies.

A common way to process form data is through a **Common Gateway Interface (CGI)** script. When a browser collects data, the data is sent to a Hypertext Transfer Protocol (HTTP) server (a gateway) specified in the HTML form. The server then starts a program (which also is specified in the HTML form) that can process the collected data. The gateway can process the input however you choose. It may return customized HTML based on the user's input, log the input to a file, or e-mail the input to someone.

The **<form> tag** includes parameters that allow you to specify a path to the server-side script or application that processes the form data and indicate which HTTP method to use when transmitting data from the browser to the server. The two HTTP methods are GET and POST, and both of these methods are attributes of the <form> tag. The **GET method** sends the data with a URL. This method is not widely used because it places a limitation on the amount and format of the data that is transmitted to the application. Another limitation of the GET method is that the information being sent is visible in the browser's Address bar. The **POST method** is more efficient because it sends the data to the application as standard input with no limits. The POST method can send much more information than the typical GET method. With POST, the information is not sent with the URL, so the data is invisible to the site visitor.

As an example of form data processing, when a user enters information into a form and clicks the Submit button, the information is sent to the server, where the server-side script or application processes it. The server then responds by sending the requested information back to the user, or performing some other action based on the content of the form.

The specifics of setting up scripts and database applications are beyond the scope of this book. Another option for form data processing exists, however, in which a form can be set up to send data to an e-mail address. The e-mail action is not 100 percent reliable and may not work if your Internet connection has extensive security parameters. In some instances, submitting a mailto form results in just a blank mail message being displayed. Nothing is harmed when this happens, but no data is attached to and sent with the message. Additionally, some browsers display a warning message whenever a form button using mailto is processed. This book uses the e-mail action, however, because this is the action more widely available for most students and users. On the other hand, your instructor may have server-side scripting available. Verify with your instructor the action you are to use.

Between the <form> and </form> tags are the tags that create the body of the form and collect the data. These tags are <input>, <select>, and <textarea>. The most widely used is the **<input> tag**, which collects data from check boxes, radio buttons, single-line text fields, form/image buttons, and passwords. The **<select> tag** is used with list and pop-up menu boxes. The **<textarea>** tag collects the data from multi-line text fields.

If you are using Internet Explorer with Windows XP Service Pack 2 (SP2), Internet Explorer automatically blocks content such as form elements. Thus, for all instances in this project where pages containing forms are displayed in Internet Explorer, you must choose to "allow blocked content" by right-clicking the Information Bar and selecting the Allow Blocked Content command from the context menu, or modify the Internet Explorer security settings to allow form elements to display.

Copying Data Files to the Local Web Site

Your Data Disk contains files for Project 4. You use the Windows My Computer option to copy the Project 4 data files to your parks folder. The data files consist of two .htm files. See the inside back cover for instructions for downloading the Data Disk or see your instructor for information about accessing the files required for this book.

The DataFiles folder for this project is stored on Local Disk (C:). The location on your computer may be different. If necessary, verify with your instructor the location of the DataFiles folder. The following steps show how to copy the project data files to the parks local root folder.

To Copy Data Files to the Parks Web Site

1 Click the Start button on the Windows taskbar and then click My Computer.

2 Double-click Local Disk (C:) and then navigate to the location of the data files for Project 4.

3 Double-click the DataFiles folder, double-click the Proj04 folder, and then double-click the parks folder.

4 Hold down the SHIFT key and select the two data files. Right-click and click the Copy command.

5 Navigate back to the your name folder. Paste the two data files into the parks folder. Close the parks folder.

The data files are pasted into the Colorado Parks Web site folder (Figure 4-2).

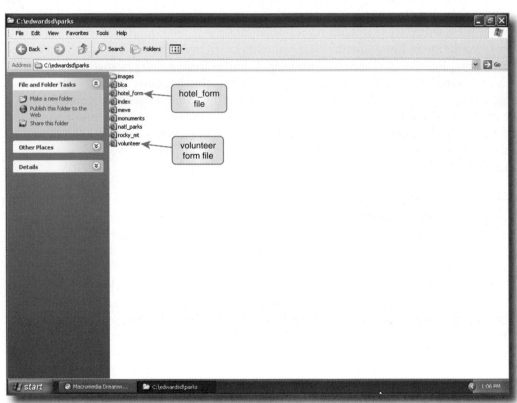

FIGURE 4-2

Starting Dreamweaver and Opening a Web Site

Each time you start Dreamweaver, it opens to the last site displayed when you closed the program. It, therefore, may be necessary for you to open the parks Web site. The **Files pop-up menu** in the Files panel lists sites you have defined. When you open the site, a list of the pages and subfolders within the site displays. The following steps illustrate how to start Dreamweaver and open the Colorado Parks Web site.

To Start Dreamweaver and Open the Colorado Parks Web Site

1 Click the Start button on the Windows taskbar.

2 Point to All Programs on the Start menu, point to Macromedia on the All Programs submenu, and then click Macromedia Dreamweaver 8 on the Macromedia submenu.

3 If necessary, display the panel groups.

4 Click the Files panel box arrow and then click Colorado Parks on the Files pop-up menu.

The Colorado Parks Web site hierarchy is displayed in the Files panel (Figure 4-3). The two new data files — volunteer.htm and hotel_form.htm — display in the list of files.

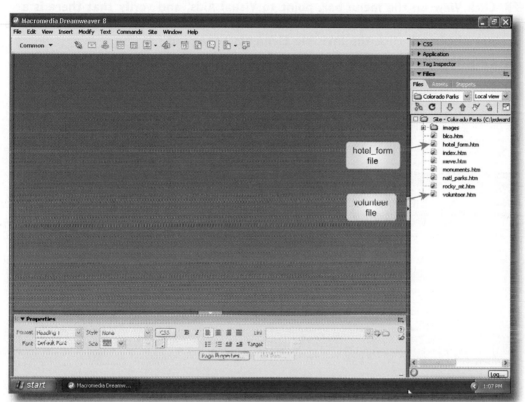

More About

File Order Display

The order in which files are displayed in the Files panel is determined by the View selected in Windows Explorer.

FIGURE 4-3

Form Design

Consistency in Web pages ties a Web site together. Using the same background image on all pages within the site is one way to achieve consistency. The background that has been used for the Colorado Parks Web site already has been added to the two HTML documents you copied from the DataFiles folder.

You open the hotel_form.htm document and then insert, center, and format a page heading. Next, you add a horizontal rule. Then you add a page title and save the Web page. The following steps show how to open the document and to insert and format the heading.

More About

Form Design

When designing a form, keep the form simple and to the point. Before you create the form, sketch it on paper. The layout should be uncomplicated and clear. For more information about form design, visit the Dreamweaver 8 More About Web page (scsite.com/dw8/more.htm) and then click Form Design.

To Insert and Format the Heading

1 Double-click hotel_form.htm in the Files panel.

2 Click the Document window, type Colorado National Parks **as the first line of the heading and then press** SHIFT+ENTER **to insert a line break. Type** Hotel Reservations Form **as the second heading line.**

3 Drag to select both lines of text, apply Heading 1, and then click the Align Center button in the Property inspector. Deselect the text and then press the ENTER key.

4 Click View on the menu bar, point to Visual Aids, and verify that there is a checkmark to the left of the Invisible Elements command. If the checkmark is not displayed, click the Invisible Elements command.

5 Click the Save button on the Standard toolbar.

6 Hide the panel groups and collapse the Property inspector.

The heading is centered and formatted (Figure 4-4). The Web page is saved in the parks folder, and the panel groups are hidden.

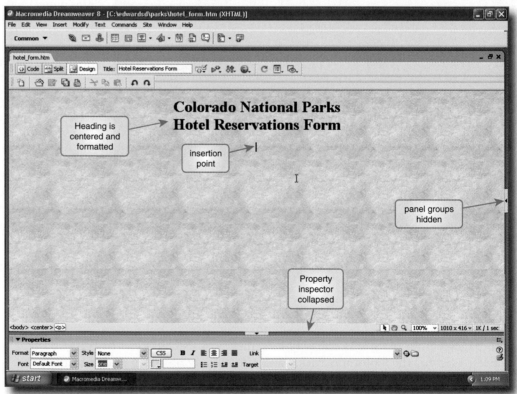

FIGURE 4-4

To add additional details to the Colorado Parks Web page, a horizontal rule is inserted below the title. Many Web designers use a horizontal rule to divide a Web page into sections and as a style element.

Horizontal Rules

A horizontal rule (or line) is useful for organizing information and visually separating text and objects. You can specify the width and height of the rule in pixels or as a percentage of the page size. The rule can be aligned to the left, center, or right, and you can add shading or draw the line in a solid color. These attributes are available in the Property inspector. The HTML tag for a horizontal rule is <hr>.

Inserting a Horizontal Rule

On the Hotel Reservations Form Web page, you insert a horizontal rule between the document heading and the form, as shown in the following steps. You change the width and the height of the rule, select no shading, and then center the rule.

To Insert a Horizontal Rule

1

• **Click Insert on the menu bar, point to HTML, and then point to Horizontal Rule (Figure 4-5).**

FIGURE 4-5

2

• **Click Horizontal Rule.**

The horizontal rule is inserted and centered below the heading. The attributes in the Property inspector change to those for the horizontal rule (Figure 4-6).

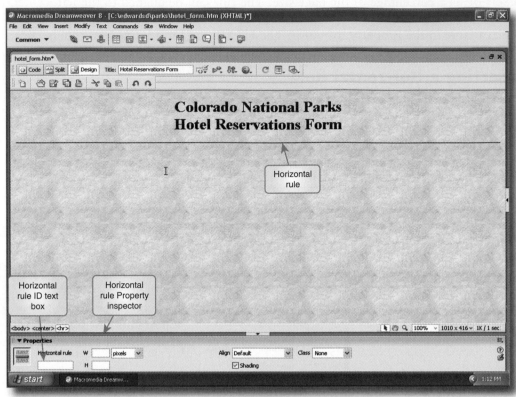

FIGURE 4-6

3

• **Click the Horizontal rule text box and type** horz_rule.

• **Click the W (Width) text box and type** 500. **Press the TAB key two times.**

• **Type** 10 **in the H (Height) text box.**

• **Click the Shading check box to deselect it.**

The width of the line is decreased, and the height of the line is increased. Shading is deselected (Figure 4-7).

4

• **Click at the end of the line and press the ENTER key. If necessary, click the Align Left button.**

• **Click the Save button.**

FIGURE 4-7

Forms and Web Pages

Web page designers create forms consisting of a collection of input fields so users can obtain useful information and enter data. When a user clicks the form Send or Submit button, the data is processed with a server-side script or is sent to a specified e-mail address. A typical form, such as the one created in this project, is composed of form objects. A **form object** can be a text box, check box, radio button, list, menu, or other buttons. Form objects are discussed in more detail later in this project.

Inserting a Form

Inserting a form is accomplished in the same manner as inserting a table or any other object in Dreamweaver. Simply position the insertion point where you want the form to start and then click the Form button on the Forms category Insert bar. Dreamweaver inserts the <form> and </form> tags into the source code and then displays a dotted red outline to represent the form in Design view. You cannot resize a form by dragging the borders. Rather, the form expands as objects are inserted into the form.

When viewed in a browser, the form outline does not display; therefore, no visible border exists to turn on or off. The following steps illustrate how to insert a form into the hotel_form.htm page.

More About

Dreamweaver and Forms

Dreamweaver makes it easy to add forms to your Web pages. The Forms category on the Insert bar contains all of the traditional form objects. When the object is entered into the form, Dreamweaver creates the JavaScript necessary for processing the form. For more information about Dreamweaver and forms, visit the Dreamweaver 8 More About Web page (scsite.com/dw8/more.htm) and then click Dreamweaver and Forms.

To Insert a Form

1

• **If necessary, display the Insert bar. Click the arrow to the right of the displayed category on the Insert bar and then point to Forms on the Insert bar pop-up menu.**

The Insert bar pop-up menu is displayed, and Forms is selected (Figure 4-8).

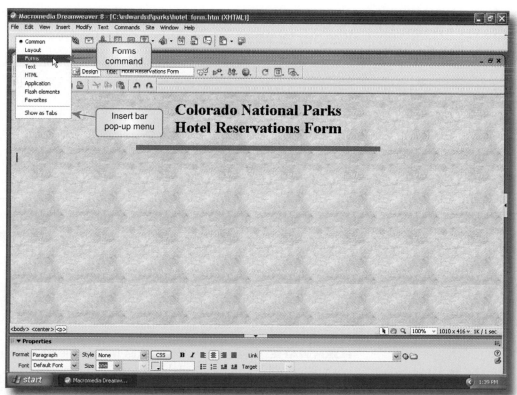

FIGURE 4-8

2

• **Click Forms and then click the Form button.**

The Forms category is displayed. The form is inserted into the Document window and is indicated by a dotted red outline. The Form Property inspector is displayed (Figure 4-9). The insertion point is blinking inside the dotted red outline.

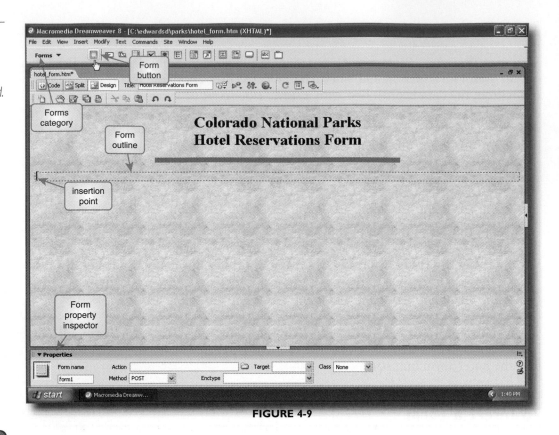

FIGURE 4-9

Property Inspector Form Properties

As you have seen, the Property inspector options change depending on the selected object. The following section describes the form-related features of the Property inspector shown in Figure 4-10.

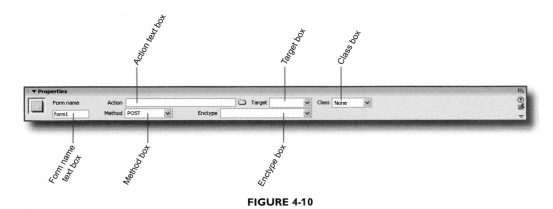

FIGURE 4-10

FORM NAME Naming a form makes it possible to reference or control the form with a scripting language, such as JavaScript or VBScript.

ACTION Contains the mailto address or specifies the URL to the dynamic page or script that will process the form.

TARGET Specifies the window or frame in which to display the data after processing if a script specifies that a new page should display. The four targets are _blank, _parent, _self, and _top. The _blank target opens the referenced link (or processed data) in a new browser window, leaving the current window untouched. The **_blank** target is the one most often used with a jump menu, which is discussed later in this project. The **_self** target opens the destination document in the same window as the one in which the form was submitted. The two other targets mostly are used with frames and are discussed in Project 7.

METHOD Indicates the method by which the form data is transferred to the server. The three options are POST, which embeds the form data in the HTTP request; GET, which appends the form data to the URL requesting the page; and **Default**, which uses the browser's default setting to send the form data to the server. Generally, the default is the GET method. The POST and GET methods were discussed earlier in this project.

ENCTYPE Specifies a **MIME (Multipurpose Internet Mail Extensions)** type for the data being submitted to the server so the server software will know how to interpret the data. The default is application/x-www-form-urlencode and typically is used in conjunction with the POST method. This default automatically encodes the form response with non-alphanumeric characters in hexadecimal format. The multipart/form-data MIME type is used with a form object that enables the user to upload a file. You can select one of these two values from the Enctype list box or manually enter a value in the Enctype list box. The text/plain value is useful for e-mail replies, but is not an option in the Enctype list box and must be entered manually. This value enables the data to be transmitted in a readable format instead of as one long string of data.

CLASS Sets style sheet attributes and/or attaches a style sheet to the current document.

Setting Form Properties

When naming the form and the form elements (discussed later in this project), use names that identify the form or form element. Be consistent with your naming conventions and do not use spaces or other special characters, except the underscore. This project uses lowercase letters to name the form and form elements. If you are using server-side scripting, be aware of and avoid reserved words that exist in the scripting language.

The following steps illustrate how to name the form and to set the other form properties, including using the mailto: action. Verify with your instructor that this is the correct action and that the form data is not to be processed with a server-side script.

More About

Interactive Forms

The mailto link is the easiest method for e-mailing form data. Generally, however, it is not recommended because many browsers do not recognize an e-mail address as a form's action. Furthermore, even if the browser accepts this attribute, the user's system and mail configuration may prevent this strategy from working. For more information about interactive forms, visit the Dreamweaver 8 More About Web page (scsite.com/dw8/more.htm) and then click Interactive Forms.

To Set the Form Properties

1

• **Double-click the Form name text box in the Property inspector. Type** hotel_form **and then press the TAB key.**

The form is named (Figure 4-11). The insertion point is blinking in the Action text box.

FIGURE 4-11

2

• **Type** mailto:
dedwards@parks.com **(use your own e-mail address).**

Your e-mail address is displayed in the Action text box (Figure 4-12).

FIGURE 4-12

3

• **Click the Target box arrow, select _self, and then press the TAB key.**

The insertion point moves to the Enctype box (Figure 4-13).

FIGURE 4-13

4

• **Type** text/plain **and press the ENTER key.**

The Enctype box displays text/plain (Figure 4-14).

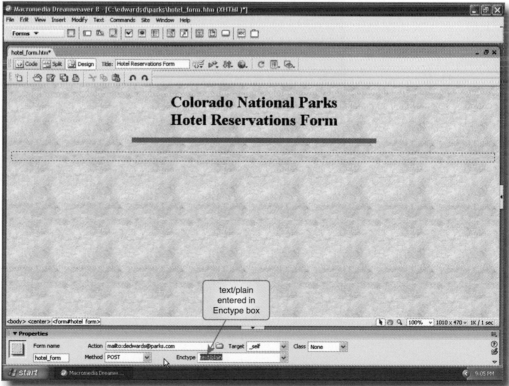

FIGURE 4-14

More About

Naming Forms

A form does not need a name to work, but a name is helpful if you use a Dreamweaver behavior or JavaScript to interact with the form.

Inserting a Table into a Form

Adding and lining up labels within a form sometimes can be a problem. The text field width for labels is measured in **monospace**, meaning that each character has the same width. Most regular fonts, however, are not monospaced; they are proportional. Two options to solve this problem are preformatted text and tables. To align labels properly using preformatted text requires the insertion of extra spaces. Using tables and text alignment, therefore, is a faster and easier method to use when creating a form.

The following steps show how to add an 11-row, 2-column table to the form.

To Insert a Table into a Form

1

• **Click inside the form (the dotted red outline).**

• **Click Insert on the menu bar and then point to Table.**

The Insert menu is displayed, and Table is selected (Figure 4-15).

FIGURE 4-15

2

• **Click Table.**

• **Type the following values in the Table dialog box: Rows -** 11, **Columns -** 2, **Table Width -** 75 **percent, Border thickness -** 4, **Cell padding -** 5, **Cell spacing -** 0, **and** Hotel reservation form for Colorado's four national parks **as the Summary text.**

The Table dialog box displays the new values (Figure 4-16).

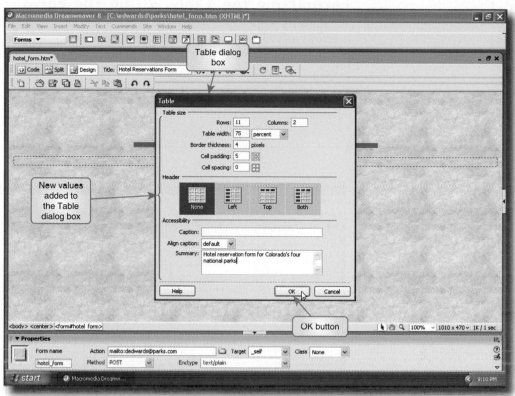

FIGURE 4-16

3

• **Click the OK button.**

• **Verify that the table is selected, click the Align box arrow in the Property inspector, and then select Center.**

The table is inserted into and centered in the form outline (Figure 4-17). The <table> tag is selected in the tag selector, and the table properties are displayed in the Property inspector.

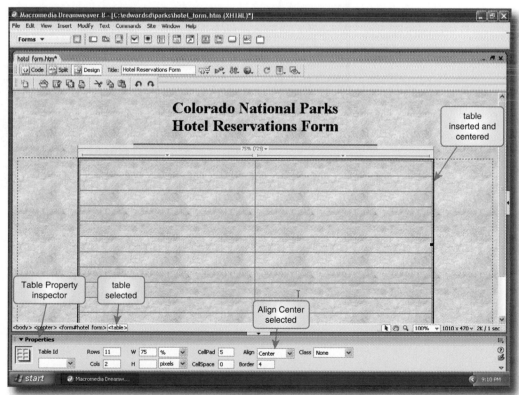

FIGURE 4-17

Other Ways

1. Click Table button on Common category on Insert bar

Formatting the Table within the Form

Adding formatting to a form creates a more attractive page. In this instance, formatting includes changing the column width, aligning the text for the labels in column 1 to the right, and changing the border color. When alignment is set to right or justified in a table cell, a dotted line displays within the cell. The following steps show how to add these formatting changes.

To Format the Form

1

• **Click the Table Id box, type** reservations **and then press the ENTER key.**

The table is named reservations (Figure 4-18).

FIGURE 4-18

2

• **Expand the Property inspector.**

• **If necessary, scroll up, click row 1, column 1, and then drag to select all of column 1. Click the W text box, type** 35%, **and then press the ENTER key.**

The column width is set to 35% (Figure 4-19).

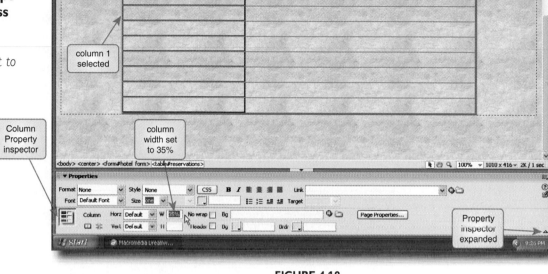

FIGURE 4-19

3

• **Click the Align Right button in the Property inspector.**

• **Click the <table> tag in the tag selector to deselect the column and to select the table. Click the Brdr color hexadecimal text box. Type** #993300 **and then press the ENTER key.**

• **Click the Save button on the Standard toolbar.**

The form is saved. The cells display dotted lines to indicate the right alignment. When text is entered into the table cells in column 1, the text will align to the right.
The table is selected, the Table Property inspector is displayed, and the form border color is changed (Figure 4-20).

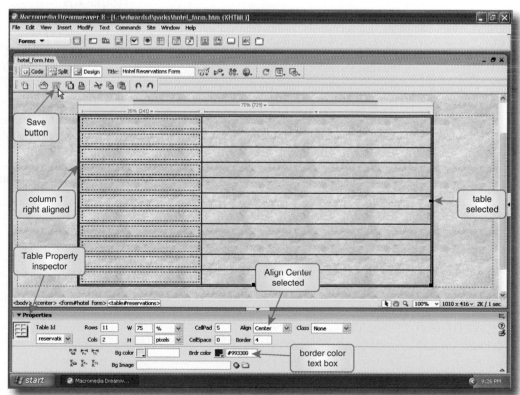

FIGURE 4-20

Form Objects

In Dreamweaver, data is entered through form input types called form objects. After you add a form to your Web page, you begin creating the form by adding form objects. Forms can contain various objects that enable user interaction and are the mechanisms that allow users to input data. Examples of form objects are text fields, check boxes, and radio buttons. Each form object should have a unique name, except the radio buttons within the same group. In that case, the radio buttons should share the same name.

The two steps used to insert a form field in a Web page are (1) to add the form field and any accompanying descriptive labels, and (2) to modify the properties of the form object. All Dreamweaver form objects are available through the Forms category on the Insert bar. Table 4-1 lists the button names and descriptions available on the Forms category (Figure 4-21).

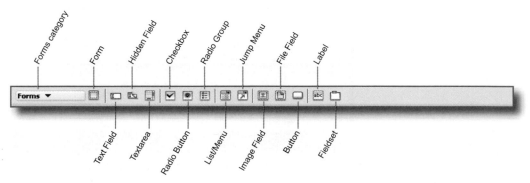

FIGURE 4-21

Table 4-1 Buttons on the Insert Bar Forms Category	
BUTTON NAME	DESCRIPTION
Form	Inserts a form into the Document window
Text Field	Accepts any type of alphanumeric text entry
Hidden Field	Stores information entered by a user and then uses that data within the site database
Textarea	Provides a multiline text entry field
Checkbox	Allows multiple responses within a single group of options and permits the user to select as many options as apply
Radio Button	Represents an exclusive choice; only one item in a group of buttons can be selected
Radio Group	Represents a group of radio buttons
List/Menu	List displays option values within a scrolling list that allows users to select multiple options; Menu displays the option values in a pop-up menu that allows users to select only a single item
Jump Menu	Special form of a pop-up menu that lets the viewer link to another document or file
Image Field	Creates a custom, graphical button
File Field	Allows users to browse to a file on their computers and upload the file as form data
Button	Performs actions when clicked; standard Submit and Reset buttons send data to the server and clear the form fields
Label	Provides a way to associate the text label for a field with the field structurally
Fieldset	Inserts a container tag for a logical group of form elements

Text Fields

A **text field** is a form object in which users enter a response. Forms support three types of text fields: single-line, multiple-line, and password. Input into a text field can consist of alphanumeric and punctuation characters. When you insert a text field into a form, the TextField Property inspector is displayed (Figure 4-22).

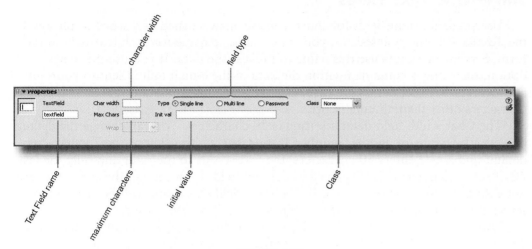

FIGURE 4-22

The following section describes the text field attributes for a single-line and password form. The multiple-line attributes are described later in this project.

TEXTFIELD Assigns a unique name to the form object.

CHAR WIDTH Specifies the maximum number of characters that can be displayed in the field.

MAX CHAR Specifies the maximum number of characters that can be entered into the field.

TYPE Designates the field as a single-line, multiple-line, or password field.

INIT VAL Assigns the value that is displayed in the field when the form first loads.

CLASS Establishes an attribute used with Cascading Style Sheets.

Typically, a **single-line text field** provides for a single word or short phrase response. A **password text field** is a single-line text box that contains special characters. When a user types in a password field, asterisks or bullets replace the text as a security precaution. Note, however, that passwords sent to a server using a password field are not encrypted and can be intercepted and read as alphanumeric text. For this reason, you always should provide encryption for data you want to keep secure. A **multiple-line text field** provides a larger text area in which to enter a response. The Property inspector for a multiple-line text field contains some minor differences than that shown in Figure 4-22. A multiple-line text field is discussed later in this project.

Inserting Text in a Form

You will notice as you insert form objects in a Web page that typically they contain no text label. **Labels** identify the type of data to be entered into the text field form object. Adding a descriptive label to the form that indicates the type of information requested provides a visual cue to the Web site visitors about the type of data they should type into the text box. Inserting text in a form is as simple as positioning the insertion point and then typing.

Single-Line Text Fields

Use single-line text fields for short, concise answers such as a word or phrase. In the TextField Property inspector, you enter a unique name for each text field in the form. Server-side scripts use this name to process the data. If you use the mailto option, the name is contained within the data in the e-mail that is sent to your e-mail address. Form object names are case sensitive and cannot contain spaces or special characters other than an underscore.

The Char width field default setting is 20 characters. You can change the default, however, by typing in another number. If the Char width is left as the 20-character default and a user enters 50 characters, the text scrolls to the right and only the last 20 of those characters are displayed in the text field. Even though the characters are not displayed, they are recognized by the form field object and will be sent to the server for processing or contained within the data if mailto is used.

Entering a value into the Max Chars field defines the size limit of the text field and is used to validate the form. If a user tries to exceed the limit, an alert is sounded. If the Max Chars field is left blank, users can enter any amount of text.

To display a default text value in a field, type the default text in the Init val text box. When the form is displayed in the browser, this text is displayed.

The following steps show how to add name, address, and e-mail single-line text boxes to the Hotel Reservations form.

To Add Descriptive Labels and Single-Line Text Fields to the Hotel Reservations Form

1

• **If necessary, scroll up and then click row 1, column 1.**

The insertion point aligns to the right in the cell (Figure 4-23).

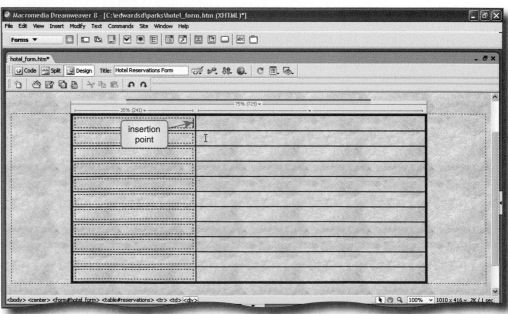

FIGURE 4-23

2

• **Type** Name **as the descriptive label and then press the TAB key.**

The insertion point displays in row 1, column 2 (Figure 4-24).

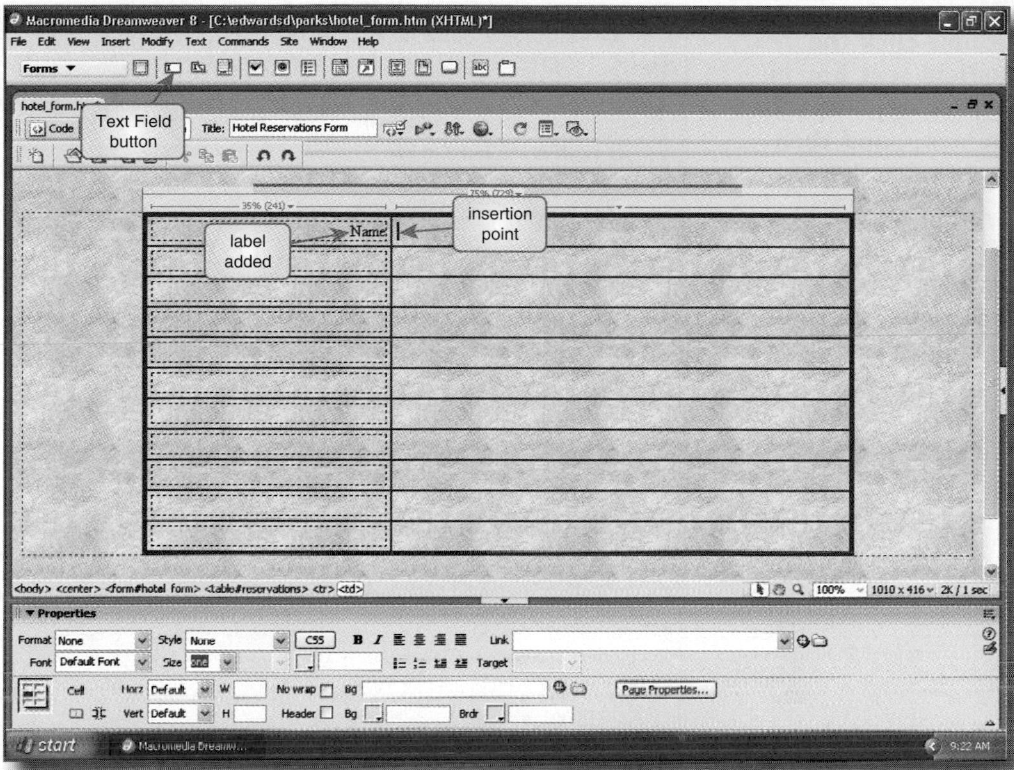

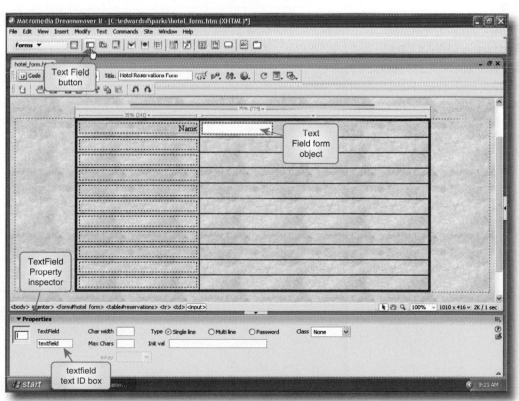

FIGURE 4-24

3

• **Click the Text Field button.**

A text field form object is inserted into the table (Figure 4-25). The Property inspector displays properties relative to the text field.

FIGURE 4-25

4

• **Double-click the TextField text box in the Property inspector, type** name, **and then press the TAB key.**

• **Type** 50 **in the Char width text box and then press the TAB key. If necessary, click Single line.**

The text field expands to a character width of 50 (Figure 4-26).

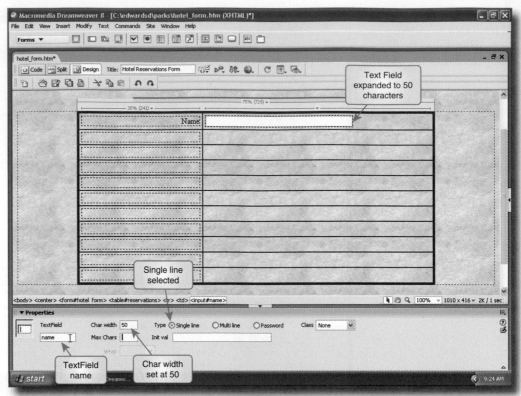

FIGURE 4-26

5

• **Click row 2, column 1, type** Address, **and then press the TAB key.**

• **Click the Text Field button on the Forms category.**

The Address label is displayed in row 2, column 1, and the text field form object is inserted into the table (Figure 4-27). The Property inspector displays TextField properties.

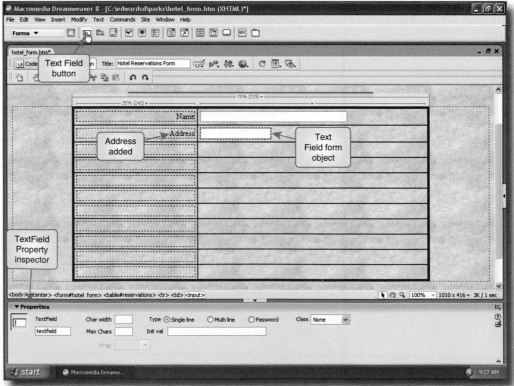

FIGURE 4-27

6

• **If necessary, scroll down. Double-click the TextField text box in the Property inspector, type** address**, and then press the TAB key.**

• **Type** 50 **in the Char width text box and then press the TAB key. If necessary, click Single line.**

The text field expands to a character width of 50 (Figure 4-28).

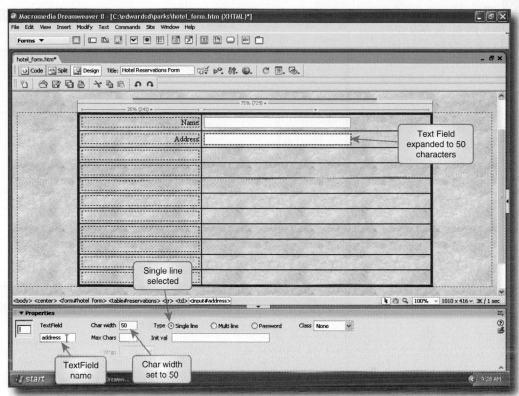

FIGURE 4-28

7

• **Click row 3, column 1, and then type** City**. Press the TAB key.**

• **Click the Text Field button on the Forms category.**

• **Type** city **as the TextField name.**

• **Type** 50 **in the Char width text box and then press the TAB key. Ensure Single line is selected.**

The label, City, is displayed in row 3, column 1. The text field expands to a character width of 50 (Figure 4-29).

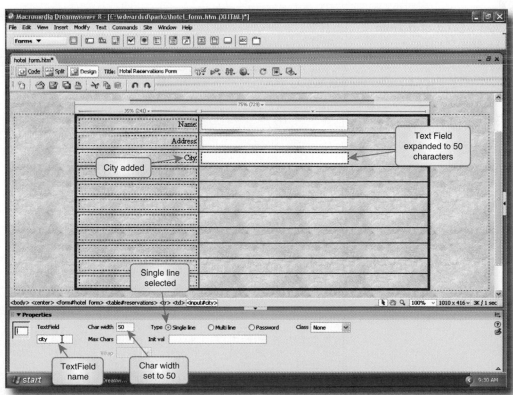

FIGURE 4-29

8

• **Click row 4, column 1. Type** State/Zip Code **as the label and then press the TAB key.**

The label, State/Zip Code, is displayed in row 4, column 1, and the insertion point is blinking in row 4, column 2 (Figure 4-30).

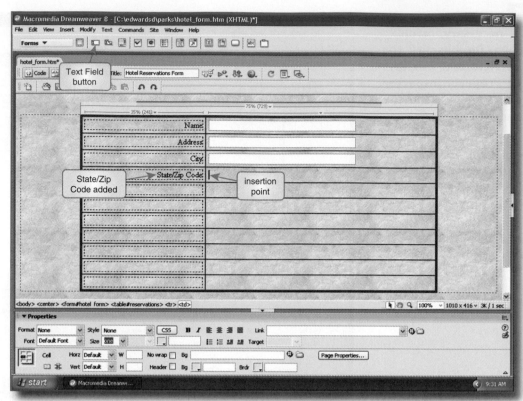

FIGURE 4-30

9

• **Type** State **and then press the SPACEBAR.**

The descriptive label for State is displayed (Figure 4-31).

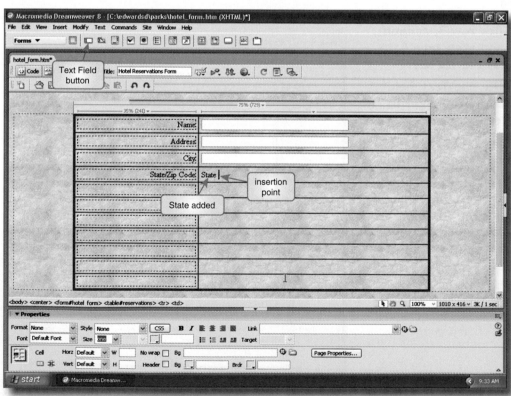

FIGURE 4-31

10

• **Click the Text Field button. Type** state **as the TextField name in the Property inspector.**

• **Type** 2 **for the Char width and Max Chars values. Press the TAB key. Ensure Single line is selected.**

The TextField name is displayed as state, and the Char width and Max Chars values are set to 2 (Figure 4-32).

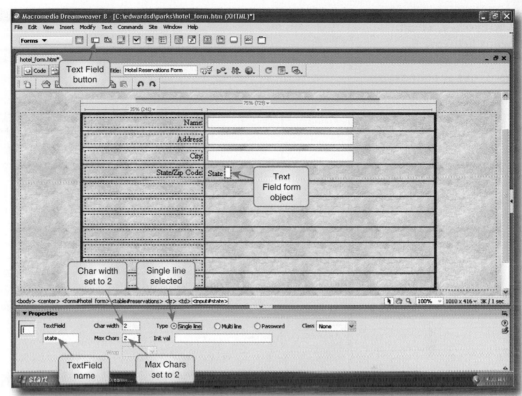

FIGURE 4-32

11

• **Click to the right of the State form object and then press the SPACEBAR. Type** Zip Code **and then press the SPACEBAR.**

• **Click the Text Field button.**

• **Type** zip **as the TextField name.**

• **Type** 10 **for the Char width and Max Chars values and then press the TAB key. Ensure Single line is selected.**

Zip Code is displayed as the descriptive label. The Char width and Max Chars values are set to 10 (Figure 4-33).

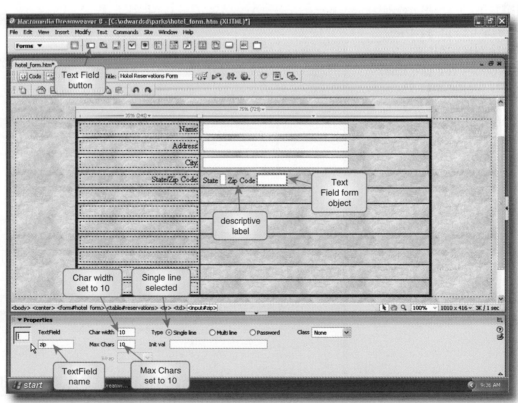

FIGURE 4-33

12

• **If necessary, scroll down. Click row 5, column 1, and then type** E-mail address.

• **Press the TAB key and then click the Text Field button.**

The descriptive label for the e-mail address is displayed, and the text field form object is added to the document (Figure 4-34).

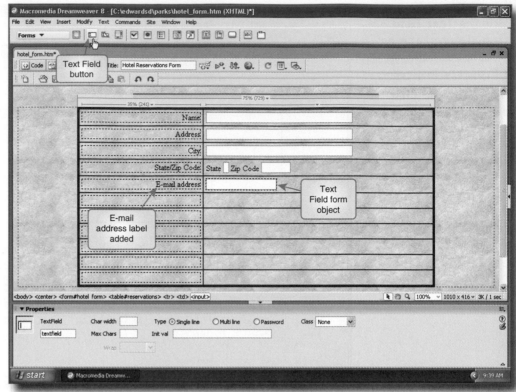

FIGURE 4-34

13

• **Type** email **as the TextField name.**

• **Type** 45 **for the Char width value and then press the ENTER key. Ensure Single line is selected.**

The text field is named, and the size of the text box form object is adjusted (Figure 4-35).

14

• **Press CTRL+S to save the page.**

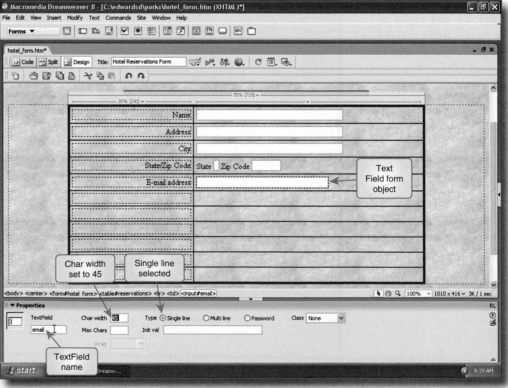

FIGURE 4-35

Other Ways

1. On Insert menu, point to Form, click Text Field

Check Boxes

Check boxes allow the Web visitor to click a box to toggle a value to either yes or no. They frequently are used to enable the visitor to select as many of the listed options as desired. Figure 4-36 displays the Property inspector for a check box. Just like a text field, each check box should have a unique name. The Checked value text box contains the information you want to send to the script or include in the mailto information to identify the data. For the Initial state, the default is Unchecked. Click Checked if you want an option to appear selected when the form first loads in the browser. The following steps illustrate how to add three check boxes to the Hotel Reservations form.

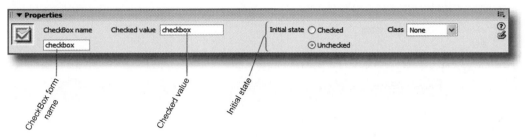

FIGURE 4-36

To Add Check Boxes

1

• **Click row 6, column 1, type** Hotels, **and then press the TAB key.**

• **Click the Checkbox button on the Forms category.**

Hotels is displayed as the descriptive label, and a check box is added to the form (Figure 4-37). The Property inspector changes to display the Checkbox properties.

FIGURE 4-37

2

• **Type** hotel1 **as the Checkbox name.**

• **Press the TAB key and then type** black_canyon **in the Checked value text box. Press the ENTER key.**

The properties for the first check box are displayed (Figure 4-38).

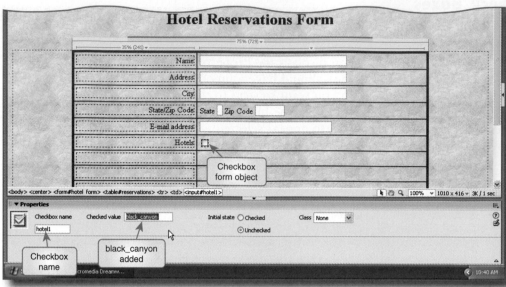

FIGURE 4-38

3

• **Click to the right of the check box form object and then press SHIFT+ENTER to add a line break.**

The insertion point is positioned below the first check box (Figure 4-39).

FIGURE 4-39

4

• **Click the Checkbox button.**

• **Type** hotel2 **as the Checkbox name. Press the TAB key and then type** mesa_verde **in the Checked value text box. Press the ENTER key.**

The second check box is added to the form, and the properties for the second check box are displayed (Figure 4-40).

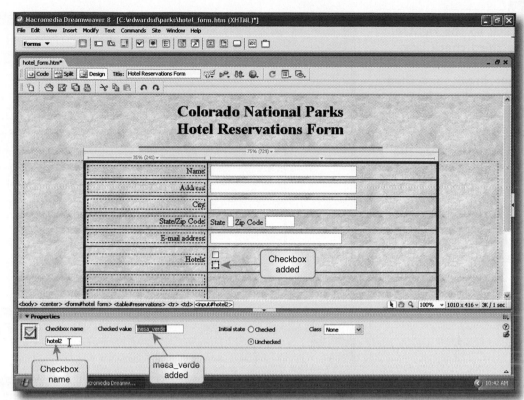

FIGURE 4-40

5

• **Click to the right of the second check box, press SHIFT+ENTER to add a line break, and then click the Checkbox button on the Forms category.**

• **Type** hotel3 **as the Checkbox name.**

• **Press the TAB key and then type** rocky_mountains **in the Checked value text box. Press the ENTER key.**

The third check box is added and the properties for the third check box are displayed (Figure 4-41).

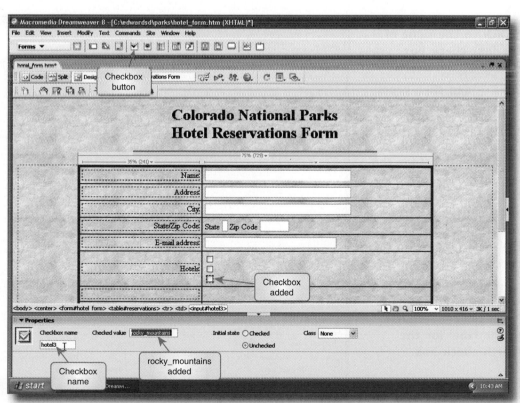

FIGURE 4-41

6

• **Click to the right of the third check box, press SHIFT+ENTER to add a line break, and then click the Checkbox button on the Forms category.**

• **Type** hotel4 **as the Checkbox name.**

• **Press the TAB key and then type** sand_dunes **in the Checked value text box. Press the ENTER key.**

The properties for the fourth check box are displayed (Figure 4-42).

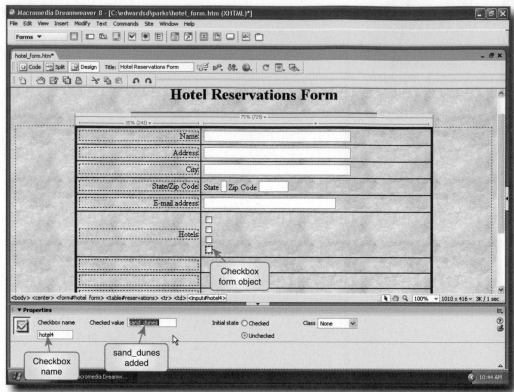

FIGURE 4-42

7

• **Click to the right of the first check box.**

• **Type** Black Canyon Royale **and then press the DOWN ARROW key.**

• **Type** Mesa Verde Pueblo **as the descriptive label for the second check box, press the DOWN ARROW key, and then type** Rocky Mountains Station **as the label for the third check box.**

• **Press the DOWN ARROW key, and then type** Sand Dunes Central **as the label for the fourth check box.**

The descriptive labels are entered for all four check boxes (Figure 4-43).

• **Click the Save button on the Standard toolbar.**

FIGURE 4-43

List/Menu

Another way to provide form field options to your Web site visitor is with lists and menus. These options provide many choices within a limited space. A **list** provides a scroll bar with up and down arrows that lets a user scroll the list, whereas a menu contains a pop-up list. Multiple selections can be made from a list, while users can select only one item from a menu. The menu option is discussed later in this project. Figure 4-44 illustrates the Property inspector for a list.

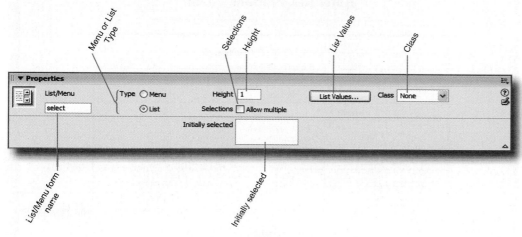

FIGURE 4-44

LIST/MENU Assigns a name to the list or menu.

TYPE Designates if the form object is a pop-up menu or a scrolling list.

HEIGHT Specifies the number of lines that display in the form; the default is 1.

SELECTIONS Designates if the user can select more than one option; not available with the menu option.

LIST VALUES Opens the List Values dialog box.

INITIALLY SELECTED Contains a list of available items from which the user can select.

CLASS An attribute used with Cascading Style Sheets.

As with all other form objects, the list should be named. You control the height of the list by specifying a number in the Height box. You can elect to show one item at a time or show the entire list. If you display the entire list, the scroll bar is not displayed. Selecting the Selections check box allows the user to make multiple selections. Clicking the List Values button opens the List Values dialog box so you can add items to a list or pop-up menu or remove them. These added items are displayed in the Initially selected box. Each item in the list has a label and a value. The label represents the text that appears in the list, and the value is sent to the processing application if the item is selected. If no value is specified, the label is sent to the processing application instead.

The following steps show how to add a scrolling list to the Hotel Reservations form.

To Create a Scrolling List

1

• **Click row 7, column 1. Type** Accommodations **and then press the TAB key. Click the List/Menu button on the Forms category.**

The label, Accommodations, is entered, and the List/Menu form object is inserted. The Property inspector displays the List/Menu properties (Figure 4-45).

FIGURE 4-45

2

• **Type** accommodations **as the List/Menu name.**

• **Click List in the Type options.**

• **Type** 2 **in the Height box.**

• **Click the Selections check box to allow multiple selections.**

The list is named, the height is set to 2, and Allow multiple selections is selected (Figure 4-46).

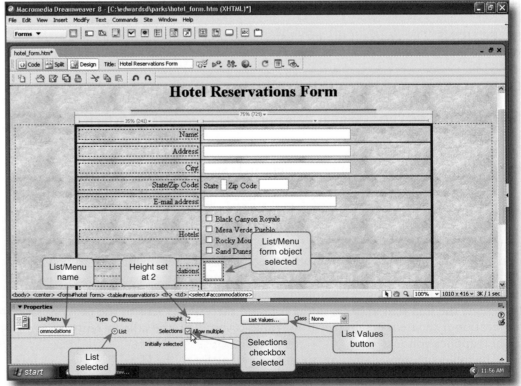

FIGURE 4-46

3

• **Click the List Values button.**

The List Values dialog box is displayed (Figure 4-47). The insertion point is blinking in the Item Label column.

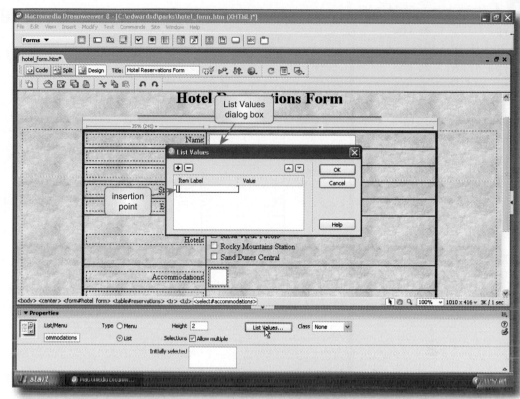

FIGURE 4-47

4

• **Type** Single **as the first Item Label, press the TAB key, and then type** single **as the Value.**

• **Press the TAB key.**

A second line is added to the Item Label list (Figure 4-48).

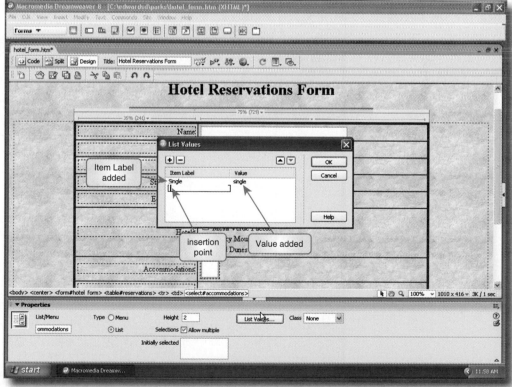

FIGURE 4-48

5

• **Type** Double **as the second Item Label.**

• **Type** double **as the Value and then press the TAB key.**

• **Type** Suite **as the third Item Label.**

• **Type** suite **as the Value and then press the TAB key.**

• **Type** Luxury Suite **as the fourth Item Label.**

• **Type** luxury_suite **as the Value.**

The items for the list are added to the List Values dialog box (Figure 4-49).

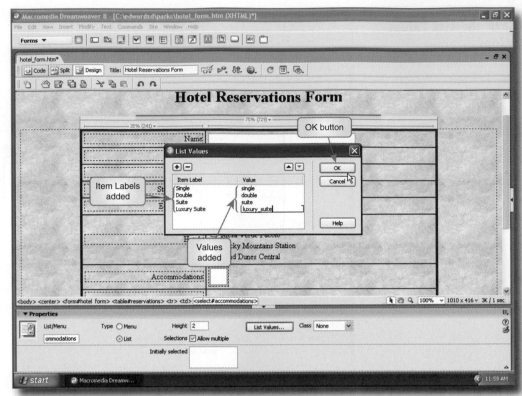

FIGURE 4-49

6

• **Click the OK button.**

The list is displayed in the Initially selected box in the Property inspector (Figure 4-50).

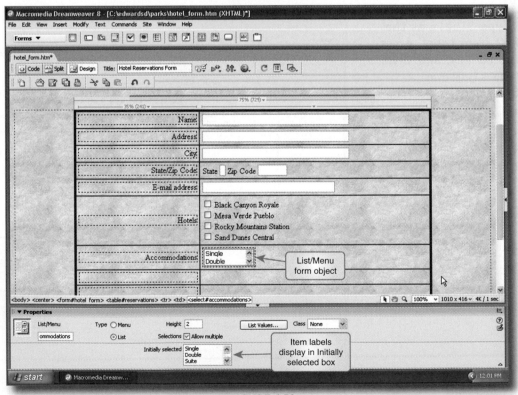

FIGURE 4-50

7

• **Click Single in the Initially selected box in the Property inspector.**

Single is designated as the default item in the list (Figure 4-51).

• **Click the Save button on the Standard toolbar.**

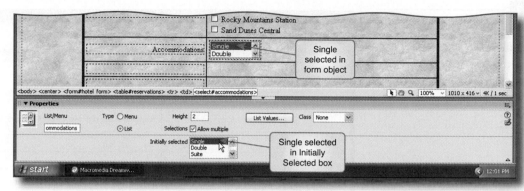

FIGURE 4-51

Other Ways

1. On Insert menu, point to Form, click List/Menu

Pop-Up Menus

You can offer your Web site visitors a range of choices by using a pop-up menu. This type of menu (also called a drop-down menu) lets a user select a single item from a list of many options. A **pop-up menu** is useful when you have a limited amount of space because it occupies only a single line of vertical space in the form. Only one option choice is visible when the menu form object displays in the browser. Clicking a down arrow displays the entire list. The user then clicks one of the menu items to make a choice. The following steps illustrate how to create a pop-up menu.

To Create a Pop-Up Menu

1

• **If necessary, scroll down and then click row 8, column 1.**

• **Type** Number of nights **and then press the TAB key.**

• **Click the List/Menu button on the Forms category.**

The descriptive label for the pop-up menu is added to the form, and the List/Menu form object is displayed. The Property inspector changes to reflect the selected form object (Figure 4-52).

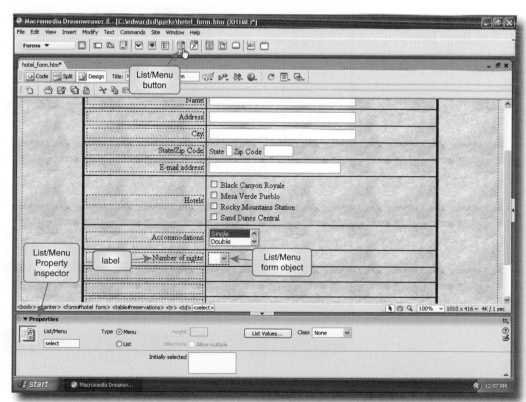

FIGURE 4-52

2

• **Type** nights **in the List/Menu text box to name the pop-up menu.**

The pop-up menu is named (Figure 4-53).

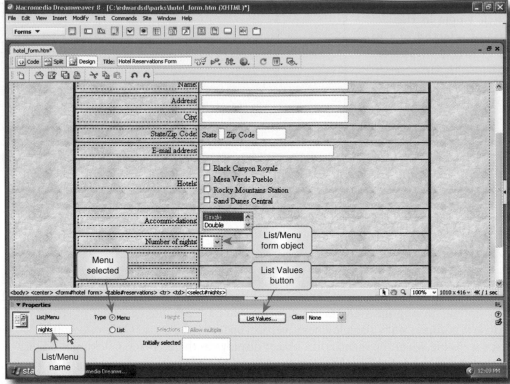

FIGURE 4-53

3

• **Click the List Values button. In the List Values dialog box, type** 1 **as the Item Label, press the TAB key, and then type** 1 **for the Value.**

• **Press the TAB key.**

The List Values dialog box is displayed (Figure 4-54). The Item Label and Value are entered.

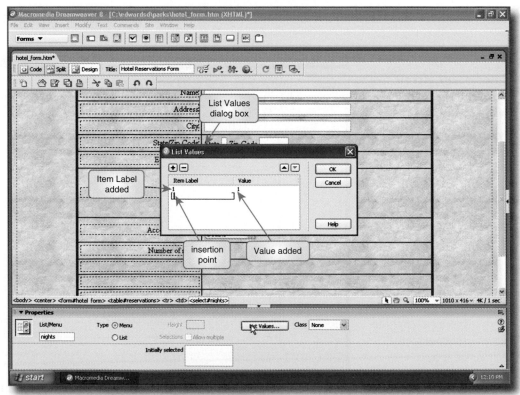

FIGURE 4-54

4

• Repeat Step 3, incrementing the number each time by 1 in the Item Label and Value fields, until the number 7 is added to the Item Label field and the Value field.

The List Values dialog box displays Item Label and Value field numbers (Figure 4-55).

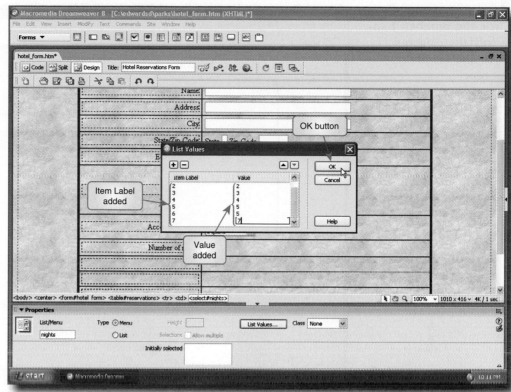

FIGURE 4-55

5

• Click the OK button.

The numbers display in the Initially selected box (Figure 4-56).

FIGURE 4-56

6

• **Click the number 1 in the Initially selected box in the Property inspector.**

The number 1 displays in the List/Menu form object as the default value (Figure 4-57).

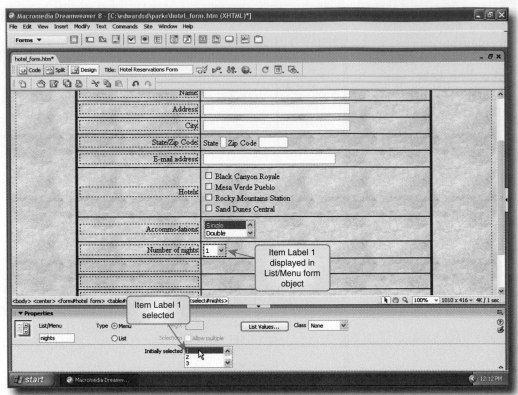

FIGURE 4-57

Jump Menus

A **jump menu** is a special type of pop-up menu that provides options that link to documents or files. You can create links to documents on your Web site, links to documents on other Web sites, e-mail links, links to graphics, or links to any other file type that can be opened in a browser. A jump menu can contain three basic components:

- An optional menu selection prompt: This could be a category description for the menu items or instructions, such as Choose one.
- A required list of linked menu items: When the user chooses an option, a linked document or file is opened.
- An optional Go button: With a Go button, the user makes a selection from the menu, and the new page loads when the Go button is clicked. Without a Go button, the new page loads as soon as the user makes a selection from the menu.

The following steps illustrate how to add a jump menu with a link to a Web site for each of the four national parks. The menu will contain a Choose one selection prompt, and the linked Web site will open in the main window.

To Insert a Jump Menu

1

• **Click row 9, column 1, type** Links, **and then press the TAB key.**

The label for the jump menu is inserted in the form (Figure 4-58).

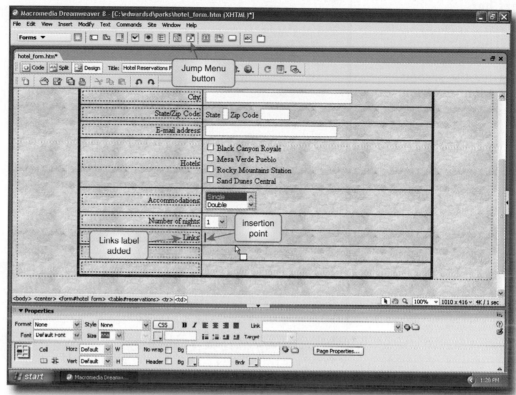

FIGURE 4-58

2

• **Click the Jump Menu button.**

• **Type** Choose one **in the Text text box and then click the Plus (+) button.**

The Insert Jump Menu dialog box is displayed (Figure 4-59). The text, Choose one, is added as the first menu item.

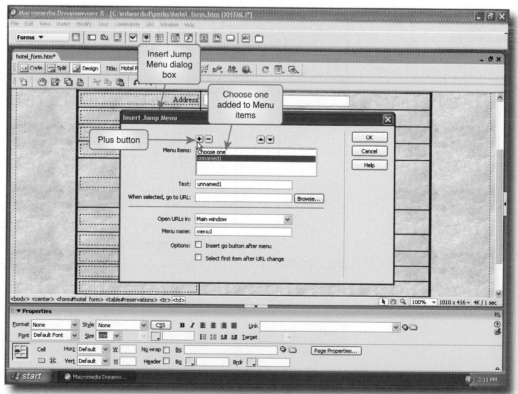

FIGURE 4-59

3

• **Double-click the Text text box.**

• **Type** Black Canyon of the Gunnison National Park **as the text for the second menu item and then press the TAB key.**

Black Canyon of the Gunnison National Park is added as the text for the second menu item (Figure 4-60). The insertion point is blinking in the When selected, go to URL text box.

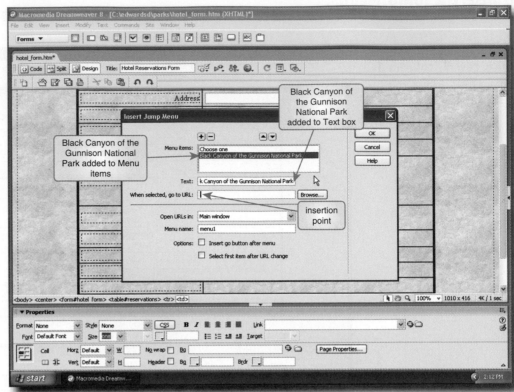

FIGURE 4-60

4

• **Type** http://www.nps.gov/blca **and then point to the Plus button.**

The URL for the Black Canyon of the Gunnison National Park Web site is added to the Insert Jump Menu dialog box (Figure 4-61).

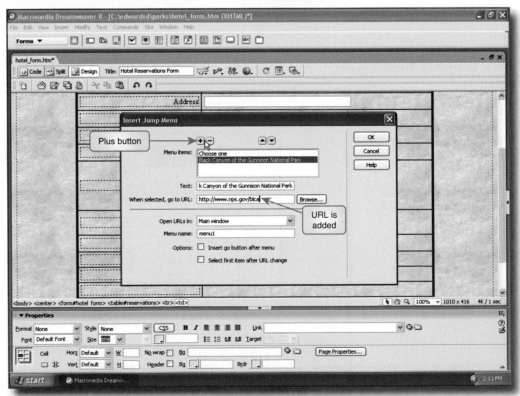

FIGURE 4-61

5

• **Click the Plus button, double-click the Text text box, type** Great Sand Dunes National Park **as the entry, and then press the TAB key.**

• **Type** http://www.nps.gov/grsa **and then point to the Plus button.**

Great Sand Dunes National Park is added as the third menu item, and the URL for the Great Sand Dunes National Park Web site is added to the Insert Jump Menu dialog box (Figure 4-62).

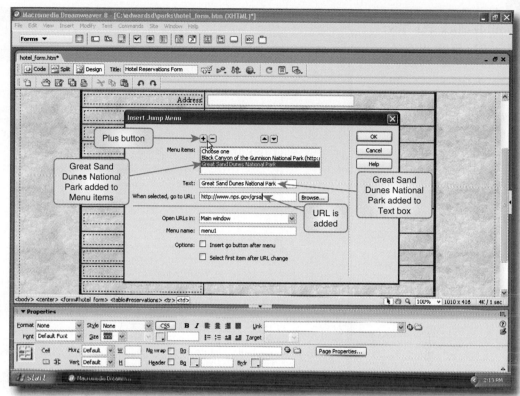

FIGURE 4-62

6

• **Click the Plus button, double-click the Text text box, type** Mesa Verde National Park **as the entry, and then press the TAB key.**

• **Type** http://www.nps.gov/meve **and click the Plus button.**

Mesa Verde National Park is added as the fourth menu item, and the URL for the Mesa Verde National Park Web site is added to the Insert Jump Menu dialog box (Figure 4-63).

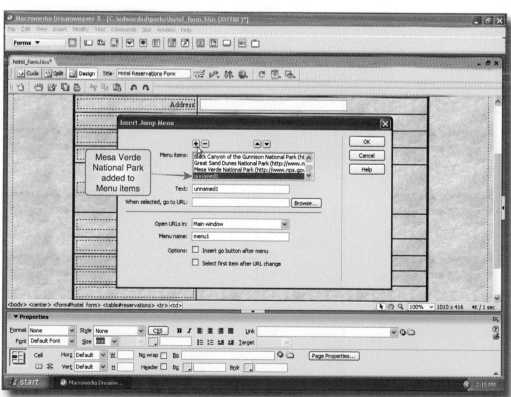

FIGURE 4-63

7

• **Double-click the Text text box, type** Rocky Mountain National Park **as the entry, and then press the TAB key.**

• **Type** http://www.nps.gov/romo **for the link.**

Rocky Mountain National Park is added as the fourth menu item, and the URL for the Rocky Mountain National Park Web site is added to the Insert Jump Menu dialog box (Figure 4-64).

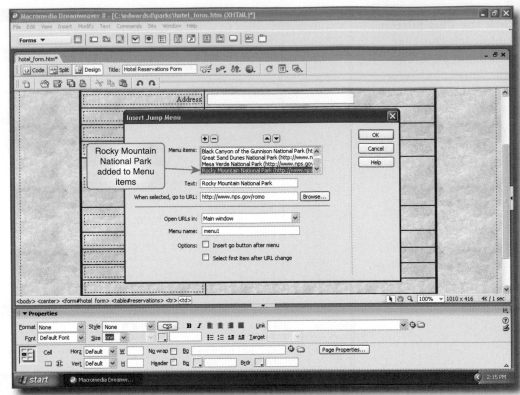

FIGURE 4-64

8

• **Double-click in the Menu name text box and type** park_web_sites.

• **Click the Select first item after URL change check box.**

The menu is named and the option Select first item after URL change is checked (Figure 4-65).

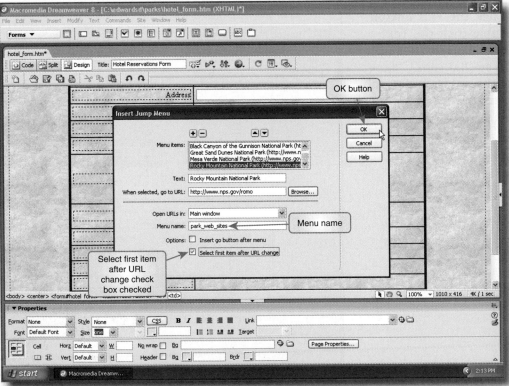

FIGURE 4-65

9

• **Click the OK button.**

• **Click Choose one in the Initially selected box in the Property inspector.**

• **Click the Save button on the Standard toolbar.**

The jump menu is added to the form and is completed (Figure 4-66).

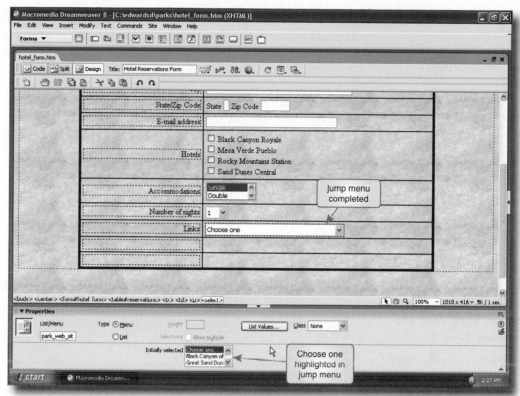

FIGURE 4-66

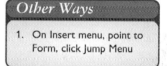

Other Ways

1. On Insert menu, point to Form, click Jump Menu

Textarea Text Fields

Earlier in this project, you added several single-line text field form objects to the Hotel Reservations form. A second type of text field is the textarea form object, which supports multiline objects. The Property inspector settings for the textarea text field are similar to those for single-line text fields except you can specify the maximum number of lines the user can enter and specify the wrap attributes. The Property inspector for a textarea text field is shown in Figure 4-67.

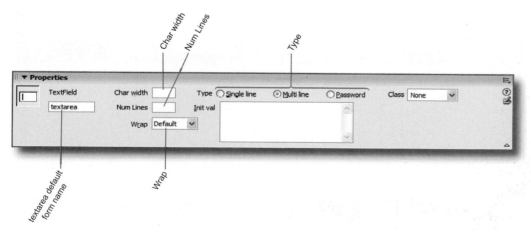

FIGURE 4-67

The Wrap pop-up menu in the Property inspector enables the Web page designer to select one of four options: Off, Default, Virtual, or Physical. Selecting **Off** or **Default** prevents the text from wrapping to the next line and requires the user to press the ENTER key to move the insertion point to the next line. **Virtual** limits word wrap to the text area. If the user's input exceeds the right boundary of the text area, the text wraps to the next line. When data is submitted for processing, however, it is submitted as one string of data. **Physical** sets word wrap in the text area and applies it to the data when it is submitted for processing.

An initial value can be added to the Init val box. When the user clicks the textarea text field, this initial value is highlighted and then deleted when the user begins to enter text. The following steps illustrate how to add a multiline text field to create a comments text area in your Hotel Reservations form.

To Add a Textarea Text Field

1

• **If necessary, scroll down. Click row 10, column 1.**

• **Type** Comments **and then press the TAB key.**

• **Click the Textarea button on the Forms category.**

The label is inserted, and the textarea form object is added to the form (Figure 4-68).

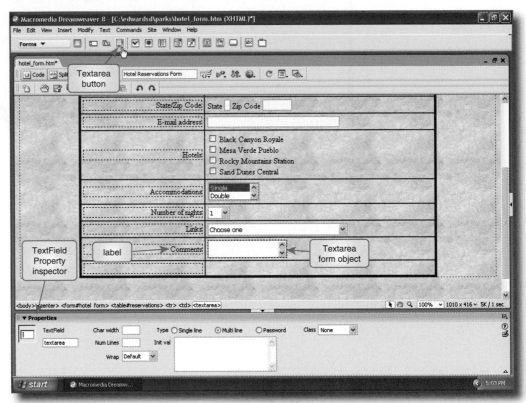

FIGURE 4-68

2

• **Type** comments **as the name for the TextField.**

• **Press the** TAB **key and type** 50 **for the Char width value. Press the** TAB **key and type** 4 **for the Num Lines value.**

• **Click the Init val box, type** Please add your comments **as the entry.**

• **Verify that Multi line is selected.**

• **Click the textarea in the form to display the initial value.**

• **Click the Save button on the Standard toolbar.**

The form is named, the character width and number of lines are set, and an initial value is entered (Figure 4-69).

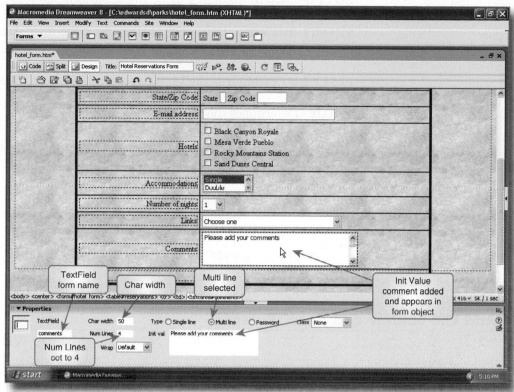

FIGURE 4-69

Form Buttons

Form buttons control form operations. HTML provides three basic types of form buttons: Submit, Reset, and Command. Submit and Reset buttons are standard features of almost every form. When the user presses the **Submit button**, the data entered into a form is sent to a server for processing or forwarded to an e-mail address. In some instances, the data is edited by JavaScript or other code prior to processing. The **Reset button** clears all the fields in the form. You also can assign to a **Command button** other processing tasks that you have defined in a script. For example, a Command button might calculate the total cost of a hotel room for a week. Command buttons require that additional code be added using Code view. The Button name Property inspector is displayed in Figure 4-70.

Other Ways

1. On Insert menu, point to Form, click Textarea

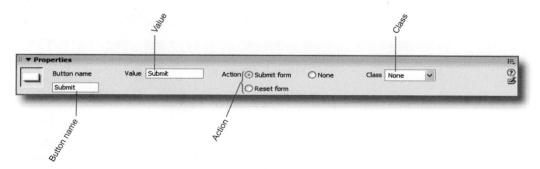

FIGURE 4-70

BUTTON NAME Assigns a name to the button. Submit and Reset are reserved names.

SUBMIT BUTTON Tells the form to submit the form data to the processing application or script or to send the data to an e-mail address.

RESET BUTTON Tells the form to reset all the form fields to their original values.

VALUE Determines the text that appears on the button.

ACTION Determines what happens when the button is clicked and how the data is to be processed. Form processing was discussed earlier in this project. The three processing options are to submit the contents of the form, to clear the contents of the form, or to do nothing.

CLASS An attribute used with Cascading Style Sheets.

The following steps illustrate how to add the Submit and Reset buttons to the Hotel Reservations form.

To Add the Submit and Reset Buttons

1

• If necessary, scroll down and then click row 11, column 1. (Figure 4-71).

FIGURE 4-71

2

• **Click the Button button on the Forms category.**

The Submit button form object is added to the form, and the Property inspector displays the Submit button attributes (Figure 4-72).

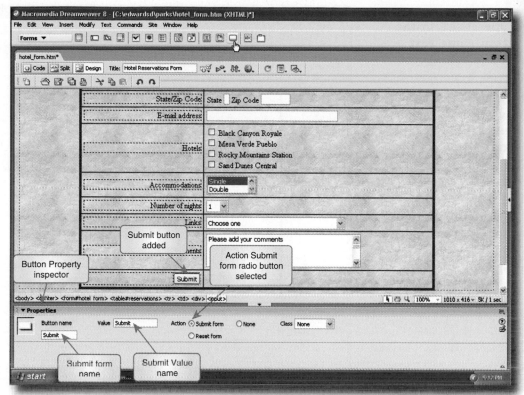

FIGURE 4-72

3

• **Click row 11, column 2, and then click the Button button on the Forms category.**

The Submit button form object is added to the form, and the Property inspector displays the Submit button attributes (Figure 4-73).

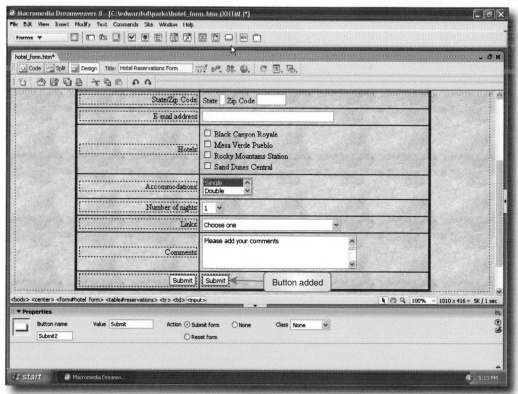

FIGURE 4-73

4

• **Type** reset **in the Button name text box and then press the TAB key.**

• **Type** Reset **in the Value text box and then click Reset form in the Action area.**

The button is renamed Reset, and the Reset form object is selected (Figure 4-74).

• **Click the Save button on the Standard toolbar.**

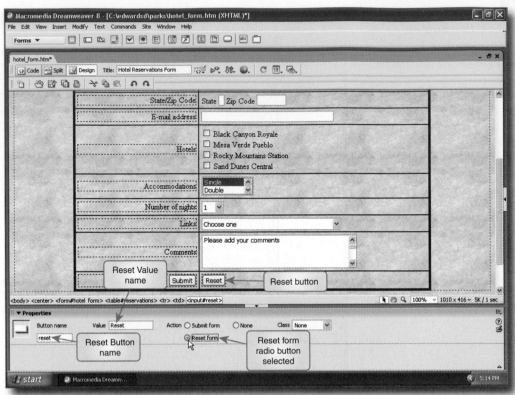

FIGURE 4-74

Radio Buttons and Radio Button Groups

Radio buttons provide a set of options from which the user can select only one button. Clicking a second button automatically deselects the first choice. Each button in a form consists of a radio button and a corresponding descriptive label. In Dreamweaver, you can insert radio buttons one at a time or insert a radio button group. When you insert an individual radio button, the Property inspector shown in Figure 4-75 is displayed. In the Property inspector's Radio Button text box, type a descriptive name. If you are inserting individual radio buttons to create a group, you must label each button. In the Checked value text box, enter the value you want sent to the server-side script or application when a user selects this radio button. For the Initial state, click Checked if you want an option to appear selected when the form first loads in the browser.

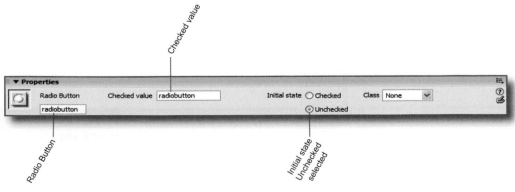

FIGURE 4-75

A radio button group is a commonly used option. If you are adding multiple radio buttons to a form, each set of radio buttons must have a unique name. When you click the Radio Group button on the Forms category, the Radio Group dialog box is displayed. Radio button groups are discussed later in this project.

Form Objects, the Label Button, and Accessibility

So far, when you added a form object to a page, you also added a descriptive label to identify the object. Traditionally, this is the way most Web page authors label form objects. The current HTML specifications, however, provide the <label> tag. This tag adds functionality to the form object by associating the descriptive label for the form object directly with that object. This is particularly helpful for the users of speech-based browsers.

The Insert bar Forms category contains a Label button. To add a label, select the specific form object to which you want to associate the label, and then click the Label button. When you click a radio button, for instance, and then click the Label button, Code view is displayed. You then manually type the descriptive text between the <label> and </label> tags. Similarly, Dreamweaver does not provide a Property inspector for labels, so any editing of labels is done in Code view.

Manual editing of the <label> tag can be time-consuming and error-prone, but Dreamweaver provides an alternative with the Accessibility options for form objects. When the Accessibility option for form objects is enabled, Dreamweaver displays the Input Tag Accessibility Attributes dialog box (Figure 4-76). Table 4-2 on the next page contains a description of the options in this dialog box. Recall that Accessibility options are turned on by clicking Edit on the menu bar and then selecting Preferences. In the Preferences dialog box, click the Accessibility category and then click the check box for Form objects. Appendix B contains an expanded discussion of accessibility options.

Q & A

Q: Why would I use the <label> tag?

A: Use the <label> tag to associate any form element with specific text to make it available for screen readers.

More About

Customizing Forms

Some organizations develop a template form for use throughout their Web sites. The Web site developer then uses this template to design a custom form for a particular need. For more information about customizing Dreamweaver forms, visit the Dreamweaver 8 More About Web page (scsite.com/dw8/more/more.htm) and then click **Customizing Forms**.

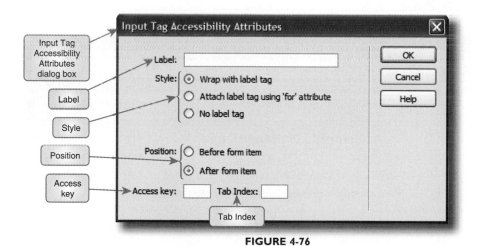

FIGURE 4-76

Table 4-2 Input Tag Accessibility Attributes

ATTRIBUTE NAME	DESCRIPTION
Label	The descriptive text that identifies the form object.
Style	Provides three options for the \<label> tag: *Wrap with label tag* wraps a label tag around the form item. *Attach label tag using 'for' attribute* allows the user to associate a label with a form element, even if the two are in different table cells. *No label tag* turns off the Accessibility option.
Position	Determines the placement of the label text in relation to the form object — before or after the form object.
Access key	Selects the form object in the browser using a keyboard shortcut (one letter). This key is used in combination with the **CTRL** key (Windows) to access the object.
Tab Index	Specifies the order in which the form objects are selected when pressing the **TAB** key. The tab order goes from the lowest to highest numbers.

Adding a Form to the Volunteer.htm Web Page

The next step is to add a form and radio button group form field to the volunteer.htm Web page. Informational text already has been added and the background image applied to this data file. You open the file and then add a form containing an e-mail form object and a radio button group.

The following steps illustrate how to open the volunteer.htm Web page.

To Open the Volunteer.htm Web Page

1 Click the expand/collapse arrow to display the panel groups.

2 Double-click volunteer.htm in the Files panel.

3 Click the expand/collapse arrow to hide the panel groups.

The volunteer.htm file is displayed in the Document window (Figure 4-77).

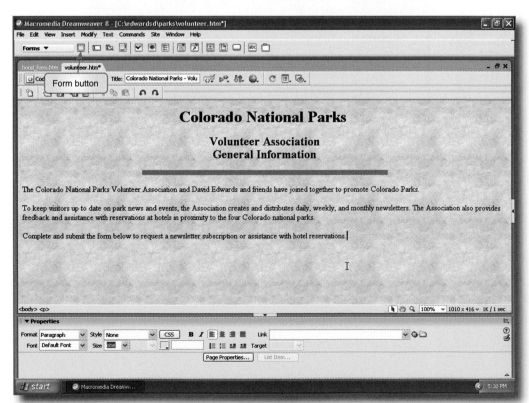

FIGURE 4-77

The following steps show how to add a form and a table to the volunteer.htm Web page.

To Add a Form and Table to the Volunteer.htm Web Page

1 If necessary, scroll down and then position the insertion point at the end of the last line of text. Press the ENTER key.

2 Click the Form button on the Forms category.

3 In the Property inspector, type newsletter as the form name.

4 Uses the mailto: format and type your e-mail address in the Action text box.

5 Select _self on the Target pop-up menu, type text/plain in the Enctype box, and then press the ENTER key.

6 Click inside the form in the Document window. Click Insert on the menu bar and then click the Table command.

7 Create a four-row, two-column table, with a width of 75%, a border thickness of 4, and a cell padding of 5. Type Colorado National Parks newsletter in the Summary text box. Click the OK button.

8 Scroll up and down as necessary.

9 Click the Table ID and type newsletter_form.

10 Select the table, click the Align pop-up menu in the Property inspector, and then center the table.

11 Enter #993300 in the Brdr color hexadecimal text box and then press the ENTER key.

12 Select row 1 and then merge the cells.

13 Click row 1, type Colorado National Park as the entry, and then press SHIFT+ENTER to insert a line break.

14 Type Newsletter Information and then select the two lines of text.

15 Apply Heading 2 and center the heading.

16 Select rows 2 through 4, column 1, and then click the Align Right button in the Property inspector.

17 Click the Save button on the Standard toolbar.

The form and table are added to the volunteer.htm Web page (Figure 4-78).

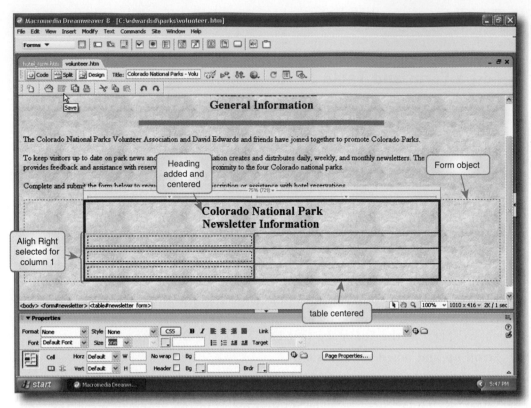

FIGURE 4-78

Inserting an E-Mail Address Text Box

Next, you adjust the column width and add descriptive text for the e-mail address and a single-line text field for user input to row 2. The following steps illustrate how to add the e-mail address and single-line text form object.

To Insert a Single-Line Text Box

1 Select rows 2 through 4, column 1, and then set the column width to 35%.

2 Click row 2, column 1, type E-mail as the entry, and then press the TAB key.

3 Click the Text Field button on the Forms category.

4 Double-click the TextField text box in the Property inspector. Type email and then press the TAB key.

5 Type 30 and then press the TAB key.

The descriptive text and text form object for the e-mail address are added to the form. A character width of 30 is set (Figure 4-79 on the next page).

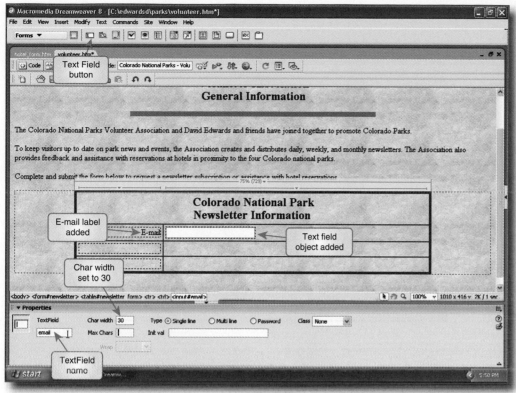

FIGURE 4-79

Radio Groups

When you are adding multiple radio buttons to a form, the **Radio Group** form object is the fastest and easiest method to use. At times, the table may extend outside the form boundaries. If this happens, ignore it. The steps on the next page show how to add descriptive text and a radio group to the Newsletter Information form.

To Add a Radio Group

1

• **Click row 3, column 1. Type** I am interested in receiving a newsletter **and then press the TAB key.**

• **Point to the Radio Group button on the Forms category.**

The descriptive text is added (Figure 4-80).

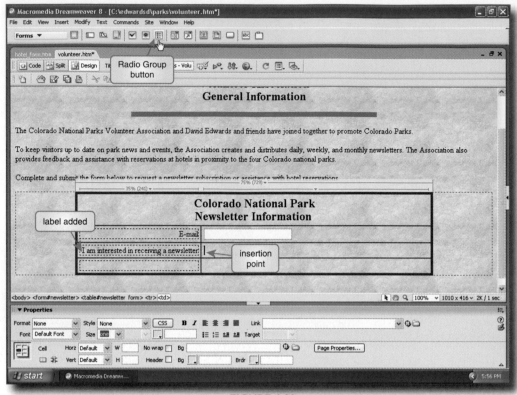

FIGURE 4-80

2

• **Click the Radio Group button.**

The Radio Group dialog box is displayed (Figure 4-81). The insertion point is blinking in the Name text box.

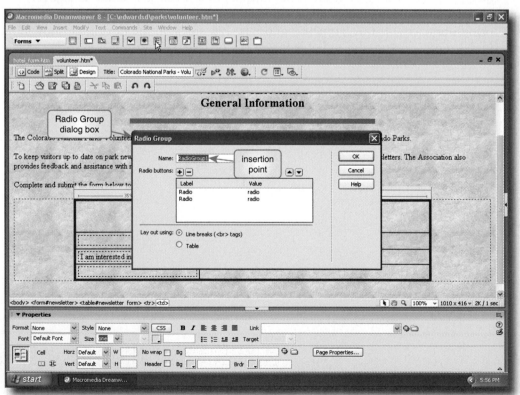

FIGURE 4-81

3

• **Type** newsletter **and then click the first instance of Radio in the Label field.**

The Radio Label is selected (Figure 4-82).

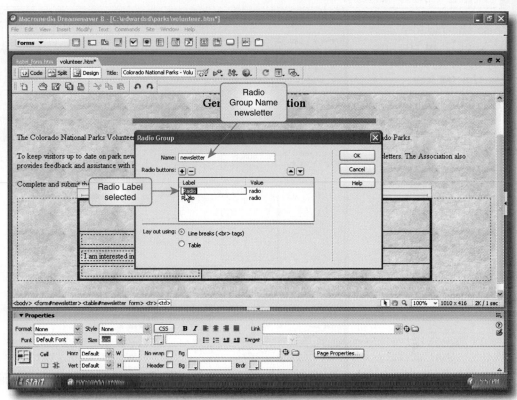

FIGURE 4-82

4

• **Type** Daily **as the Label and then press the TAB key.**

• **Type** daily **as the Value.**

The Label and Value are entered (Figure 4-83).

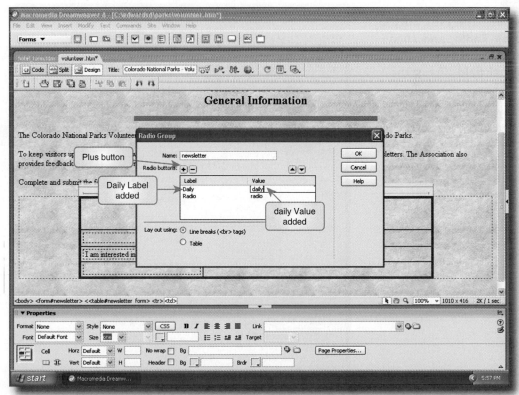

FIGURE 4-83

5

• **Press the TAB key, type** Weekly **in the Label field, and then press the TAB key.**

• **Type** weekly.

The Label and Value are entered (Figure 4-84).

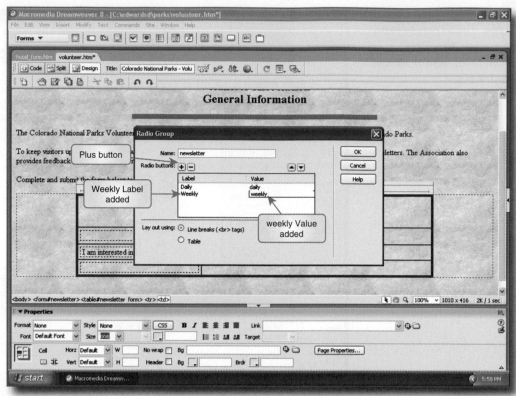

FIGURE 4-84

6

• **Click the Plus button, click Radio, and then type** Monthly **in the Label field. Press the TAB key.**

• **Type** monthly **and then, if necessary, click the Lay out using Line breaks (
 tags) radio button.**

*The text, Monthly, is entered for the Label, and monthly is entered for the Value. The Lay out using Line breaks (
 tags) radio button is selected (Figure 4-85).*

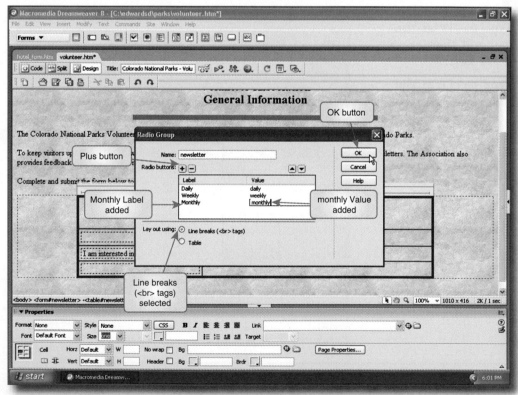

FIGURE 4-85

7

• **Click the OK button.**

The radio group and labels are inserted into the form (Figure 4-86).

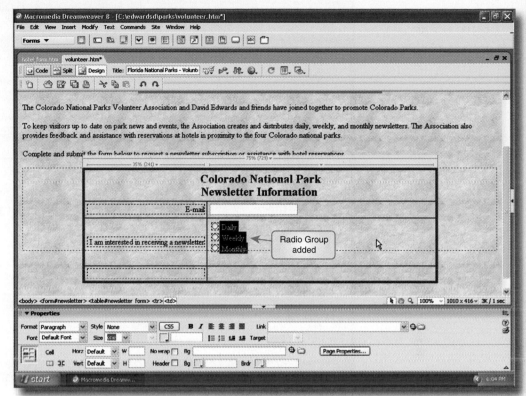

FIGURE 4-86

The final step is to add the Submit and Reset buttons to the form. The following steps show how to add these two buttons.

To Add the Submit and Reset Buttons to the Volunteer.htm Form

1 If necessary, scroll down. Click row 4, column 1, and then click the Button button on the Forms category.

2 Click row 4, column 2, and then click the Button button on the Forms category.

3 Type Reset as the Button name and then press the TAB key.

4 Type Reset in the Value text box and then click Reset form in the Action area.

5 Click the Save button on the Standard toolbar.

The properties are set, and the Submit and Reset buttons are added to the form (Figure 4-87 on the next page).

Other Ways

1. On Insert menu, point to Form, click Radio Group

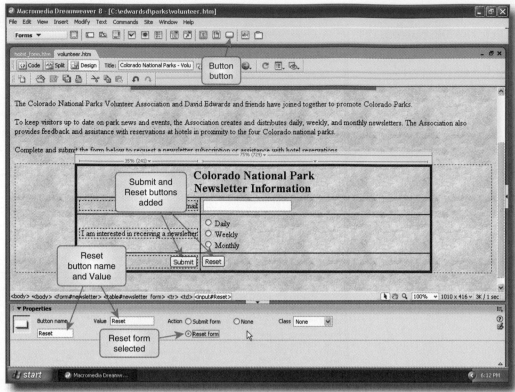

FIGURE 4-87

Adding Links

Project 2 discussed the different types of links, including relative links, absolute links, named anchors, and e-mail links. The following steps illustrate how to add links to the volunteer.htm and hotel_form.htm Web pages and how to add links from the natl_parks.htm Web page to the volunteer.htm and hotel_form.htm Web pages.

To Add Links to the Volunteer.htm, Hotel_Form.htm, and Natl_Parks.htm Web Pages

1 Display the panel groups and open the natl_parks.htm Web page.

2 Scroll to the end of the Web page and then add a line break after the Home link. Press the END key.

3 Type Colorado National Parks Volunteer Association. **Add a line break, and then type** Colorado National Parks Hotel Reservations.

4 Select the text Colorado National Parks Volunteer Association and create a link to the volunteer.htm Web page. Select the text Colorado National Parks Hotel Reservations and create a link to the hotel_form.htm Web page.

5 Save the natl_parks.htm Web page and then press the F12 key to display the page in your browser (Figure 4-88a on the next page). Verify that the links work and close the browser. Close the natl_parks.htm Web page.

6 Click the volunteer.htm tab and then scroll to the bottom of the page. Type Home and then add a line break.

7 Type Colorado National Parks as the entry.

8 Select the Home text and then create a link to the index.htm Web page.

9 Select the Colorado National Parks text and then create a link to the natl_parks.htm Web page.

10 Save the volunteer.htm Web page.

11 Press the F12 key to display the Web page in your browser and then verify that the links work (Figure 4-88b on the next page). Close the browser.

12 Click the hotel_form.htm tab and then, if necessary, scroll to the bottom of the page. Type Home and then add a line break.

13 Type Colorado National Parks as the entry.

14 Select the Home text and then create a link to the index.htm Web page.

15 Select the Colorado National Parks text and then create a link to the natl_parks.htm Web page.

16 Save the hotel_form.htm Web page.

17 Press the F12 key to display the Web page in your browser and then verify that the links work (Figure 4-88c on the next page). Close the browser.

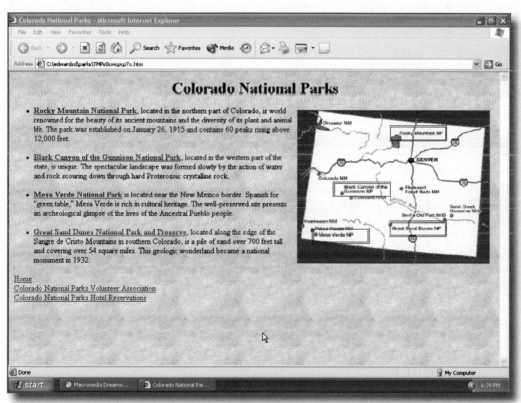

FIGURE 4-88a

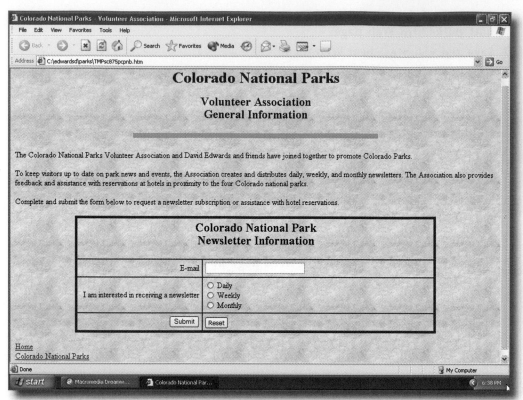

FIGURE 4-88b

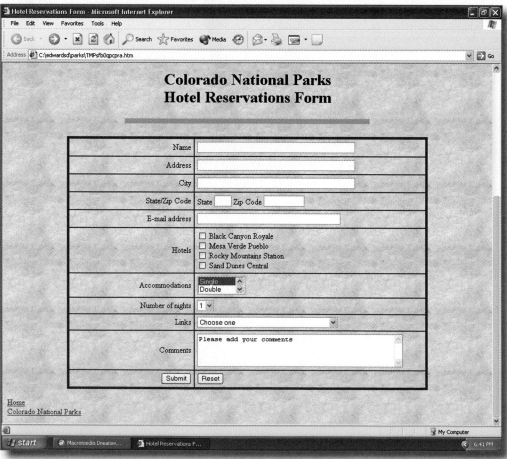

FIGURE 4-88c

Behaviors

A **behavior** is a combination of an event and an action. Behaviors are attached to a specific element on the Web page. The element can be a table, an image, a link, a form, a form object, and so on. When a behavior is initiated, Dreamweaver uses JavaScript to write the code. **JavaScript** is a scripting language written as a text file. After a behavior is attached to a page element, and when the event specified occurs for that element, the browser calls the action (the JavaScript code) that is associated with that event. A scripting language, such as JavaScript, provides flexibility, interaction, and power to any Web site.

Using Behaviors with Forms

To create this type of user interaction with almost any other software program requires that you write the JavaScript. When you attach a behavior in Dreamweaver, however, the JavaScript is produced and inserted into the code for you. Dreamweaver provides two form-related behaviors: Validate Form and Set Text of Text Field. These behaviors are available only if a text field has been inserted into the form.

The **Validate Form** behavior verifies that the user has entered data into each designated field. The form is checked when the user clicks the Submit button. If omissions or other errors occur, a Microsoft Internet Explorer (or other browser) dialog box is displayed. The errors then must be corrected before the form can be submitted successfully.

The **Set Text of Text Field** action replaces the content of a form's text field with the content you specify when creating the behavior. For example, this behavior could be used to insert the current date. The Behaviors panel is displayed in Figure 4-89. The following steps show how to add the Validate Form behavior to the Hotel Reservations form.

More About

Form Validation

Additional form validation behaviors can be added to Dreamweaver by downloading and installing the JavaScript Integration Kit for Flash 8 and Dreamweaver 8 from the Macromedia Exchange. This extension contains several advanced form validations that check field entries such as credit card numbers, ZIP codes, and dates. For more information about form validation, visit the Dreamweaver 8 More About Web page (scsite.com/dw8/more.htm) and then click Form Validation.

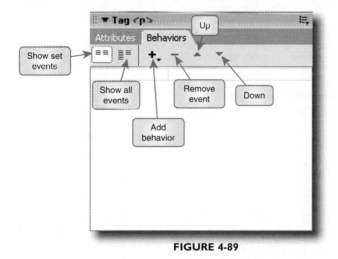

FIGURE 4-89

To Add the Validate Form Behavior

1

• **Display the panel groups and hide the Property inspector.**

• **If necessary, click the hotel_form.htm tab.**

• **Click Window on the menu bar and then point to Behaviors.**

The Window menu is displayed (Figure 4-90).

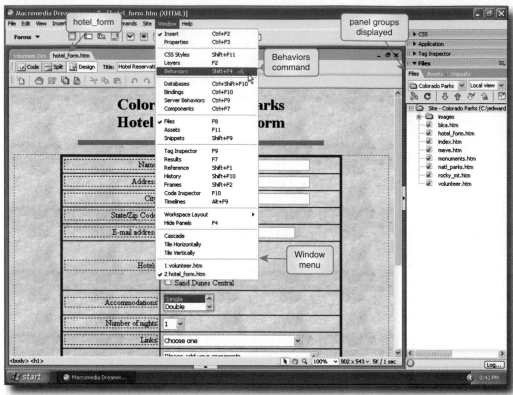

FIGURE 4-90

2

• **Click Behaviors.**

The Behaviors panel is displayed (Figure 4-91).

FIGURE 4-91

3

• **If necessary, click anywhere inside the form. Click <form#hotel_ form> in the tag selector. Click the Add Behavior button in the Behaviors panel and then point to Validate Form on the pop-up menu.**

The form is selected (Figure 4-92). If form#hotel_form does not display in the tag selector, verify that the insertion point is in the form and not in the table.

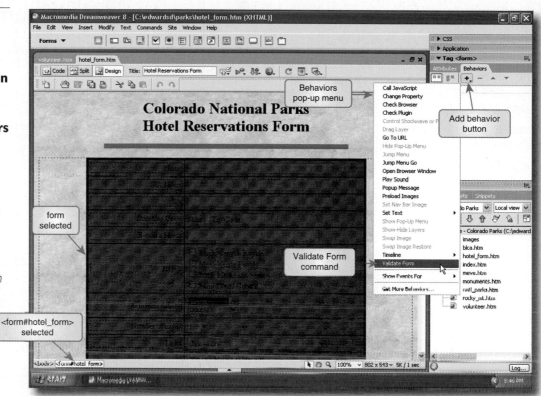

FIGURE 4-92

4

• **Click Validate Form.**

The Validate Form dialog box is displayed (Figure 4-93). Each of the text fields in the hotel_form.htm document is listed in the Named fields list. The text "name" in form "hotel_form" field is selected, and the Anything radio button is selected.

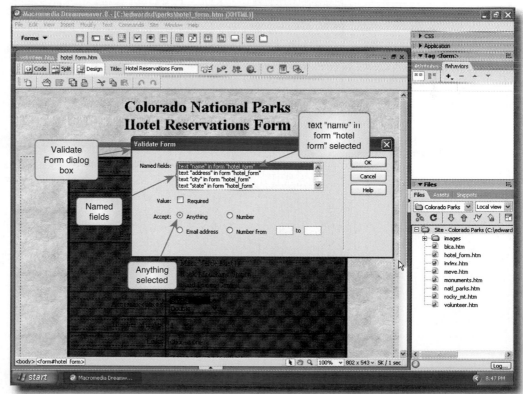

FIGURE 4-93

5

• **Click the Value Required check box.**

The Value Required check box is selected for the "name" field. An (R) is inserted to the right of the field name (Figure 4-94).

FIGURE 4-94

6

• **Click the text "address" in form "hotel_form" field and then click Value Required for the "address" field.**

The Value Required check box is selected for the "address" field. An (R) is inserted to the right of the field name (Figure 4-95).

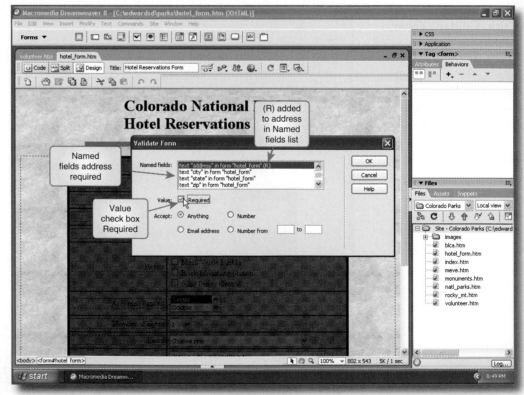

FIGURE 4-95

7

• **Repeat the above step for the city, state, and zip fields.**

The Value Required check box is selected for the "city", "state", and "zip" fields. An (R) is inserted to the right of each of the field names (Figure 4-96).

FIGURE 4-96

8

• **Click the text "email" in the form "hotel_form" field. Click the Value Required check box and the Email address radio button.**

The Value Required check box and the Email address radio button are selected (Figure 4-97).

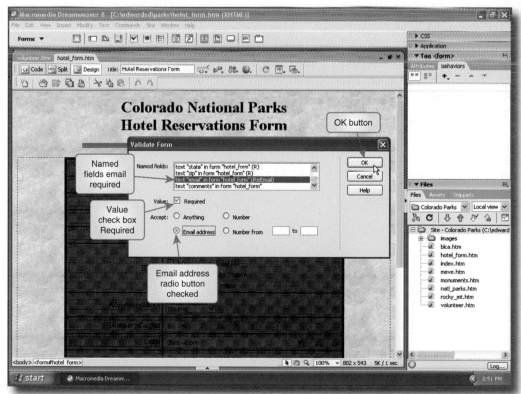

FIGURE 4-97

9

• **Click the OK button.**

• **Click anywhere in the Document window to deselect the form.**

• **Click the Save button on the Standard toolbar.**

The Event and Action are displayed in the Behaviors panel. No visible changes are evident in the Document window (Figure 4-98).

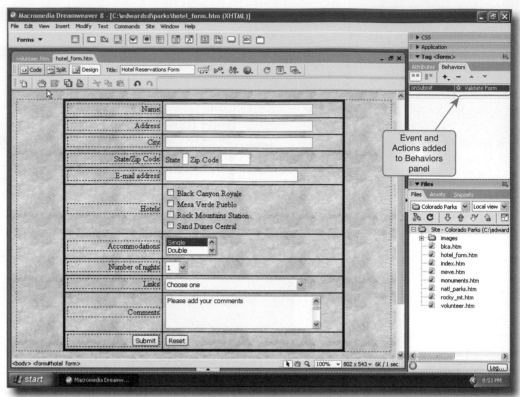

FIGURE 4-98

Viewing and Testing the Forms

To ensure that the form objects work correctly, they are viewed through the browser and each of the form objects is tested. The following steps illustrate how to view and test the hotel_form.htm and volunteer.htm forms.

To View and Test the Hotel_Form.htm Form

1

• **Press the F12 key.**

The hotel_form.htm page is displayed in the browser (Figure 4-99).

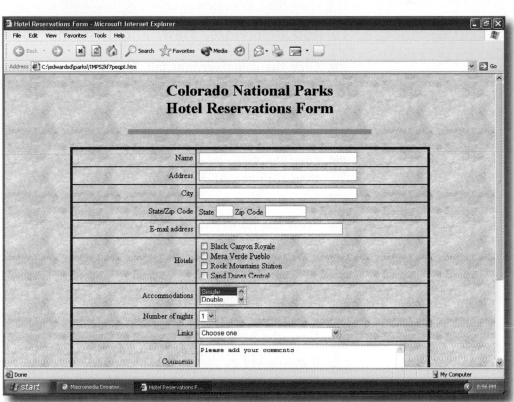

FIGURE 4-99

2

• **Complete the form, typing data in each field, and then click the Submit button.**

A Microsoft Internet Explorer dialog box is displayed (Figure 4-100).

3

• **Read the information in the dialog box, and then click the OK button.**

The form is processed, and the data is e-mailed to you. In some instances, your e-mail message may not include the data attachment. This is determined by the e-mail program, server, and security set up on your computer.

• **Close the browser and return to Dreamweaver.**

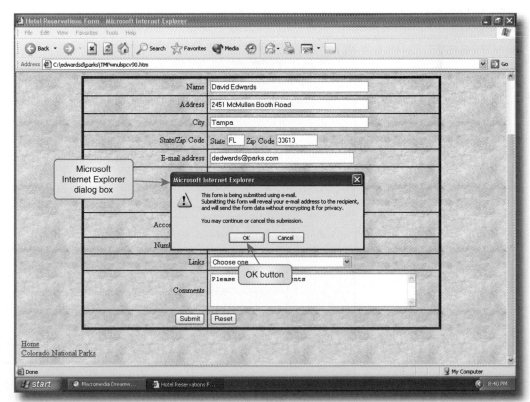

FIGURE 4-100

The steps below illustrate how to add behaviors to and how to view and test the volunteer.htm form.

To Add Behaviors, View, and Test the Volunteer.htm Form

1 Click the volunteer.htm tab. Click inside the form, but not in the table, and then click <form#newsletter> in the tag selector. Verify that form#newsletter is selected in the tag selector.

2 Click the Add behavior button on the Behaviors panel and then click Validate Form on the pop-up menu.

3 Click the Value Required check box and the Email address radio button and then click the OK button.

4 Save the form.

5 Press the F12 key to display the form in your browser (Figure 4-101).

6 Click the E-mail address form object and then type your e-mail address.

7 Click the Weekly radio button and then click the Submit button.

8 Click the OK button in the Microsoft Internet Explorer dialog box to e-mail the data.

9 Close the browser and return to Dreamweaver.

10 If instructed to do so, upload your Web site to a remote server. Appendix C contains information on uploading to a remote server. A remote folder is required before you can upload to a remote server. Generally, the remote folder is defined by the Web server administrator or your instructor.

Figure 4-101 shows the Volunteer Association Web page as it is displayed in the browser in Step 5.

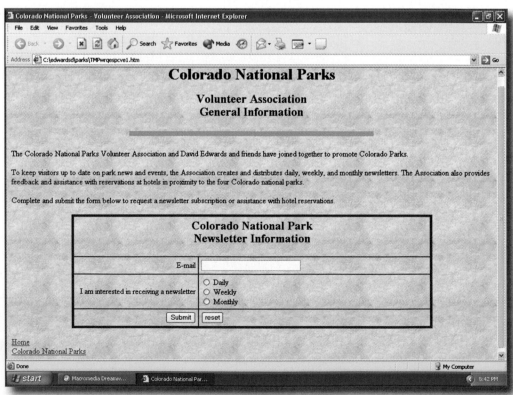

FIGURE 4-101

Quitting Dreamweaver

After you have created your forms, tested and verified that the forms work, and uploaded the Web site to a remote server, Project 4 is complete. The following step shows how to close the Web site, quit Dreamweaver 8, and return control to Windows.

To Close the Web Site and Quit Dreamweaver

1 **Click the Close button on the upper-right corner of the Dreamweaver title bar.**

The Dreamweaver window, the Document windows, and the parks Web site all close. If you have unsaved changes, Dreamweaver will prompt you to save the changes. Clicking the Yes button in the Dreamweaver 8 dialog box saves the changes.

Project Summary

Project 4 introduced you to forms and to Web page design using forms. You created two forms and added a table to each of the forms to format them. In the Hotel Reservations form, you added the following form objects: text fields, check boxes, a list and pop-up menu, a jump menu, a text area, and Submit and Reset buttons. You added a text field, radio group buttons, and Submit and Reset buttons to the Newsletter Information form. You then used the Behaviors panel to attach the Validate Form behavior to both forms. Finally, you viewed and tested the forms in your browser.

What You Should Know

Having completed this project, you now should be able to perform the tasks below. The tasks are listed in the same order they were presented in the project. For a list of keyboard commands for topics introduced in this project, see the Quick Reference for Windows at the back of this book and refer to the Shortcut column.

1. Copy Data Files to the Parks Web Site (DW 318)
2. Start Dreamweaver and Open the Colorado Parks Web Site (DW 318)
3. Insert and Format the Heading (DW 320)
4. Insert a Horizontal Rule (DW 321)
5. Insert a Form (DW 323)
6. Set the Form Properties (DW 326)
7. Insert a Table into a Form (DW 328)
8. Format the Form (DW 330)
9. Add Descriptive Labels and Single-Line Text Fields to the Hotel Reservations Form (DW 334)
10. Add Check Boxes (DW 341)
11. Create a Scrolling List (DW 346)
12. Create a Pop-Up Menu (DW 349)
13. Insert a Jump Menu (DW 353)
14. Add a Textarea Text Field (DW 358)
15. Add the Submit and Reset Buttons (DW 360)
16. Open the Volunteer.htm Web Page (DW 364)
17. Add a Form and Table to the Volunteer.htm Web Page (DW 365)
18. Insert a Single-Line Text Box (DW 366)
19. Add a Radio Group (DW 368)
20. Add the Submit and Reset Buttons to the Volunteer.htm Form (DW 371)
21. Add Links to the Volunteer.htm, Hotel_Form.htm, and National.htm Web Pages (DW 372)
22. Add the Validate Form Behavior (DW 376)
23. View and Test the Hotel_Form.htm Form (DW 381)
24. Add Behaviors, View, and Test the Volunteer.htm Form (DW 382)
25. Close the Web Site and Quit Dreamweaver (DW 383)

Learn It Online

Instructions: To complete the Learn It Online exercises, start your browser, click the Address bar, and then enter the Web address `scsite.com/dw8/learn`. When the Dreamweaver 8 Learn It Online page is displayed, follow the instructions in the exercises below. Each exercise has instructions for printing your results, either for your own records or for submission to your instructor.

1 Project Reinforcement TF, MC, and SA

Below Dreamweaver Project 4, click the Project Reinforcement link. Print the quiz by clicking Print on the File menu for each page. Answer each question.

2 Flash Cards

Below Dreamweaver Project 4, click the Flash Cards link and read the instructions. Type 20 (or a number specified by your instructor) in the Number of playing cards text box, type your name in the Enter your Name text box, and then click the Flip Card button. When the flash card is displayed, read the question and then click the answer box arrow to select an answer. Flip through Flash Cards. If your score is 15 (75%) correct or greater, click Print on the File menu to print your results. If your score is less than 15 (75%) correct, then redo this exercise by clicking the Replay button.

3 Practice Test

Below Dreamweaver Project 4, click the Practice Test link. Answer each question, enter your first and last name at the bottom of the page, and then click the Grade Test button. When the graded practice test is displayed on your screen, click Print on the File menu to print a hard copy. Continue to take practice tests until you score 80% or better.

4 Who Wants To Be a Computer Genius?

Below Dreamweaver Project 4, click the Computer Genius link. Read the instructions, enter your first and last name at the bottom of the page, and then click the PLAY button. When your score is displayed, click the PRINT RESULTS link to print a hard copy.

5 Wheel of Terms

Below Dreamweaver Project 4, click the Wheel of Terms link. Read the instructions, and then enter your first and last name and your school name. Click the PLAY button. When your score is displayed, right-click the score and then click Print on the shortcut menu to print a hard copy.

6 Crossword Puzzle Challenge

Below Dreamweaver Project 4, click the Crossword Puzzle Challenge link. Read the instructions, and then enter your first and last name. Click the SUBMIT button. Work the crossword puzzle. When you are finished, click the Submit button. When the crossword puzzle is redisplayed, click the Print Puzzle button to print a hard copy.

7 Tips and Tricks

Below Dreamweaver Project 4, click the Tips and Tricks link. Click a topic that pertains to Project 4. Right-click the information and then click Print on the shortcut menu. Construct a brief example of what the information relates to in Dreamweaver to confirm that you understand how to use the tip or trick.

8 Newsgroups

Below Dreamweaver Project 4, click the Newsgroups link. Click a topic that pertains to Project 4. Print three comments.

9 Expanding Your Horizons

Below Dreamweaver Project 4, click the Expanding Your Horizons link. Click a topic that pertains to Project 4. Print the information. Construct a brief example of what the information relates to in Dreamweaver to confirm that you understand the contents of the article.

10 Search Sleuth

Below Dreamweaver Project 4, click the Search Sleuth link. To search for a term that pertains to this project, select a term below the Project 4 title and then use the Google search engine at google.com (or any major search engine) to display and print two Web pages that present information on the term.

Apply Your Knowledge

1 Creating a Form for Andy's Lawn Service

Instructions: The Andy's Lawn Service Web site currently contains five pages. You will add a sixth page with a form containing a table. You add to this page a heading and a form with single-line text fields and textarea fields, a list, Submit and Reset buttons, and links to and from the Andy's Lawn Service services page. The new page added to the Web site is shown in Figure 4-102. Software and hardware settings determine how a Web page is displayed in a browser. Your Web page may display differently than the one shown in Figure 4-102. Appendix C contains instructions for uploading your local site to a remote server.

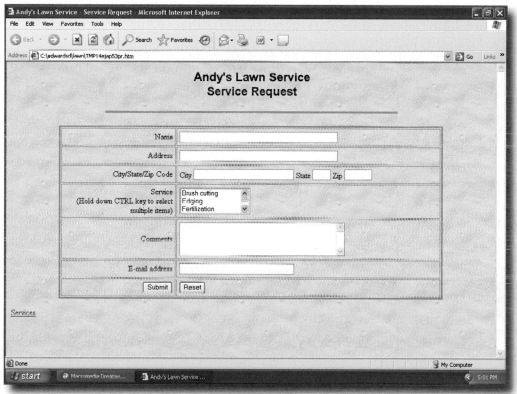

FIGURE 4-102

1. Start Dreamweaver. Select Lawn Service from the Files pop-up menu in the Files panel and open a new HTML file. Save the file as services_form.htm.
2. Apply the lawnbg.jpg background image, which can be found in the images folder.
3. Display the Insert bar and then click the Forms category.
4. Click the upper-left corner of the Document window. Type Andy's Lawn Service and then press the SHIFT+ENTER keys. Type Service Request and then press the ENTER key.
5. Select both lines. Apply Heading 2 and then center the two lines of text. Change the font of the heading to Arial, Helvetica, sans-serif.
6. Click at the end of the heading and then press the ENTER key. Click Insert on the menu bar, point to HTML, and then click Horizontal Rule. Specify a width of 600 pixels, a height of 4, center alignment, and no shading.

(continued)

Apply Your Knowledge

Creating a Form for Andy's Lawn Service *(continued)*

7. Click below the horizontal rule. Click the Form button on the Forms category. Double-click the Form name text box in the Property inspector and then type services as the form name. Click the Action text box and then type mailto:dave@hometown.com (substitute your e-mail address). Click the Target box arrow and then select _self. Click the Enctype box and then type text/plain as the entry.

8. Click inside the form. Click Insert on the menu bar and then click Table. Insert a seven-row, two-column table with a width of 80%, a border thickness of 3, a cell padding of 5, and a cell spacing of 2.

9. If necessary, select the table. Click the Align box arrow in the Property inspector and then click Center.

10. Select column 1 and then click the Align Right button. Set the column W (width) to 30%. Select the table. Click the Brdr color hexadecimal text box and then type #FF9900 as the border color.

11. Click row 1, column 1; type Name as the entry; and then press the TAB key.

12. Click the Text Field button on the Forms category. In the Property inspector, type name as the form object name. Press the TAB key and then type 50 as the Char width.

13. Click row 2, column 1; type Address as the entry; and then press the TAB key. Insert a TextField form object in row 2, column 2. Type address as the form object name, and then specify a Char width of 50.

14. Click row 3, column 1; type City/State/Zip Code as the entry; and then press the TAB key.

15. Type City and then press the SPACEBAR. Insert a TextField form object named city with a Char width of 30. Click to the right of the text field and then press the SPACEBAR.

16. Type State and then press the SPACEBAR. Insert a TextField form object named state with a Char width of 2. Click to the right of the text field and then press the SPACEBAR.

17. Type Zip and then press the SPACEBAR. Insert a TextField form object named zip with a Char width of 5.

18. Click row 4, column 1; type Service as the entry; and then press SHIFT+ENTER. Type (Hold down CTRL key to select multiple items) as the entry.

19. Click row 4, column 2, and then click the List/Menu button on the Forms category. Type service as the List/Menu form object name, click the List radio button in the Property inspector Type area, specify a height of 3, click the Allow multiple check box in the Selections area, and then click the List Values button. Type each Item Label and Value as shown in Table 4-3. Press the TAB key to move from field to field.

20. Click the OK button; click row 5, column 1; type Comments as the entry; and then press the TAB key. Insert a textarea form object named comments, with a Char width of 40. Type 4 for the Num Lines value.

21. Click row 6, column 1; type E-mail address as the entry; and then press the TAB key. Insert a TextField form object named email, with a Char width of 35.

22. Click row 7, column 1, and then insert a Submit button. Click row 7, column 2, and then insert a button. Type Reset in the Value text box, and then click the Reset form radio button in the Action area.

23. If necessary, display the Behaviors panel. Click form#services in the tag selector and then click the Add behavior button in the Behaviors panel. Click Validate Form on the Action menu.

24. In the Validate Form dialog box, click the Required check box for all fields in the Named fields list box. In the Accept area, make sure the Anything radio button is selected for all fields except the email field. For the email field, click Email address. Click the OK button in the Validate Form dialog box.

25. Click below the form. Type Services as the entry, select the text, and then create a link to the services.htm Web page. Title the page Andy's Lawn Service - Service Request, and then click the Save button on the Standard toolbar.

Apply Your Knowledge

26. Open the services.htm Web page and then scroll down to the bottom of the page. Click to the right of the last bulleted list item and press the ENTER key twice. Click the Align Center button in the Property inspector. Type Service Request Form and then create a link to the services_form.htm Web page. Save the Web page.

27. Press F12 to display the services.htm Web page in your browser. Click the Service Request Form link to display the services_form.htm Web page. Input data into the form and then click the Submit button to test the form. Then test the link to the services.htm Web page. Close the browser.

28. Print a copy of the form, if instructed to do so. Upload the services_form.htm and services.htm Web pages to the lawn Web site on a remote server, if instructed to do so. Close Dreamweaver.

Table 4-3 Lawn Services List Values	
ITEM LABEL	VALUE
Brush cutting	brush
Edging	edge
Fertilization	fertilize
Mowing/Trimming	mow
Irrigation	irrigate
Landscaping	landscape
Mulching	mulch
Pruning	prune
Weed/Insect control	weed

1 Creating a Web Form for the CandleWix Web Site

Problem: Martha has decided she would like to conduct a survey to determine which candles her Web site visitors like best and their favorite locations to burn the candles. She wants to include a comments section and provide a copy of the results to those visitors who are interested. To create the survey, she has requested that you add a form to the CandleWix site. The completed form is shown in Figure 4-103. Appendix C contains instructions for uploading your local site to a remote server.

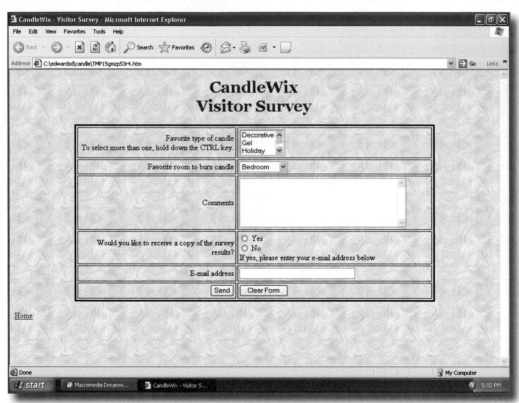

FIGURE 4-103

Instructions: Perform the following tasks:

1. Start Dreamweaver. Select CandleWix from the Files pop-up menu in the Files panel and open a new HTML file. Save the file as survey_form.htm.
2. Apply the candlebg.gif background image, which can be found in the images folder.
3. Title the Web page, "CandleWix - Visitor Survey".
4. Click the upper-left corner of the Document window. Add and center the two-line heading, CandleWix Visitor Survey, as shown in Figure 4-103. Apply Heading 1 and then apply the Georgia, Times New Roman, Times, serif font. Change the color of the heading to #990000. Click below the heading.
5. If necessary, click the Forms category on the Insert bar and then click the Form button. Type survey as the form name. Type mailto:david@hometown.com (substitute your e-mail address) as the action. Select _self in the Target box. Click the Enctype box and then type text/plain as the entry.

In the Lab

6. Click inside the form and then insert a table with the following attributes: 6 rows, 2 columns, width of 75%, border thickness of 3, cell padding of 3, and cell spacing of 3. Center the table in the form and then specify a width of 45% for column 1.

7. Select the table and click the Brdr color hexadecimal text box and then type #000000 as the border color. Select column 1 and then click the Align Right button.

8. Click row 1, column 1; type Favorite type of candle as the entry; and then enter a line break. Type To select more than one, hold down the CTRL key. and then press the TAB key.

9. Click the List/Menu button on the Forms category. Type favorite as the List/Menu name, click List in the Type area, type 3 in the Height box, and then click the Allow multiple check box.

10. Click the List Values button. Type each Item Label and Value as shown in Table 4-4. Press the TAB key to move from field to field. Click the OK button when you're finished entering the list values.

Table 4-4 CandleWix List Values

ITEM LABEL	VALUE
Decorative	decorative
Gel	gel
Holiday	holiday
Pillar	pillar
Scented	scented
Texture	texture
Votive	votive

11. Click row 2, column 1. Type Favorite room to burn candle and then press the TAB key. Click the List/Menu button on the Forms category. Type burn as the menu name. If necessary, click Menu in the Type area, and then click the List Values button. Type each Item Label and Value as shown in Table 4-5. Press the TAB key to move from field to field. Select Bedroom in the Initially selected list box.

Table 4-5 CandleWix Menu Values

ITEM LABEL	VALUE
Bedroom	bedroom
Dining room	dining room
Bathroom	bathroom
Kitchen	kitchen

12. Click row 3, column 1; type Comments as the entry; and then press the TAB key. Insert a Textarea form object named comments, with a Char width of 40 and Num Lines of 6.

13. Click row 4, column 1. Type Would you like to receive a copy of the survey results? and then press the TAB key.

(continued)

Creating a Web Form for the CandleWix Web Site (*continued*)

14. Insert a Radio Group form object named group results. Click the first instance of Radio below Label, type Yes as the Label, and then press the TAB key. Type yes for the Value and then press the TAB key. Type No for the second Label field, press the TAB key, and then type no for the second Value. Click the OK button.

15. Position the insertion point to the right of No and then insert a line break. Type If yes, please enter your e-mail address below and then press the TAB key.

16. Type E-mail address and then press the TAB key. Insert a TextField form object named email and then set a Char width of 35.

17. Click row 6, column 1, and then insert a Button form object named send. Type Send in the Value text box.

18. Click row 6, column 2, and then insert a Button form object named clear. Type Clear Form in the Value text box, and then click Reset form in the Action area.

19. Click below the form. Type Home as the entry, select the text, and then add a link to the index.htm Web page. Click the Save button on the Standard toolbar. Press the F12 key to view the Web page in your browser. Input data into the form and then click the Send button to test the form.

20. Open the index.htm Web page and then scroll down to the bottom of the page. Click at the end of the Products link and press the ENTER key. Type Survey and create a link to the survey_form.htm Web page.

21. Click at the end of the subheading, Welcome to CandleWix, and then press the ENTER key. Click Insert on the menu bar, point to HTML, and then click Horizontal Rule. Change the width to 550 pixels, and specify no shading and center alignment.

22. Save the Web page and then test the link in your browser. Print a copy of the form, if instructed to do so. Upload the survey_form.htm and index.htm Web pages to the candle Web site on a remote server, if instructed to do so.

2 Creating a Form Web Page for the Credit Protection Web Site

Problem: Monica recently received several e-mails asking for suggestions on how to spend money wisely. She has created three informational articles and would like to provide these articles to her Web site visitors. Monica asks you to create a form so she can provide this information. The form is shown in Figure 4-104. Appendix C contains instructions for uploading your local site to a remote server.

In the Lab

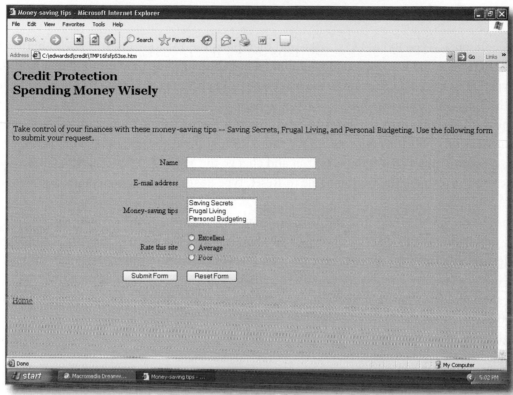

FIGURE 4-104

1. Use the Windows My Computer option to copy the data file from the DataFiles folder to your credit folder.
2. Start Dreamweaver. Display the Credit Protection site in the Files panel.
3. Double-click tips_form.htm to open the Web page.
4. Click to the right of the last sentence and then press the ENTER key. If necessary, click the Forms category on the Insert bar and then click the Form button. Name the form guest_comments. Type mailto:dave@hometown.com (substitute your e-mail address). Select _self in the Target box. Click the Enctype box and then type text/plain as the entry.
5. Click inside the form and then insert a table with the following attributes: 5 rows, 2 columns, width of 75%, border thickness of 0, cell padding of 7, and a cell spacing of 3. Center the table in the form and specify a width of 30% for column 1.
6. Select column 1 and then click the Align Right button.
7. Click row 1, column 1; type Name as the entry; and then press the TAB key. Add a single-line text field named name, with a Char width of 40.
8. Click row 2, column 1; type E-mail address as the entry; and then press the TAB key. Add a TextField form object named email, with a Char width of 40.
9. Click row 3, column 1; type Money-saving tips as the entry; and then press the TAB key. Insert a List/Menu form object named saving, with a Type of List and a Height of 3. Click the Allow multiple check box.
10. In the List Values box, type each Item Label and Value as shown in Table 4-6 on the next page. Press the TAB key to move from field to field.

(continued)

In the Lab

Creating a Form Web Page for the Credit Protection Web Site *(continued)*

11. Click row 4, column 1. Type Rate this Site and then press the TAB key. Insert a Radio button named excellent. Type excellent in the Checked value text box. Click to the right of the radio button and then press the SPACEBAR. Type Excellent and then press the SHIFT+ENTER keys. Insert a Radio button named average. Type average in the Checked value text box. Click to the right of the radio button and then press the SPACEBAR. Type Average and then press the SHIFT+ENTER keys. Insert a Radio button named poor. Type poor in the Checked value text box. Click to the right of the radio button, press the SPACEBAR, and then type Poor.

12. Click row 5, column 1. Insert the Submit button and change the Value to Submit Form. Click row 5, column 2. Insert another button, change the button name to Reset, type Reset Form as the Value, and then click Reset form in the Action area.

13. At the bottom of the page, add a link to the index.htm Web page.

14. If necessary, press SHIFT+F4 to display the Behaviors panel. Select the form. Click the Add behavior button and then select the Validate form command to open the Validate Form dialog box. Require a value in the name field, and accept only email addresses in the email field.

15. Insert a left-aligned horizontal rule under the second line in the heading. The horizontal rule should have a width of 400 pixels, a height of 3, and shading applied.

16. Title the Web page Money-saving tips.

17. Save the form.

18. Open the index.htm Web page, scroll down to the bottom of the page, click at the end of the "Tips and Hints on Saving" link, and then press the SHIFT+ENTER keys. Type Information Request as the entry, select the text, and then create a link to the tips_form.htm Web page.

19. View the Web pages in your browser. Input data into the form and then click the Submit Form button to test the form. Close the browser. Print a copy of the form, if instructed to do so. Upload the tips_form.htm and index.htm Web pages to the credit Web site on a remote server, if instructed to do so.

Table 4-6 Credit Protection List Values	
ITEM LABEL	VALUE
Saving Secrets	saving
Frugal Living	frugal
Personal Budgeting	budget

3 Creating a Guest Book Form for the Lexington, NC Web Site

Problem: The Lexington, NC Web site provides information about the city, but does not provide a means of response from your visitors. The city manager would like visitors to comment on the Web site and the city and asks that you add a guest book to the site. The Web page is shown in Figure 4-105. Appendix C contains instructions for uploading your local site to a remote server.

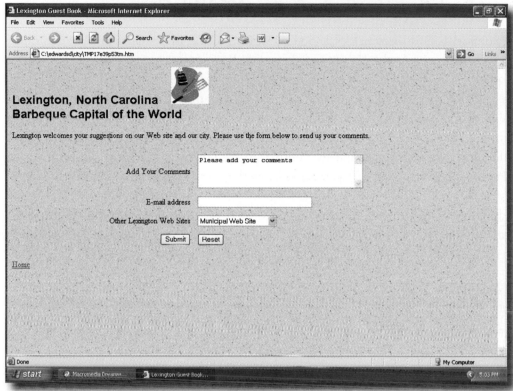

FIGURE 4-105

Instructions: Perform the following tasks:

1. Use the Windows My Computer option to copy the file from the DataFiles folder to your city folder.
2. Start Dreamweaver. Open the Lexington, NC Web site.
3. Double-click guest_form.htm to open the data file. Click at the end of the last line of text.
4. If necessary, click the Forms category on the Insert bar. Insert a form named guests. Type mailto:dave@hometown.com (substitute your e-mail address). Select _self in the Target box. Click the Enctype box and then type text/plain as the entry.
5. Click inside the form and then insert a table with the following attributes: 4 rows, 2 columns, width of 75%, border thickness of 0, cell padding of 5, and cell spacing of 5. Center-align the table.
6. Select column 1 and then click the Align Right button.
7. Click row 1, column 1; type Add Your Comments as the entry; and then press the TAB key. Insert a textarea form object named comments, with a Char width of 40 and Num Lines of 4. Type Please add your comments for the Init val. If necessary, click the Multi line radio button.
8. Click row 2, column 1; type E-mail address as the entry; and then press the TAB key. Insert a TextField form object named email, with a Char width of 35.
9. Click row 3, column 1; type Other Lexington Web Sites; and then press the TAB key. Insert a Jump Menu form object. Type the text and URL values as shown in Table 4-7 on the next page. Press the TAB key to move from field to field and click the Plus button to add additional menu items.
10. Type city as the jump menu name.

(continued)

Creating a Guest Book Form for the Lexington, NC Web Site *(continued)*

11. Click row 4, column 1, and then insert the Submit button form object. Click row 4, column 2, and then insert a button. Type Reset as the Value, and then click Reset form.
12. Add a link to the Lexington, NC Web site index.htm page.
13. If necessary, click SHIFT+F4 to display the Behaviors panel. Click the Add behavior button and validate the form. A value should be required for all fields, and only email addresses should be accepted for the email field.
14. Save the form.
15. Open the index.htm Web page and then scroll down to the bottom of the page. Insert a vertical bar to the right of the Police Department link. Type Comments as the entry, select the text, and then create a link to the guest_form.htm Web page. Print a copy of the form if instructed to do so.
16. View the Web pages in your browser. Input data into the form and then click the Submit button to test the form. Upload the guest_form.htm and index.htm Web pages to the city Web site on a remote server, if instructed to do so.

Table 4-7 Text and URLs	
TEXT	**WHEN SELECTED, GO TO URL**
Municipal Web Site	http://www.lexingtonnc.net
Lexington, NC Tourism	http://www.visitlexingtonnc.com
The Barbecue Festival	http://www.barbecuefestival.com

Cases and Places

The difficulty of these case studies varies:
■ are the least difficult and ■■ are the most difficult. The last exercise is a group exercise.

1 ■ Your sports Web site is receiving more hits each day. You have received many e-mails asking for statistics and other information. You decide to start a weekly newsletter and want to add a form so your visitors can subscribe to the newsletter. Add a background image to the page and add a title to the page. Insert a form and name the form appropriately. Add a horizontal rule below the heading on your page. Next, add a table to your form. Include text fields for name and e-mail address and a text area for comments. Add descriptive text asking if the visitor would like to subscribe to the newsletter and then include a radio group with Yes and No options. Add Submit and Reset buttons. Create links to and from the home page. Save the page in your sports Web site. Open the pages in your browser and then check your links and forms. For a selection of images and backgrounds, visit the Dreamweaver 8 Media Web page (scsite.com/dw8/media) and then click Media below Project 4.

2 ■ You would like to add some interactivity to your hobby Web site. You decide to do this by adding a survey. First, add a background image to the page and then add an appropriate title. Add a horizontal rule below the heading on your page. Insert a form and then add a table to your form. Add a four-pixel border to the form. Add a list form object that contains a list of hobbies. Ask your viewers to select their favorite hobbies. Create an e-mail text field for those visitors who would like a copy of your survey results. Add Submit and Reset buttons. Create links to and from the home page. Save your Web pages, open the pages in your browser, and then check your links and forms. Upload the page to a remote site, if instructed to do so. For a selection of images and backgrounds, visit the Dreamweaver 8 Media Web page (scsite.com/dw8/media) and then click Media below Project 4.

3 ■■ Add an informational form to your music hobby Web site and then add a background to the page. Add a horizontal rule below the heading on your page. Insert a form and a table. Include form objects for name, address, telephone number, and e-mail address. Include a menu with at least five choices and then add the Submit and Reset buttons. Rename the buttons. Fill in all relevant attributes in the Property inspector for each object. Create links to and from the home page. Save your Web pages, open the pages in your browser, and then check your links and forms. Upload the page to a remote site. For a selection of images and backgrounds, visit the Dreamweaver 8 Media Web page (scsite.com/dw8/media) and then click Media below Project 4.

Cases and Places

4 ■■ Your campaign for political office is progressing well. Create a new Web site and name it office_form. Add two pages with forms to the new site. The first page should contain a form asking for opinions and comments about your political views. The second form should contain form objects requesting donations and campaign volunteers. Add a horizontal rule below the headings on each of your two pages. Create links to and from the home page. Save your pages, open your pages in your browser, and then check your links and forms. Upload the office_form Web site to a remote server. For a selection of images and backgrounds, visit the Dreamweaver 8 Media Web page (scsite.com/dw8/media) and then click Media below Project 4.

5 ■■ **Working Together** Last week, the student government officers selected three possible vacation sites to visit. Now they would like to have a form page for students to provide feedback about each of the three sites. Each student in your group creates a page with introductory text and a form listing each of the three student trip locations. Provide form objects so the Web site visitors can vote on which trip they would like to take and offer feedback regarding the number of days, minimum and maximum costs, and other related information. Integrate the three pages into one. Add a horizontal rule below the heading on your page. Create links to and from the home page. Save your Web pages, open the pages in your browser, and then check your links and forms. For a selection of images and backgrounds, visit the Dreamweaver 8 Media Web page (scsite.com/dw8/media) and then click Media below Project 4.

Templates and Style Sheets

PROJECT

5

CASE PERSPECTIVE

The Colorado National Parks Web site offers visitors many interesting and informative Web pages. David, however, would like to add additional enhancements to the site. He asks you and Tracy for ideas and suggestions. After numerous discussions and the exchange of ideas, several proposals are put forward. One idea is to do a photo page containing various images from one of the national monuments. To add variety to the Web site, however, Tracy suggests that a new Web page be developed that will spotlight a different national monument each month. David expresses concern that changing this page each month will become quite a chore.

Tracy explains that instead of redeveloping the entire page each month, the team can use a template. She also explains that style sheet attributes can be added to the template to provide consistency in the heading, park description, and display of images and links. All team members agree to add the Web page and develop a template.

As you read through this project, you will learn about templates and style sheets, how to create a cascading style sheet (CSS), and how to apply CSS attributes to a template. In addition, you will learn how to create a Web page from a template.

Templates and Style Sheets

Objectives

You will have mastered the material in this project when you can:

- Describe a template
- Create a template
- Describe the different types of style sheets
- Create a Cascading Style Sheet
- Apply Cascading Style Sheet attributes to a template
- Create a Web page from a template

Introduction

Project 5 introduces the addition of a Dreamweaver template to the Colorado National Parks Web site. Designing a Web site is a complex process that requires the author to make decisions about the structure of the site and the appearance and content of each Web page within the site. Templates are an important element of many Web sites and are used in a variety of ways. For example, a Web site developer can use a template to provide a basic framework for the structured organization of the entire Web site. Or an educational institution could have a template for student home pages. The student supplies the content for the Web page. The template then takes care of the rest of the job and displays the page in a format that promotes consistency between student Web pages. Another example is the content within an e-commerce catalog page. Using a template, the content developer easily can add and delete new products, change prices, and make other modifications.

Project Five — Creating Templates and Style Sheets

In this project, you learn how to create a Dreamweaver template, create a style sheet, and apply styles to the template. Using the template, you then create a Web page highlighting one of Colorado's national monuments.

First, you create a single page that has all the elements you want to include in your Web page, and then you save the page as a template. After creating the template, you create the style sheet and then apply the style sheet attributes to the template. Next, you use the template, containing the style sheet attributes, to create a Web page featuring one of Colorado's monuments — Dinosaur National Monument — shown in Figure 5-1. This Web page contains a logo and four designated regions that can be edited. The editable regions are as follows: a heading, a short description, and two tables. You use styles to apply font and color attributes to the heading and the description and to apply fonts, font color attributes, a background, and a border to the two tables. The first table contains template cells for monument images. You also will add a short description of each image. The second table contains cells for links. In this project, you add a relative link to your home page, the Colorado National Parks and Monuments index page, and an absolute link to the Dinosaur National Monument Web site.

FIGURE 5-1

Workspace Organization

Organization and preparation lead to a more productive work setting. Successful Web developers prepare their Dreamweaver workspace to provide an effective work environment. As you learn to use additional Dreamweaver tools, including templates and style sheets, you will become even more proficient working in the Dreamweaver environment.

Copying Data Files to the Local Web Site

Your Data Disk contains images for Project 5. You use the Windows My Computer option to copy the Project 5 images to your parks\images folder. See the inside back cover for instructions for downloading the Data Disk, or see your instructor for information about accessing the files required for this book.

The DataFiles folder for this project is stored on Local Disk (C:). The location on your computer may be different. If necessary, verify with your instructor the location of the DataFiles folder. The following sections show how to copy the files to the parks local root folder.

To Copy Data Files to the Parks Web Site

1 Click the Start button on the Windows taskbar and then click My Computer.

2 Double-click Local Disk (C:) and then navigate to the location of the data files for Project 5.

3 Double-click the DataFiles folder and then double-click the Proj05 folder.

4 Double-click the parks folder and then double-click the images folder.

5 Click the first image file in the list, hold down the SHIFT key, and then click the last image file in the list.

6 Right-click the selected files to display the context menu.

7 Click the Copy command and then click the My Computer Back button the number of times necessary to navigate to the your name folder.

8 Double-click the your name folder, double-click the parks folder, and then double-click the images folder.

9 Right-click in the open window to display the context menu.

10 Click the Paste command to paste the image files into the images folder (Figure 5-2).

11 Click the images window Close button.

The image files are pasted into the Colorado National Parks Web site images folder (Figure 5-2 on the following page).

Starting Dreamweaver and Closing Open Panels

Each time you start Dreamweaver, it opens to the last site displayed when you closed the program. Therefore, you may need to open the parks Web site. The **Files pop-up menu** in the Files panel lists sites you have defined. When you open the site, a list of pages and subfolders within the site are displayed. The following section illustrates how to start Dreamweaver and open the Colorado National Parks Web site.

FIGURE 5-2

To Start Dreamweaver and Open the Colorado Parks Web Site

1 Click the Start button on the Windows taskbar.

2 Point to All Programs on the Start menu, point to Macromedia on the All Programs submenu, and then click Macromedia Dreamweaver 8 on the Macromedia submenu.

3 If necessary, display the panel groups and expand the Property inspector.

4 If necessary, click the Files panel box arrow and then point to Colorado Parks on the Files pop-up menu.

5 Click Colorado Parks (Figure 5-3 on the next page).

Dreamweaver opens, and the Colorado Parks Web site hierarchy is displayed in the Files panel (Figure 5-3 on the following page).

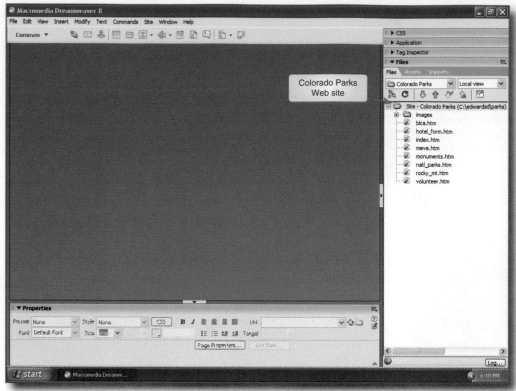

FIGURE 5-3

Understanding Templates

Templates exist in many forms. A stencil, for instance, is a type of template. Or you may have used a template in Microsoft Office or other software applications to create documents with a repeated design. In Web site development with Dreamweaver, a **template** is a predesigned Web page that contains the definition of the appearance of the page, including items such as the default font, font size, logos and images, and backgrounds. A template provides an alternative to separately creating similar-type pages on your Web site. Instead, you create a basic layout and navigation system and use it as a template for each similar page. A template page functions as a pattern for other pages. Using a template can save time and can help create a consistent and standardized design.

Planning is an important element in creating a template. Organizing the information and deciding how to structure the template will make it user-friendly and a more effective site-design tool. The first step is to determine the look of the page, including backgrounds, fonts, and logos. Other elements to consider are heading styles and the inclusion of links, tables, graphics, and other media.

Creating a Template

Dreamweaver provides three methods to create a template: (1) create a template from an existing file, (2) create a template from a new document Basic page, or (3) use the File menu New command and select the Template page category in the New Document dialog box. To create a template from an existing file, you open the file, use the Save as Template command on the File menu, and then define the editable regions. To create a template from a new document Basic page, use the Save as Template command on the File menu. In this project, you use the third method — selecting the Template page category in the New Document dialog box.

The following steps show how to create a new template document.

To Create a New Template Document

1

• **Click New on the File menu.**

The New Document dialog box is displayed (Figure 5-4).

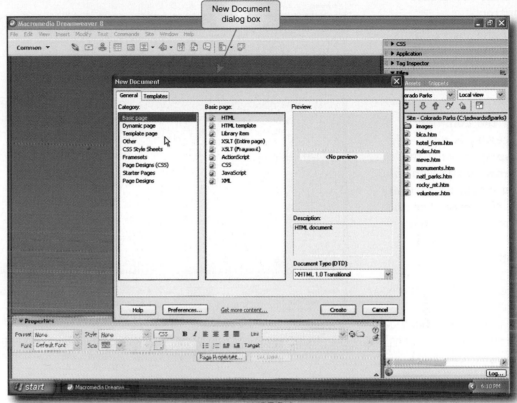

FIGURE 5-4

2

• **Click Template page in the Category list and then click HTML template in the Template page list.**

Template page is selected in the Category list, and HTML template is selected in the Template page list (Figure 5-5).

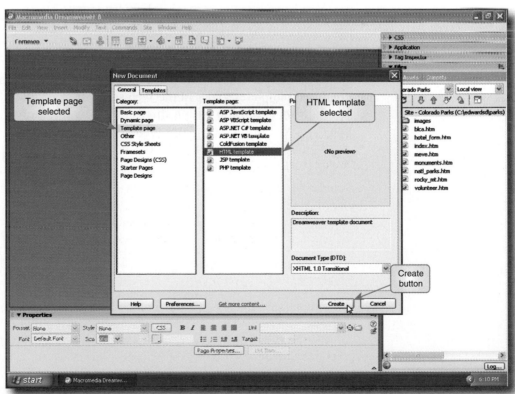

FIGURE 5-5

3

- Click the Create button.

- If the Insert bar is not displayed, click Window on the Insert bar and then click Insert.

- If the Common category is not displayed, click the arrow to the right of the displayed category on the Insert bar and then click Common on the Insert bar pop-up menu.

A template document window is displayed, and [<<Template>> Untitled-1 (XHTML)] is displayed on the title bar (Figure 5-6).

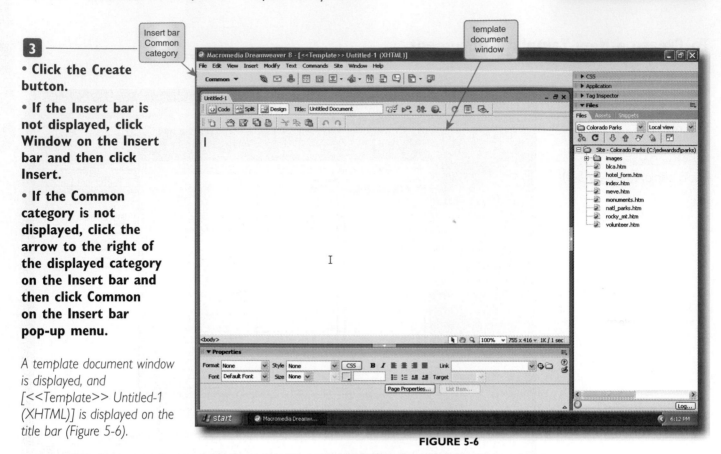

FIGURE 5-6

You have created a new template document. The next step is to save the template.

Saving a Template

When the first template for a Web site is saved, Dreamweaver automatically creates a Templates folder in the Web site local root folder and then saves the template with a **.dwt extension** within that folder. Any additional templates added to the Web site are saved in the Templates folder automatically.

The following section illustrates how to save the Web page as a template and to have Dreamweaver create the Templates folder.

To Save the Web Page as a Template

1

• **Click File on the menu bar and then click Save.**

A Dreamweaver Warning box is displayed.

2

• **Click OK.**

The Save As Template dialog box is displayed (Figure 5-7). Untitled-1 is selected in the Save as text box.

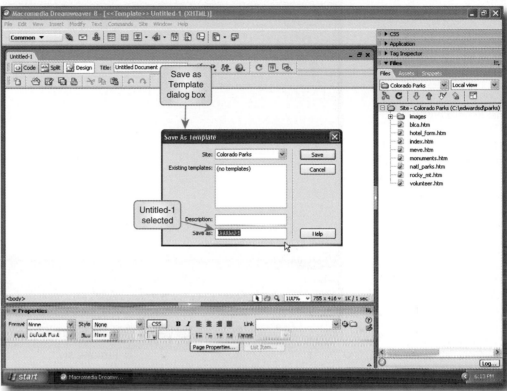

FIGURE 5-7

3

• **Type** spotlight_monuments **in the Save as text box.**

The spotlight_monuments name is displayed in the Save as text box (Figure 5-8).

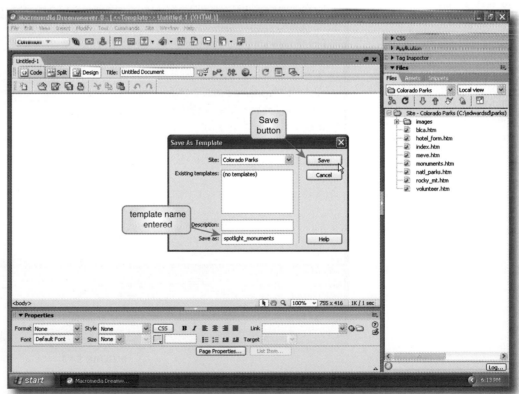

FIGURE 5-8

4

• **Click the Save button.**

The template is saved. A Templates folder is created automatically in the Colorado Parks Files panel (Figure 5-9). If the Templates folder does not display, click the Files panel Refresh button.

FIGURE 5-9

5

• **Click the plus sign to the left of the Templates folder.**

The folder expands. The template name, spotlight_monuments.dwt, is displayed in the Templates folder (Figure 5-10). The .dwt extension indicates it is a template file.

FIGURE 5-10

The Dreamweaver Template

A **Dreamweaver template** is a special type of HTML document. When you create a template, Dreamweaver inserts special code into the template. A **template instance**, which is a Web page based on a template, looks identical to the template. The difference, however, is that you can make changes only to designated parts of the template instance. The designated parts of the page to which you can make changes are called editable regions. An editable region can be any part of a page: a heading, a paragraph, a table, a table cell, and so on. You designate the editable regions when you design the template. Once the designation is complete, other parts of the page are locked.

One of the more powerful benefits that templates provide to the Dreamweaver developer is the ability to update multiple pages at once. After a new document is created from a template, the document remains attached to the original template unless it specifically is separated. Therefore, you can modify a template and immediately update the design in all of the documents based on it.

The purpose of the template created in this project is to use it as a foundation to spotlight a different monument each month. The next section shows how to begin creating the spotlight template page.

To Add a Background Image and Title to the Template Page

1 Click **Modify** on the menu bar and then click **Page Properties**.

2 Click the **Browse** button to the right of the **Background image** box.

3 If necessary, navigate to the images folder. Click **bg.jpg** and then click the **OK** button in the Select Image Source dialog box.

4 Click the **OK** button in the Page Properties dialog box.

5 Click the **Title** text box, delete **Untitled Document**, and type `Spotlight on Colorado National Monuments` as the entry.

6 Press the **ENTER** key. If necessary, click the **Document** window.

The background image and title are applied to the Spotlight template page (Figure 5-11 on the next page). The insertion point is blinking at the top of the page.

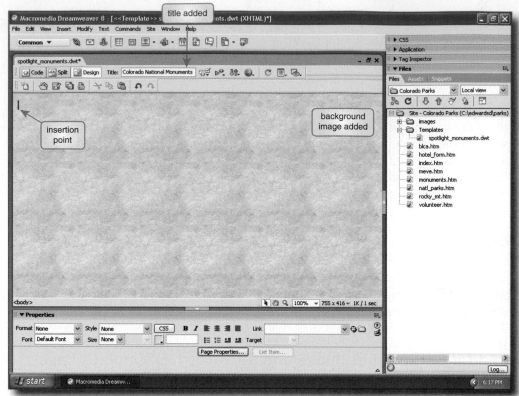

FIGURE 5-11

Editable and Noneditable Regions

When a template first is created, Dreamweaver automatically locks most parts of the template document. The title, however, is not locked. The template author defines which regions of a template-based document will be editable by inserting editable regions or editable parameters in the template. Dreamweaver supports four different types of regions in a template: editable regions, repeating regions, optional regions, and editable tag attributes. The following section describes these four regions.

EDITABLE REGION An **editable region** is the basic building block of a template and is an unlocked region. A template author can define any area of a template as editable. Thus, this is a section a content developer can edit; it can be a heading, a paragraph, a table, or another type of section. A template can have, and usually does contain, multiple editable regions. For a template to be functional, it should contain at least one editable region; otherwise, pages based on the template cannot be edited.

REPEATING REGION A **repeating region** is a section in a document that is set to repeat. Repeating regions enable the template author to control the layout of regions that are repeated on a page. The two types of repeating template objects are repeating table and repeating region. For instance, a list of catalog products may include a name, description, price, and picture in a single row. You can repeat the table row to allow the content developer to create an expanding list, while still enabling the template author to keep the design under his or her control. A repeating region is a section of a template that can be duplicated as often as desired in a template-based page. By default, the repeating region does not include an editable region, but the template author can insert an editable region into the repeating region. A repeating region generally is used with a table, but also can be defined for other page elements.

OPTIONAL REGION   An **optional region** lets the content developer show or hide content on a page-by-page basis. For example, the template author may want to include an optional region that would contain special promotional products.

EDITABLE TAG ATTRIBUTE   An **editable tag** attribute lets the content developer unlock a tag attribute in a template and edit the tag in a template-based page. For instance, the template developer could unlock the table border attribute, but keep locked other table attributes such as padding, spacing, and alignment.

The following steps show how to add a logo image to the template. This logo, once added, becomes part of the template and is a noneditable item. When a content developer uses this template, the logo image will remain as is and cannot be deleted or aligned to another position.

To Add the Logo Image to the Template

1

• **Click the Assets tab in the panel groups. If necessary, click the Images icon. Scroll down and click the logo.gif file.**

The Assets panel is displayed, and logo.gif is selected (Figure 5-12).

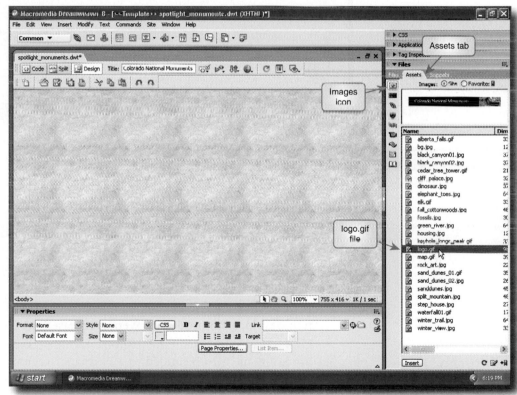

FIGURE 5-12

2

• **Drag the logo.gif image to the top-left corner of the Document window.**

• **Click the Alt text box, type** Colorado National Monuments logo **as the entry, and then press the ENTER key.**

• **Click to the right of the image to deselect it and then press the ENTER key.**

The logo.gif image is displayed in the Document window, and the insertion point is at the left margin below the image (Figure 5-13).

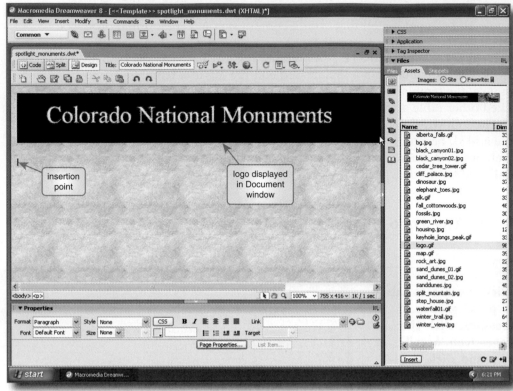

FIGURE 5-13

Designing the Template

When you are creating a template, one of the best methods is to finalize a single page that includes all the elements you want in the template. Then, save the document as a template and mark all of the editable regions. Consider the following when designing your template page:

- Include as much content as possible. Structure and design will enable the content developer to produce a Web page based on the template more quickly.
- Use prompts in the editable regions to inform the content developer as to the type of content to be added to a particular region.
- Give your editable regions meaningful names.
- Use placeholders if possible, particularly for images.

The following steps show how to add prompts for two editable regions in the template page. The prompt for the first editable region is the heading and includes instructions to add the monument name; the prompt for the second editable region is the instruction to add a short description of the monument.

To Add the Monument Name and Monument Description Prompts for the First Two Editable Regions

1

• **Collapse the panel groups.**

• **Type** Spotlight on [name of national monument] **as the heading prompt.**

The heading text, Spotlight on [name of national monument], appears in the Document window below the logo image (Figure 5-14).

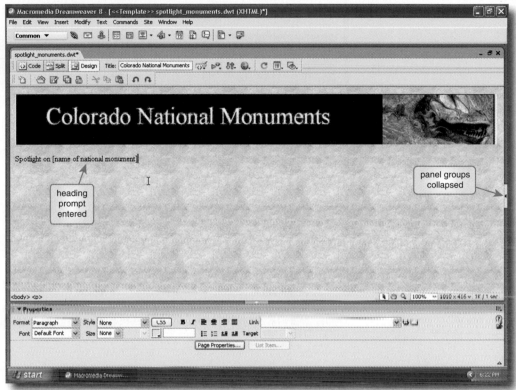

FIGURE 5-14

2

• **Click the Format box arrow in the Property inspector and apply Heading 2 to the spotlight prompt.**

Heading 2 is applied to the heading text prompt (Figure 5-15).

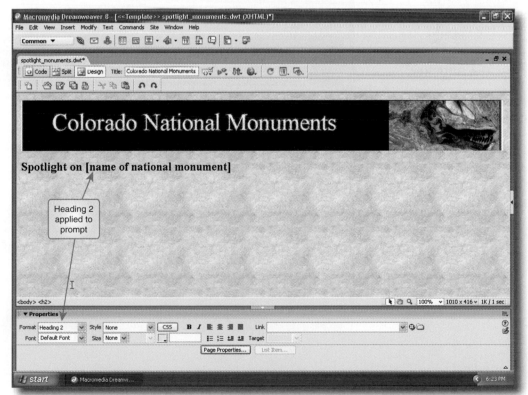

FIGURE 5-15

3

• **Press the ENTER key.**

The insertion point is blinking at the left, below the prompt (Figure 5-16).

FIGURE 5-16

4

• **Type** Add short description of monument **as the prompt for the second editable region.**

• **Bold the text and then press the ENTER key.**

The insertion point is blinking at the left below the description prompt (Figure 5-17).

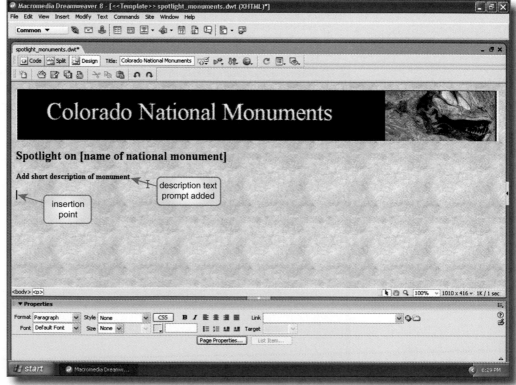

FIGURE 5-17

Adding Tables for Images and Links

The third editable region will consist of a one-row, two-column centered table that will contain centered images and a short description immediately below each image. The table is editable, so depending on the monument to be spotlighted and the number of available images, the content developer can add additional rows and columns to the table as needed. Instructions for the table are contained in row 1, column 1, and an image placeholder is contained in row 1, column 2. A placeholder provides the Web page developer with a guide as to what is to be placed in the cell and the required format, such as right, left, or centered.

A second table will become the fourth editable region. This one-row, two-column centered table will contain cells for a relative link to the Colorado National Monuments index page and an absolute link to the Dinosaur National Monument Web page. This second table also is editable, which will permit the content developer to modify or add additional links as needed.

The following section illustrates how to add the first table as the third editable region.

To Add and Center a Table as the Third Editable Region

1

• **Click Insert on the menu bar and then click Table.**

• **Enter the following data in the Insert Table dialog box: 1 for Rows, 2 for Columns, 70 percent for Table width, 0 for Border thickness, 5 for Cell padding, and 5 for Cell spacing. Type** Spotlight on Colorado national monuments **as the Summary text.**

The table data is entered (Figure 5-18).

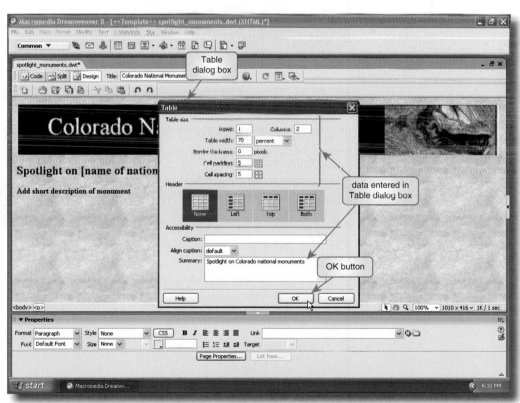

FIGURE 5-18

2

• **Click the OK button.**

• **Click the Align box arrow in the Property inspector, and then click Center to center the table.**

The table is centered in the Document window (Figure 5-19).

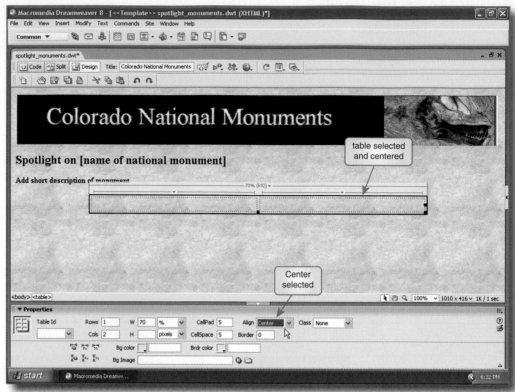

FIGURE 5-19

3

• **Click the left cell in the table and then drag to select both cells in the table.**

Both cells are selected (Figure 5-20).

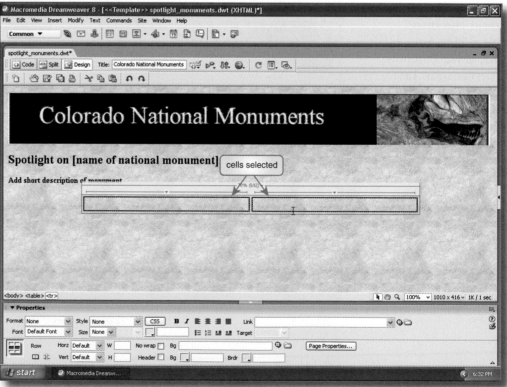

FIGURE 5-20

4

• **Click the Horz box arrow in the Property inspector and then click Center. Click the Vert box arrow and then click Middle.**

The specified attributes are applied to the table cells (Figure 5-21). No changes are evident in the Document window at this time.

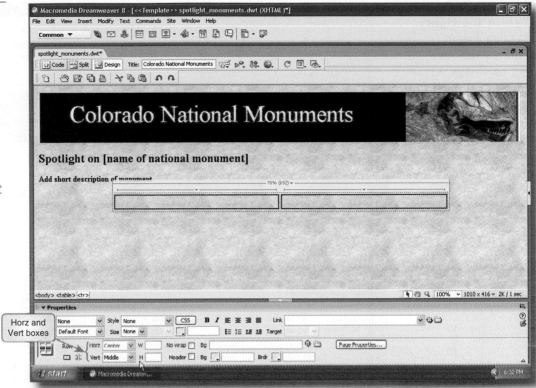

FIGURE 5-21

5

• **Click the left cell in the table and then type** Add additional columns and rows as necessary. Add images and short descriptions of image to each cell in the table **as the prompt.**

The prompt is entered into the left cell (Figure 5-22).

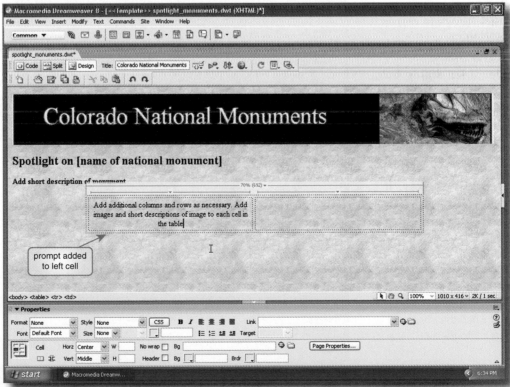

FIGURE 5-22

6

• **Click in the right cell. Click Insert on the menu bar, point to Image Objects, and then point to Image Placeholder.**

The Insert menu and Image Objects submenu are displayed, and Image Placeholder is selected (Figure 5-23).

FIGURE 5-23

7

• **Click Image Placeholder.**

• **In the Image Placeholder dialog box, type** add_image **in the Name text box as the prompt.**

• **Press the TAB key. Type** 64 **for the Width.**

• **Press the TAB key. If necessary, type** 32 **for the Height.**

The Image Placeholder dialog box is displayed. The Width is changed to 64 and the Height is 32. Alternate text will be added when the image is inserted into the cell.

FIGURE 5-24

8

• **Click the OK button.**

• **Click <table> in the tag selector and type** spotlight **in the Table ID box. Press the ENTER key.**

The image placeholder is added to the table cell and the table is named (Figure 5-25).

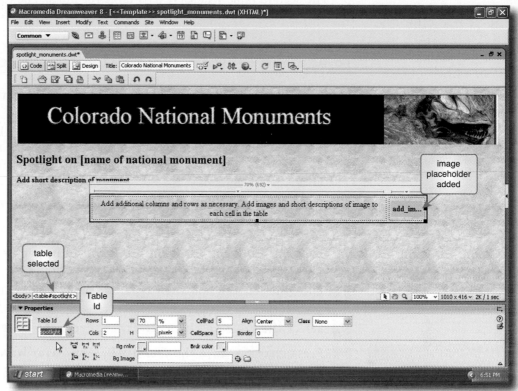

FIGURE 5-25

9

• **Click to the right of the table and then press the ENTER key two times.**

The insertion point is blinking at the left margin below the table (Figure 5-26).

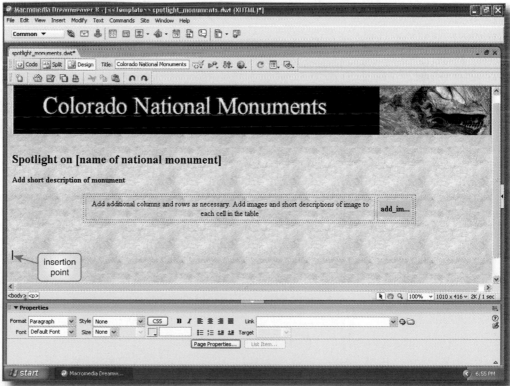

FIGURE 5-26

The second table will serve as a table for links. The following steps show how to add the link table as the fourth editable region.

To Add and Center a Table as the Fourth Editable Region

1 Click Insert on the menu bar and then click Table to display the Insert Table dialog box.

2 Enter the following data in the Insert Table dialog box: 1 for Rows, 2 for Columns, 50 percent for Table width, 0 for Border thickness, 5 for Cell padding, and 0 for Cell spacing. Type Web site links as the Summary text. Click the OK button.

3 Click the Align box arrow in the Property inspector, and then center the table.

4 Click the left cell and then drag to select both cells in the table.

5 Click the Horz box arrow in the Property inspector and then click Center. Click the Vert box arrow and then click Middle.

6 Click the left cell and then type Add additional columns as necessary for links as the prompt.

7 Select the table and name it links. Press the ENTER key.

8 Press CTRL+S to save the file. If a Dreamweaver warning box appears, click the OK button.

The second table is added, centered, and named, and a prompt is added to the table. (Figure 5-27).

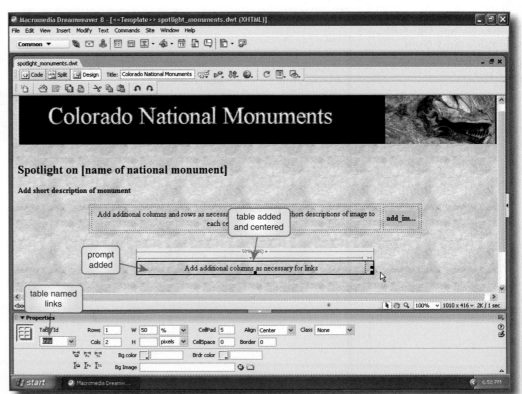

FIGURE 5-27

Adding Editable Regions

As previously discussed on pages DW 408–409, Dreamweaver supports four different regions in a template: editable regions, repeating regions, optional regions, and editable tag attributes. All Dreamweaver region objects, along with other template-related objects, are available through the Templates pop-up menu on the Common category of the Insert bar. Figure 5-28 shows the Templates pop-up menu. Table 5-1 lists the commands and descriptions on the Templates pop-up menu.

FIGURE 5-28

Table 5-1 Commands on the Templates Pop-Up Menu	
COMMAND NAME	DESCRIPTION
Make Template	Displays the Save As Template dialog box; features in the dialog box include selecting a Web site in which to save the template, a list of existing templates, and a Save As box to name the template.
Make Nested Template	Creates a template whose design and editable regions are based on another template; useful for sites in which all pages share certain elements and subsections of those pages share a subset of page elements.
Editable Region	Creates an unlocked region; the basic building block of a template.
Optional Region	Designates a region that can be used to show or hide content on a page-by-page basis; use an optional region to set conditions for displaying content in a document.
Repeating Region	Creates a section of a template that can be duplicated as often as desired in a template-based page.
Editable Optional Region	Designates a region that can be used to show or hide content on a page-by-page basis.
Repeating Table	Defines a table and then defines the location of editable regions in each cell in the table.

Displaying the Insert Bar Templates Commands

The Templates pop-up menu is located on the Insert bar Common category. Commands on this menu are helpful when creating editable regions.

Marking Existing Content as an Editable Region

As discussed previously, an editable region is one that the content developer can change. Editable template regions control which areas of a template-based page can be edited. Each editable region must have a unique name. Dreamweaver uses the name to identify the editable region when new content is entered or the template is applied. The next section shows how to make the heading an editable region.

To Create the First Editable Region

1

• **If necessary, click Window on the menu bar and then click Insert.**

• **If the Common category is not displayed, click the arrow to the right of the displayed category on the Insert bar and then click Common on the Insert bar pop-up menu.**

• **Click the Property inspector expander arrow to hide the Property inspector.**

• **If necessary, scroll to the top and then click to the left of the heading prompt.**

The insertion point is blinking to the left of the heading text prompt (Figure 5-29).

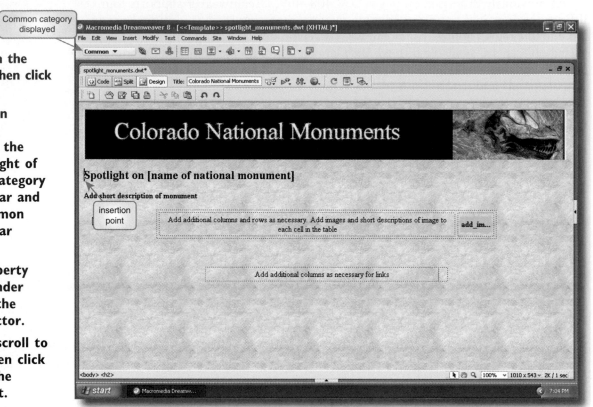

FIGURE 5-29

2

• **Click the <h2> tag in the Tag selector.**

The prompt for the title and the <h2> tag are selected (Figure 5-30).

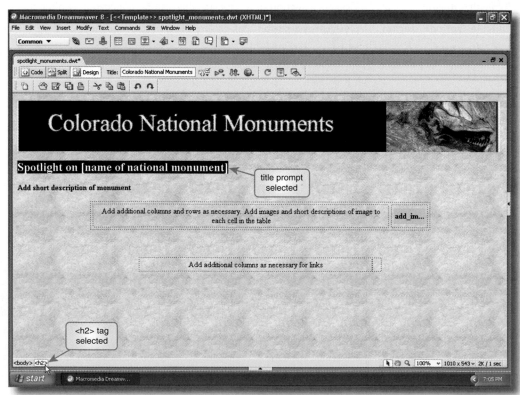

FIGURE 5-30

3

• **Click the Templates pop-up menu arrow and point to Editable Region.**

The Templates pop-up menu is displayed, and Editable Region is selected (Figure 5-31).

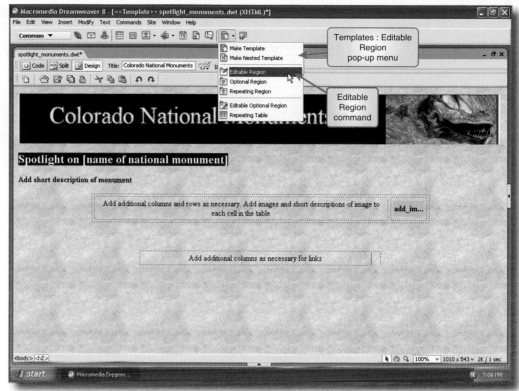

FIGURE 5-31

4

• **Click Editable Region.**

• **Type** monument_name **in the Name text box.**

The New Editable Region dialog box is displayed, and monument_name is typed in the Name text box (Figure 5-32).

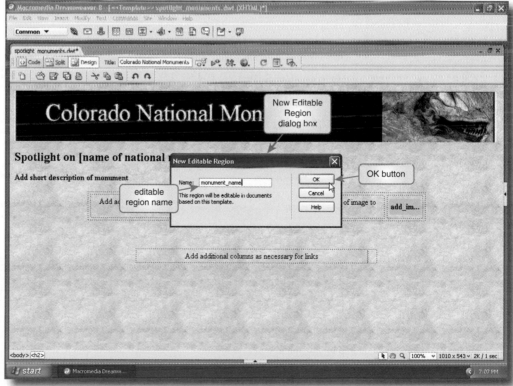

FIGURE 5-32

5

• Click the OK button.

The editable region name is added. The editable region is enclosed in a selected-rectangular outline in the template (Figure 5-33).

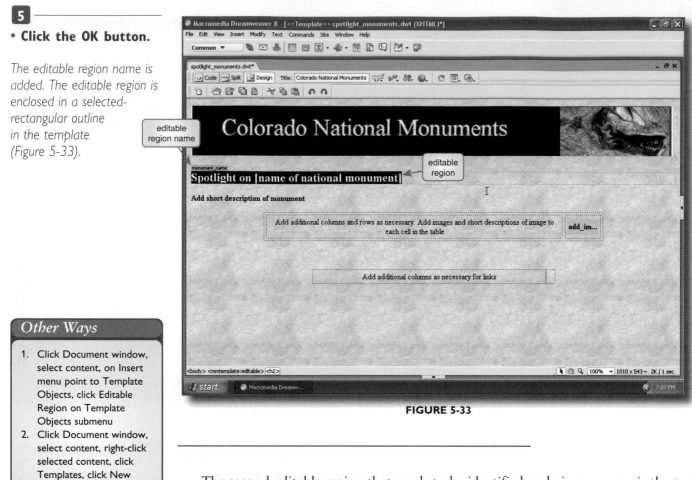

FIGURE 5-33

Other Ways

1. Click Document window, select content, on Insert menu point to Template Objects, click Editable Region on Template Objects submenu
2. Click Document window, select content, right-click selected content, click Templates, click New Editable Region on the Templates submenu

The second editable region that needs to be identified and given a name is the text area that will provide a short description of the featured monument. The following steps illustrate how to make the monument description section an editable region.

To Create the Second Editable Region

1

• Click to the left of the prompt, Add short description of monument, in the Document window.

The insertion point is blinking to the left of the prompt (Figure 5-34).

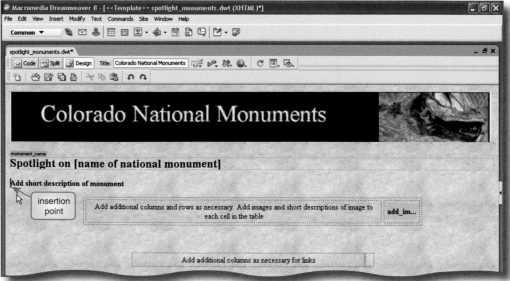

FIGURE 5-34

2

• **Click the <p> tag in the tag selector. Click the Templates pop-up menu arrow and then click Editable Region.**

The New Editable Region dialog box is displayed (Figure 5-35).

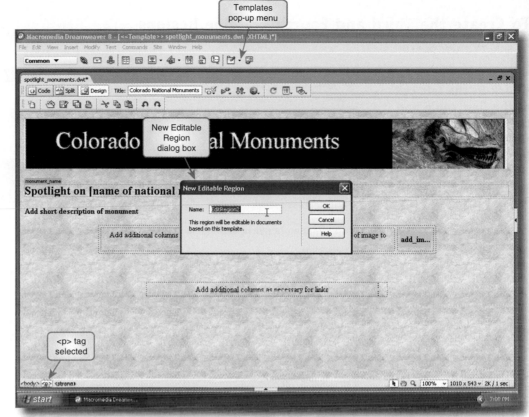

FIGURE 5-35

3

• **Type** monument_description **in the Name text box and then click the OK button.**

The editable region name, monument_description, is added. The editable region is enclosed in a selected-rectangular outline in the template (Figure 5-36).

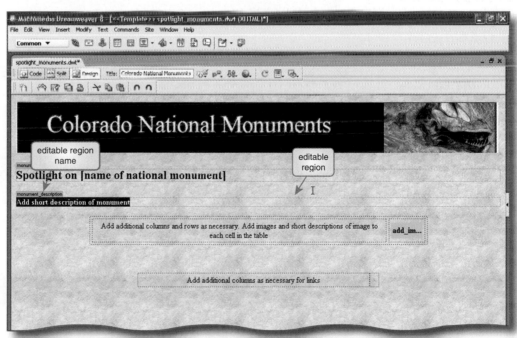

FIGURE 5-36

The third and fourth editable regions are the two tables that were added to the template. The following steps show how to make both tables editable regions.

To Create the Third and Fourth Editable Regions

1

• **Click in the left cell of the first table and then click the <table#spotlight> tag in the tag selector.**

The table is selected (Figure 5-37).

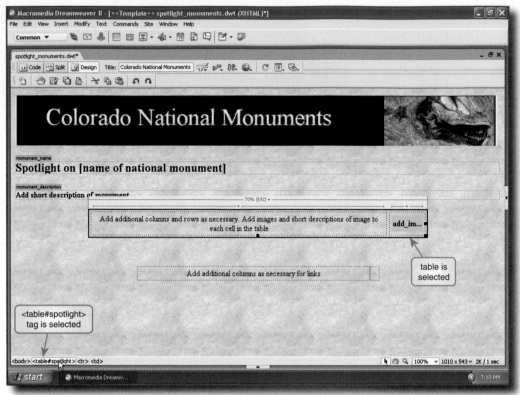

FIGURE 5-37

2

• **Click the Editable Region command on the Templates pop-up menu.**

• **Type** monument_images **in the Name text box, and then click the OK button.**

The editable region name, monument_images, is added. The editable region is enclosed in a selected-rectangular outline in the template (Figure 5-38).

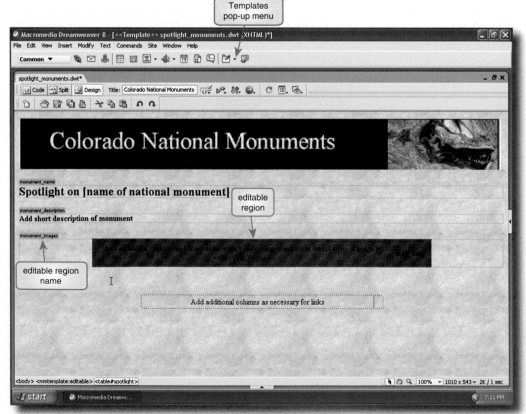

FIGURE 5-38

3

• **If necessary, scroll down to display the second table, click in the left cell of the second table, click the <table#links> tag in the tag selector, and then click the Editable Region command on the Templates pop-up menu.**

The table is selected, and the New Editable Region dialog box is displayed (Figure 5-39).

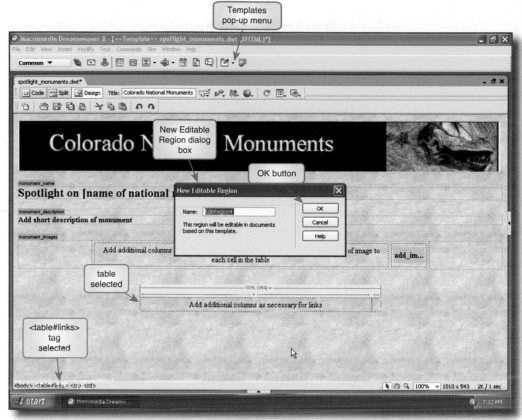

FIGURE 5-39

4

• **Type** links **in the Name text box and then click the OK button.**

The editable region name, links, is added. The editable region is enclosed in a selected-rectangular outline in the template (Figure 5-40). If a warning dialog box is displayed, indicating you have placed an editable region inside a <p> tag, click OK to continue.

• **Click the Save button.**

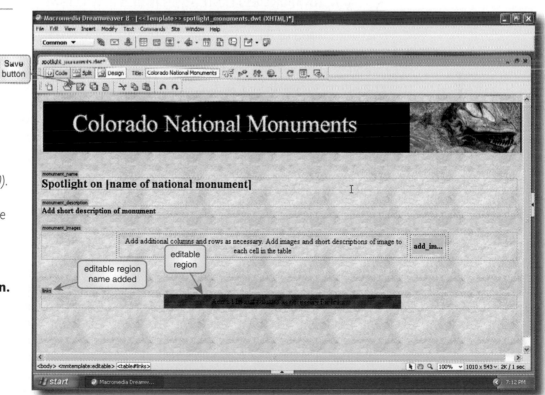

FIGURE 5-40

You have completed adding the editable regions to the template. Next, you create a style sheet and apply the style attributes to the text and tables contained within the template.

Introduction to Style Sheets

If you have used styles in a word processing program such as Microsoft Word, then the concept of styles within HTML and Dreamweaver will be familiar. A **style** is a rule describing how a specific object is formatted. A style sheet (discussed later in this section) is a file that contains a collection of these rules or styles. One style sheet, for example, can control the typography, color, and other layout elements for an entire Web site.

Dreamweaver supports two types of styles: HTML styles and Cascading Style Sheets (CSS).

HTML Styles

Thus far, when you have formatted text, you have selected the text in the Document window and then applied font attributes using the Property inspector. You selected and then formatted each text element individually: the heading, character, word, paragraph, and so on. **HTML styles**, however, are a Dreamweaver feature that a Web page developer can use to apply formatting options quickly and easily to text in a Web page. HTML styles use HTML tags such as the <font> and <b> tags to apply the formatting. Once you have created and saved an HTML style, you can apply it to any document in the Web site.

One advantage of HTML styles is that they consist only of font tags, and therefore display in just about all browsers, including Internet Explorer 3.0 and earlier versions. One of the main disadvantages of HTML styles, however, is that changes made to an HTML style are not updated automatically in the document. If a style is applied and then the style is modified, the style must be reapplied to the text to update the formatting. To use HTML styles, you must deselect the Use CSS instead of HTML Tags option in the General category of the Preferences dialog box.

The HTML 4.0 specification released by the World Wide Web Consortium (W3C) in early 1998 discourages the use of HTML formatting tags in favor of Cascading Style Sheets (CSS). This project, therefore, focuses on Cascading Style Sheets.

Cascading Style Sheets

Cascading Style Sheets, also called **CSS** and **style sheets**, are a collection of formatting rules that control the appearance of content in a Web page. Cascading Style Sheets are the cornerstone of Dynamic HTML (DHTML). **DHTML** is an extension to HTML that enables a Web page to respond to user input without sending a request to the Web server. Compared with HTML styles, style sheets provide the Web site developer with more precision and control over many aspects of page design.

In previous lessons, you used styles that were created for you by Dreamweaver. For instance, in Project 1, when you applied a font color to a page heading, style 1 was created. In later projects, you applied this same style to the headings for other pages.

Dreamweaver contains three different selectors: Class, Tag, and Advanced. Selectors are types of rules that Dreamweaver uses to define a style. A CSS style rule contains two parts: the **selector**, which is the name of the style, and the **declaration**, which defines the style elements. An example of a selector is h2 (defining the HTML h2 tag) and an example of a declaration is 24pt Courier, defining the font size and type to apply to the h2 tag.

- Class: Also considered a custom style, class is the most flexible way to define a style. In a **custom style**, you specify all the attributes you want the style to include. The name of a custom style always begins with a period. This type of style can be applied to any text within the document.
- Tag: The tag style provides the option to make global changes to existing Web pages by modifying the properties or attributes of an HTML tag. When this option is selected in the New CSS Rule dialog box, the Tag pop-up menu provides a selection of over 90 HTML tags listed in alphabetical order.
- Advanced: Also known as pseudo-class, this type of style commonly is applied to hyperlinks to create a rollover effect. For example, when the mouse pointer moves over or hovers over a link, the link changes color. Dreamweaver provides the a:active, a:hover, a:link, and a:visited link options through the pop-up menu. You are not limited to these four options. You can enter one or more of any HTML tag in the Selector text box and apply a single attribute or a combination of attributes to that tag.

After creating a style, you can apply it instantly to text, margins, images, and other Web page elements. Some of the advantages of style sheets include the following:

- Precise layout control
- Smaller, faster downloading pages
- Browser-friendly — nonsupporting CSS browsers ignore the code
- All attached Web pages can be updated at one time

The capability of updating every element with a designated style simultaneously is one of the main benefits of style sheets. For example, suppose you create a custom text style defined as 24-point Times New Roman bold. Later, you decide to change the text color to red. All elements formatted with that style instantly are changed and display in red.

Conflicting Styles

The term **cascading** refers to the capability of applying multiple style sheets to the same Web page. When more than one style is applied to the same Web page, an order of preference is involved. Styles are used as described and applied in the following preference order:

- An **external style sheet** is a single style sheet that is used to create uniform formatting and contains no HTML code. An external style sheet can be linked to any page within the Web site or imported into a Web site. Using the Import command creates an @import tag in the HTML code and references the URL where the published style sheet is located. This method does not work with Netscape Navigator.
- An **internal style sheet**, or **embedded style sheet**, contains styles that apply to a specific page. The styles that apply to the page are embedded in the <head> portion of the Web page.
- A specified element within a page can have its own style.

In some instances, two styles will be applied to the same element. When this occurs, the browser displays all attributes of both styles unless an attribute conflict exists. For example, one style may specify Arial as the font and the other style may specify Times New Roman. When this happens, the browser displays the attribute of the style closest to the text within the HTML code.

More About

HTML Styles

Use the HTML Styles panel to record the HTML styles you use in your Web site, and then you can share the styles with other users, local sites, or remote sites. For more information about HTML styles, visit the Dreamweaver 8 More About Web page (scsite.com/dw8/more.htm) and then click HTML Styles.

More About

External Style Sheets

External style sheets are separate files and exist independently of any HTML pages within the Web site. Any and all Web pages within a Web site can access a common set of properties by linking to the same external style sheet. For more information about external style sheets, visit the Dreamweaver 8 More About Web page (scsite.com/dw8/more.htm) and then click Style Sheets.

The CSS Styles Panel

To develop a style sheet, you start with the **CSS Styles panel** (Figure 5-41), which is part of the Design panel group. Styles are created and controlled through the CSS Styles panel. A **custom style** is a style you can create and name and specify all the attributes you want the style to include. The name of a custom style always begins with a period.

At the bottom of the CSS Styles panel are four buttons. These buttons are used for the following tasks:

- The **Attach Style Sheet** button opens the Link External Style Sheet dialog box. Select an external style sheet to link to or import into your current document.

- The **New CSS Rule** button opens the New CSS Rule dialog box. Use the New CSS Rule dialog box to define a type of style.

- The **Edit Style Sheet** button opens the CSS Style Definition dialog box. Edit any of the styles in the current document or in an external style sheet.

- The **Delete CSS Rule** button removes the selected style from the CSS Styles panel, and removes the formatting from any element to which it was applied.

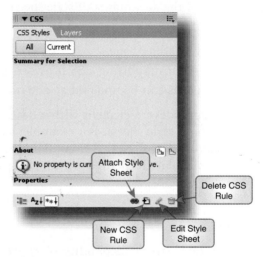

FIGURE 5-41

The following steps show how to display the Design panel group and the CSS Styles panel. You also will increase the width of the panel groups to display a better view of the style elements.

To Display the Design Panel Group

1

• **Click the expand/ collapse arrow to expand the panel groups.**

• **Move the mouse pointer over the vertical bar until it turns to a two-headed arrow.**

• **Drag the vertical bar about ½ inch to the left to increase the width of the panel groups.**

The panel groups are expanded and the width increased (Figure 5-42).

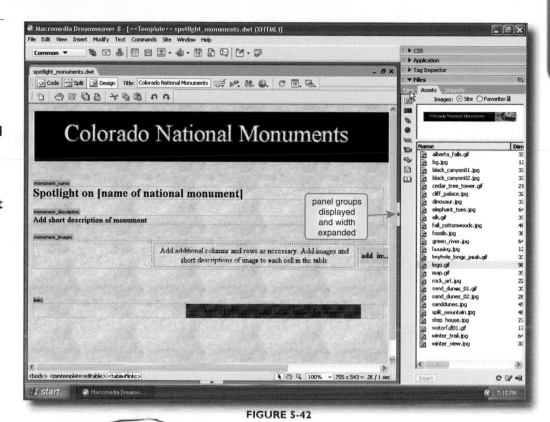

FIGURE 5-42

2

• **Click Window on the menu bar and then click CSS Styles.**

The CSS Styles panel is displayed (Figure 5-43).

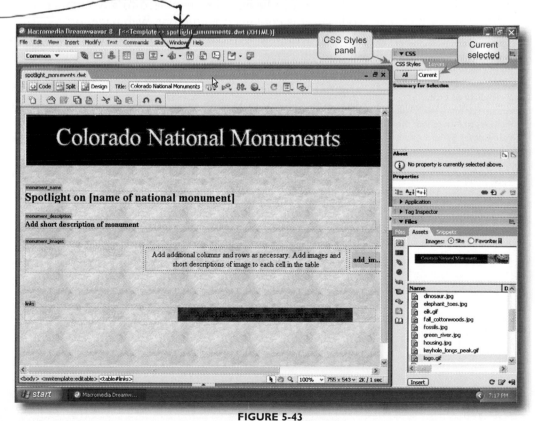

FIGURE 5-43

Other Ways

1. Press SHIFT+F11

Defining Style Attributes

Dreamweaver makes it easy to add style attributes to the style sheet. This is done through the CSS Rule Definition dialog box (Figure 5-44) The CSS Rule Definition dialog box contains eight categories with more than 70 different CSS attributes. As you are defining a style, select a category to access the attributes for that category. Styles from more than one category can be applied to the same element. Tables 5-4 through 5-11 on pages DW 462–464 contain a description of each attribute in each of the eight categories.

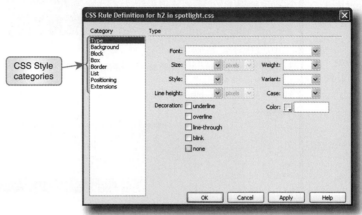

FIGURE 5-44

Adding a Style and Saving the Style Sheet

Recall that styles and style sheets are applied in a variety of formats: an external style sheet can be linked or imported to any number of Web pages, an embedded style sheet is contained within one Web page, or you can apply a style to a specific element within a Web page. The spotlight style sheet you create in the following steps is an external style sheet that is linked to the spotlight template page. When you apply the first style, a Document window with a .css extension opens behind the original Document window. This window contains the code for the applied styles; it does not display in Design view. When you complete adding styles, you also save and close the .css window.

In this project, the original Document window is a template. The Document window, however, does not have to be a template. It also can be a basic page or a frame to which you can apply styles. The following steps show how to create the heading style and then save the style sheet.

To Add a Style and Save the Style Sheet

1

• Click the Files panel tab.

• Click to the left of the text, Spotlight on [name of national monument], in the monument_name editable region and then click the <h2> tag in the tag selector.

The heading prompt is selected in the Document window, and the <h2> tag is selected in the tag selector (Figure 5-45).

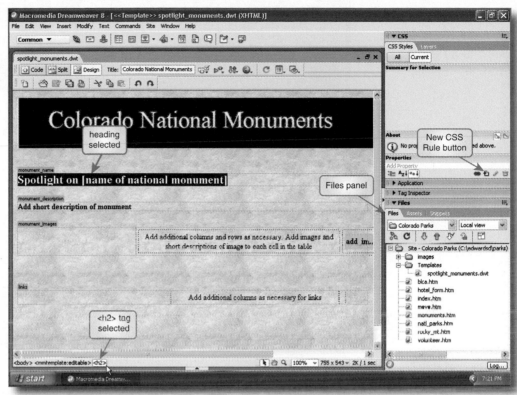

FIGURE 5-45

2

• Click the New CSS Rule button.

• Click the Tag (redefines the look of a specific tag) radio button to select it.

• Click the Tag box and type h2 as the tag name.

• Verify that (New Style Sheet File) is selected in the Define in: section.

The New CSS Rule dialog box is displayed. The Tag (redefines the look of a specific tag) and Define in (New Style Sheet File) radio buttons are selected. The h2 tag name is displayed in the Tag box (Figure 5-46).

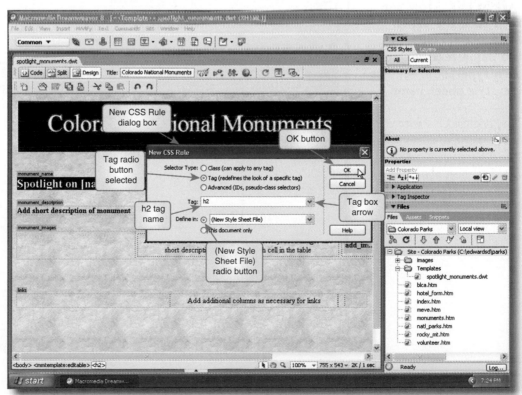

FIGURE 5-46

3

• **Click the OK button.**

The Save Style Sheet File As dialog box is displayed (Figure 5-47). The parks folder is displayed in the Save in box.

FIGURE 5-47

4

• **If necessary, click the Save in box arrow and then click the parks folder name. Click the File name text box and then type** spotlight **as the style sheet name.**

The parks folder is selected and is displayed in the Save in text box (Figure 5-48). The style sheet name, spotlight, is displayed in the File name text box.

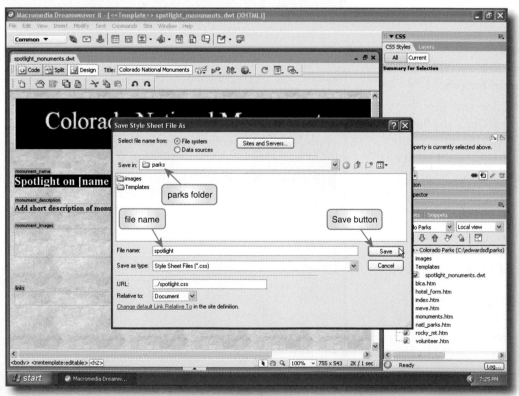

FIGURE 5-48

5

• **Click the Save button.**

The CSS Rule Definition dialog box is displayed. The Type category is selected (Figure 5-49).

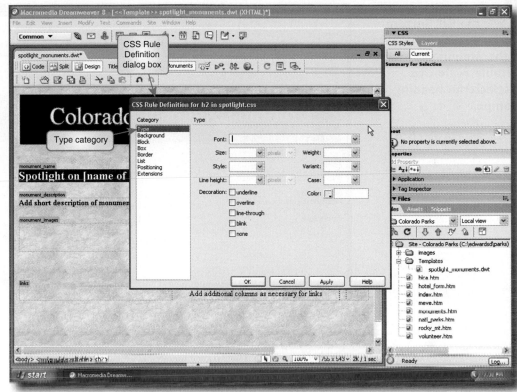

FIGURE 5-49

6

• **Click the Font box arrow; click Arial, Helvetica, sans-serif in the Font list; and then press the TAB key.**

• **Click the Size box arrow, click 24 in the Size list, and then press the TAB key two times.**

• **Click the Weight box arrow, click bolder, and then press the TAB key.**

• **Click the Style box arrow and then click italic.**

• **Click the Color text box, type #420000, and then press the TAB key.**

The style definitions are entered as shown in Figure 5-50. The shade of maroon in the Color box matches the maroon color in the logo.

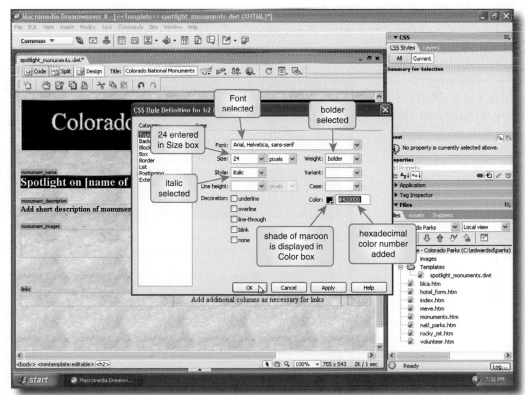

FIGURE 5-50

7

• **Click the OK button and then click anywhere in the monument_name editable region to deselect the heading prompt.**

The heading prompt in the Document window changes to reflect the new style of the applied attributes. The spotlight.css tab displays in the Document window. The new Properties for "h2" CSS style and the style attributes are displayed in the CSS Styles panel (Figure 5-51).

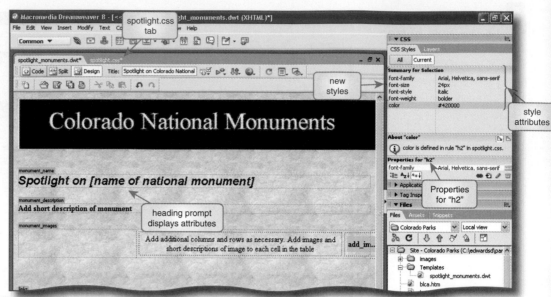

FIGURE 5-51

Next, you create a style for the paragraph text. The following section illustrates how to redefine the HTML paragraph tag for the monument_description editable region.

To Create a Style for the Paragraph Text

1

• **Click to the left of the prompt, Add short description of monument, and then click the <p> tag in the tag selector.**

The prompt is selected (Figure 5-52).

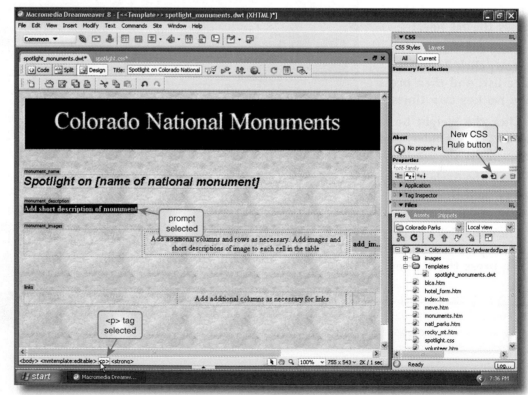

FIGURE 5-52

2

• **Click the New CSS Rule button in the CSS Styles panel.**

The New CSS Rule dialog box is displayed. The p tag is selected in the Tag box, and spotlight.css is displayed in the Define in box (Figure 5-53).

FIGURE 5-53

3

• **Click the OK button.**

The CSS Rule Definition dialog box is displayed (Figure 5-54).

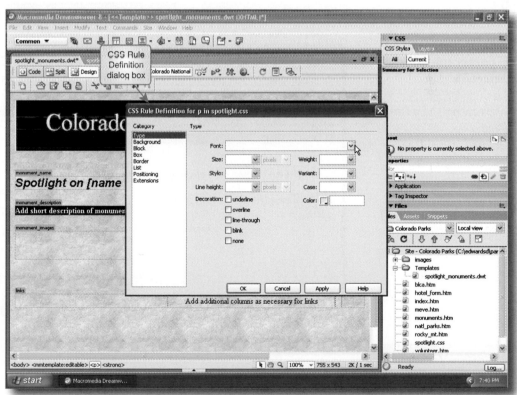

FIGURE 5-54

4

• **Click the Font box arrow and then click Arial, Helvetica, sans-serif.**

• **Click the Size box arrow and then click 12.**

• **Click the Weight box arrow and then click bold.**

• **Click the Color text box and then type #420000 for the color. Press the TAB key.**

The CSS Rule Definition attributes for Type are added (Figure 5-55).

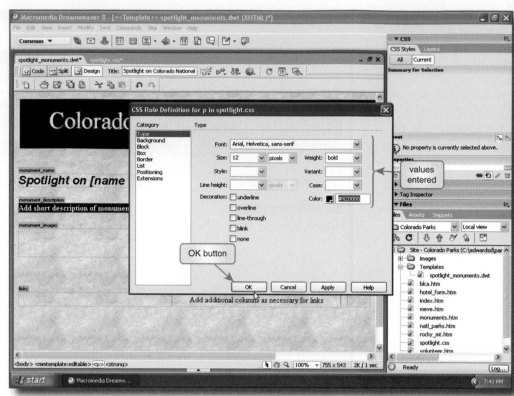

FIGURE 5-55

5

• **Click the OK button.**

• **Click to the right of the paragraph to deselect it.**

The text changes to reflect the new attributes. The new style is displayed as p in the CSS Styles panel (Figure 5-56).

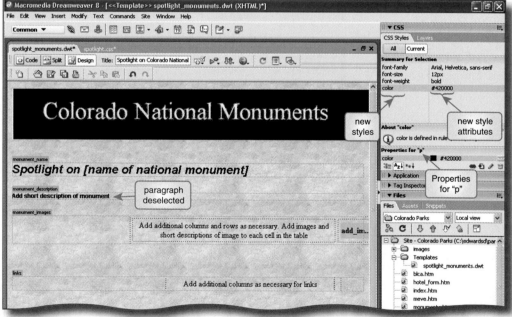

FIGURE 5-56

Adding a background, border, and text color to the tables is your next goal. To accomplish this, you use the Type, Background, and Border categories in the CSS Style Definition dialog box. The following steps show how to select a font, a background color of maroon, and a shade of tan for the border.

To Add a Background, Border, and Text Color to a Table

1

• **Click in the first cell of the monument_images table.**

• **Click the <table#spotlight> tag in the tag selector.**

The monument_images table is selected (Figure 5-57).

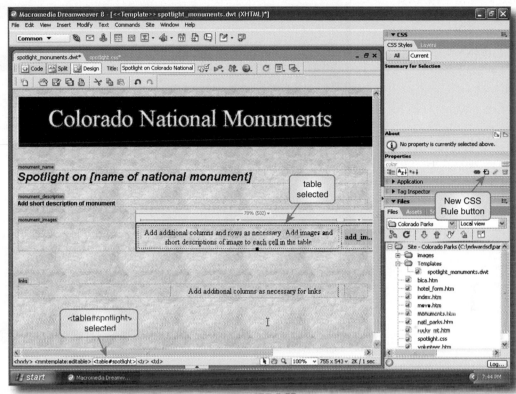

FIGURE 5-57

2

• **Click the New CSS Rule button in the CSS Styles panel.**

• **If necessary, click the Tag (redefines the look of a specific tag) radio button.**

• **If necessary, select and delete the text #spotlight in the Tag box and then type** table.

The New CSS Rule dialog box is displayed (Figure 5-58). The table tag appears in the Tag box, the Tag (redefines the look of a specific tag) radio button is selected, and spotlight.css is displayed in the Define in box.

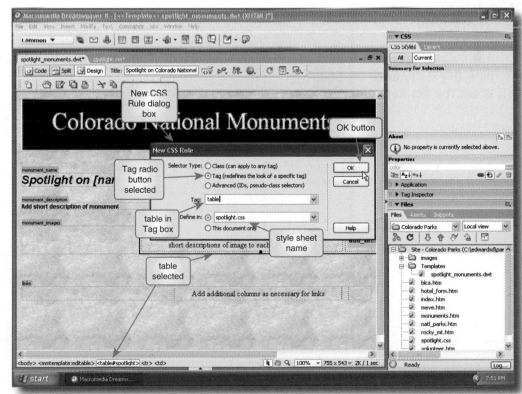

FIGURE 5-58

3

• **Click the OK button.**

The CSS Rule Definition for table in spotlight.css dialog box is displayed (Figure 5-59). The Type category is selected.

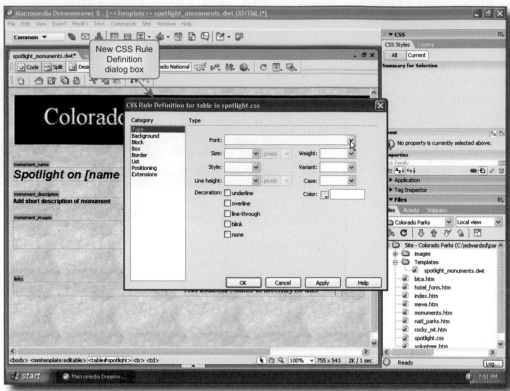

FIGURE 5-59

4

• **Click the Font box arrow and then click Arial, Helvetica, sans-serif.**

• **Click the Color text box, type** #FFFFFF, **and then press the TAB key.**

The font is displayed as Arial, Helvetica, sans-serif, and the hexadecimal #FFFFFF is displayed in the Color text box (Figure 5-60). The color is white.

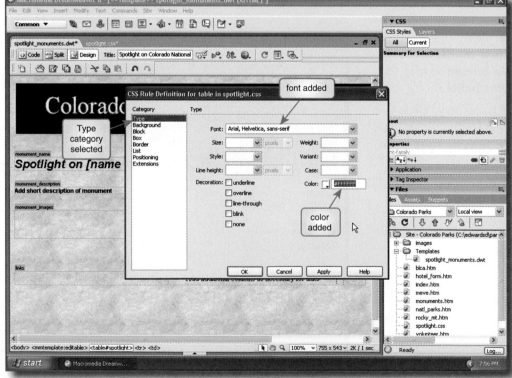

FIGURE 5-60

5

• **Click Background in the Category list.**

• **Click the Background color text box, type** #420000 **as the color, and then press the TAB key.**

The background color is displayed in the Background color box (Figure 5-61).

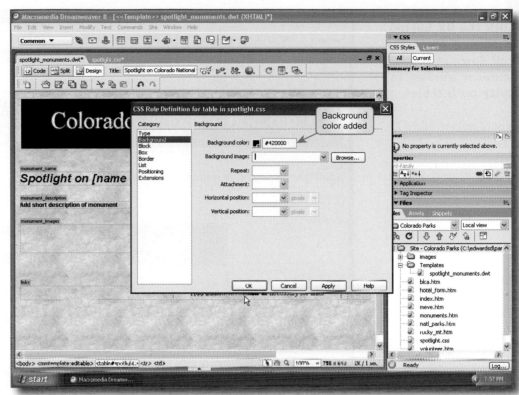

FIGURE 5-61

6

• **Click Border in the Category list.**

• **Verify that the Same for all check boxes are selected for Style, Width, and Color.**

• **Click the Top box arrow and then click groove in the Top pop-up menu.**

• **Click the Width box arrow and then click thick in the Width pop-up menu.**

• **Click the top text box in the Color area and then type** #CC9900 **for the border color. Press the TAB key.**

The attributes are defined and will apply to both tables (Figure 5-62).

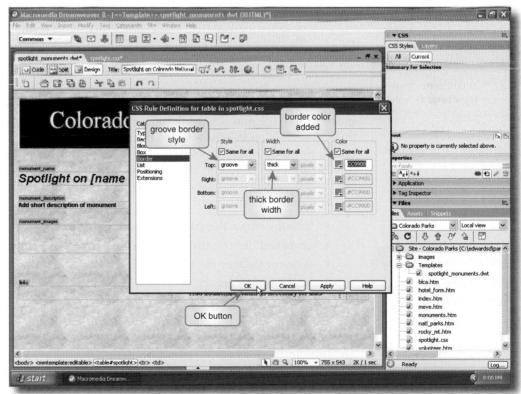

FIGURE 5-62

7

• **Click the OK button and then, if necessary, scroll down in the Document window to display both tables.**

The attributes are added to both tables, and the table style is added to the spotlight.css style sheet in the CSS Styles panel (Figure 5-63).

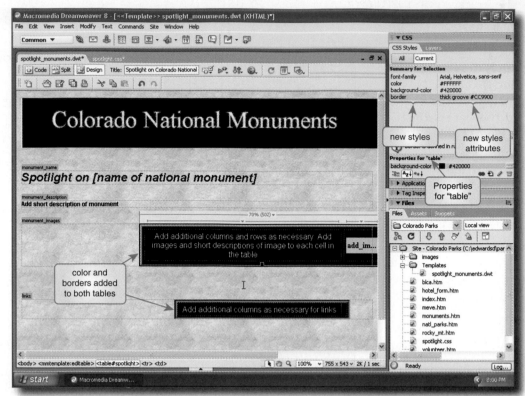

FIGURE 5-63

Style Sheets and Links

When you selected the <table> tag for the monument_images table and applied the attributes, these attributes were added to all tables in the template. Now you will add two links to the links table — a relative link to the Colorado National Monuments index Web page and an absolute link to the Dinosaur National Monument page. Style sheets provide new ways to display links, which enable the content developer to match the style of the links with that of the rest of the Web page. For example, all of the attributes available in the Selector Type category in the New CSS Rule dialog box also can be applied to links. When you are defining the style for links, four attributes are available—a:link, a:visited, a:hover, and a:active.

- **a:link** defines the style of an unvisited link.
- **a:visited** defines the style of a link to a Web site that you have visited.
- **a:hover** defines the style of a link when the mouse pointer moves over the link.
- **a:active** defines the style of a clicked link.

Using the Advanced Selector Type and attributes from the Selector pop-up menu, you specify that the links will use white for the text color and will not contain an underline when displayed in the browser. The check boxes within the Decoration attribute in the CSS Style Definition dialog box provide options to add an underline, an overline, or a line through the text, or to make the text blink. The default setting for regular text is none. The default setting for links is underline. When you set the link attribute to none, you remove the underline from links. You also can specify that when the mouse pointer moves over a link, the underline is displayed. This indicates to the Web page visitor that the link is available. The Decoration attribute is supported by both Microsoft Internet Explorer and Netscape Navigator. The following steps show how to add the attributes for formatting of the links as they will display in a browser.

To Modify the A:Link Attribute

1

- **Select the links table.**
- **Click the New CSS Rule button in the CSS Styles panel.**
- **Click the Advanced (IDs, pseudo-class selectors) radio button.**
- **If necessary, click the Define in spotlight.css radio button.**
- **Click the Selector box arrow, and then point to a:link.**

The New CSS Rule dialog box is displayed, and a:link is selected in the pop-up menu (Figure 5-64).

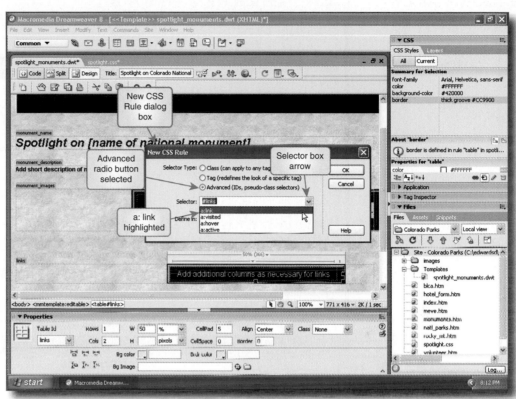

FIGURE 5-64

2

- **Click a:link.**

The a:link attribute is displayed in the Selector box (Figure 5-65).

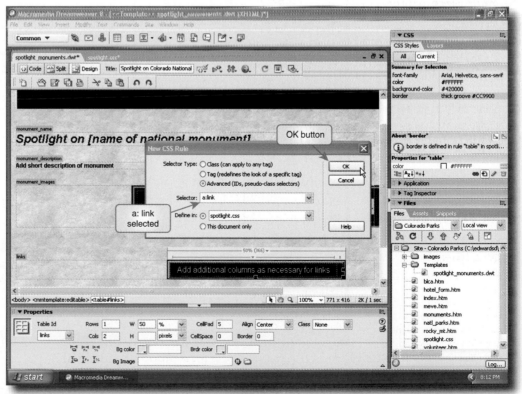

FIGURE 5-65

• **Click the OK button.**

The CSS Rule Definition dialog box is displayed (Figure 5-66).

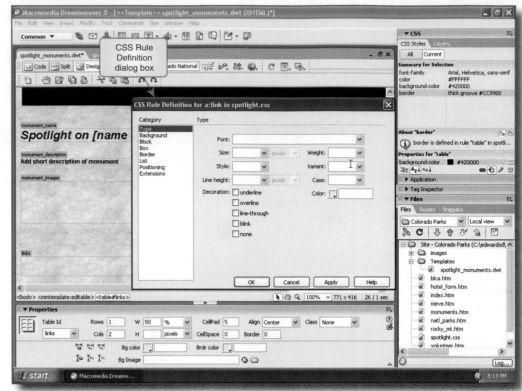

FIGURE 5-66

• **Click none to select the none Decoration attribute.**

• **Click the Color text box, type #FFFFFF, and press the TAB key.**

The a:link style is added to the spotlight.css style sheet (Figure 5-67). The link color is white.

5

• **Click the OK button.**

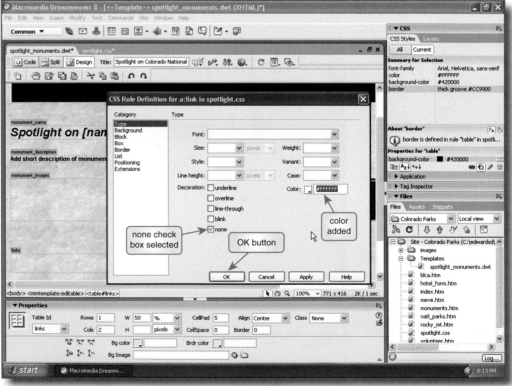

FIGURE 5-67

The link attribute is added to the template, and the next step is to add the visited attribute. After a Web site visitor clicks a link, it will display as tan.

To Add the A:Visited Attribute

1 Verify that the links table is selected.

2 Click the New CSS Rule button in the CSS Styles panel to display the New CSS Rule dialog box.

3 Click the Advanced (IDs, pseudo-class selectors) radio button.

4 Verify that the Define in spotlight.css radio button is selected.

5 Click the Selector box arrow and then click a:visited.

6 Click the OK button to display the CSS Rule Definition dialog box.

7 Click the none check box to select the none Decoration attribute.

8 Type #CC9900 in the Color text box and then press the TAB key (Figure 5-68).

9 Click the OK button.

The a:visited style is added to the spotlight.css style sheet, and the visited link color is tan (Figure 5-68).

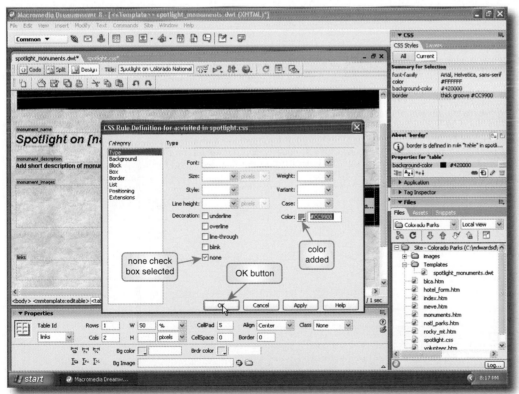

FIGURE 5-68

The final attribute to be added is the a:hover attribute. Many Web site visitors are accustomed to having links identified by underlines. Because the links in this template are designed to not include underlines, the a:hover attribute is applied to the links. Thus, when the mouse pointer moves over a link, an underline is not displayed. Note, however, that the hover attribute is not displayed by all browsers. The following steps illustrate how to add the a:hover attribute.

Add the A:Hover Attribute

1 Verify that the links table is selected.

2 Click the New CSS Rule button in the CSS Styles panel to display the New CSS Rule dialog box.

3 If necessary, click the Advanced (IDs, pseudo-class selectors) radio button.

4 Click the Selector box arrow and then click a:hover.

5 Click the OK button to display the CSS Rule Definition for a:hover in spotlight.css dialog box.

6 Type #FFCC66 in the Color text box and then press the TAB key. Click the none check box to select the None Decoration attribute (Figure 5-69).

7 Click the OK button and then click the Save button on the Standard toolbar.

8 If a Dreamweaver warning dialog box appears, click No. At this point, the template is not attached to any documents.

9 Close the spotlight_monuments template.

10 Click the Save button on the spotlight.css document and then close the style sheet.

The CSS styles are defined for the spotlight_monuments template, as shown in Figure 5-69.

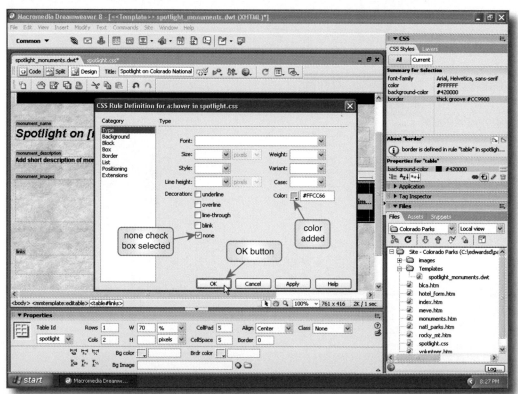

FIGURE 5-69

Style Sheet Maintenance

After a style is created, it can be edited, deleted, or duplicated. You apply these commands through the CSS Styles panel. You can view the CSS rules through Current mode, which relates to the currently selected element, or All mode, which relates to the full document. Figure 5-70 shows an expanded view of the CSS panel in Current mode. In Figure 5-70, for example, the rules you applied to the heading "h2" on pages DW 431–434 are displayed. Note that Current mode contains three panes—Summary for Selection, Rules, and Properties.

Figure 5-71 on the next page shows an expanded view of the CSS panel in All mode and displays a list, All Rules, with table selected. The table element is selected and rules for "table" are displayed. All mode contains two panes—All Rules and Properties.

You can make changes to any of these properties either in All mode or Current mode. Select the property and then click the Edit Style button to display the CSS Rule Definition dialog box. Make your changes and then click the OK button.

Below the Properties pane are three buttons that you can use to change the view in the Properties pane. Clicking the Category View button divides the CSS properties into eight categories. Click the Plus button or Minus button to expand or collapse these categories. The List View button displays all Dreamweaver CSS properties in alphabetical order. Set Properties View (default view) displays only set properties.

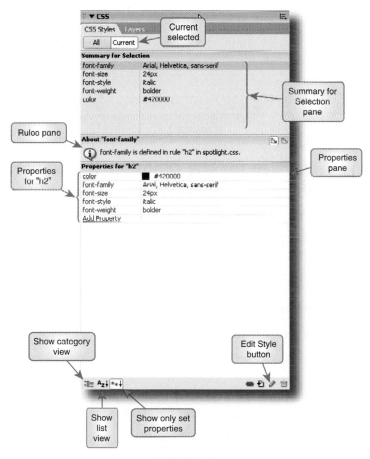

FIGURE 5-70

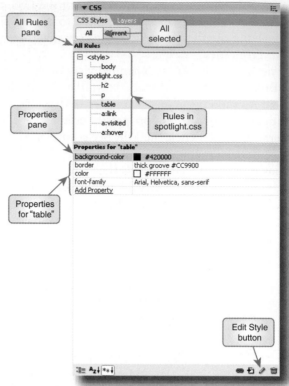

FIGURE 5-71

Creating the Web Page for the Dinosaur National Monument

The template has been created, and styles have been added to the template. The following steps show how to open a basic page and then save the page as an HTML document.

To Create the Dinosaur National Monument Spotlight Web Page

1 Click the CSS panel expand/collapse arrow to collapse the panel.

2 Click File on the menu bar and then click New.

3 Click Basic Page in the New Document dialog box Category and then click the Create button.

4 Click the Save button on the Standard toolbar and then save the page in the parks folder. Use dinosaur.htm as the file name.

5 If necessary, collapse the Property inspector.

The dinosaur document is saved in the parks folder (Figure 5-72 on the next page).

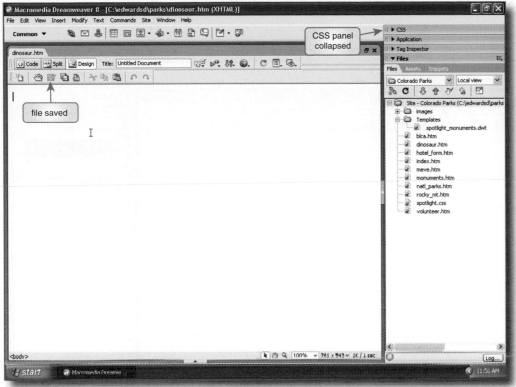

FIGURE 5-72

To apply a template to a document, you use the Assets panel. The following steps illustrate how to display the Assets panel and apply the template to the Dinosaur National Monument Web page.

To Apply a Template to the Dinosaur National Monument Web Page

1

• **Click the Assets panel tab in the Files group panel.**

• **If necessary, click the Templates icon in the Assets panel.**

• **Click spotlight_monuments.**

The Assets panel is displayed, and the template is selected in the Assets panel (Figure 5-73).

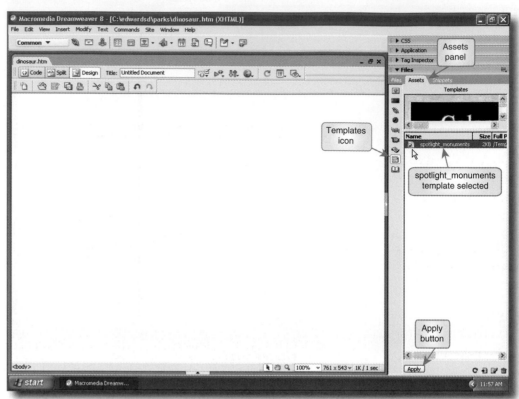

FIGURE 5-73

2

• **Click the Apply button.**

• **Collapse the panel groups.**

The template is applied to the dinosaur document. The template name, Template:spotlight_monuments, is displayed in the upper-right corner of the Document window (Figure 5-74). The panel groups are collapsed.

Other Ways

1. Click Document window; on Modify menu point to Templates, click Apply Template to Page on Templates submenu, select a template from list, click Select button
2. Click Document window; from Assets panel, drag template to Document window

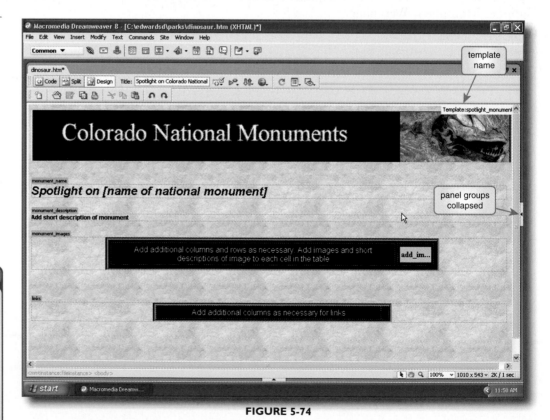

FIGURE 5-74

Now you use the template to create the Dinosaur National Monument Web page. You first add the name of the monument and then add a short description of the monument. The following steps show how to add the monument name and monument description.

To Add the Monument Name and Monument Description to the Dinosaur National Monument Web Page

1

• **If necessary, click anywhere on the document. Move the mouse pointer over the page and note that in the non-editable sections, the pointer changes to a circle with a line through the middle. This icon indicates that this is a non-editable area.**

• **Select the text and brackets, [name of national monument], in the monument_name editable region.**

The text and brackets, [name of national monument], are selected (Figure 5-75).

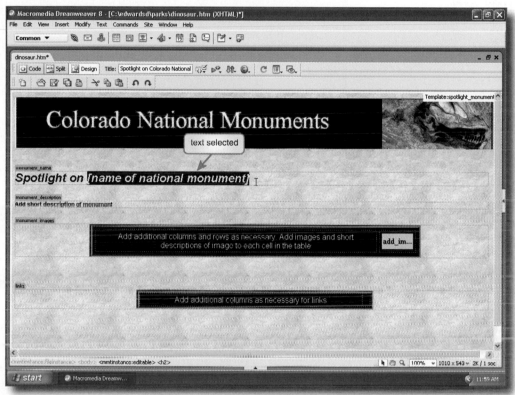

FIGURE 5-75

2

• **Type** Dinosaur National Monument **as the monument name.**

The monument name, Dinosaur National Monument. is added to the dinosaur.htm Web page (Figure 5-76).

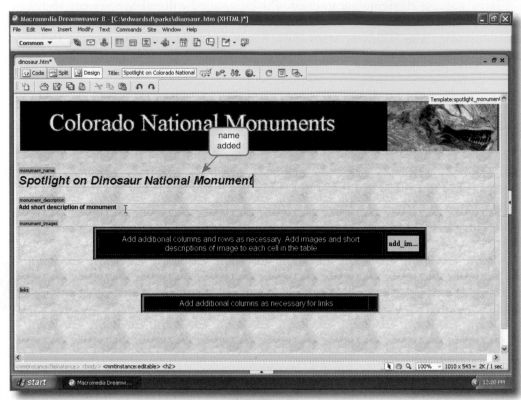

FIGURE 5-76

3

• **Select the prompt, Add short description of monument, in the monument_description editable region. Type the following text:** Dinosaur National Monument spans the Colorado/Utah border in the northwest corner of Colorado. The Quarry Area contains a collection of some 1,600 fossilized dinosaur bones from 11 different dinosaur species. Visitors can view the bone displays by visiting the Douglas Quarry and Visitor Center. Program events and nature tours are available through the Center.

The description is added to the monument_description editable region (Figure 5-77).

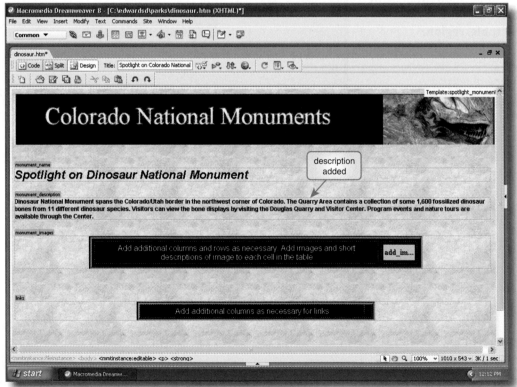

FIGURE 5-77

The Dinosaur National Monument Web page table will contain six images, in three rows and two columns. The monument_images editable table currently contains only one row and two columns. The following steps show how to add two additional rows.

To Add Rows to the Monument_images Table

1

• **Click in the left cell of the monument_images table. Click Modify on the menu bar, point to Table, and then point to Insert Rows or Columns.**

The Modify menu and Table submenu are displayed (Figure 5-78).

FIGURE 5-78

• **Click Insert Rows or Columns.**

The Insert Rows or Columns dialog box is displayed (Figure 5-79). The number of rows displayed may be different on your screen.

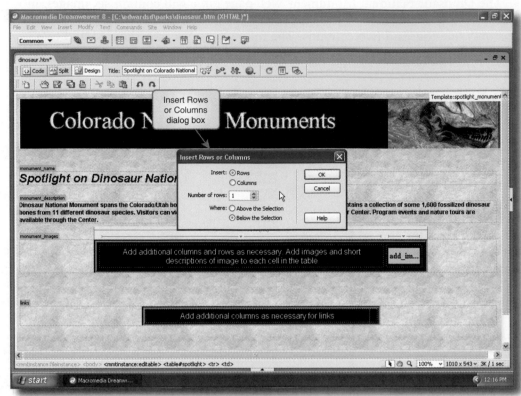

FIGURE 5-79

• **Double-click the Number of rows text box and then type** 2 **for the number of rows.**

The number of rows is changed to 2 (Figure 5-80).

FIGURE 5-80

4

• **Click the OK button.**

The additional two rows are added to the monument_images table (Figure 5-81).

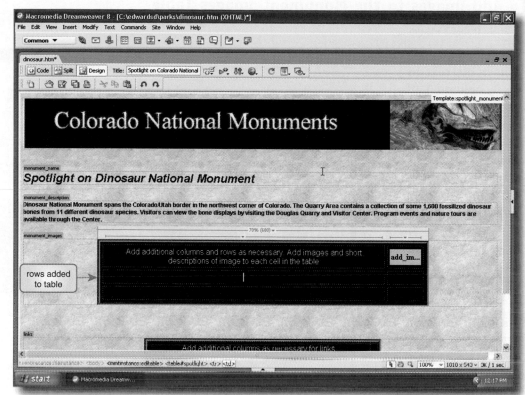

rows added
to table

FIGURE 5-81

Expanded Tables Mode

Inserting an image into a table cell and then clicking to the right or left of the image is somewhat awkward in Dreamweaver. Recall that you used Expanded Tables mode in Project 3 to temporarily add cell padding and spacing to all tables in a document and increase the tables' borders to make editing easier. This mode enables you to select items in tables or precisely place the insertion point. You return to Standard mode when you complete adding images and text to the table.

The following steps illustrate how to add the six images and a short description of each image. To add an image, you drag the image from the Files panel to a table cell. You use Expanded Tables mode to assist with insertion point placement. You add a <br> tag by holding down the SHIFT key and pressing the ENTER key. Then you type the image description.

To Add Images to the Monument_images Table

 1

• **Select the text in row 1, column 1 of the monument_images table and then press the DELETE key.**

• **Press the F6 key to switch to Expanded Tables mode.**

• **If a Getting Started in Expanded Tables Mode dialog box displays, read the information and then click the OK button.**

• **Display the panel groups.**

• **If necessary, click the Assets tab.**

The table is displayed in Expanded Tables mode, and the prompt is deleted from the first cell (Figure 5-82).

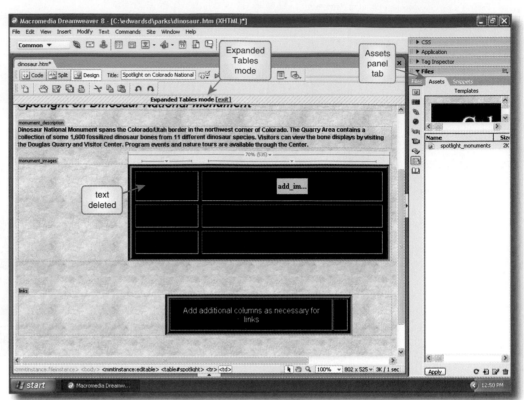

FIGURE 5-82

2

• **Click the Images icon in the Assets panel.**

• **Drag the elephant_toes.jpg file to row 1, column 1 of the monument_images table.**

• **Click to the right of the image.**

The image is displayed in the cell. The insertion point is blinking to the right of the image (Figure 5-83).

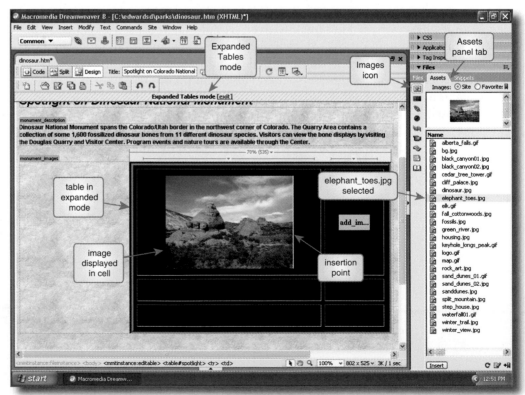

FIGURE 5-83

3

• **Hold down the SHIFT key and then press the ENTER key. You will not see the insertion point until you begin typing.**

• **Type** Elephant Toes Mountain **as the description.**

The text, Elephant Toes Mountain, is added to the cell (Figure 5-84).

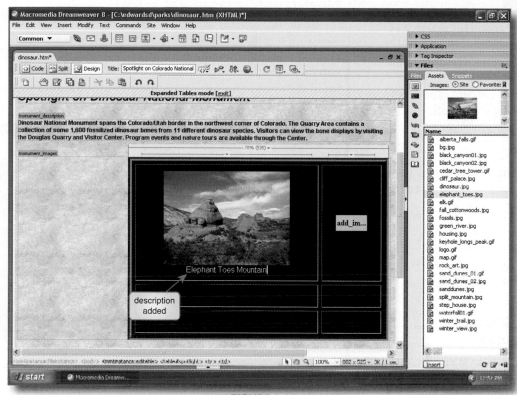

FIGURE 5-84

4

• **Press the TAB key to move the insertion point to row 1, column 2.**

The image placeholder is selected (Figure 5-85).

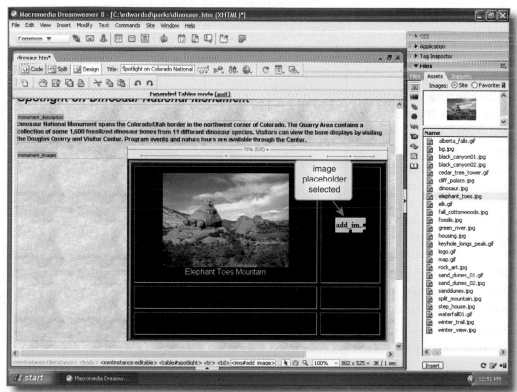

FIGURE 5-85

5

• **Press the DELETE key to delete the image placeholder and then drag the fall_cottonwoods.jpg file to the cell.**

• **Click to the right of the image.**

• **Hold down the SHIFT key and then press the ENTER key.**

• **Type** Fall cottonwoods along the river **as the description.**

The image is displayed in the cell, and the description is added below the image (Figure 5-86).

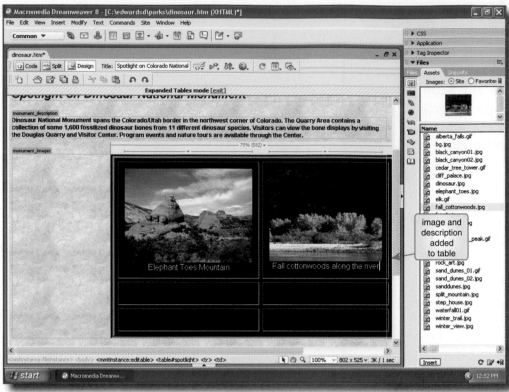

FIGURE 5-86

6

• **Add the four other images and descriptions to the monument_images table as indicated in Table 5-2 on the next page. Scroll as necessary.**

• **Drag each image to the appropriate table cell, click to the right of the image, hold down SHIFT and press the ENTER key, and then type the description.**

• **Press the TAB key to move from cell to cell.**

• **Press the F6 key to exit from Expanded Tables mode.**

The images and descriptions are added to the monument_image table (Figure 5-87).

FIGURE 5-87

Table 5-2 Dinosaur Monument Image File Names and Descriptions

CELL	IMAGE	IMAGE DESCRIPTION
Row 1, Column 1	elephant_toes.jpg	Elephant Toes Mountain
Row 1, Column 2	fall_cottonwood.jpg	Fall cottonwoods along the river
Row 2, Column 1	rock_art.jpg	Rock art
Row 2, Column 2	green_river.jpg	Green River Overlook
Row 3, Column 1	winter_trail.jpg	Jones Hole Trail
Row 3, Column 2	split_mountain.jpg	Split Mountain near Cub Creek

7

• **Hide the panel groups.**

• **Display the Property inspector.**

• **Click each image and add the ALT Text as indicated in Table 5-3 (Figure 5-88)**

Alt text is added for each image (Figure 5-88).

FIGURE 5-88

Table 5-3 Dinosaur Monument

IMAGE	ALT TEXT
elephant_toes.jpg	Elephant Toes Mountain
fall_cottonwood.jpg	Fall cottonwoods
rock_art.jpg	Rock art
green_river.jpg	Green River Overlook
winter_trail.jpg	Jones Hole Trail
split_mountain.jpg	Split Mountain

Other Ways

1. Click table cell; on Insert menu click Image, select file name in Select Image Source dialog box, click OK button

To complete the Dinosaur National Monument Web page, you add two links in the links table. The first link is a relative link to the Colorado National Parks index page. The second link is an absolute link to the Dinosaur National Monument Web page. Thus far, when creating links, you used the default and did not specify a target. The target for your links, therefore, has been to open the linked document in the same browser window.

When you create the link to the Dinosaur National Monument Web page, however, the page opens in a new browser window. Recall from Project 2 that the Target option in the Property inspector specifies the frame or window in which the linked page is displayed. When the _blank target is specified, the linked document opens in a new browser window. The other three choices in the Target option are _parent, _self, and _top. These options are discussed in detail in Project 7, when you create a framed Web site. The following steps show how to add the two links to the links table.

To Add Links to the Links Table

1

• **Scroll down to display the links table. Select the text in the left cell of the links table and then press the DELETE key.**

The text is deleted from the cell (Figure 5-89).

FIGURE 5-89

2

• **Type** Home **as the text link in the left cell and then select the text.**

• **Click the Link text box in the Property inspector, type** index.htm **as the link, and then press the TAB key.**

The link to the home page is added and centered in the cell (Figure 5-90). The link is not underlined because the selected Decoration style is None.

3

• **Click the right cell in the links table. Type** Dinosaur National Monument **as the text for the link and then select the text.**

• **Click the Link text box in the Property inspector and then type** http://www.nps.gov/dino

• **Click the Target box arrow and select _blank.**

The text is displayed in the table, and the link is added to the Link text box (Figure 5-91). The linked page will open in a new window when the link is clicked.

4

• **Click the Save button on the Standard toolbar.**

The dinosaur.htm Web page is saved.

FIGURE 5-90

FIGURE 5-91

The following steps illustrate how to complete the updating of the Colorado Parks Web site by adding a link from the Colorado National Monuments page to the Dinosaur National Monument page.

To Add a Link from the Monuments Page to the Dinosaur National Monument Page

1 Expand the panel groups and open the monuments.htm page. If necessary, click the Files tab.

2 Scroll to the bottom of the page and then click to the right of the Home link. Press the END key.

3 Hold down the SHIFT key and then press the ENTER key.

4 Type Featured Monument as the link text.

5 Select the text and then drag dinosaur.htm from the Files panel to the Property inspector Link text box.

6 Click the Save button on the Standard toolbar.

7 Press the F12 key to preview the dinosaur.htm page in your browser. Scroll down and then click the Featured Monument link to view the Dinosaur National Monument Web page, as shown in Figure 5-92.

8 Verify that the Dinosaur National Monument Web page links work.

9 If instructed to do so, print a copy of the Dinosaur National Monument Web page and submit it to your instructor.

10 If instructed to do so, upload your Web site to a remote server. Appendix C contains information on uploading to a remote server. A remote folder is required before you can upload to a remote server. Generally, the remote folder is defined by the Web server administrator or your instructor.

11 Close the browser.

The Dinosaur National Monument Web page is displayed in the browser after you complete step 7 (Figure 5-92 on the next page).

FIGURE 5-92

Quitting Dreamweaver

After you have created your Web page based on a template with applied styles, and tested and verified that the links work, Project 5 is complete. The following steps show how to close the Web site, quit Dreamweaver 8, and return control to Windows.

To Close the Web Site and Quit Dreamweaver

1 Click the Close button on the upper-right corner of the Dreamweaver title bar.

The Dreamweaver window, the Document window, and the Colorado National Parks Web site all close. If you have unsaved changes, Dreamweaver will prompt you to save the changes. Clicking the Yes button in the Dreamweaver 8 dialog box saves the changes.

CSS Style Definition Category Descriptions

The following tables list the attributes and descriptions of the eight categories available through the CSS Rule Definition dialog box. Not all browsers support all properties; browser support is indicated in the Description column. The phrase, both browsers, refers to Microsoft Internet Explorer and Netscape Navigator.

Table 5-4 Type Style Properties

ATTRIBUTES	DESCRIPTION
Font	Sets the font family for the style; supported by both browsers.
Size	Defines the size of the text. Enter or select a number and then select a unit of measurement. Selecting pixels prevents Web site visitors from adjusting the text size in their Web browsers. Supported by both browsers.
Weight	Defines the thickness of the font. Thirteen different choices are available; normal and bold are the most common and work in all browsers that support CSS.
Style	Specifies normal, italic, or oblique as the font style; supported by both browsers.
Variant	Specifies small-caps or normal. Dreamweaver does not display this attribute in the Document window. Not supported by Netscape Navigator.
Line Height	Refers to the amount of space between lines of text; also called leading. Normal allows the line height for the font size to be calculated automatically. Supported by both browsers.
Case	Capitalizes the first letter of each word in the selection or sets the text to all uppercase or lowercase; supported by both browsers.
Decoration	Adds an underline, overline, or line-through to the text, or makes the text blink; supported by both browsers.
Color	Sets the text color; supported by both browsers.

Table 5-5 Background Style Properties

ATTRIBUTES	DESCRIPTION
Background Color	Sets the background color for an element — a character, a word, a paragraph, or even the Web page itself; supported by both browsers.
Background Image	Adds a background image to either a Web page or a table; supported by both browsers.
Repeat	Repeats the background image; supported by both browsers.
Attachment	Determines whether the background image is fixed at its original position or scrolls along with the content; not supported by Netscape Navigator.
Horizontal and Vertical Positions	Specifies a position for selected text or other Web page elements; can be used to align a background image to the center of the page, both vertically and horizontally, or to align the element relative to the Document window; not supported by Netscape Navigator.

Table 5-6 Block Style Properties

ATTRIBUTES	DESCRIPTION
Word Spacing	Sets the spacing between words; not displayed in the Document window. The bigger the number, the more space between the words. Supported by both browsers.
Letter Spacing	Sets the spacing between letters or characters; supported by both browsers.
Vertical Alignment	Specifies the vertical alignment of the element to which it is applied; is displayed in the Document window only when applied to an image; supported by both browsers.
Text Align	Sets the text alignment within the element; supported by both browsers.
Text Indent	Specifies the amount of space the first line of text is indented; supported by both browsers.
Whitespace	Determines how the browser displays extra white space; supported by Netscape Navigator and Internet Explorer 5.5 and higher.
Display	Specifies whether an element is displayed, and, if so, how it is displayed; supported by both browsers.

Table 5-7 Box Style Properties

ATTRIBUTES	DESCRIPTION
Width and Height	Sets the width and height of an element; supported by both browsers.
Float	Sets on which side other elements, such as text, layers, and tables, will float around an element; supported by both browsers.
Clear	Prevents an element from wrapping around an object with a right or left float; supported by both browsers.
Padding	Specifies the amount of space between the content of an element and its border (or margin if there is no border); supported by both browsers.
Margin	Specifies the amount of space between the border of an element (or the padding if there is no border) and another element; supported by both browsers.
Same for All	Sets the same padding or margin attributes to the Top, Right, Bottom, and Left of the Padding and element to which it is applied; supported by both browsers.

Table 5-8 Border Style Properties

ATTRIBUTES	DESCRIPTION
Style	Sets the style appearance of the border. Appearance may be rendered differently in different browsers. Supported by both browsers.
Width	Sets the thickness of the element; supported by both browsers.
Color	Sets the color of the border; supported by both browsers.
Same For All	Applies the same style, thickness, or color to the Top, Bottom, Right and Left of the element to which is it is applied; supported by both browsers.

Table 5-9 List Style Properties

ATTRIBUTES	DESCRIPTION
Type	Sets the appearance of bullets or numbers; supported by both browsers.
Bullet Image	Specifies a custom image for the bullet; supported by both browsers.
Position	Sets whether list item text wraps and indents (outside) or whether the text wraps to the left margin (inside); supported by both browsers.

Table 5-10 Positioning Style Properties (Used with Layers)

ATTRIBUTES	DESCRIPTION
Type	Determines how the browser should position the element (absolute, relative, or static); supported by both browsers.
Visibility	Determines the initial display condition of the layer; supported by both browsers.
Width	Sets the width of the layer; supported by both browsers.
Z-Index	Determines the stacking order of the layer; supported by both browsers.
Height	Sets the height of the layer; supported by both browsers.
Overflow	Determines what happens if the content of a layer exceeds its size; CSS layers only.
Placement	Specifies the location and size of the layer (Left, Top, Right, or Bottom); supported by both browsers.
Clip	Defines the part of the layer that is visible (Left, Top, Right, or Bottom); supported by both browsers.

Table 5-11 Extensions Style Properties

ATTRIBUTES	DESCRIPTION
Page Break	Creates a page break during printing either before or after the object controlled by the style; supported by both browsers.
Visual Effect (Cursor and Filter)	Cursor changes the pointer image when the pointer is over the object controlled by style; supported by both browsers. Filter applies special effects to the object controlled by the style; supported by both browsers.

What You Should Know

Having completed this project, you now should be able to perform the tasks below. The tasks are listed in the same order they were presented in the project. For a list of keyboard commands for topics introduced in this project, see the Quick Reference for Windows at the back of this book and refer to the Shortcut column.

1. Copy Data Files to the Parks Web Site (DW 400)
2. Start Dreamweaver and Open the Colorado National Parks Web Site (DW 401)
3. Create a New Template Document (DW 403)
4. Save the Web Page as a Template (DW 405)
5. Add a Background Image and Title to the Template Page (DW 407)
6. Add the Logo Image to the Template (DW 409)
7. Add the Monument Name and Monument Description Prompts for the First Two Editable Regions (DW 411)
8. Add and Center a Table as the Third Editable Region (DW 413)
9. Add and Center a Table as the Fourth Editable Region (DW 418)
10. Create the First Editable Region (DW 420)
11. Create the Second Editable Region (DW 422)
12. Create the Third and Fourth Editable Regions (DW 424)
13. Display the Design Panel Group (DW 429)
14. Add a Style and Save the Style Sheet (DW 431)

15. Create a Style for the Paragraph Text (DW 434)

16. Add a Background, Border, and Text Color to a Table (DW 437)

17. Modify the A:Link Attribute (DW 441)

18. Add the A:Visited Attribute (DW 443)

19. Add the A:Hover Attribute (DW 444)

20. Create the Dinosaur National Monument Spotlight Web Page (DW 446)

21. Apply a Template to the Dinosaur National Monument Web Page (DW 448)

22. Add the Monument Name and Monument Description to the Dinosaur National Monument Web Page (DW 449)

23. Add Rows to the Monument_images Table (DW 451)

24. Add Images to the Monument_images Table (DW 454)

25. Add Links to the Links Table (DW 458)

26. Add a Link from the Monuments Page to the Dinosaur National Monument Page (DW 460)

27. Close the Web Site and Quit Dreamweaver (DW 461)

Learn It Online

Instructions: To complete the Learn It Online exercises, start your browser, click the Address bar, and then enter the Web address scsite.com/dw8/learn. When the Dreamweaver 8 Learn It Online page is displayed, follow the instructions in the exercises below. Each exercise has instructions for printing your results, either for your own records or for submission to your instructor.

1 Project Reinforcement TF, MC, and SA

Below Dreamweaver Project 5, click the Project Reinforcement link. Print the quiz by clicking Print on the File menu for each page. Answer each question.

2 Flash Cards

Below Dreamweaver Project 5, click the Flash Cards link and read the instructions. Type 20 (or a number specified by your instructor) in the Number of playing cards text box, type your name in the Enter your Name text box, and then click the Flip Card button. When the flash card is displayed, read the question and then click the ANSWER box arrow to select an answer. Flip through the Flash Cards. If your score is 15 (75%) correct or greater, click Print on the File menu to print your results. If your score is less than 15 (75%) correct, then redo this exercise by clicking the Replay button.

3 Practice Test

Below Dreamweaver Project 5, click the Practice Test link. Answer each question, enter your first and last name at the bottom of the page, and then click the Grade Test button. When the graded practice test is displayed on your screen, click Print on the File menu to print a hard copy. Continue to take practice tests until you score 80% or better.

4 Who Wants To Be a Computer Genius?

Below Dreamweaver Project 5, click the Computer Genius link. Read the instructions, enter your first and last name at the bottom of the page, and then click the PLAY button. When your score is displayed, click the PRINT RESULTS link to print a hard copy.

5 Wheel of Terms

Below Dreamweaver Project 5, click the Wheel of Terms link. Read the instructions, and then enter your first and last name and your school name. Click the PLAY button. When your score is displayed, right-click the score and then click Print on the shortcut menu to print a hard copy.

6 Crossword Puzzle Challenge

Below Dreamweaver Project 5, click the Crossword Puzzle Challenge link. Read the instructions, and then enter your first and last name. Click the SUBMIT button. Work the crossword puzzle. When you are finished, click the Submit button. When the crossword puzzle is redisplayed, click the Print Puzzle button to print a hard copy.

7 Tips and Tricks

Below Dreamweaver Project 5, click the Tips and Tricks link. Click a topic that pertains to Project 5. Right-click the information and then click Print on the shortcut menu. Construct a brief example of what the information relates to in Dreamweaver to confirm you understand how to use the tip or trick.

8 Newsgroups

Below Dreamweaver Project 5, click the Newsgroups link. Click a topic that pertains to Project 5. Print three comments.

9 Expanding Your Horizons

Below Dreamweaver Project 5, click the Expanding Your Horizons link. Click a topic that pertains to Project 5. Print the information. Construct a brief example of what the information relates to in Dreamweaver to confirm you understand the contents of the article.

10 Search Sleuth

Below Dreamweaver Project 5, click the Search Sleuth link. To search for a term that pertains to this project, select a term below the Project 5 title and then use the Google search engine at google.com (or any major search engine) to display and print two Web pages that present information on the term.

Apply Your Knowledge

1 Creating a Template and Style Sheet for Andy's Lawn Service

Instructions: Start Dreamweaver. See the inside back cover of this book for instructions for downloading the Data Disk, or see your instructor for information on accessing the files in this book.

The proprietors of Andy's Lawn Service would like to add a page to their Web site that features native plants for different areas of the country. They want something that can be modified easily, so a template is used. To create this template and then add styles, you copy six images from the DataFiles folder to the Lawn Service Web site images folder. You begin the process by creating a template, then you define styles. When this is completed, you apply this template to a new blank page and create a page for Florida native plants. Finally, you add a link to and from the Andy's Lawn Service home page. When you create this template, you select the This document only option in the New CSS Style dialog box. Because this template is applied to one document, an external style sheet is not created.

The template is shown in Figure 5-93a; the Web page is shown in Figure 5-93b on the next page. Software and hardware settings determine how a Web page is displayed in a browser. Your Web pages may display differently than the ones shown in Figures 5-93a and 5-93b. Appendix C contains instructions for uploading your local site to a remote server.

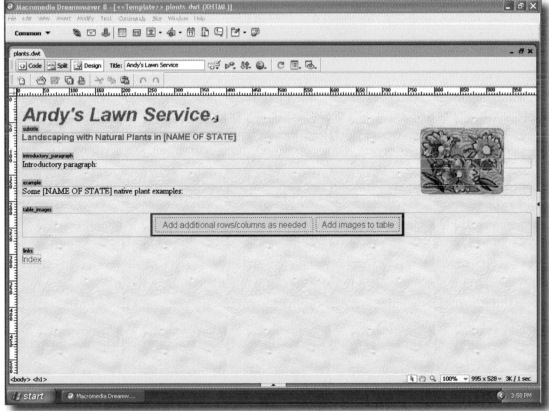

FIGURE 5-93a

(continued)

Apply Your Knowledge

Creating a Template and Style Sheet for Andy's Lawn Service *(continued)*

FIGURE 5-93b

1. Use the Windows My Computer option to copy the data files from the DataFiles folder to your lawn/images folder.
2. Start Dreamweaver. If necessary, display the panel groups. Select Lawn Service from the Files pop-up menu in the Files panel. Click File on the menu bar and then click New. Select Template page in the New Document dialog box General category and HTML template in the Template page column, and then click the Create button. Click Save on the menu bar and type plants for the file name.
3. To begin creating the template, click Modify on the menu bar and then click Page Properties. Apply the lawnbg.jpg background image. Type Andy's Lawn Service as the Web page title.
4. In the Document window, type Andy's Lawn Service as the entry. Apply Heading 1 and then press the ENTER key.
5. Type Landscaping with Natural Plants in [NAME OF STATE] as the entry. Apply Heading 3 and then press the ENTER key.
6. Type Introductory paragraph: and then press the ENTER key.
7. Type Some [NAME OF STATE] native plant examples: and then press the ENTER key.
8. Insert a one-row, two-column table with a width of 50 percent, border of 0, cell padding of 5, and cell spacing of 5. Type Landscaping with natural plants as the Summary text, and then center-align the table.
9. If necessary, click the Property inspector expander arrow to expand the Property inspector. Drag the background_table.gif file to the Bg Image text box. Click to the right of the table in the Document window and then press the ENTER key.

Apply Your Knowledge

10. Type Index and then select the text. Drag the index.htm file name to the Property inspector Link box.

11. Drag the logo.gif image to the right of the heading. If the Image Tag Accessibility Attributes dialog box is displayed, click the OK button. Select the image. Set a V Space of 4 and H Space of 50. Type Landscaping as the Alt text. Right-align the logo.gif image.

12. Click the Editable Region button on the Template pop-up menu. Create the five editable regions indicated in Table 5-12 on the next page.

13. Click the CSS panel arrow to display the CSS Styles panel.

14. Click anywhere in the heading, Andy's Lawn Service, and then click the <h1> tag in the tag selector. Click the New CSS Rule button in the CSS Styles panel. In the New CSS Rule dialog box, verify that Tag (redefines the look of a specific tag) and h1 are selected in the Tag box and that Define in This document only is selected, and then click the OK button. In the CSS Rule definition for h1 dialog box, set the following values in the Type category: Arial, Helvetica, sans-serif for the Font; 36 pixels for the Size; bolder for the Weight; oblique for the Style; and #996600 for the Color. Click the OK button.

15. Click anywhere in the first paragraph prompt, Landscaping with Natural Plants in [NAME OF STATE], and then click the <h3> tag in the tag selector. Click the New CSS Rule button in the CSS Styles panel. In the New CSS Rule dialog box, verify that Tag (redefines the look of a specific tag) and h3 are selected in the Tag box and that Define in This document only is selected, and then click the OK button. Set the following values in the Type category: Arial, Helvetica, sans-serif for the Font; 16 pixels for the Size; 600 for the Weight; and #996633 for the Color. Click the OK button.

16. Click anywhere in the table and then click the <table> tag in the tag selector. Click the New CSS Rule button in the CSS Styles panel. In the New CSS Rule dialog box, verify that Tag (redefines the look of a specific tag) and table are selected in the Tag box and that Define in This document only is selected, and then click the OK button. Set the following values in the Type category: Arial, Helvetica, sans-serif for the Font; 16 pixels for the Size; #996600 for the Color; and none for the Decoration. Set the following values in the Border category: outset for the Style and #996633 for the Color. Click the OK button. Click row 1, column 1, and then type Add additional rows/columns as needed as the entry. Then click row 1, column 2, and type Add images to table as the entry.

17. Click anywhere in the table and then click the <tr> tag in the tag selector. Click the New CSS Rule button in the CSS Styles panel. In the New CSS Rule dialog box, verify that Tag (redefines the look of a specific tag) and tr are selected in the Tag box and that Define in This document only is selected, and then click the OK button. Set the following values in the Block category: middle for Vertical alignment and center for Text align. Click the OK button.

18. Select the text, Index, and then click the New CSS Rule button in the CSS Styles panel. In the New CSS Rule dialog box, click Advanced (IDs, pseudo-class selectors) and Define in This document only. If necessary, click the Selector arrow and then click a:link. Click the OK button. Set the following values in the Type category: Arial, Helvetica, sans-serif for the Font; 16 pixels for the Size; and #996633 for the Color. Click the OK button, and then save and close the template. If the Dreamweaver 8 dialog box is displayed, click the OK button.

19. Open a new Basic Page Document window and save the page as native_plants.htm in the lawn folder.

20. Click the Assets tab in the Files panel group and then click the Templates button. Click the Apply button to apply the template to the native_plants.htm page.

21. Use Table 5-13 on the next page as a guide to add content to each of the editable regions. Title the document Native Plants.

(continued)

Apply Your Knowledge

Creating a Template and Style Sheet for Andy's Lawn Service *(continued)*

22. Save the document. Open the services.htm file. Scroll to the bottom of the page and then click to the right of the Services Form Request link. Press the END key, insert a line break, and then type Native Plants as the link text. Add a link to the native_plants.htm page. Save the services.htm page.

23. Press the F12 key to view the page in your browser. Click the Native Plants link. Print a copy of the template and Web page if instructed to do so. Upload the page to the lawn Web site on a remote server, if instructed to do so.

Table 5-12 Andy's Lawn Service Editable Regions

REGION TEXT	REGION NAME
Landscaping with Natural Plants in [NAME OF STATE]	subtitle
Introductory paragraph	introductory_paragraph
Some [NAME OF STATE] native plant examples:	example
The table	table_images
Index	links

Table 5-13 Andy's Lawn Service Page Content

REGION TEXT	REGION NAME
Landscaping with Natural Plants in Florida	Subtitle
Native plants are plants that are indigenous to a specific area. Some people believe native plants to be weeds, but native plants are beautiful and hardy. Once established, they require less maintenance than conventional plants.	introductory_paragraph
Some Florida native plant examples:	Examples
(Note: Press TAB to move from cell to cell) Row 1, column 1: plant01.gif Row 1, column 2: plant02.gif Row 2, column 1: plant03.gif Row 2, column 2: plant04.gif	table_images

1 Creating a Template for the CandleWix Web Site

Problem: The CandleWix Web site is receiving a large number of hits every day, and Martha is receiving increasingly more orders each day. She foresees a time when she will need to expand the Web site and is considering a standard design for her pages. Martha is not sure exactly how a template works within a Web site and has requested that you put together an example. You know that she has been considering beeswax for candle making, so you decide to create the page using this topic. The template is shown in Figure 5-94a and the example is shown in Figure 5-94b on the next page. The template contains five tables — one non-editable table and four editable tables. Your Web pages may display differently than the ones shown in Figures 5-94a and 5-94b. Appendix C contains instructions for uploading your local site to a remote server.

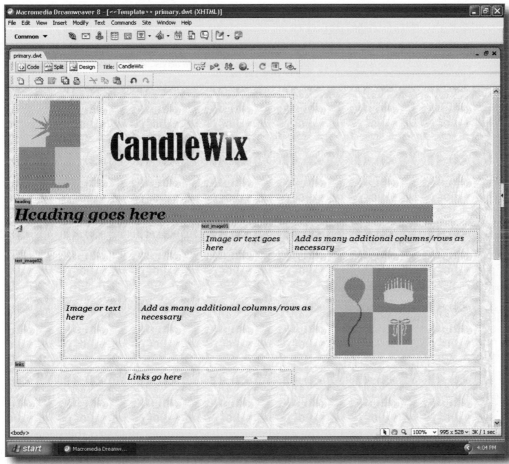

FIGURE 5-94a

(continued)

In the Lab

Creating a Template for the CandleWix Web Site *(continued)*

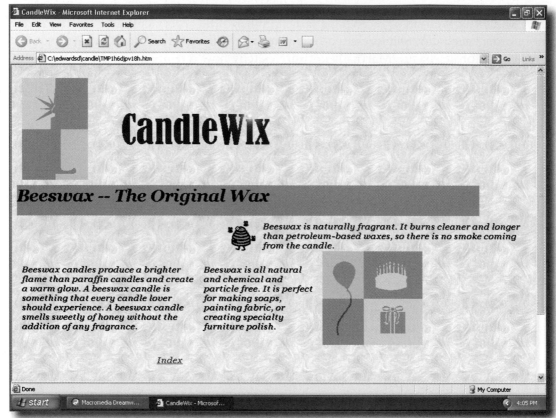

FIGURE 5-94b

Instructions: Perform the following tasks:

1. Use the Windows My Computer option to copy the data files from the DataFiles folder to your candle/images folder.

2. Start Dreamweaver. If necessary, display the panel groups. Select CandleWix from the Files pop-up menu in the Files panel. Click File on the menu bar and then click New. Select Template page in the New Document dialog box General category and HTML template in the Template Page column, and then click the Create button. Click Save on the menu bar and type primary for the file name.

3. Use the Page Properties dialog box to add the candlebg.gif background image to the page.

4. Create a one-row, two-column table with a table width of 60 percent, border of 0, cell padding of 5, and cell spacing of 5. Type CandleWix logo table as the Summary text. This is a noneditable table. Select the table cells and set Vert to Middle. Drag the candle1.gif image to the first cell and then type logo_image as the Alt text. Drag the logo.gif image to the second cell and type logo as the Alt text.

5. Click to the right of the table and then press the ENTER key. Add a one-row, one-column table with a width of 90 percent, border of 0, cell padding of 0, and cell spacing of 0. Type Table heading as the Summary text. Click in the table and type Heading goes here as the prompt. Apply Heading 1 to the text. Click the Bg color hexadecimal text box and type #CC9966 as the entry. Click to the right of the table and press the ENTER key.

In the Lab

6. Add a one-row, two-column table with a width of 60 percent, border thickness of 0, cell padding of 5, and cell spacing of 5. Type `General information` as the Summary text. Align the table to the right. Select the table cells and set Vert to Middle. In the first cell, type `Image or text goes here` as the text prompt, and in the second cell, type `Add as many additional columns/rows as necessary` as the text prompt. Click to the right of the table and then press the ENTER key two times.

7. Add a third editable table with one row and three columns. Use a width of 80 percent, border thickness of 0, cell padding of 5, and cell spacing of 5. Center the table. In the first cell, type `Image or text here` as the prompt, and in the second cell, type `Add as many additional columns/rows as necessary` as the prompt. Drag the candle2.gif image to the third cell. Click outside the table and then press the ENTER key.

8. Insert a fourth editable table — a one-row, one-column table with a width of 60 percent, border thickness of 0, cell padding of 5, and cell spacing of 5. Select the cell and set Horz to Center and Vert to Middle. Type `Links go here` in the table cell.

9. Create four editable regions in the template — the first with the heading and then the three tables. Name the heading editable region heading, name the first table text_image01, the second table text_image02, and the third table links.

10. Click anywhere in the heading prompt and then click the <table> tag in the tag selector. Click the New CSS Rule button in the CSS Styles panel. In the New CSS Rule dialog box, verify that Tag (redefines the look of a specific tag) and table are selected in the Tag box and that Define in (New Style Sheet File) is selected, and then click the OK button. Name the style sheet primary.css. In the CSS Style Definition dialog box, set the font to Georgia, Times New Roman, Times, serif; the size to 16; the style to italic; and the weight to bolder. Save the template and style sheet.

11. Open a new Basic page and save it as beeswax.htm. Click the Assets tab in the Files panel group. Apply the template to the new Document window.

12. Select the text and then type `Beeswax — The Original Wax` in the heading editable region.

13. Delete the text and then drag the bee.gif image to the left cell in the first editable table — text_image01. Type bee as the image Alt text. In the right cell of the first table, select the text, and then type `Beeswax is naturally fragrant. It burns cleaner and longer than petroleum-based waxes, so there is no smoke coming from the candle.`

14. Select the text in the left cell of the text_image02 table and then type `Beeswax candles produce a brighter flame than paraffin candles and create a warm glow. A beeswax candle is something that every candle lover should experience. A beeswax candle smells sweetly of honey without the addition of any fragrance.` Select the text in the center cell of the second table and then type `Beeswax is all natural and chemical and particle free. It is perfect for making soaps, painting fabric, or creating specialty furniture polish.`

15. Select the text in the links table, type `Index` as the entry, and then drag the index.htm file to the Link text box in the Property inspector. Save the page.

16. Open the index.htm file. Scroll to the bottom of the page and then click to the right of the Survey link. Press the ENTER key and then type `Candlemaking` as the link text. Create a link to the beeswax.htm page. Save the index page.

17. Press the F12 key to view the page in your browser. Click the Candlemaking link. Print a copy of the template and Web page if instructed to do so. Upload the page to the candle Web site on a remote server, if instructed to do so.

2 Creating a Template for the Credit Protection Web Site

Problem: Monica has decided to add additional Web pages emphasizing the ABCs of Credit. She would like to have a uniform format for these pages and has asked you to create a template. She has provided you with content for the first page. The template is shown in Figure 5-95a and the Web page is shown in Figure 5-95b on the next page. Appendix C contains instructions for uploading your local site to a remote server.

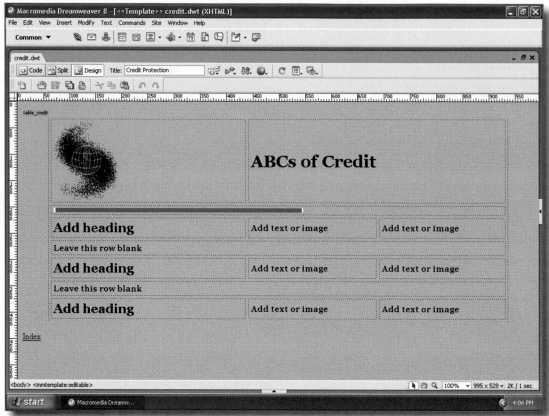

FIGURE 5-95a

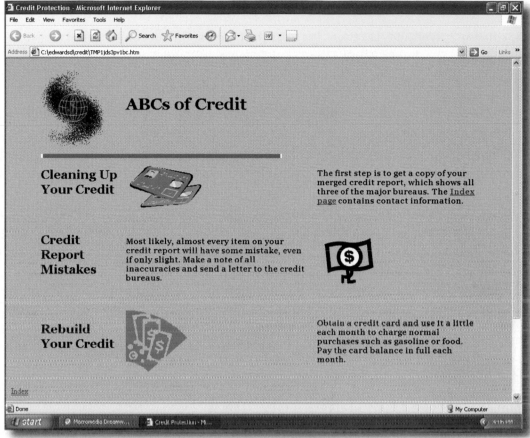

FIGURE 5-95b

Instructions: Perform the following tasks:

1. Use the Windows My Computer option to copy the data files from the DataFiles folder to your credit/images folder.

2. Start Dreamweaver. Select Credit Protection from the Files pop-up menu in the Files panel. Click File on the menu bar and then click New. Select Template page in the New Document dialog box General category and HTML template in the Template page column. Click Save on the menu bar and type credit for the file name. If necessary, display the panel groups. Title the template Credit Protection. Use the Page Properties dialog box to add the creditbg.jpg background image to the page.

3. Insert a seven-row, three-column table with a width of 90 percent, border thickness of 0, cell padding of 5, cell spacing of 5, and summary text of ABCs of Credit. Center the table. Drag the logo.gif image to the first cell in the first row. Merge the last two cells in row 1. Type ABCs of Credit in the merged cells and apply the Heading 1 format.

4. Merge all three cells in row 2. Drag the line.gif image to the merged row.

5. Merge all three cells in row 4 and then type Leave this row blank in the cell. Repeat this instruction in row 6.

6. Click row 3, column 1, type Add heading as the entry, and then apply Heading 2 to this text. Repeat this instruction in column 1 of rows 5 and 7.

(continued)

In the Lab

Creating a Template for the Credit Protection Web Site *(continued)*

7. Click row 3, column 2; type Add text or image as the entry; and then copy this text. Paste the text into row 3, column 3; row 5, columns 2 and 3; and row 7, columns 2 and 3.

8. Click outside of the table, press the ENTER key, and then type Index as the entry. Create a link from this text to the index.htm page.

9. Click anywhere in the table and then click the <table> tag in the tag selector. Use the Editable Regions menu item on the Templates pop-up menu to name the editable region table_credit.

10. Open the CSS Styles panel and then click the Add CSS Rule button. In the New CSS Rule dialog box, verify that Tag (redefines the look of a specific tag) and table are selected in the Tag box and that Define in (New Style Sheet File) is selected, and then click the OK button. Name the style sheet credit_info.css and save it in your credit folder. Apply the following attributes in the Type category: Georgia, Times New Roman, Times, serif for the Font; 16 for the Size; and bold for the Weight. Click the Save button and close the template.

11. Open a new Basic page and save it as credit_info.htm. Click the Assets panel tab and then click the Apply button. Delete the text, Leave this row blank, from all cells.

12. Select the text in row 3, column 1; type Cleaning Up Your Credit as the entry; and then select the text in row 3, column 3. Type The first step is to get a copy of your merged credit report, which shows all three of the major bureaus. The Index page contains contact information. Select the text, Index page, and add a link to the index.htm page. Delete the text in row 3, column 2, and drag the credit_card.gif image to the cell.

13. Select the text in row 5, column 1, type Credit Report Mistakes as the entry, and then select the text in row 5, column 2. Type Most likely, almost every item on your credit report will have some mistake, even if only slight. Make a note of all inaccuracies and send a letter to the credit bureaus. Delete the text in row 5, column 3 and then drag the money3.gif image to the cell.

14. Select the text in row 7, column 1; type Rebuild Your Credit as the entry; and then select the text in row 7, column 3. Type Obtain a credit card and use it a little each month to charge normal purchases such as gasoline or food. Pay the card balance in full each month. Delete the text in row 7, column 2, and then drag the rebuild.gif image to the cell.

15. Save the document and the credit_info.css page. Open the index.htm file. Scroll to the bottom of the page, click to the right of the Information Request link, and then press the END key. Insert a line break and then type Credit Information as the link text. Create a link to the credit_info.htm page. Press the ENTER key and save the page.

16. Press the F12 key to view the page in your browser. Click the Credit Information link. Print a copy of the template and Web page, if instructed to do so. Upload the page to the credit Web site on a remote server, if instructed to do so.

3 Creating a Template for the Lexington, NC Web Site

Problem: The Lexington, NC Web site provides information about the city, but provides very little information about activities. The mayor wants to let visitors know about upcoming attractions and events. She wants the page to have a structured format and would like it to be changed easily. You will use a template to accomplish this task. The template is shown in Figure 5-96a, and the Web page is shown in Figure 5-96b on page DW 478.

In the Lab

6. Merge all three cells in row 1. Type Upcoming Events and then center the text. Apply Heading 3 to the text.

7. Click row 2, column 1; type Add Event Name as the entry; and then add this same text to rows 3 and 4, column 1.

8. Click row 2, column 2; type Add Date as the entry; and add this same text to rows 3 and 4, column 2.

9. Click row 2, column 3; type Add Location as the entry; and add this same text to rows 3 and 4, column 3.

10. Click to the right of the second table and then press the ENTER key two times. Add a third table with one row and two columns, with a width of 50 percent, border thickness of 0, cell padding of 5, and cell spacing of 5. Center the table. Select the row and then select Center in the Horz box.

11. Click the first cell in the third table and then type Index as the entry. Select the text, Index, and create a link to the Lexington, NC Web site index.htm page. Click the second cell and then type Lexington, NC Info as the entry. Create an absolute link from this text to http://www.lexingtonnc.net.

12. Click anywhere in the second table and then select the <table> tag in the tag selector. Click the Templates pop-up menu and then click the Editable Region command. Name the new editable region event_table.

13. Click the <table> tag in the tag selector. Click the New CSS Rule button. Verify that Tag (redefines the look of a specific tag) and table are selected in the Tag box and that Define in (New Style Sheet File) is selected. Click the OK button and name the style sheet events.css. Add the following attributes: Arial, Helvetica, sans-serif for the Font; 16 for the Size; normal for the Weight; and oblique for the Style. Click the OK button.

14. Click anywhere in the third table and then click the <table> tag in the tag selector. Click the Templates pop-up menu and then click the Editable Region command. Name the new editable region links.

15. Click the <table> tag in the tag selector. Click the New CSS Rule button and then click the Advanced (IDs, contextual selectors, etc) radio button. Add the following attributes for the a:link: Arial, Helvetica, sans-serif for the Font; 14 for the Size; normal for the Weight; and oblique for the Style. Click the Decoration attribute underline check box.

16. For the a:visited link, apply the same attributes, but add #663300 for the Color and none for the Decoration. Save and close the template and style sheet.

17. Open a new Basic page and save it as events.htm. Apply the template. Add the data in Table 5-14 to the second table as the Upcoming Events.

18. Save the document. Open the index.htm file. Scroll to the bottom of the page and then click to the right of the Comments link. Press the SPACEBAR, add a vertical line, press the SPACEBAR, type Events as the link text, and then press the SPACEBAR again. Create a link to the events.htm page, and then save the page.

19. Press the F12 key to view the page in your browser. Click the Upcoming Events link. Print a copy of the template and Web page, if instructed to do so. Upload the page to the city Web Site on a remote server, if instructed to do so.

Table 5-14 Lexington, NC Upcoming Events Text

LEFT CELL	MIDDLE CELL	RIGHT CELL
The Bob Timberlake Gallery	Open all year	1714 East Center Street
Quicksilver Bluegrass Festival	May 6, 7, and 8	TBA
Barbecue Festival	October 23	Main Street

Cases and Places

The difficulty of these case studies varies:
■ are the least difficult and ■■ are the most difficult. The last exercise is a group exercise.

1 ■ Your sports Web site has become very popular. You have received many e-mails asking for statistics and other information. You decide to add a Web page that will contain statistics and will be updated on a weekly basis. Add a background image to the page and add a title to the page. Create the template using tables. Add descriptive prompts and then create editable regions. Add styles to the headings and text. Then create a page, apply the template, and save the page in your sports Web site. Create links to and from the home page. For a selection of images and backgrounds, visit the Dreamweaver 8 Media Web page (scsite.com/dw8/media) and then click Media below Project 5.

2 ■ You have decided to add a do-it-yourself section to your hobby Web site and want to use a consistent format and look for the page. You decide to use a template to create this new section. Create the template using a logo, tables, and links. Add descriptive prompts to the editable regions and apply styles to enhance the text and text size. Create the first do-it-yourself Web page and apply the template. Create links to and from the home page. Upload the pages to a remote server, if instructed to do so. For a selection of images and backgrounds, visit the Dreamweaver 8 Media Web page (scsite.com/dw8/media) and then click Media below Project 5.

3 ■■ Create a template for your music hobby Web site and then add a background to the page. Insert logos, tables, and other appropriate elements. Add a background image to a table. Apply a border to the table. Use the CSS Styles panel and apply styles to the elements on the page. Create a new Web page featuring a new topic for your Web site and apply the template. Create links to and from the home page. Upload the page to a remote server, if instructed to do so. For a selection of images and backgrounds, visit the Dreamweaver 8 Media Web page (scsite.com/dw8/media) and then click Media below Project 5.

Cases and Places

4 ■■ Your campaign for political office is progressing well, and you are one of the top two candidates. You have decided to add a new section to your Web site featuring your campaign supporters. To provide consistency and control, you use a template for this site. After completing the template, attach styles. Next, create two new pages for the site and then apply the template. Create links to and from the home page. Upload the new pages to a remote server, if instructed to do so. For a selection of images and backgrounds, visit the Dreamweaver 8 Media Web page (scsite.com/dw8/media) and then click Media below Project 5.

5 ■■ **Working Together** Each member of the group decides to create a template for the three vacation sites previously selected. Include on the templates headings, tables, links, and graphics. Present the three templates to the group and determine which one best meets the needs of the Web site. Next, add appropriate styles, including styles from the Type, Background, and Border categories. Include at least two images and a logo on the template. Create the three vacation site Web pages and apply the template. Then create links to and from the home page. Upload the new pages to a remote server, if instructed to do so. For a selection of images and backgrounds, visit the Dreamweaver 8 Media Web page (scsite. com/dw8/media) and then click Media below Project 5.

Layers, Image Maps, and Navigation Bars

PROJECT

6

CASE PERSPECTIVE

David recently attended a business workshop and was fascinated by some of the Web sites demonstrated by other workshop attendees. He particularly was impressed with some of the options offered through the use of layers and behaviors. He describes to you and Tracy some of the features of layers, including flexibility and precise positioning. The concept that impressed David the most, however, was the ability to add behaviors to show and hide different objects on a Web page.

Another feature that David specifically liked on some of the demonstrated Web sites was a navigation bar. He felt this gave the Web page a more professional look. You and Tracy both agree that layers, behaviors, and a navigation bar would be good additions to the Web site.

Colorado has a variety of national parks, monuments, historic sites, and recreation areas located throughout the state. Many visitors to the area have a limited vacation time of one or two weeks and cannot possibly visit all of these sites within a short time. Tracy suggests that a new page could be added to the Web site that would help vacationers better plan their trips. The page would use layers to display some bullet-point information about sites of interest located in the northern, central, and southern parts of the state. She further suggests that you develop a navigation bar and add it to the index page. You agree that these are both good suggestions, and you are eager to get started with these modifications and additions.

As you read through this project, you will learn about layers and how to use layers to design a Web page. You also learn how to create an image map and a navigation bar, add a date object, and control various elements through Dreamweaver's Behaviors panel.

Layers, Image Maps, and Navigation Bars

PROJECT

6

Objectives

You will have mastered the material in this project when you can:

- Explain the concept of layers
- Insert, select, resize, and move a layer
- Name a layer
- Align layers
- Describe an image map

- Create an image map
- Add and edit behaviors
- Describe a navigation bar
- Create a navigation bar
- Insert a Date object

Introduction

Project 6 introduces three unique Dreamweaver features: layers, image maps, and navigation bars. Web developers have long dreamed of being able to position graphics, text, and other HTML objects at specific pixel coordinates. Tables provide some placement control, but not absolute precision. Layers, however, can be positioned anywhere on the page. They remain in the same position relative to the top and left margins of the window regardless of how a user resizes the browser window.

An image map is the second feature discussed in this project. An image map is a picture that is divided into regions, called hotspots. When a user clicks a hotspot, an assigned action occurs. You can create multiple hotspots in an image, and you can have more than one image map on a single Web page.

The third feature introduced in this project is the navigation bar. Navigation bars often provide an easy way to move among the pages and files on a site. The linking elements within a navigation bar can consist of text, images, and/or a combination of text and images. To complement the Colorado Parks Web site with these new elements, you modify the index page by adding an interactive navigation bar. As you complete the activities in this project, you will find that adding these features to a Web page offers greater interactivity and excitement for the user.

If you are using Internet Explorer with Windows XP Service Pack 2 (SP2), Internet Explorer automatically blocks active content such as that contained in this and other projects. Thus, for all instances where Web pages containing active content are displayed in Internet Explorer, you must choose to "allow blocked content" by right-clicking the Information Bar and selecting the Allow Blocked Content command from the context menu. Or you can modify the Internet Explorer security settings to allow elements such as image maps and layers to be displayed.

Project Six — Layers, Image Maps, and Navigation Bars

In this project, you learn how to use and apply three favorite Dreamweaver tools to the Colorado Parks Web site. You begin the project by adding a new page to the Web site, containing interactive layers and an image map (Figure 6-1a). Four separate layers are added to the page, and images then are embedded in each layer. One layer contains a Colorado map, which serves as the image map. Clicking different spots on the image map displays a list of the parks and other attractions in northern, central, and southern Colorado. Next, you revise the index page by deleting the existing links and adding a navigation bar (Figure 6-1b on the next page). The navigation bar adds a more professional look by bringing all of the links together in one location at the top of the Web page. When the mouse pointer moves over an image link within the navigation bar, the image changes color to indicate that this is an active link. Each image also has alternate text to address accessibility issues.

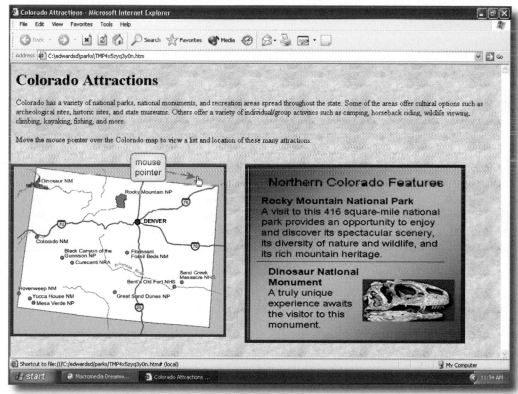

FIGURE 6-1a

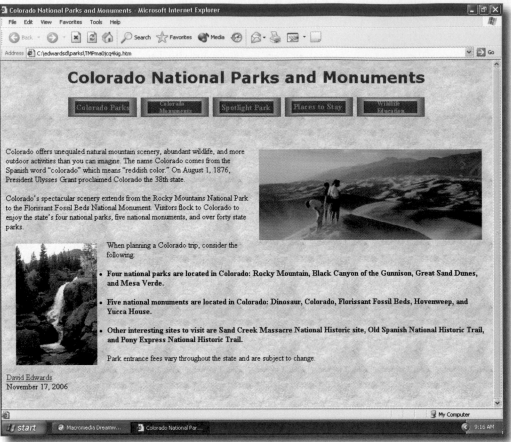

FIGURE 6-1b

Workspace Organization

Organization and preparation lead to a more productive work setting. Successful Web developers prepare their Dreamweaver workspace to provide an effective work environment. As you learn to use additional Dreamweaver tools, including layers, image maps, and navigation bars, you will become even more proficient working in the Dreamweaver environment.

Copying Data Files to the Local Web Site

Your Data Disk contains images for Project 6. You use the Windows My Computer option to copy the Project 6 data file and the images to your parks folder. See the inside back cover for instructions for downloading the Data Disk or see your instructor for information about accessing the files required for this book.

The DataFiles folder for this project is stored on Local Disk (C:). The location on your computer may be different. If necessary, verify with your instructor the location of the DataFiles folder. The following steps show how to copy the files to the parks folder.

To Copy Images and a Data File to the Parks Web Site

1 Click the Start button on the Windows taskbar and then click My Computer.

2 Double-click Local Disk (C:) and then navigate to the location of the data files for Project 6.

3 Double-click the DataFiles folder and then double-click the Proj06 folder.

4 Double-click the parks folder and then double-click the images folder.

5 Click the first image file in the list, hold down the SHIFT key, and then click the last image file in the list.

6 Right-click the selected files to display the context menu.

7 Click the Copy command and then click the My Computer Back button the number of times necessary to navigate to the your name folder.

8 Double-click the your name folder, double-click the parks folder, and then double-click the images folder.

9 Right-click in the open window to display the context menu.

10 Click the Paste command to paste the image files into the images folder (Figure 6-2).

11 Navigate to the Proj06 parks folder. Double-click the parks folder.

12 Click the colorado_attractions.htm file, and then right-click to display the context menu.

13 Click the Copy command and then navigate to the your name folder.

14 Double-click the your name folder, double-click the parks folder, and then right-click to display the context menu.

15 Click the Paste command to paste the data file into the parks folder.

16 Close the My Computer window.

The image files are pasted in the Colorado Parks Web site images folder (Figure 6-2) and the data file into the parks folder.

FIGURE 6-2

Starting Dreamweaver and Closing Open Panels

Each time you start Dreamweaver, it opens to the last site displayed when you closed the program. Therefore, it may be necessary for you to open the parks Web site. The Files pop-up menu in the Files panel lists sites you have defined. When you open the site, a list of pages and subfolders within the site is displayed. The next steps illustrate how to start Dreamweaver and open the Colorado Parks Web site.

To Start Dreamweaver and Open the Colorado Parks Web Site

1 Click the Start button on the Windows taskbar.

2 Point to All Programs on the Start menu, point to Macromedia on the All Programs submenu, and then click Macromedia Dreamweaver 8 on the Macromedia submenu.

3 Click the Files panel box arrow and click Colorado Parks on the Files pop-up menu. If necessary, click the plus sign to open the site folder.

Dreamweaver opens, and the Colorado Parks Web site hierarchy is displayed in the Files panel (Figure 6-3). Note that the Insert bar Common Category is displayed in Figure 6-3. You may have a different category displayed on your screen. If the Insert bar does not display on your screen, you will open it later in this project.

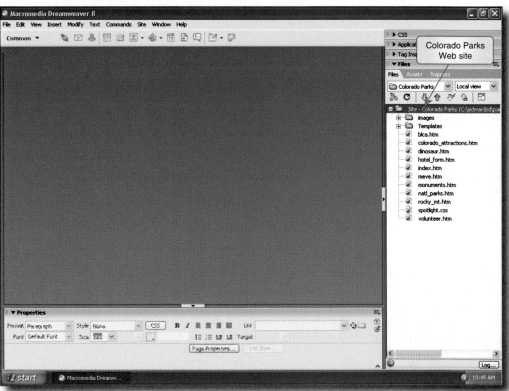

FIGURE 6-3

Understanding Layers

A **layer** is similar to a table — it is a container that holds other types of content, such as images, text, form objects, and even other layers (nested layers). Anything you can put in an HTML document, you also can put in a layer. Layers can be stacked on top of one another, placed side by side, or overlapped. They easily can be moved, dragged, or resized. Web site developers use layers for page layout much as they use tables. A layer, however, provides more flexibility than a table because it can be placed in an exact spot anywhere on the page with pixel-perfect precision. It remains in this position (relative to the top and left margins of the page) regardless of how the Web page visitor resizes the browser window or views the text size. This is called **absolute positioning** and is possible because layers are positioned using a standard x-, y-, and z-coordinate system, similar to what you would use to create a graph on graph paper. Instead of having the point of origin be in the bottom-left corner, however, the x- and y-coordinates correspond to a layer's top and left positions within the page. The z-coordinate, also called the **z-index**, determines a layer's stacking order when more than one layer is added to a page.

Netscape does not fully support layers. If designing for Netscape, it is best to convert the layers to tables. To convert layers to tables, click the Modify menu, point to Convert, and then select the Layers to Table command.

Layers and DHTML

Layers are a component of dynamic HTML (DHTML) — an extension of HTML that gives Web page developers the capability of precisely positioning objects on the Web page. DHTML combines layers, Cascading Style Sheets (CSS), and JavaScript coding, enabling the creation of dynamic page elements. Additionally, because a layer uses both DHTML and CSS, it offers a wide range of flexibility and control. Some possible effects you can accomplish using DHTML are as follows:

- Add images that are hidden from view initially and then display them when a user clicks a button or hotspot
- Create pop-up menus
- Position objects side by side
- Drag and drop objects
- Create animations
- Provide feedback to right and wrong answers

A disadvantage of using layers is that older browsers do not support them. Internet Explorer 4.0 and Netscape Navigator 4.0 (and later) support layers under the original W3C Cascading Style Sheets-Positioning (CSS-P) specifications. Browsers older than version 4.0, however, ignore the layer code and display the content in the normal flow of the page (no absolute positioning). Also, even though current browsers support layers, Internet Explorer and Netscape Navigator implement DHTML differently, and, therefore, some discrepancy in the display of layers exists. Navigator 4.0 in particular has a difficult time with layers and often displays them incorrectly. Dreamweaver, however, contains a Netscape 4 Resize Fix option, which is available through the Layers category in the Preferences dialog box.

Dreamweaver provides two options for creating layers: the Draw Layer button located on the Layout category in the Insert bar, and the Layout Objects submenu available through the Insert menu. In this project, you use the Draw Layer button on the Layout category on the Insert bar, modify attributes through the Layer Property inspector, and control visibility through the Layers panel. Displaying Dreamweaver's layout tools, such as the rulers or the grid, helps with precise positioning. In this project, you use the rulers.

The following steps show how to open the colorado _attractions.htm page and to display the rulers.

Q: How would I change the stacking order of several layers?

A: Press the F2 key to open the Layers panel. Drag a layer up or down to the desired stacking order.

To Open the Colorado Attractions Page and Display the Rulers

1

• **Double-click the colorado_attractions. htm file.**

The colorado_attractions.htm file opens in the Document window (Figure 6-4). The insertion point is blinking at the top of the page, to the left of the heading.

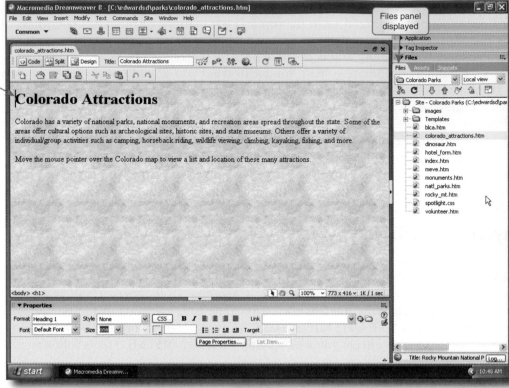

FIGURE 6-4

2

• **If necessary, Click View on the menu bar, point to Rulers, and then point to Show on the Rulers submenu.**

The View menu and Rulers submenu are displayed (Figure 6-5).

FIGURE 6-5

3

• **Click Show.**

*Dreamweaver displays
the rulers in the Document
window (Figure 6-6). The
ruler-origin icon is displayed in
the upper-left corner, where
the rulers meet in the
Document window.*

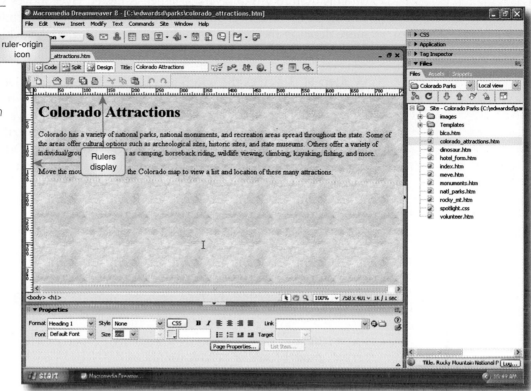

FIGURE 6-6

Layer Property Inspector

When you insert a layer into a Web page and the layer is selected, Dreamweaver displays the Layer Property inspector (Figure 6-7). The following section describes the layer properties that are available through the Layer Property inspector.

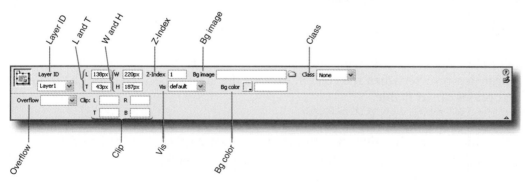

FIGURE 6-7

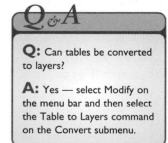

Q: Can layers be converted to tables?

A: Yes — select Modify on the menu bar and then select the Layers to Table command on the Convert submenu.

Q: Can tables be converted to layers?

A: Yes — select Modify on the menu bar and then select the Table to Layers command on the Convert submenu.

LAYER ID Assigns a unique name to identify the layer in the Layers panel and in JavaScript code. Layer names must start with a letter and can contain only standard alphanumeric characters.

L AND T Specifies the position of the layer's top-left corner relative to the top-left corner of the page, or the top-left corner of the parent layer if the layer is nested. A nested layer, or child layer, is a layer whose code is contained in another layer. Nesting often is used to group layers together. A nested layer moves with its parent layer and can be set to inherit visibility from its parent. Parent and child layers are discussed in more detail in the section on nesting, overlapping, and stacking layers, later in this project.

W AND H Specifies the width and height of the layer in Design view. In Design view, if the content of the layer exceeds the specified size, the bottom edge of the layer stretches to accommodate the content. When the layer appears in a browser, however, the bottom edge does not stretch unless the Overflow property is set to visible. The default unit for position and size is pixels (px). Other units include pc (picas), pt (points), in (inches), mm (millimeters), cm (centimeters), and % (percentage of the parent layer's corresponding value). The abbreviations must follow the value without a space: for example, 3mm indicates 3 millimeters.

Z-INDEX Determines the stacking order of the layer. In a browser, higher-numbered layers appear in front of lower-numbered ones. The z-index values can be positive or negative. The stacking order can be changed through the Layers panel.

VIS Specifies whether the layer is visible initially or not. The following options are available:

- **default** does not specify a visibility property. When no visibility is specified, most browsers default to inherit.

- **inherit** uses the visibility property of the layer's parent.

- **visible** displays the layer contents, regardless of the parent's value.

- **hidden** hides the layer contents, regardless of the parent's value. Note that hidden layers created with ilayer (a tag unique to Netscape Navigator) still take up the same space as if they were visible.

BG IMAGE Specifies a background image for the layer.

BG COLOR Specifies a background color for the layer. Leave this option blank to specify a transparent background.

CLASS Lets you apply CSS rules to the selected object.

OVERFLOW Works only with the <div> and <span> tags and controls how layers appear in a browser when the content exceeds the layer's specified size. The following options are available:

- **visible** indicates that the extra content appears in the layer.
- **hidden** specifies that the extra content is not displayed in the browser.
- **scroll** specifies that the browser should add scroll bars to the layer whether or not they are needed.
- **auto** causes the browser to display scroll bars for the layer only when the layer's contents exceed its boundaries.

CLIP Defines the visible area of a layer. Specify left, top, right, and bottom coordinates to define a rectangle in the coordinate space of the layer (counting from the top-left corner of the layer). The layer is clipped so that only the specified rectangle is visible.

Using the Rulers as a Visual Guide

In Project 3, you learned how to display and use the rulers. Now you use the rulers as a visual guide and create a layer that will be a container for the Colorado map image. When you draw the layer in the Document window, a rectangular image appears, representing the layer. (If the layer borders do not display in the Document window, they can be turned on through the Visual Aids submenu accessed through the View menu.) The rectangular image, however, is not displayed when the page is viewed in a browser. Instead, only the content of what is contained within the layer is displayed in the browser.

The default rulers appear on the left and top borders of the Document window, marked in pixels. The **ruler origin** is the 0 point, or the location on the page where the horizontal and vertical lines meet and read 0. The 0 point is represented by the **ruler-origin icon**, which is located in the Document window when the page is displayed in Design view and the rulers are displayed (see Figure 6-6 on page DW 491). Generally, this location is the upper-left corner of the Document window.

Using the rulers as a drawing guideline can be somewhat difficult to manage if done from the default 0 point. To make measuring easier, however, you can move the 0 point anywhere within the Document window. To move the 0 point, move the mouse pointer to the upper-left corner where the vertical and horizontal lines meet, and then click and drag the cross hairs to the desired location. When you move the 0 point, the cross hairs are displayed in the Document window and follow the mouse pointer. The mouse pointer position is indicated with a dotted line on both the vertical and horizontal ruler lines.

Relocating the 0 point does not affect the page content. You can relocate the 0 point as many times as necessary. You also can reset the ruler origin by right-clicking anywhere on the rulers and then selecting Reset Origin on the context menu.

The Layer-Code Marker

When you insert a layer, a **layer-code marker** appears in the Document window. This small yellow square indicates that a layer is on the page. For the layer-code marker to display, the Anchor points for layers check box must be selected through the Invisible Elements category in the Preferences dialog box. When the Invisible Elements option is turned on, the markers may cause the elements on the page in the Document window to appear to shift position. These markers, however, are not displayed in the browser. When you view the page in your browser, the layers and other objects are displayed in the correct positions.

The layer-code marker is similar in appearance to the invisible element marker that displayed when you inserted images into a Web page in Project 2. In Project 2, dragging the image marker to another position in the Document window also moved the image to another position. Normally, the position of HTML objects in the Document window and in the browser is determined by their order in the HTML source code. They are displayed in a top-to-bottom sequence that mirrors their order in the source code.

Dragging or moving the layer-code marker, however, generally does not reposition the layer and has no effect on the way a Web page displays the layer in a browser. When you move a layer-code marker, you are not moving the layer; instead, you are repositioning the layer's code in the HTML of the page. Moving a layer-code marker, therefore, can affect how the code is interpreted and the order in which the layer content is loaded. It is possible to have a layer's content displayed at the top of the Web page while the source code is at the end of the page.

If your Web page contains tables, do not drag the layer-code marker into a table cell. This can cause display problems in some browsers. You can drag a layer, however, to overlap a table or make a label display so it appears to be inside the table cell, as long as the layer-code marker itself is not in the table cell. When you use the Draw Layer button to create the layer, Dreamweaver will not put the code into a table cell. The following steps illustrate how to create and select a layer.

To Create and Select a Layer for the Colorado Map Image

1

• **If necessary, display the Insert bar and then select the Layout category from the Insert bar pop-up menu.**

• **Click below the last line of text in the Document window.**

• **Click the ruler-origin icon and drag it to the insertion point.**

The insertion point is blinking below the last line of text in the Document window. Notice that the cross hair increases in size as you drag the ruler. The vertical ruler 0 point now is to the left of the insertion point (Figure 6-8).

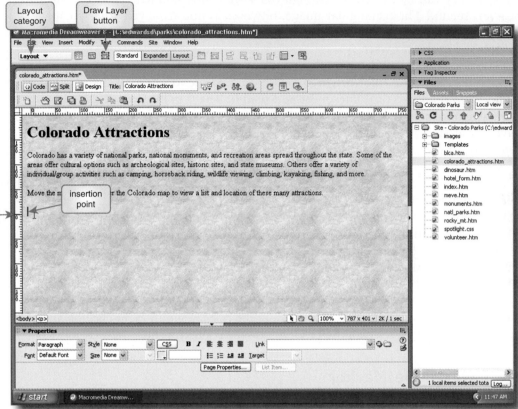

FIGURE 6-8

2

• **Click the Draw Layer button on the Insert bar Layout category and then move the pointer to the insertion point.**

The layer pointer (in the shape of a plus sign) is displayed in the Document window (Figure 6-9).

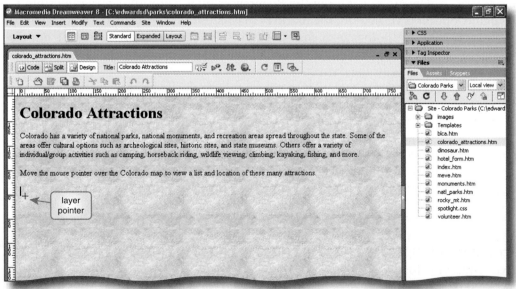

FIGURE 6-9

3

• **Using the rulers as a guide, draw a layer approximately 440 pixels wide and 350 pixels high. If the layer outline does not appear in the Document window, click View on the menu bar, point to Visual Aids, and then click Layer Outlines on the Visual Aids submenu.**

• **Scroll to the top of the Document window.**

• **Right-click anywhere on the rulers and click Reset Origin on the context menu.**

• **Click the layer outline to select it.**

• **If necessary, scroll to the top of the page (Figure 6-10). If the layer-code marker does not display, click Edit on the menu bar, select Preferences, and then click the Invisible Elements category. Click the Anchor points for layers check box and then click the OK button.**

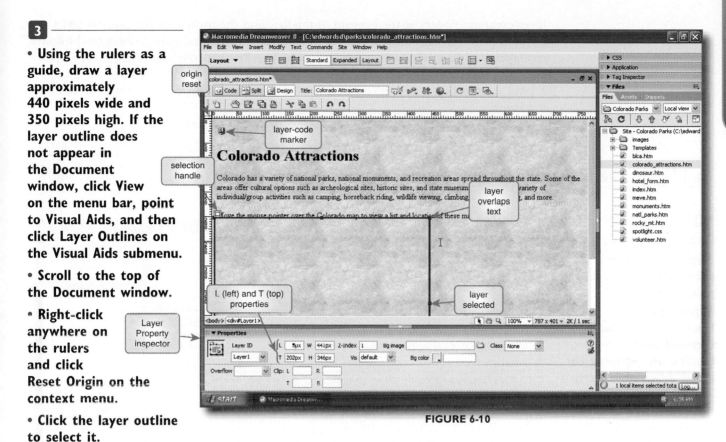

FIGURE 6-10

The layer is displayed and selected. The vertical 0 point returns to its original position. In most instances, the layer will overlap some of the text (Figure 6-10). The layer code marker is displayed at the top of the page, and the Layer Property inspector is displayed.

Other Ways

1. On Insert menu, click Layout Objects, click Layer

In addition to moving a layer by positioning the mouse pointer on a layer outline, you also can drag the **selection handle** that appears above the layer in the upper-left corner (see Figure 6-10).

The Layers Panel

The **Layers panel**, part of the CSS panel group, is helpful in managing the layers in your document. Use the Layers panel to prevent overlaps, to change the visibility of layers, to nest or stack layers, and to select one or more layers. All of the layers on a Web page are listed in the panel. The Layers panel contains three columns: Visibility, Name, and Z-Index. The Visibility column uses eye icons. A **closed-eye icon** indicates that a layer is hidden; an **open-eye icon** indicates that a layer is visible. The absence of an eye icon indicates that the layer is in its default state — that it is showing, but not defined as showing in the HTML code. The middle column displays the names of the layers. Clicking a layer name in the Layers panel is another way to select a layer. In the Z-Index column, layers are displayed in order of their z-index values. The first layer created appears at the bottom of the list, and the most recently created layer at the top of the list. Nested layers are displayed as indented names connected to parent layers (as discussed later in this project). The Prevent overlaps check box, when clicked, prevents layers from overlapping. When the Prevent overlaps option is on, a layer cannot be created in front of, moved or resized over, or nested within an existing layer.

The following step illustrates how to display the Layers panel.

To Display the Layers Panel

1

• **Press the F2 key to display the Layers panel. Move the mouse pointer over the Application panel until the mouse pointer changes to a two-headed arrow. Drag the panel down about two inches or so.**

The Layers panel is displayed and is part of the CSS group panel (Figure 6-11). The other panels are moved down so that more of the Layers panel displays. The Layers panel on your screen may be in a different location.

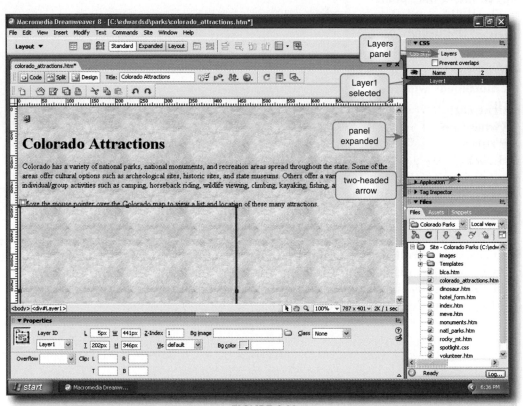

FIGURE 6-11

The default name for layers is Layer1, Layer2, and so on. The next step is to use the Property inspector to rename the layer, to adjust the layer width and height properties, and to specify the layer visibility.

To Name the Layer and Adjust the Layer Properties

1

• **Double-click the Layer ID text box in the Property inspector and then type** col_map **as the layer name. If necessary, double-click the W box and change the width to 440px. Then, if necessary, double-click the H box and change the height to 350px.**

• **Click the Vis box arrow and then click visible.**

• **Press the TAB key.**

The property changes for the col_map layer are made in the Property inspector. The col_map name appears in the Layers panel with the open-eye icon indicating that the layer is visible (Figure 6-12). Your measurements and layer position are approximate and most likely will not match those in Figure 6-12. Later in this project, you will adjust the L and T attributes.

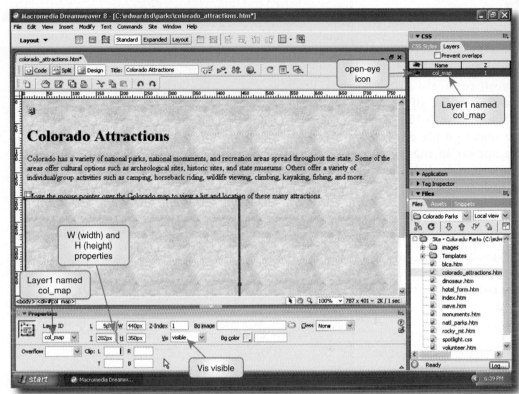

FIGURE 6-12

Other Ways

1. Double-click layer name in Layers panel

Adding Objects to Layers

As indicated previously, a layer is a container that can hold objects. The objects can be anything that can be added to an HTML page and include such items as images, text, form objects, and even other layers (nested layers). Objects, including images, can be inserted onto layers through the Insert menu. Images also can be dragged from the Files or Assets panels onto the layer. The following steps show how to add the Colorado map image to the col_map layer.

To Add an Image to the Col_map Layer

1

• **Click the Assets panel tab and, if necessary, click the Images icon.**

• **Scroll to locate and click the map2.gif image (Figure 6-13). If the map2.gif file does not appear in the Assets panel, click the Refresh button.**

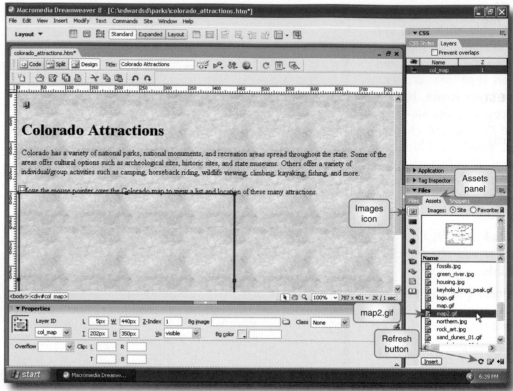

FIGURE 6-13

2

• **Drag the map2.gif image onto the layer.**

• **Click the Image ID box and type** colorado_map**. Click the Alt text box and type** Colorado Map**. Press the TAB key.**

• **Click the Save button on the Standard toolbar (Figure 6-14).**

The Colorado map image is selected and displayed in the layer. The Property inspector displays image properties (Figure 6-14).

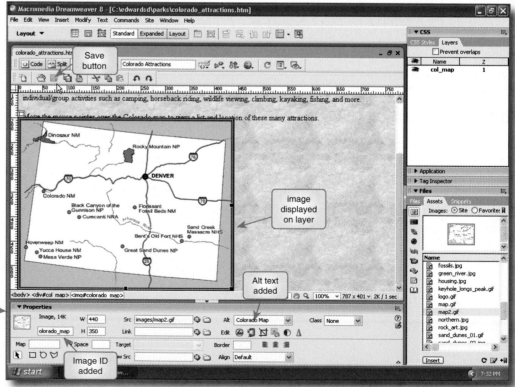

FIGURE 6-14

3

* **Press F12 and view the Web page in your browser. Note the space between the text and the image.**
* **Close the browser.**

Nesting, Overlapping, and Stacking Layers

Several methods are available to manage and manipulate layers. As noted previously, layers can be nested, overlapped, or stacked one on top of another.

Nesting is used to group layers. This process also is referred to as creating a parent-child relation. A nested layer, also called a **child layer**, is similar in concept to a nested table or a nested frame. Having a nested layer, however, does not necessarily mean that one layer resides within another layer. Rather, it means that the HTML code for one layer is written inside the code for another layer. The nested layer can be displayed anywhere on the page. It does not even have to touch the **parent layer**, which is the layer containing the code for the other layers. The primary advantage of nested layers is that the parent layer controls the behavior of its child layers. If the parent layer is moved on the screen, the nested layers move with it. Additionally, if you hide the parent layer, you also hide any nested layers. In the Layers panel, nested layers are indented below the parent layer.

To create a nested layer, draw the layer inside an existing layer while holding down the CTRL key. To unnest a nested layer, drag the layer-code marker to a different location in the Document window, or, in the Layers panel, drag the nested layer to an empty spot.

Layers also can overlap and/or be stacked one on top of another. Layers that float on top of each other have a **stacking order**. In the HTML source code, the stacking order, or z-index, of the layers is determined by the order in which they are created. The first layer you draw is 1, the second is 2, and so on. The layer with the highest number appears on top or in front of layers with lower numbers. Stacking layers provides opportunities for techniques such as hiding and displaying layers and/or parts of a layer, creating draggable layers, and creating animation.

Two different methods are available through the Layers panel to change the z-index for a layer and set which layer appears in front of or behind another layer. First, you can click the layer name and then drag it up or down in the list. A line appears, indicating where the layer will be placed. The second method is to click the number of the layer you want to change in the Z column, and then type a higher number to move the layer up or a lower number to move the layer down in the stacking order. After you change the z-index, Dreamweaver automatically rearranges the layers from highest to lowest, with the highest number on top. You also can turn off the overlapping feature in the Layers panel. When the Prevent overlaps check box is selected, layers cannot be overlapped or stacked.

The following steps illustrate how to draw three stacked layers, one on top of the other. The placement of the layers in Figures 6-15 through 6-24 on pages DW 500– DW 505 is approximate. Later in this project, you align and position the layers.

More About

Absolute Positioning

Absolute positioning is the more common and widely used CSS positioning method. Dreamweaver uses this method. Two other methods, however, also are available: static positioning and relative positioning. Relative positioning places the layer using the coordinates entered in the Placement boxes relative to the object's position in the text flow of the document. This option is not displayed in the Document window. Static positioning places the layer at its location in the text flow.

More About

Z-Index

The term z-index comes from the coordinate system used in algebra. The z-index is the third coordinate that works with x and y and is required to describe three-dimensional space.

To Create Stacked Layers

1

• **Click the expander arrow to collapse the panel groups.**

The panel groups are collapsed (Figure 6-15).

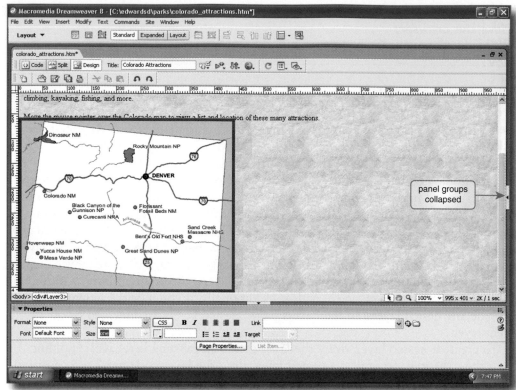

FIGURE 6-15

2

• **Click the ruler-origin icon and drag it about 25 pixels to the right of the col_map layer.**

• **Click the Draw Layer button on the Insert bar, and then use the rulers as a visual guide to draw a layer measuring approximately 440px in width and 350px in height to the right of the col_map layer.**

The layer is drawn and appears to the right of the col_map layer (Figure 6-16).

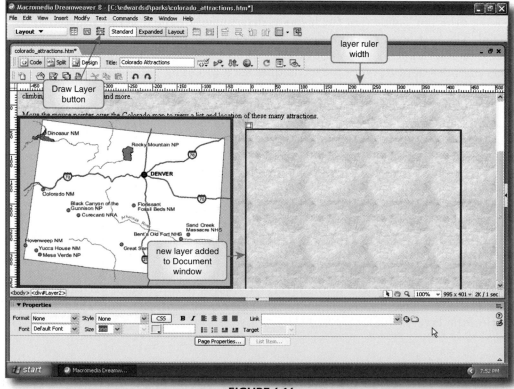

FIGURE 6-16

3

- **Right-click anywhere on the rulers and then click Reset Origin on the context menu.**

- **Move the mouse pointer over any border of the layer outline and then click the border.**

- **Click the Layer ID text box and then type** northern_colorado **as the layer ID. If necessary, change the W to 440px and the H to 350px in the Property inspector. Click the Vis box arrow and then click hidden.**

- **Press the TAB key.**

The properties for the northern_colorado layer are added and are displayed in the Property inspector. The origin point for the rulers is reset to 0 (Figure 6-17). You will align the T and L properties later in this project. Pressing the TAB key activates the action for the selected box.

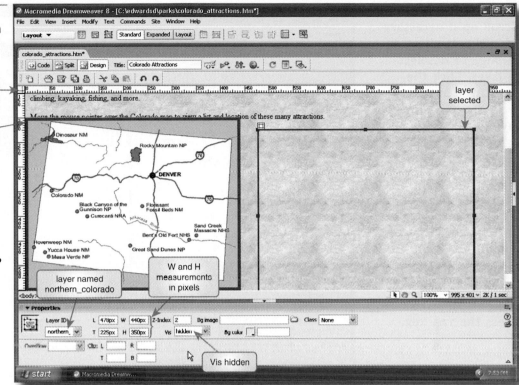

FIGURE 6-17

4

- **If necessary, scroll up to see the top of the layer. Click anywhere on the page to deselect the layer.**

- **Click the Draw Layer button on the Insert bar and then draw a second layer directly on top of the northern_colorado layer.**

- **Select the layer. Add and modify the following properties in the Property inspector: Layer ID – central_colorado, W – 440px, H – 350px, and Vis – hidden.**

- **Press the TAB key.**

The properties are modified and added for the central_colorado layer, and are displayed in the Property inspector (Figure 6-18). You will align the T and L properties later in this project.

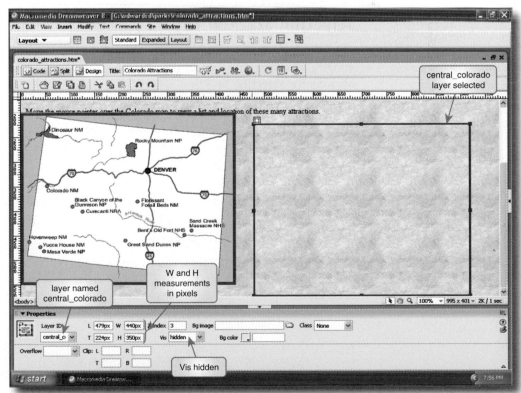

FIGURE 6-18

5

• **Scroll up if necessary and click anywhere on the page to deselect the layer. Click the Draw Layer button on the Insert bar and then draw a third layer on top of the central_colorado layer.**

• **Select the layer. Add and modify the following attributes in the Property inspector: Layer ID – southern_colorado, W – 440px, H – 350px, and Vis – hidden.**

• **Press the TAB key.**

The properties are added and modified for the southern_colorado layer, and are displayed in the Property inspector (Figure 6-19). You will align the T and L properties later in this project.

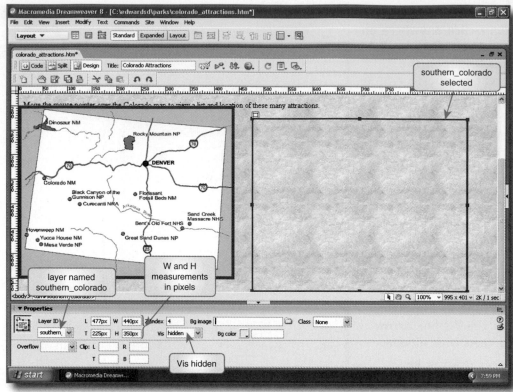

FIGURE 6-19

Selecting Stacked Layers

The next step is to add images to each of the layers, but before you add the images, you first must select the correct layer. Dreamweaver provides the following options for selecting layers:

- Click the name of the desired layer in the Layers panel.
- Click a layer's selection handle. If the selection handle is not visible, click anywhere inside the layer to make the handle visible.
- Click a layer's border.
- Press CTRL+SHIFT+CLICK. If multiple layers are selected, this deselects all other layers and selects only the one that you clicked.
- Click the layer-code marker (in Design view) that represents the layer's location in the HTML code.

When layers are stacked, the easiest way to select a layer is to click the name in the Layers panel. The next steps illustrate how to select layers and add images to each layer.

To Select Layers and Add Images

1

• **Click the expander arrow to expand the panel groups.**

The southern_colorado layer is selected in the Layers panel and the Document window. Closed-eye icons are displayed to the left of the three hidden layers. An open-eye icon displays to the left of the col_map layer (Figure 6-20).

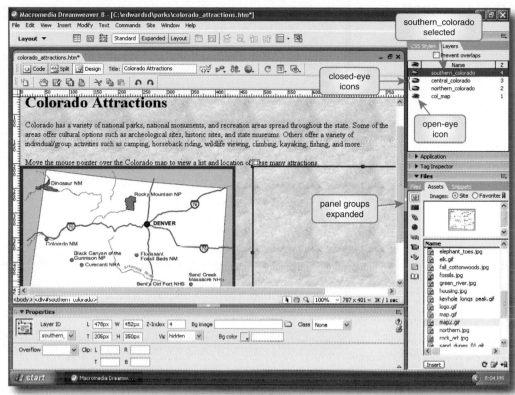

FIGURE 6-20

2

• **Scroll to the right in the Document window.**

• **Scroll in the Assets panel and locate the southern.jpg file. Drag the southern.jpg image onto the southern_colorado layer.**

• **Click the Image ID box and type** so_col.

• **Click the Alt text box and type** Southern Colorado Features. **Press the TAB key.**

The southern.jpg image is displayed in the southern_colorado layer (Figure 6-21).

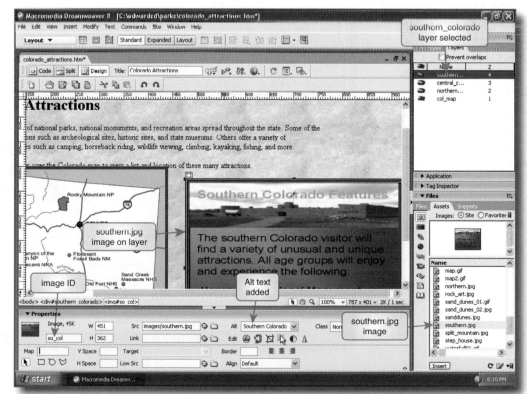

FIGURE 6-21

3

• **Click central_colorado in the Layers panel.**

The central_colorado layer is selected in the Layers panel and the Document window (Figure 6-22).

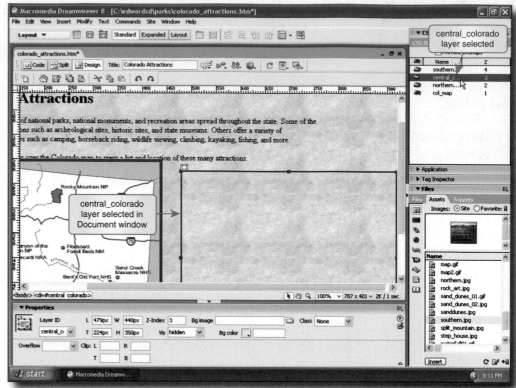

FIGURE 6-22

4

• **If necessary, scroll up in the Assets panel and locate the central.jpg file. Drag the central.jpg image into the central_colorado layer.**

• **Click the Image ID box and type** cen_col. **Click the Alt text box and type** Central Colorado Features.

The central.jpg image is displayed in the central_colorado layer (Figure 6-23).

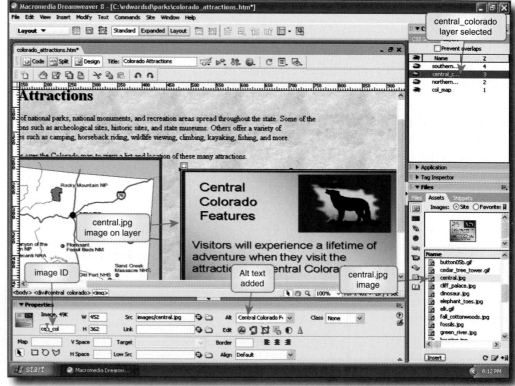

FIGURE 6-23

5

• Click northern_colorado in the Layers panel.

• Locate the northern.jpg image in the Assets panel and drag the image onto the northern_colorado layer.

• Click the Image ID box and type nor_col. Click the Alt text box and type Northern Colorado Features. Press the TAB key.

The northern.jpg image is displayed in the northern_colorado layer (Figure 6-24).

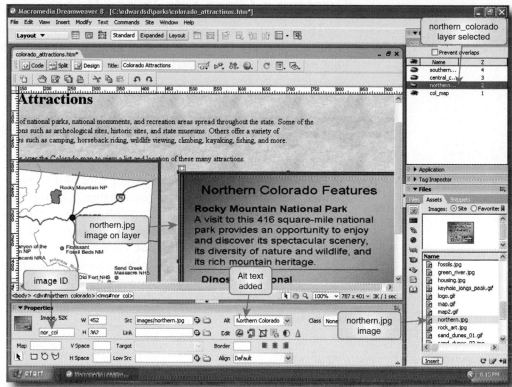

FIGURE 6-24

Image Maps

Image maps are an exciting and interesting way to liven up your Web site. An **image map** is an image that has one or more hotspots placed on top of it. A **hotspot** is a designated area on an image map that the user clicks to cause an action to occur. You can create a hotspot on an image map to link to different parts of the same Web page, to link to other Web pages within the Web site or outside the Web site, or to display content within a hidden layer.

Two types of image maps exist: server-side and client-side. The way in which **map data** is stored and interpreted depends on the type of map. Map data is the description in the HTML code of the mapped regions or hotspots within the image. A Web server interprets the code or map data for **server-side maps**. When a visitor to a Web page clicks a hotspot in a server-side image map, the browser transfers data to a program running on a Web server for processing. The code for **client-side maps** is stored as part of the Web page HTML code. The Web browser, therefore, interprets the code for client-side maps. When a visitor to a Web page clicks a hotspot in a client-side image map, the browser processes the HTML code without interacting with the Web server. The code for client-side maps is processed faster because it does not have to be sent to a server.

You can add both client-side image maps and server-side image maps to the same document in Dreamweaver. Browsers that support both types of image maps give priority to client-side image maps. When you create an image map in the Document window, Dreamweaver automatically creates the code for client-side image maps. To include a server-side image map in a document, you must write the appropriate HTML code in Code view. In this project, you create a client-side image map.

Creating a Client-Side Image Map

The first step in creating the image map is to place the image on the Web page. In this project, the image is a Colorado map. Earlier in this project, you placed the image on the col_map layer. It is not necessary to place an image on a layer to create an image map. You can insert the image anywhere on the page, just as you previously have inserted images in earlier projects. Placing the image in a layer, however, provides absolute positioning. Using this method, you can be assured that the image map will display properly in all browsers supporting CSS-P.

When you create an image map and add a hotspot, you are creating an area that is clickable on the image. To define a hotspot, use one of three shapes: a rectangle, a circle (or oval), or a polygon. Select the tool you want to use and then drag the pointer over the image to create the hotspot. Use the **Rectangular Hotspot Tool** to create a rectangular-shaped hotspot. Use the **Oval Hotspot Tool** to define an oval or circular hotspot area. Use the **Polygon Hotspot Tool** to define an irregularly shaped hotspot. Click the **Pointer Hotspot Tool** (arrow) to close the polygon shape.

When an image is selected, the Property inspector for images is displayed. The Map name text box and hotpot tools are available in the lower portion of the Property inspector (Figure 6-25a).

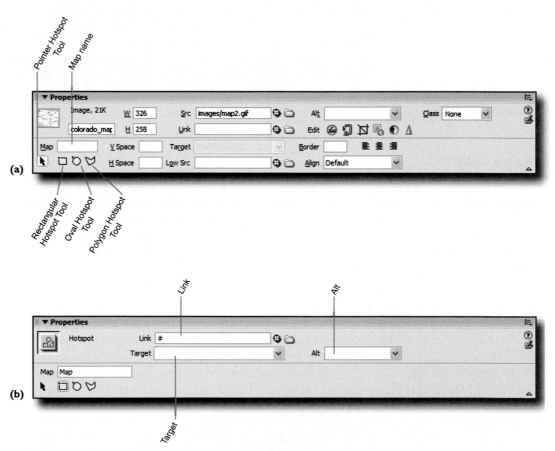

FIGURE 6-25

The **Map name** and the **hotspot tools** allow you to label and create a client-side image map. The other properties in the Image Property inspector are described in Project 2 on pages DW 144 – DW 145.

After you create a hotspot, Dreamweaver displays the Property inspector for a hotspot (Figure 6-25b). If you are linking to other locations within the same Web page or to Web pages outside of your existing Web site, the link or URL is inserted into the Link text box. On the Target pop-up menu, choose the window in which the file should open in the Target field. If the Web site contains frames, a list of the frame names is contained on the pop-up menu. You also can select from the reserved target names: _blank, _parent, _self, and _top. See page DW 592 in Project 7 for a discussion about these target names. The target option is not available unless the selected hotspot contains a link.

In this image map, you will not link to another Web site or Web page. Instead, you add behaviors to the hotspots to link to and to display hidden layers. Behaviors are discussed later in this project. Clicking the top third of the Colorado map displays an image listing some of the more popular features in northern Colorado. Clicking the middle portion of the map displays an image listing some of the more popular features in central Colorado. Clicking the lower third of the map displays an image listing some of the more popular features in southern Colorado.

If Windows SP2 is installed on your computer, the Internet Explorer security settings can prevent the display of active content such as the layers associated with the hotspots. To display the content, right-click the information bar at the top of the Internet Explorer window, and choose to allow blocked content.

Earlier in this project, you used the View menu to select Visual Aids, and then verified that Layer Borders was selected. This same menu also contains an Image Maps command. To see a visual of the hotspot on the image, the Image Maps command must be active. The following steps illustrate how to verify that the Image Maps command is selected and how to create three rectangular hotspots on the Colorado map image.

To Create Hotspots on the Colorado Map Image

1

• **Collapse the panel groups.**

• **If necessary, scroll up to display the top of the col_map layer. Click the map2.gif image in the col_map layer.**

The map2.gif image is selected. The Image Property inspector is displayed and the panel groups are collapsed (Figure 6-26).

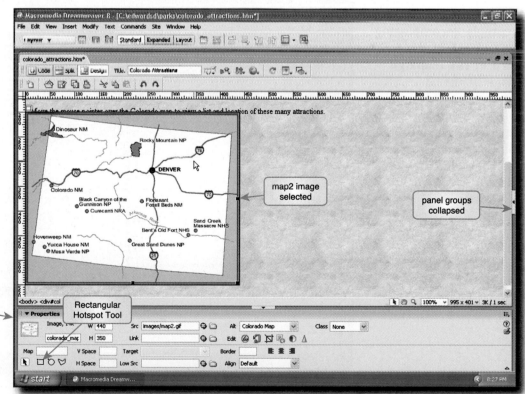

FIGURE 6-26

2

• **Click the Rectangular Hotspot Tool and then move the cross hair pointer to the upper-left corner of the map2.gif image.**

The cross hair pointer is located in the upper-left corner of the map2.gif image (Figure 6-27).

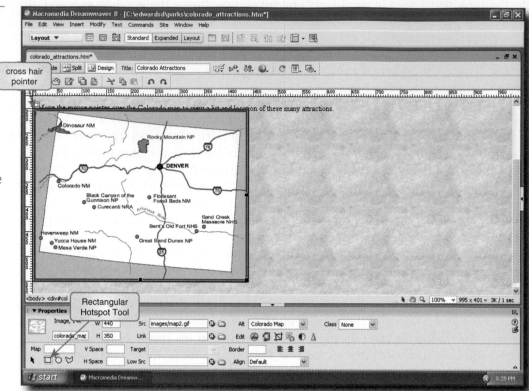

FIGURE 6-27

3

• **Drag to draw a rectangle encompassing approximately the top third of the map2.gif image. If the rectangular hotspot does not appear, click View on the menu bar, point to Visual Aids, and then click Image Maps on the Visual Aids submenu.**

A rectangular hotspot is drawn on the map2.gif image (Figure 6-28). Dreamweaver displays the Hotspot Property inspector.

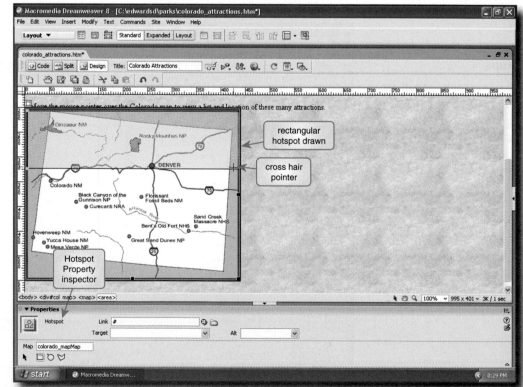

FIGURE 6-28

4

• **Draw two more hotspots on the map2.gif image by dragging the cross hair pointer over the middle third of the image and then over the lower third of the image.**

• **Click anywhere in the window to cancel the cross hair pointer, and then, if necessary, scroll down.**

The second and third hotspots are drawn in the middle and lower thirds of the map2.gif image (Figure 6-29). The cross hair pointer is canceled.

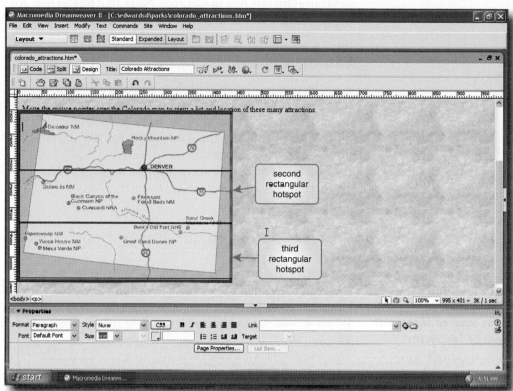

FIGURE 6-29

Behaviors — Combo event + action

In Project 4, you learned about the Behaviors panel and about using behaviors with forms. Recall that a behavior is a combination of an event and an action. Behaviors are attached to a specific element on a Web page. The element can be a table, an image, a link, a form, a form object, and even a hotspot on an image map. Some of the actions you can attach to hotspots (or other elements) include Show Pop-Up Menu, Play Sound, Drag Layer, Swap Image, and Show-Hide Layers.

Dreamweaver contains three standard events designed expressly for working with layers: Drag Layer, Set Text of Layer, and Show-Hide Layers. **Drag Layer** is used to set up an interactive process in which the user can drag or rearrange elements of the design. **Set Text of Layer** is used to change a layer's content dynamically; using this action, the user can swap the content of one layer for new content. **Show-Hide Layers** is used to make visible or to hide a layer and the layer's content.

Actions to invoke these events are **onMouseOut**, which initiates whatever action is associated with the event when the mouse is moved out of an object; **onMouseOver**, which initiates whatever action is associated with the event when the mouse is moved over the object; **onClick**, which initiates whatever action is associated with the event when the object is clicked; and **onDblClick**, which initiates whatever action is associated with the event when the object is double-clicked. These actions are selected through the Behaviors panel. The default is onMouseOver. To change the action for an event, click the existing event in the Behaviors panel. An arrow then is displayed to the right of the event, listing the four actions. Click the arrow to display a pop-up menu and to select another action: onClick, onDblClick,

More About

Behaviors

Use Dreamweaver behaviors to allow visitors to interact with a Web page. Simply specify the action and the event that triggers that action. For more information about behaviors, visit the Dreamweaver 8 More About Web page (scsite.com/dw8/more.htm) and then click Behaviors.

onMouseOut, or onMouseOver. Note that the arrow for the pop-up menu does not display until the existing event is clicked.

Adding Behaviors

Selecting a hotspot and then clicking the Add behavior (+) pop-up menu in the Behaviors panel displays a menu of actions that can be attached to the hotspot. When you choose an action on this menu, Dreamweaver displays a dialog box in which you can specify the parameters for the action. In this project, you use the Show-Hide Layers action.

The following steps show how to attach the Show-Hide Layers action to each of the three image map hotspots.

To Add the Show-Hide Layers Action to the Image Map Hotspots

1

• **Display the panel groups and collapse the Property inspector.**

• **Press SHIFT+F4 to display the Behaviors panel. If necessary, collapse the Files panel.**

The Behaviors panel is displayed and is part of the Tag panel group (Figure 6-30). Your panel may display in a different location on your screen.

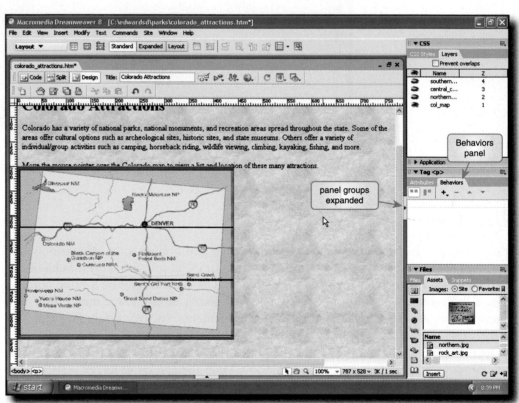

FIGURE 6-30

2

• **If necessary, scroll up and then click the top rectangular hotspot on the map2.gif image.**

The top rectangular hotspot is selected on the map2.gif image (Figure 6-31).

Hotspot handle

rectangular hotspot selected

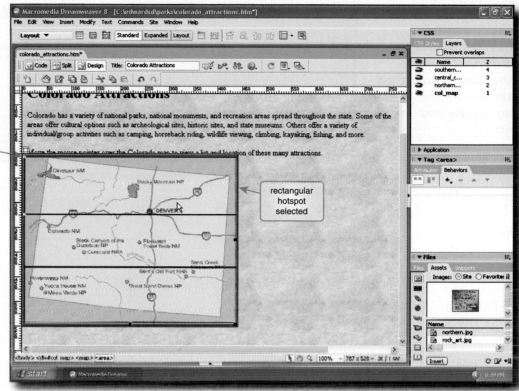

FIGURE 6-31

3

• **Click the Plus (+) button to display the Actions pop-up menu in the Behaviors panel. Point to Show-Hide Layers.**

Dreamweaver displays the Actions pop-up menu, and the Show-Hide Layers command is selected (Figure 6-32).

Plus (+) button

Actions pop-up menu

Show-Hide Layers command

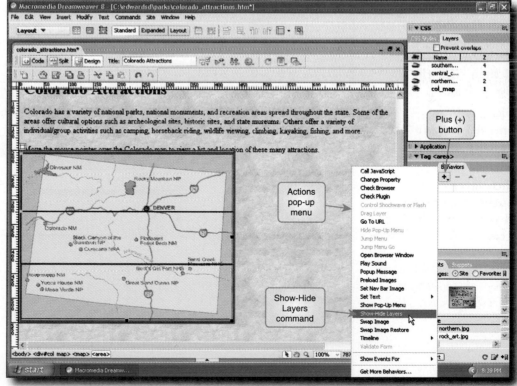

FIGURE 6-32

4

• **Click Show-Hide Layers. If necessary, click layer "col_map" in the Named layers list in the Show-Hide Layers dialog box to select it.**

Dreamweaver displays the Show-Hide Layers dialog box (Figure 6-33). The order of the layers in your dialog box may be different.

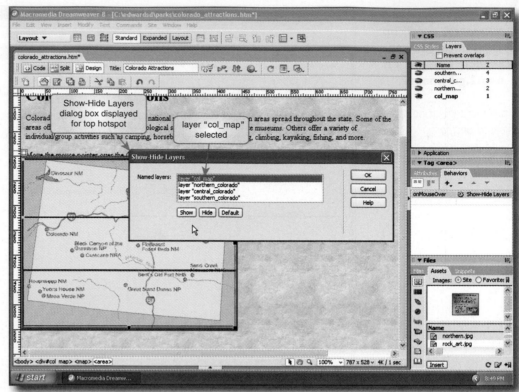

FIGURE 6-33

5

• **Click the Show button. Click layer "northern_colorado" and then click the Show button.**

• **Click layer "central_colorado" and then click the Hide button.**

• **Click layer "southern_colorado" and then click the Hide button.**

The selected Show-Hide Layers behaviors are added to each of the layers (Figure 6-34).

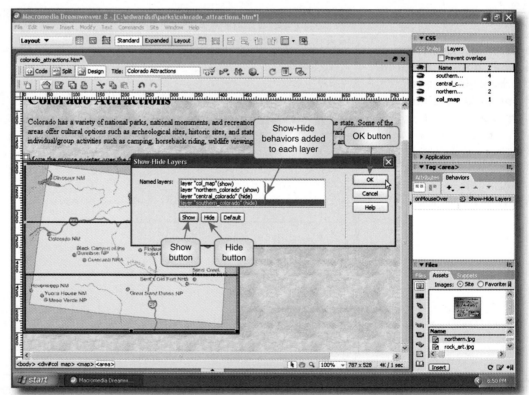

FIGURE 6-34

6

• **Click the OK button.**

• **Click the middle hotspot on the map2.gif image, click the Plus (+) button in the Behaviors panel, and then click Show-Hide Layers on the Actions pop-up menu.**

The middle hotspot is selected in the map2.gif image. Dreamweaver displays the Show-Hide Layers dialog box (Figure 6-35). The order of the layers in your dialog box may be different.

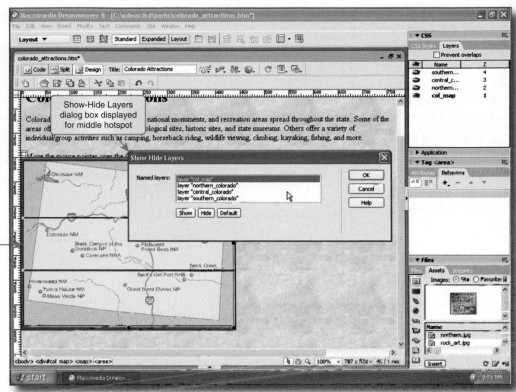

FIGURE 6-35

7

• **If necessary, click layer "col_map" and then click the Show button. Click layer "northern_colorado" and then click the Hide button. Click layer "central_colorado" and then click the Show button. Click layer "southern_colorado" and then click the Hide button.**

The selected Show-Hide Layers behaviors are added to each of the layers (Figure 6-36).

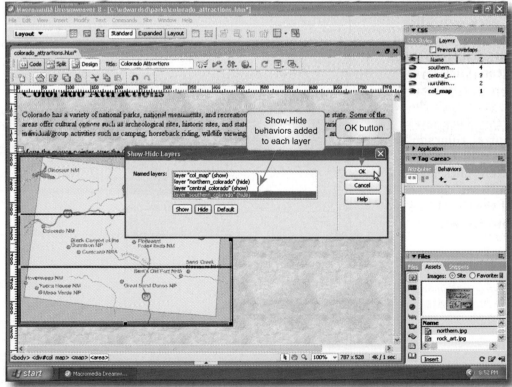

FIGURE 6-36

8

• **Click the OK button.**

• **If necessary, scroll down in the Document window and then click the third hotspot on the map2.gif image.**

• **Click the Plus (+) button in the Behaviors panel, and then click Show-Hide Layers on the Actions pop-up menu.**

The lower hotspot is selected in the map2.gif image. Dreamweaver displays the Show-Hide Layers dialog box (Figure 6-37). The order of the layers in your dialog box may be different.

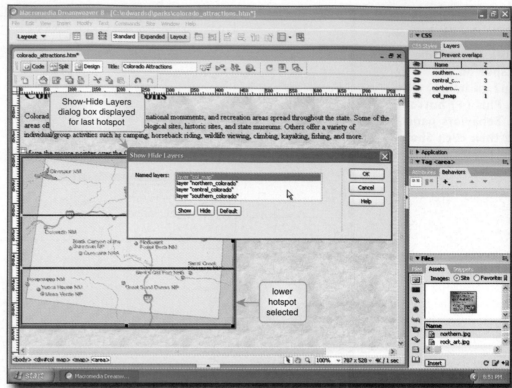

FIGURE 6-37

9

• **If necessary, click layer "col_map" and then click the Show button. Click layer "northern_colorado" and then click the Hide button. Click layer "central_colorado" and then click the Hide button. Click layer "southern_colorado" and then click the Show button.**

The selected Show-Hide Layers behaviors are added to each of the layers (Figure 6-38).

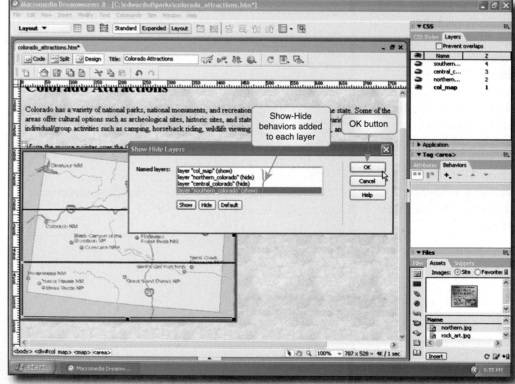

FIGURE 6-38

10

- **Click the OK button.**
- **Click the Save button on the Standard toolbar and then press the F12 key to display the Web page in your browser.**
- **If necessary, maximize the browser window.**
- **Move the mouse pointer over the hotspots on the map2.gif image to display each of the hidden layers.**

As you move the mouse pointer over each hotspot on the Colorado map image, the images appear to the right. The layer with the image for Northern Colorado Features is displayed in Figure 6-39.

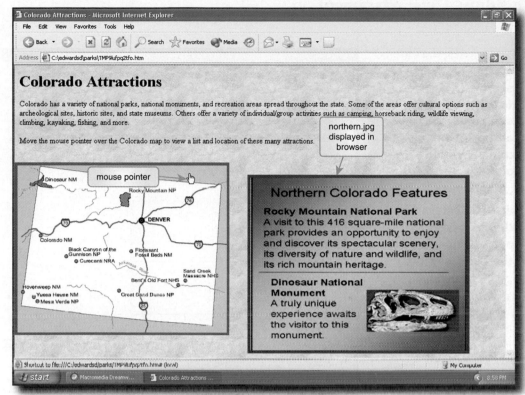

FIGURE 6-39

11

- **Close the browser window and return to Dreamweaver.**

Positioning Layers

When you displayed the Colorado map image and the images in the browser, you may have noticed that quite a bit of space appeared between the images and the paragraph above the images. You can position a layer anywhere on the page. In some instances, to eliminate extra space, it is necessary to drag the image over existing text. Even though the text is covered in the Document window, it is displayed correctly in the browser.

This sometimes can be a trial-and-error process. You can select and drag the layer by the selection handle or you can move the layer pixel by pixel by selecting the image, holding down the SHIFT key, and then pressing one of the arrow keys.

The following steps show how to adjust the position of the col_map layer.

To Adjust Layer Placement

1

• **Display the Property inspector. If necessary, click col_map in the Layers panel and then scroll up in the Document window to display the top of the col_map layer.**

• **Click the T text box in the Property inspector and type** 205 **as the pixel number.**

• **Press the TAB key and then click anywhere in the Document window.**

The Layer Property inspector is displayed. The col_map layer is selected in the Layers panel. The col_map layer is moved down in the Document window and still overlaps part of the text (Figure 6-40). The text will not be overlapped when displayed in the browser. Some of the Layer properties may be different on your screen than those in Figure 6-40. You will adjust other properties later in this project.

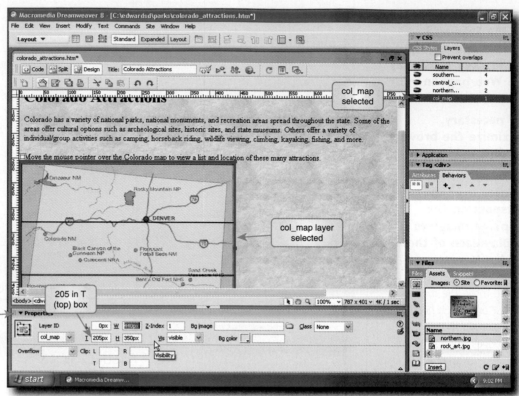

FIGURE 6-40

2

• **Press the F12 key to view the Web page in your browser. Verify that none of the text is covered and that the image is positioned nicely within the Web page.**

Central Colorado Features is displayed in Figure 6-41.

3

• **Close the browser to return to Dreamweaver.**

• **Make any necessary adjustments in the Document window to adjust the placement of the col_map layer.**

• **Click the Save button.**

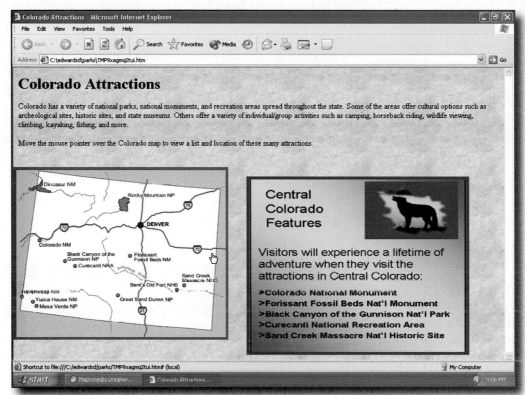

FIGURE 6-41

Selecting, Aligning, and Resizing Multiple Layers

Dreamweaver contains yet another command that you can use to lay out your Web page: the **Arrange command**. This command, which is accessed through the Modify menu, lets you align layers to their left, right, top, or bottom edges. The Arrange command also provides an option to make the width and/or height of selected layers the same. When you are using the Arrange command, the layer you select last controls the alignment selection. For instance, if you first select northern_colorado, then central_colorado, and finally southern_colorado, the alignment placement is determined by southern_colorado. Likewise, if you select the option to make the width and/or height of selected layers the same, the last layer selected is the one whose values are used as the values for the other layers.

To align two or more layers, you first must select the layers. To select multiple layers in the Layers panel, you select one layer, hold down the SHIFT key, and then click the other layers you want to align. A second method for selecting multiple layers is to click

More About

Positioning Layers

Control the absolute positioning of layers on a Web page by setting five attributes: Left, Top, Width, Height, and Z-Index. For more information about positioning layers, visit the Dreamweaver 8 More About Web page (scsite.com/dw8 /more.htm) and then click Positioning Layers.

the border of one layer, hold down the SHIFT key, and then click the border of any other layers. When multiple layers are selected, the handles of the last selected layer are highlighted in black. The resize handles of the other layers are highlighted in white.

Layers do not have to be stacked or overlapped to be aligned. The three layers you are going to align, however, are stacked one on top of the other. Thus, the best method for selecting the three layers is through the Layers panel.

The final steps for this Web page are to use the Align command to align the tops of the three hidden layers with the col_map layer, make the three hidden layers the same height and width if necessary, and then align the three layers to the left. Finally, you add a link from the natl_parks.htm Web page to this new colorado_attractions.htm page. The next steps illustrate how to complete the alignment options and add the link.

More About

Resizing Layers

To resize a layer one pixel at a time, hold down the CTRL key while pressing an arrow key.

To Select and Align Multiple Layers

1

• **Select the southern_colorado layer in the Layers panel. Hold down the SHIFT key and then select the central_colorado, northern_colorado, and col_map layers.**

All four layers are selected in the Layers panel. The col_map layer should be the last one selected. The Property inspector for Multiple Layers is displayed (Figure 6-42).

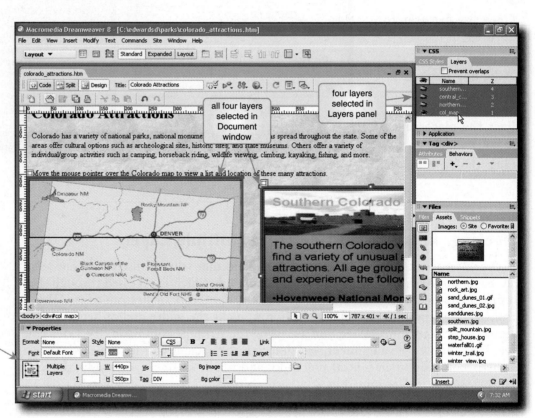

FIGURE 6-42

Dreamweaver Project 6

2

• **Click Modify on the menu bar, point to Arrange, and then point to Align Top on the Arrange submenu.**

The Modify menu and Arrange submenu are displayed (Figure 6-43).

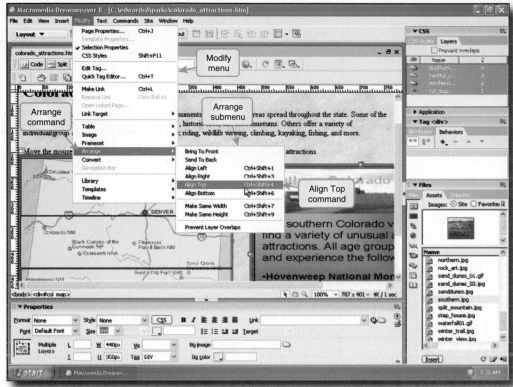

FIGURE 6-43

3

• **Click Align Top. If necessary, scroll down in the Document window.**

All four layers are aligned at the top (Figure 6-44).

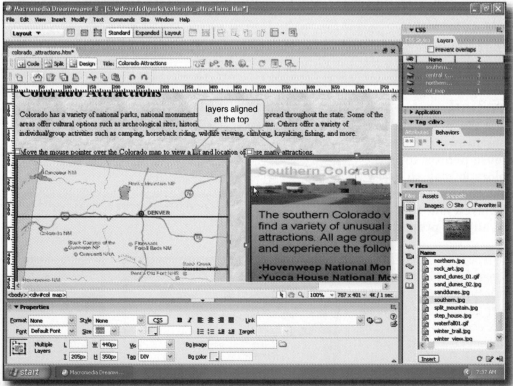

FIGURE 6-44

4

• **Hold down the SHIFT key and then click col_map in the Layers panel.**

The col_map layer is deselected (Figure 6-45). The other three layers still are selected.

5

• **Click Modify on the menu bar, point to Arrange, and then click Align Left on the Arrange submenu.**

• **Click Modify on the menu bar, point to Arrange, and then click Make Same Width on the Arrange submenu.**

• **Click Modify on the menu bar, point to Arrange, and then click Make Same Height on the Arrange submenu.**

The three stacked layers are aligned at the left and are now the same width and height. No apparent changes appear in the Document window.

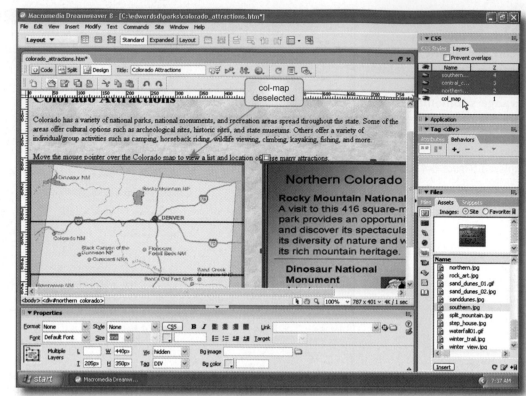

FIGURE 6-45

6

• **Press the F12 key to view the Web page in your browser. Move the mouse pointer over the Colorado map to verify that the images are displayed and that they are aligned properly.**

The browser is displayed (Figure 6-46). In Figure 6-46, the mouse pointer is over the lower portion of the Colorado map, and the image for Southern Colorado is displayed.

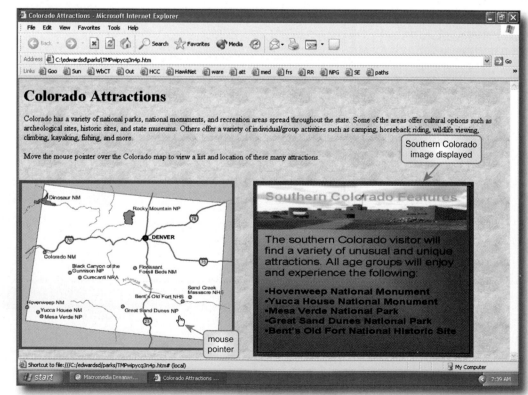

FIGURE 6-46

7

• **Close the browser and return to Dreamweaver.**

• **Click View on the menu bar, point to Rulers, and then click Show on the Rulers submenu to hide the rulers.**

• **Press F2 to collapse the CSS group and then press SHIFT+F4 to collapse the Tag Inspector group.**

• **Press F8 to display the Files panel. Open the natl_parks.htm file and scroll to the bottom of the page. Click to the right of the Colorado National Parks Hotel Reservations link and press SHIFT+ENTER. Type** Colorado Attractions Map **as the entry, create a link to the colorado_attractions.htm page, and then save the natl_parks.htm file (Figure 6-47).**

• **Press F12 to view the Web page and test the link. Close the browser and then close the natl_parks.htm page.**

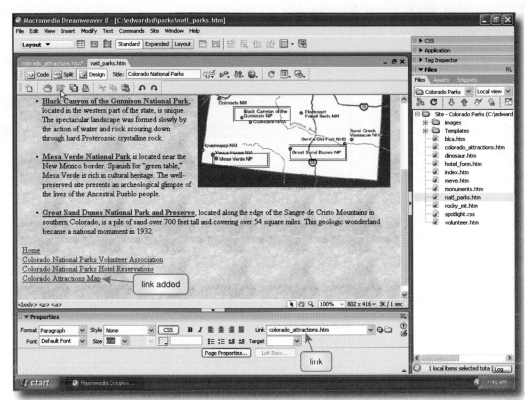

FIGURE 6-47

The Netscape Resize Fix

The Netscape 4 browser has a known compatibility problem that causes layers to lose their positioning coordinates when a visitor resizes a browser window.

Dreamweaver provides a fix for this through the Preferences dialog box by adding JavaScript code that forces the page to reload each time the browser window is resized, thus reassigning the layers to the correct positions. This option may be activated on your system. If not, the following steps show how to set the fix.

To Set the Netscape Resize Fix

1

• Click Edit on the menu bar and then click Preferences.

• Click the Layers category and then click the Add resize fix when inserting layer check box to select it. If necessary, click the Nest when created within a layer check box to select it.

The Add resize fix when inserting layer check box is selected (Figure 6-48).

2

• Click the OK button. The Netscape Resize Fix source code is added. No visible changes are displayed in the Document window.

• If necessary, click the Save button on the Standard toolbar and then close the colorado_attractions.htm page.

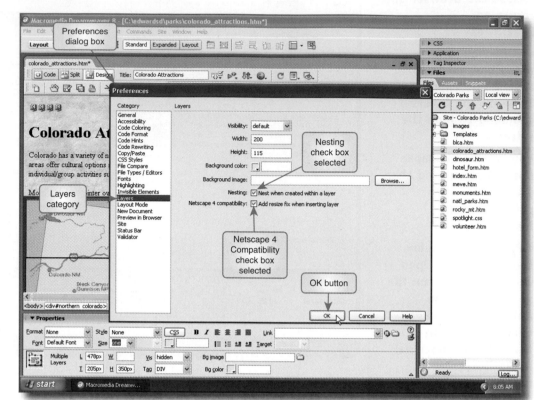

FIGURE 6-48

More About

Navigation Bar

Dreamweaver's navigation bar feature provides a visually interesting option that allows visitors to navigate the Web site easily. A navigation bar often extends along the top or side of a Web page and can include text, images, or animations that link to other sections or pages in the site. For more information about navigation bars, visit the Dreamweaver 8 More About Web page (scsite.com/dw8/more.htm) and then click Navigation Bars.

The Navigation Bar and Date Object

In earlier projects, you used text to add links to your Web pages. Dreamweaver provides another quick-and-easy method to provide navigation: a navigation bar. A **navigation bar** (or **nav bar**) is a set of interactive buttons that the Web site visitor uses as links to other Web pages, Web sites, or frames. The Insert Navigation Bar dialog box provides an option to insert the navigation bar horizontally or vertically. Many Web site developers consider a navigation bar to be a convenient, customized alternative to a browser's Back and Forward buttons.

Dreamweaver also provides the **Date object**, which inserts the current date in a format of your preference and provides the option of updating the date (with or without the time) whenever you save the file.

Preparing the Index Page and Adding the Date Object

You add these two objects (Date object and navigation bar) to the index page. You open the index.htm page, delete the existing links, and then insert a navigation bar to replace these links. Additionally, you delete the static date and replace it with the Date object.

The following step illustrates how to open and prepare the index.htm page for the navigation bar and Date object.

To Open and Prepare the Index.htm Page

1

• **If necessary, click the Files panel tab.**

• **Double-click index.htm in the Files panel to open the index.htm file.**

Dreamweaver displays the index.htm page in the Document window (Figure 6-49).

2

• **Collapse the Property inspector and the panel groups.**

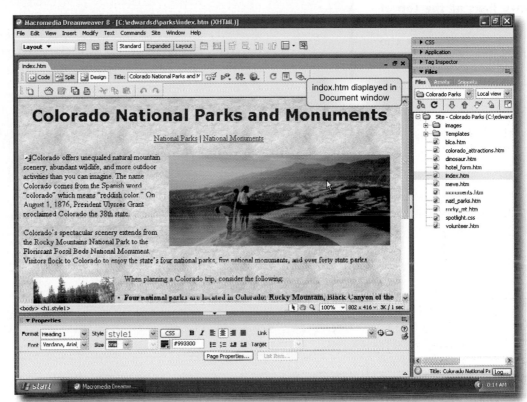

index.htm displayed in Document window

FIGURE 6-49

The index page contains two links at the top of the page. The first step in modifying the index page is to delete these links.

To further update the page, you remove the static date placed at the bottom of the page and replace it with a new format using the Dreamweaver Date object. The next steps show how to delete the existing links and insert the Date object.

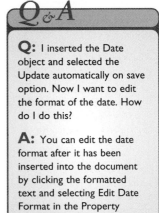

Q: I inserted the Date object and selected the Update automatically on save option. Now I want to edit the format of the date. How do I do this?

A: You can edit the date format after it has been inserted into the document by clicking the formatted text and selecting Edit Date Format in the Property inspector.

To Delete Existing Links and Insert the Date Object

1

• Move the insertion point to the left of the two links at the top of the index.htm page and then drag to select the links.

The two links are selected (Figure 6-50).

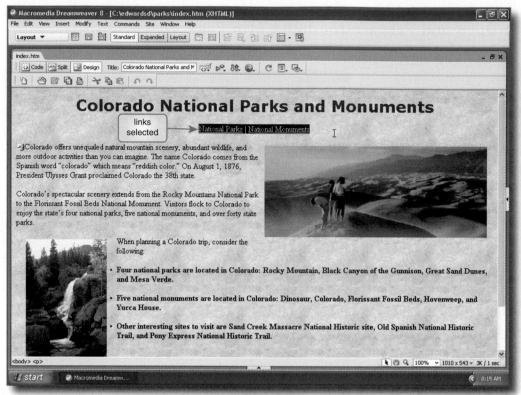

FIGURE 6-50

2

• Press the DELETE key to remove the two links.

The links are deleted (Figure 6-51).

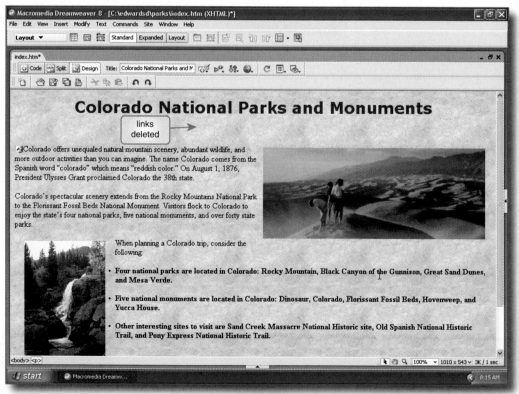

FIGURE 6-51

3

• **Scroll to the bottom of the page.**

• **Select the date below your e-mail address link and then press the DELETE key.**

The date is deleted. The insertion point is blinking below your linked e-mail address (Figure 6-52). The insertion point, however, may be just a tiny speck.

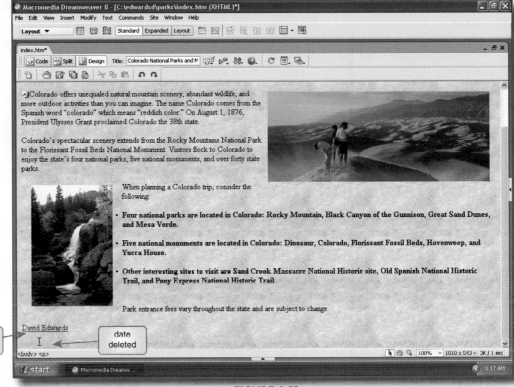

insertion point

date deleted

FIGURE 6-52

4

• **Click Insert on the menu bar and then point to Date.**

The Insert menu is displayed (Figure 6-53).

Insert menu

Date command

FIGURE 6-53

5

• **Click Date.**

Dreamweaver displays the Insert Date dialog box. The March 7, 1974 Date format is selected, which is the one you will use (Figure 6-54). The dates and times shown in the Insert Date dialog box neither are the current date nor reflect the dates/times that visitors will see when they display your site. They are examples of the formats in which you can display this information.

6

• **Click the Update automatically on save check box.**

The Update automatically on save check box is selected (Figure 6-54).

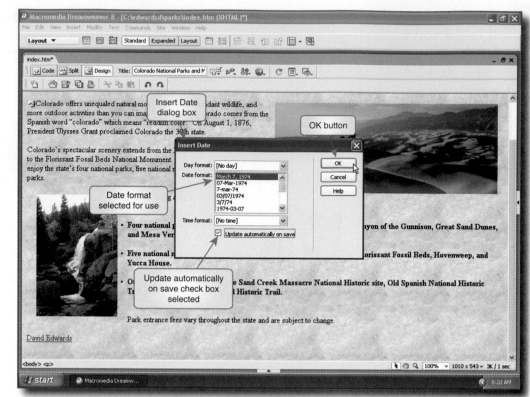

FIGURE 6-54

7

• **Click the OK button.**

The current date is inserted (Figure 6-55). The date on your Web page will be different from that displayed in Figure 6-55.

8

• **Click the Save button on the Standard toolbar.**

Other Ways

1. Click Common category on Insert bar, click the Date button on Common category, select Date format in Insert Date dialog box, click OK button

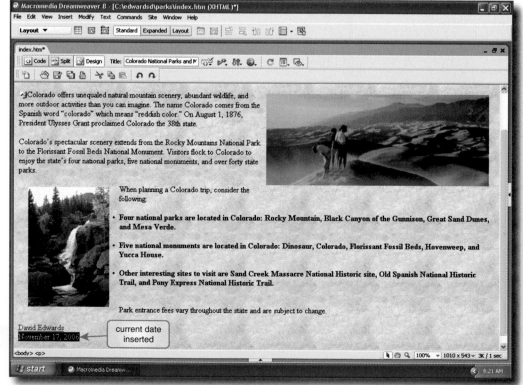

FIGURE 6-55

Creating a Navigation Bar

You create a navigation bar using icon or button elements. Each element is a slightly different shape or a different color. An element in a navigation bar is called a **rollover** if animation takes place when you move the mouse pointer over the element or click the element. The original image is swapped out for a different one, thus creating a simple animation.

Each element in a Dreamweaver navigation bar can have up to four different states. It is not necessary, however, to include images for all four states. The four possible images and states are as follows:

- **Up**: the image that is displayed when the visitor has not clicked or interacted with the element.
- **Over**: the image that appears when the mouse pointer is moved over the Up image.
- **Down**: the image that appears after the element is clicked.
- **Over While Down**: the image that appears when the pointer is rolled over the Down image after the element is clicked.

Dreamweaver also provides several features that contribute to the versatility of the navigation bar. Some of these features are:

- The navigation bar can be placed within a table or directly integrated into the HTML code.
- An Alternate text text box is available for use with nongraphical browsers and as an accessibility option.
- You can copy the navigation bar to other Web pages.
- A Preload images check box is available; select Preload images to download the images when the page loads.
- Check the Show "Down image" check box to display the selected element initially in its Down state when the page is displayed, instead of in its default Up state.

Modifying a navigation bar is easy. After you create the navigation bar, you can add or remove images by using the Navigation Bar command on the Modify menu. You can use this command to change an image or set of images, to change which file opens when an element is clicked, to select a different window or frame in which to open a file, and to reorder the images.

The Colorado Parks navigation bar contains five links. You specify three different states for each link — Up, Over, and Down. The same image is used for the Over and Down states. The following steps illustrate how to create the navigation bar.

Q & A

Q: If I create a navigation bar, are the button images part of the Dreamweaver program?

A: No — you must create a set of images for the display states of each navigation element.

Q & A

Q: Why do I need to add alternate text for each button in a navigation bar?

A: Alternate text appears in place of images for text-only browsers or for browsers that have been set to download images manually. Screen readers read alternate text, and some browsers display alternate text when the user mouses over the navigation bar element.

To Create the Navigation Bar

1

• **Scroll up to the top of the page in the Document window and then click below the heading. Click Insert on the menu bar, point to Image Objects, and then point to Navigation Bar on the Image Objects submenu.**

The Insert menu and Image Objects submenu are displayed (Figure 6-56).

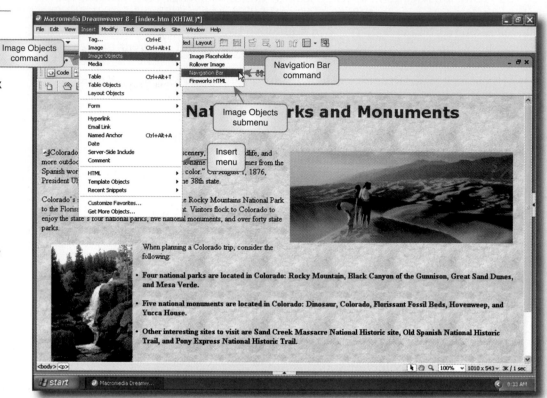

FIGURE 6-56

2

• **Click Navigation Bar.**

Dreamweaver displays the Insert Navigation Bar dialog box (Figure 6-57). The insertion point is blinking in the Element name text box.

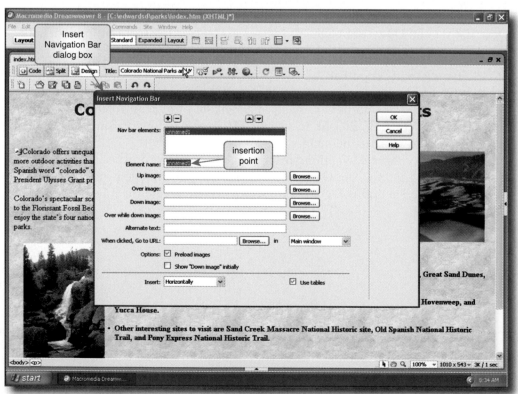

FIGURE 6-57

3

• **Type** colorado_parks **in the Element name text box. If necessary, click the Use tables check box to select it and verify that Horizontally is selected in the Insert pop-up menu. Point to the Browse button for the Up image text box.**

The name colorado_parks is displayed in the Element name text box and the Use tables check box is selected (Figure 6-58).

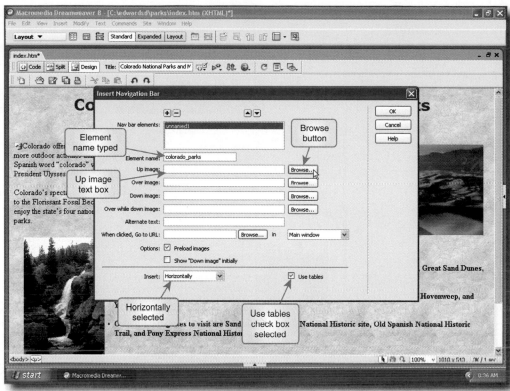

FIGURE 6-58

4

• **Click the Browse button to the right of the Up image text box. If necessary, double-click the images folder in the Select image source dialog box.**

Dreamweaver displays the Select image source dialog box (Figure 6-59).

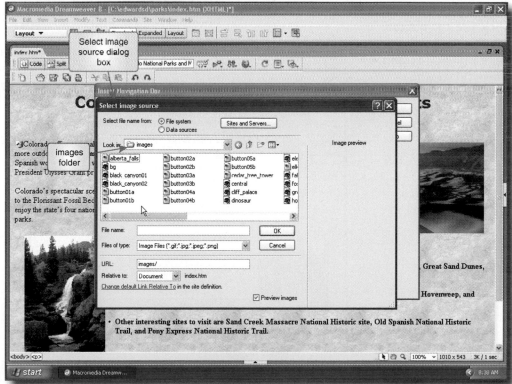

FIGURE 6-59

5

• **Click the button01a file.**

The button01a.gif image is selected (Figure 6-60). The Image preview area shows how the button will look.

FIGURE 6-60

6

• **Click the OK button in the Select image source dialog box and then point to the Browse button to the right of the Over image text box.**

The path to the button01a.gif image is inserted into the Up image text box (Figure 6-61).

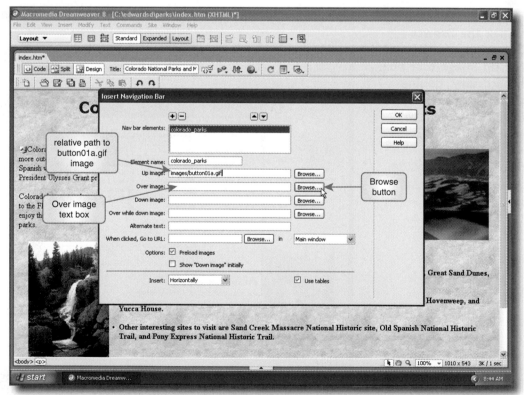

FIGURE 6-61

7

• **Click the Browse button to the right of the Over image text box and then click button01b.**

The button01b file is selected (Figure 6-62).

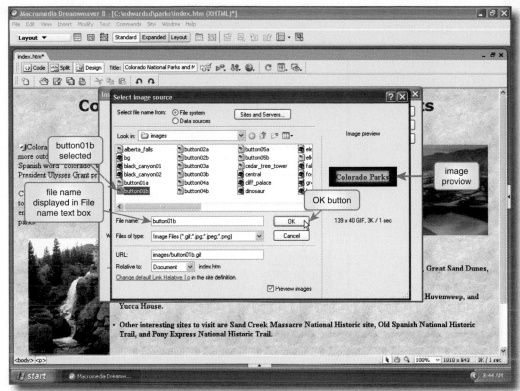

FIGURE 6-62

8

• **Click the OK button. Point to the Browse button to the right of the Down image text box.**

The path to the button01b.gif image is inserted into the Over image text box (Figure 6-63).

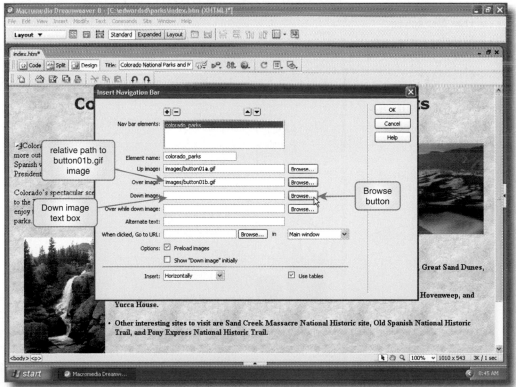

FIGURE 6-63

9

• **Click the Browse button to the right of the Down image text box. Click button01b, and then click the OK button.**

The path to the button01b.gif image is inserted into the Down image text box (Figure 6-64).

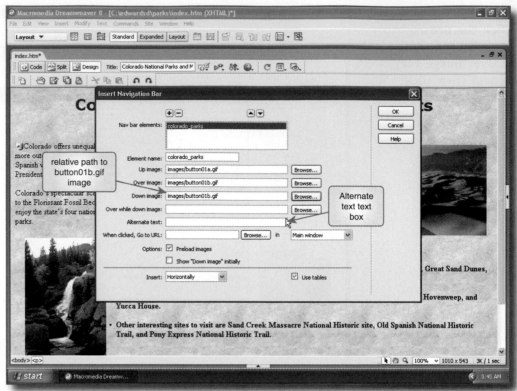

FIGURE 6-64

10

• **Click the Alternate text text box and then type** Colorado Parks **as the alternate text. Point to the Browse button to the right of the When clicked, Go to URL text box.**

Colorado Parks is displayed in the Alternate text text box (Figure 6-65).

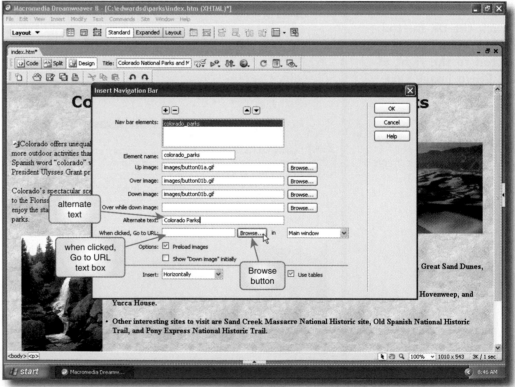

FIGURE 6-65

11

• **Click the Browse button. If necessary, navigate to the parks folder. Click the natl_parks file and then point to the OK button in the Select HTML file dialog box.**

Dreamweaver displays the Select HTML file dialog box (Figure 6-66). The natl_parks.htm file is selected.

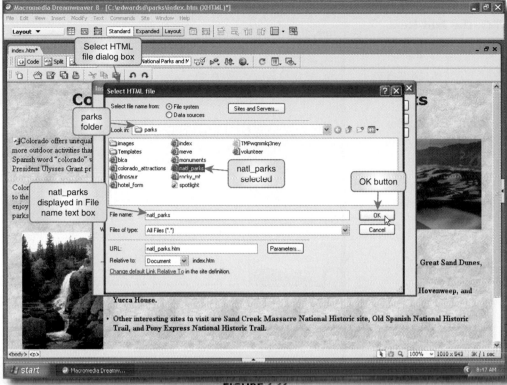

FIGURE 6-66

12

• **Click the OK button in the Select HTML file dialog box. Point to the Add Item button.**

The link to the natl_parks.htm file is displayed in the When clicked, Go to URL text box (Figure 6-67).

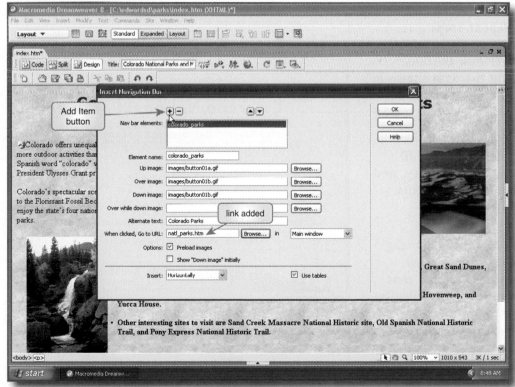

FIGURE 6-67

13

• **Click the Add Item button.**

The data for the first button for the navigation bar is added, and the Modify Navigation Bar dialog box is ready for the next button (Figure 6-68).

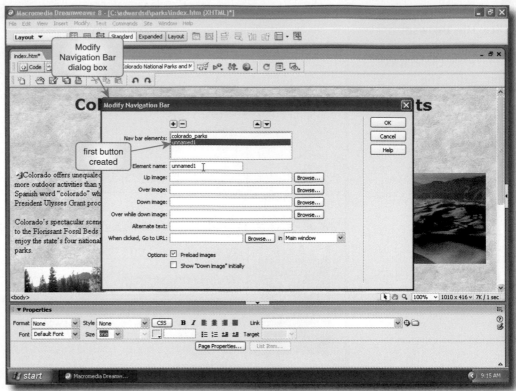

FIGURE 6-68

14

• **Repeat Steps 3 through 13 to add the other four buttons, using the data shown in Table 6-1 on DW 535.**

• **If necessary, display the Property inspector.**

• **Click the Table ID box, type** nav_bar **and then press the ENTER key.**

• **Click the `<table#nav_bar>` tag in the tag selector. Center the table that contains the navigation bar.**

• **Click the CellPad text box and type** 4. **Press the TAB key.**

The navigation bar is created and is centered in the Document window. It is displayed within a table (Figure 6-69).

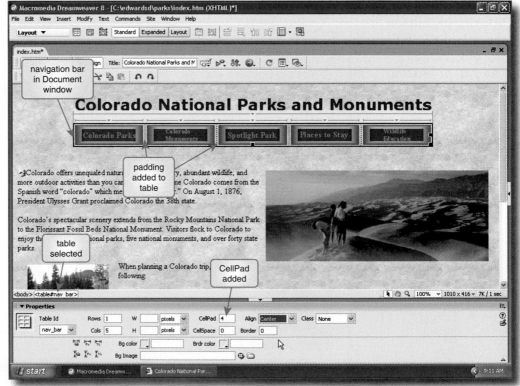

FIGURE 6-69

Table 6-1 Navigation Bar Buttons

ELEMENT NAME	UP IMAGE	OVER IMAGE	DOWN IMAGE	ALTERNATE TEXT	URL
monuments	button02a.gif	button02b.gif	button02bgif	Colorado Monuments	monuments.htm
spotlight	button03a.gif	button03b.gif	button03b.gif	Featured Monument	dinosaur.htm
places_to_stay	button04a.gif	button04b.gif	button04b.gif	Hotel Information	hotel_form.htm
wildlife_education	button05a.gif	button05b.gif	button05b.gif	Wildlife Education	http://www.wildlife.state.co.us/education/coexisting_with_wildlife/

15

• **Press the F12 key to view the navigation bar in your browser, and test each of the links.**

The navigation bar is displayed in the browser window (Figure 6-70).

16

• **If instructed to do so, print a copy of the colorado_attractions.htm page and the revised index.htm page, hand them in to your instructor, and upload the revised Web pages to a server. Close the browser and then click the Save All button on the Standard toolbar.**

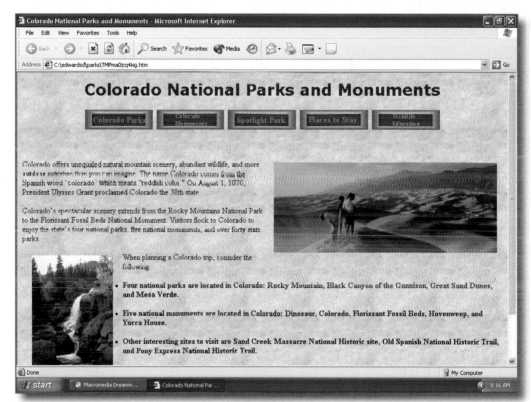

FIGURE 6-70

Quitting Dreamweaver

Now that you have added a new page with layers and an image map and modified the index page by adding a Date object and a navigation bar, Project 6 is complete. The following step shows how to close the Web site, quit Dreamweaver 8, and return control to Windows.

To Close the Web Site and Quit Dreamweaver

1 **Click the Close button in the upper-right corner of the Dreamweaver title bar.**

The Dreamweaver window, the Document window, and the Colorado Parks Web site all close.

Project Summary

Project 6 introduced you to layers, image maps, navigation bars, and the Date object. You added single layers and stacked layers. You selected and aligned several layers. Next, you created an image map and then added hotspots that displayed hidden layers. Then, you modified the existing index page by deleting links and replacing those links with a navigation bar. You also inserted a Date object on the index page.

What You Should Know

Having completed this project, you now should be able to perform the tasks below. The tasks are listed in the same order they were presented in the project. For a list of keyboard commands for topics introduced in this project, see the Quick Reference for Windows at the back of this book and refer to the Shortcut column.

1. Copy Images and a Data File to the Parks Web Site (DW 486)
2. Start Dreamweaver and Open the Colorado Parks Web Site (DW 488)
3. Open the Colorado Attractions Page and Display the Rulers (DW 490)
4. Create and Select a Layer for the Colorado Map Image (DW 494)
5. Display the Layers Panel (DW 496)
6. Name the Layer and Adjust the Layer Properties (DW 497)
7. Add an Image to the Col_map Layer (DW 498)
8. Create Stacked Layers (DW 500)
9. Select Layers and Add Images (DW 503)
10. Create Hotspots on the Colorado Map Image (DW 507)
11. Add the Show-Hide Layers Action to the Image Map Hotspots (DW 510)
12. Adjust Layer Placement (DW 516)
13. Select and Align Multiple Layers (DW 518)
14. Set the Netscape Resize Fix (DW 522)
15. Open and Prepare the Index.htm Page (DW 523)
16. Delete Existing Links and Insert the Date Object (DW 524)
17. Create the Navigation Bar (DW 528)
18. Close the Web Site and Quit Dreamweaver (DW 536)

Learn It Online

Instructions: To complete the Learn It Online exercises, start your browser, click the Address bar, and then enter the Web address scsite.com/dw8/learn. When the Dreamweaver 8 Learn It Online page is displayed, follow the instructions in the exercises below. Each exercise has instructions for printing your results, either for your own records or for submission to your instructor.

1 Project Reinforcement TF, MC, and SA

Below Dreamweaver Project 6, click the Project Reinforcement link. Print the quiz by clicking Print on the File menu for each page. Answer each question.

2 Flash Cards

Below Dreamweaver Project 6, click the Flash Cards link and read the instructions. Type 20 (or a number specified by your instructor) in the Number of playing cards text box, type your name in the Enter your Name text box, and then click the Flip Card button. When the flash card is displayed, read the question and then click the answer box arrow to select an answer. Flip through Flash Cards. If your score is 15 (75%) correct or greater, click Print on the File menu to print your results. If your score is less than 15 (75%) correct, then redo this exercise by clicking the Replay button.

3 Practice Test

Below Dreamweaver Project 6, click the Practice Test link. Answer each question, enter your first and last name at the bottom of the page, and then click the Grade Test button. When the graded practice test is displayed on your screen, click Print on the File menu to print a hard copy. Continue to take practice tests until you score 80% or better.

4 Who Wants To Be a Computer Genius?

Below Dreamweaver Project 6, click the Computer Genius link. Read the instructions, enter your first and last name at the bottom of the page, and then click the PLAY button. When your score is displayed, click the PRINT RESULTS link to print a hard copy.

5 Wheel of Terms

Below Dreamweaver Project 6, click the Wheel of Terms link. Read the instructions, and then enter your first and last name and your school name. Click the PLAY button. When your score is displayed, right-click the score and then click Print on the shortcut menu to print a hard copy.

6 Crossword Puzzle Challenge

Below Dreamweaver Project 6, click the Crossword Puzzle Challenge link. Read the instructions, and then enter your first and last name. Click the SUBMIT button. Work the crossword puzzle. When you are finished, click the Submit button. When the crossword puzzle is redisplayed, click the Print Puzzle button to print a hard copy.

7 Tips and Tricks

Below Dreamweaver Project 6, click the Tips and Tricks link. Click a topic that pertains to Project 6. Right-click the information and then click Print on the shortcut menu. Construct a brief example of what the information relates to in Dreamweaver to confirm that you understand how to use the tip or trick.

8 Newsgroups

Below Dreamweaver Project 6, click the Newsgroups link. Click a topic that pertains to Project 6. Print three comments.

9 Expanding Your Horizons

Below Dreamweaver Project 6, click the Expanding Your Horizons link. Click a topic that pertains to Project 6. Print the information. Construct a brief example of what the information relates to in Dreamweaver to confirm that you understand the contents of the article.

10 Search Sleuth

Below Dreamweaver Project 6, click the Search Sleuth link. To search for a term that pertains to this project, select a term below the Project 6 title and then use the Google search engine at google.com (or any major search engine) to display and print two Web pages that present information on the term.

Apply Your Knowledge

1 Adding Layers to the Andy's Lawn Service Web Site

Instructions: Start Dreamweaver. See the inside back cover of this book for instructions for downloading the Data Disk, or see your instructor for information on accessing the files in this book.

The proprietors of Andy's Lawn Service would like to make some additions to their Web site. First, they would like to add a navigation bar to the main page. Second, they would like to have an additional informational page that provides tree-pruning tips. You begin the process by adding a navigation bar to the index.htm page. Next, you open a data file and add layers to show some tree-pruning procedures. The modified index.htm page and the new tree-pruning page are shown in Figures 6-71a and 6-71b. Software and hardware settings determine how a Web page is displayed in a browser. Your Web page may display differently than the ones shown in Figures 6-71a and 6-71b. Appendix C contains instructions for uploading your local site to a remote server.

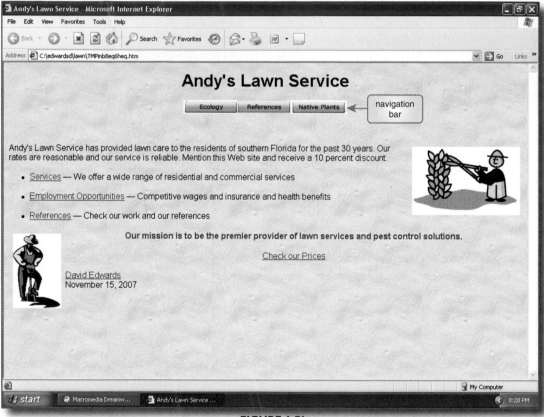

FIGURE 6-71a

Apply Your Knowledge

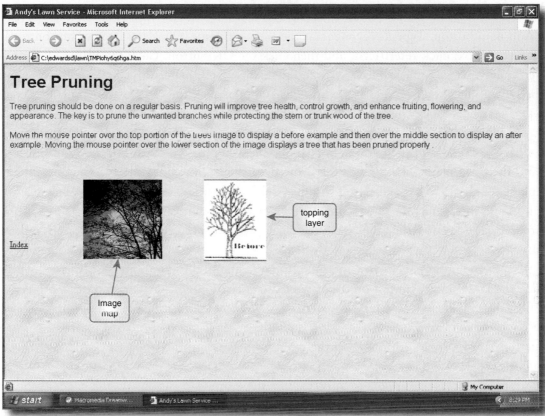

FIGURE 6-71b

1. If necessary, display the Property inspector, Standard toolbar, and panel groups. Select Lawn Service on the Files pop-up menu in the Files panel.
2. Use the Windows My Computer option to copy the data files and the images from the DataFiles folder to your lawn folder and lawn/images folder.
3. Open the index.htm page and, if necessary, display the rulers. Click to the right of the Andy's Lawn Service heading and press the ENTER key.
4. Click Insert on the menu bar, point to Image Objects, and then click Navigation Bar on the Image Objects submenu. Verify that the Preload image is selected, that Horizontally is selected, and that the Use tables check box is selected in the Insert Navigation Bar dialog box.
5. Type Ecology as the Element name. Click the Browse button to the right of the Up image text box. Navigate to the yourname/lawn/images folder, click ecol01.gif, and then click the OK button. Click the Browse button to the right of the Over image text box. Click ecol02.gif, and then click the OK button. Click the Browse button to the right of the Down image text box, click ecol02.gif, and then click the OK button. Click the Alternate text text box and then type Ecological Information as the entry. Click the When clicked, Go to URL text box and then type http://www.eap.mcgill.ca/Publications/EAP68.htm as the linked text.

(continued)

Apply Your Knowledge

Adding Layers to the Andy's Lawn Service Web Site *(continued)*

6. Click the Add item button. Type References as the Element name. Click the Browse button to the right of the Up image text box, click refer01.gif, and then click the OK button. Click the Browse button to the right of the Over image text box, click refer02.gif, and then click the OK button. Click the Browse button to the right of the Down image text box, click refer02.gif, and then click the OK button. Type References in the Alternate text text box. Click the When clicked, Go to URL text box and then type references.htm.

7. Click the Add Item button. Type NativePlants as the Element name. Click the Browse button to the right of the Up image text box and then add plants01.gif. Click the Browse button to the right of the Over image text box and then add plants02.gif. Click the Browse button to the right of the Down image text box and then add plants02.gif. Type Native Plants in the Alternate text text box. Click the When clicked, Go to URL text box and then type native_plants.htm. Click the OK button.

8. If necessary, select and center the table. Save the page, press the F12 key, and then test each link. Close the index.htm page.

9. Open the tree_pruning.htm page. Click the ruler-origin icon and drag it about 25 pixels below the last paragraph. Click the Draw Layer button on the Layout category on the Insert bar, and draw a layer approximately 150 by 150 pixels in size. Make any necessary W and H adjustments in the Property inspector. Type map in the Layer ID text box. Press the TAB key and change the L property to 150px. Press the TAB key again and change the T property to 220px. Drag the trees.gif image onto the layer. Click the Overflow box arrow and then click hidden.

10. Add three more layers. Use the rulers to approximate the L and T positions on the page, as indicated in Table 6-2. Name the layers and drag images onto each layer, using the data as indicated in the table. Set the Overflow property after you drag the images onto each layer. Make any other necessary adjustments in the Property inspector.

Table 6-2 Layer Properties

LAYER ID PROPERTIES	L AND T PROPERTIES	W AND H PROPERTIES	VIS PROPERTY	OVERFLOW	IMAGE
before	380px, 220px	160px, 170px	hidden	hidden	before.gif
after	380px, 220px	180px, 200px	hidden	hidden	after.gif
topping	380px, 220px	175px, 170px	hidden	hidden	topping.gif

11. Add three rectangular hotspots to the trees.gif image. Each hotspot should cover about one-third of the image (the first hotspot should cover the top third of the image, the second hotspot should cover the middle third of the image, and the third hotspot should cover the bottom third of the image). Display the Behaviors panel. Select the top hotspot, click the Add behavior button in the Behaviors panel, and then click Show-Hide Layers on the Add behavior pop-up menu. In the Show-Hide Layers dialog box, show layer "map" and layer "before." Hide layer "after" and layer "topping." Click the OK button. Click the middle hotspot and then click the Add behavior button in the Behaviors panel. Click Show-Hide Layers on the Add behavior pop-up menu. Show layer "map" and layer "after." Hide layer "before" and layer "topping." Click the OK button. Click the bottom hotspot, click the Add behavior button in the Behaviors panel, and then click Show-Hide Layers on the Add behavior pop-up menu. Show layer "map" and layer "topping." Hide layer "before" and layer "after." Click the OK button to close the Show-Hide Layers dialog box.

12. Click the Save button and then press the F12 key to view the Web page in your browser. Move the mouse pointer over the map image and verify that each layer is displayed in its proper spot. Close the browser to return to Dreamweaver.

13. Open the services.htm page. Click to the right of the Native Plants link and press the SHIFT+ENTER keys. Type Tree Pruning and create a link to the tree_pruning.htm page. Click the Save button and then press the F12 key to view the Web page in your browser. Test the Tree Pruning link. Close the browser to return to Dreamweaver.

14. Print a copy of the index, services, and tree-pruning Web pages, if instructed to do so. Upload the pages to the lawn Web site on a remote server, if instructed to do so.

In the Lab

1 Creating a New Index Page for the CandleWix Web Site

Problem: The CandleWix Web site has become very popular. Martha would like to redesign the index page and give it a more professional look. She has requested that you help her with this project by adding a navigation bar, rearranging some of the text by using layers, adding an automatic Date object so the current date is displayed on the page, and aligning existing layers. You agree to help her. The revised Web page is shown in Figure 6-72. Appendix C contains instructions for uploading your local site to a remote server.

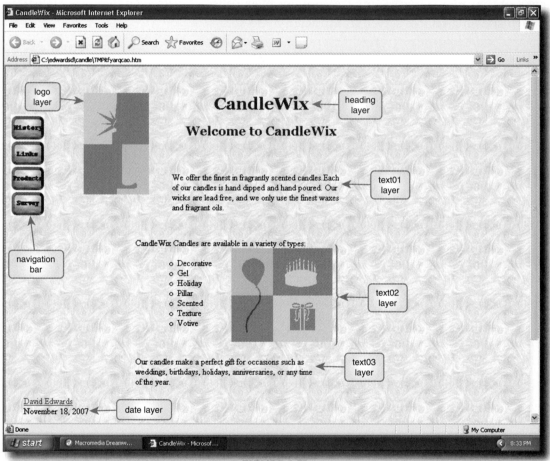

FIGURE 6-72

Instructions: Perform the following tasks:

1. Use the Windows My Computer option to copy the images from the DataFiles folder to your candle/images folder.

2. Select CandleWix on the Files pop-up menu in the Files panel. If necessary, display the panel groups.

3. Create a new file and name it index01.htm. Later in this project, you will save this file as index.htm, so that it will replace the current index.htm page. If necessary, display the Insert bar Layout category. Add the candlebg.gif image to the background. The insertion point is blinking at the top left of the page. Press the ENTER key two times.

4. The first task is to add a vertical navigation bar with four links. Click Insert on the menu bar, point to Image Objects, then click Navigation Bar on the Image Objects submenu. Verify that the Preload images and Use tables check boxes are selected and that Vertically is selected in the Insert box.

5. Use the data in Table 6-3 to complete the Insert Navigation Bar dialog box.

Table 6-3 Navigation Bar Data

ELEMENT NAME	UP IMAGE	OVER IMAGE	DOWN IMAGE	ALTERNATE TEXT	WHEN CLICKED, GO TO URL NAME
history	history01.gif	history02.gif	history02.gif	Company history	history.htm
links	links01.gif	links02.gif	links02.gif	Instruction links	http://www.candleandsoap.about.com/cs/candlemaking1/
products	products01.gif	products02.gif	products02.gif	Products for sale	products.htm
survey	survey01.gif	survey02.gif	survey02.gif	Survey	survey_form.htm

6. After all data is entered, click the OK button to insert the navigation bar.

7. Next, you add a layer for the logo. Display the rulers and then move the ruler-origin point about 150px to the right and approximately 50px from the top. Click the Draw Layer button on the Insert bar and then draw a layer with an approximate width of 120px and height of 150px. Make any necessary size adjustments in the Property inspector. Name the layer logo. Click the Vis box arrow and then click visible. Drag the candle1.gif image onto the layer. Right-click anywhere on the rulers and select Reset Origin on the context menu.

8. Next, you add five new layers: one for the heading, three for the text data contained on the original index page, and a layer for your e-mail address and date at the end of the page. Open the original index.htm page to use as a guide.

9. Using the data from Table 6-4 on the next page, draw the heading layer. Make any L and T, and W and H adjustments in the Property inspector. Click the index.htm page tab and copy the heading text. Click the index01.htm page tab and paste the heading text onto the heading layer.

10. Using the data from Table 6-4, repeat Step 9 to add the four remaining layers and to copy and paste the text from the index page.

11. Delete the existing date in the date layer. Click Insert on the menu bar and then click Date. Select the first option in the Insert Date dialog box. Click the Update automatically on save check box and then click the OK button.

12. Select the text02 layer in the Layers panel. Hold down the SHIFT key and select the text03 layer. Click Modify on the menu bar, click Arrange, and then click Align Left to align both layers to the left.

13. Title the page CandleWix.

14. Close the index.htm file. If prompted to save the file, click No. Save the index01.htm file as index.htm by clicking the File menu and then clicking Save As. Type index.htm in the File name text box of the Save As dialog box, then click Save. Click the Yes button in response to the Macromedia Dreamweaver alert dialog box. The Web page is saved as index.htm.

15. Right-click the index01.htm file in the Files panel to display the context menu. Point to Edit and then click Delete. Click the Yes button in response to the Macromedia Dreamweaver alert dialog box.

16. Press the F12 key to view the page in your browser. Click each of the links in the navigation bar to verify that they work. Print a copy of the Web page, if instructed to do so. Upload the page to the candle Web site on a remote server, if instructed to do so.

(continued)

In the Lab

Creating a New Index Page for the CandleWix Web Site *(continued)*

Table 6-4 Layer Properties

LAYER ID	L AND T PROPERTIES	W AND H PROPERTIES	VIS PROPERTY	OVERFLOW PROPERTY	IMAGE/TEXT
heading	340px, 50px	300px, 100px	visible	visible	CandleWix Welcome to CandleWix
text01	320px, 200px	325px, 90px	visible	visible	We offer the finest in fragrantly scented candles. Each of our candles is hand dipped and hand poured. Our wicks are lead free, and we use only the finest waxes and fragrant oils.
text02	200px, 325px	450px, 80px	visible	visible	CandleWix candles are available in a variety of types: • Decorative • Gel • Holiday • Pillar • Scented • Texture • Votive
text03	250px, 550px	350px, 65px	visible	visible	Our candles make a perfect gift for occasions such as weddings, birthdays, holidays, anniversaries, or any time of the year.
date	35px, 625px	130px, 50px	visible	visible	Your name and Date object

2 Modifying the Questions Web Page for the Credit Protection Web Site

Problem: Monica would like to add more interaction to the Credit Protection Web site and has asked you for ideas. You suggest that the questions.htm page could be revised so that when a question is pointed to, the answer to the question is displayed. Monica likes your suggestion, and you agree to revise the page. The revised page is shown in Figure 6-73; it displays the answer to a question that is pointed to. Appendix C contains instructions for uploading your local site to a remote server.

In the Lab

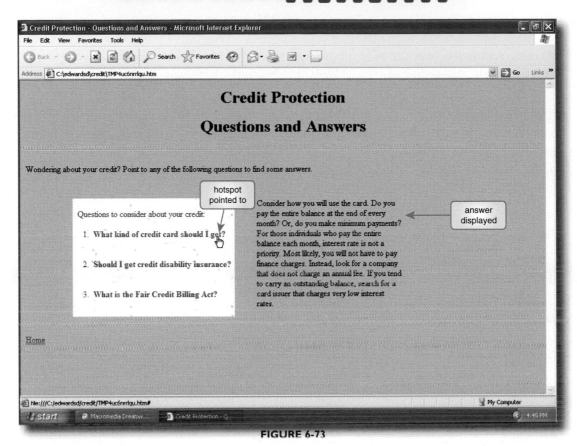

FIGURE 6-73

Instructions: Perform the following tasks:

1. Use the Windows My Computer option to copy the data files and images from the DataFiles folder to your credit folder and credit/images folder. The data files contain a questions.htm file, which will replace the existing questions.htm file. Click the Yes button in response to the Confirm File Replace dialog box.

2. Start Dreamweaver. Select Credit on the Files pop-up menu in the Files panel. If necessary, display the panel groups and the Insert bar Layout category.

3. Open the questions.htm file. Display the rulers. Position the insertion point below the horizontal line and type Wondering about your credit? Point to any of the following questions to find some answers. Press the ENTER key two times.

4. Click the Draw Layer button on the Insert bar and use the rulers as a guide to draw a layer with the following properties: Layer ID – questions, L – 100px, T – 225px, W – 305px, H – 220px, Vis – visible. Drag the questions.gif image from the Files panel onto the questions layer.

5. Draw three more layers. Use the rulers as a guide to draw the layers. Use Table 6-5 on the next page to enter the properties for each layer. After you create each layer, type the text as listed in the Text column.

6. Select the questions layer and then draw a rectangular hotspot over the first question. With the hotspot selected, click the Add behavior button in the Behaviors panel and then click Show–Hide Layers on the Add behavior pop-up menu. Show layer "questions" and layer "quest01." Hide layers "quest02" and "quest03."

(continued)

In the Lab

Modifying the Questions Web Page for the Credit Protection Web Site *(continued)*

7. Draw a second rectangular hotspot over the second question. With the hotspot selected, click the Add behavior button in the Behaviors panel and then click Show-Hide Layers on the Add behavior pop-up menu. Show layer "questions" and layer "quest02." Hide layers "quest01" and "quest03."

8. Draw a third rectangular hotspot over the third question. With the hotspot selected, click the Add behavior button in the Behaviors panel and then click Show-Hide Layers on the Add behavior pop-up menu. Show layer "questions" and layer "quest03." Hide layers "quest01" and "quest02."

9. Press CTRL+S to save the questions.htm Web page.

10. Press the F12 key to view the page in your browser. Roll over each of the hotspots to verify that they work correctly. Print a copy of the Web page, if instructed to do so. Upload the page to the credit Web site on a remote server, if instructed to do so.

Table 6-5 Layer Properties				
LAYER ID	**L AND T IN PX**	**W AND H IN PX**	**VIS**	**TEXT**
quest01	450/225	280/205	hidden	Consider how you will use the card. Do you pay the entire balance at the end of every month? Or, do you make minimum payments? For those individuals who pay the entire balance each month, interest rate is not a priority. Most likely, you will not have to pay finance charges. Instead, look for a company that does not charge an annual fee. If you tend to carry an outstanding balance, search for a card issuer that charges very low interest rates.
quest02	450/225	275/145	hidden	Credit disability insurance pays off your credit card bills if you become unable to work. Many credit card and direct mail companies offer this type of insurance. The insurance is generally very expensive. If you are in good health, a broader policy would probably be a better option.
quest03	450/225	285/160	hidden	The Fair Credit Billing Act is a federal law that determines how billing errors and disputes involving credit and charge cards are handled. If you check the back of your monthly statement, generally you will find information about this process. If the company violates any provision of the law, you can sue to recover any damages.

3 Creating a Layered Page for the Lexington, NC Web Site

Problem: John wants to add some interactivity to the Lexington Web site. You suggest to John that a navigation bar on the index page would be a good addition and that a different layout for the recipes page would enhance the overall site. John likes your ideas, and you are ready to get started. The revised pages are shown in Figures 6-74a and 6-74b on page DW 548.

In the Lab

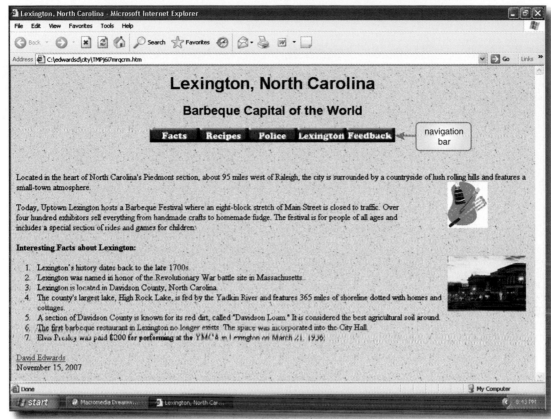

FIGURE 6-74a

(continued)

Creating a Layered Page for the Lexington, NC Web Site *(continued)*

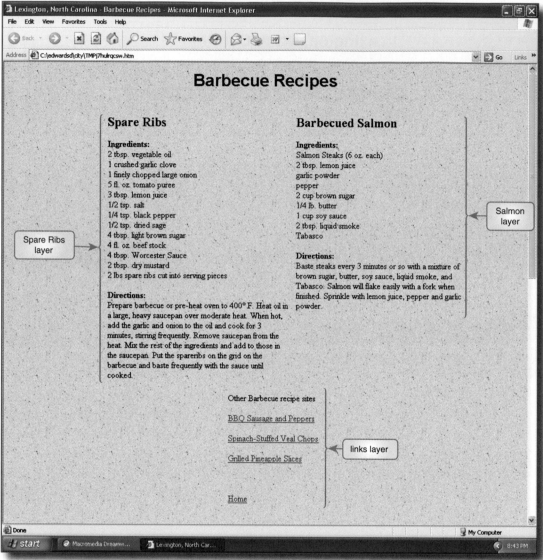

FIGURE 6-74b

Instructions: Perform the following tasks:

1. Use the Windows My Computer option to copy the images from the DataFiles folder to your city/images folder.
2. If necessary, display the panel groups. Select Lexington, NC on the Files pop-up menu in the Files panel.
3. Open the index.htm page. If necessary, display the rulers. Delete the links at the end of the page. Click at the end of heading 2 and then press the ENTER key. If necessary, center the insertion point.
4. Click the Insert menu, point to Image Objects, and then click Navigation Bar on the Image Objects submenu. In the Insert Navigation Bar dialog box, verify that Horizontally and Use tables are selected. Use the data in Table 6-6 to create the navigation bar.

In the Lab

ELEMENT NAME	UP IMAGE	OVER IMAGE	DOWN IMAGE	ALTERNATE TEXT	WHEN CLICKED, GO TO URL
facts	facts01.gif	facts02.gif	facts02.gif	Lexington facts	facts.htm
recipes	recipes01.gif	recipes02.gif	recipes02.gif	Recipes	recipes.htm
police	police01.gif	police02.gif	police02.gif	Police department	police.htm
lexington	lexington01.gif	lexington02.gif	lexington02.gif	Lexington city Web site	http://www.lexingtonnc.net/
feedback	feedback01.gif	feedback02.gif	feedback02.gif	Feedback form	guest_form.htm

Table 6-6 Data for Navigation Bar

5. Center the navigation bar. Press the F12 key and verify that the navigation bar links work. Click the Save button on the Standard toolbar and then close the index.htm page.

6. Open the recipes.htm Web page. Delete the two horizontal rules. Select and cut the Spare Ribs recipe. If necessary, display the rulers and then move the origin point about 125px to the right and down about 100px. Draw a layer with the following properties: Layer ID – spareribs, L – 200px, T – 100px, W – 345px, H – 500px, Vis – visible.

7. Click in the layer and then click the Paste button on the Standard toolbar to paste the recipe onto the layer.

8. Click to the right of the spareribs layer and draw a second layer with the following properties: Layer ID – salmon, L – 560px, T – 100px, W – 345px, H – 380px, Vis – visible.

9. Select and cut the Barbecued Salmon recipe and then paste it into the layer.

10. Click below the first two layers and then draw a third layer with the following properties: Layer ID – links, L – 430px, T – 625px, W – 295px, H – 200px, Vis – visible. Click in the links layer. Type Other Barbecue recipe sites and then press the ENTER key. Cut and paste the links into this layer.

11. Press the F12 key to view the page in your browser. Print a copy of the Web pages, if instructed to do so. Upload the page to the city Web site on a remote server, if instructed to do so. Save and close the Web page.

Cases and Places

The difficulty of these case studies varies:
■ are the least difficult and ■■ are the most difficult. The last exercise is a group exercise.

1 ■ You would like to add some interactivity to your sports Web site. You have looked at some other Web sites and are impressed with navigation bars. You decide to modify the index page and add a navigation bar to your sports Web site. You also decide to add the Date object so the date will be updated automatically when you save the page. Create a navigation bar for your sports site. Determine if a vertical or horizontal bar will best fit your needs. Then insert the Date object at the end of the page. For a selection of images and backgrounds, visit the Dreamweaver 8 Media Web page (scsite.com/dw8/media) and then click Media below Project 6.

2 ■ Your hobby Web page has become very popular and you want to give it a more professional look. One object you can add is a navigation bar. Determine if a vertical or horizontal bar will best suit your particular Web page. Next, use layers to create a new layout for one of your pages. Determine which page in your Web site you will revise and then add at least four layers to the page. Name each layer and place it appropriately on the page. Add images and/or text to the layers. Upload the page to a remote site if instructed to do so. For a selection of images and backgrounds, visit the Dreamweaver 8 Media Web page (scsite.com/dw8/media) and then click Media below Project 6.

3 ■■ You are receiving a lot of e-mail about what a great Web site you have for your music hobby. You decide to make it more interactive by adding a navigation bar on the index page, adding a layer with an image map, and then adding two additional layers. Create the navigation bar and then create the three layers — the first one with the image map and the other two displaying images related to your music site. Add hotspots to your image map to show and hide the two images. Upload the revised pages to a remote site. For a selection of images and backgrounds, visit the Dreamweaver 8 Media Web page (scsite.com/dw8/media) and then click Media below Project 6.

Cases and Places

4 ▪▪ Polls indicate that you are the favorite to win the race for office. You want to add a new page to the site that will provide some interactivity and give the page a professional look. Add a navigation bar to the index page. Next, add another page with additional text information and then add a layer for an image map. Add at least two additional layers with pictures of yourself campaigning. Add hotspots to the image map to hide and show the pictures. Upload the revised and new pages to a remote server. For a selection of images and backgrounds, visit the Dreamweaver 8 Media Web page (scsite.com/dw8/media) and then click Media below Project 6.

5 ▪▪ **Working Together** The student trips Web site still is receiving numerous hits, and the debate about which location to pick for the trip is continuing. Add a new page to the Web site. Include a navigation bar that will link to various Web sites which provide information about three different possible vacation spots. Then, add at least four layers to the Web site. The first layer will contain a map of the United States. The other three layers will contain pictures of possible trip locations. Add hotspots to the image map on the individual states and then add the Show-Hide Layers action. Upload the new pages to a remote server. For a selection of images and backgrounds, visit the Dreamweaver 8 Media Web page (scsite.com/dw8/media) and then click Media below Project 6.

Page Layout with Frames

PROJECT

7

CASE PERSPECTIVE

The Colorado Parks Web site is very popular and is receiving numerous hits each day. David received 43 e-mail messages last week asking for more general information about Colorado State Parks. The messages included questions about the cost to visit a park, accessibility options, and programs for kids. David shares the e-mail messages with you and Tracy and explains that answering these messages is very time-consuming. He asks if either of you have any suggestions or solutions for how he can respond in a more efficient way.

Tracy suggests that adding additional pages to the existing Web site could be one solution. Everyone agrees that this is a good idea, but David expresses concern that the main Web site focuses on different parks and monuments and this is a more general topic. You suggest that a new Web site be created and that it be linked to/from the main Web site. Tracy further suggests that frames be used to keep this Web site compact and easy to navigate. The team agrees that this is the best solution and that a framed Web site containing general information about Colorado parks is a good addition.

As you read through this project, you will learn about the advantages and disadvantages of frames, the difference between a frame and a frameset, how to create a frameset and frames, and how to add a navigation bar using Flash buttons.

Page Layout with Frames

Objectives

You will have mastered the material in this project when you can:

- Describe the advantages and disadvantages of using frames on a Web page
- Describe frameset layout and properties
- Create a frameset and frames
- Define frames and describe how they work
- Delete a frame

- Set the properties for a frame and for a frameset
- Apply and modify the properties of a frame
- Add static content to a frame using the main content frame
- Add Flash buttons as navigation elements
- Save the frame and frameset

Introduction

You learned in Projects 3 and 6 that you can use tables and layers to control the arrangement or layout of items on a Web page. Frames are another layout option and a unique way to design the presentation of your Web pages and Web sites. This project focuses on creating a Web site using frames and examines the advantages and disadvantages of using a framed Web site.

Web designers use frames to present information in a more flexible and useful fashion. A **frame** is an area that acts as an independent browser window and acts independently of other regions in the window. Frames divide a Web page into multiple, scrollable regions, or panes. Each frame contains its own source document. For instance, using frames, you could have four different HTML documents displaying in a single window.

When the pages in a Web site share many of the same links and images, creating and maintaining these links for each page involves considerable duplication. With frames, you can create a Web page to display the common links in one frame and display the linked target Web pages in another frame. Some typical uses of frames include:

- Displaying a navigation bar consisting of links in one frame and displaying the corresponding Web pages in another
- Placing a number of images in one frame and displaying the accompanying descriptions and details in another
- Placing a list of vocabulary words in one frame and displaying their definitions in another.

With frames, a Web page designer can place elements the user always should see, such as navigation buttons and title graphics, in static frames that do not change. As the user navigates the site, the static frame's contents remain fixed, even as new pages display in adjoining frames. Another example is a side-by-side frame design that allows a user to enter a query and view the answer in the same browser window. One frame contains the query and the other one displays the results.

Although most Web browsers support frames, some Web site visitors may have older browsers that do not support frames or may prefer a no-frames version. Dreamweaver lets you add a <noframes> tag to specify the content to display in text-based browsers and in older graphical browsers that do not support frames. When a browser that does not support frames loads the frameset file, the browser displays only the content enclosed by the <noframes> tag.

Project Seven — Colorado Parks Web Page Layout with Frames

In this project, you learn to use frames to create and display general information for a new local site that will be linked to the main Colorado Parks Web site.

The frameset, which is an HTML file that defines the layout and properties of a set of frames, will display three frames. The top frame is a single-row, single-column static frame that contains a title image or logo. The second row contains two columns with a left frame and a right frame. The left frame is the navigation frame, or navigate_frame, and contains Flash buttons that link to content files. The right frame is the main frame, which will display the linked content files. When a visitor clicks one of the buttons in the left frame, related park information is displayed in the right frame. The navigate_frame contains five Flash buttons. Clicking any of the first four buttons displays the associated page in the right frame (Figures 7-1a through 7-1d on pages DW 556–557). The Home button breaks out of the frames and returns the visitor to the main Colorado Parks Web site index page.

Borders separate the frames. The right frame is scrollable and contains a scroll bar when the content extends beyond the screen. Each button in the navigate_frame contains text to meet Web design accessibility standards.

If you are using Internet Explorer with Windows XP Service Pack 2 (SP2), Internet Explorer automatically blocks content such as Flash buttons. Thus, for all instances in this project where pages containing Flash buttons are displayed in Internet Explorer, you must either choose to allow blocked content by right-clicking the Information Bar and choosing the Allow Blocked Content command from the context menu, or modify the Internet Explorer security settings to allow Flash elements to display.

More About

Windows Service Pack 2 (SP2)

If you are using Windows SP2, some changes to the operating system and to Internet Explorer may affect Macromedia Dreamweaver. For more information about Windows SP2, visit the Dreamweaver 8 More About Web page (scsite.com/dw8/more.htm) and then click Windows Service Pack 2.

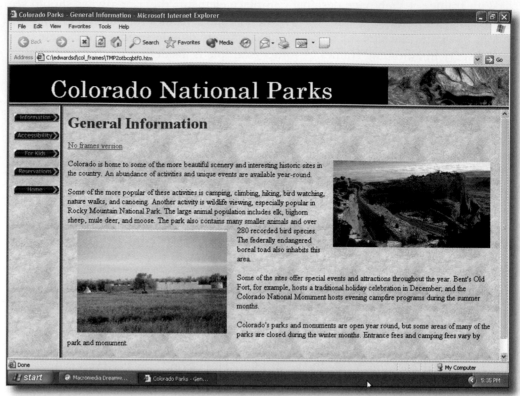

FIGURE 7-1a

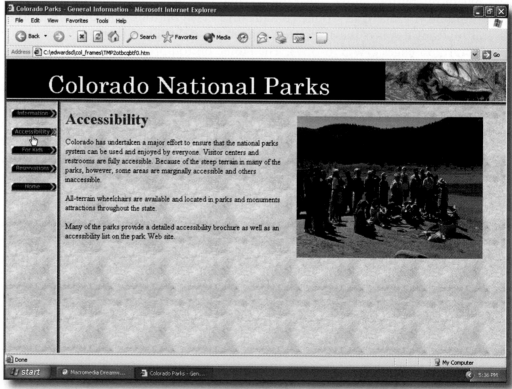

FIGURE 7-1b

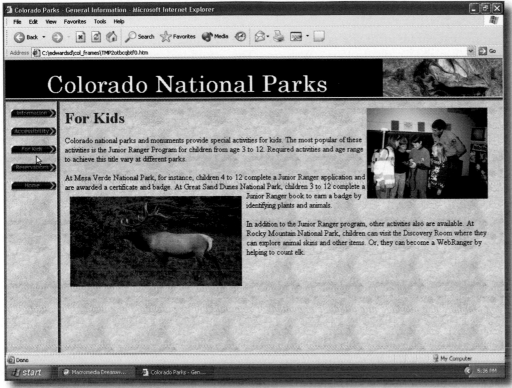

FIGURE 7-1c

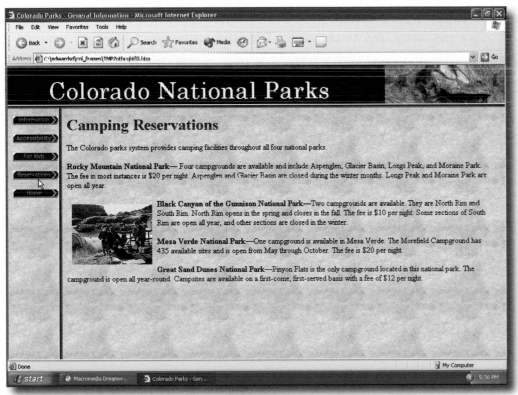

FIGURE 7-1d

Workspace Organization

Creating a separate local site is the best way to organize and control the number of pages within the Colorado Parks Web site. This new local site, named Parks Frames, will be linked to the main Colorado Parks Web site. After creating your local site, you use the My Computer option to copy Project 7 data files to the site. The following steps show how to create a local site.

To Use Site Definition to Create a Local Web Site

1 Start Dreamweaver.

2 Click Site on the menu bar and then click New Site to display the Site Definition dialog box.

3 If necessary, click the Advanced tab. Verify that Local Info is selected in the Category column.

4 Type Parks Frames as the site name.

5 Click the folder icon to the right of the Local root folder text box.

6 Navigate to the your name folder and then double-click the your name folder.

7 Click the Create New Folder icon.

8 Type col_frames as the name of the new folder and then press the ENTER key.

9 Double-click the col_frames folder name.

10 Click the Select button.

11 Click the folder icon to the right of the Default images folder text box.

12 Navigate to the your name folder and then double-click the col_frames folder.

13 Click the Create New Folder icon.

14 Type images as the name of the new folder and then press the ENTER key.

15 Double-click the images folder name.

16 Click the Select button.

17 Verify that the Refresh local file list automatically and Enable cache check boxes are selected in the Site Definition dialog box (Figure 7-2).

18 Click the OK button.

19 The Dreamweaver window is displayed, and the Parks Frames site is displayed in the Files panel.

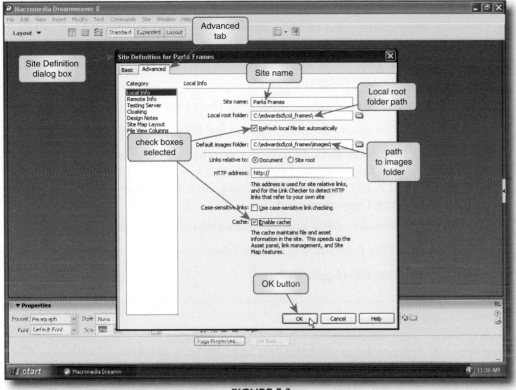

FIGURE 7-2

The Parks Frames Web site you create in this project requires additional HTML files and images. These files and images need to be copied from the DataFiles folder to the ParksFrames Web site.

Copying Data Files to the Local Web Site

Your Data Disk contains data files and images for Project 7. You use the Windows My Computer option to copy the Project 7 images to your col_frames\images folder and to copy the data files to your col_frames folder. See the inside back cover for instructions for downloading the Data Disk or see your instructor for information about accessing the files required for this book.

The DataFiles folder for this project is stored on Local Disk (C:). The location on your computer may be different. If necessary, verify with your instructor the location of the DataFiles folder. The following steps illustrate how to copy the files to the frames\images folder.

To Copy Data Files to the Parks Frames Web Site

1 Click the Start button on the Windows taskbar and then click **My Computer**.

2 Double-click **Local Disk (C:)** and then navigate to the location of the data files for Project 7.

3 Double-click the **DataFiles** folder and then double-click the **Proj07** folder.

4 Double-click the **col_frames** folder and then double-click the **images** folder.

5 Click the first image file in the list, hold down the SHIFT key, and then click the last image file in the list.

6 Right-click the selected files to display the context menu.

7 Click the Copy command and then click the My Computer Back button the number of times necessary to navigate back to the your name folder.

8 Double-click the your name folder, double-click the col_frames folder, and then double-click the images folder.

9 Right-click in the open window to display the context menu.

10 Click the Paste command to paste the image files into the images folder.

11 Click the My Computer Back button the number of times necessary to return to the col_frames folder. Hold down the SHIFT key, select the no_frames sub-folder, and then select the data files. Right-click to display the context menu and then click the Copy command.

12 Click the My Computer Back button and navigate to the your name folder.

13 Paste the data files into the col_frames folder.

14 Click the Close button (Figure 7-3).

More About

Frames versus Tables

When creating your page design, you may be unsure about whether to use frames or tables. Frames are used more frequently for navigation, but can be difficult to create and implement. For more information about frames versus tables, visit the Dreamweaver 8 More About Web page (scsite.com/dw8/more.htm) and then click Frames versus Tables.

The data files are pasted into the Parks Frames Web site root folder (Figure 7-3).

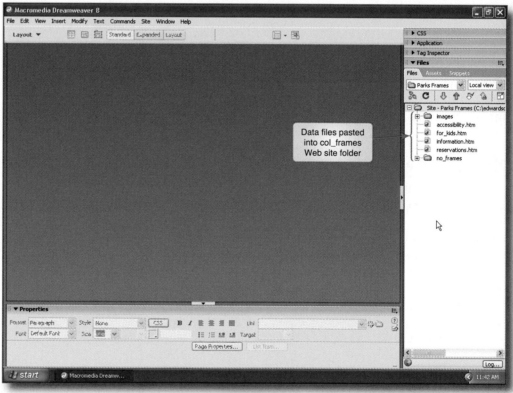

FIGURE 7-3

Advantages and Disadvantages of Frames

Frames became a standard on Web pages with the release of Netscape Navigator 2.0 and were added to the HTML specification with HTML 4.0. After being added to the specification, they experienced immediate popularity and became widely used as a design tool. Designing with frames, however, can be difficult. The complexity of designing with frames is particularly challenging for inexperienced Web site authors.

As a result, poorly designed frame-based Web sites became fairly common. This resulted in a controversy among Web site developers and users regarding the value and use of frames for Web site development.

When frames are well designed and used for specific purposes, however, they can be very useful. Some advantages of using frames include the following:

- Navigation-related graphics do not have to be reloaded for every page in the Web site.
- Each frame can have its own scroll bar, permitting the visitor to scroll the frames independently.
- Static content remains fixed.
- Content and navigation can be separated from each other in a clear way.

Users who dislike frames generally have encountered sites that use frames poorly or unnecessarily. Or they may dislike frames because of the following disadvantages:

- Some browsers, and Netscape in particular, do not support the file:// protocol. The link to the home or index page in this project, therefore, will not work in Netscape unless modified in the code.
- Frames may be difficult to navigate for visitors with disabilities.
- Printing pages with frames may be a problem.
- Pages that are displayed in the main frame are displayed in a smaller window than they would be if they were displayed in a full browser window, and are difficult to bookmark or to add to favorites.

Several of the disadvantages, however, are compensated for in the more recent versions of the major browsers. For example, when a user views a frame-based site in a browser, right-clicking in a particular frame displays a context menu with a number of commands, including Add to Favorites, View Source, and Print. Selecting the Print command displays the Print dialog box, which includes options to print just the selected frame, to print all frames individually, to print the page as laid out on the screen, to print all linked documents, and to print a table of links.

Frameset and Frame Basics

Creating a framed Web site is more complex than creating a Web page without frames. The <body> tag is not used to create a framed page. Instead, a **frameset** defines the layout of the frames when they are displayed on the screen. A frameset requires a combination of two HTML tags: <frameset> and <frame>. When the frameset is created, Dreamweaver automatically includes the <noframes> tag for those viewers using browser versions that do not support frames. Most Web site developers also include a no-frames option link for those users whose browsers do not support frames or for those who prefer a no-frames version.

Frameset Layout

Frames on a page function independently of one another. A separate HTML document is loaded into each frame. As discussed above, creating a framed Web page requires an accompanying file called a frameset. The frameset is an underlying HTML document that defines the layout and properties of a set of frames and then displays navigation elements, title graphics, content documents, and so on, inside the defined frames.

The frameset can be compared to a sectioned box, such as a desk drawer organizer. Each section of the box is designed to hold specific items, such as pens, pencils, or

More About

Designing with Frames

Many Web sites consist of a narrow left frame and a wide right frame. The navigation links are displayed in the left frame, and the site's main content is displayed in the right. Other site designs may split the window vertically. In these cases, the site's title and navigation links typically appear in a narrow top frame and the main content appears in a wider lower frame. For more information about frame design, visit the Dreamweaver 8 More About Web page (scsite.com/dw8/more.htm) and then click Frame Design.

paper clips. The design of each section of the box determines what should be placed within that section. The frameset works in a similar way. The <frame> tags within a frameset provide information to the browser about what the frameset's set of frames displays and what documents are displayed in the frames. Some frames may contain static documents such as title graphics, while the content in other frames changes based on the provided navigation options.

Creating the Frameset

Dreamweaver provides two methods for creating a frameset; you can design it yourself or you can use a predefined frameset. You design a frameset using the following steps:

- Display a new Document window.
- Click Modify on the menu bar, select Frameset, and then select Split Frame Left, Split Frame Right, Split Frame Up, or Split Frame Down on the Frameset submenu.

To split the frame into smaller sections, use one of the following methods:

- Click the frame and then select Split Frame Left, Split Frame Right, Split Frame Up, or Split Frame Down on the Frameset submenu.
- To split a frame or set of frames vertically or horizontally, drag a frame border from the edge of the Design view into the middle of the Design view.
- To split a frame using a frame border that is not at the edge of the Design view, press the ALT key and then drag the desired frame border.
- To divide a frame into four frames, drag a frame border from one of the corners of the Design view into the middle of a frame.

The second method for creating a frameset in Dreamweaver is to use a predefined frameset. A **predefined frameset** provides a visual representation of how the framed window will display. You can use a predefined frameset without modifications, or you can use the predefined frameset as a starting point and then modify the frameset using one or more of the options listed previously for splitting frames.

Dreamweaver provides two methods to create a predefined frameset: the Frames pop-up menu in the Layout category of the Insert bar and the New Document dialog box. The Insert bar Frames pop-up menu generally is used to create a predefined frameset and, at the same time, display an existing document in one of the frames. The New Document dialog box is used to create a new empty predefined frameset.

In this project, you use the New Document dialog box to create a predefined nested frameset, such as the one shown in the expanded Frames panel in Figure 7-4 on the next page. Notice in this figure that Dreamweaver names the frames in the Frames panel: topFrame, leftFrame, and mainFrame. The primary frameset is selected as indicated by the <frameset> tag in the tag selector and the dark border surrounding the frame in the Frames panel. In the Property inspector, Row is selected.

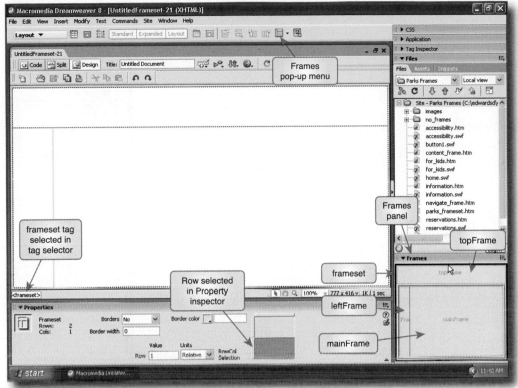

FIGURE 7-4

A frameset inside another frameset is called a **nested frameset**. Most framesets contain nested framesets, and most Web pages that use frames use nested frames. Most predefined framesets in Dreamweaver also use nesting. A single frameset file can contain multiple nested framesets. Any set of frames in which different numbers of frames are in different rows or columns creates a nested frameset.

The most common frame layout has one frame in the top row and two frames in the second row. Generally, the top frame contains a title graphic or logo. The left frame in the second row usually is a navigation frame, and the right frame generally is the main frame that displays the linked content. In this case, the second row is the nested frameset. As shown in Figure 7-5 on the next page, the tag selector displays a second or nested <frameset> tag, a dark border surrounds the frame's second row in the Frames panel, and a dotted border surrounds the nested frameset. In the Property inspector, Column is selected.

You copied the images and files necessary to begin creating the new framed Web site to the frames local root folder. You begin the project by using a visual aid to make the frame borders visible in the Document window. Then you create, name, and save the frameset. The following steps illustrate how to create the frameset.

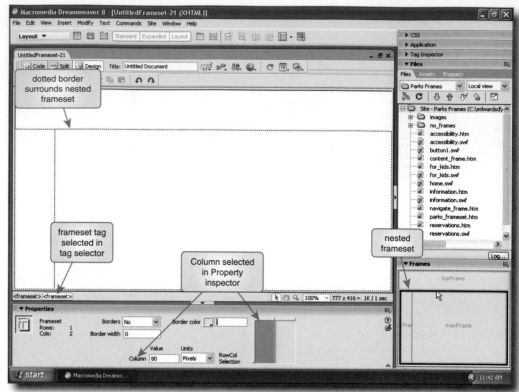

FIGURE 7-5

To Create the Frameset

1

• **Click File on the menu bar and then click New. Point to Framesets in the Category list.**

The New Document dialog box is displayed (Figure 7-6).

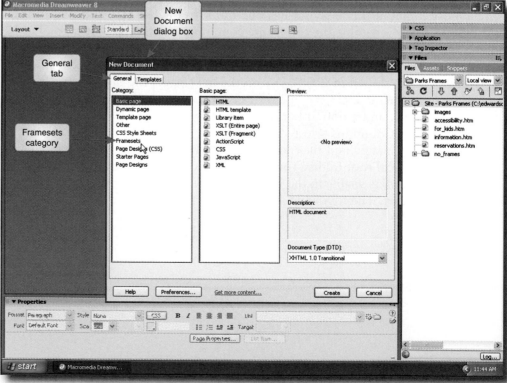

FIGURE 7-6

2

• **Click Framesets. Point to Fixed Top, Nested Left in the Framesets column.**

The Framesets category is displayed within the New Document dialog box. The Framesets category contains 15 predefined framesets. The Fixed Bottom frameset is selected, as indicated by the preview and description displayed in the right pane (Figure 7-7). Your selection might be different.

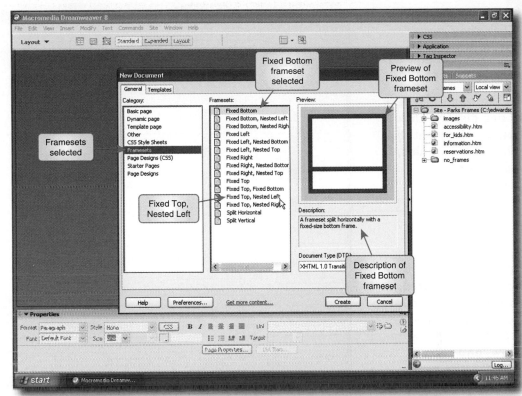

FIGURE 7-7

3

• **Click Fixed Top, Nested Left in the Framesets column.**

The Fixed Top, Nested Left frameset is selected. A preview and description of the selected frameset are displayed in the right pane (Figure 7-8).

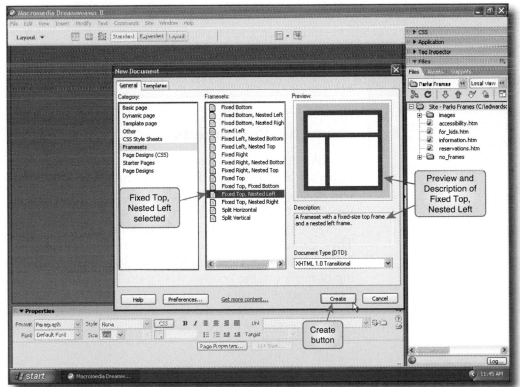

FIGURE 7-8

4

• **Click the Create button. If necessary, expand the Property inspector.**

• **If the frame borders do not display, click View on the menu bar, point to Visual Aids, and then click Frame Borders on the Visual Aids submenu. If the Property inspector is not expanded so that both panes are displayed, hide the panel groups, click the Property inspector expander arrow, and then redisplay the panel groups.**

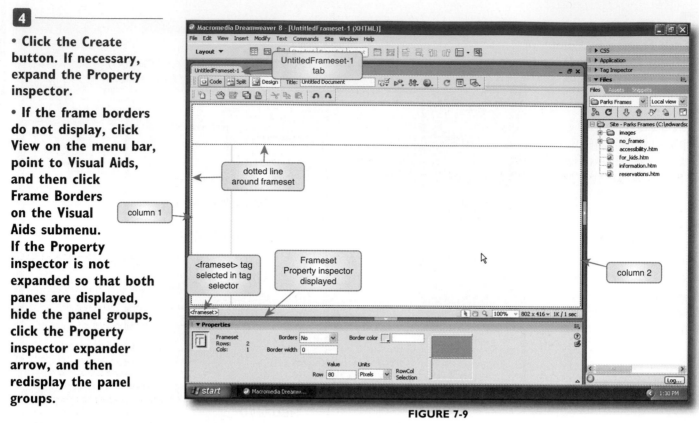

FIGURE 7-9

UntitledFrameset-1 is displayed in the Document window (Figure 7-9). The dotted border around the frameset indicates that the frameset is selected. The Property inspector displays attributes relevant to the frameset in both panes. The tag selector displays the <frameset> tag. The number of the untitled frameset may be different on your computer.

Other Ways

1. On Insert bar, click Layout category, click Frames button pop-up menu, select frameset

Frameset Properties

Like many other objects in Dreamweaver, the frameset has its own Property inspector that displays a frameset's properties when that frameset is selected in the Document window. Clicking the expander arrow in the lower-right corner expands the Property inspector to show additional attributes.

Dreamweaver determines the default attributes used for each predefined frameset. These default attributes are applied automatically to each frame. In the Fixed Top, Nested Left example, the mainFrame default is no borders, no scroll bars, and no resizing of frames in the browser. Using the Property inspector, however, these attributes can be changed easily and additional attributes can be applied. The following section describes the frameset-related features of the Property inspector (Figure 7-10 on the next page). The Property inspector for frames is discussed later in this project.

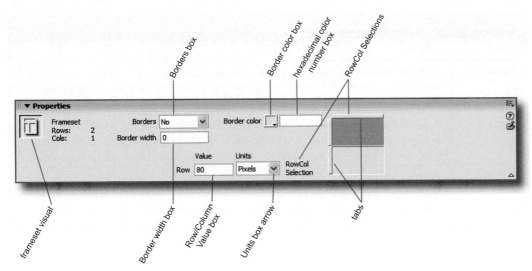

FIGURE 7-10

FRAMESET VISUAL A visual representation of a frameset is displayed in the upper-left corner of the Property inspector. This visual is generated automatically and cannot be altered through the Property inspector.

BORDERS **Borders** determines if borders should appear around the frames when the document is viewed in a browser. Clicking the Borders box arrow to the right of the Borders box displays three options: Yes, No, and Default. Selecting Yes causes borders to display around the frames when the Web page is viewed in a browser. Selecting No causes borders not to display in the browser. Selecting Default allows the user's browser to determine how borders are displayed.

BORDER WIDTH In the **Border width** box, a number specifies a width for all the borders in the frameset.

BORDER COLOR Use the color box to select a border color, or type the hexadecimal value for a color in the related text box.

FRAMESET COLUMN SIZES AND ROW SIZES The **RowCol Selection** box on the right side of the Property inspector is a visual representation of the frameset. On the top and left sides of the box are tabs. Click a tab on the left side of the RowCol Selection area to select a row, or click a tab on the top to select a column. When the row is selected, you can enter a height for the selected row. When a column is selected, you can enter a width for the selected column. When you click the Units box arrow, three options are displayed: Pixels, Percent, and Relative. Table 7-1 on the next page contains information about these three size options.

In Figures 7-9 and 7-10, the RowCol Selection in the Property inspector contains rows, which indicates that the frameset is selected. Recall that this frameset contains a nested frameset. If the nested frameset is selected, then the Property inspector displays two columns instead of two rows in the RowCol Selection area.

More About

Inserting a Predefined Frameset

Dreamweaver's predefined framesets make it easy for you to select the type of frameset you want to create. For a predefined frameset to be inserted, the Dreamweaver Document window must be open in Design view.

Table 7-1	Frameset Row and Column Size Measurements
UNIT	**RESULT**
Pixels	Sets the size of the row or column to an absolute value. This option is the best choice for a frame that always should be the same size, such as a title frame or navigation frame.
Percent	A percentage-based frame stretches and shrinks based on the width of the browser window. Frames with Units set to Percent are allocated space after frames with Units set to Pixels, but before frames with Units set to Relative.
Relative	Relative specifies that the selected column or row be allocated the leftover space after pixels and percent frames have had space allocated; the remaining space is divided proportionally among the frames with sizes set to Relative.

More About

Selecting Framesets and Frames in the Document Window

In the Document window, clicking a frame border selects the frameset that contains the frame. When a frameset is selected, all the borders of the frames within the frameset are outlined with a dotted border. To select a frame in the Document window, hold down the ALT key and then click inside the frame. When a frame is selected, its borders are outlined with a dotted border.

Selecting and Naming Frames and the Frameset

Selecting framesets and frames can be somewhat complex. Dreamweaver provides two basic ways to select a frame or frameset: select the frame or frameset directly in the Document window or use the Frames panel.

Displaying the Frames Panel

The easiest method to select a frame or frameset is to use the Frames panel. In the Frames panel, clicking within a frame or on a frame border selects that frame. Clicking the frameset border selects the frameset. The following step shows how to display the Frames panel.

To Display the Frames Panel

1

• **If necessary, expand the panel groups. Click Window on the menu bar and then click Frames.**

The Frames panel is displayed (Figure 7-11). A dark border appears around the frameset in the Frames panel. The <frameset> tag is displayed in the tag selector, indicating that the frameset is selected. Each frame within the Frames panel has a name: topFrame, leftFrame, and mainFrame. Dreamweaver automatically names these frames. To view the leftFrame name fully in the Frames panel, the panel groups must be expanded.

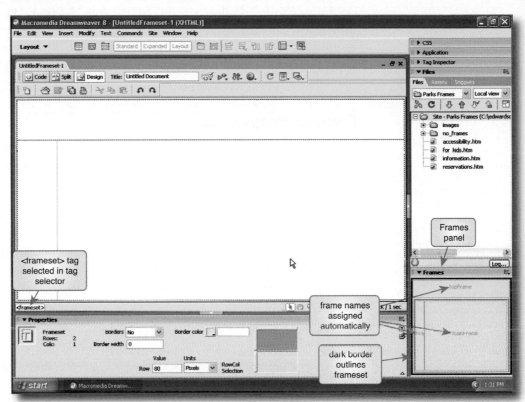

FIGURE 7-11

Other Ways

1. Press SHIFT+F2

Frames and Framesets

The frameset and the frame documents must be saved before you can preview framed pages in a browser. As indicated earlier in this project, when you create a frameset using a predefined frameset, the frames are given names such as topFrame and leftFrame in the Frames panel. These are not the default names Dreamweaver uses, however, when you select one of the Save commands. Instead, the first frameset file is named UntitledFrameset-1, while the first document in a frame is named UntitledFrame-1, and so on. You can use the default names to save the frameset and frames, but you might find it less confusing if you give meaningful names to the frameset and the frames. Frames and framesets also should be given titles. You add a title to a frame or frameset the same way you added a title to previous HTML documents: by typing the title in the Title text box on the Document toolbar. In this project, you use the same title for all the framesets and frames: Colorado Parks - General Information.

Dreamweaver provides several options for saving your documents. You can save the frameset file and each framed document individually, or you can save the frameset file and all documents appearing in the frames at once. To save the frameset file and all frame documents at one time, click File on the menu bar and then click Save All. This saves the frameset and frames with the default name. In this project, you name and save the frameset and each frame separately.

More About

Defining Row and Column Size

You can mix pixel, percent, and relative point sizes when defining row and column size measurements. Deciding which to use, however, is a hotly contended issue. For more information about pixels versus points, visit the Dreamweaver 8 More About Web page (scsite.com/dw8/more.htm) and then click Pixels versus Points.

Selecting a Frame

To save a frame or to make changes to the properties of a frame, you first select the frame. You can select a frame by clicking the frame border in the Document window or by using the Frames panel. When you select a frame, a dotted border appears around the frame in both the Frames panel and the Document window's Design view. Placing the insertion point in a document that is displayed in a frame is not the same as selecting a frame.

Frames Properties

Like other objects in Dreamweaver, a frame has a specific Property inspector. When you select a frame within the Document window or in the Frames panel, the Property inspector displays the frame's properties. Clicking the expander arrow in the lower-right corner expands the Property inspector to show additional attributes.

When a frame is created, the default attributes are applied automatically. Using the Property inspector, however, you easily can change these attributes and apply additional attributes. The following section describes the frame-related features of the Property inspector (Figure 7-12).

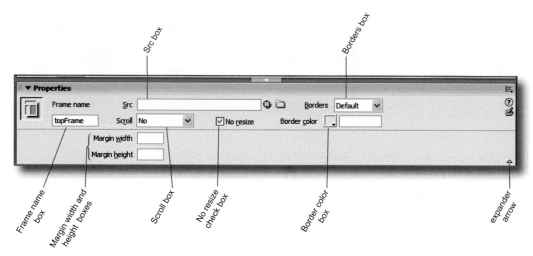

FIGURE 7-12

FRAME NAME The **Frame name** is used by a link's target attribute or by a script to refer to the frame. A frame name must be a single word and must start with a letter (not a numeral). An underscore (_) is allowed, but hyphens (-), periods (.), and spaces cannot be used. Frame names are case-sensitive.

SRC The **Src** box specifies the source document to display in the frame.

SCROLL The **Scroll** box specifies whether scroll bars appear in the frame. Setting this option to Default allows each browser to use its default value of Auto. This causes scroll bars to display only when needed to display the full contents of the current frame.

NO RESIZE The **No resize** check box specifies whether the user can change the frame size by dragging the frame borders.

BORDERS The Borders box displays or hides the borders of the current frame when it is viewed in a browser. Choosing a Borders option for a frame overrides the frameset border settings. Most browsers default to showing borders unless the parent frameset has Borders set to No.

BORDER COLOR The **Border color** box specifies a color for the frame borders. The selected color applies to all borders that touch the frame, and overrides the specified border color of the frameset.

MARGIN WIDTH The **Margin width** box sets the width in pixels of the space between the frame borders and the content.

MARGIN HEIGHT The **Margin height** box sets the height in pixels of the space between the frame borders and the content.

Naming and Saving the Frames

The frameset that you created contains three frames. These three frames need to be named and saved. When naming and saving a frame, remember that a frame is not a data file and is considered a holder for a content document. A frame contains a document, image, or another file. You can use the default name of UntitledFrame-xx.htm to save the frame, but providing meaningful names to frames causes less confusion. In this project, the topFrame is named title_frame, the leftFrame is named navigate_frame, and the mainFrame is named content_frame. Frames are saved with an .htm extension. The following steps show how to name and save the three frames.

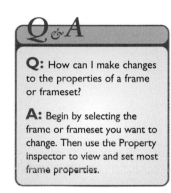

Q: How can I make changes to the properties of a frame or frameset?

A: Begin by selecting the frame or frameset you want to change. Then use the Property inspector to view and set most frame properties.

To Name and Save the Three Frames

1

• **Click the topFrame in the Document window.**

The insertion point is displayed in the topFrame (Figure 7-13). The UntitledFrame number may be different on your computer.

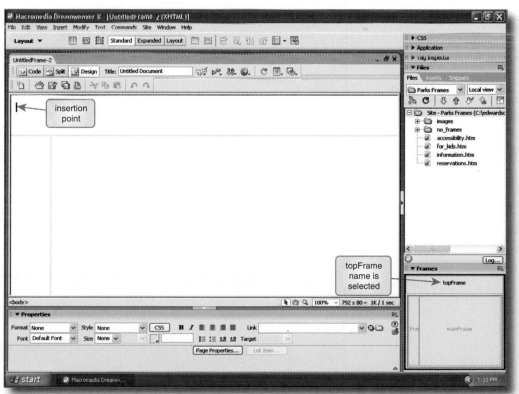

FIGURE 7-13

2

• **Click File on the menu bar and then point to Save Frame As (Figure 7-14).**

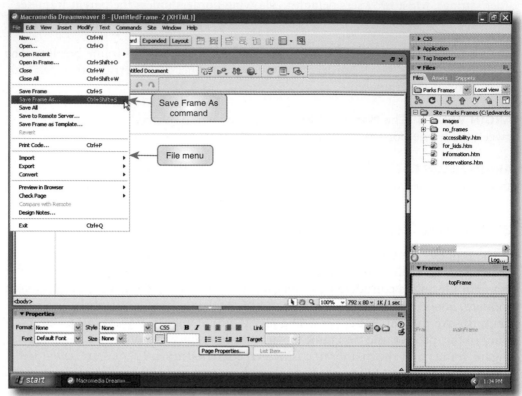

FIGURE 7-14

3

• **Click Save Frame As.**

The Save As dialog box is displayed (Figure 7-15). The root folder, col_frames, is displayed in the Save in box. The default name is displayed in the File name text box. The number in the file name on your computer may be different.

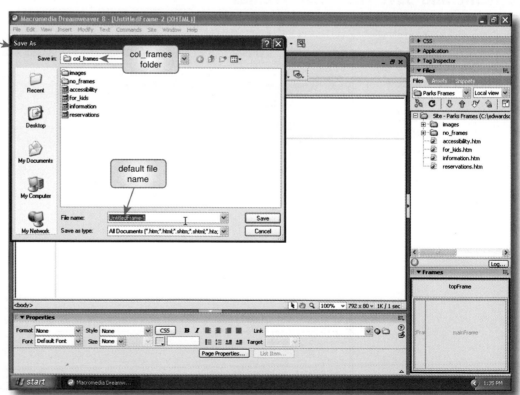

FIGURE 7-15

4

• **Type** title_frame **in the File name text box (Figure 7-16).**

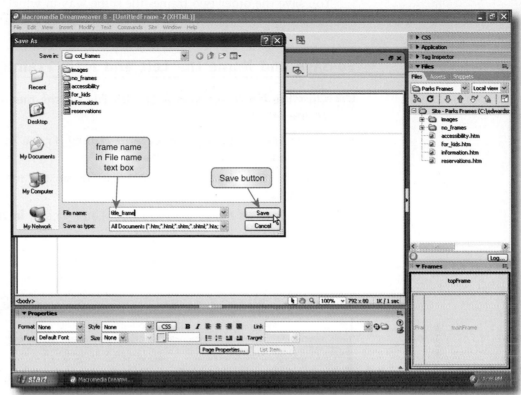

FIGURE 7-16

5

• **Click the Save button.**

The frame is saved as title_frame.htm and is displayed in the Files panel (Figure 7-17). The file name also is displayed on the frame tab and the title bar.

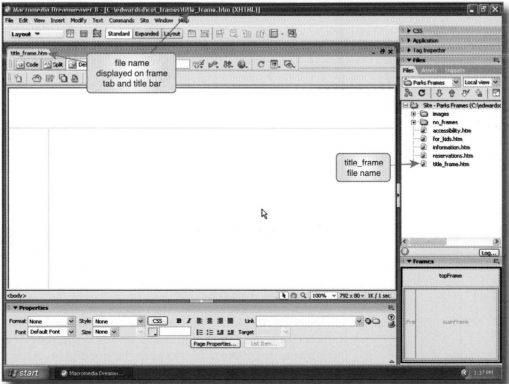

FIGURE 7-17

You save the other two frames the same way in which you saved the title frame. The following steps illustrate how to save the other two frames: left and main.

To Save and Name the Left and Main Frames

1 Click the left frame in row 2, click File on the menu bar, and then click Save Frame As.

2 In the Save As dialog box, type navigate_frame in the File name text box and then click the Save button.

3 Click the right frame in row 2. Click File on the menu bar and then click Save Frame As.

4 In the Save As dialog box, type content_frame in the File name text box and then click the Save button.

The navigate_frame.htm and content_frame.htm file names are displayed in the Files panel (Figure 7-18).

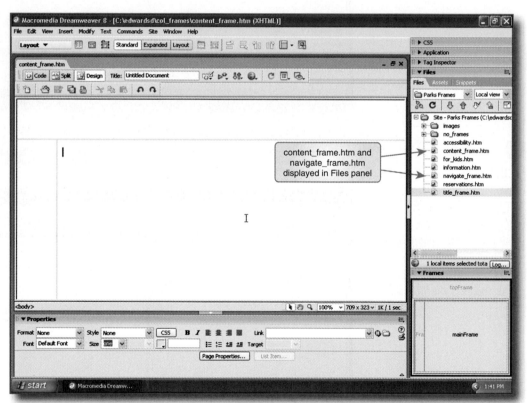

FIGURE 7-18

Deleting a Frame

Deleting a frame is simple. Drag a frame border off the page or to the edge of the frameset. If a document in a frame that is being removed contains unsaved content, Dreamweaver prompts you to save the document. After a frame is deleted, you will not be able to undo the deletion.

Naming and Saving the Frameset

Just as you named the frames, you also must save and name the frameset. The following steps show how to name and save the frameset.

To Name and Save the Frameset

1

• **Click the outside border of the frameset in the Frames panel. Verify that <frameset> is selected in the tag selector. Select Untitled Document in the Title text box on the Document toolbar and then type** Colorado Parks - General Information **as the title.**

The Colorado Parks - General Information title is displayed in the Title text box, and the frameset is selected (Figure 7-19).

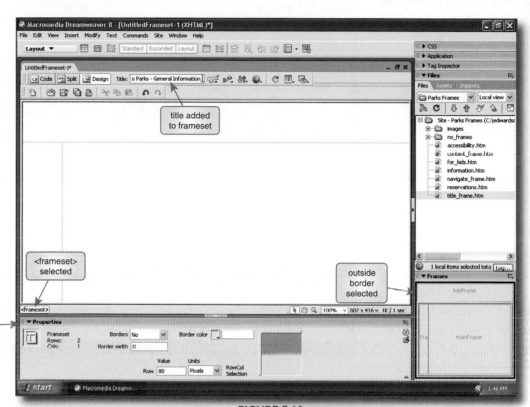

FIGURE 7-19

2

• **Click File on the menu bar and then point to Save Frameset As (Figure 7-20).**

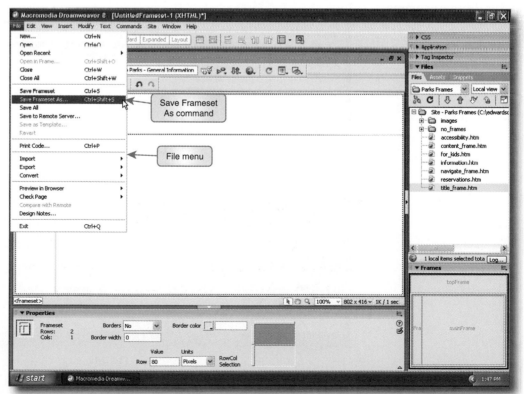

FIGURE 7-20

3

• **Click Save Frameset As.**

The Save As dialog box is displayed (Figure 7-21). If necessary, navigate to the root folder, col_frames, so it is displayed in the Save in box. The default file name, UntitledFrameset-1, is displayed in the File name text box, and the insertion point is blinking at the end of the file name. The number in the file name on your computer may be a number other than 1.

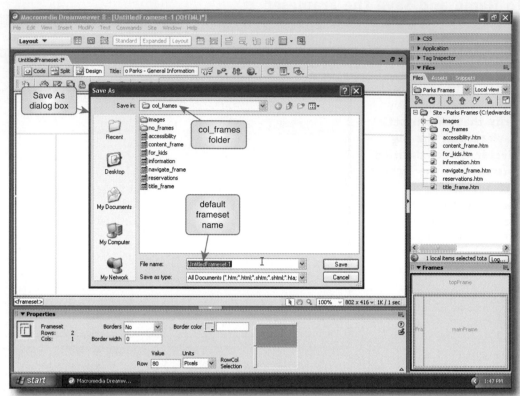

FIGURE 7-21

4

• **Type** parks_frameset **as the frameset name.**

The parks_frameset file name is displayed in the File name text box (Figure 7-22).

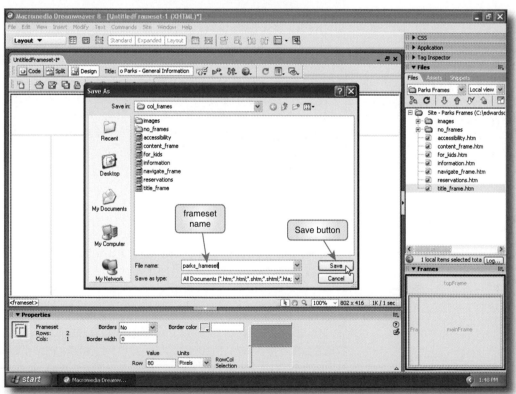

FIGURE 7-22

5

• **Click the Save button. If necessary, scroll in the Files panel.**

The frameset is saved in the col_frames root folder (Figure 7-23).

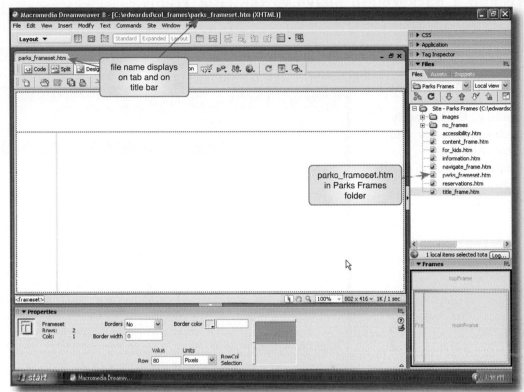

FIGURE 7-23

Formatting the Frames

Backgrounds, text, tables, images, and other elements can be added to a frame in a manner similar to the way in which they are added to a regular Document window. To each of the frames you add the same background that you used in the main Colorado Parks Web site you developed in Projects 1 through 6. The title_frame also contains a title graphic, and the navigate_frame contains buttons to load content into the main frame (content-frame).

The Title_Frame

One of the advantages of frames is that they can reduce the amount of duplicate information on each page, thus saving download time. A title image, for instance, can be inserted into a frame and remains static as new content is viewed in the main frame. The following steps illustrate how to apply a background image to the title frame and to give the frame a title.

To Add a Background Image to the Title_Frame

1

• **Click in the title_frame (topFrame) in the Document window. Click Modify on the menu bar and then click Page Properties. Point to the Browse button.**

The Page Properties dialog box is displayed (Figure 7-24).

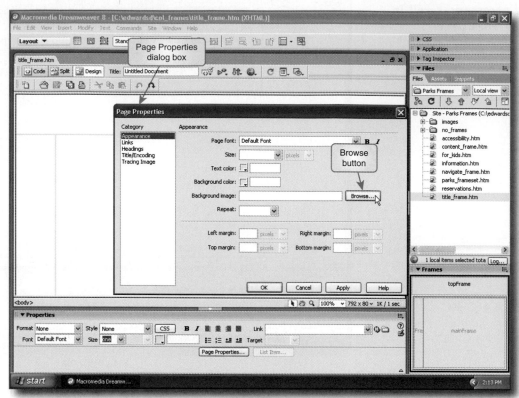

FIGURE 7-24

2

• **Click the Browse button. If necessary, double-click the images folder and then click the bg.jpg file.**

The Select Image Source dialog box is displayed (Figure 7-25). The bg.jpg file is selected.

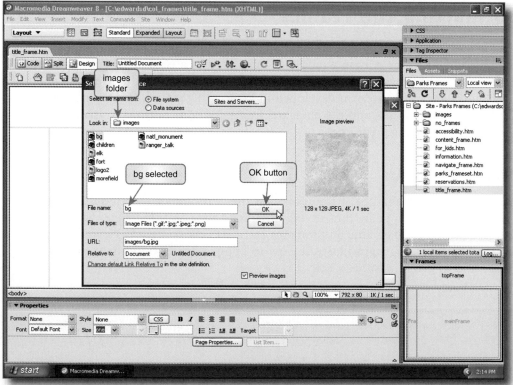

FIGURE 7-25

3

• **Click the OK button.**

The path and bg.jpg file name are displayed in the Background image text box in the Page Properties dialog box (Figure 7-26).

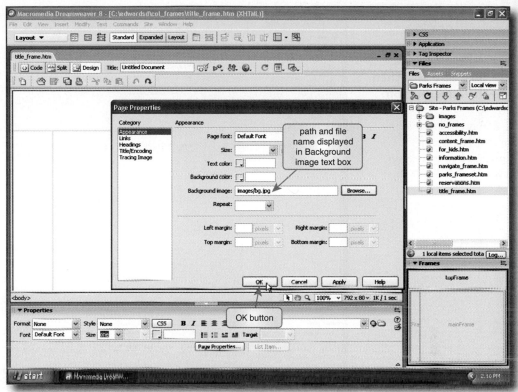

FIGURE 7-26

4

• **Click the OK button.**

The background image is applied to the frame (Figure 7-27).

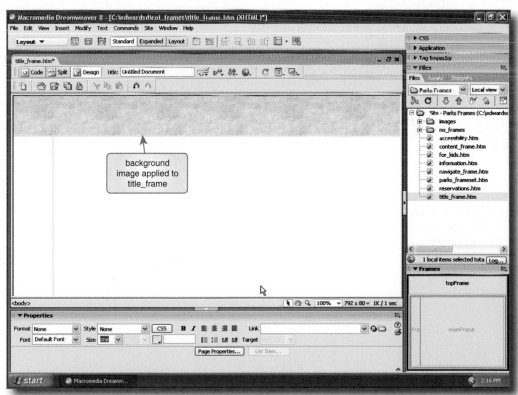

FIGURE 7-27

5

• **Type** Colorado
Parks - General
Information **in the
Title text box and then
click the Save button.**

*The title is displayed in the
Title text box on the
Document toolbar and on
the title bar (Figure 7-28).*

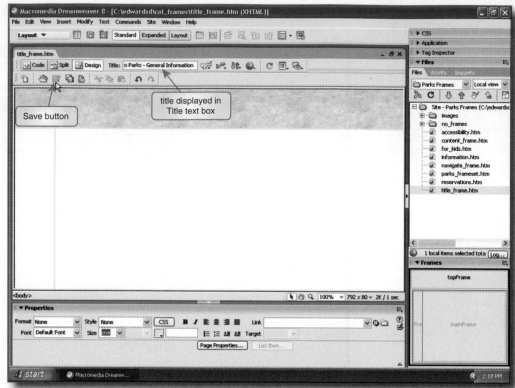

FIGURE 7-28

More About

Inserting an Image into a Frame

Regular images, as well as
background images, also can
be inserted into a frame. If
the image is smaller than the
frame, a blank space appears
around the image. For more
information about images
and frames, visit the
Dreamweaver 8 More About
Web page (scsite.com/dw8/
more.htm) and then click
Frames and Images.

Adding an Image to the Title_Frame.htm File

The next step is to add an image to the title_frame and then adjust the margin
height so the image will display correctly when viewed in a browser. Placing a 0 in
the Margin height box assures that the image will display properly in a browser.
After making these changes, you will need to resave the frame.

To Add a Title Image to the Title_Frame

1

• **If necessary, expand the images folder. Click the logo2.gif image. If necessary, click the Reset button in the Files panel to display the logo2.gif file.**

The logo2.gif image is selected (Figure 7-29).

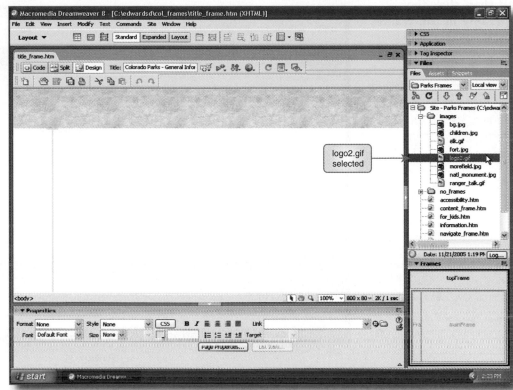

FIGURE 7-29

2

• **Drag the logo2.gif Image to the title_frame.**

The logo2.gif image is selected and displayed in the title_frame.htm frame (Figure 7-30).

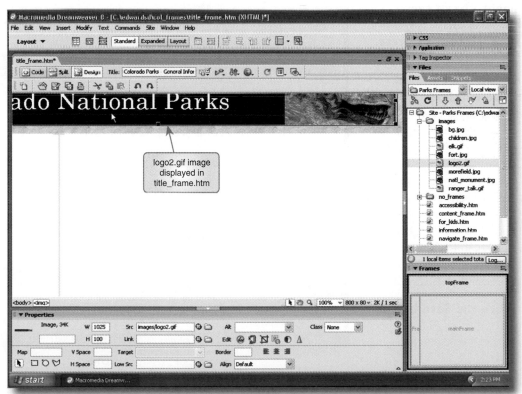

FIGURE 7-30

3

• **Click the Save button and then click the topFrame in the Frames panel.**

The title_frame.htm (topFrame) frame is selected and a dotted border surrounds the frame. The Property inspector displays frame attributes (Figure 7-31).

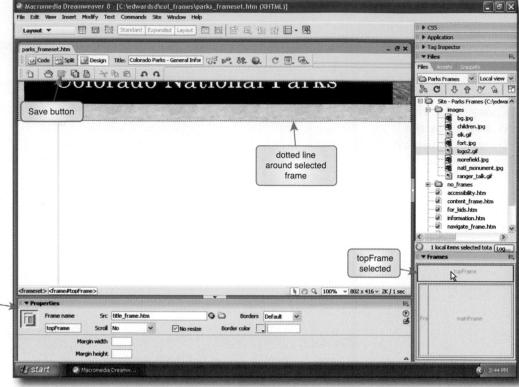

FIGURE 7-31

4

• **Click the Margin height box in the Property inspector. Type 0 and then press the TAB key.**

• **Verify that the No resize checkbox is selected.**

The Margin height value is changed to 0 (Figure 7-32). No changes are evident in the Document window. Changing the margin height affects how the image is displayed in the browser.

5

• **Click the Save button.**

The title_frame.htm file is saved.

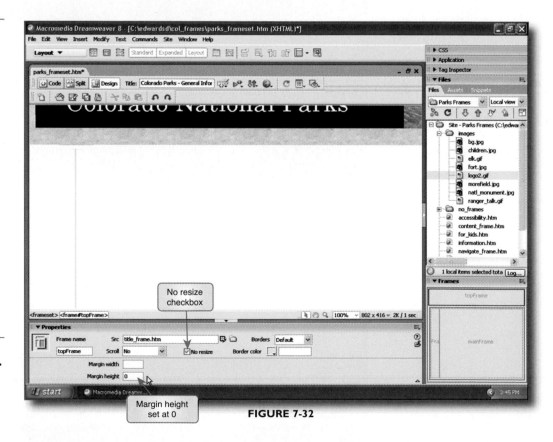

FIGURE 7-32

The Navigate_Frame

In the navigate_frame (leftFrame), buttons provide links to each of the four content pages and to the Colorado Parks main Web site. The content_frame (mainFrame) uses most of the Web page display area and shows the content of the page. To display another page in the content_frame.htm frame, simply click another button in the navigate_frame.htm frame. Displaying the content in the content_frame.htm frame requires that text or image links be added to one of the frames. Image links with text in the form of Flash buttons will be inserted into the navigate_frame.htm frame. First, however, you add the background image and title to the navigate_frame.htm frame.

To Add a Background Image and a Frame Title to the Navigate_Frame

1 Click in the navigate_frame (leftFrame) in the Document window.

2 Click Modify on the menu bar and then click Page Properties.

3 Click the Browse button, select the bg.jpg image, and then click the OK button in the Select Image Source dialog box.

4 Click the OK button.

5 Type Colorado Parks - General Information as the title in the Title text box.

6 Click the Save button (Figure 7-33).

More About

Setting a Frame Property

Frames and framesets can have different property settings. Setting a frame property overrides the setting for that property in a frameset.

The title is added and the background image is applied to the navigate_frame.htm frame. The file is saved (Figure 7-33).

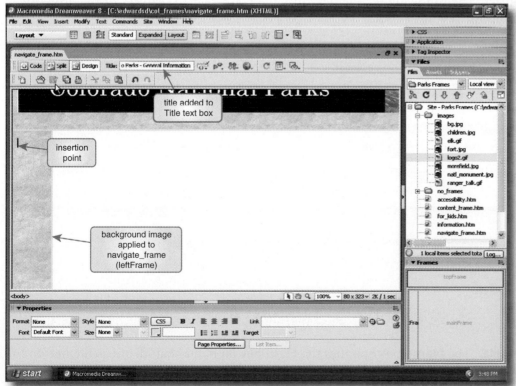

FIGURE 7-33

Flash Buttons

In Project 6, you added a navigation bar that contained Flash buttons. The Macromedia Flash program is used to develop graphics and animations. In most instances, creating these graphics and animations requires that the Flash program be installed on your computer. Dreamweaver, however, comes with Flash objects that you can use without having the Flash program.

You can use the Flash objects to create and insert Flash buttons in your documents while working in Design view or in Code view. You also can use the objects to create Flash text. You must save your document before inserting a Flash button or text object.

Flash can generate three different file types, as follows:

FLASH FILE (.FLA) This is the source file for any project and is created in the Flash program. Opening an .fla file requires the Flash program. Using Flash, you then can export the .fla file as an .swf or .swt file, which can be viewed in a browser.

FLASH MOVIE FILE (.SWF) This is a compressed version of the Flash (.fla) file, optimized for viewing on the Web. The .swf file can be played back in browsers and previewed in Dreamweaver, but cannot be edited in Flash. This is the type of file you create when using the Flash button and text objects in Dreamweaver.

FLASH TEMPLATE FILE (.SWT) This file type enables you to modify and replace information in a Flash movie file. The Flash button object uses .swt files.

The Flash Player is available as both a Netscape Navigator plug-in and an ActiveX control for Microsoft Internet Explorer and is incorporated in the latest versions of Netscape Navigator, Microsoft Internet Explorer, and the America Online browser.

When a Flash button is saved in Dreamweaver, it has an .swf extension. This file can be played back in browsers and previewed in Dreamweaver. When a Flash object is selected, the Property inspector displays properties specific to the Flash object. The following section describes the Flash-related features of the Property inspector (Figure 7-34).

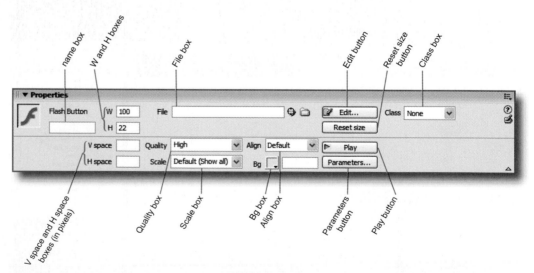

FIGURE 7-34

NAME The **Name** box specifies the Flash button name that identifies the button for scripting. It is not necessary to enter a name.

W AND H The **W** and **H** boxes indicate the width and height of the Flash object in pixels. You also can specify the width and height as a percentage. In that case, the % sign must follow the value without a space (for example, 3%).

FILE The **File** box contains the path to the Flash object file and the file name.

EDIT Clicking the **Edit** button displays the Insert Flash Button dialog box, or a related dialog box if the object is other than a button.

RESET SIZE The **Reset size** button resets the selected button to its original size.

V SPACE AND H SPACE The **V space** and **H space** boxes specify the number of pixels of white space above, below, and on both sides of the button.

QUALITY The **Quality** box contains options that set the quality parameter for the object and embed tags that define the button. The options are High, Low, Auto Low, and Auto High. **Low** emphasizes speed over appearance, whereas **High** favors appearance over speed. **Auto Low** emphasizes speed at first, but improves appearance when possible. **Auto High** emphasizes both qualities at first, but sacrifices appearance for speed, if necessary.

SCALE The **Scale** box options define how the button (movie) is displayed within the area defined for the movie by the width and height values. The options are Default (Show all), No Border, and Exact Fit.

ALIGN The **Align** box options define how the object is aligned on the page. The align options are the same as those for images discussed in Project 2.

BG The **Bg** box contains a palette of colors you can use to specify a background color for the object. The color also is represented by the hexadecimal value in the adjacent box.

PLAY/STOP The **Play/Stop** button lets you preview the Flash object in the Document window. Click the green Play button to see the object in Play mode; click the red Stop button to stop the movie.

PARAMETERS The **Parameters** button opens a dialog box for entering additional parameters. These values are for special parameters that can be defined for Shockwave and Flash movies, ActiveX controls, Navigator plug-ins, and Java applets.

CLASS The Class box styles are a type of CSS style that can be applied to any text in a document, regardless of which tags control the text.

Inserting Flash Buttons into the Navigate_Frame

You insert five Flash buttons into the navigate_frame. The first four buttons display content in the content_frame. This content is generated from the four HTML documents you copied from the Data Files folder. The four documents (information, accessibility, for_kids, and reservations) already are formatted and the background image has been added to each one. The fifth button returns to the main frame content. The following steps illustrate how to insert the first Flash button into the navigate_frame (leftFrame).

To Insert a Flash Button into the Navigate_Frame

1

• **Click Insert on the menu bar, point to Media, and then point to Flash Button on the Media submenu.**

The Insert menu is displayed, and Flash Button is selected on the Media submenu (Figure 7-35).

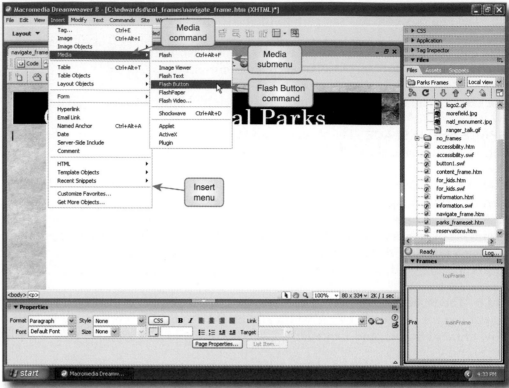

FIGURE 7-35

2

• **Click Flash Button.**

The Insert Flash Button dialog box is displayed (Figure 7-36).

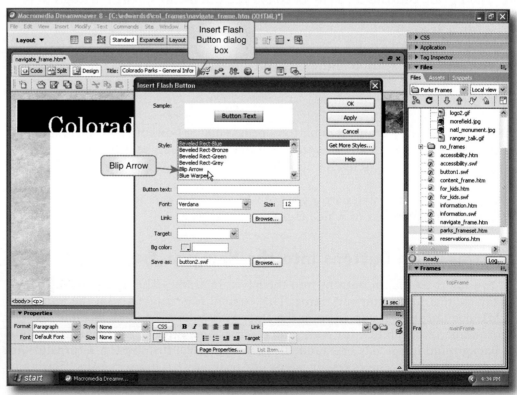

FIGURE 7-36

3

• **Click Blip Arrow. Click the Button text text box and then type** Information **as the text to display on the first button. Double-click the Size box and then type** 12 **as the new value. Point to the Browse button to the right of the Link box.**

The Blip Arrow button sample is displayed in the Sample area, Information is displayed in the Button text text box, and the font size is changed to 12 (Figure 7-37).

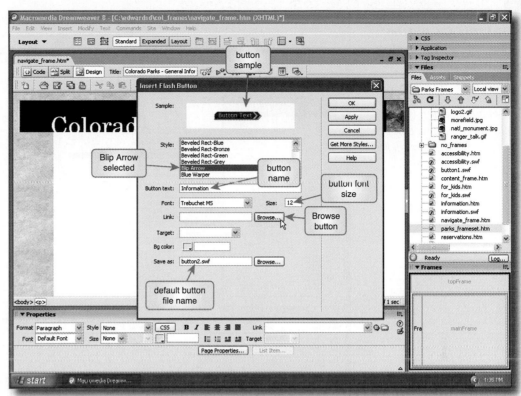

FIGURE 7-37

4

• **Click the Browse button. When the Select file dialog box is displayed, click information.htm in the Look in list. If necessary, click the Relative to box arrow and then select Document.**

The Select file dialog box is displayed (Figure 7-38). The col_frames folder is displayed in the Look in box. The information.htm file is selected, information is displayed in the File name text box, and information.htm is displayed in the URL box.

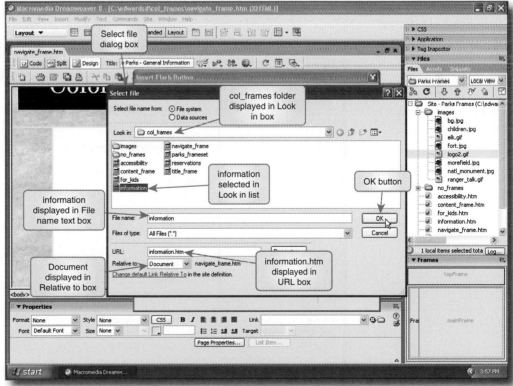

FIGURE 7-38

5

• **Click the OK button in the Select file dialog box. Point to the Target box arrow.**

The information.htm link is displayed in the Link box in the Insert Flash Button dialog box (Figure 7-39).

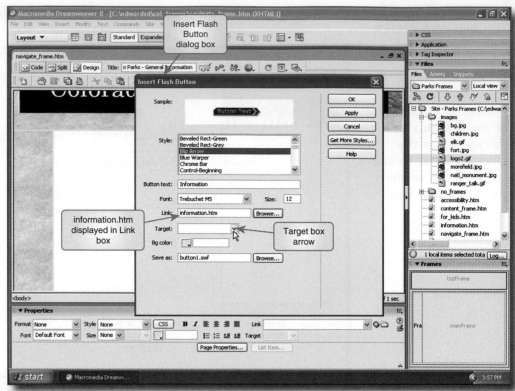

FIGURE 7-39

6

• **Click the Target box arrow and then point to mainFrame.**

The mainFrame target is selected (Figure 7-40).

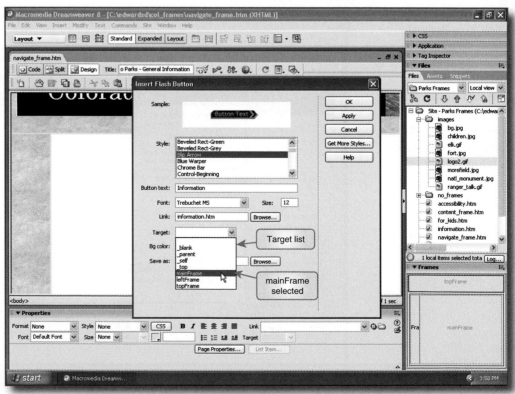

FIGURE 7-40

7

• **Click mainFrame.**

• **Click the Save as text box and type** information.swf **as the file name.**

• **Point to the OK button.**

The mainFrame frame is selected as the target frame (Figure 7-41).

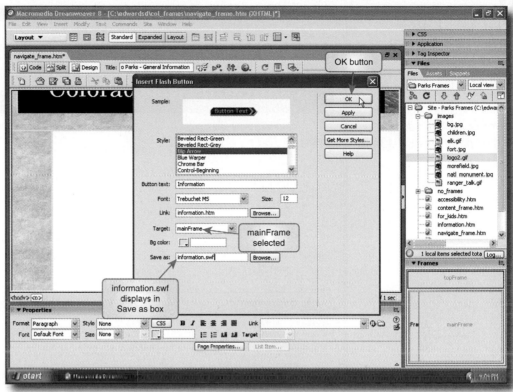

FIGURE 7-41

8

• **Click the OK button to insert the Flash button.**

The Flash button is inserted into the navigate_frame and is selected (Figure 7-42). The navigate_frame currently is not wide enough to display the entire button. Later in this project, you will learn how to adjust the width of the frame so the whole button is displayed.

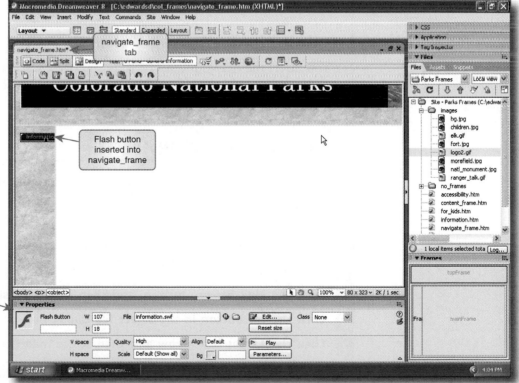

FIGURE 7-42

9

• **Click below the button to deselect it and then press the ENTER key.**

A blank line space is inserted between the button and the insertion point (Figure 7-43).

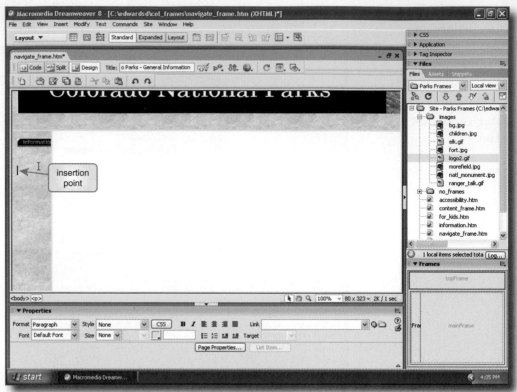

FIGURE 7-43

Inserting the Remaining Buttons

You insert the Accessibility, For Kids, and Reservations buttons using the same steps you used to add the Information button. The next steps show how to insert the Accessibility button.

To Insert the Accessibility Button

1 Click Insert on the menu bar, point to Media, and then click Flash Button on the Media submenu.

2 Click Blip Arrow.

3 Click the Button text text box. Type `Accessibility` as the button text.

4 Change the font size to 12.

5 Click the Link Browse button, and then click accessibility.htm.

6 Click the OK button in the Select file dialog box.

7 Click the Target box arrow and then select mainFrame.

8 Click the Save as text box and type `accessibility.swf` as the file name.

9 Click the OK button to insert the Accessibility button into the navigate_frame.

10 Click below the button and then press the ENTER key.

The Accessibility button is inserted into the navigate_frame, and a blank line is inserted below the button (Figure 7-44).

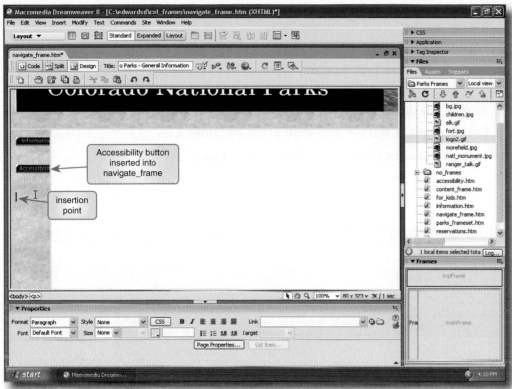

FIGURE 7-44

The following steps illustrate how to add the For Kids button.

To Insert the For Kids Button

1 Click Insert on the menu bar, point to Media, and then click Flash Button on the Media submenu.

2 Click Blip Arrow. Click the Button text text box. Type For Kids as the button name. Change the font size to 12.

3 Click the Link Browse button, click for_kids.htm, and then click the OK button in the Select file dialog box.

4 Click the Target box arrow and then select mainFrame.

5 Click the Save as text box and type for_kids.swf as the file name.

6 Click the OK button to insert the For Kids button into the navigate_frame.

7 Click below the button and then press the ENTER key.

You have inserted the first three buttons. The following steps show how to insert the Reservations button.

To Insert the Reservations Button

1 Click Insert on the menu bar, point to Media, and then click Flash Button on the Media submenu.

2 Click Blip Arrow. Click the Button text text box. Type Reservations as the button text. Change the font size to 12.

3 Click the Link Browse button, click reservations.htm, and then click the OK button in the Select file dialog box.

4 Click the Target box arrow and then select mainFrame.

5 Click the Save as text box and type reservations.swf as the file name.

6 Click the OK button to insert the Reservations button into the navigate_frame.

7 Click below the button and then press the ENTER key.

8 Click the Save button on the Standard toolbar.

The first four buttons are inserted (Figure 7-45). The navigate_frame.htm frame is saved.

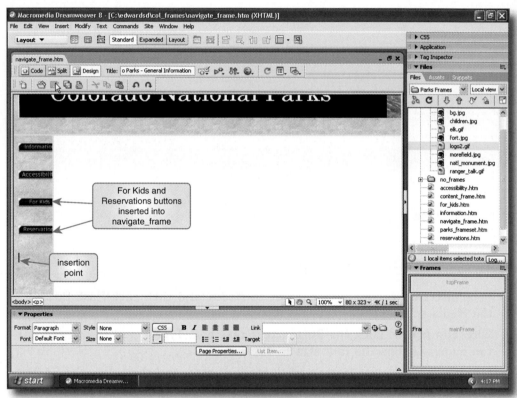

FIGURE 7-45

More About

Linking to Web Pages

If you are linking to a page outside of your Web site, always use target="_top" or target="_blank" to ensure that the page does not appear to be part of your site.

Thus far, the target for your links has been the mainFrame. The last button to be added to the navigate_frame is the Home button. When clicked, this button will cause the main index page of the Colorado Parks Web site to display on the screen. Other possible targets within the same frameset include leftFrame and topFrame. Targets outside the frameset include _blank, _parent, _self, and _top. The following section describes these targets.

• The **_blank** target opens the linked document in a new browser window, leaving the current window untouched.

• The **_parent** target opens the linked document in the parent frameset of the frame the link appears in, replacing the entire frameset.

• The **_self** target opens the link in the current frame, replacing the content in that frame.

• The **_top** target opens the linked document in the current browser window, replacing all frames.

To create the Home button, you use an absolute link. If you published the main Colorado Parks Web site to a remote server in a previous project, use the remote server Web site address for the index page as the link. Otherwise, use the path to the location of the C:/yourname/parks/index.htm file. To further create this link, you select _blank as the target. Selecting this option opens the linked document in a new browser window, leaving the current window untouched. The following steps illustrate how to create a link to the main Web site index page.

To Insert the Home Button

1

• **Click Insert on the menu bar, point to Media, and then click Flash Button on the Media submenu. Click Blip Arrow. Click the Button text text box and then type** Home **as the button text. Change the font size to 12.**

Home is displayed in the Button text text box, and the font size is changed to 12 (Figure 7-16).

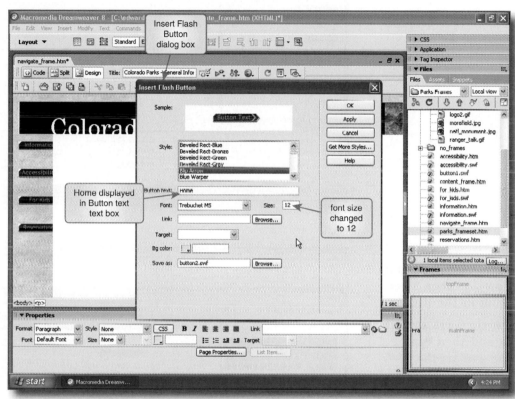

FIGURE 7-46

2

• **If you are linking to a remote server, copy and paste the URL to the main Colorado Parks Web site into the Link box. If you are linking to the C:/yourname/ parks/index.htm file, type that path in the Link box.**

The path to the index.htm file for the main Colorado Parks Web site appears in the Link box (Figure 7-47).

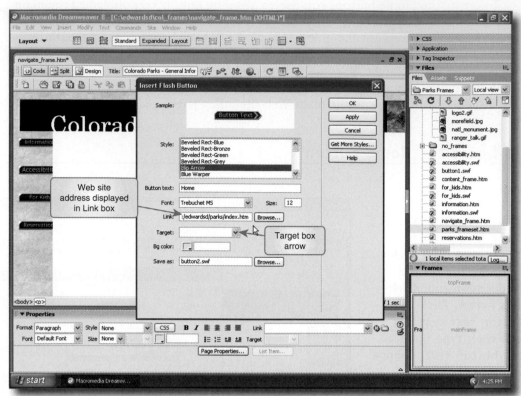

FIGURE 7-47

3

• **Click the Target box arrow and then select _blank in the list.**

Click the Save as text box and then type home.swf **as the file name.**

The Target box displays _blank (Figure 7-48).

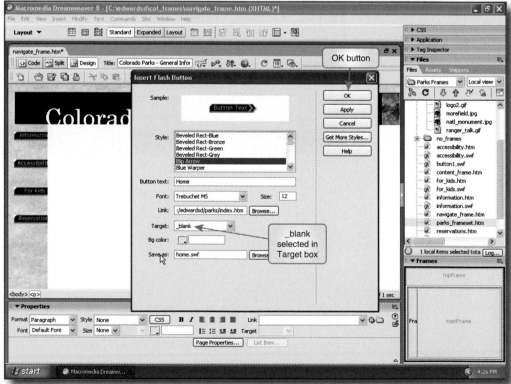

FIGURE 7-48

4

• **Click the OK button and then click the Save button on the Standard toolbar.**

The five buttons are added to the navigate_frame (Figure 7-49), and the navigate_frame is saved.

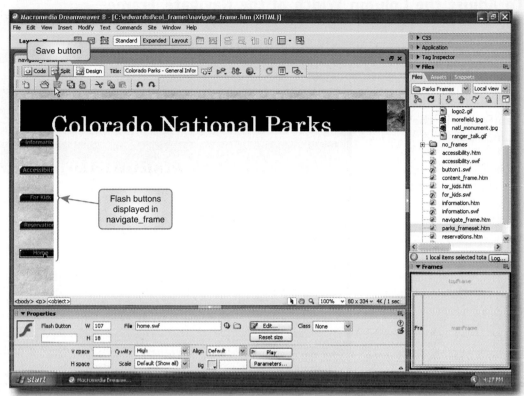

FIGURE 7-49

Adjusting Column Width

The Flash buttons are partially displayed in the navigate_frame. You can adjust the size of the buttons or you can adjust the column width. In this project, you adjust the column width and use pixels as the measurement for the width. Using pixels ensures that the column width does not change when displayed in a browser. The navigate_frame is in the nested frameset. You can adjust the column width by dragging the right border of the frame or you can adjust the column width through the Property inspector. To adjust the column width through the Property inspector, first you must select the nested frameset. The following steps show how to select the nested frameset and to adjust the column width of the navigate_frame.

To Adjust the Column Width of the Navigate_Frame

1

• **Click the border surrounding the leftFrame and the mainFrame in the Frames panel.**

The nested frameset is selected. A second <frameset> tag is selected in the tag selector. The Property inspector for the frameset is displayed. A dotted border surrounds the selected frames (Figure 7-50).

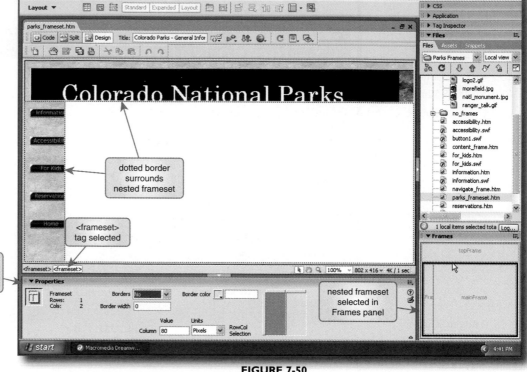

FIGURE 7-50

2

• **If necessary, click the tab on the first column in the Property inspector. Double-click the Column Value box, type 105 as the entry, and then press the ENTER key.**

The column width is expanded to 105 pixels (Figure 7-51).

3

• **Click the Save button on the Standard toolbar to save the navigate_frame.htm file and the changes to the frameset.**

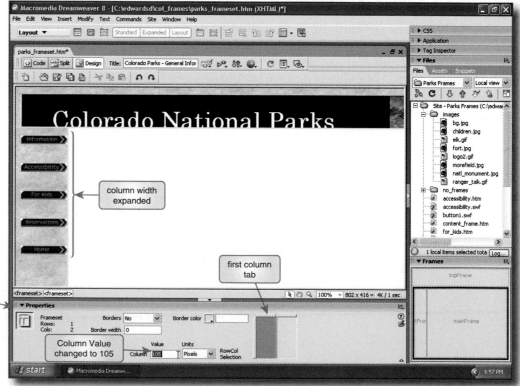

FIGURE 7-51

The Content_Frame

The content_frame (mainFrame) is where the content is displayed when one of the Flash navigation buttons is clicked. The four content pages are information, accessibility, for_kids, and reservations. The following steps illustrate how to add the background image and title to the content_frame page.

To Add a Background Image and Frame Title to the Content_Frame

1 Click the content_frame (mainFrame) in the Document window.

2 Click Modify on the menu bar and then click Page Properties.

3 Click the Browse button to the right of the Background Image box, navigate to and select the bg.jpg image, and then click the OK button in the Select Image Source dialog box.

4 Click the OK button in the Page Properties dialog box.

5 Type Colorado Parks - General Information as the title.

6 Click the Save button on the Standard toolbar.

The background image is applied to the content_frame, and the title is added. (Figure 7-52).

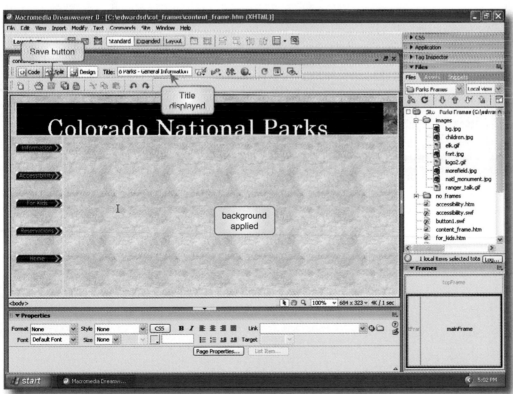

FIGURE 7-52

Linking and Targeting

You created the links and targets for the navigation buttons when you created the buttons. To display default content in the content_frame, however, requires that content be added in a manner similar to adding the title graphic and navigate_frame content. The default content is the information.htm file. The next steps show how to add the default content to the content_frame.

To Link and Target the Default Content

1

• **Click the mainFrame in the Frames panel.**

A dotted border appears around the mainFrame in the Document window. The Frames Property inspector is displayed (Figure 7-53).

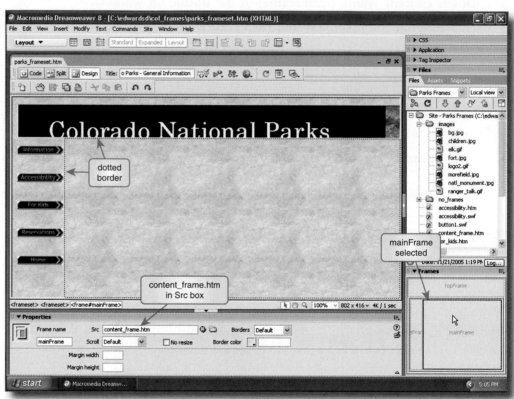

FIGURE 7-53

2

• **Double-click content_frame.htm in the Src box in the Property inspector.**

The text, content_frame.htm, is selected in the Src box (Figure 7-54).

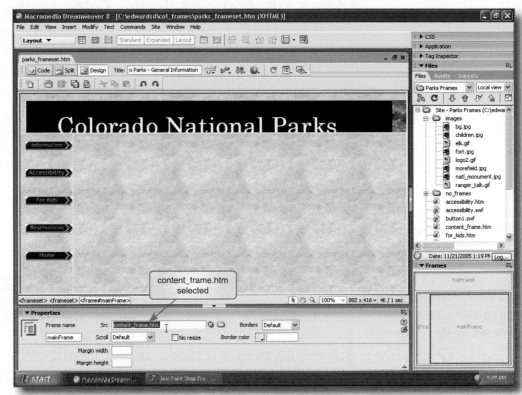

FIGURE 7-54

3

• **Type** information.htm **and then press the ENTER key.**

4

• **If a Dreamweaver Warning box is displayed, click the Yes button.**

The contents of the information.htm file are displayed in the mainFrame (Figure 7-55).

5

• **Click File on the menu bar and then click Save All.**

All the framesets and frames are saved.

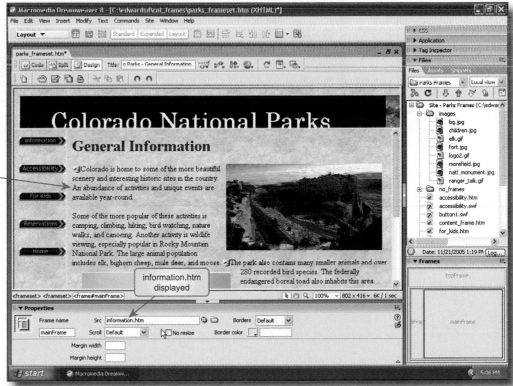

FIGURE 7-55

Adding a Border and Border Color to the Framesets

The Borders feature in the Property inspector determines whether borders should appear around the frames when a document is viewed in a browser. You can add a border to an individual frame or to the frameset. If the frameset contains one or more nested framesets, then each nested frameset must be selected and the border added to it. The Border width specifies a width for all the borders in the frameset, and the Border Color sets a color for the borders. Border colors and widths selected for an individual frame override the border color and border width of the frameset properties. Use the color picker to select a color, or type the hexadecimal value for a color. The following steps illustrate how to add a border and border color to the main frameset.

To Add a Border and Border Color to the Frameset

1

• **Click the border around the outer frameset in the Frames panel.**

A dark border surrounds the entire frame in the Frames panel, and a dotted border surrounds the frameset and frames in the Document window (Figure 7-56). The Property inspector for the frameset is displayed, and <frameset> is selected in the tag selector.

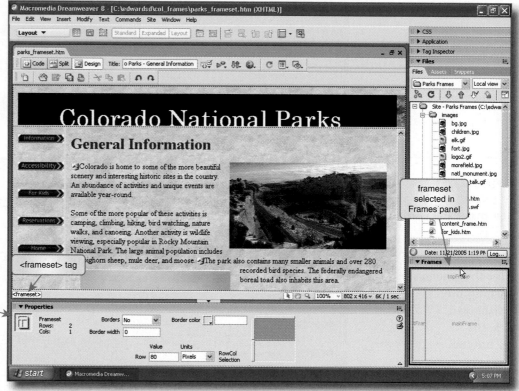

FIGURE 7-56

2

• **Type** No frames version **as the text for the link.**

The text, No frames version, is displayed in the information.htm Document window (Figure 7-63). It is displayed as style1.

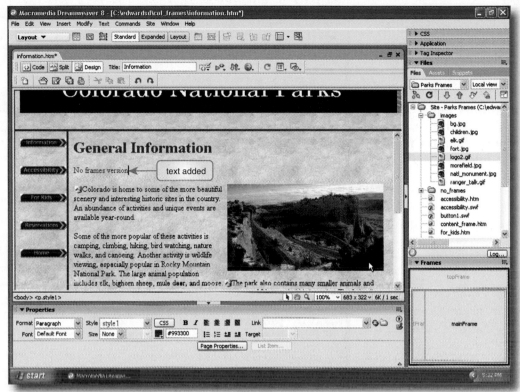

FIGURE 7-63

3

• **Select the text, No frames version.**

The text, No frames version, is selected (Figure 7-64).

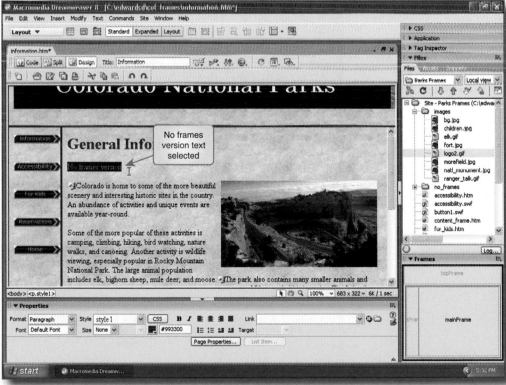

FIGURE 7-64

4

• **If necessary, scroll in the Files panel to display the no_frames folder. Click the plus sign to the left of the no_frames folder and then click the information.htm file in that folder.**

The no_frames folder is open, and the information.htm file is selected (Figure 7-65).

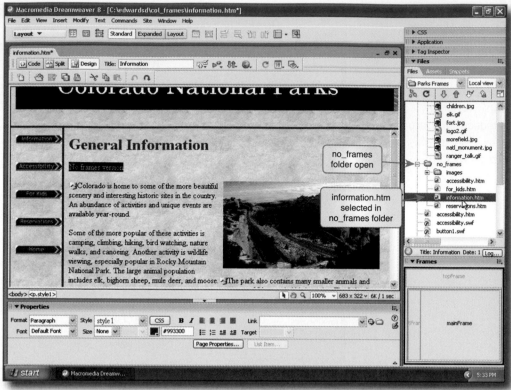

FIGURE 7-65

5

• **Drag the information.htm file to the Link box in the Property inspector and then press the ENTER key.**

The link, no_frames/information.htm, is displayed in the Link box (Figure 7-66).

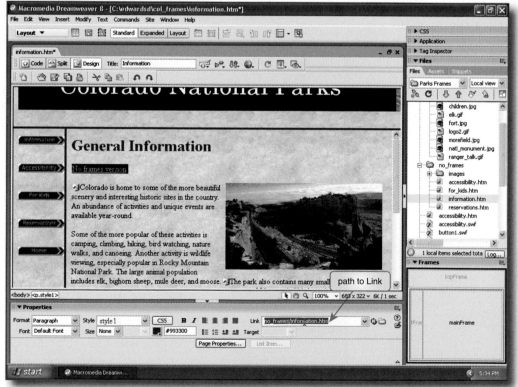

FIGURE 7-66

6

• **Click the Target box arrow and then select _top. Click the Save button on the Standard toolbar.**

The _top option is selected in the Target box, and the file is saved (Figure 7-67).

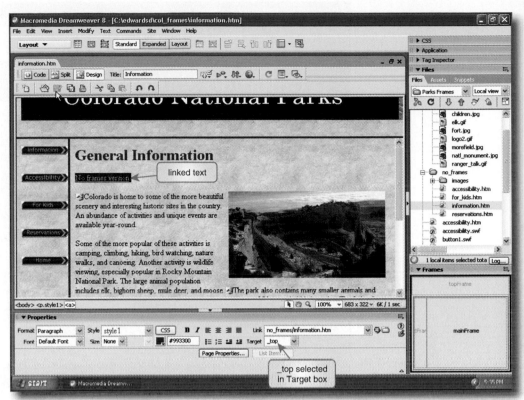

FIGURE 7-67

The last step is to view the Web site and verify that the links work. The next steps show how to display the pages in your browser.

To View the Web Site and Verify Links

1 Press the F12 key to preview the Parks Frames Web site.

2 Click each of the navigation buttons to verify that they work (Figures 7-68a through 7-68d on pages DW 608 and DW 609).

3 If necessary, click Information and then click the No frames version link.

4 Click the browser Back button to return to the framed version.

5 If instructed to do so, upload the Web site to a remote server.

6 If instructed to do so, right-click in each frame, print a copy of each frame, and hand in the copies to your instructor.

7 Close the browser.

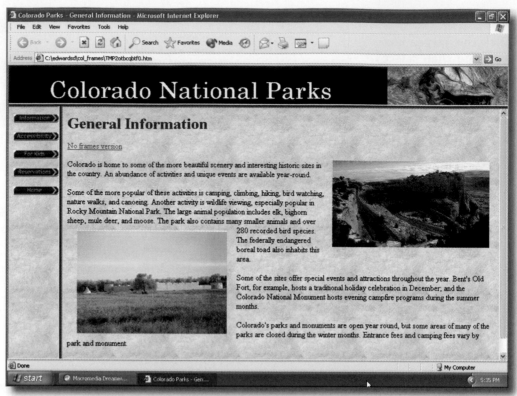

FIGURE 7-68a

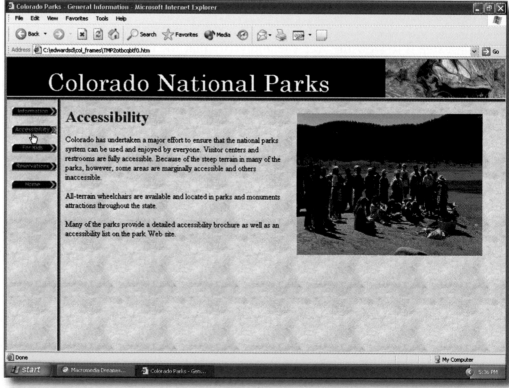

FIGURE 7-68b

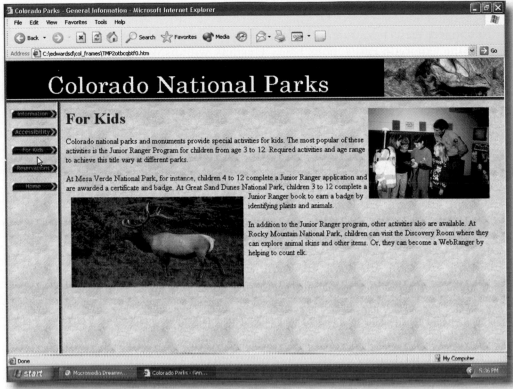

FIGURE 7-68c

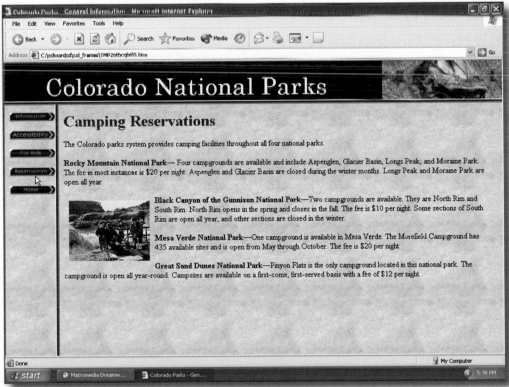

FIGURE 7-68d

Adding a Link to the Colorado Parks Web Site Index Page

To connect the Colorado Parks Web site to the Parks_Frames Web site, you add a link to the Colorado Parks index page. This link will display at the end of the page. The following steps illustrate how to add the link.

To Add a Link from the Colorado Parks Web Site to the Parks_Frames Web Site

1 Open the Colorado Parks Web site and then open the index.htm page.

2 Scroll to the bottom of the page and then click to the right of the last sentence on the page. Press the ENTER key.

3 Type General Information and then create an absolute link from the text, General Information, to the col_frames/parks_frameset.htm file in the Parks Frames Web site. If a warning box displays, click No to proceed.

4 If you are publishing to a remote site, copy and paste the Colorado Parks Web site address into the Link box.

5 If you are saving your work to a local computer or server, use the Browse for File icon in the Property inspector to create the link path.

6 Click the Save button on the Standard toolbar.

7 Press F12 to preview the file in your browser. Click the General Information link.

8 Close the browser.

Quitting Dreamweaver

After you have created your framed Web site, verified that the navigation works, and uploaded it to a remote server, Project 7 is complete. The following step shows how to close the Web site, quit Dreamweaver 8, and return control to Windows.

To Close the Web Site and Quit Dreamweaver

1 Click the Close button on the right corner of the Dreamweaver title bar.

The Dreamweaver window, the Document window, and the Parks Frames Web site all close. If you have unsaved changes, Dreamweaver prompts you to save the changes. Clicking the Yes button in the Dreamweaver 8 dialog box saves the changes.

Project Summary

Project 7 introduced you to frames and to Web page design using frames. You created a framed Web site that included two framesets — one a nested frameset. You named the framesets and the frames and modified the frameset and frame properties. You added navigation links in the form of Flash buttons to display content in the main frame. Finally, you added a link for a no-frames version of the Web site for those visitors who do not want to use frames.

What You Should Know

Having completed this project, you now should be able to perform the tasks below. The tasks are listed in the same order they were presented in the project. For a list of keyboard commands for topics introduced in this project, see the Quick Reference for Windows at the back of this book and refer to the Shortcut column.

1. Use Site Definition to Create a Local Web Site (DW 558)
2. Copy Data Files to the Parks_Frames Web Site (DW 559)
3. Create the Frameset (DW 564)
4. Display the Frames Panel (DW 569)
5. Name and Save the Three Frames (DW 571)
6. Save and Name the Left and Main Frames (DW 574)
7. Name and Save the Frameset (DW 575)
8. Add a Background Image to the Title_Frame (DW 578)
9. Add a Title Image to the Title_Frame (DW 581)
10. Add a Background Image and a Frame Title to the Navigate_Frame (DW 583)
11. Insert a Flash Button into the Navigate_Frame (DW 586)
12. Insert the Accessibility Button (DW 590)
13. Insert the For Kids Button (DW 591)
14. Insert the Reservations Button (DW 591)
15. Insert the Home Button (DW 593)
16. Adjust the Column Width of the Navigate_Frame (DW 596)
17. Add a Background Image and Frame Title to the Content_Frame (DW 597)
18. Link and Target the Default Content (DW 598)
19. Add a Border and Border Color to the Frameset (DW 600)
20. Apply the Border and Border Color to the Nested Frameset (DW 603)
21. Add a No-Frames Link (DW 604)
22. View the Web Site and Verify Links (DW 607)
23. Add a Link from the Colorado Parks Web Site to the Parks_Frames Web Site (DW 610)
24. Close the Web Site and Quit Dreamweaver (DW 610)

Learn It Online

Instructions: To complete the Learn It Online exercises, start your browser, click the Address bar, and then enter the Web address scsite.com/dw8/learn. When the Dreamweaver 8 Learn It Online page is displayed, follow the instructions in the exercises below. Each exercise has instructions for printing your results, either for your own records or for submission to your instructor.

1 Project Reinforcement TF, MC, and SA

Below Dreamweaver Project 7, click the Project Reinforcement link. Print the quiz by clicking Print on the File menu for each page. Answer each question.

2 Flash Cards

Below Dreamweaver Project 7, click the Flash Cards link and read the instructions. Type 20 (or a number specified by your instructor) in the Number of playing cards text box, type your name in the Enter your Name text box, and then click the Flip Card button. When the flash card is displayed, read the question and then click the ANSWER box arrow to select an answer. Flip through the Flash Cards. If your score is 15 (75%) correct or greater, click Print on the File menu to print your results. If your score is less than 15 (75%) correct, then redo this exercise by clicking the Replay button.

3 Practice Test

Below Dreamweaver Project 7, click the Practice Test link. Answer each question, enter your first and last name at the bottom of the page, and then click the Grade Test button. When the graded practice test is displayed on your screen, click Print on the File menu to print a hard copy. Continue to take practice tests until you score 80% or better.

4 Who Wants To Be a Computer Genius?

Below Dreamweaver Project 7, click the Computer Genius link. Read the instructions, enter your first and last name at the bottom of the page, and then click the PLAY button. When your score is displayed, click the PRINT RESULTS link to print a hard copy.

5 Wheel of Terms

Below Dreamweaver Project 7, click the Wheel of Terms link. Read the instructions, and then enter your first and last name and your school name. Click the PLAY button. When your score is displayed, right-click the score and then click Print on the shortcut menu to print a hard copy.

6 Crossword Puzzle Challenge

Below Dreamweaver Project 7, click the Crossword Puzzle Challenge link. Read the instructions, and then enter your first and last name. Click the SUBMIT button. Work the crossword puzzle. When you are finished, click the Submit button. When the crossword puzzle is redisplayed, click the Print Puzzle button to print a hard copy.

7 Tips and Tricks

Below Dreamweaver Project 7, click the Tips and Tricks link. Click a topic that pertains to Project 7. Right-click the information and then click Print on the shortcut menu. Construct a brief example of what the information relates to in Dreamweaver to confirm that you understand how to use the tip or trick.

8 Newsgroups

Below Dreamweaver Project 7, click the Newsgroups link. Click a topic that pertains to Project 7. Print three comments.

9 Expanding Your Horizons

Below Dreamweaver Project 7, click the Expanding Your Horizons link. Click a topic that pertains to Project 7. Print the information. Construct a brief example of what the information relates to in Dreamweaver to confirm that you understand the contents of the article.

10 Search Sleuth

Below Dreamweaver Project 7, click the Search Sleuth link. To search for a term that pertains to this project, select a term below the Project 7 title and then use the Google search engine at google.com (or any major search engine) to display and print two Web pages that present information on the term.

Apply Your Knowledge

1 Creating a Framed Web Site for Andy's Lawn Service

Instructions: See the inside back cover of this book for instructions for downloading the Data Disk, or see your instructor for information on accessing the files in this book.

Andy's Lawn Service recently started selling lawn mowers and other lawn equipment and would like to investigate the possibility of selling this equipment on the Internet. Its goal is to create a framed Web site displaying four of the more popular lawn mowers. The Web site will contain five pages: the index page and a page describing each of the four lawn mowers. The frameset will contain three frames: topFrame, leftFrame, and mainFrame. The top frame (named title) displays the title, the left frame contains the navigation text, and the main frame displays the linked content, as shown in Figures 7-69a through 7-69e on pages DW 613 – DW 615. Appendix C contains instructions for uploading your local site to a remote server.

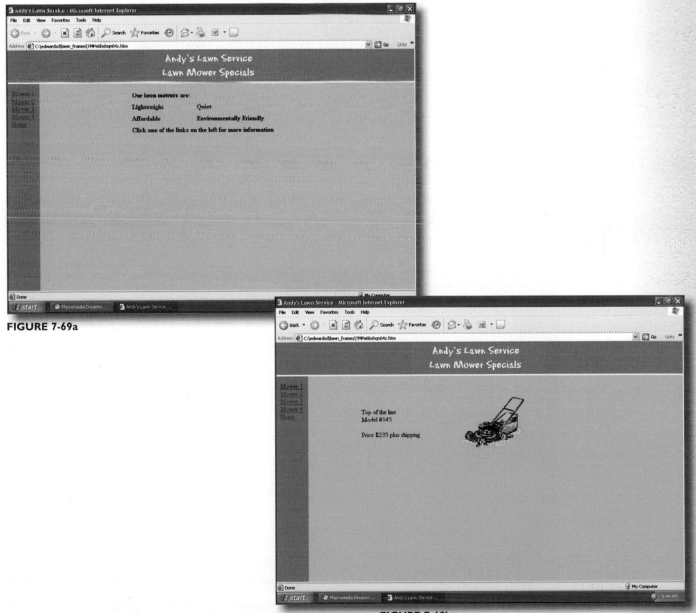

FIGURE 7-69a

FIGURE 7-69b

(continued)

Apply Your Knowledge

Creating a Framed Web Site for Andy's Lawn Service *(continued)*

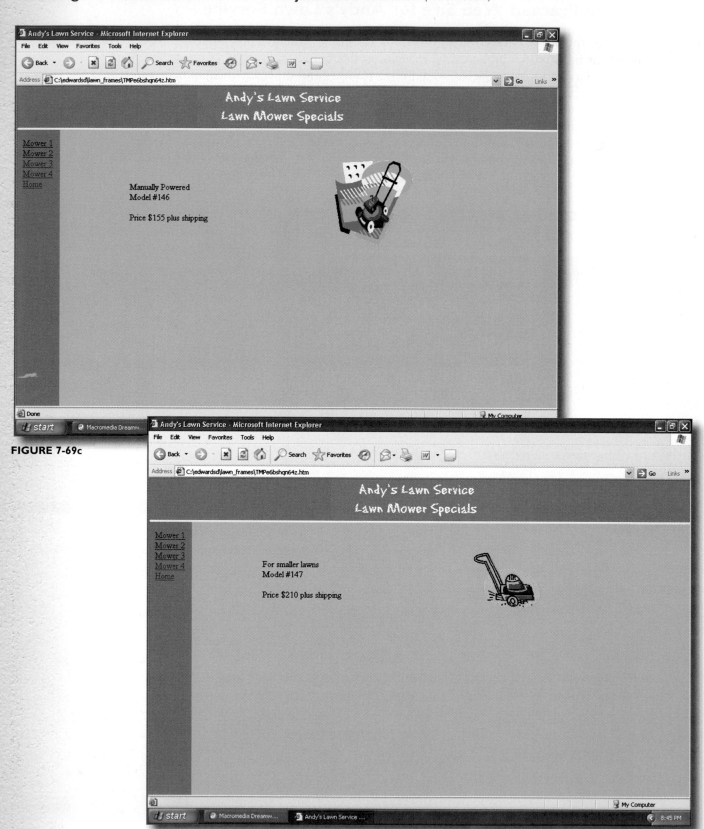

FIGURE 7-69c

FIGURE 7-69d

Apply Your Knowledge

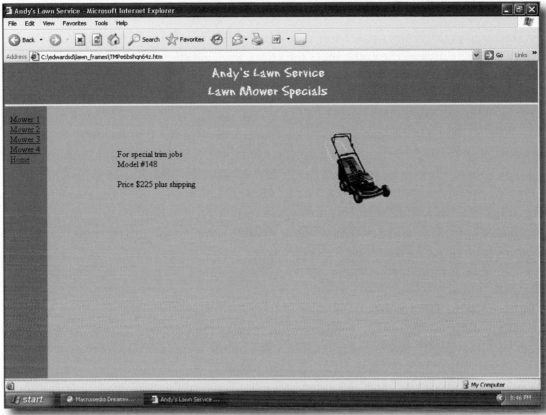

FIGURE 7-69e

1. Start Dreamweaver. If necessary, display the panel groups, and then display the Frames panel.
2. Create a new Web site. Name the Web site Lawn Service Frames. Store your Web site in a new folder called lawn_frames. The path for the new Web site will be C:\yourname\lawn_frames\. Add an images folder. The path for the images will be C:\yourname\lawn_frames\images\.
3. Use the Windows My Computer option to copy the data files and the images from the Data Files to your lawn_frames local root folder.
4. Click File on the menu bar, click New, and then click Framesets in the Category column of the General tab in the New Document dialog box. Select Fixed Top, Nested Left and then click the Create button to create the frameset.
5. Title the document Andy's Lawn Service. Save the frameset as index.htm in the lawn_frames local root folder.
6. Click in the topFrame, click Modify on the menu bar, and then click Page Properties. In the Background color hexadecimal box, type #3399FF and then click the OK button. Type Andy's Lawn Service in the Title text box for the topFrame.
7. Drag the title.gif file to the topFrame and then center the title.gif file. Click the topFrame in the Frames panel to display the Frames Property inspector. Click the Margin height box and then type 0 as the entry. Click in the topFrame in the Document window and then save the topFrame. Use title.htm as the frame name.
8. Click in the mainFrame in the Document window. Type Andy's Lawn Service in the Title text box. Click the Page Properties button in the Property inspector. In the Background color hexadecimal box, type #66CCFF and then click the OK button. Save the mainFrame. Use main.htm as the file name.

(continued)

Creating a Framed Web Site for Andy's Lawn Service *(continued)*

9. Click the mainFrame in the Frames panel and then double-click main.htm in the Src box in the Property inspector. Type content.htm as the entry, press the ENTER key, and then click the Save button.

10. Click in the leftFrame. Type Andy's Lawn Service in the Title text box. Click the Page Properties button, type #3399FF in the Background color hexadecimal box, and then click the OK button. Save the frame as navigate.htm in the lawn_frames local root folder.

11. Create a five-row, one-column table in the navigate frame. Use 0 for the Cell Padding, Cell Spacing, and Border thickness, and use 100 Percent for the Width. Center the table. Type Mower 1 in row 1, type Mower 2 in row 2, type Mower 3 in row 3, type Mower 4 in row 4, and type Home in row 5.

12. Select the text, Mower 1, in column 1. Drag the file, mower01.htm, from the Files panel to the Link box in the Property inspector. Click the Target box arrow and then select mainFrame.

13. Repeat Step 12 for rows 2, 3, and 4, dragging the related files (mower02.htm through mower04.htm) to the Link box. Select mainFrame as the target for each file.

14. Select Home in the fifth column and then drag content.htm to the Link box. Select mainFrame as the target. Save the navigate frame.

15. Select the frameset in the Frames panel.

16. Click the Borders arrow in the Property inspector and then set the Borders attribute to Yes. Double-click the Border width box and then type 2 as the entry. Click File on the menu bar and then click Save All. If instructed to do so, upload your Web sites to a remote server.

17. Open the Lawn Service Web site, open the index.htm page, scroll to the bottom of the page, and then click to the right of the last bulleted item. Press the ENTER key. Type Lawn mowers for sale and then insert two line breaks between the two bulleted items. Create an absolute link from the text, Lawn mowers for sale, to the index.htm file in the Lawn Service Frames Web site. Set the Target to _blank. If you are publishing to a remote site, copy and paste the Lawn Service Frames Web site address into the Link box. If you are saving your work to a local computer or server, use the Browse for File icon in the Property inspector to create the link path. Click the Save button on the Standard toolbar. If the Macromedia Dreamweaver dialog box displays, click the OK button. If instructed to do so, upload your Web site changes to a remote server.

18. Press the F12 key to view the Lawn Service index.htm page in your browser. Click the Lawn mowers for sale link to display the Lawn Service Frames Web site. Click each of the navigation buttons to verify that they work. Print copies of each frame, if instructed to do so.

In the Lab

1 Adding a Framed Web Page to CandleWix

Problem: Martha has received several e-mails asking how to make candles. She has some specialty recipes for votive and pillar candles and would like to put these online. Martha has requested that you add a left and right framed page to the CandleWix site. The navigation will be Flash buttons in the right frame. The recipe formulas will be displayed in the left frame. The right frame also will contain a link to the CandleWix home page. The framed Web site is shown in Figures 7-70a through 7-70c.

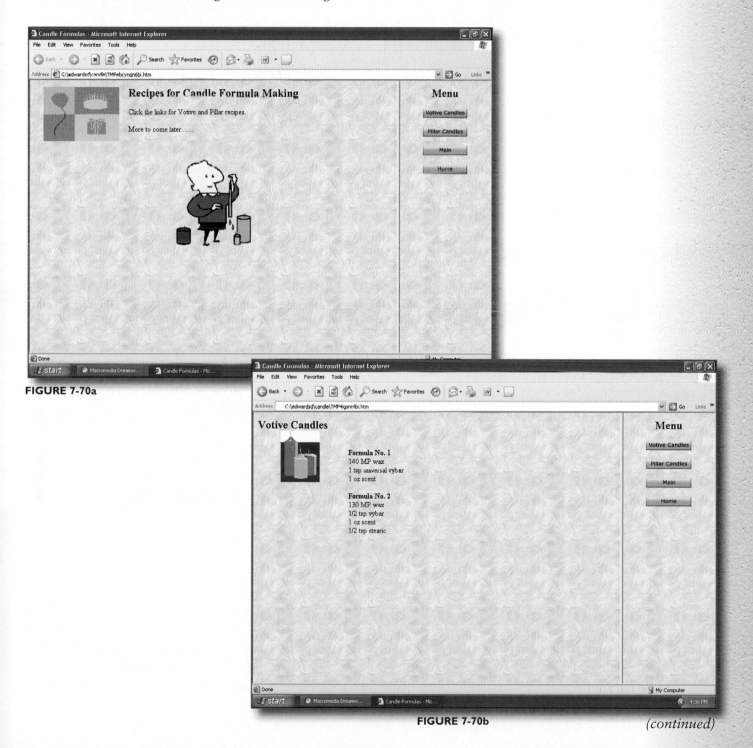

FIGURE 7-70a

FIGURE 7-70b

(continued)

In the Lab

Adding a Framed Web Page to CandleWix (continued)

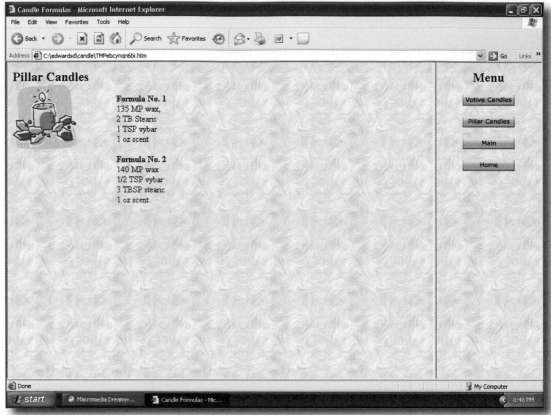

FIGURE 7-70c

Instructions: Perform the following tasks:

1. Use the Windows My Computer option to copy the images and the data files to your candle folder.
2. Start Dreamweaver. If necessary, display the panel groups. Select CandleWix from the Files pop-up menu in the Files panel.
3. Create a predefined frameset. Use the Fixed Right frameset. Add the title Candle Formulas to the frameset. Save the frameset as recipes.htm in the candle root folder.
4. Click the rightFrame and then save the frame as navigate.htm in the candle root folder. Add the candlebg.gif image as the background image. Add the title, Candle Formulas, to the frame.
5. Click the mainFrame and then save the frame as main.htm. Add the candlebg.gif as the background image. Title the frame Candle Formulas.
6. Click the mainFrame in the Frames panel.
7. Double-click main.htm in the Src box in the Property inspector, type content.htm as the entry, and then press the TAB key. If necessary, press the ENTER key when the Macromedia Dreamweaver dialog box is displayed.
8. Select the frameset in the Frames panel to display the Property inspector for the frameset. If necessary, click the second column tab. Type 20 as the value in the Column text box and then change the Units to Percent.
9. Click the rightFrame. Type Menu and then center the text. Apply Heading 2. Press the ENTER key.
10. Click Insert on the menu bar, point to Media, and then click Flash Button on the Media submenu. Select the Beveled Rect-bronze button.

11. Type Votive Candles as the button text. Select votive.htm as the link, mainFrame as the target, and then click the OK button.

12. Click to the right of the first button and then press the ENTER key. Repeat Step 10 to create another button.

13. Type Pillar Candles as the button text and then select pillar.htm as the link, mainFrame as the target, and then click the OK button.

14. Click to the right of the second button and then press the ENTER key. Repeat Step 10 to create another button.

15. Type Main as the button text and then select content.htm as the link, mainFrame as the target, and then click the OK button.

16. Click to the right of the third button and then press the ENTER key. Repeat Step 10 to create another button.

17. Type Home as the button text and then select index.htm as the link, _blank as the target, and then click the OK button.

18. Select the frameset in the Frames panel to display the Frameset Property inspector. Click the Borders pop-up menu and then select Yes. Type 3 as the border width and #CC9999 in the Border color hexadecimal box.

19. Click File on the menu bar and then click Save All.

20. Open the index.htm page. Click before the word Votive in the Votive bullet point, press the END key, and then press ENTER. Click the Unordered List button. Type Recipes and then create a link to recipes.htm. Change the target to _blank. Click the Save button.

21. Press the F12 key to view the index page and then click the Recipes link. Test each button. Print copies of each frame, if instructed to do so. Upload the Web site to a remote server, if instructed to do so.

2 Creating a Framed Layout for the Credit Protection Web Site

Problem: The Credit Protection Web site has become very popular. Monica recently received several e-mails asking for suggestions on how to spend money wisely. Monica asks you to create a new Web site with frames so she can share some of this information. The framed Web site is shown in Figures 7-71a through 7-71d on pages DW 620 and DW 621.

Instructions: Perform the following tasks:

1. Start Dreamweaver. If necessary, display the panel groups.

2. Create a new Web site. Name the Web site Credit Frames and then create a folder named credit_frames. The path will be C:\yourname\credit_frames\. Create a default images folder for the site. The path for the images will be C:\yourname\credit_frames\images\.

3. Use the Windows My Computer option to copy the data files to the credit_frames Web site.

4. Create a predefined frameset. Use the Fixed Left, Nested Top frameset. Title the frameset Spending Wisely. Save the frameset as index.htm in the credit_frames local root folder.

5. Click the topFrame. Apply the creditbg.jpg image as the background image and then type Spending Wisely as the title. Save the frame as title.htm. Create a one-row, two-column table in the title frame (topFrame). Drag title01.gif to the first column and title02.gif to the second column. Adjust the table size so the images display proportionally. Select the topFrame in the frames panel and then add a Margin height of 0. Save the title frame.

6. Click the mainFrame. Apply the same background to the mainFrame as you did to the title frame. Title the frame Spending Wisely and save the frame as main.htm.

7. Click the mainFrame in the Frames panel.

(continued)

Creating a Framed Layout for the Credit Protection Web Site *(continued)*

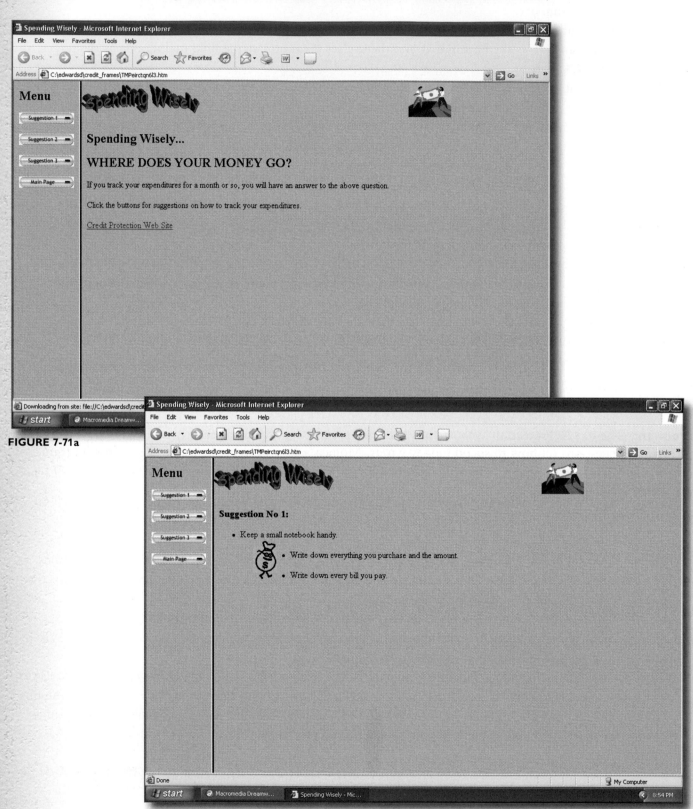

FIGURE 7-71a

FIGURE 7-71b

In the Lab

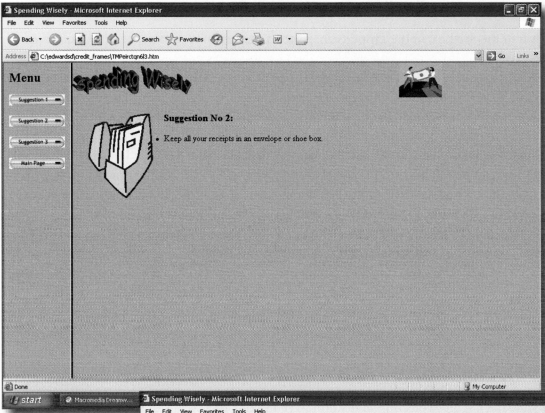

FIGURE 7-71c

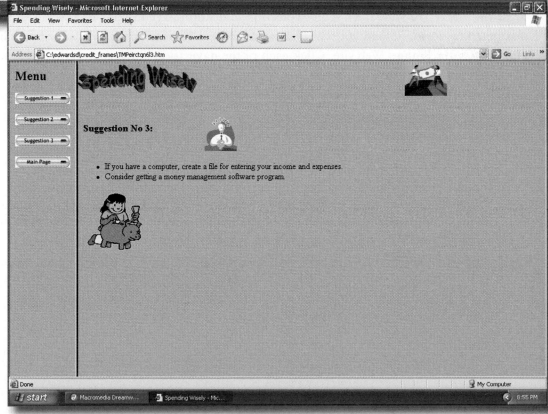

FIGURE 7-71d

(continued)

In the Lab

Creating a Framed Layout for the Credit Protection Web Site *(continued)*

8. Double-click main.htm in the Src box in the Property inspector, type content.htm as the entry, and then click the Save button.

9. Click the leftFrame. Apply the same background to the leftFrame as you did to the topFrame and mainFrame. Title the frame Spending Wisely. Save the frame as navigate.htm.

10. Type Menu at the top of the leftFrame, and apply Heading 2. Press the ENTER key. Add four Flash buttons. The text for the first Flash button is Suggestion 1; for the second, Suggestion 2; for the third, Suggestion 3; and for the fourth, Main Page. Use the Chrome Bar button with a font size of 10. The links for buttons 1, 2, and 3 are money01.htm, money02.htm, and money03.htm, respectively. The link for the Main Page button is content.htm. The target for all four buttons is the mainFrame. Adjust the width of the leftFrame to accommodate the button size and then press CTRL+S to save the frame.

11. Add a three-pixel border to the frameset. Use hexadecimal #330000 for the border color. Click File on the menu bar and then click Save All. If instructed to do so, upload your Web site to a remote server.

12. Open the Credit Protection Web site, open the index.htm page, and then scroll to the bottom of the page. Click to the right of the Credit Information link, press the SHIFT+ENTER keys, and then type Spending Wisely as the entry. Create an absolute link from the text, Spending Wisely, to the index.htm file in the Credit Frames Web site. Set the Target to _blank. If you are publishing to a remote site, copy and paste the Credit Frames Web site address into the Link box. If you are saving your work to a local computer or server, use the Browse for File icon in the Property inspector to create the link path. Click the Save button on the Standard toolbar.

13. Press the F12 key to view the Credit Protection index.htm page in your browser. Test each button and link. If instructed to do so, upload your Web site changes to a remote server. Click the Spending Wisely link to display the Credit Frames Web site. Click each of the navigation buttons to verify that they work. Print copies of each frame, if instructed to do so.

3 Adding a Framed Page to the Lexington, NC Web Site

Problem: The mayor has requested that John Davis further enhance the Lexington, NC Web site and has suggested that an employment section be added. John agrees that this is an excellent idea and meets with you to discuss this new addition. You suggest that a framed-based section be added to the main Web site. John supports the idea and provides you with the information to begin creating the site. The Web site is displayed in Figures 7-72a through 7-72d on pages DW 623 and DW 624.

In the Lab

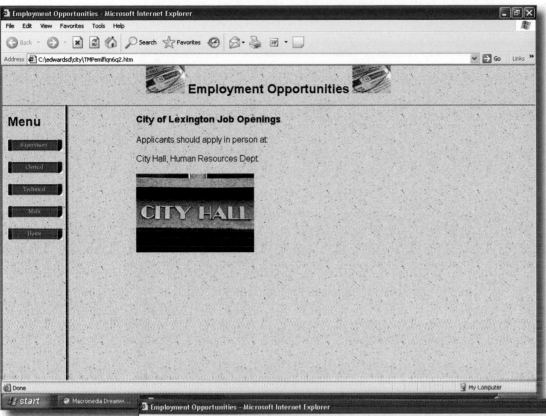

FIGURE 7-72a

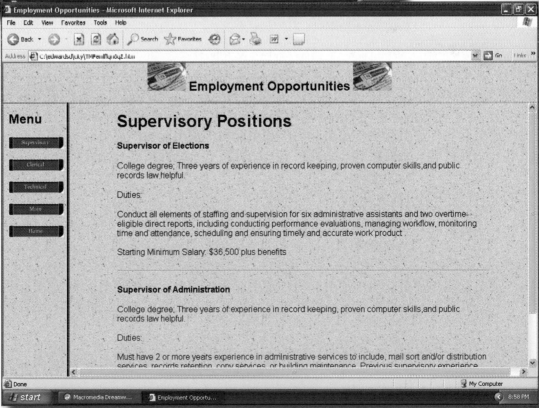

FIGURE 7-72b

(continued)

Adding a Framed Page to the Lexington, NC Web Site *(continued)*

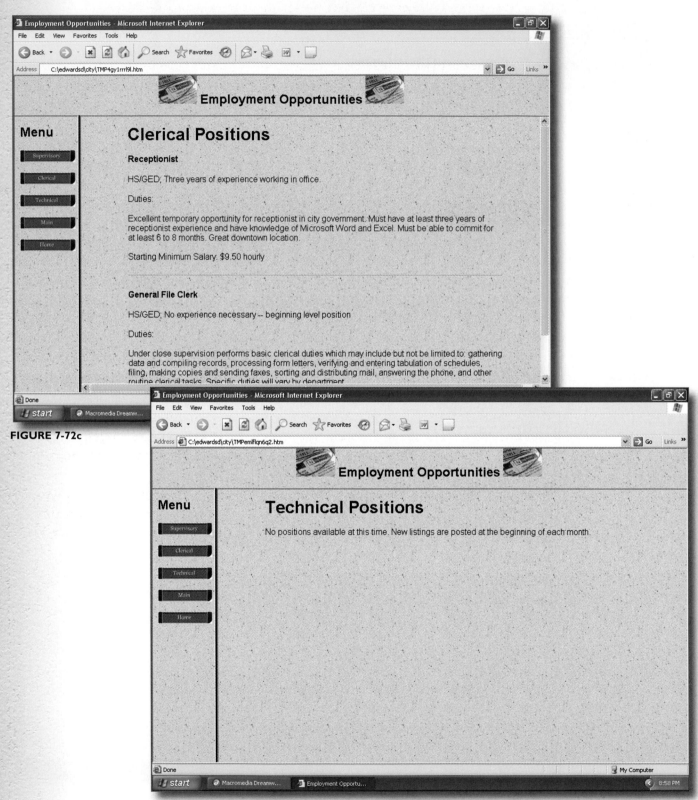

FIGURE 7-72c

FIGURE 7-72d

In the Lab

Instructions: Perform the following tasks:

1. Use the Windows My Computer option to copy the data files to the C:\yourname\city folder.

2. Start Dreamweaver. If necessary, display the panel groups. Select Lexington, NC in the Files pop-up menu in the Files panel.

3. Create a predefined frameset. Use the Fixed Top, Nested Left frameset. Type Employment Opportunities in the Title text box on the Document toolbar. Save the frameset as employment.htm in the city local root folder.

4. Click the topFrame. Click the Align Center button in the Property inspector. Drag the help_wanted.gif image to the insertion point. Click to the right of the image and press the SPACEBAR. Type Employment Opportunities, apply Heading 2 as the style, and change the font to Arial, Helvetica, sans-serif. Click to the right of the heading, press the SPACEBAR, and then drag the help_wanted.gif to the insertion point. Select the topFrame and then add a margin height of 0. Apply the citybg.gif background image. Save the topFrame as title.htm.

5. Click the mainFrame. Add the citybg.gif background image to the mainFrame. Save the frame as main.htm.

6. Click the mainFrame in the Frames panel.

7. Drag content.htm to the Src box. Click the File menu and then click Save Frameset.

8. Click the leftFrame. Type Menu at the top of the leftFrame, apply Heading 2, and change the font to Arial, Helvetica, sans-serif. Press the ENTER key. Add the citybg.gif image to the background. Save the frame as navigate.htm.

9. Add five Flash buttons to the leftFrame. The text for the first Flash button is Supervisory; for the second, Clerical; for the third, Technical; for the fourth, Main; and for the fifth, Home. Use the Corporate-Orange button with a font size of 10. The document links for the first three buttons have the same names as the buttons (supervisory.htm, etc.). The document link for the Main button is content.htm. The target for all buttons, except the Home button, is the mainFrame. The link for the Home button is index.htm, and the target is _blank. Adjust the width and height of the frames to accommodate the text and images.

10. Select the nested frameset and then apply a three-pixel black border. Click File on the menu bar and then click Save All.

11. Open the index.htm page. Scroll to the bottom of the page and then click to the right of the last list item. Press the ENTER key, click the Ordered List button in the Property inspector, and then type Employment Opportunities. Create a relative link to employment.htm. Select _blank in the Target pop-up menu. Click the Save button.

12. Press the F12 key to view the Web site in your browser. Click the Employment Opportunities link. Test each button. Print copies of each frame, if instructed to do so. If instructed to do so, upload your Web site changes to a remote server.

Cases and Places

The difficulty of these case studies varies:
■ are the least difficult and ■■ are the most difficult. The last exercise is a group exercise.

1 ■ Your sports Web site has become very popular. You have decided to add two pages showing uniform types for football and baseball. To show these, you will use a right and left frame. The left frame will contain the links. When the user clicks the link, a picture of the uniform type will be displayed in the right frame. Add a background image to the pages and add a title to each page. Create a link to the home page. Save the page in your sports Web site. For a selection of images and backgrounds, visit the Dreamweaver 8 Media Web page (scsite.com/dw8/media) and then click Media below Project 7.

2 ■ Modify your hobby Web site by adding a two-framed Web page. The left frame should contain three navigation links. Use buttons or text. The first link loads general information about your hobby into the content frame. The second link loads a page with an introductory paragraph and a minimum of three links to other related Web sites. The third link displays the index page in a separate window. Create a link to your home page. Add a four-pixel border to the frame. Upload the Web site changes to a remote site, if instructed to do so. For a selection of images and backgrounds, visit the Dreamweaver 8 Media Web page (scsite.com/dw8/media) and then click Media below Project 7.

3 ■ Create a new site for your music hobby. Name the site music_frames. Select one of the predefined framesets. Add three pages of content and a title graphic. Use buttons or text in the navigate_frame to access and display the content pages in the main frame. Name your frames and framesets and add titles to all frames. Add a background to all frames. Upload the entire Web site to a remote site. For a selection of images and backgrounds, visit the Dreamweaver 8 Media Web page (scsite.com/dw8/media) and then click Media below Project 7.

4 ■■ Your campaign for political office is very successful. Create a new Web site and name it office_frames. Use a predefined frameset. Create three content pages with information highlighting at least three major accomplishments over the past 12 months. Create a static title frame and add your logo to this frame. Create a navigate_frame using Flash buttons — one of each for the content pages. Add a three-pixel border to the frame. Upload the framed Web site to a remote server. For a selection of images and backgrounds, visit the Dreamweaver 8 Media Web page (scsite.com/dw8/media) and then click Media below Project 7.

5 ■■ **Working Together** The student trips Web site is receiving hundreds of hits each day, and the student government officers have selected three possible sites to visit. Create a trip_frames Web site using a predefined frameset. Create four content pages: one with general information and the other three highlighting the three possible student trip locations. Include at least one image on each of the content pages. Create a static title frame and a navigate_frame. Add a background image to all frames. Create a link to the home page to break out of the framed Web site. Upload the framed Web site to a remote server. For a selection of images and backgrounds, visit the Dreamweaver 8 Media Web page (scsite.com/dw8/media) and then click Media below Project 7.

Animation and Behaviors

CASE PERSPECTIVE

Adding interactivity to Web pages makes visiting and surfing Web sites interesting. David thinks it would be a good idea to add some animation to the Colorado Parks Web site. Now that he understands how to use layers and behaviors, he wants to add animation using these Dreamweaver features. He comes to you for help in utilizing these more advanced concepts. You explain that Dreamweaver provides the capability of adding animation by using layers through the Timelines panel.

The next decision is where within the Web site to add the animation and what will be the focus of the animated page. Tracy suggests that this be a project similar to the spotlight page previously added to the site. Instead of a static page, however, this Web page will contain a slide show where the viewer controls the display of images of various state parks. Tracy further suggests adding another page to the site. The second page will contain a map focused on the state and include the names and locations of the parks and other attractions. The map will contain an image such as a motor home that will move across the state from park to park and/or attraction. Everyone on the team agrees that both of these pages will be a great addition to the site.

As you read through this project, you will learn about timelines and how to use timelines to create linear and nonlinear animations. You also will learn to control timelines by applying different behaviors.

Animation and Behaviors

Objectives

You will have mastered the material in this project when you can:

- Describe a timeline
- Describe the Timelines panel
- Create a nonlinear timeline
- Add a behavior to a layer
- Add a play button to a timeline

- Create a linear timeline
- Add a layer to a timeline
- Show and hide a layer
- Play an animation

Introduction

In Project 6, you applied some simple animation techniques when you learned about layers and behaviors and how to show and hide layers. Project 8 continues with the layer feature and introduces the integration of layers and timelines using the Dreamweaver Timelines panel. You can use timelines in three ways:

- To alter a layer's position, size, visibility, and depth
- To apply Dreamweaver's JavaScript behaviors
- To change the source for any image and replace it with another

Using this feature, the layers and images can be manipulated over time. Thus, adding layers and applying behaviors to the layers within a timeline provide the Web site designer with the ability to add interactivity and animation to a Web site.

A timeline is similar to a strip of movie film. Just like movies, animation requires movement and time. A timeline is made up of frames. Each frame represents a moment in time, similar to that in a movie or video. A collection of frames makes a timeline. The Web site developer also can control the speed of the timeline, or how fast the frames play. The default is 15 **fps**, or frames per second. If you decrease the number of fps, the animation takes longer to play; increase the number of fps and the animation plays faster.

Because timelines depend on layers, they require version 4 or later browsers. In addition, some features work only in Microsoft Internet Explorer. Layers and images are the only items that can be added to a Dreamweaver timeline, and only layers can be positioned. Using the timeline feature to add animation is a valuable tool that captures the interest of Web site visitors.

Project Eight — Creating Timeline Animation

In this project, you learn how to use Dreamweaver's Timelines panel and how to add animation to the Colorado Parks Web site. You begin the project by adding a new page to the Web site and then adding a layer containing a map of Colorado (Figure 8-1a). A second layer then is added to the page, and an image of a motor home is embedded in the layer. Clicking a Forward button on the page moves the motor home image over the map from one park location to another. This animation is created by dragging the image to create a nonlinear **animation path**. Dreamweaver automatically records the path, but does not record the timing of the drag operation. You specify these movements through the Timelines panel. Therefore, when you are creating the animation path, you can take your time to make sure that the path is what you want.

The second page added to the Web site is a slide show presentation (Figure 8-1b). The Web site visitor controls the display of the slide show by clicking a Start button. The six slides within the slide show display a variety of Rocky Mountain wildflowers. You create this second animation using a linear, or straight-line, animation technique.

Exercises in this project use **active content**, which is content in a Web page that is interactive or dynamic. This type of content can be a security risk. In Windows XP SP2, Microsoft introduced a set of security technologies for protection from viruses and worms. When previewing a file, before Internet Explorer runs active content, the Information Bar is displayed, informing users about the potential security risk of running active content. Macromedia has worked with Microsoft to ensure security within Macromedia Flash, Shockwave, and Authorware Players, so users can acknowledge the warning and run content by clicking through the Information Bar prompts. If your computer uses a different operating system or does not use SP2, the Information Bar will not display.

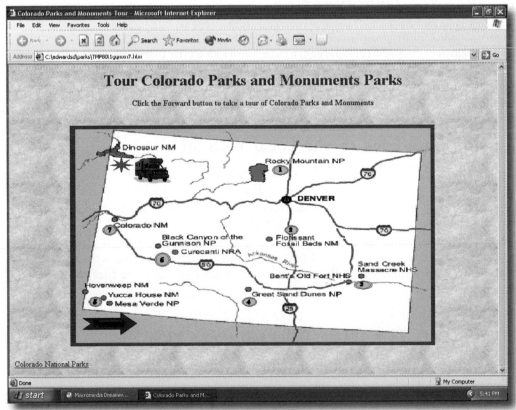

FIGURE 8-1a

FIGURE 8-1b

Workspace Organization

Organization and preparation lead to a more productive work setting. Successful Web developers prepare their Dreamweaver workspace to provide an effective work environment. As you learn to use additional Dreamweaver tools, including timelines and behaviors, you will become even more proficient working in the Dreamweaver environment.

Copying Data Files to the Local Web Site

Your Data Disk contains data files and images for Project 8. You use the Windows My Computer option to copy the Project 8 files to your parks folder. See the inside back cover for instructions for downloading the Data Disk, or see your instructor for information about accessing the files required for this book.

The DataFiles folder for this project is stored on Local Disk (C:). The location on your computer may be different. If necessary, verify with your instructor the location of the DataFiles folder. The following steps show how to copy the files to the parks local root folder.

To Copy Data Files to the Colorado Parks Web Site

1 Click the Start button on the Windows taskbar and then click My Computer.

2 Double-click Local Disk (C:) and then navigate to the location of the data files for Project 8.

3 Double-click the DataFiles folder and then double-click the Proj08 folder.

4 Double-click the parks folder and then double-click the images folder.

5 Click the first image file in the list, hold down the SHIFT key, and then click the last image file in the list.

6 Right-click the selected files to display the context menu.

7 Click the Copy command and then click the My Computer Back button the number of times necessary to navigate back to the your name folder.

8 Double-click the your name folder, double-click the parks folder, and then double-click the images folder.

9 Right-click in the open window to display the context menu.

10 Click the Paste command to paste the image files into the images folder.

11 Click the My Computer Back button the number of times necessary to return to the parks DataFiles folder. Hold down the SHIFT key and then select the two data files. Right-click to display the context menu, and then click the Copy command.

12 Click the My Computer Back button and navigate to the your name folder.

13 Paste the data files into the parks folder.

14 Click the Close button.

Starting Dreamweaver and Closing Open Panels

Each time you start Dreamweaver, it opens to the last site that was displayed when you closed the program. Therefore, it may be necessary for you to open the Colorado Parks Web site. The **Files pop-up menu** in the Files panel lists sites you have defined. When you open the site, a list of pages and subfolders within that site are displayed. The following steps illustrate how to start Dreamweaver and open the Colorado Parks Web site.

To Start Dreamweaver and Open the Colorado Parks Web Site

1 Click the Start button on the Windows taskbar.

2 Point to All Programs on the Start menu, point to Macromedia on the All Programs submenu, and then click Macromedia Dreamweaver 8 on the Macromedia submenu.

3 Click the Files panel box arrow on the Files pop-up menu, and then click Colorado Parks.

Dreamweaver opens, and the Colorado Parks Web site hierarchy is displayed in the Files panel (Figure 8-2 on the next page).

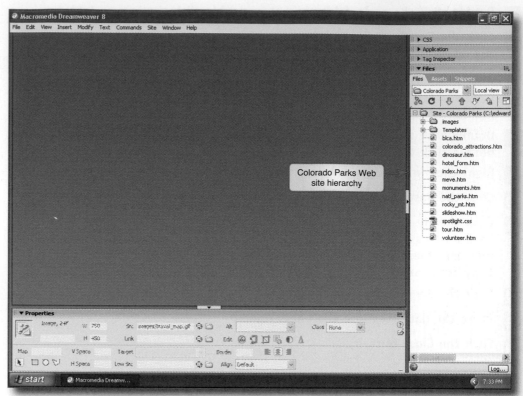

FIGURE 8-2

Preparing the Web Page

Creating an animation in Dreamweaver requires some Document window preparation before you create the actual animation. To prepare the Web page requires that you add images and a layer.

To begin the preparation for the tour.htm page, you first add a map of Colorado. The map contains the name and location of each park and monument. The starting point is marked with a star and numbered circles are included as a guideline for creating a nonlinear animation path. Creating the animation path is discussed later in this project. Animations are built around images and layers. Creating this animation requires that you add a layer for the map and then add a second layer that will contain an image of a motor home. The second layer that contains the motor home image moves along the map from attraction to attraction.

To Add the Colorado Map Image and Layer

1

• **Double-click tour.htm in the Files panel. If necessary, click below the introductory paragraph. If necessary, close the Insert bar and display the Property inspector.**

• **Click Insert on the menu bar, point to Layout Objects, and then click Layer.**

• **Click the layer selection handle and type the following properties: Layer ID,** map**; L,** 125px**; and T,** 125px.

• **Press F2 to display the Layers panel.**

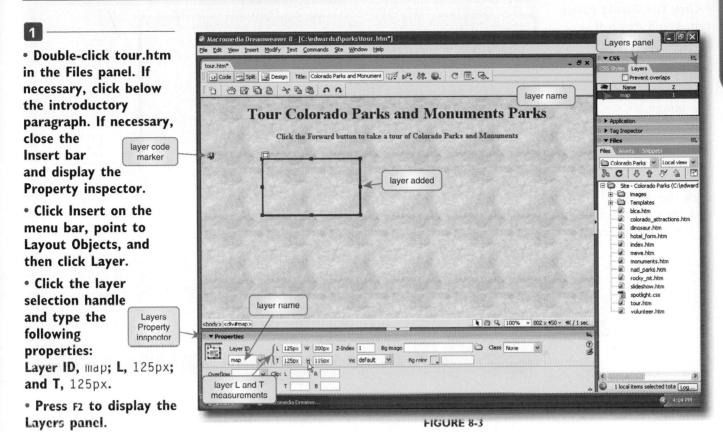

FIGURE 8-3

The tour.htm page is displayed in the Document window, the layer is displayed on the page below the introductory paragraph, and the Layers panel is displayed (Figure 8-3).

2

• **Click the Assets panel tab, scroll down if necessary, and then drag the travel_map.gif image onto the layer. If necessary, select the image.**

• **Click the Image ID box in the Property inspector and type** travel_map. **Then click the Alt box and type** Colorado Map **as the alternate text.**

The travel_map.gif image is displayed on the layer and is selected. The Property inspector for images is displayed. The Image ID box contains the image name and the Alt box contains the text, Colorado Map (Figure 8-4). If the travel_map.gif image does not appear in the Assets panel, click the Files panel tab, and then click the Refresh button.

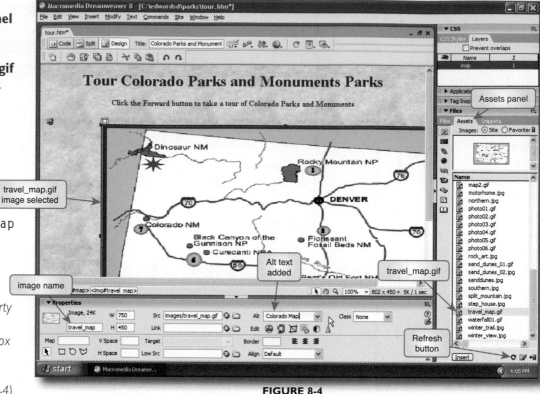

FIGURE 8-4

3

• **Click anywhere on the Web page background to deselect the image and/or layer.**

• **Click Insert on the menu bar, point to Layout Objects, and then click Layer. If necessary, use the Document window horizontal and vertical scroll bars to display the layer.**

A second layer is added to the Document window, and Layer2 is displayed in the Layers panel (Figure 8-5). Your layer may have a different number.

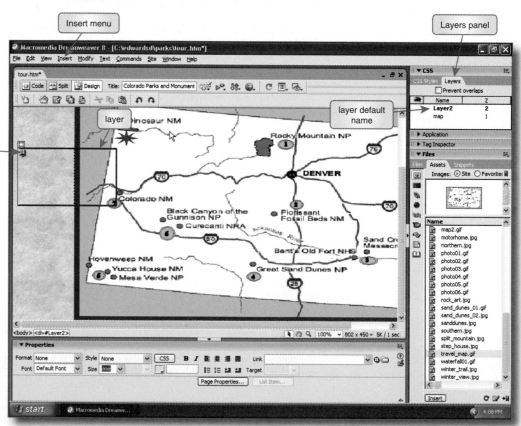

FIGURE 8-5

4

• **Select the layer.**

• **Click the Layer ID name in the Layers panel. Type** motorhome **as the layer name and then press the ENTER key.**

The layer is named motorhome, and the layer is selected (Figure 8-6).

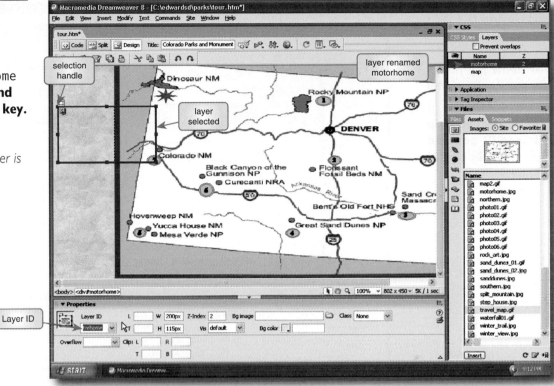

FIGURE 8-6

5

• **Click the motorhome layer selection handle and then drag the layer so it is near the star on the map.**

The motorhome layer is displayed on the map (Figure 8-7).

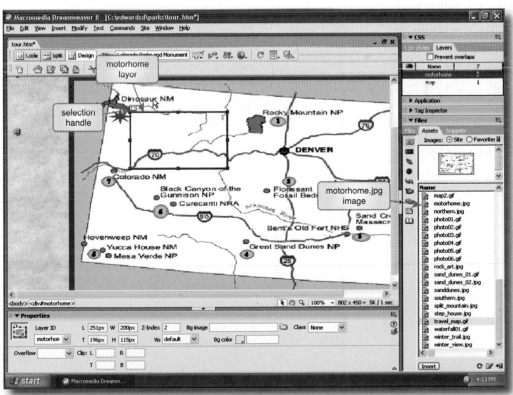

FIGURE 8-7

6

• **Click inside the motorhome layer and then drag the motorhome.jpg image from the Assets panel onto the layer.**

• **Type** motor_home **in the Image ID box and** Motor Home **in the Alt text box.**

The motorhome.jpg image is displayed in the layer (Figure 8-8).

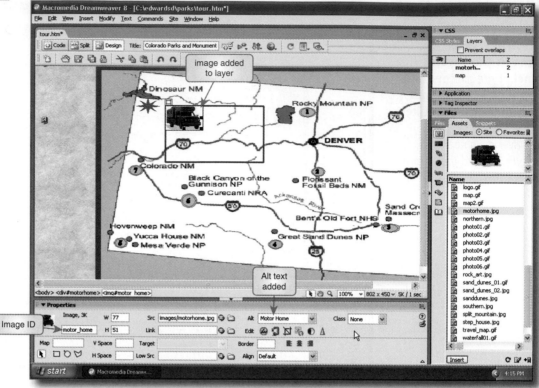

FIGURE 8-8

7

• **Click the expander arrow to collapse the panel groups.**

• **Select the motorhome layer, click a resize handle, and then resize the layer to fit the motorhome.jpg image.**

• **If necessary, click the layer selection handle and adjust the layer so that it is in close proximity to the star starting point.**

The panel groups are collapsed, and the layer is resized and placed close to the star starting point (Figure 8-9).

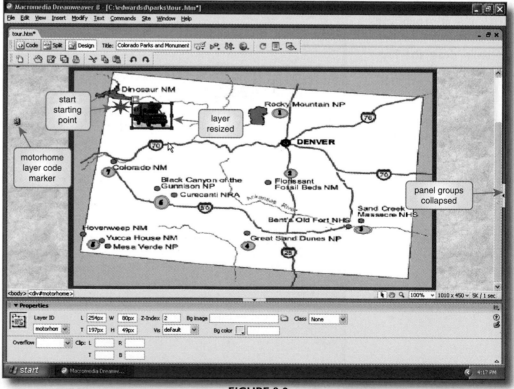

FIGURE 8-9

Other Ways

1. On Window menu, click Insert, click Draw Layer button on Layout category

Introduction to Timelines

Timelines use dynamic HTML (DHTML) to change the position of a layer or the source of an image over time, or to call behavior actions automatically after the page has loaded. (See page DW 426 for a detailed discussion of DHTML.) The timeline is the critical component for creating animation on a Web page. This Dreamweaver feature lets the Web site developer create animations that do not require plug-ins, ActiveX controls, or Java applets. As the Web site developer, you can choose to control the animation or you can add controls that let the Web site visitor control the animation.

More About

Timelines

To display a list of commands that can be applied to timelines, click the Timelines panel menu pop-up menu. For more information about timelines, visit the Dreamweaver 8 More About Web page (scsite.com/dw8/more.htm) and then click Timelines.

Timeline Features

A timeline is composed of a series of frames. A **frame** is one cell or one point of time in a timeline. The total number of frames in the timeline determines the length of the presentation. You can create multiple animations on a Web page. The animations all can be contained within one timeline or spread out over several timelines. A single timeline can contain up to 32 individual layers.

As you create the animation, Dreamweaver converts the timeline commands into JavaScript and thereby creates the animation. Layers and images are the only objects that can be added to a timeline. Anything you add to a layer, however, can be animated, whether it is text, images, forms, tables, or other objects. A basic animation moves from one point on the timeline to another. Any animation created in the timeline must have a start point and a stop point. These start and stop points are marked on the timeline by small circles and are called **keyframes**. Keyframes are discussed in more detail throughout this project.

The Timelines Panel

The Web site developer uses the Timelines panel to create animation. The Timelines panel resembles a spreadsheet somewhat, showing units of time as columns and animated objects as rows. Figure 8-10a shows an overall view of the Timelines panel, and Figure 8-10b shows a view of the playback options and command buttons for viewing an animation.

The following section describes the Timelines panel (Figure 8-10a).

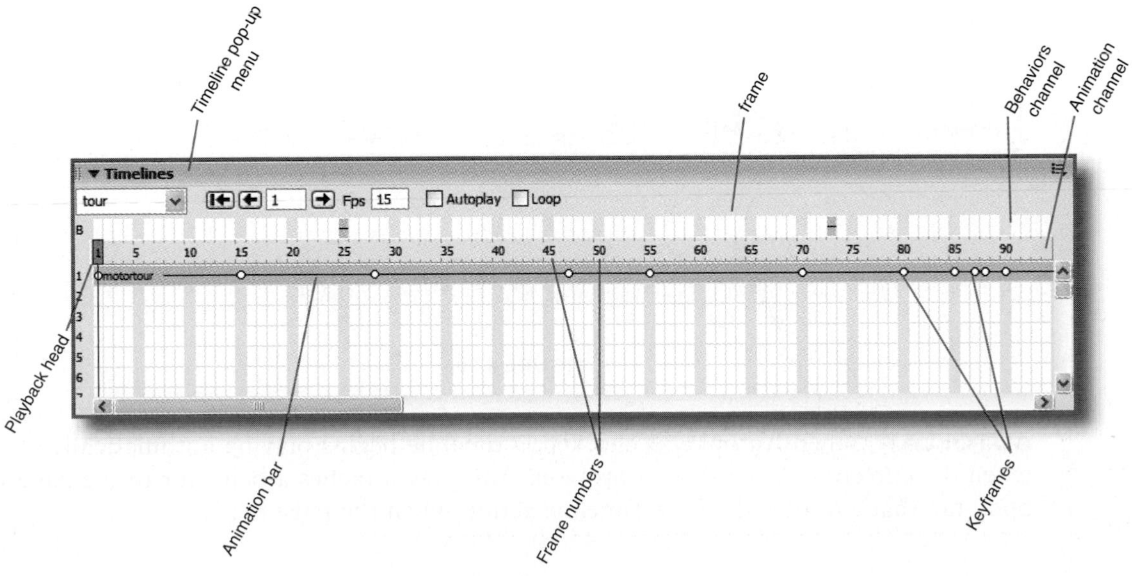

FIGURE 8-10a

ANIMATION BAR The animation bar shows the duration of each object's animation. A single row can include multiple bars representing different objects. Different bars cannot control the same object in the same frame.

ANIMATION CHANNEL The Animation channel contains the bars for animating layers and images.

BEHAVIORS CHANNEL The Behaviors channel executes behaviors along a channel at a particular frame in the timeline.

FRAME A frame is one cell or one point of time in a timeline. The total number of frames in the timeline determines the length of the presentation.

FRAME NUMBERS The frame numbers indicate the sequential numbering of frames. The number between the Back and Play buttons is the current frame number. The Web site developer controls the duration of an animation by setting the total number of frames and the number of frames per second (fps). The default setting is 15 fps.

KEYFRAME A keyframe contains specific properties (such as position) for an object; small circles indicate keyframes.

PLAYBACK HEAD The playback head indicates which frame of the timeline currently is displayed in the Document window.

TIMELINE POP-UP MENU The Timeline pop-up menu contains the names of a document's recent timelines. The Timeline pop-up menu text box contains the name of the document's timeline currently selected and displayed in the Timelines panel.

    The timeline contains several playback options and command buttons. You can use the command buttons to preview and control an animation in the Document window. The following section describes the playback options and command buttons (Figure 8-10b) within the Timelines panel. The buttons are similar to the controls on a DVR.

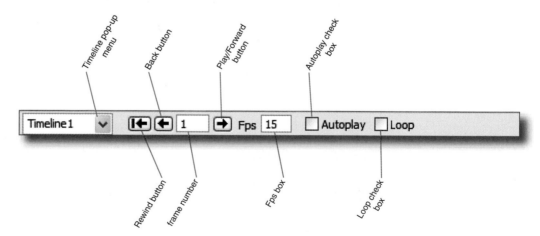

FIGURE 8-10b

AUTOPLAY When Autoplay is checked, a timeline begins playing automatically when the current page loads in a browser. Autoplay attaches a behavior to the page's body tag that executes the Play Timeline action when the page loads.

BACK The Back button moves the playback head one frame to the left. You can play the timeline backward by clicking the Back button and holding down the mouse button.

LOOP When the Loop check box is selected, the current timeline loops indefinitely while the page is open in a browser. Loop inserts the Go to Timeline Frame behavior in the Behaviors channel after the last frame of the animation.

PLAY/FORWARD The Play/Forward button moves the playback head one frame to the right. You can play the timeline forward by clicking the Play button and holding down the mouse button.

REWIND The Rewind button moves the playback head to the first frame in the timeline.

Nonlinear Animations

The most common kind of timeline animation involves moving a layer along a path. Using layers and the Timelines panel, you can create linear, or straight-line, animations and nonlinear animations. A **nonlinear animation** is one that does not follow a straight path. Creating a linear, or straight-line, animation is discussed later in this project.

To create a layer with a complex path for a nonlinear animation, it is easier to drag the layer rather than to create individual keyframes. Earlier in this project, you added a Colorado map image to the tour.htm Web page, added a layer, added an image to the layer, and then resized the layer. The object of the animation is to create a path where the motorhome image moves across the Colorado map to the various parks and monuments and then returns to its original position. The numbered circles are used as guidelines for this animated movement.

To create this animation, you drag the layer containing the motorhome image. This is a freeform exercise, so the path on which you drag the image will vary somewhat from the path shown in Figures 8-15a through 8-15c on DW 642-643.

The following steps show how to add the nonlinear animation path to the tour.htm Web page. As you are creating this animation, you may find it necessary to expand and collapse the Timelines panel and the panel groups to provide maximum Document window visibility. You also may find that at times you will have to scroll horizontally and vertically within the Document window to redisplay the motorhome image. When you are dragging this image, a thin gray line will indicate the path you are creating. Recall that Dreamweaver automatically records the path, but does not record the timing of the drag operation. You control the timing through the Timelines panel.

To Create a Nonlinear Animation

1

• **Press ALT+F9 to display the Timelines panel. If necessary, expand the Timelines panel.**

• **Close the Property inspector.**

The Timelines panel is displayed and the Property inspector is closed (Figure 8-11). (The Timelines panel also is available through the Windows menu.)

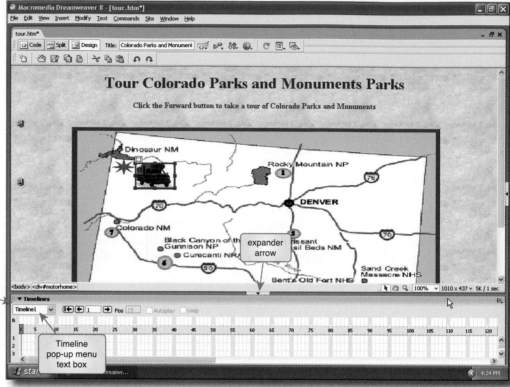

FIGURE 8-11

2

• **Double-click the Timeline pop-up menu text box.**

3

• **Type** tour **as the timeline name and then press the TAB key.**

The timeline is renamed tour (Figure 8-12).

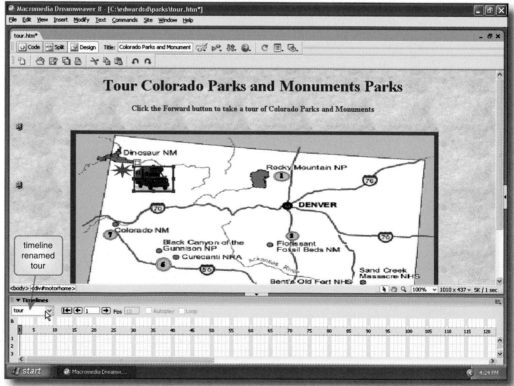

FIGURE 8-12

4

• **If necessary, adjust the vertical scroll placement to display the map.**

• **If necessary, select the motorhome layer (not the image) or click the motorhome layer selection handle in the Document window and then right-click the selected motorhome layer or motorhome selection handle.**

• **Point to Record Path on the context menu.**

The motorhome layer is selected, and the context menu is displayed (Figure 8-13).

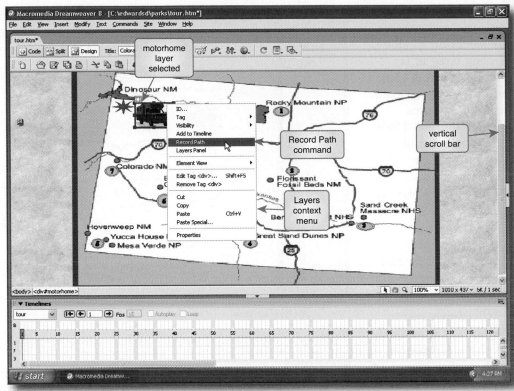

FIGURE 8-13

5

• **Click Record Path.**

The motorhome layer is selected, and the Record Path command is active (Figure 8-14). Frame 1 is selected in the playback head.

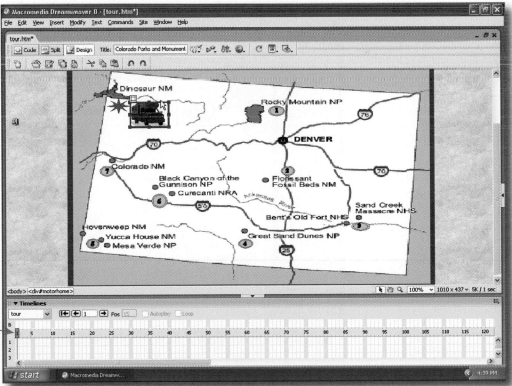

FIGURE 8-14

6

• **Click the motorhome layer selection handle and then drag it to circle 1 (Figure 8-15a); then down to circle 2 and right again to circle 3 (Figure 8-15b); left to circle 4 and down and left to circle 5; up and to the right to circle 6; left to circle 7 (Figure 8-15c); and then up to the starting point star (Figure 8-15d). Do not release the mouse button while dragging.**

• **If a Dreamweaver dialog box is displayed, read the information and then click the OK button.**

A timeline has been added to the Animation channel in the Timelines panel. Figure 8-15a shows the motorhome layer and the line created as the layer was dragged to the first stop. Figure 8-15b shows the motorhome after it is dragged to circle 3. Figure 8-15c on DW 643 shows the motorhome after is dragged to circle 5. Figure 8-15d is for illustration purposes only and displays all the stops along the route. The path on which the motorhome is dragged is freeform; your line will not be identical to the one shown here.

If you need to start over, return the playback head to frame 1.

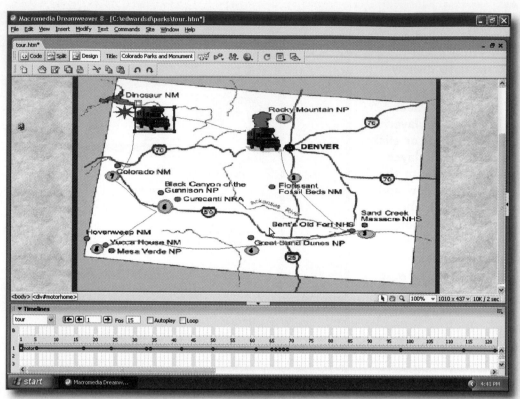

FIGURE 8-15a

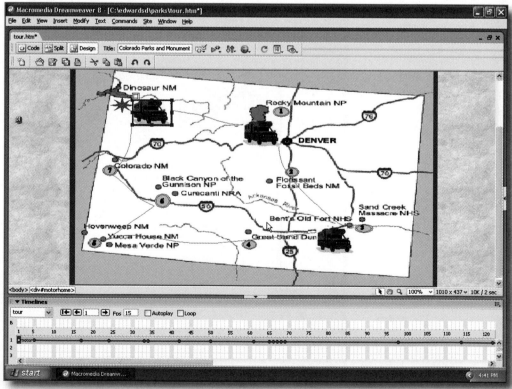

FIGURE 8-15b

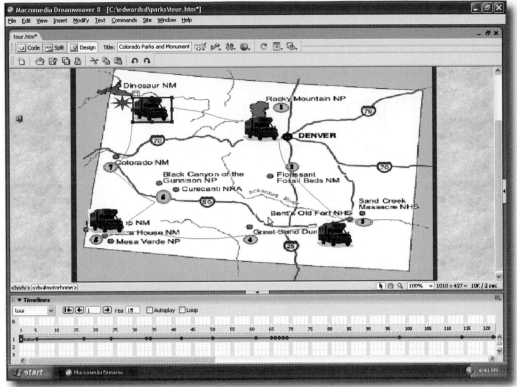

FIGURE 8-15c

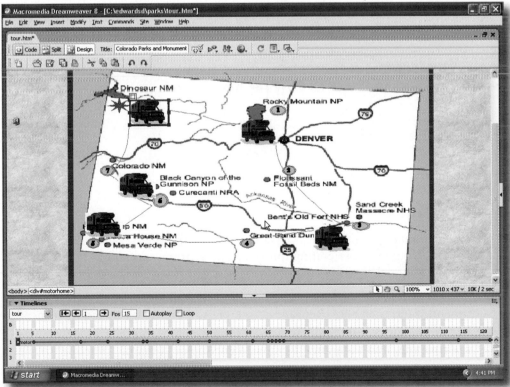

FIGURE 8-15d

7

• **Click the Autoplay check box in the Timelines panel.**

• **Drag the horizontal scrollbar to the right to view the rest of the timeline.**

• **If a Dreamweaver dialog box is displayed, read the information, and then click the OK button.**

Notice that the timeline extends beyond the screen and is selected in the Animation channel. Several keyframes are shown on the timeline. These keyframes are added when you hesitate or drag the timeline in a nonlinear line. The timeline on your screen will be somewhat different from the one shown here, and the keyframes will be in different frames.

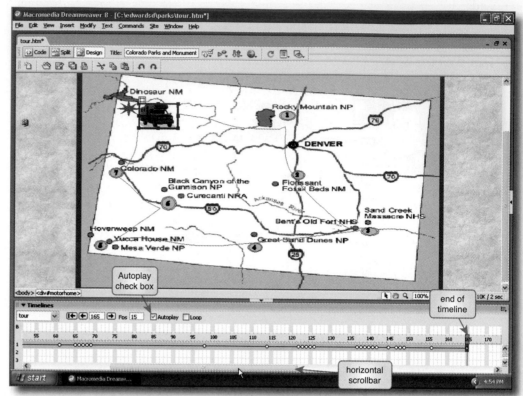

FIGURE 8-16

8

• **Click the Save button on the Standard toolbar.**

• **Press the F12 key to view the animation in your browser. Close the browser and return to Dreamweaver.**

The motorhome image travels across the map and returns to its original position.

Editing a Timeline

As you are creating a timeline, occasionally you will need to edit different features. The following provides editing information for frames, timelines, behaviors, and animation channels:

- To add or remove a frame in the timeline, click the frame, right-click the timeline, and then click Remove Frame or Add Frame on the context menu.
- To remove or rename a timeline, click the timeline to select it, right-click the timeline, and then click Remove Timeline or Rename Timeline on the context menu.
- To remove a behavior from the Timelines panel, right-click the behavior in the Behaviors channel and then click Remove Behavior on the context menu.
- To remove a keyframe, select the keyframe, right-click the keyframe, and select Remove Keyframe on the context menu.
- To remove an Animation channel, select it in the Timelines panel, right-click the Animation channel, and then click Delete on the context menu.

In addition to using the context menu, you also can select the object in the timeline, and then click the Timelines Options pop-up menu.

Adding Behaviors to the Timeline

In Project 6, you learned about behaviors and how to add behaviors to show and hide objects. These behaviors are ready-to-use Dreamweaver-created JavaScript functions. The available functions vary based on the selected object. You also can add behaviors to your timelines. Examples of behaviors you can add to a timeline include playing sound, showing pop-up messages, showing and hiding layers, starting and stopping timelines, and other events. For example, to add a pop-up message, select the object, click the Add behavior (+) button in the Behaviors panel, and then click Popup Message. Type the message in the Popup Message dialog box and then click the OK button.

The steps show how to add Stop Timeline behaviors to the tour timeline. You add a Stop Timeline behavior at each of the seven circles listed in the previous steps. Keep in mind that this is a freeform exercise and that the frame numbers in the Timelines panel in the following figures most likely will not match those on your screen.

To Add the Stop Timeline Behavior

1

• **Drag the horizontal scrollbar to the left to display frame 1.**

• **If necessary, click the motorhome layer to display the selection handle.**

• **Click a frame in the Animation channel that moves the motorhome layer close to circle 1. In Figure 8-17, this is frame 30, but your frame number may be different.**

• **Use the Document window vertical scroll bar as necessary to reposition the image so the motorhome layer is displayed.**

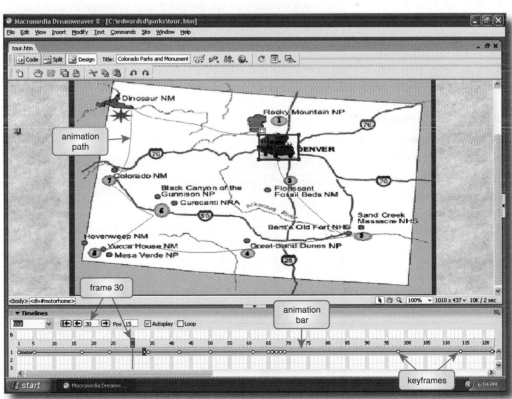

FIGURE 8-17

The motorhome layer moves based on the selected frame number and is positioned in close proximity to circle 1. The playback head is in frame 30 in the Animation channel (Figure 8-17). The location of the motorhome layer and the frame number on your screen most likely will be different.

2

• Press **SHIFT+F4** to display the Behaviors panel. If necessary, collapse the Files panel and move the mouse pointer over the Tag title bar and drag to increase the height of the Behaviors panel

• Point to the frame number in the timeline Behaviors channel that is the same number as the one in the Animation channel on your screen. In Figure 8-19, this is frame 30. Most likely the frame number on your screen will be a different number.

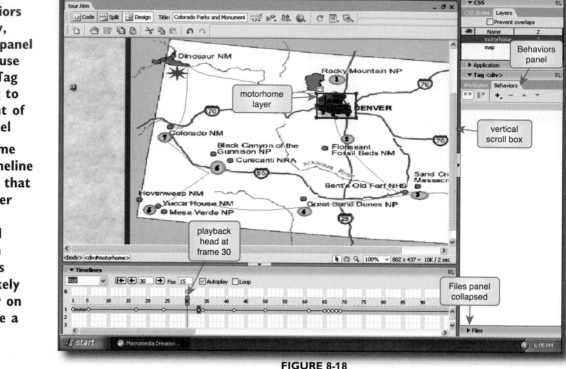

FIGURE 8-18

The panel groups are expanded, and the Behaviors panel is displayed (Figure 8-18). When expanding and collapsing panels, it may appear that the motorhome layer changes positions. Recall, however, that a layer enables absolute positioning of objects and elements on a page. When the panel groups are collapsed, the motorhome layer will return to its correct position.

3

• Click your selected frame in the Behaviors channel and then point to the Add behavior (+) button in the Behaviors panel.

Frame 30 is selected in the Behaviors channel (Figure 8-19). Most likely the frame number on your screen will be different.

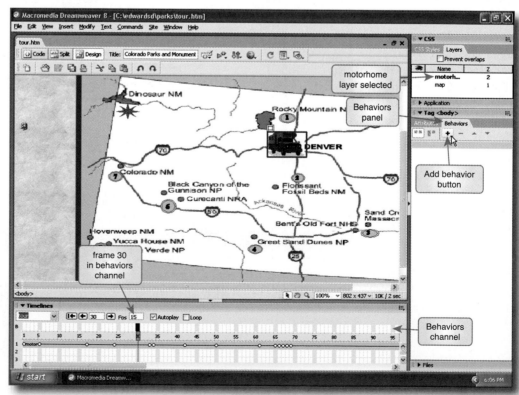

FIGURE 8-19

4

• **Click the Add behavior (+) button, point to Timeline on the Add behavior pop-up menu, and then point to Stop Timeline on the Timeline submenu.**

The Add behavior pop-up menu is displayed, and the Stop Timeline command is highlighted (Figure 8-20).

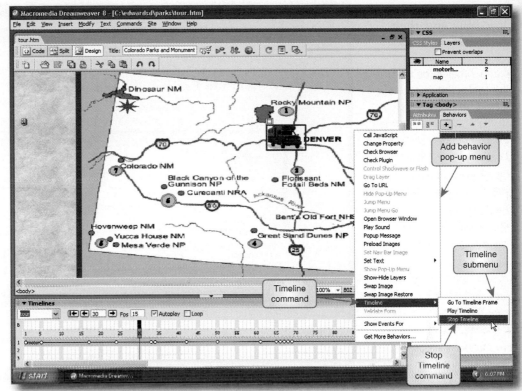

FIGURE 8-20

5

• **Click Stop Timeline.**

• **In the Stop Timeline dialog box, click the Stop Timeline box arrow and then point to tour.**

The Stop Timeline dialog box is displayed, and tour is highlighted (Figure 8-21).

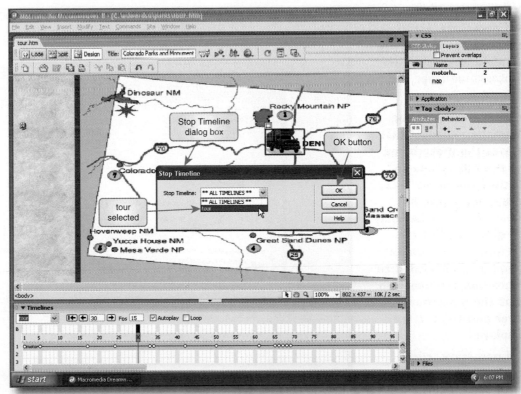

FIGURE 8-21

6

• **Click tour and then click the OK button.**

The Stop Timeline behavior is added to the Behaviors panel, and a minus sign is displayed in frame 30 in the Behaviors channel. The event and action are displayed in the Behaviors panel (Figure 8-22). Most likely the frame number for the Behaviors channel on your screen will be different.

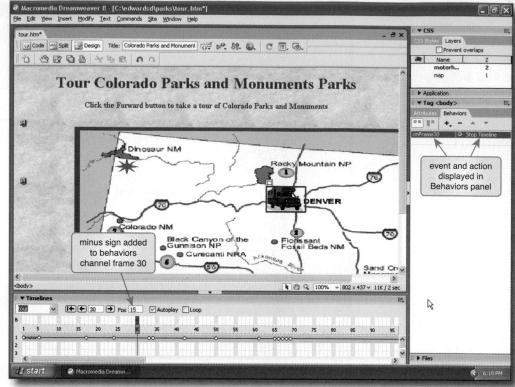

FIGURE 8-22

7

• **If necessary, scroll down in the Document window to display the motorhome layer and the circle 2.**

• **Click a frame in the Animation channel that moves the motorhome layer so it is close to circle 2. In Figure 8-23, this is frame 50, but your frame number may be different. Use the vertical and horizontal scroll bars as needed to reposition the image so that the motorhome layer and circle 2 are displayed.**

• **If necessary, click other frame numbers until the motorhome layer is in close proximity to the circle 2 on your screen.**

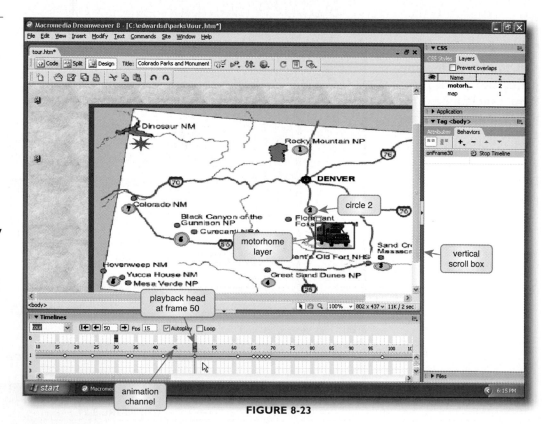

FIGURE 8-23

The motorhome layer is positioned in close proximity to circle 2 (Figure 8-23). The playback head is located at frame 50. Most likely the frame number of your screen will be different.

8

• **Click your selected frame in the Behaviors channel. In Figure 8-24, this is frame 50, but your frame number most likely will be different.**

• **Click the Add behavior (+) button in the Behaviors panel.**

• **Point to Timeline and then click Stop Timeline.**

• **Click the Stop Timeline box arrow in the Stop Timeline dialog box, click tour, and then click the OK button.**

The Stop Timeline behavior is added to the Behaviors panel, and a minus sign is displayed in frame 50 (or your selected frame) in the Behaviors channel (Figure 8-24).

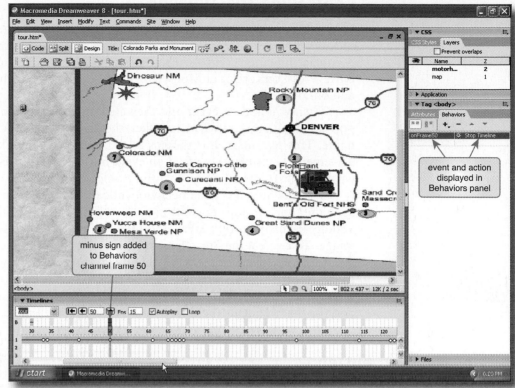

event and action displayed in Behaviors panel

minus sign added to Behaviors channel frame 50

FIGURE 8-24

9

• **Repeat Steps 7 and 8 using Table 8-1 for the list of the other five circle names and the star and the approximate frame numbers to stop the motorhome layer. The frame numbers listed in the table are example values. Modify the frame numbers to fit your timeline. Use the horizontal and vertical scroll boxes as needed to scroll to display the rest of the animation bar in the Animation channel.**

The Stop Timeline behavior is added to each frame close to one of the designated park names.

Table 8-1 Park Names and Frame Numbers	
PARK NAMES	**APPROXIMATE FRAME NUMBER***
Circle 3	Frame 75
Circle 4	Frame 95
Circle 5	Frame 120
Circle 6	Frame 140
Circle 7	Frame 150
Star	Frame 165

*Your frame numbers most likely will be different.

Controlling the Timeline

In Project 6, you learned about the onMouseOver event. In addition to the onMouseOver event, Dreamweaver provides access to several other events that you can assign as animation controls. These events include onClick, onDblClick, onKeyDown, onKeyPress, onKeyUp, onMouseDown, onMouseOut, onMouseUp, onAbort, onError, and onLoad.

When you add an event and then click the event name in the Behaviors panel, a pop-up menu appears when you click the arrow button next to the selected event name. This pop-up menu contains a list of all the events that can trigger the action. This menu is visible only when an event in the behavior list is selected. Different events appear depending on the object selected.

With the Stop Timeline behaviors added to the timeline, a method is needed to start the timeline and move from park to park. This is done by adding another layer, adding an image to that layer, and then adding the Start Timeline behavior to the image. To control the Start Timeline behavior, the user clicks the image. The default event for the selected object is onLoad. The goal here, however, is to allow the user to control the timeline by clicking the mouse. You, therefore, change the event from onLoad to onClick. The following steps illustrate how to add the Forward button and the Start Timeline behavior to the tour.htm Web page.

To Add a Forward Button

1

• **Click Insert on the menu bar, point to Layout Objects, and then click Layer.**

2

• **Use the vertical and horizontal scroll bars to scroll as necessary to view the new layer in the Document window.**

A new layer and new layer code-marker are inserted in the Document window (Figure 8-25).

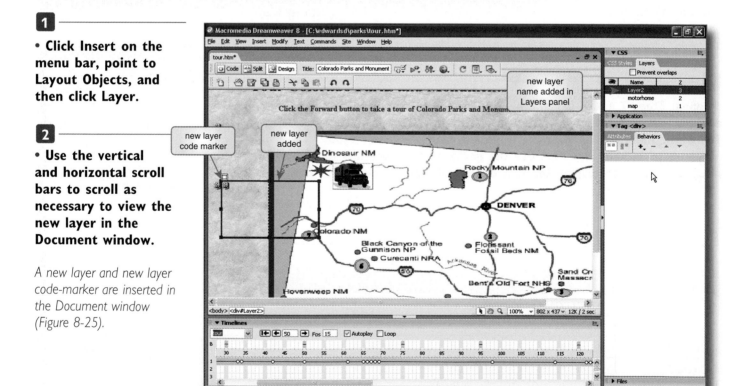

FIGURE 8-25

3

• **If necessary, select the layer. Double-click the Layer1 name in the Layers panel and rename the layer forward.**

• **Click the forward layer selection handle and then drag the layer onto the travel_map.gif image as shown in Figure 8-26.**

The layer is renamed forward and is displayed on the travel_map.gif image.

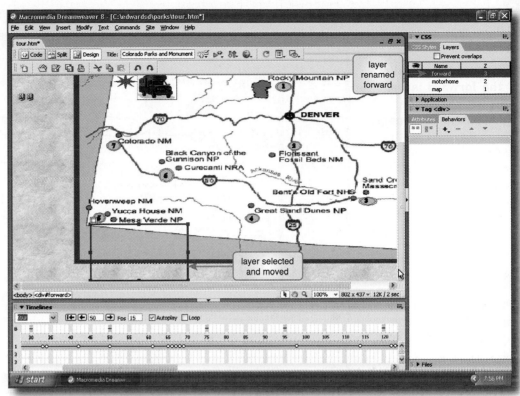

FIGURE 8-26

4

• **Double-click the Files panel title bar and then, if necessary, click the Assets tab.**

• **Drag the forward.gif image onto the forward layer.**

The forward image is displayed in the forward layer (Figure 8-27).

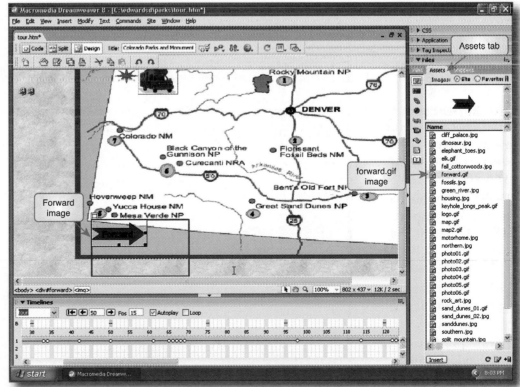

FIGURE 8-27

5

• **Select the forward layer.**

• **Click a resize handle on the forward layer and then resize the layer around the image.**

The forward layer is resized and selected (Figure 8-28).

6

• **Press CTRL+F3 to display the Property inspector. Set L at 150 and T at 500.**

• **Close the Property inspector.**

Left and top attributes were set for the forward image layer. The Property inspector is closed.

7

• **Click anywhere in the animation channel (or any empty frame) to deselect the behavior in the Behaviors panel.**

• **If necessary, double-click the Tag Inspector panel title bar in the panel groups to display the Behaviors panel.**

• **Click the forward image (not the layer).**

• **Click the Add behavior (+) button in the Behaviors panel, point to Timeline, and then click Play Timeline.**

• **Click the OK button in the Play Timeline dialog box.**

The onClick event and the Play Timeline action are added to the Behaviors panel (Figure 8-29).

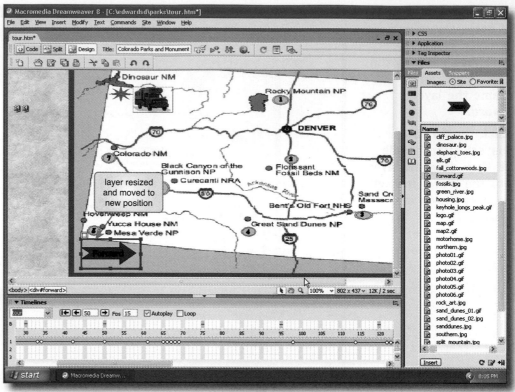

FIGURE 8-28

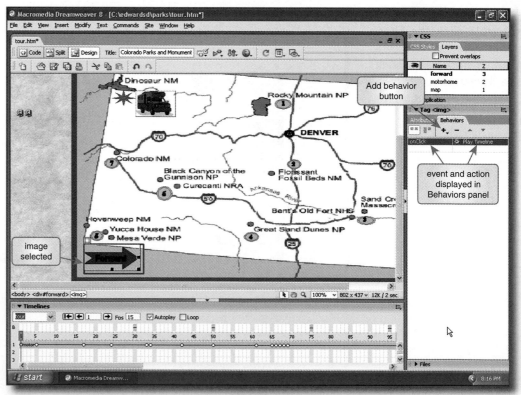

FIGURE 8-29

8

• **Click the Loop check box. If a warning dialog box is displayed, read the information, and then click the OK button.**

• **Deselect the Autoplay check box.**

The behavior for the Loop action is added to the Behaviors panel, and the Autoplay check box is deselected (Figure 8-30). Most likely, the Events frame number in the Behaviors panel on your screen will be different.

9

• **Press the F12 key to view the animation in your browser. Click the Forward button to move the motorhome image along the animation path. Close the browser and return to Dreamweaver.**

The motorhome image moves along the animation path and returns to the starting point.

10

• **Save and then close the tour Web page.**

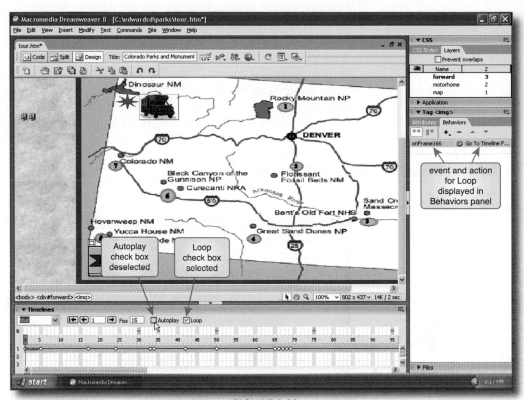

FIGURE 8-30

To integrate the Web page into the Colorado Parks Web site, later in this project you create a link to the natl_parks.htm page. You also create a link from the natl_parks.htm page to this page (tour.htm) and to the slideshow.htm page you create next.

Linear, or Straight-Line, Path Animations

The animation you just created uses a nonlinear path. Your next objective is to create a slide show using a **linear**, or **straight-line**, **path animation**. You accomplish this primarily through the Timelines panel, by adding keyframes at various points along the timelines. As discussed previously, keyframes are marked on the timeline by small circles. A keyframe is the main tool for controlling an animation. Using a keyframe, you can change the properties of an object in a timeline. In this exercise, you change the Show-Hide properties.

The slide show will contain six layers to display six different types of Colorado wildflowers. You use the Show-Hide behavior to display and hide the wildflower images, or slides. All images are the same size and use absolute positioning. The

More About

Creating Simple Animations

Do not create animations that demand more than current browsers can support. Browsers always play every frame in a timeline animation, even when system or Internet performance decreases. Therefore, create simple animations.

Web site visitor cycles through the images by clicking a Start button. The image sequence loops, and, at the end of the loop, the Start button returns the visitor to the beginning slide.

To begin creating your slide show, you add six layers and six images. The images are positioned on top of each other, and each is aligned to the same coordinates. Using same-sized images and absolute positioning provides for a smooth transition between slides and keeps the user's attention focused on a single spot. The following steps show how to create the layers and add images to each layer.

To Add the First Layer and Image

1

• **Close the Timelines panel.**

• **Click the Tag Inspector expand/collapse button, and, if necessary, expand the CSS Panel title bar.**

• **Open slideshow.htm.**

• **Press CTRL+F3 to display the Property inspector. If necessary, click below the heading and then click the Align Left button in the Property inspector.**

The slideshow.htm page is displayed in the Document window. The insertion point is at the left in the Document window (Figure 8-31).

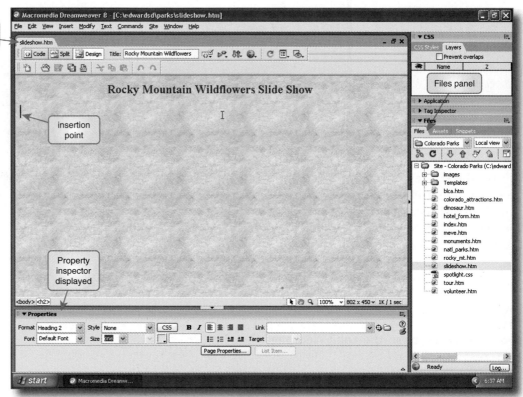

FIGURE 8-31

2

• **Click Insert on the menu bar, point to Layout Objects, and then click Layer.**

A layer is inserted into the Document window. The layer-code marker is displayed in the upper-left corner, and the insertion point is blinking inside the layer (Figure 8-32).

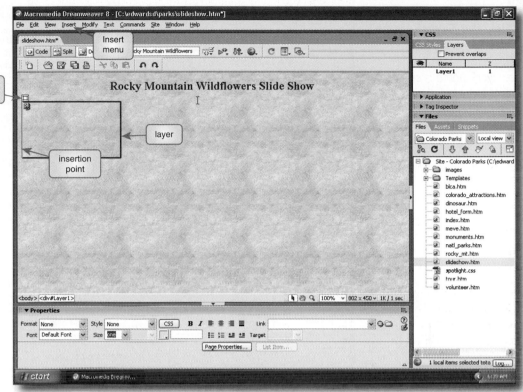

FIGURE 8-32

3

• **Click the Assets tab. Drag the photo01.gif image onto the layer.**

• **Click the Image ID box and name the image bluecolumbine. Click the Alt text box and type** Blue Columbine.

The photo01.gif image is displayed in Layer1. The image is named bluecolumbine and Alt text is added (Figure 8-33).

FIGURE 8-33

4

• **Click the Layer1 name in the Layers panel.**

The Layer1 name is selected in the Layers panel, and the Property inspector for layers is displayed (Figure 8-34).

FIGURE 8-34

5

• **In the Property inspector, add the following attributes: Layer ID, photo01; L, 200px; and T, 100px.**

The properties are added for the photo01 layer, and the Layer1 name changes to photo01 in the Layers panel (Figure 8-35).

FIGURE 8-35

6

• **Click the Visibility column to the left of the photo01 layer in the Layers panel until the closed-eye icon is displayed.**

• **If necessary, click the Document window to hide the layer and image.**

The closed-eye icon is displayed (Figure 8-36). Later in this project, you will change this closed-eye icon to the open-eye icon.

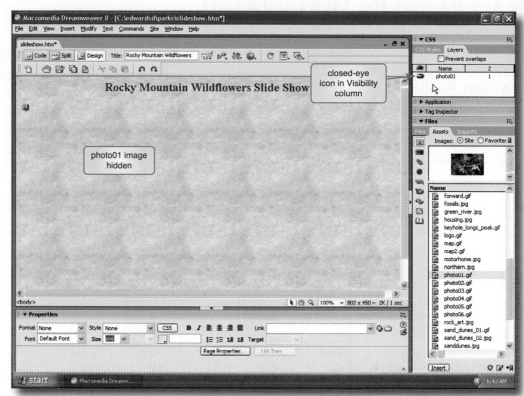

FIGURE 8-36

The first layer and image for the slide show have been added to the Document window. Next, you add five more layers, add an image to each layer, and then change the properties for each of the layers.

To Add the Next Five Layers and Images

1

• Click Insert on the menu bar, point to Layout Objects, and then click Layer.

• Drag the photo02.gif image onto the layer.

• Click the Image ID box and name the image globeflower. Click the Alt text box and type Globe Flower.

Layer1 is displayed in the Layers panel. The photo02.gif image is displayed in the Document window, the image is named, and Alt text is added (Figure 8-37).

FIGURE 8-37

2

• Select the Layer1 name in the Layers panel. Add the following attributes in the Layer Property inspector: Layer ID, photo02; L, 200px; and T, 100px.

The properties are added for the photo02 layer, and the layer name changes to photo02 in the Layers panel (Figure 8-38).

FIGURE 8-38

3

• **Click the Visibility column to the left of the photo02 layer in the Layers panel until the closed-eye icon is displayed. If necessary, click the Document window to hide the layer and image.**

The closed-eye icon is displayed for the photo02 layer in the Layers panel. The globeflower image no longer appears in the Document window.

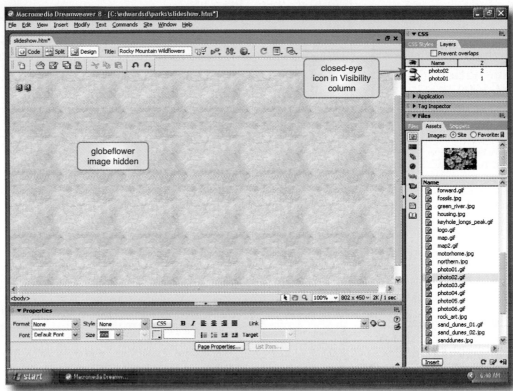

FIGURE 8-39

4

• **Four more layers must be added to prepare for the slide show. Repeat Steps 1 through 3 to add the next four layers. Table 8-2 on the next page contains the attributes for each image and for each layer. Apply the closed-eye icon to all of the layers.**

• **Click the Save button on the Standard toolbar.**

All six layers are added and are hidden and the file is saved (Figure 8-40).

The slideshow.htm file is saved.

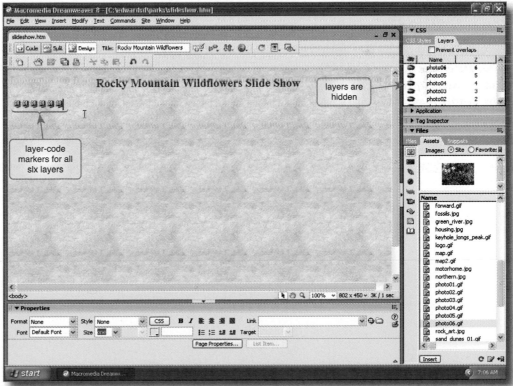

FIGURE 8-40

Table 8-2 Image and Layer Attributes

IMAGE NAME	ALT TEXT	LAYER ID	L AND T
alpineforgetmenot	Alpine Forget-me-not	photo03	200px and 100px
sunflower	Sunflower Wooly Actinea	photo04	200px and 100px
mountainhareball	Mountain Hareball	photo05	200px and 100px
wildflowers	Mountain Wildflowers	photo06	200px and 100px

More About

Animation Speeds

Slow down an animation by increasing the length of the animation bar. Click the last keyframe on the bar and drag right. To speed up an animation, decrease the length of the animation bar.

Next, you display the Timelines panel and then name the timeline. Recall that the Timelines panel shows how the properties of layers and images change over time. The following steps show how to accomplish this task.

To Display and Name the Timeline

1

• **Close the Property inspector. Press ALT+F9 to display the Timelines panel.**

• **If necessary, move the mouse pointer over the horizontal line below the Layers panel until the pointer turns into a two-headed arrow. Drag the mouse pointer down until all six layers display.**

The Timelines panel is displayed, and the Property inspector is closed (Figure 8-41).

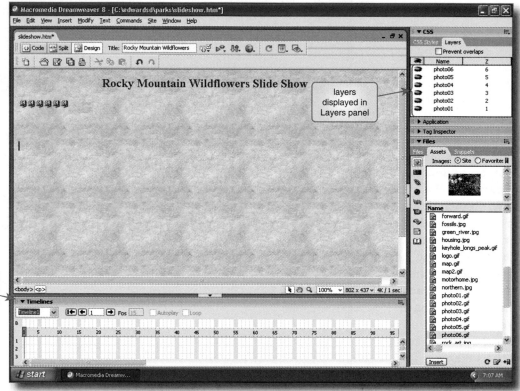

FIGURE 8-41

2

- **Click the Timelines pop-up menu text box. Delete the default text entry, type** slideshow, **and then press the TAB key.**

The timeline is named, and the name is displayed in the Timelines pop-up menu text box (Figure 8-42).

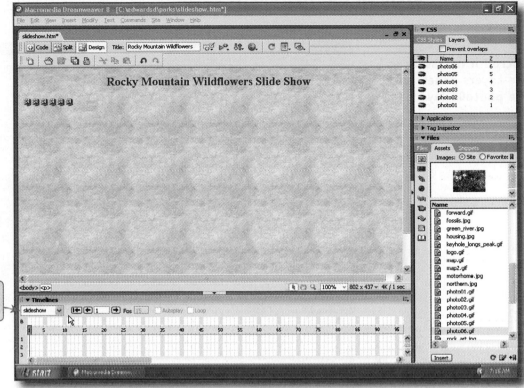

timeline is named slideshow

FIGURE 8-42

Adding Layers to a Timeline

The next step is to add the six layers to the timeline. The timeline for each layer is on a separate Animation channel. The steps on the following pages illustrate how to add the six layers to the timeline.

To Add the Layers to the Timeline

1

• **Scroll if necessary in the Layers panel. Click the photo01 layer.**

The photo01 layer is selected in the Layers panel. The bluecolumbine image is displayed in the Document window (Figure 8-43).

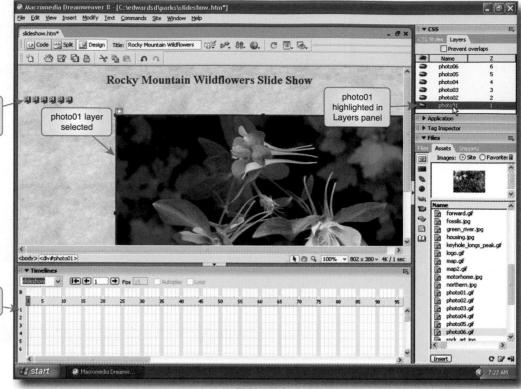

layer-code marker for photo01 layer

photo01 layer selected

photo01 highlighted in Layers panel

Animation channel 1

FIGURE 8-43

2

• **Drag the photo01 layer-code marker to Animation channel 1, frame 1, in the Timelines panel. If a Dreamweaver dialog box is displayed, read the information and then click the OK button.**

The photo01 layer is selected in Animation channel 1 (Figure 8-44).

photo01 layer added to Animation channel

photo01 timeline

FIGURE 8-44

3

• **Click the photo02 layer in the Layers panel.**

The photo02 layer is selected in the Layers panel (Figure 8-45).

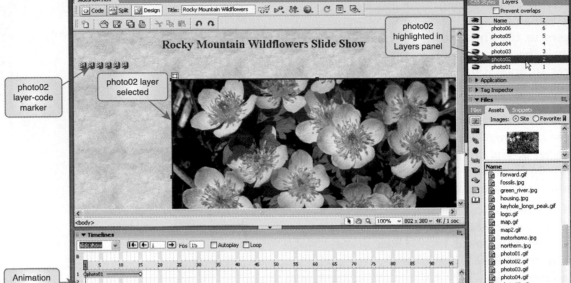

FIGURE 8-45

4

• **Drag the photo02 layer-code marker to Animation channel 2, frame 1, in the Timelines panel. If a Dreamweaver dialog box is displayed, click the OK button.**

The photo02 layer is displayed and selected in Animation channel 2 (Figure 8-46).

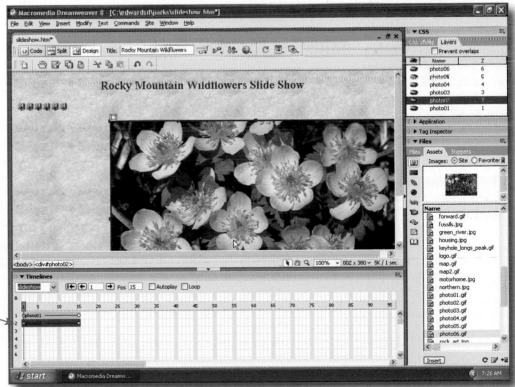

FIGURE 8-46

5

• Repeat Steps 3 and 4, selecting and dragging the remaining four layers to the Timelines panel: the photo03 layer to Animation channel 3, the photo04 layer to Animation channel 4, the photo05 layer to Animation channel 5, and the photo06 layer to Animation channel 6.

• If the photos cover the layer markers, click the open and closed eye icons to hide the layers.

The photo06 timeline is selected (Figure 8-47).

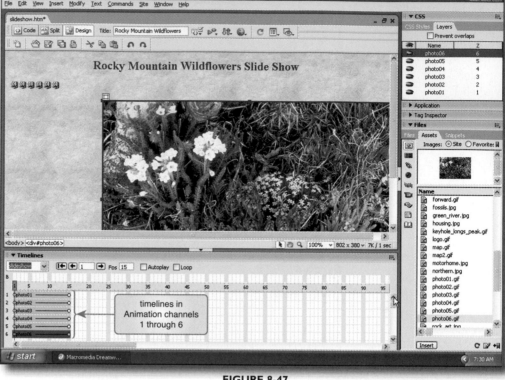

FIGURE 8-47

Adjusting the Number of Frames

The slide show is not a self-running animation. Instead, the Web site user controls the slide show by clicking a button. Thus, the time, or fps, is not relevant. The number of frames within each of the timelines, therefore, can be set to a minimum. Keyframes are added to the timeline to show and hide each layer, and a pause is added between the show and hide events. The pause is added through the Behaviors channel. Because fps are not relevant and because you want to create the most efficient slide show, the number of frames for each timeline is set to the lowest number required to create the slide show.

As discussed previously, a keyframe is required to hide and then show each of the six images within the layers. Keyframe number 3, for instance, is used to hide the photo01 layer and to display the photo02 layer. Another keyframe is required to stop the display of each layer, and an ending keyframe is required. Therefore, to determine the minimum number of frames, multiply the number of images in your sequence by 2 and then add 1. In this instance, the slide show contains six slides, which makes the number of required frames 13. You adjust the number of frames by dragging the last keyframe for each of the timelines to the left. The following steps illustrate how to adjust the number of keyframes for each timeline.

To Adjust the Number of Keyframes

1

• **Click the keyframe at frame 15 in the photo01 animation bar in the Timelines panel.**

The playback head moves to frame 15, and the keyframe circle is selected (Figure 8-48).

FIGURE 8-48

2

• **Drag the keyframe to frame 13.**

The playback head moves to frame 13 (Figure 8-49).

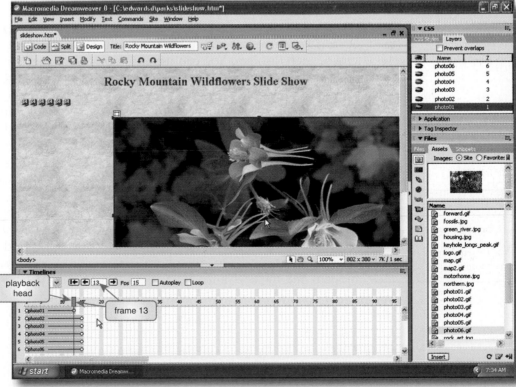

FIGURE 8-49

3

• Repeat Steps 1 and 2 for the other five layers.

All six timelines are adjusted to 13 frames (Figure 8-50).

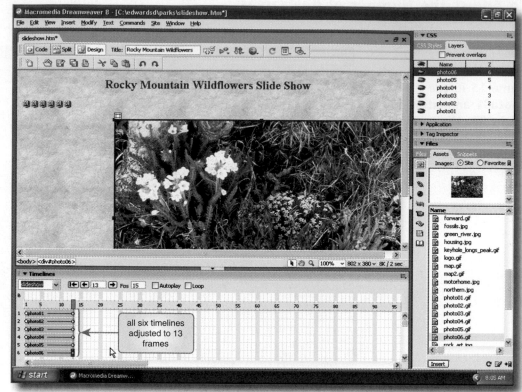

FIGURE 8-50

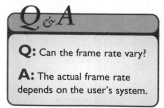

Q: Can the frame rate vary?

A: The actual frame rate depends on the user's system.

Adding Keyframes to Show and Hide Layers

Recall that you use a keyframe to define the properties of an object in a timeline. A start keyframe and a stop keyframe automatically are added to the beginning and end of each timeline. You can use keyframes to change an object's position or to show and hide layers. As the slide show plays, for instance, the layers are displayed and then hidden.

When using keyframes to show and hide layers, as within a slide show, visualize the keyframes as a stairstep process. To display the slide show, a layer is turned on and then turned off. When the layer is turned off, the next layer is turned on, and so on. The slide show starts with the bluecolumbine layer displayed at frame 1 and the other five layers hidden. Showing and hiding layers is accomplished through the Visibility column in the Layers panel, using the open-eye and closed-eye icons. Therefore, for the photo01 timeline, the keyframe at frame 1 shows the layer (the open-eye icon in the Layers panel). The keyframes at frame 1 for the other five layers show closed-eye icons. To hide the photo01 layer and to show the photo02 layer, the keyframe at frame 3 for the photo01 layer is a closed-eye icon (i.e., the layer is hidden) and the keyframe at frame 3 for the photo02 layer is an open-eye icon.

When the photo01 layer is hidden, the next layer (the photo02 layer) is displayed. Continuing with the slide show, the keyframe at frame 5 for the photo02 layer is a closed-eye icon and the keyframe at frame 5 for the photo03 layer is an open-eye icon, and so on. When one layer is hidden, the next one is turned on. In between layers being shown and hidden, a behavior is added to the even-numbered frames to stop the slide show. Clicking the Play button resumes the slide show presentation.

In the following steps, keyframes are added to the timeline to show and hide layers. When the timeline is executed and a keyframe is encountered, then the visibility of the selected layer is turned on or off. The next steps show how to add keyframes to show or hide a selected layer. The keyframes are added at odd-numbered frames for each of the timelines.

More About

Animation Sequences

After you have an animation sequence that you like, you can copy it and paste it into another area of the current timeline, into another timeline in the same document, or into a timeline in another document. You also can copy and paste multiple sequences at once.

To Add Keyframes to Show and Hide Layers

1

• **Click the keyframe in frame 1 in the photo01 timeline in the Timelines panel.**

• **If necessary, click the Visibility column for the photo01 layer in the Layers panel until the open-eye icon is displayed.**

The playback head is in frame 1 and the open-eye icon appears for the photo01 layer (Figure 8-51). The open-eye icon for keyframe 1 displays the first slide (Blue Columbine) when the slide show opens in the browser window.

FIGURE 8-51

2

• **Drag the playback head to frame 3.**

The playback head is at frame 3 (Figure 8-52).

FIGURE 8-52

3

• **Click and then right-click the photo01 timeline at frame 3. Point to Add Keyframe on the context menu.**

The context menu displays, and Add Keyframe is highlighted (Figure 8-53).

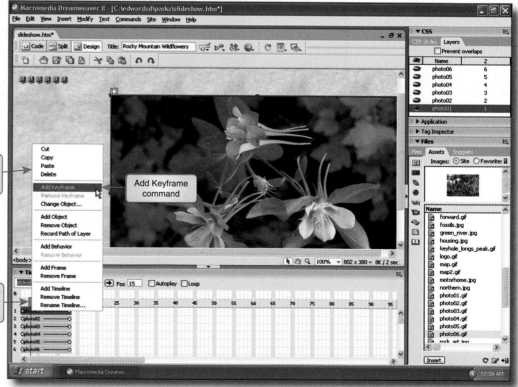

FIGURE 8-53

4

- **Click Add Keyframe.**
- **Click the Visibility column for the photo01 layer in the Layers panel until the closed-eye icon is displayed.**

A keyframe is added to the photo01 layer at frame 3. This keyframe setting hides the photo01 layer (Blue Columbine) when the animation plays and the layer advances to frame 3 (Figure 8-54).

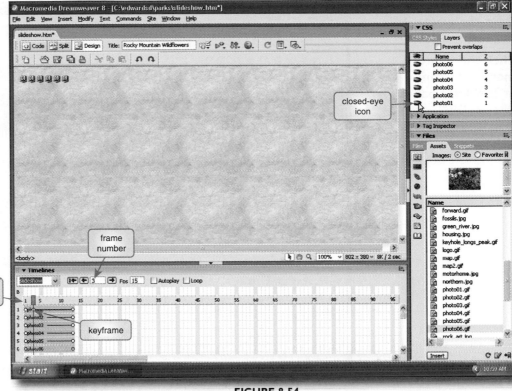

FIGURE 8-54

5

- **Click the photo02 timeline at frame 3 in the Timelines panel. Right-click to display the context menu and then click Add Keyframe.**
- **Click the Visibility column for the photo02 layer in the Layers panel until the open-eye icon is displayed.**

The open-eye icon is displayed to the left of the photo02 layer in the Layers panel. A keyframe is added to the photo02 timeline at frame 3 (Figure 8-55). This keyframe setting displays the Globe Flower image during the slide show presentation.

FIGURE 8-55

6

• **Drag the playback head to frame 5.**

• **Click the photo02 timeline at frame 5 in the Timelines panel.**

The photo02 timeline is selected in the Timelines panel (Figure 8-56).

FIGURE 8-56

7

• **Right-click the photo02 timeline at frame 5 and then click Add Keyframe.**

• **Click the Visibility column for the photo02 layer in the Layers panel until the closed-eye icon is displayed.**

A keyframe is added to the photo02 timeline at frame 5 (Figure 8-57). This keyframe setting hides the Globe Flower image during the slide show presentation.

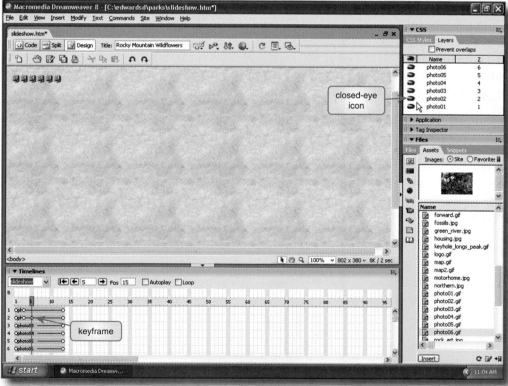

FIGURE 8-57

8

• **Click the photo03 timeline at frame 5 in the Timelines panel.**

The photo03 timeline is selected at frame 5 (Figure 8-58).

FIGURE 8-58

9

• **Right-click the photo03 timeline and then click Add Keyframe.**

• **Click the Visibility column for the photo03 layer in the Layers panel until the open-eye icon is displayed.**

A keyframe is added to the photo03 timeline at frame 5 (Figure 8-59). This keyframe setting shows the Alpine Forget-me-not image during the slide show presentation.

FIGURE 8-59

10

• **Click frame 7 in the photo03 timeline in the Timelines panel, right-click, and then click Add Keyframe.**

• **Click the Visibility column for the photo03 layer in the Layers panel until the closed-eye icon is displayed.**

A keyframe is added to the photo03 timeline at frame 7 (Figure 8-60). This keyframe setting hides the Alpine Forget-me-not image during the slide show presentation.

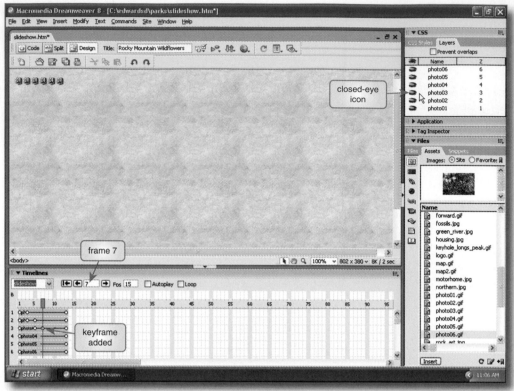

FIGURE 8-60

11

• **Click frame 7 in the photo04 timeline in the Timelines panel, right-click, and then click Add Keyframe.**

• **Click the Visibility column in the photo04 layer in the Layers panel until the open-eye icon is displayed.**

A keyframe is added to the photo04 timeline at frame 7 (Figure 8-61). This keyframe setting shows the Sunflower Wooly Actinea image during the slide show presentation.

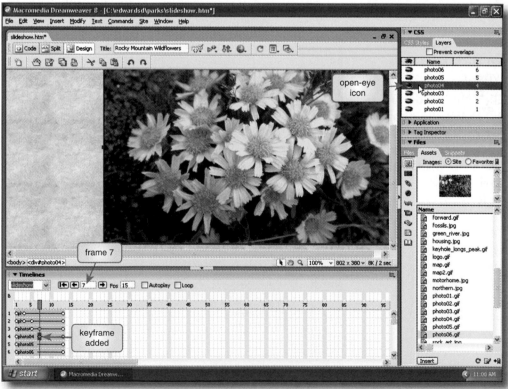

FIGURE 8-61

Click the photo04 timeline at frame 9 in the Timelines panel, right-click, and then click Add Keyframe.

Click the Visibility column in the photo04 layer in the Layers panel until the closed-eye icon is displayed.

A keyframe is added to the photo04 timeline at frame 9 (Figure 8-62). This keyframe setting hides the Sunflower Wooly Actinea image during the slide show presentation.

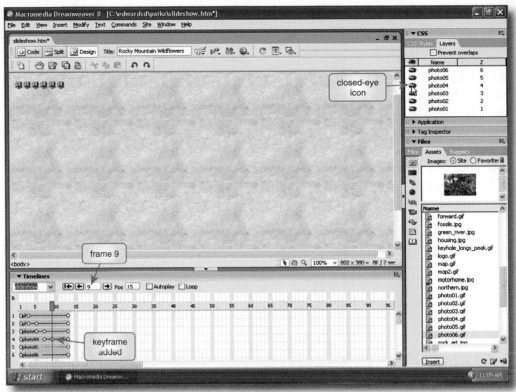

FIGURE 8-62

Click the photo05 timeline in the Timelines panel at frame 9, right-click, and then click Add Keyframe.

Click the Visibility column in the photo05 layer in the Layers panel until the open-eye icon is displayed.

A keyframe is added to the photo05 layer at frame 9 (Figure 8-63). This keyframe setting shows the Mountain Hareball image during the slide show presentation.

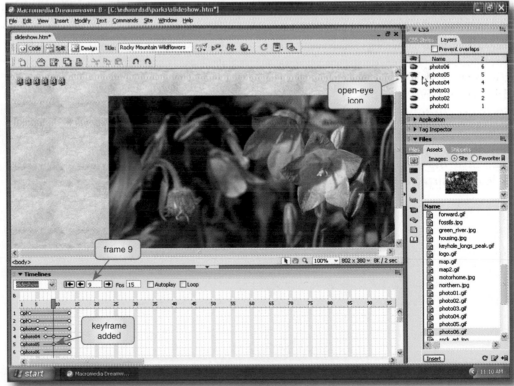

FIGURE 8-63

14

• **Click the photo05 timeline at frame 11 in the Timelines panel, right-click, and then click Add Keyframe.**

• **Click the Visibility column in the photo05 layer in the Layers panel until the closed-eye icon is displayed.**

A keyframe is added to the photo05 layer at frame 11 (Figure 8-64). This keyframe setting hides the Mountain Hareball image during the slide show presentation.

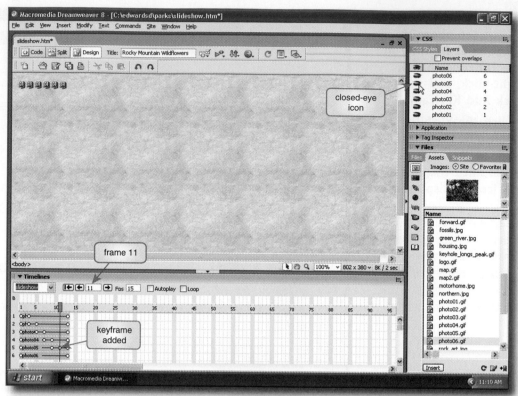

FIGURE 8-64

15

• **Click the photo06 timeline at frame 11 in the Timelines panel, right-click, and then click Add Keyframe.**

• **Click the Visibility column in the photo06 layer in the Layers panel until the open-eye icon is displayed.**

A keyframe is added to the photo06 layer at frame 11 (Figure 8-65). This keyframe setting shows the Alpine Wildflowers image during the slide show presentation.

FIGURE 8-65

• **Click the photo06 timeline at frame 13 in the Timelines panel.**

• **If necessary, click the Visibility column in the photo06 layer in the Layers panel until the closed-eye icon is displayed.**

This keyframe setting hides the Alpine Wildflowers image during the slide show presentation (Figure 8-66). The closed-eye icon is displayed for all six layers at this point.

FIGURE 8-66

• **Click the keyframe in frame 13 in the photo01 timeline in the Timelines panel.**

• **Click the Visibility column in the photo01 layer in the Layers panel until the open-eye icon is displayed.**

The visibility setting is added to keyframe 13 of the photo01 layer (Figure 8-67). This keyframe setting redisplays the first image (Blue Columbine) at the end of the slide show presentation so the viewer is not left with a blank screen.

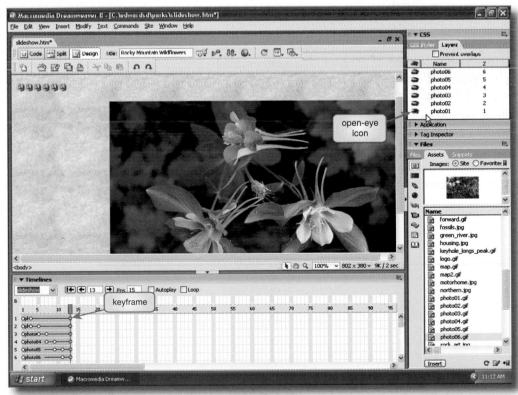

FIGURE 8-67

18

• **Click the Autoplay check box in the Timelines panel. If a Dreamweaver dialog box is displayed, read the information and then click the OK button.**

• **Click the Save button on the Standard toolbar.**

• **Press the F12 key to view the presentation in your browser.**

The presentation cycles through quickly. It ends with the first image, Blue Columbine (Figure 8-68).

19

• **Close the browser window and return to Dreamweaver.**

FIGURE 8-68

Other Ways

1. Click a frame; on Modify menu, point to Timeline; click Add Keyframe on Timeline submenu

---

Using Behaviors to Pause the Slides

The next step is to add a pause between each slide. Adding a pause stops the timeline from playing. Adding pauses between slides is accomplished through the Timelines panel Behaviors channel. Simply click the desired frame number in the Behaviors channel and apply the Stop Timeline behavior. The Stop Timeline behavior is added to even-numbered frames for this timeline. The Play Timeline behavior is added through the Start button. You add the Start button later in this project. The following steps show how to add the pauses.

To Use Behaviors to Pause between Slides

1

• Press SHIFT+F4 to display the Behaviors panel. If necessary, collapse the Files panel.

• Click frame 2 in the Behaviors channel in the Timelines panel.

The Behaviors panel is displayed, and frame 2 in the Behaviors channel is selected (Figure 8-69).

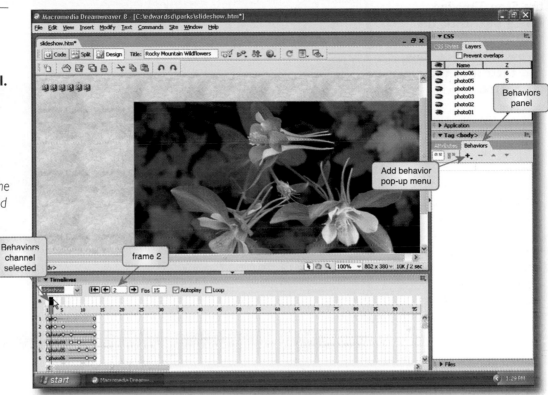

FIGURE 8-69

2

• Click the Add behavior (+) button in the Behaviors panel, point to Timeline, and then point to Stop Timeline.

The Add behavior pop-up menu is displayed (Figure 8-70).

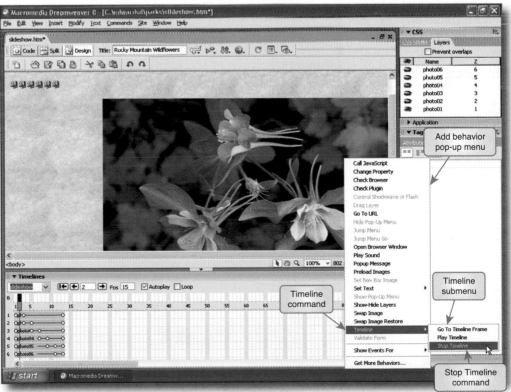

FIGURE 8-70

3

• **Click Stop Timeline. In the Stop Timeline dialog box, click the Stop Timeline box arrow, click slideshow, and then click the OK button.**

The Stop Timeline behavior is added to frame 2 in the Behaviors channel. The event and action are displayed in the Behaviors panel (Figure 8-71).

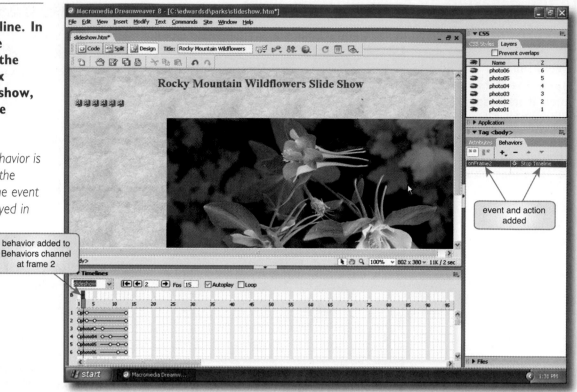

behavior added to Behaviors channel at frame 2

event and action added

FIGURE 8-71

4

• **Click frame 4 in the Behaviors channel. Click the Add behavior (+) button in the Behaviors panel, point to Timeline, and then click Stop Timeline.**

• **Click the Stop Timeline box arrow, click slideshow, and then click the OK button.**

The Stop Timeline behavior is added to frame 4 in the Behaviors channel. The event and action are displayed in the Behaviors panel for frame 4 (Figure 8-72).

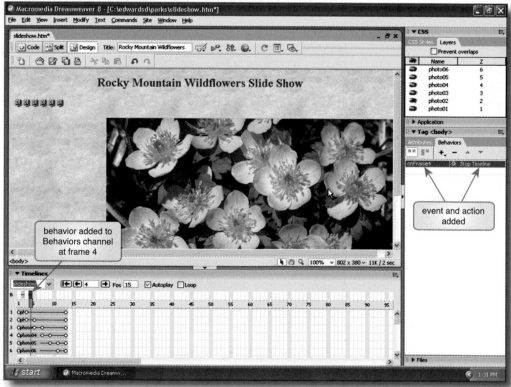

behavior added to Behaviors channel at frame 4

event and action added

FIGURE 8-72

5

• **Repeat Step 4 to add the Stop Timeline behavior to frames 6, 8, 10, and 12 in the Timelines panel Behaviors channel.**

The Stop Timeline behavior is added to frames 6, 8, 10, and 12 (Figure 8-73).

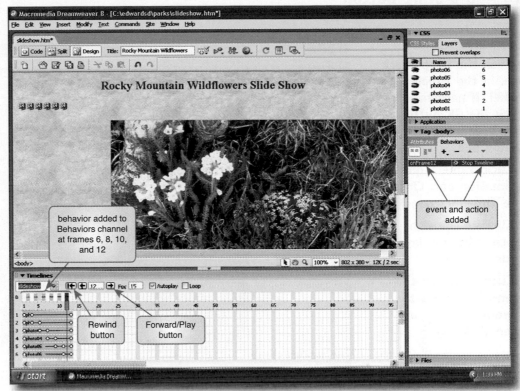

FIGURE 8-73

Previewing a Timeline in the Timelines Panel

After creating a timeline, you can preview it in Dreamweaver by using the Timelines panel playback options (see page DW 638). Recall that the Rewind button moves the playback head to the first frame in the timeline. The Back button moves the playback head one frame to the left. Clicking the Back button and holding down the mouse button plays the timeline backward. The Play/Forward button moves the playback head one frame to the right. Clicking the Play/Forward button and holding down the mouse button plays the timeline forward. The following step illustrates how to preview your timeline in Dreamweaver.

To Preview a Timeline in the Timelines Panel

1 In the Timelines panel, click the Rewind button to move the playback head to the first frame. Click the Play/Forward button in the Timelines panel. As you click forward to each frame, verify in the Layers panel that the eye icon is appropriately closed or opened for each of the layers and that the minus sign displays for the Stop Timeline action in the correct frames.

Adding a Start Button

To provide the Web site visitor with the ability to control the slide show requires that a Start button be added to the Web page. Clicking the button the first time starts the image sequence. Clicking the button again advances the sequence to the next image. Adding a Start button requires that a layer be added to the Web page and that the button be contained within the layer. The following steps show how to add the layer and then add the Start button.

Q: How are animations created within Dreamweaver?

A: Dreamweaver uses JavaScript to create animations. Behaviors place JavaScript code in documents to allow visitors to interact with a Web page, to change the page in various ways, or to cause certain tasks to be performed.

To Add a Start Button

1

• Click the Loop check box in the Timelines panel. If necessary, click the OK button in the Dreamweaver dialog box.

• Click frame 1 on the animation bar. Close the Timelines panel.

• Click to the right of the photo06 layer-code marker.

• Click Insert on the menu bar, point to Layout Objects, and then click Layer.

A layer is added and is displayed (Figure 8-74).

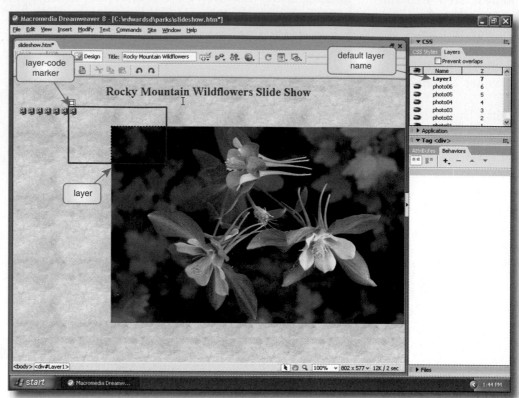

FIGURE 8-74

2

• Double-click the Files panel title bar. Drag the start.gif image onto the layer.

• Press CTRL+F3 to display the Property inspector.

• If necessary, display the Layers panel. Select the layer. Name the layer start, and set L at 200px and T at 500px.

• Click the Visibility column for the start layer in the Layers panel until the open-eye icon is displayed.

• Press CTRL+F3 to hide the Property inspector and then scroll down to view the layer and image.

The layer with the start.gif image is placed on the Web page at the designated location (Figure 8-75).

FIGURE 8-75

3

• **Resize the layer to fit the image.**

• **Expand the Tag Inspector group to display the Behaviors panel.**

• **Click the image within the start layer, click the Add behavior (+) button in the Behaviors panel, point to Timeline, and then click Play Timeline.**

• **Click the OK button in the Play Timeline dialog box.**

The start layer is resized to fit the image, and the onClick event and Play Timeline action are added to the Behaviors panel (Figure 8-76).

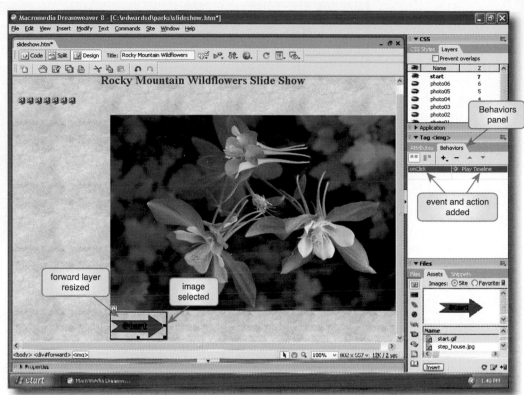

FIGURE 8-76

Next, you add a link from the motorhome page and from the slide show page to the Colorado State Parks page. The steps show how to add the first link, from the slide show page to the Colorado State Parks page.

To Add a Link from the Slideshow.htm Page to the Natl_Parks.htm Page

1 Display the Property inspector.

2 Click to the right of the start layer-code marker.

3 Press the ENTER key 13 times, type Colorado National Parks, and then select the text you just typed.

4 Double-click the Files panel title bar and then click the Files tab.

5 Drag the natl_parks.htm file to the Link box and then press the ENTER key (Figure 8-77 on the next page).

6 Save the slideshow.htm page.

7 Press the F12 key and then check the link to verify that it works.

8 Close the browser to return to Dreamweaver and then close the slideshow.htm page.

The link is added to the Colorado National Parks page as shown in Step 5 (Figure 8-77).

More About

Changing Events

Each action has a default setting or event. To change the event, click the event and then click the pop-up menu to display a list of all events that can trigger the action.

More About

Behaviors

Use Dreamweaver's Show-Hide Layers and Drag Layer behaviors to create interactive events or games. For more information about Dreamweaver behaviors, visit the Dreamweaver 8 More About Web page (scsite.com/dw8/more.htm) and then click Behaviors.

FIGURE 8-77

The following steps show how to add a link from the tour page to the Colorado National Parks page.

To Add a Link from the Tour.htm Page to the Natl_Parks.htm Page

1 Open the tour.htm page.

2 Click to the right of the third layer-code marker.

3 Press the ENTER key twelve times or more as necessary, type Colorado National Parks, and then select the text you just typed.

4 Drag the natl_parks.htm file to the Link box and then press the ENTER key (Figure 8-78).

5 Save the tour.htm page.

6 Press the F12 key and then check the link to verify that it works.

7 Close the browser to return to Dreamweaver and then close the tour.htm page.

The link is added to the Colorado National Parks page, as shown in Step 4 (Figure 8-78).

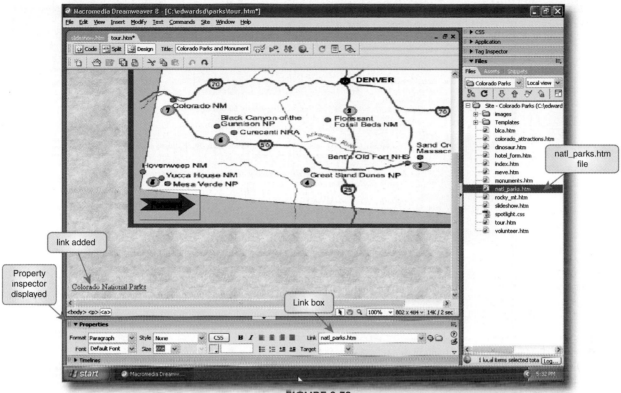

FIGURE 8-78

Linking to the Tour and Slide Show Pages

To add the two new pages to the Colorado Parks Web site, a link is created from the index.htm page to the two new pages—tour.htm and slideshow.htm. The following steps show how to create the links.

To Add Links from the Index.htm Web Page

1 Open the index.htm page.

2 Scroll to the bottom of the page, click to the right of the link, General Information, press the END key, and then press SHIFT+ENTER.

3 Type Colorado Parks Slide Show as the entry, press the END key, and then press SHIFT+ENTER.

4 Type Colorado Tour as the entry.

5 Select the text, Colorado Parks Slide Show, and then drag the slideshow.htm file from the Files panel to the Property inspector Link text box.

6 Select the text, Colorado Tour, and then drag the tour.htm file from the Files panel to the Property inspector Link text box (Figure 8-79 on the next page).

7 Save the index.htm page and then press the F12 key. Test the links and then close the browser.

Links are added to the two new Web pages, as shown in Step 6 (Figure 8-79).

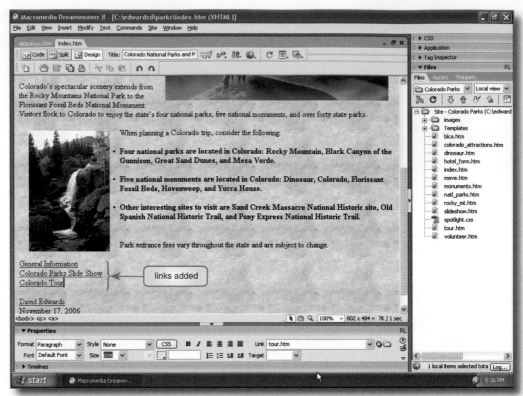

FIGURE 8-79

Quitting Dreamweaver

After you have created your animated Web pages containing a slide show and a tour of Colorado, and tested and verified that the animations and links work, Project 8 is complete. The following step shows how to close the Web site, quit Dreamweaver 8, and return control to Windows.

To Close the Web Site and Quit Dreamweaver

1 Click the Close button on the upper-right corner of the Dreamweaver title bar.

The Dreamweaver window, the Document window, and the Colorado Parks Web site all close. If you have unsaved changes, Dreamweaver will prompt you to save the changes. Clicking the Yes button in the Dreamweaver 8 dialog box saves the changes.

Project Summary

Project 8 introduced you to animation using Dreamweaver's Timelines panel. You created two animations: the first one a tour of Colorado parks and the second a slide show depicting images of some of the wildflowers located in Colorado parks. Next, you added behaviors to start and stop the animations and events to show and hide objects. You then added a Play button to both pages to provide the Web site visitor with user control.

What You Should Know

Having completed this project, you now should be able to perform the tasks below. The tasks are listed in the same order they were presented in the project. For a list of keyboard commands for topics introduced in this project, see the Quick Reference for Windows at the back of this book and refer to the Shortcut column.

1. Copy Data Files to the Colorado Parks Web Site (DW 630)
2. Start Dreamweaver and Open the Colorado Parks Web Site (DW 631)
3. Add the Colorado Map Image and Layer (DW 633)
4. Create a Nonlinear Animation (DW 640)
5. Add the Stop Timeline Behavior (DW 645)
6. Add a Forward Button (DW 650)
7. Add the First Layer and Image (DW 654)
8. Add the Next Five Layers and Images (DW 658)
9. Display and Name the Timeline (DW 660)
10. Add the Layers to the Timeline (DW 662)
11. Adjust the Number of Keyframes (DW 665)
12. Add Keyframes to Show and Hide Layers (DW 667)
13. Use Behaviors to Pause Between Slides (DW 677)
14. Preview a Timeline in the Timelines Panel (DW 679)
15. Add a Start Button (DW 680)
16. Add a Link from the Slideshow.htm Page to the Natl_Parks.htm Page (DW 681)
17. Add a Link from the Tour.htm Page to the Natl_Parks.htm Page (DW 682)
19. Add Links from the Index.htm Web Page (DW 683)
20. Close the Web Site and Quit Dreamweaver (DW 684)

Learn It Online

Instructions: To complete the Learn It Online exercises, start your browser, click the Address bar, and then enter the Web address scsite.com/dw8/learn When the Dreamweaver 8 Learn It Online page is displayed, follow the instructions in the exercises below. Each exercise has instructions for printing your results, either for your own records or for submission to your instructor.

1 Project Reinforcement TF, MC, and SA

Below Dreamweaver Project 8, click the Project Reinforcement link. Print the quiz by clicking Print on the File menu for each page. Answer each question.

2 Flash Cards

Below Dreamweaver Project 8, click the Flash Cards link and read the instructions. Type 20 (or a number specified by your instructor) in the Number of playing cards text box, type your name in the Enter your Name text box, and then click the Flip Card button. When the flash card is displayed, read the question and then click the ANSWER box arrow to select an answer. Flip through the Flash Cards. If your score is 15 (75%) correct or greater, click Print on the File menu to print your results. If your score is less than 15 (75%) correct, then redo this exercise by clicking the Replay button.

3 Practice Test

Below Dreamweaver Project 8, click the Practice Test link. Answer each question, enter your first and last name at the bottom of the page, and then click the Grade Test button. When the graded practice test is displayed on your screen, click Print on the File menu to print a hard copy. Continue to take practice tests until you score 80% or better.

4 Who Wants To Be a Computer Genius?

Below Dreamweaver Project 8, click the Computer Genius link. Read the instructions, enter your first and last name at the bottom of the page, and then click the PLAY button. When your score is displayed, click the PRINT RESULTS link to print a hard copy.

5 Wheel of Terms

Below Dreamweaver Project 8, click the Wheel of Terms link. Read the instructions, and then enter your first and last name and your school name. Click the PLAY button. When your score is displayed, right-click the score and then click Print on the shortcut menu to print a hard copy.

6 Crossword Puzzle Challenge

Below Dreamweaver Project 8, click the Crossword Puzzle Challenge link. Read the instructions, and then enter your first and last name. Click the SUBMIT button. Work the crossword puzzle. When you are finished, click the Submit button. When the crossword puzzle is redisplayed, click the Print Puzzle button to print a hard copy.

7 Tips and Tricks

Below Dreamweaver Project 8, click the Tips and Tricks link. Click a topic that pertains to Project 8. Right-click the information and then click Print on the shortcut menu. Construct a brief example of what the information relates to in Dreamweaver to confirm that you understand how to use the tip or trick.

8 Newsgroups

Below Dreamweaver Project 8, click the Newsgroups link. Click a topic that pertains to Project 8. Print three comments.

9 Expanding Your Horizons

Below Dreamweaver Project 8, click the Expanding Your Horizons link. Click a topic that pertains to Project 8. Print the information. Construct a brief example of what the information relates to in Dreamweaver to confirm you that you understand the contents of the article.

10 Search Sleuth

Below Dreamweaver Project 8, click the Search Sleuth link. To search for a term that pertains to this project, select a term below the Project 8 title and then use the Google search engine at google.com (or any major search engine) to display and print two Web pages that present information on the term.

Apply Your Knowledge

1 Creating a Slide Show for Andy's Lawn Service

Instructions: Start Dreamweaver. See the inside back cover of this book for instructions for downloading the Data Disk, or see your instructor for information on accessing the files in this book.

The proprietors of Andy's Lawn Service Web site would like to add a slide show to their Web site that shows examples of the plants that they sell. To create this slide show, you copy six images from the DataFiles folder to the Lawn Service Web site images folder and one data file to the lawn folder. You begin the process by creating five layers and adding an image to each layer. When this is completed, you use the Timelines panel to add the start and stop timeline events. Next, you add a Start button. Finally, you add links to and from the Andy's Lawn Service Services page. The first slide is shown in Figure 8-80. Software and hardware settings determine how a Web page is displayed in a browser. Your Web page may display differently than the one shown in Figure 8-80. Appendix C contains instructions for uploading your local site to a remote server.

FIGURE 8-80

1. Use the Windows My Computer option to copy the six images from the DataFiles lawn/images folder to your lawn/images folder and the data file to your lawn folder.
2. Select Lawn Service on the Files pop-up menu in the Files panel. Open the slideshow.htm file. If necessary, display the Property inspector, Standard toolbar, and panel groups.
3. Click below the introductory paragraph. Click Insert on the menu bar, point to Layout Objects, and then click Layer.
4. Drag the slide01.gif image onto the layer. Click the layer selection handle to select the layer and display the Layer Property inspector. Add the following attributes to the Property inspector: Layer ID, slide01; L, 250; and T, 175.

(continued)

Apply Your Knowledge

Creating a Slide Show for Andy's Lawn Service *(continued)*

5. Click the Vis pop-up menu and select hidden.
6. Using the data in Table 8-3, repeat Steps 3 through 5 to add the next four layers to the Web page and to add images to the layers.

Table 8-3 Slide Data				
SLIDE IMAGE	LAYER ID	L	T	VIS
Slide02.gif	slide02	250	175	hidden
Slide03.gif	slide03	250	175	hidden
Slide04.gif	slide04	250	175	hidden
Slide05.gif	slide05	250	175	hidden

7. Press ALT+F9 to display the Timelines panel. Select the text in the Timelines pop-up menu text box and then type flowers to name the timeline.
8. Drag the layer-code marker for the slide01 layer to frame 1 in Animation channel 1 in the Timelines panel. Then, drag the layer-code marker for the slide02 layer to frame 1 in Animation channel 2, and so on until all five layers have been added to the Timelines panel. If a Dreamweaver dialog box is displayed, read the information, and then click the OK button.
9. Drag the keyframe at the end of each timeline to change the number of frames to 11.
10. Click keyframe 1 in the slide01 timeline in the Timelines panel and change the closed-eye icon in the Layers panel to the open-eye icon. Click the slide01 timeline at frame 3 in the Timelines panel and then right-click to display the context menu. Click Add Keyframe and then click the Visibility column in the Layers panel for slide01 to display the closed-eye icon.
11. Click the slide02 timeline at frame 3 in the Timelines panel. Right-click to display the context menu and then click Add Keyframe. Click the Visibility column in the Layers panel for slide02 to display the open-eye icon. Click the slide02 timeline at frame 5 in the Timelines panel. Right-click to display the context menu and then click Add Keyframe. Click the Visibility column in the Layers panel for slide02 to display the closed-eye icon.
12. Click the slide03 timeline at frame 5 in the Timelines panel. Right-click to display the context menu and then click Add Keyframe. Click the Visibility column in the Layers panel for slide03 to display the open-eye icon. Click the slide03 timeline at frame 7 in the Timelines panel. Add a keyframe and then click the Visibility column in the Layers panel for slide03 to display the closed-eye icon.
13. Click the slide04 timeline at frame 7 in the Timelines panel. Add a keyframe and then click the Visibility column in the Layers panel for slide04 to display the open-eye icon. Click the slide04 timeline at frame 9 in the Timelines panel. Add a keyframe and then click the Visibility column in the Layers panel for slide04 to display the closed-eye icon.
14. Click the slide05 timeline at frame 9 in the Timelines panel, and add a keyframe. Click the Visibility column in the Layers panel for slide05 to display the open-eye icon. Click the slide05 timeline at frame 11 in the Timelines panel. Verify that the Visibility column in the Layers panel displays the closed-eye icon.
15. Click the slide01 timeline at frame 11 in the Timelines panel. Click the Visibility column in the Layers panel for slide01 to display the open-eye icon.

16. Use the playback options in the Timelines panel to play the animation in the Document window. Verify that the open and closed-eye icons are correct. When the animation is playing to verify the icons, only one open-eye icon should display; this should be the icon for the layer currently displayed. All other icons in the Layers panel Visibility column should be closed-eye icons.

17. Press SHIFT+F4 to display the Behaviors panel.

18. Click frame 2 in the Behaviors channel, click the Add behavior (+) button in the Behaviors panel, point to Timeline, and then click Stop Timeline to add the Stop Timeline behavior. If the Stop Timeline dialog box is displayed, select the flowers timeline in the Stop timeline box, and then click the OK button.

19. Repeat Step 18 and add the Stop Timeline behavior to frames 4, 6, 8, and 10 in the Timelines panel Behaviors channel. If necessary, click the Autoplay check box to deselect the check box and click the Loop check box to select the check box. If a Dreamweaver 8 dialog box is displayed, click the OK button. Click frame 1 in Animation channel 1. Collapse the Timelines panel.

20. Insert another layer in the Document window. Drag the start_button.gif image to the layer and resize the layer around the image.

21. If necessary, select the layer and then add the following attributes: Layer ID, start; L, 350; and T, 350.

22. Select the start_button.gif image within the layer and then click the Add behavior (+) button in the Behaviors panel. Point to Timeline and then apply the Play Timeline behavior. If the Play Timeline dialog box is displayed, click the OK button. If necessary, change the event to onClick in the Behaviors panel.

23. Save the Web page.

24. Press the ENTER key to move the insertion point below the layers you just added. If necessary, scroll to the bottom of the page. Type Services as the link text and create a link to the services.htm page. Save the document. Press the F12 key to view the slide show in your browser. Click the Start button to move from slide to slide. Close the browser.

25. Open the services.htm page. Select the text, Landscaping, in the bulleted list, and then create a link to the slideshow.htm page. Save the services.htm page.

26. Press the F12 key to view the page in your browser. Click the Landscaping link. Print a copy of the slideshow.htm page, if instructed to do so. Upload the page to the lawn Web Site on a remote server, if instructed to do so.

27. Quit Dreamweaver.

In the Lab

1 The CandleWix Web Site

Problem: Martha would like to add a Web page with some interactivity to the CandleWix Web site. She wants to advertise a sale for some of her special candles. You suggest a page with a nonlinear animation, in which the special for-sale candles are displayed one by one on the same page (Figure 8-81 on the next page). The first candle is set on the left side of the screen, below the heading; the second animates in from the left of the screen to the middle of the screen; and the third image animates in from the left to the right side of the screen. Martha likes this idea, and you agree to create the page. As you are completing this exercise, expand and collapse the panels as necessary. Because this is a freeform exercise, the placement on your screen is approximate. Appendix C contains instructions for uploading your local site to a remote server. *(continued)*

In the Lab

The CandleWix Web Site *(continued)*

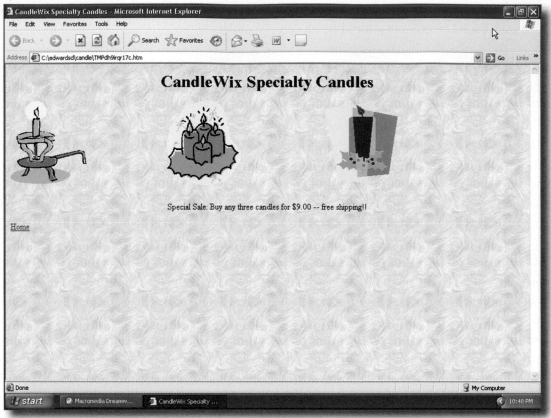

FIGURE 8-81

Instructions: Perform the following tasks:

1. Use the Windows My Computer option to copy the data file to your candle folder.

2. Start Dreamweaver. If necessary, display the panel groups and Standard toolbar. Select CandleWix on the Files pop-up menu in the Files panel. Open the candlesale.htm file.

3. If necessary, use the View menu to display the rulers. If necessary, move the insertion point to the left margin below the heading. Use the Insert menu to insert a layer. Drag the candle3.gif image onto the layer and then resize the layer to fit the image.

4. Display the Layers and Timelines panels. In the Timelines panel, name the timeline candlesale. In the Layers panel, rename the layer sale01. Click the layer-code marker and then drag it to frame 1, Animation channel 1, in the Timelines panel. If necessary, slightly move the layer and image to access the layer-code marker. The candle will display in this location, so there is no need to drag it to create a nonlinear animation.

5. Use the Insert menu to add a second layer. This layer will be created on top of the first layer. Drag the candle4.gif image onto the layer. Resize the layer to fit the image. In the Layers panel, rename the layer sale02.

6. Verify that the playback head is in frame 1 in the Timelines panel. If necessary, select the layer and then right-click the selection handle. Click Record Path on the context menu and then, using the rulers as a guide, drag the layer and image to the right approximately 300 pixels. The timeline for the sale02 layer is displayed in Animation channel 2 of the Timelines panel.

7. If necessary, move the playback head to frame 1. Insert a third layer and then drag the candle5.gif image onto the layer. Resize the layer to fit the image. Double-click Layer1 in the Layers panel and then rename the layer sale03.

8. If necessary, select the layer and then right-click the selection handle. Click Record Path on the context menu and then, using the rulers as a guide, drag the layer and image to the right approximately 600 pixels. The timeline for the sale03 layer is displayed in Animation channel 3 in the Timelines panel.

9. Move the playback head to frame 1 and then click the keyframe for sale01. Click the Visibility column in the Layers panel until the open-eye icon displays. Click the keyframe in frame 1 for the sale02 layer and then click the Visibility column in the Layers panel until the closed-eye icon displays. Click the keyframe in frame 1 for the sale03 layer and then click the Visibility column in the Layers panel until the closed-eye icon is displayed. For frame 1, sale01 has an open-eye icon and sale02 and sale03 have closed-eye icons.

10. Click the ending keyframe for sale01. The frame number will be somewhere around 15. If necessary, click the Visibility column for sale01 until the open-eye icon is displayed. Click the same frame number (somewhere around 15) in the sale02 Animation channel. If a keyframe does not exist in this location, right-click to display the context menu and then click Add Keyframe. Click the Visibility column for sale02 until the open-eye icon is displayed.

11. Click the ending keyframe for sale02, and, if necessary, change the eye icon to an open-eye icon.

12. Click the same frame number (somewhere around 20) in the sale03 Animation channel. Right-click to display the context menu and then click Add Keyframe. Click the Visibility column for sale03 until the open-eye icon is displayed. Click the ending keyframe for sale03, and, if necessary, change the eye icon to an open-eye icon. All three layers now should display open-eye icons. Click the Autoplay check box in the Timelines panel. Create a link to the Home page, and then save the candlesale page.

13. Press the F12 key to view the candlesale page in your browser. The candle02 layer should move across the page, followed by the candle03 layer. All three layers should be visible at the end of the animation. Close your browser to return to Dreamweaver.

14. Open the products.htm page. Scroll to the end of the page and then create a link following the Home link. Click to the right of the Home link, press the SPACEBAR, type |, press the SPACEBAR again, and then type Special Sale. Select the text Special Sale and link it to the candlesale.htm page. Save the products.htm page.

15. Press the F12 key to view the products.htm page in your browser. Verify that the links work. If necessary, close the browser and make any necessary adjustments to your animated Web page. Print a copy of the Web page, if instructed to do so. Upload the page to the candle Web site on a remote server, if instructed to do so.

2 Creating a Slide Show for the Credit Protection Web Site

Problem: Monica recently gave a PowerPoint presentation on stock market investing. She has received several requests asking for a copy of her presentation. To accommodate the requests, she would like to add this presentation to the Web site. Monica saved each slide as a JPEG image and has asked if you can create a Web page with the slide show images. You assure her that you can create the slide show. The first screen is shown in Figure 8-82 on the next page. As you are completing this exercise, expand and collapse the panels as necessary. Appendix C contains instructions for uploading your local site to a remote server.

(continued)

In the Lab

Creating a Slide Show for the Credit Protection Web Site *(continued)*

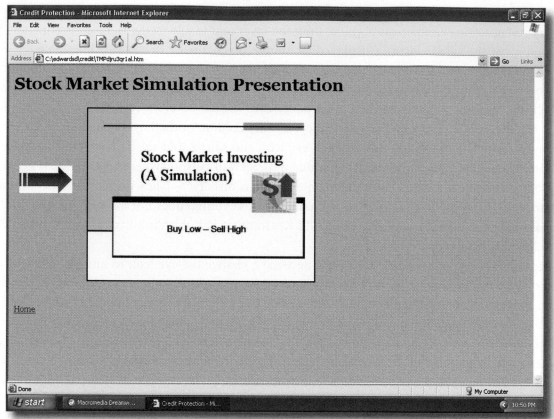

FIGURE 8-82

Instructions: Perform the following tasks:

1. Use the Windows My Computer option to copy the data file and images to your credit folder.
2. Start Dreamweaver. If necessary, display the panel groups and Standard toolbar. Select Credit Protection on the Files pop-up menu in the Files panel. Open the credit_slides.htm file.
3. If necessary, move the insertion point to the left below the heading. Insert a layer. Drag the slide1.jpg image onto the layer.
4. Click Layer1 in the Layers panel to select the layer. Click the Visibility column in the Layers panel until the closed-eye icon is displayed. In the Layer Property inspector, add stock01 as the Layer ID, and set L to 150 and T to 80. Click the layer-code marker and drag it to frame 1, Animation channel 1, in the Timelines panel. Name the timeline stockmarket.
5. Insert three more layers. Use the data in Table 8-4 to create the layers and to add the images for each layer.

Table 8-4 Slide Data				
SLIDE IMAGE	LAYER ID	L	T	EYE ICON
slide2.jpg	stock02	150	80	closed
slide3.jpg	stock03	150	80	closed
slide4.jpg	stock04	150	80	closed

6. Drag the layer-code marker for the stock02 layer to Animation channel 2, the layer-code marker for the stock03 layer to Animation channel 3, and the layer-code marker for the stock04 layer to Animation channel 4.

7. Drag the keyframe at the end of each timeline to change the number of frames to 9.

8. Click keyframe 1 in the stock01 Animation channel of the Timelines panel and then change the eye icon in the Layers panel to the open eye. The closed-eye icon should be displayed in the Layers panel for the other three layers.

9. Click the stock01 animation channel at frame 3. Add a keyframe and then change the eye icon in the Layers panel to the closed eye.

10. Click the stock02 Animation channel at frame 3. Add a keyframe and then, if necessary, change the eye icon in the Layers panel to the open eye.

11. Click the stock02 Animation channel at frame 5. Add a keyframe and then change the eye icon in the Layers panel to the closed eye.

12. Click the stock03 Animation channel at frame 5. Add a keyframe and then change the eye icon in the Layers panel to the open eye. Click the stock03 Animation channel at frame 7. Add a keyframe and then change the eye icon in the Layers panel to the closed eye.

13. Click the stock04 Animation channel at frame 7. Add a keyframe and then change the eye icon in the Layers panel to the open eye. Click the stock04 Animation channel at frame 9 and verify that the eye icon in the Layers panel is closed.

14. Click the stock01 Animation channel at frame 9 and then change the eye icon in the Layers panel to the open eye.

15. Click frame 2 in the Behaviors channel in the Timelines panel. Click the Add behavior (+) button in the Behaviors channel and then add the Stop Timeline behavior.

16. Repeat Step 15 for frames 4, 6, and 8. Click frame 1 in Animation channel 1.

17. Create another layer and then drag the next.jpg image onto the layer. Resize the layer to fit the image. Set the following properties in the Layer Property inspector: Layer ID, next; L, 20; T, 190. Select the image and then click the Add behavior (+) button in the Behaviors panel. Apply the Play Timeline command. If necessary, change the event to onClick in the Behaviors panel.

18. Click the Autoplay and Loop check boxes. Save the credit_slides.htm file.

19. Open the saving.htm page. Scroll to the bottom of the page and click to the right of the Theft link. Add a vertical line and then a link to the credit_slides.htm page. Type Stock Market Simulation as the linked text. Save the document. Press the F12 key to view the page in your browser. Click the link to display the slide show page. Click the Next button and review the slide show. Print a copy of the Web page, if instructed to do so. Upload the page to the credit Web site on a remote server, if instructed to do so.

3 Creating an Animation Page for the Lexington, NC Web Site

Problem: John wants to add some animation to the Lexington, NC Web site. You suggest to him that an animated map through the city and around the outlying areas would enhance the overall site. John likes your ideas, and you are ready to get started. The Web page with the map is shown in Figure 8-83 on the next page. Appendix C contains instructions for uploading your local site to a remote server.

(continued)

Creating an Animation Page for the Lexington, NC Web Site *(continued)*

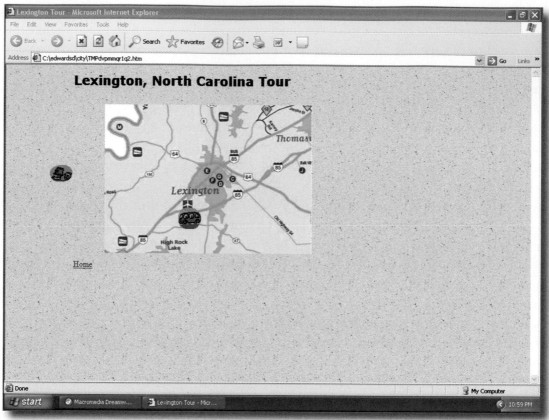

FIGURE 8-83

Instructions: Perform the following tasks:

1. Use the Windows My Computer option to copy the data file and images to your city folder.
2. Start Dreamweaver. If necessary, display the panel groups and Standard toolbar. Select Lexington, NC on the Files pop-up menu in the Files panel.
3. Open the tour.htm page. Insert a layer and then drag the map.jpg image onto the layer. Select the layer and apply the following properties in the Layer Property inspector: Layer ID, map; L, 190; T, 75.
4. Insert a second layer and then drag the bus.gif image onto the new layer. Resize the layer to accommodate the size of the bus.gif. image. Name the layer bus. Drag the bus layer onto the map so the bus.gif image is placed on Interstate 85, just below the airport icon. Right-click the bus layer and then click Record Path on the context menu.
5. Drag the bus.gif image to the right along Interstate 85 until you get to Route 64. Drag the image up and to the left along Route 64 until you reach 150. Drag down along 150 back to Interstate 85, and then along Interstate 85 until you return to the location just below the airport.
6. Name the timeline tour and then add Stop Timeline behaviors at frames near the intersection of Interstate 85 and Route 64, the intersection of Routes 64 and 150, the intersection of Route 150 and Interstate 85, and the location on Interstate 85 just below the airport. Click frame 1 in Animation channel 1.

7. Insert another layer. Drag the go.gif button onto the layer and resize the layer to accommodate the image size. Apply the following properties to the layer: Layer ID, go; L, 85; T, 190. Click the image, click the Add behavior (+) button in the Behaviors panel, and then apply the onMouseOver Play Timeline event and action. If necessary, change the event to onMouseOver in the Behaviors panel.

8. Click the Loop check box. Save the tour.htm page.

9. Open the index.htm page. Scroll to the bottom and then add a link to the tour.htm page to the right of the Employment Opportunities link. Type City Tour as the linked text. Separate the two links with a vertical bar.

10. Press the F12 key to view the index.htm page in your browser. Click the City Tour link to open the tour.htm page. Move the mouse pointer over the go.gif image to play the animation. Print a copy of the Web page, if instructed to do so. Upload the page to the city Web site on a remote server, if instructed to do so.

Cases and Places

The difficulty of these case studies varies:
■ are the least difficult and ■■ are the most difficult. The last exercise is a group exercise.

1 ■ Your sports Web site is receiving more hits each day. You decide to add a slide show page highlighting some of the more popular players. Add a background image to the page and then add a title to the page. Insert three layers and then add images to the layers. Use the Timelines panel and Autoplay to create the slide show. Create links to and from the home page. Save the page in your sports Web site. For a selection of images and backgrounds, visit the Dreamweaver 8 Media Web page (scsite.com/dw8/media) and then click Media below Project 8.

2 ■ You would like to add some interactivity to your hobby Web site. You decide to do this by adding an animation. First, add a background image to the page and then add an appropriate title. Insert four layers and four images. All four images should be the same size. Create a Forward button to advance the slide show from slide to slide. Create links to and from your home page. Upload the page to a remote site, if instructed to do so. For a selection of images and backgrounds, visit the Dreamweaver 8 Media Web page (scsite.com/dw8/media) and then click Media below Project 8.

3 ■■ Add a new page to your music hobby Web site and then add a background to the page. Add a large image that contains images of five musical instruments, musicians, or other applicable musical features. Add a layer and an image that will move from instrument to instrument (or other musical feature). Use Dreamweaver's Record Path command to move the image from instrument to instrument using the Timelines Autoplay feature. Create links to and from your home page. Upload the page to a remote site. For a selection of images and backgrounds, visit the Dreamweaver 8 Media Web page (scsite.com/dw8/media) and then click Media below Project 8.

4 ■■ Your campaign for political office is going very well. Create a new Web page and name it campaign_trail. Add an appropriate background. Next, add a map image showing locations you have visited recently. Add a layer and then add your picture to the layer. Click Dreamweaver's Record Path command and then drag the layer from location to location. Add a Forward button. Add Play Timeline and Stop Timeline behaviors where appropriate. Create links to and from your index page. Upload the revised Web site to a remote server. For a selection of images and backgrounds, visit the Dreamweaver 8 Media Web page (scsite.com/dw8/media) and then click Media below Project 8.

5 ■■ **Working Together** Recently, the student government officers selected three possible vacation sites to visit. Working with your team, create three slide shows displaying two images from each of these vacation sites. All images should be the same size. Use the T and L properties within the Layer Property inspector to center the layers. Add Stop Timeline and Play Timeline behaviors where appropriate. Add another layer with a Forward button. Create links to and from the index page. Display the three slide shows and determine which one best suits the needs of your team. Upload the selected slide show to a remote server. For a selection of images and backgrounds, visit the Dreamweaver 8 Media Web page (scsite.com/dw8/media) and then click Media below Project 8.

MACROMEDIA
Dreamweaver 8

Media Objects

PROJECT

CASE PERSPECTIVE

After visiting other Web sites for new ideas for the Colorado Parks Web site, David has found that many Web sites start with a splash page, which adds visual appeal and interest for visitors. Generally, splash pages contain videos, audio, and/or other media. This is an element that the Colorado Parks Web site does not include. David asks how difficult it would be to add a splash page to the Web site. You explain to him that it would involve some technical issues, but that Dreamweaver provides the capability of easily adding these types of features.

David brings the team together to determine the content of the splash page. Tracy suggests that some Flash text, a background sound, and a Flash movie be added and that the natl_parks.htm page be modified to contain an embedded sound file and a video file. The video, titled Tracking Kids with GPS, focuses on using technology to keep track of children. This technology is especially useful in areas such as state and national parks.

With the addition of these media objects, the Web site culminates with the best features that Dreamweaver has to offer. David and Tracy are grateful for your guidance and assistance, which have made the development of their site possible.

As you read through this project, you will learn about media and media objects. You also will learn how to insert Flash text and Flash movies into a Web page, how to add a background sound, and how to embed a sound. Additionally, you will learn how to insert video and Shockwave movies into a Web page and how to insert an applet. Finally, you will use the Dreamweaver Results panel to learn how to validate a Web page, check links, and check target browsers.

 # Media Objects

Objectives

You will have mastered the material in this project when you can:

- Describe media objects
- Insert Flash text into a Web page
- Insert a Flash movie into a Web page
- Add a background sound to a Web page
- Embed a sound file in a Web page
- Insert a video into a Web page
- Check for plug-ins
- Describe Shockwave and how to insert a Shockwave movie into a Web page

- Describe a Java applet and how to insert an applet into a Web page
- Describe the ActiveX control and how it differs from plug-ins
- Use the Results panel to validate a Web page, check links, and check target browsers

Introduction

Media objects, also called **multimedia**, are files that can be displayed or executed within HTML documents or in a stand-alone fashion. Examples include graphics such as GIFs and JPEGs, video, audio, Flash objects (SWF), Shockwave objects (DIR or DCR), PDFs (Adobe's Portable Document Format), Java applets, and other objects that can be viewed through a browser using a helper application or using a plug-in. A **helper application** is a program such as the Flash player or Shockwave viewer. These two examples are Macromedia programs and are handled easily through Dreamweaver. A **plug-in** is a program application that is installed on your computer and used to view plug-in programs through the Web browser. Once a plug-in is installed, its functionality is integrated into the HTML file, and the Web browser generally recognizes the plug-in application.

Project Nine — Designing with Interactive Media

In this project, you learn how to add interactive media to a Web page. Interactive media, or multimedia, is not suitable for all Web sites. You most likely have visited Web sites that contained so many bits and pieces of multimedia that, instead of being a constructive part of the site, the multimedia elements were detrimental to the Web experience. Therefore, when adding this type of element to your Web page, you need to consider the value of each element and how it will enhance or detract from your site.

Consider the following guidelines for adding interactive media to your Web site:

- Provide entertainment
- Assist Web site visitors with navigation
- Direct attention to certain elements
- Provide feedback
- Illustrate and/or demonstrate a particular element or part of the Web page

In Project 9, you learn how to add interactive media to the Colorado Parks Web site. You add a **splash page** that will contain Flash text, a Flash movie, and a background sound. A splash page generally consists of a default home page that displays the Web site logo or some other Web site promotion. Many splash pages use various types of interactive media — from Flash movies to animated graphics — and are good mood setters. After one or two visits to the splash page, however, the frequent Web site visitor most likely would prefer to skip the page and move on to the main Web site. Therefore, a link is added to the splash page that, when clicked, will take the visitor directly to the Web site's index page. The splash page with the link is shown in Figure 9-1a.

Next, you add an embedded sound and a video to the natl_parks.htm page (Figure 9-1b on the next page). These two elements use the Windows Media Player as the helper application to display the media within the browser window.

Finally, you use the Results panel to validate a Web page, check links, and check target browsers.

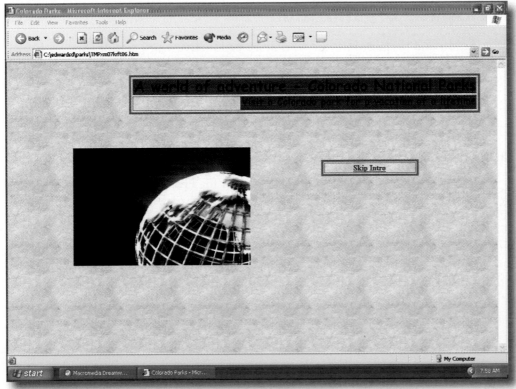

FIGURE 9-1a

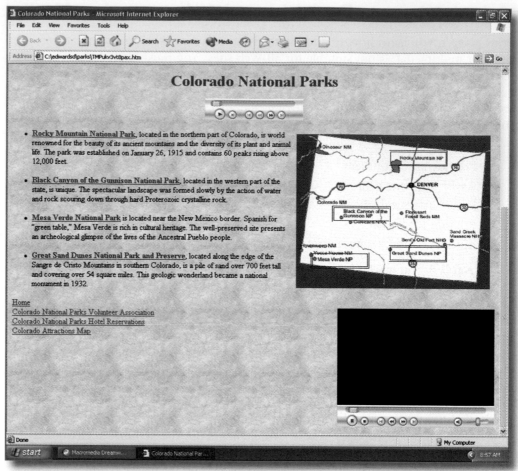

FIGURE 9-1b

Workspace Organization

Organization and preparation lead to a more productive work setting. Successful Web developers prepare their Dreamweaver workspaces to provide an effective work environment. As you learn to use additional Dreamweaver tools, including multimedia elements, you will become even more proficient working in the Dreamweaver environment.

Copying Data Files to the Local Web Site

Your Data Disk contains data files and images for Project 9. You use the Windows My Computer option to copy the Project 9 files to your parks folder. See the inside back cover for instructions for downloading the Data Disk or see your instructor for information about accessing the files required for this book.

The DataFiles folder for this project is stored on Local Disk (C:). The location on your computer may be different. If necessary, verify with your instructor the location of the DataFiles folder. The following steps illustrate how to copy the files to the parks local root folder.

To Copy Data Files to the Colorado Parks Web Site

1 Click the Start button on the Windows taskbar and then click My Computer.

2 Double-click Local Disk (C:) and then navigate to the location of the data files for Project 9.

3 Double-click the DataFiles folder, double-click the Proj09 folder, and then double-click the parks folder.

4 Right-click the media folder to display the context menu and then copy the media folder to the your name\parks folder using the Copy and Paste commands on the context menu.

5 Click the Back button and navigate to the DataFiles folder. Double-click the DataFiles folder, double-click the Proj09 folder, and then double-click the parks folder. Use the context menu to copy the splash.htm file.

6 Navigate to the your name/parks folder and use the context menu to paste the splash.htm file into the folder.

7 Close the My Computer window.

Starting Dreamweaver and Closing Open Panels

Each time you start Dreamweaver, it opens to the last site displayed when you closed the program. It therefore may be necessary for you to open the Colorado Parks Web site. The **Files pop-up menu** in the Files panel lists sites you have defined. When you open a site, a list of the pages and subfolders within the site are displayed. The following steps illustrate how to start Dreamweaver and open the Colorado Parks Web site.

To Start Dreamweaver and Open the Colorado Parks Web Site

1 Click the Start button on the Windows taskbar.

2 Point to All Programs on the Start menu, point to Macromedia on the All Programs submenu, and then click Macromedia Dreamweaver 8 on the Macromedia submenu.

3 If necessary, display the panel groups, and close the Property inspector.

4 Click the Files panel box arrow on the Files pop-up menu and then click Colorado Parks.

5 Open the splash.htm page.

6 If necessary, press CTRL+F2 to display the Insert bar and then select the Common category.

Dreamweaver opens, the Colorado Parks Web site hierarchy is displayed in the Files panel, and two tables and a layer are displayed in the splash.htm page (Figure 9-2 on the next page).

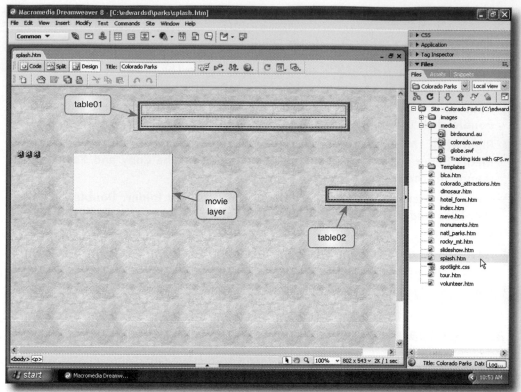

FIGURE 9-2

Media Objects

Dreamweaver provides two methods to insert media objects: the Media pop-up menu on the Insert bar and the Insert menu. The Media pop-up menu, located on the Insert bar Common category, contains buttons for inserting these special configurable objects (Figure 9-3). You use the Insert bar to complete the steps in this project. Table 9-1 describes the buttons on the Media pop-up menu on the Insert bar. Recall from Project 1 that when you select an option from a pop-up menu in some categories, that option becomes the default action for the button. The icon displayed for the Media pop-up menu in Figure 9-3 is a default icon. After you select an option from this pop-up menu, the default Media pop-up icon is no longer is available.

FIGURE 9-3

Table 9-1 Commands on the Media Pop-Up Menu

COMMAND NAME	DESCRIPTION
Flash	Places a Flash movie at the insertion point, using the <OBJECT> and <EMBED> tags. A dialog box is displayed in which you can browse to an SWF file. An SWF file is a compressed version of a Flash (.fla) file, and is optimized for viewing on the Web.
Flash Button	Places a Flash button at the insertion point; a Flash button allows a Flash movie to be inserted into the Web page.
Flash Text	Places a Flash Text button at the insertion point; a Flash Text button lets you create and insert a Flash movie that contains just text.
Flash Paper	Converts printable files into Flash documents or PDF files.
Flash Video	Inserts Flash video into a Web page.
Shockwave	Places a Macromedia Shockwave movie at the insertion point, using the <OBJECT> and <EMBED> tags.
Applet	Places a Java applet at the insertion point. A dialog box is displayed in which you can specify the file that contains the applet's code, or click Cancel to leave the source unspecified. The Java applet is displayed only when the document is viewed in a browser.
param	Inserts a tag that allows you to pass parameters to an applet or object.
ActiveX	Places an ActiveX control at the insertion point. Use the Property inspector to specify a source file and other properties for the ActiveX control.
Plugin	Inserts a file at the insertion point, using an <EMBED> tag that requires a Netscape Navigator plug-in for playback. A dialog box is displayed in which you can specify the source file.

Macromedia Flash

The **Macromedia Flash program** is an excellent way to create and add animation and interactivity to a Web page. It is a collection of tools for animating and drawing graphics, adding sound, creating interactive elements, and playing movies. It quickly is becoming a standard for Web animation. Objects within Flash are created using vector graphics. Recall from Project 2 that mathematical formulas are used to describe vector images and produce relatively small file sizes. By contrast, GIF and JPEG graphics use **bitmap technology,** which includes data for every pixel within an object. Bitmap technology therefore produces large file sizes. Thus, vector images are a more efficient method of delivering graphics over the Internet because they are displayed faster on a downloading Web page.

Creating **Flash files** (also called Flash movies) requires that the developer use the Flash program. Learning to use this program and developing Flash movies can be time-consuming. A search of the Internet, however, produces many Web sites with free and/or nominally-priced Flash animations that can be downloaded and added to your Dreamweaver Web page.

Most media objects require a helper program or plug-in before they can be displayed in the browser. For instance, the **Flash player** is required to view Flash files. Plug-ins are discussed in more detail later in this project. The Flash player is available as both a plug-in for Netscape Navigator and an ActiveX control for Microsoft

---

More About

Flash Movies

When you insert a Flash movie into a document, Dreamweaver uses both the <OBJECT> tag (defined by Internet Explorer for ActiveX controls) and the <EMBED> tag (defined by Netscape Navigator) to get the best results in all browsers.

Internet Explorer, and it is incorporated in the latest versions of Netscape Navigator, Microsoft Internet Explorer, and America Online. Macromedia also provides this player as a free download at the Macromedia Web site. You will learn more about plug-ins and ActiveX controls later in this project.

Flash Objects

Recall that Dreamweaver comes with two Flash objects you can use without having the Flash program. These two objects are Flash buttons and Flash text. In Project 7, you created a framed Web site and added Flash buttons to the navigation frame. In this project, you add Flash text. Also, recall from Project 7 that an object created with the Flash program can generate three different files, as follows:

1. **Flash file (.fla)** This is the source file for any project and is created in the Flash program. Opening an .fla file requires the Flash program. Using Flash, you then can export the .fla file as an .swf or .swt file that can be viewed in a browser.

2. **Flash movie file (.swf)** This is a compressed version of the Flash (.fla) file, and is optimized for viewing on the Web. This file can be played back in browsers and previewed in Dreamweaver, but cannot be edited in Flash. This is the type of file you create when using the Flash button and text objects in Dreamweaver.

3. **Flash template file (.swt)** This file type enables you to modify and replace information in a Flash movie file. Flash template files are used in the Flash button object.

Flash text is self-contained. Therefore, when creating Flash text, you can use fonts that are not installed on the Web site visitor's computer. In this project, the Comic Sans MS font is used to create the Flash text file. If this font is not available on your computer, use another font of your own choosing or as directed by your instructor.

Adding Flash Text

To begin creating your splash page, you open the splash.htm data file and then add Flash text. The page includes layers containing tables to facilitate page layout and to add borders to the Flash text object and other objects. The splash page contains three layers, which are named as follows: movie, title, and intro. The title and intro layers each contain tables. The title table named table01 contains two rows, or two cells. You first insert the Flash text into the table cells of table01. The following steps show how to add the Flash text to table01 in the title layer.

Q: What is an external editor?

A: You can associate each file type that Dreamweaver does not handle directly with one or more external editors found on your system. The editor that launches when you double-click the file in the Files panel is called the primary editor. You can set which editor is associated with a particular file type in the File Types/ Editors preferences.

To Add Flash Text

1

• **Collapse the panel groups. Click the first cell in table01.**

The splash.htm file contains three layers: movie, title, and intro. The title layer contains table01. The alignment for the first cell in table01 is left-aligned and the alignment for the second cell is right-aligned.

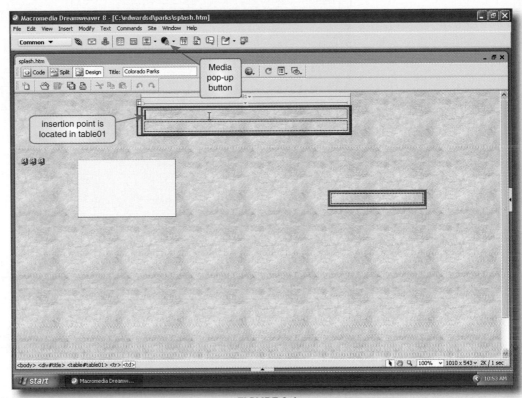

FIGURE 9-4

2

• **Click the Media pop-up button on the Insert bar and then point to Flash Text.**

The Flash Text command on the Media pop-up menu is selected (Figure 9-5). The Media pop-up button on your computer may display a different icon than that in Figure 9-5.

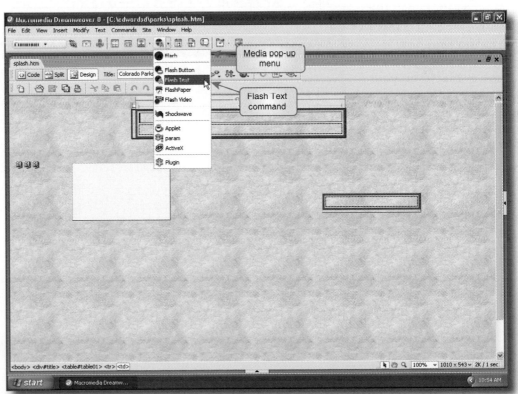

FIGURE 9-5

3

• **Click Flash Text.**

The Insert Flash Text dialog box is displayed (Figure 9-6).

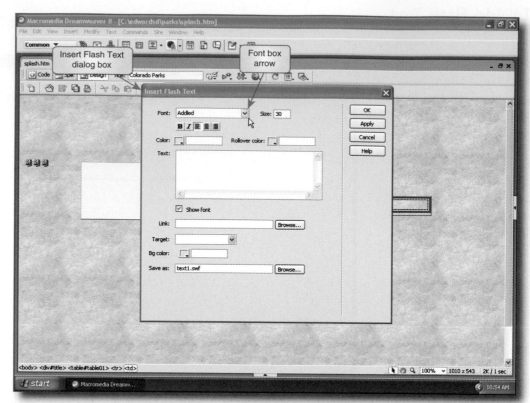

FIGURE 9-6

4

• **Click the Font box arrow, scroll down, and then click Comic Sans MS in the Font list. If the Comic Sans MS font is not available on your computer, select another font of your own choosing or as directed by your instructor.**

Comic Sans MS is selected in the Font box (Figure 9-7).

FIGURE 9-7

5

• **If necessary, double-click the Size text box and type** 30.

• **Click the Bold button.**

• **Double-click the Color hexadecimal text box, type** #000000, **if necessary, and then press the TAB key.**

• **In the Rollover color hexadecimal text box, type** #F8E4BF **and then press the TAB key. Type** A world of adventure - Colorado National Parks **in the Text box.**

• **Click the Bg color hexadecimal text box. Type** #993333 **and then press the TAB key.**

• **Type** media/heading01 **in the Save as text box.**

• **Click the OK button.**

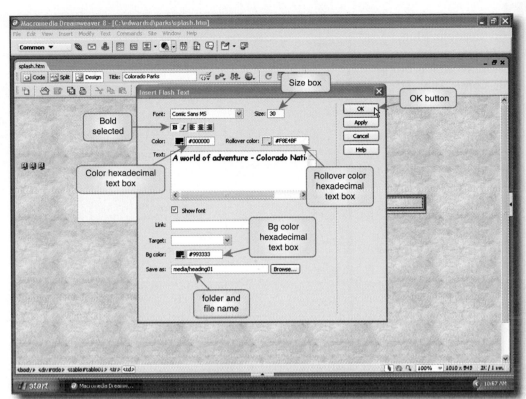

FIGURE 9-8

The attributes are added for the Flash text (Figure 9-8). The heading01 is saved as an .swf file in the media subfolder.

6

• **Click the second cell in table01 and then click the Flash Text command on the Media pop-up menu.**

In the second cell of table01, the insertion point is right-aligned, and the Insert Flash Text dialog box is displayed (Figure 9-9).

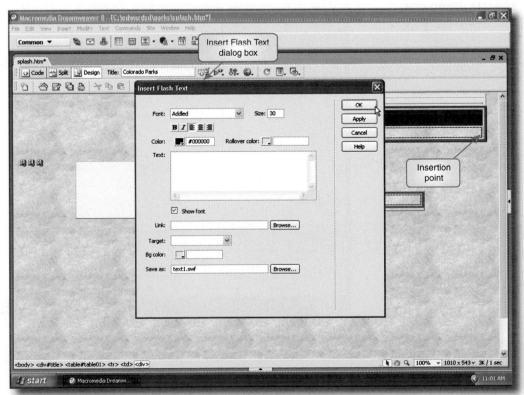

FIGURE 9-9

7

• **Add the following attributes to the Insert Flash Text dialog box— Font: Comic Sans MS; Size: 20; Bold text; Color: #000000; Rollover color: #F8E4BF; Text: Visit a Colorado park for a vacation of a lifetime; Bg color: #993333; and Save as: media/heading02.**

The attributes are added to the Insert Flash Text dialog box (Figure 9-10). Note that all of the text in the Text text box may not be visible at the same time.

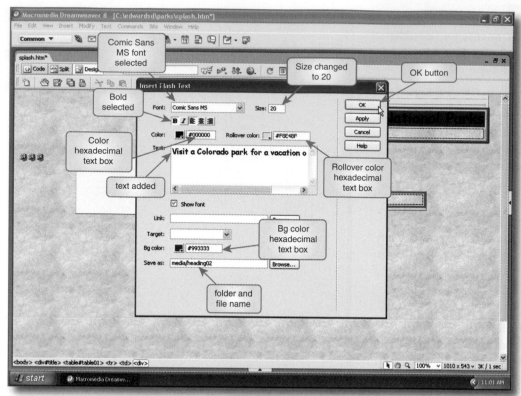

FIGURE 9-10

8

• **Click the OK button. Press CTRL+S to save the Web page. Display the Property inspector.**

The Flash text is displayed, the Web page is saved, and the Property inspector is displayed (Figure 9-11). Width and height on your screen may differ from that shown in Figure 9-11.

9

• **Press F12 to view the page in the browser. Move the mouse pointer over each line of text to verify that the text changes color.**

• **Close the browser.**

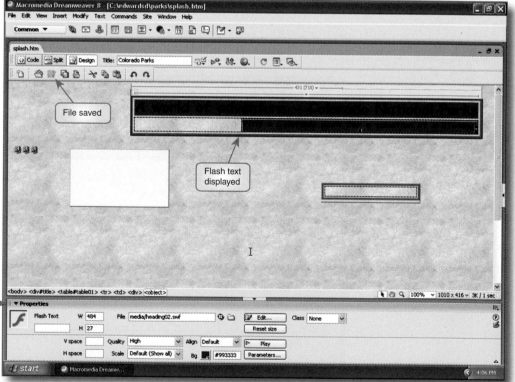

FIGURE 9-11

<table>
<tr><td>Other Ways</td></tr>
<tr><td>1. On Insert menu, point to Media, click Flash Text</td></tr>
</table>

Editing Flash Text

You edit Flash text through the Property inspector. If you select Flash text, the Flash Text Property inspector displays Flash attributes (Figure 9-12). The following section describes the Flash Text Property inspector.

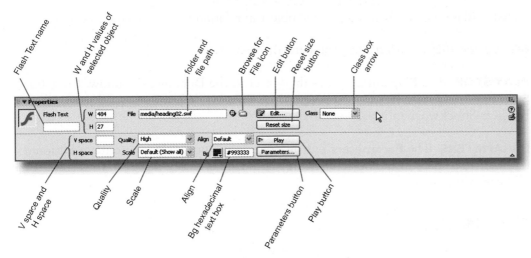

FIGURE 9-12

FLASH TEXT NAME The **Flash Text name** is an identifier used to identify the Flash text object for scripting.

W AND H The **W** and **H** boxes indicate the width and height of the object in pixels. You can specify the size in the following units: pc (picas), pt (points), in (inches), mm (millimeters), cm (centimeters), or % (percentage of the parent object's value). The abbreviations must follow the value without a space (for example, 3mm).

FILE The **File** text box allows you to include a file name that specifies the path to the Flash object file. Click the Browse for File icon to browse to a file, or type a path name in the File text box.

EDIT The **Edit** button opens the Flash object dialog box for edits to the selected Flash object. If Flash is not installed on your computer, this button is disabled.

RESET SIZE The **Reset size** button returns the selected object to its original size.

CLASS Used for scripting with Cascading Style Sheets.

V SPACE AND H SPACE The values entered into the **V space** and **H space** boxes add space, in pixels, along the sides of the object. V space adds space along the top and bottom of the object. H space adds space along the left and right of the object.

QUALITY **Quality** controls antialiasing (smoothing the jagged edges) during play-back of the movie. A movie looks better with a Quality setting of High, but that requires a faster processor to render it correctly on the screen. Low emphasizes speed over appearance, whereas High favors appearance over speed. Auto Low emphasizes speed at first, but improves appearance when possible. Auto High emphasizes both qualities at first, but sacrifices appearance for speed if necessary.

SCALE **Scale** determines how the object fits into the dimensions set in the W and H fields. The Default setting displays the entire object. The other options are No border and Exact fit. No border fits the object into the set dimensions so that no borders show and so that the original aspect ratio is maintained. Exact fit scales the object to the set dimensions, regardless of the aspect ratio.

ALIGN **Align** sets the alignment of the object in relation to other elements on the page.

BG **Bg** specifies a background color for the text area.

PLAY/STOP The **Play** button plays the object in the Document window. Click the **Stop** button to stop the object from playing. This toggle button is used primarily for Flash or Shockwave movies.

PARAMETERS The **Parameters** button opens a dialog box for entering additional parameters to pass to the object. The object must have been designed to receive these additional parameters.

Flash Movies

The earliest Web pages were plain, consisting mostly of text with links on a gray or white background. Eventually, typefaces changed, and colors and static images were added. In 1997, Macromedia purchased a software program known as FutureSplash and changed the name to Flash. Flash is a multimedia program developed especially for the Internet and the World Wide Web, and it has changed the look of and added interactivity to Web pages. Today, it is a popular program for creating movies, Web graphics, and other multimedia elements.

Adding a Flash Movie

Dreamweaver makes it easy to insert a Flash movie into a Web page. Simply position the insertion point in the Document window at the location where you would like the movie to display. Then click the Flash button on the Media pop-up menu and select the file name. Flash movies end with .swf extensions. When you insert a movie, Dreamweaver adds the code for the movie. After the movie is inserted into the Document window, a gray rectangle is displayed on the page. This rectangle represents the width and height of the movie. The width and height are determined when the developer creates the movie. The Flash logo is displayed in the center of the gray rectangle.

When a Flash movie is inserted and selected, Dreamweaver displays the Flash Property inspector. Most of the properties for a Flash movie are identical to those for Flash text (described earlier in this project). The following section describes the Flash movie Property inspector properties that are different from those for Flash text (Figure 9-13).

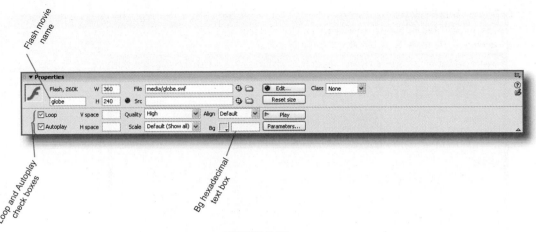

Flash movie name

Loop and Autoplay check boxes

Bg hexadecimal text box

FIGURE 9-13

FLASH MOVIE NAME The **Flash movie name** is an identifier used to identify the Flash movie object for scripting.

LOOP When the **Loop** check box is checked, the movie plays continuously; when unchecked, the movie plays once and stops.

AUTOPLAY When the **Autoplay** check box is checked, the movie plays automatically when the page loads.

BG **Bg** specifies a background color for the movie area. This color also appears while the movie is not playing (while loading and after playing).

To Add a Flash Movie

1

• **If necessary, scroll down and then click the movie layer.**

The insertion point is blinking in the layer (Figure 9-14).

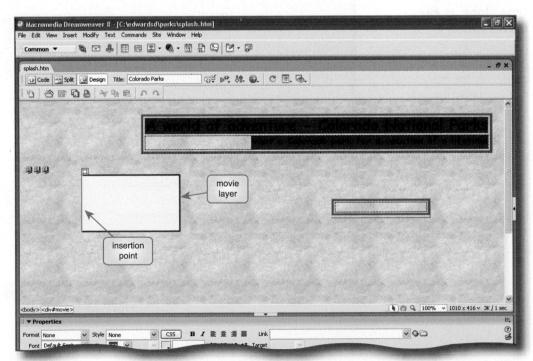

movie layer

insertion point

FIGURE 9-14

2

• **Display the panel groups and then click the Assets tab. Click the Flash icon in the Assets panel and then drag globe.swf to the movie layer.**

The Flash movie is inserted into the layer (Figure 9-15).

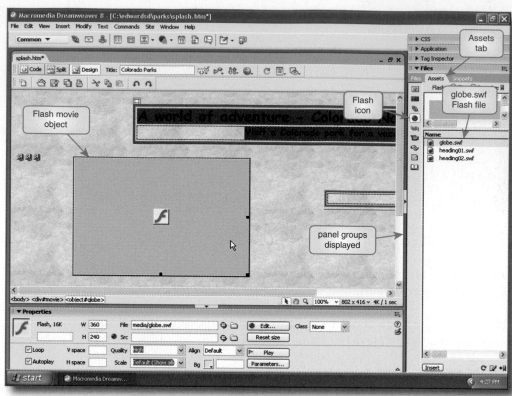

FIGURE 9-15

3

• **Hide the panel groups.**

• **Click the Flash text box in the Property inspector and then type globe as the movie name.**

The movie name, globe, appears in the Flash name text box in the Property inspector (Figure 9-16).

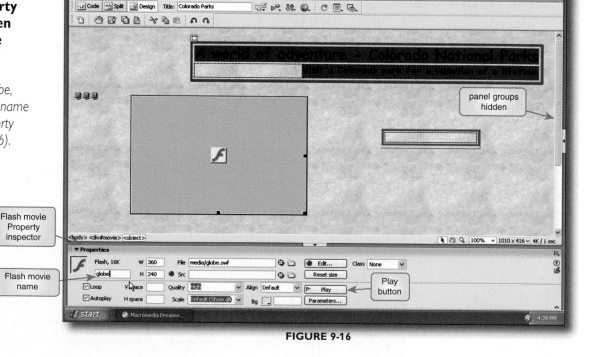

FIGURE 9-16

4

• **Click the Play button in the Property inspector.**

The movie plays in the Document window (Figure 9-17). Notice that the Play button is a toggle button, and as soon as you clicked it, the button label changed to Stop.

5

• **Click the Stop button in the Property inspector.**

The movie stops playing.

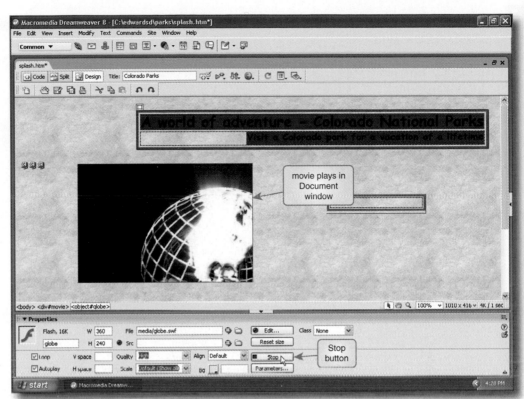

FIGURE 9-17

Other Ways

1. On Insert menu, point to Media, click Flash
2. Press CTRL+ALT+F

Adding a Link to Go to the Index Page

A splash page adds interest to a Web site, but may annoy frequent visitors. It is always best, therefore, to provide a link for the visitor to go directly to the index and/or home page. The following steps add a link in table02 to the index page.

To Add a Link to Go to the Index Page

1

• **Scroll up in the Document window and then click table02.**

The insertion point is blinking in the center of table02 (Figure 9-18).

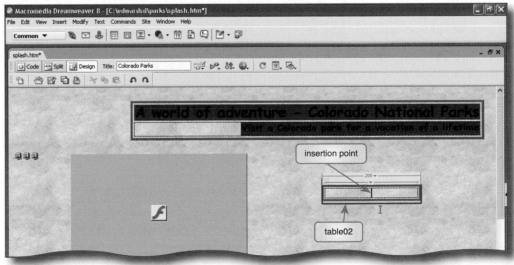

FIGURE 9-18

• **Type** Skip Intro **and then select the text. Click the BOLD button. Click the hexadecimal text box and type** #993333. **Press the TAB key.**

The text, Skip Intro, is displayed and selected in table02 (Figure 9-19).

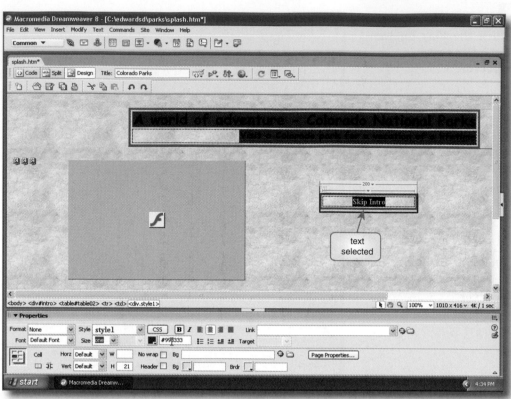

FIGURE 9-19

3

• **Display the panel groups and then click the Files tab. If necessary, scroll down in the Files panel and then drag index.htm to the Link box in the Property inspector. Press the ENTER key and then click anywhere on the page.**

The link to the index.htm Web page is added (Figure 9-20).

• **Click the Save button on the Standard toolbar and then press the F12 key to view the page in your browser.**

• **Click the link to verify that it works.**

• **Close the browser and return to Dreamweaver.**

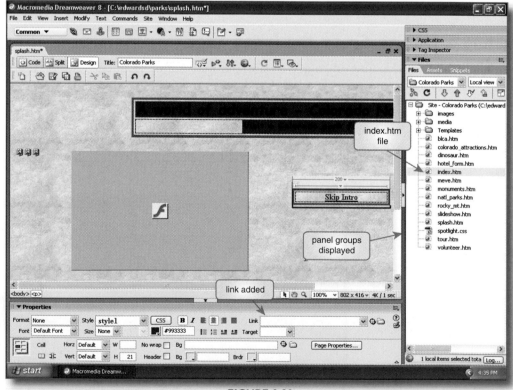

FIGURE 9-20

Audio on the Web Page

Adding sound to your Web page can add interest and set a mood. Background music can enhance your theme. Attaching sounds to objects, such as the sound of clicking buttons, can provide valuable feedback to the Web site visitor. Sound, however, can be expensive in terms of the Web site size and download time, particularly for those visitors with base-band access. Another consideration is that adding sound to a Web page can be a challenging and confusing task. Most computers today have some type of sound card and some type of sound-capable plug-in that works with the browser. The difficult part, though, is generating the desirable sounds. As you work with sound, you will discover that the Web supports several popular sound file formats, along with their supporting plug-ins; a standard format does not exist. The trick is to find the one most widely used. Table 9-2 contains a list and description of the commonly used sound file formats.

Table 9-2 Sound File Formats	
FILE NAME EXTENSION	**DESCRIPTION**
.aif (Audio Interchange File Format, or AIFF)	The AIFF format can be played by most browsers and does not require a plug-in; you also can record AIFF files from a CD, tape, microphone, and so on. The large file size, however, limits the length of sound clips that you can use on your Web pages.
.midi or .mid (Musical Instrument Digital Interface, or MIDI)	The MIDI format is for instrumental music. MIDI files are supported by many browsers and do not require a plug-in. The sound quality is good, but it can vary depending on a visitor's sound card. A small MIDI file can provide a long sound clip. MIDI files cannot be recorded and must be synthesized on a computer with special hardware and software.
.mp3 (Motion Picture Experts Group Audio, or MPEG-Audio Layer-3, or MP3)	The MP3 format is a compressed format that allows for substantially smaller sound files, yet the sound quality is very good. You can stream the file so that a visitor does not have to wait for the entire file to download before hearing it. To play MP3 files, visitors must download and install a helper application or plug-in such as QuickTime, Windows Media Player, or RealPlayer.
.ra, .ram, .rpm (RealAudio)	The RealAudio format has a very high degree of compression, with smaller file sizes than the MP3 format. Whole song files can be downloaded in a reasonable amount of time. The files also can be streamed, so visitors can begin listening to the sound before the file has been downloaded completely. The sound quality is poorer than that of MP3 files. Visitors must download and install the RealPlayer helper application or plug-in to play these files.
.wav (Waveform Extension, or WAV)	WAV-formatted files have good sound quality, are supported by many browsers, and do not require a plug-in. The large file size, however, severely limits the length of sound clips that you can use on your Web pages.

ActiveX versus Plug-ins

A Web browser basically is an HTML decoder. Recall that a plug-in is a program that is used to view plug-in applications through the Web browser. A plug-in adds functionality to the browser — it is not a stand-alone program and cannot start and run on its own. To work correctly, plug-in programs must be present in the browser's Plugins folder. Both Internet Explorer and Netscape include Plugins folders within their own application folders. When the browser encounters a file with an extension of .swf, for example, it looks for and attempts to start the Flash player plug-in.

Several years ago, Netscape developed the capability of incorporating plug-ins within the browser by creating the nonstandard HTML tag, <EMBED>. This tag never was made part of the W3C's official HTML specifications, but it became widely used.

Some of the more popular plug-ins are Adobe's Acrobat Reader, RealAudio and RealVideo, Apple's QuickTime, Macromedia's Flash and Shockwave, and VRML (Virtual Reality Modeling Language). Using these plug-ins, Web site visitors can use their browsers to view specialized content, such as animation, virtual reality, streaming audio and video, and formatted content. These plug-in programs and information are available for download at their related Web sites.

In contrast, **ActiveX** is a set of technologies developed by Microsoft and is an outgrowth of OLE (object linking and embedding). An **ActiveX control** is a control that uses ActiveX technologies and currently is limited to Windows environments. ActiveX objects use the <OBJECT> tag instead of the <EMBED> tag. When you insert media using ActiveX, you must specify a ClassID or ActiveX control and, in many instances, add parameters. Parameters are discussed in more detail later in this project.

As a result, two ways exist to insert media content into browsers: as plug-ins using the <EMBED> tag and as ActiveX objects using the <OBJECT> tag. Until recently, both Internet Explorer and Netscape supported Netscape-style plug-ins, but newer versions of Internet Explorer support only ActiveX controls, although Internet Explorer still supports the <EMBED> tag for ActiveX content.

When adding media to a Web page, the Web page developer must try to predict how Web site visitors will have their browsers configured. One of the more common problems is that a particular plug-in may not be available on a visitor's computer. Fortunately, Dreamweaver helps by offering support for both plug-ins and ActiveX controls.

Windows Media Player is one of the more popular platforms for playing audio and video. This player is Internet Explorer's default multimedia player. It plays the standard audio formats, including AIFF, AU, MIDI, WAV, and MP3. The WAV format (.wav), for example, is one of the more popular sound formats on the Internet. A compatibility issue exists, however, with the default Netscape installation and the .wav format. If you are using Netscape to view pages that contain the .wav format, most likely you will need to download a compatible plug-in.

Adding Sound to the Splash Page

As with any other technology, you first determine what you want to accomplish by adding a sound. Your sound should serve a clear and useful purpose or have an entertaining or instructional value. Web site developers primarily use one of three methods to add sound to a Web page: linking to an audio file, adding a background sound, or embedding an audio file. The simplest and easiest way to add sound to a Web page is through linking. The link can be any object, such as text, an image, or a table. The object is selected and then a link to a sound file is created. Clicking the link opens the user's designated player, such as Windows Media Player, in a separate window. You might consider using the linking method, for example, to provide instructional enhancement.

If you want to appeal to novelty, a background sound can serve this purpose. A background sound starts to play as soon as the Web page opens in the browser. In most instances, when you add a background sound, keep the sound short, do not loop the sound, and do provide your visitor with an option to stop the sound.

Embedding a sound file integrates the audio into the Web page. The sound player, along with controls, is inserted directly into the Web page. This process lets Web site visitors choose whether they want to listen to the audio and how many times they want to hear it.

In the next steps, you add the colorado.wav background sound to the splash page. When the Web site visitor opens the page, the colorado.wav file plays in the background, and the visitor has no control over the sound.

More About

Embed a Sound

When you embed a sound in a Web page, you can set the volume, the way the player looks on the page, and the beginning and ending points of the sound file. For more information about Dreamweaver and embedding sound, visit the Dreamweaver 8 More About Web page (scsite.com/dw8/more.htm) and then click Embedding Sound.

More About

ActiveX Controls

ActiveX is a set of rules for how applications should share information. ActiveX controls have full access to the Windows operating system. For more information about ActiveX controls, visit the Dreamweaver 8 More About Web page (scsite.com/dw8/more.htm) and then click ActiveX.

To Add a Background Sound and Set Parameters

1

• **Hide the Property inspector. Click below the movie layer.**

The insertion point is blinking at the left margin below the movie layer, and the Property inspector is hidden (Figure 9-21).

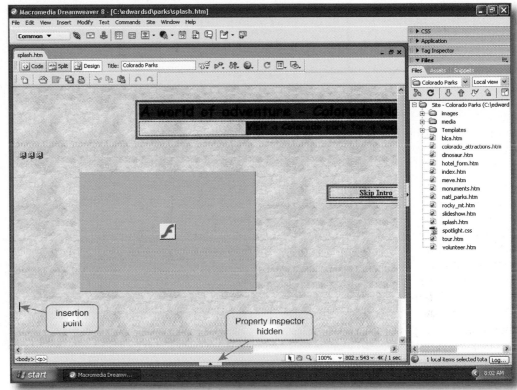

FIGURE 9-21

2

• **Click the Media pop-up button and then point to Plugin on the Media pop-up menu.**

The Media pop-up menu is displayed, and Plugin is selected (Figure 9-22).

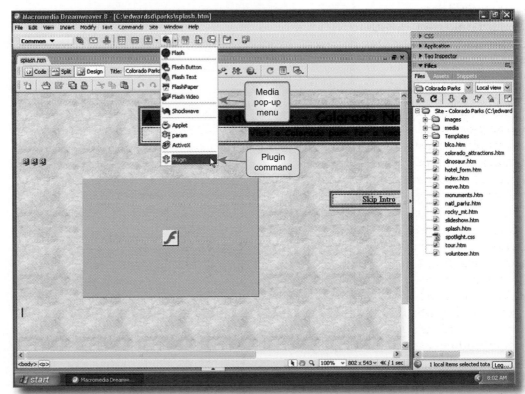

FIGURE 9-22

3

• **Click Plugin.**

The Select File dialog box is displayed (Figure 9-23).

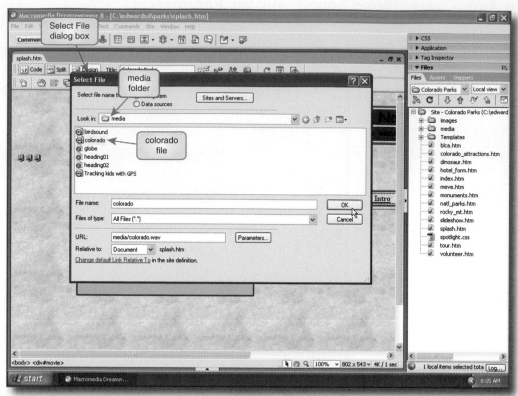

FIGURE 9-23

4

• **If necessary, navigate to and select the media folder and then click colorado in the list of files.**

The Colorado file is selected (Figure 9-24).

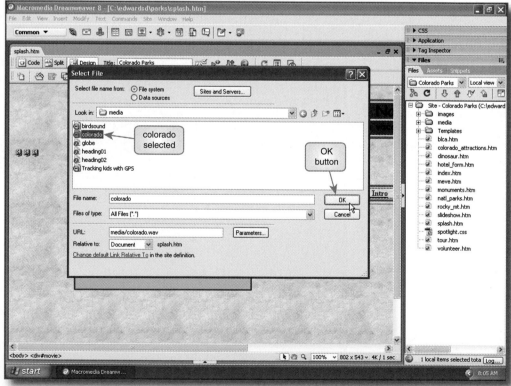

FIGURE 9-24

5

• **Click the OK button.**

A 32 × 32 pixel placeholder is displayed (Figure 9-25). This placeholder indicates the location of the plugin within the code.

FIGURE 9-25

6

• **Verify that the placeholder is selected. Display the Property inspector and then type** 2 **in the W text box.**

• **Press the TAB key and then type** 2 **in the H text box. Press the ENTER key.**

The placeholder is resized and appears as a dot on the Web page (Figure 9-26).

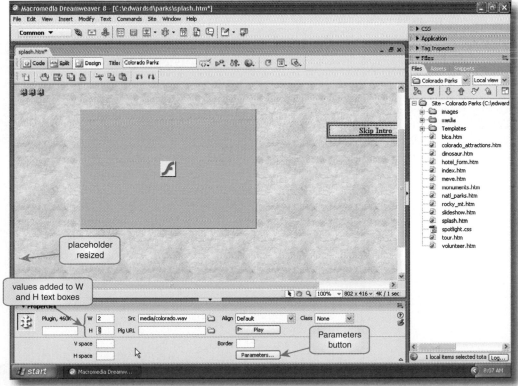

FIGURE 9-26

7

• **Click the Parameters button.**

The Parameters dialog box is displayed (Figure 9-27).

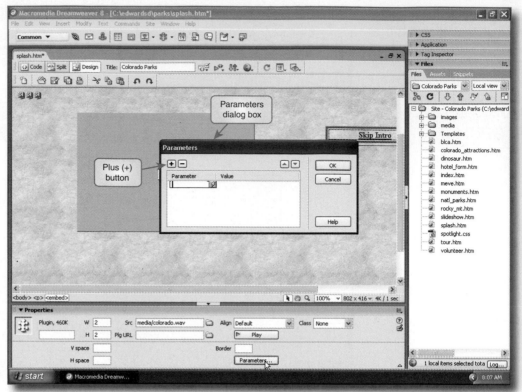

FIGURE 9-27

8

• **Type** hidden **in the Parameter column. Press the TAB key two times.**

The hidden parameter is added, and the insertion point is in the Value column (Figure 9-28).

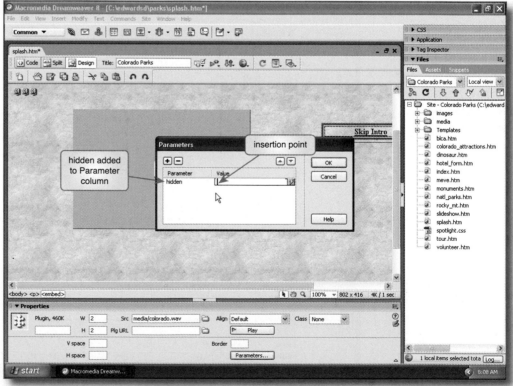

FIGURE 9-28

9

• **Type** true **in the Value column and then press the TAB key two times.**

The true parameter is added, and the insertion point is in the Parameter column (Figure 9-29).

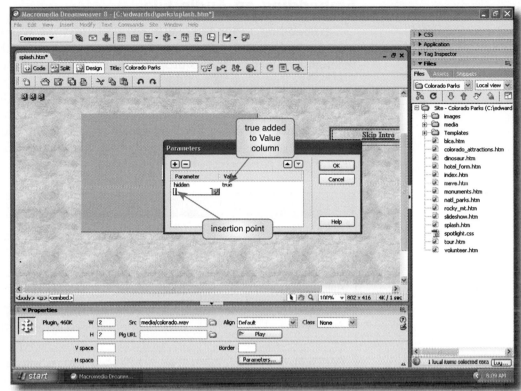

FIGURE 9-29

10

• **Type** autoplay **and then press the TAB key two times. Type** true **in the Value column.**

• **Press the TAB key two times. Type** loop **in the Parameter column, press the TAB key two times, and then type** false **in the Value column.**

The autoplay and loop parameters and the true and false values are added to the Parameters dialog box (Figure 9-30).

11

• **Click the OK button.**

• **Save the file.**

• **Press the F12 key to open the browser and verify that the audio works. A speaker or headphones must be attached to the computer for you to hear the audio. Close the browser.**

• **Close the splash.htm page.**

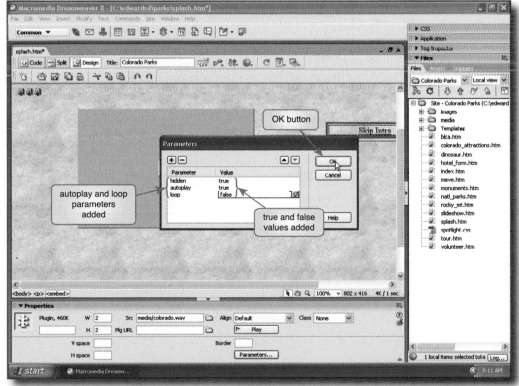

FIGURE 9-30

Embedding an Audio File

Embedding a sound in a Web page provides the Web site visitor with control over the audio player. The content developer determines the amount of control through parameters. In this project, you embed an audio player into the natl_parks.htm page. When the user clicks a control, a bird sound is heard through the Windows Media Player. An ActiveX control is used, thereby requiring specific parameters. A parameter defines the characteristics of something. For example, AutoRewind, AutoStart, and font specifications are considered to be parameters. Table 9-3 contains a list of frequently used parameters. This list is an example only; several other parameters also are available.

Table 9-3 ActiveX Parameters		
PARAMETER	**DEFAULT**	**DESCRIPTION**
AutoStart	True	Defines whether the player should start automatically
AnimationAtStart	True	Defines whether an animation should show while the file loads
AutoRewind	False	Defines whether the player should rewind automatically
ClickToPlay	True	Defines whether the player should start when the user clicks the play area
DisplayBackColor	False	Shows a background color
EnablePositionControls	True	Provides the user with position controls
EnableFullScreenControls	False	Provides the user with screen controls
Filename	N/A	Indicates the URL of the file to play
InvokeURLs	True	Links to a URL
Mute	False	Mutes the sound
ShowControls	True	Defines whether the player controls should show
ShowAudioControls	True	Defines whether the audio controls should show
ShowDisplay	False	Defines whether the display should show
Volume	-200	Specifies the volume

ActiveX controls also require a ClassID. Dreamweaver uses the ClassID to define the object when generating the code for the ActiveX control. This hexadecimal ID is added through the ActiveX Property inspector. Once added, it will become an option within the ClassID pop-up menu. The following section describes the ActiveX Property inspector (Figure 9-31).

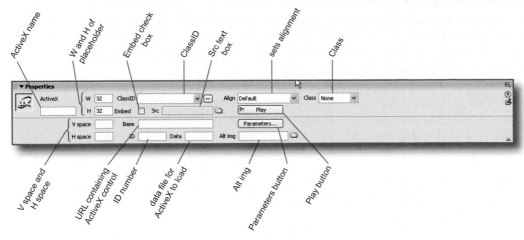

FIGURE 9-31

ACTIVEX NAME BOX The name in the ActiveX name box identifies the ActiveX object for scripting purposes.

W AND H W and H are the width and height, respectively, of the image, in pixels. Dreamweaver automatically inserts the dimensions when an image is inserted into the page. You can specify the image size in the following units: pc (picas), pt (points), in (inches), mm (millimeters), cm (centimeters), and combinations, such as 2in+5mm. Dreamweaver converts the values to pixels in the HTML source code.

CLASSID The **ClassID value** identifies the ActiveX control to the browser. Enter a value or choose one on the pop-up menu. When the page is loaded, the browser uses the ClassID to locate the ActiveX control required for the ActiveX object associated with the page. For all versions of Windows Media Player from version 7 on, use the following ClassID: CLSID:22d6f312-b0f6-11d0-94ab-0080c74c7e95. You assign this number in the ActiveX Property inspector.

EMBED Checking the **Embed** check box adds an <EMBED> tag within the <OBJECT> tag for the ActiveX control. If the ActiveX control has a Netscape Navigator plug-in equivalent, the <EMBED> tag activates the plug-in. Dreamweaver assigns the values you enter as ActiveX properties to their Netscape Navigator plug-in equivalents.

ALIGN Align sets the alignment of an ActiveX object on the page.

PARAMETERS The **Parameters** button opens a dialog box for entering additional parameters to pass to the ActiveX object.

SRC The **Src** value defines the data file to be used for a Netscape Navigator plug-in if the Embed check box is selected. If a value is not entered, Dreamweaver attempts to determine the value from the ActiveX properties already entered.

V SPACE AND H SPACE The **V space** and **H space** values add space, in pixels, along the sides of the object. V space adds space along the top and bottom of an object. H space adds space along the left and right of an object.

BASE The **Base value** specifies the URL containing the ActiveX control. Internet Explorer downloads the ActiveX control from this location if the control has not been installed already in the visitor's system. If the Base parameter is not specified and if the Web site visitor does not have the relevant ActiveX control installed, the browser cannot display the ActiveX object.

ALT IMG The **Alt img** parameter indicates an image to be displayed if the browser does not support the <OBJECT> tag. This option is available only when the Embed check box is not selected.

DATA The **Data** parameter specifies a data file for the ActiveX control to load. Many ActiveX controls, such as Shockwave and RealPlayer, do not use this parameter.

ID This option specifies the data file ID.

PLAY/STOP The Play/Stop button plays and stops the movie, sound, or other selected media in the Document window.

CLASS Used for scripting with cascading style sheets.

To Embed an Audio File

The following steps illustrate how to embed an audio file in the natl_parks.htm Web page. A speaker or headphones are required to hear the sound.

To Embed an Audio File

1

• **Open the natl_parks.htm page and then hide the panel groups.**

• **Click to the right of the heading text, Colorado National Parks, and then press the ENTER key.**

• **Click the Media pop-up button and then point to ActiveX.**

The insertion point is centered and below the heading text (Figure 9-32).

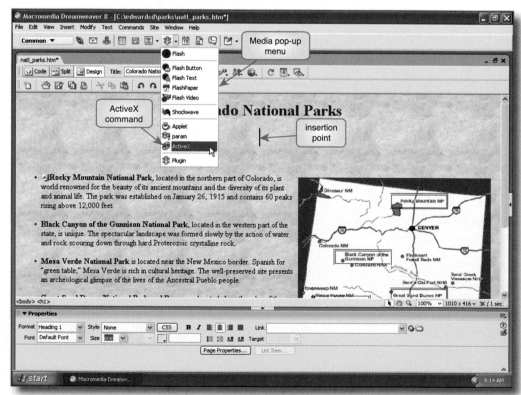

FIGURE 9-32

2

• **Click ActiveX.**

A placeholder marks the location where the ActiveX control will appear on the page in Internet Explorer, and the ActiveX Property inspector is displayed (Figure 9-33).

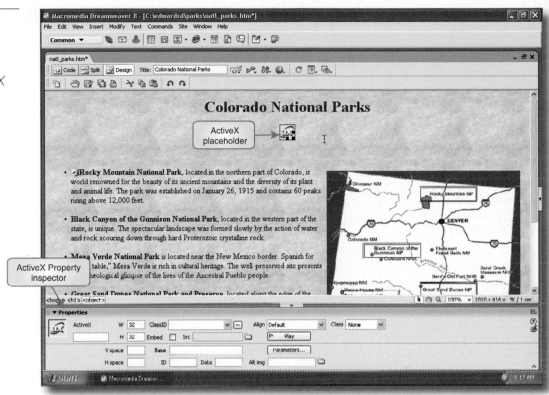

FIGURE 9-33

3

• **Click the ActiveX name box in the Property inspector and then name the ActiveX control birdsound.**

• **Change the W value to 200 and the H value to 45. Type** CLSID:22d6f312-b0f6-11d0-94ab-0080c74c7e95 **in the ClassID text box.**

• **Press the ENTER key.**

The ActiveX name, W and H values, and ClassID number are added to the ActiveX Property inspector (Figure 9-34). Once you type in the ClassID number, it becomes part of the pop-up menu. It will not be necessary to add the number again. It is suggested you check the number to verify that it is correct.

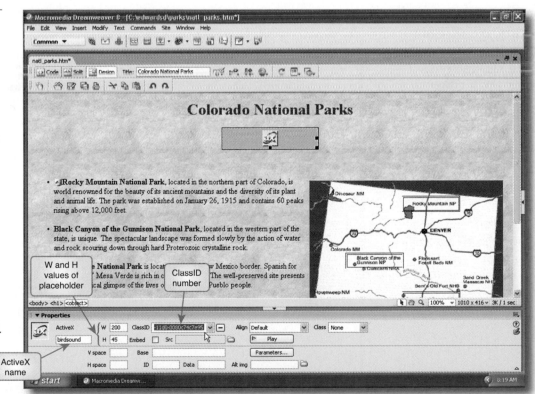

FIGURE 9-34

4

• **Click the Embed check box and then click the Browse for File icon to the right of the Src text box.**

• **If necessary, when Dreamweaver displays the Select Netscape Plug-In File dialog box, click the Look in box arrow and then, if necessary, navigate to the media folder.**

The Select Netscape Plug-In File dialog box is displayed and the media folder is open (Figure 9-35).

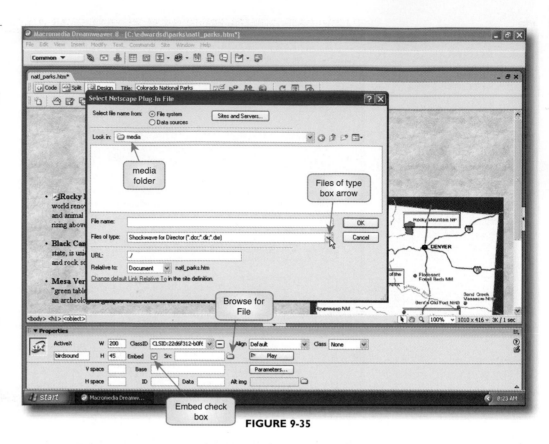

FIGURE 9-35

5

• **Click the Files of type box arrow and then click All Files. Click the birdsound file. Verify that Document is selected in the Relative to box.**

The birdsound file is selected (Figure 9-36).

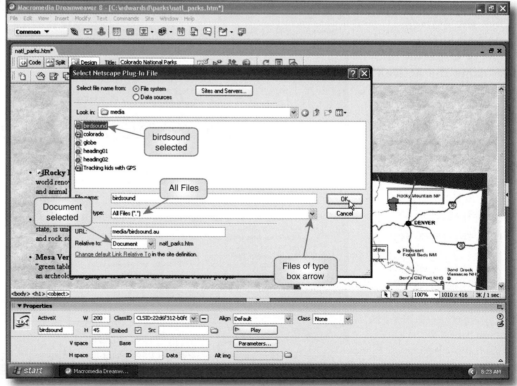

FIGURE 9-36

6

• **Click the OK button.**

The link to the source file is created (Figure 9-37). When viewed in a browser, this rectangle will contain the audio controls.

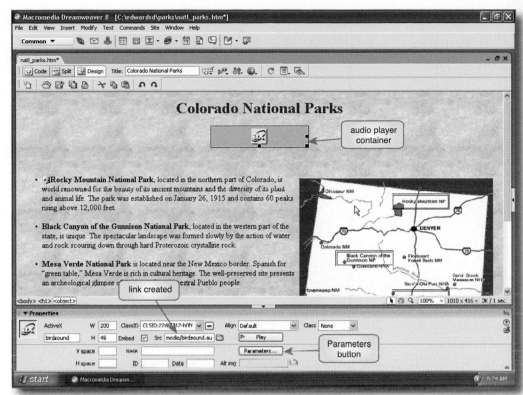

FIGURE 9-37

7

• **Click the Parameters button in the Property inspector.**

• **if necessary, click the Plus (+) button to display the insertion point in the Parameter column.**

The Parameters dialog box is displayed, and the insertion point is in the Parameter column (Figure 9-38).

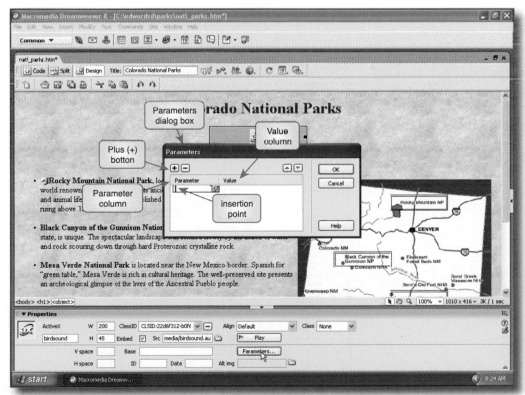

FIGURE 9-38

8

• **Type** FileName **and then press the** TAB **key two times. Type** media/birdsound.au **in the Value column.**

The first parameter and value are added to the Parameters dialog box (Figure 9-39).

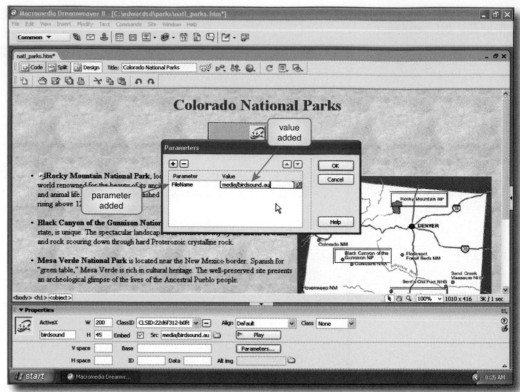

FIGURE 9-39

9

• **Press the** TAB **key two times.**

• **Use Table 9-4 to add the other parameters and values to the Parameters dialog box.**

The parameters are added to the Parameters dialog box (Figure 9-40).

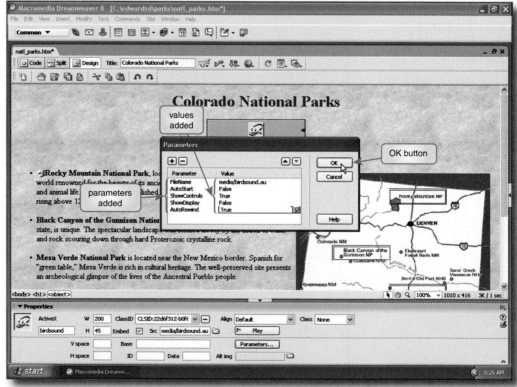

FIGURE 9-40

Table 9-4 Parameters and Values	
PARAMETER	VALUE
AutoStart	False
ShowControls	True
ShowDisplay	False
AutoRewind	True

10

• **Click the OK button.**

• **Click the Save button on the Standard toolbar.**

The ActiveX control for the Media player is displayed in the Document window (Figure 9-41).

11

• **Press the F12 key to view the Web page in your browser. Click the Play button to listen to the audio. A speaker or headphones are necessary to hear the sound. If a Dreamweaver dialog box is displayed, read the information and then click the OK button.**

The Windows Media Player audio control is displayed (Figure 9-42). If the sound control bar does not display in the browser, see your instructor.

12

• **Close the browser.**

Other Ways

1. On Insert menu, point to Media, click ActiveX

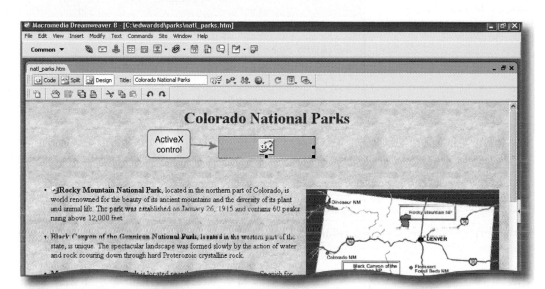

FIGURE 9-41

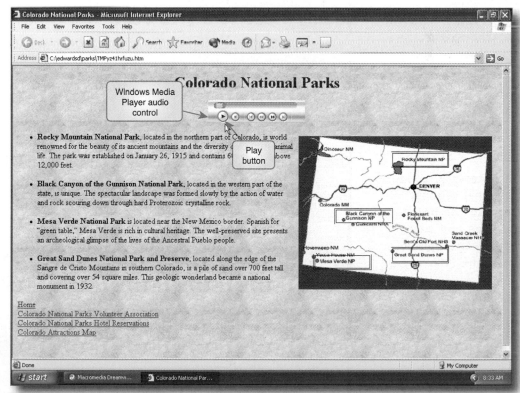

FIGURE 9-42

More About

Adding Video

When adding video, you can let
the user download it or the
video can be streamed so that
it plays while downloading. For
more information about
Dreamweaver and video, visit
the Dreamweaver 8 More
About Web page (scsite.com/
dw8/more.htm) and then click
Streaming Video.

Earlier in this project, you inserted a Flash movie into the splash page. Inserting the Flash movie was a fairly simple process because Flash also is a Macromedia product. Therefore, Dreamweaver comes with built-in controls to display a Flash movie. Movies, however, come in several other formats, and most likely occasions will arise when you will want to insert a movie in another format. Table 9-5 contains a description of video file formats that are used on the Internet. All formats display in both Internet Explorer and Netscape.

Table 9-5 Video File Formats

FILE NAME EXTENSION	DESCRIPTION
.avi (Audio Video Interleave, or AVI)	The AVI format is supported by all computers running Windows.
.mpg or .mpeg (Moving Pictures Expert Group, or MPEG)	The MPEG format is one of the more popular formats on the Internet. It is cross-platform, running on Windows and Macintosh computers.
.mov (QuickTime, developed by Apple)	QuickTime is a common format on the Internet for both Windows and Macintosh computers. Playing QuickTime movies on a Windows computer requires the QuickTime Player.
.rm or .ram (RealVideo, developed by RealMedia)	The RealVideo format allows the streaming of video, which reduces downloading time.
.swf (Flash SWF)	The SWF format requires the Macromedia Flash player.
.wmv, .wvx (Windows Media Format, or WMF)	The WMF format allows the streaming of video, uses the Windows Media Player, and plays on both Windows and Macintosh computers.

Adding Video to a Web Page

The following steps show how to add a Windows Media Player video file to the natl_parks.htm Web page.

To Add Video to a Web Page

1

• **If necessary, collapse the panel groups. Scroll to the bottom of the page and then click to the right of the Home link.**

The insertion point is blinking to the right of the Home link (Figure 9-43).

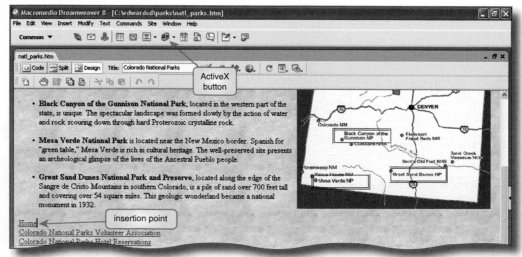

FIGURE 9-43

2

• **Click the ActiveX button on the Common category Insert bar.**

The ActiveX control is displayed and selected in the Document window (Figure 9-44).

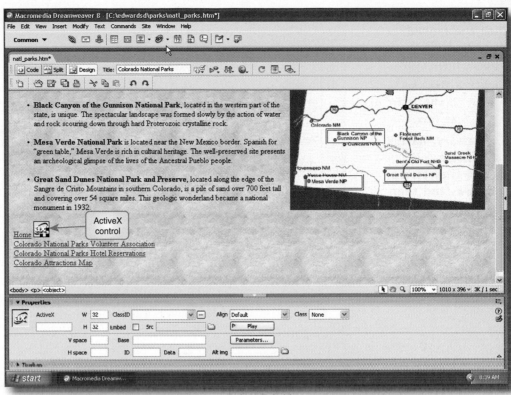

FIGURE 9-44

3

• **Click the ActiveX name box in the Property inspector and then type** gps **as the name.**

• **Press the TAB key and then change the W value to 320. Press the TAB key and then change the H value to 240.**

• **Click the ClassID box arrow and then select the ClassID value you entered earlier in this project.**

• **Click the Align box arrow and align the ActiveX control to the right.**

The name, W and H, ClassID, and Align properties are added to the Property inspector (Figure 9-45).

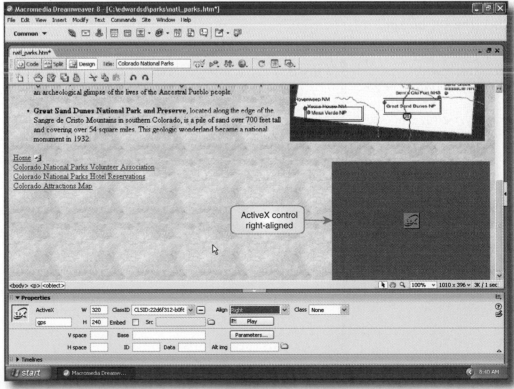

FIGURE 9-45

4

• **Click the Embed check box in the Property inspector.**

• **Click the Browse for File icon to the right of the Src text box.**

• **If necessary, navigate to the media folder, click the Files of type box arrow, and then select All Files. Click the Tracking kids with GPS file.**

The Select Netscape Plug-In File dialog box is displayed (Figure 9-46).

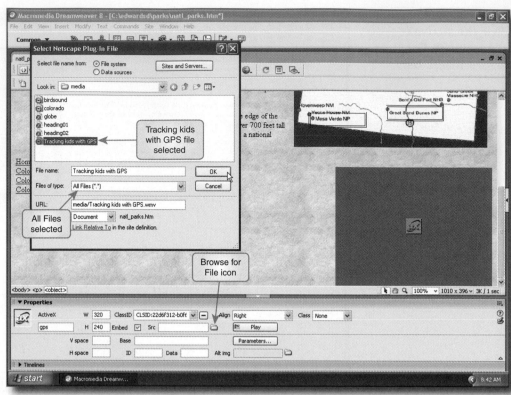

FIGURE 9-46

5

• **Click the OK button.**

The file name and path are added to the Src text box (Figure 9-47).

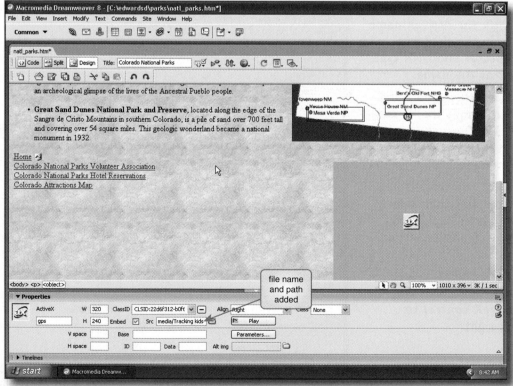

FIGURE 9-47

6

• **Click the Parameters button in the Property inspector and then click the Plus (+) button.**

The Parameters dialog box is displayed, and the insertion point is blinking in the Parameter text box (Figure 9-48).

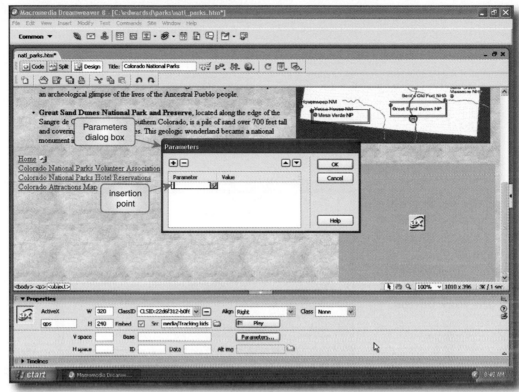

FIGURE 9-48

7

• **Apply the steps you used on pages DW 727 – 729 to add the parameters and values shown in Table 9-6 on the next page to the Parameters dialog box.**

The parameters and values are added to the Parameters dialog box (Figure 9-49).

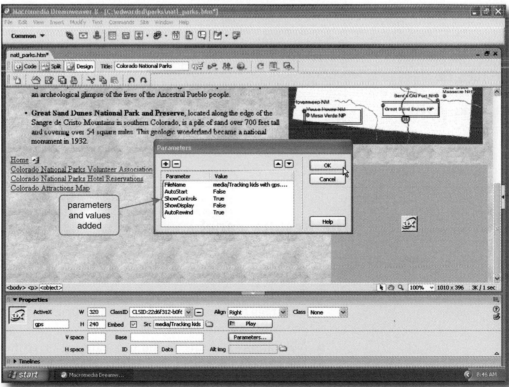

FIGURE 9-49

Table 9-6 Parameters and Values	
PARAMETER	VALUE
FileName	media/Tracking kids with gps.wmv
AutoStart	False
ShowControls	True
ShowDisplay	False
AutoRewind	True

• **Click the OK button.
Save the page. Press
the F12 key to display
the page in your
browser. Scroll down to
display the video file.
Click the Play button.**

*The video placeholder is
displayed (Figure 9-50). If you
are using Netscape as your
browser, most likely the movie
starts to play when the page
is displayed in the browser.*

9

• **Close the browser
to return to
Dreamweaver. Close the
natl_parks page.**

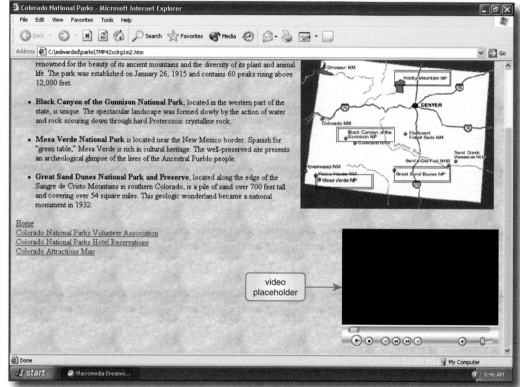

FIGURE 9-50

The Results Panel

Dreamweaver's Results panel (Figure 9-51 on the next page) provides several options to help maintain your site. These options are described below:

- **Search**   Use this option to search for and replace text, source code, and specific tags for the current document, open documents, selected files in a site, or the entire current local site.

- **Validation**   Use this option to locate tag or syntax errors. You can validate the current document or a selected tag.

- **Target Browser Check**   The Target Browser Check feature checks the code in your documents to see if any of the tags, attributes, CSS properties, or CSS values are unsupported by your target browser.

- **Link Checker**   The Link Checker searches for broken links and unreferenced files in a portion of a local site or throughout an entire local site. External links are not checked.

- **Site Reports** Site reports provide information on workflow or HTML attributes, including accessibility, for the current document, selected files, or the entire site. This option primarily is used by Web teams.
- **FTP Log** This option keeps track of all FTP activity. If an error occurs when you are transferring a file using FTP, the site FTP log can help you determine the problem.
- **Server Debug** This option is a tool to assist with server problems, and is used primarily with dynamic data.

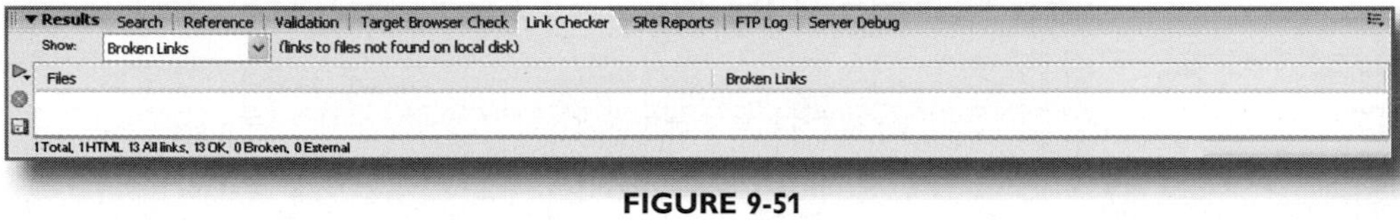

▼ Results	Search	Reference	Validation	Target Browser Check	Link Checker	Site Reports	FTP Log	Server Debug

Show: Broken Links ∨ (links to files not found on local disk)

Files   Broken Links

1 Total, 1 HTML, 13 All links, 13 OK, 0 Broken, 0 External

FIGURE 9-51

Using the Link Checker

It is important that you check and verify that your links work. Links are not active within Dreamweaver; that is, you cannot open a linked document by clicking the link in the Document window. You can check any type of link by displaying the page in a browser. Using a browser is the only available validation option for absolute or external links and e-mail links. For relative or internal links, Dreamweaver provides the Link Checker feature. Use the Link Checker to check internal links in a document, a folder, or an entire site.

A large Web site can contain hundreds of links that can change over time. Dreamweaver's **Link Checker** searches for broken links and unreferenced files in a portion of a local site or throughout an entire local site. This feature is limited, however, because it verifies internal links only. A list of external links is compiled, but not verified. As previously discussed, external links must be checked through a browser.

The Link Checker does have advantages, however. When you use this feature, the Link Checker displays a statistical report that includes information about broken links, orphaned files, and external links. An **orphaned file** is a file that is not connected to any page within the Web site. The orphaned file option is for informational purposes only. The orphaned file report, however, is particularly valuable for a large site, because it displays a list of all files that are not part of the Web site. Deleting unused files from a Web site increases disk space and streamlines your site. You can use the Link Checker to check links throughout your entire site from any Web page within the site. After you run the Link Checker, you can fix broken links in the Property inspector or directly in the Link Checker panel. In this exercise, you fix a broken link in the Property inspector.

The following steps show how to use the Link Checker to verify the internal links for the natl_parks.htm page. The link to the Colorado Parks Slide Show is changed from slideshow.htm to slide_show.htm intentionally to illustrate how the Link Checker works and how to make corrections. Your results may be different from the ones shown below. The following steps illustrate how to change a file name and to verify internal links using the Link Checker.

To Verify Internal Links with the Link Checker

1

• Display the panel group and then open the index.htm page.

• Click slideshow.htm in the Files list to select the name and then press the F2 key.

• Type slide_show.htm to rename the file and then press the ENTER key.

• If the Update Files dialog box is displayed, click the Don't Update button.

• Press the F5 key to refresh the panel groups and then hide the panel groups.

• Click File on the menu bar, point to Check Page, and then point to Check Links.

FIGURE 9-52

The File menu is displayed, and Check Links is selected (Figure 9-52).

2

• Click Check Links.

The Results panel group is displayed, and the Link Checker panel is selected. The statistical report shows information about the links in the site, including 1 Total, 1 HTML, 37 All links, 33 OK, 1 Broken, and 3 External (Figure 9-53). External links are not verified. Your report may include different results.

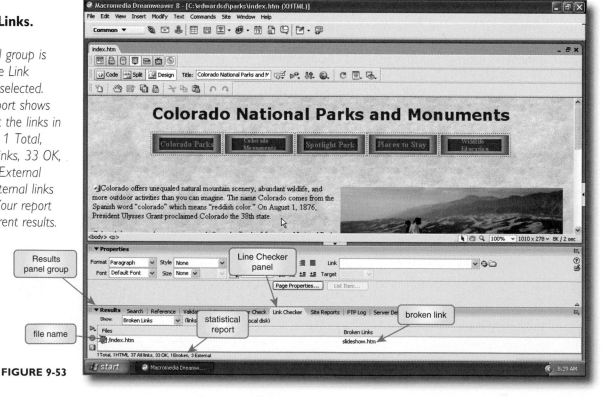

FIGURE 9-53

3

• **Double-click index.htm in the Results panel.**

The Colorado Parks Slide Show linked text is selected, and slideshow.htm is displayed in the Link box (Figure 9-54).

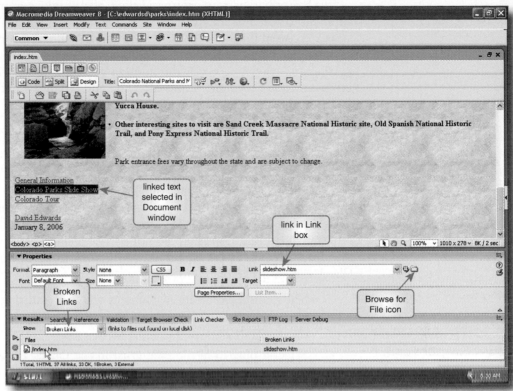

FIGURE 9-54

4

• **Double-click the Link box in the Property inspector and type** slide_show.htm **as the new link. Press the ENTER key.**

• **Click the Check Links arrow and then click Check Links in Current Document.**

• **Save the index file.**

The link is modified to slide_show.htm in the Property inspector. The broken link is removed from the Link Checker panel, and the statistical report is updated automatically (Figure 9-55).

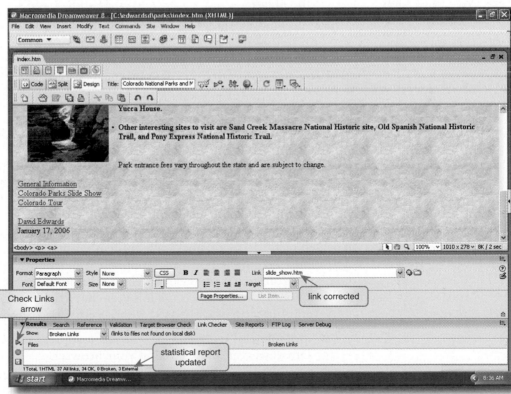

FIGURE 9-55

Other Ways

1. Press SHIFT+F8

In the previous steps, you used the Check Links command on the Check Page submenu of the File menu to check the links. The Check Page submenu also contains Check Accessibility, Check Target Browsers, Validate Markup, and Validate XML commands. These options all are for a single page.

Dreamweaver also provides another option to check links sitewide or to change a link sitewide. The Check Links Sitewide and Change Link Sitewide commands are accessed through the Site menu.

Checking for Plug-ins

If a visitor accesses a Web page and does not have the appropriate plug-in, it is helpful to provide a link where the visitor can download the plug-in. This is done through the Check Plugin behavior. This is particularly helpful for RealMedia, RealAudio, and other media applications that are not part of a standard Windows installation (like Windows Media Player). The following steps provide information on how to add the Check Plugin behavior.

1. Select an object in the Document window and then open the Behaviors panel.
2. Click the Action (+) button in the Behaviors panel and then click Check Plugin on the Actions pop-up menu.
3. Select a plug-in in the Plugin list in the Check Plugin dialog box, or click the Enter option button and then type the exact name of the plug-in in the adjacent text box.
4. In the If Found, Go To URL text box, specify a URL for visitors who have the plug-in.
5. In the Otherwise, Go to URL text box, specify an alternative URL for visitors who do not have the plug-in.
6. Click the Always go to first URL if detection is not possible check box to select it. Click the OK button.

Shockwave

Another popular media type is **Shockwave**. Macromedia's Director program is used to create Shockwave files. Director often is referred to as an authoring tool or development platform. A developer can use a combination of graphics, video, sound, text, animation, and other elements to create interactive multimedia. After the developer creates the multimedia, it can be compressed into a Shockwave file and then added to a Web page. To play Shockwave content within your browser, the Shockwave player must be installed on your computer. You can download the latest version of the player from the Macromedia Web site. Information on Macromedia's Web site indicates that more than 280 million users have the Shockwave player installed.

Several file formats associated with Director and Shockwave are described below.

-   **.dcr (Shockwave)** The .dcr file is a compressed file that can be previewed in Dreamweaver and viewed in your browser.
-   **.dir** The .dir file is the source file created by Director. These files usually are exported through Director as .dcr files.
-   **.dxr** The .dxr file is a locked Director file.
-   **.cst** The .cst file contains additional information that is used in a .dxr or .dir file.
-   **.cxt** The .cxt file is a file locked for distribution purposes.

The software that plays Shockwave movies is available both as a Netscape Navigator plug-in and as an ActiveX control. When you insert a Shockwave movie into a Web page, Dreamweaver uses both the <OBJECT> tag (for the ActiveX control) and the <EMBED> tag (for the plug-in) to get the best results in all browsers. When you make changes in the Property inspector for the movie, Dreamweaver maps your entries to the appropriate parameters for both the <OBJECT> and <EMBED> tags.

Inserting a Shockwave file is similar to inserting a Flash movie. The following steps explain how to insert a Shockwave file into the Dreamweaver Document window.

1. Click the Document window where you want to insert the movie.
2. Click the Shockwave command on the Media pop-up menu on the Insert bar.
3. Select a movie file in the Select File dialog box.
4. Enter the W and H values of the movie in the W and H text boxes in the Property inspector.
5. Add any necessary parameters.

Java Applets

An **applet** is a small program written in **Java**, which is a programming language for the Web. The applet can be downloaded by any computer. The applet also runs in HTML and usually is embedded in an HTML page on a Web site. Thus, it can be executed from within a browser. Hundreds, or even thousands, of applets are available on the Internet — many of them for free. Some general categories of applets include text effects, audio effects, visual effects, navigation, games, and utilities. Inserting a Java applet is similar to inserting a Flash or Shockwave movie. The following steps explain how to insert a Java applet into the Dreamweaver Document window.

1. Click the Document window where you want to insert the applet.
2. Click the Applet command on the Media pop-up menu on the Insert bar.
3. Select an applet file in the Select File dialog box.
4. Set all necessary properties in the Property inspector.
5. Add any necessary parameters.

Quitting Dreamweaver

After you have added the Flash text, Flash movie, audio, and video, and verified that the media objects work, Project 9 is complete. To close the Web site, quit Dreamweaver 8, and return control to Windows, complete the following step.

To Close the Web Site and Quit Dreamweaver

1 Click the Close button on the upper-right corner of the Dreamweaver title bar.

The Dreamweaver window, the Document window, and the Colorado Parks Web site are closed. If you have unsaved changes, Dreamweaver will prompt you to save the changes. Clicking the Yes button in the Dreamweaver 8 dialog box saves the changes.

Project Summary

Project 9 introduced you to Dreamweaver's media objects. You added a splash page with Flash text, a Flash movie, and a link to an audio file. Then you added a link to the index page from the splash page. Next, you opened the state_parks.htm page and embedded an audio file with controls. Then you added a video to the page. You also learned about the Results panel group and how to use the Link Checker. Finally, you learned the general procedure for adding Shockwave movies and Java applets to Web pages.

What You Should Know

Having completed this project, you now should be able to perform the tasks below. The tasks are listed in the same order they were presented in the project. For a list of keyboard commands for topics introduced in this project, see the Quick Reference for Windows at the back of this book and refer to the Shortcut column.

1. Copy Data Files to the Colorado Parks Web Site (DW 701)
2. Start Dreamweaver and Open the Colorado Parks Web Site (DW 701)
3. Add Flash Text (DW 705)
4. Add a Flash Movie (DW 711)
5. Add a Link to Go to the Index Page (DW 713)
6. Add a Background Sound and Set Parameters (DW 717)
7. Embed an Audio File (DW 724)
8. Add Video to a Web Page (DW 730)
9. Verify Internal Links with the Link Checker (DW 736)
10. Close the Web Site and Quit Dreamweaver (DW 739)

Learn It Online

Instructions: To complete the Learn It Online exercises, start your browser, click the Address bar, and then enter the Web address scsite.com/dw8/learn When the Dreamweaver 8 Learn It Online page is displayed, follow the instructions in the exercises below. Each exercise has instructions for printing your results, either for your own records or for submission to your instructor.

1 Project Reinforcement TF, MC, and SA

Below Dreamweaver Project 9, click the Project Reinforcement link. Print the quiz by clicking Print on the File menu for each page. Answer each question.

2 Flash Cards

Below Dreamweaver Project 9, click the Flash Cards link and read the instructions. Type 20 (or a number specified by your instructor) in the Number of playing cards text box, type your name in the Enter your Name text box, and then click the Flip Card button. When the flash card is displayed, read the question and then click the ANSWER box arrow to select an answer. Flip through the Flash Cards. If your score is 15 (75%) correct or greater, click Print on the File menu to print your results. If your score is less than 15 (75%) correct, then redo this exercise by clicking the Replay button.

3 Practice Test

Below Dreamweaver Project 9, click the Practice Test link. Answer each question, enter your first and last name at the bottom of the page, and then click the Grade Test button. When the graded practice test is displayed on your screen, click Print on the File menu to print a hard copy. Continue to take practice tests until you score 80% or better.

4 Who Wants To Be a Computer Genius?

Below Dreamweaver Project 9, click the Computer Genius link. Read the instructions, enter your first and last name at the bottom of the page, and then click the PLAY button. When your score is displayed, click the PRINT RESULTS link to print a hard copy.

5 Wheel of Terms

Below Dreamweaver Project 9, click the Wheel of Terms link. Read the instructions, and then enter your first and last name and your school name. Click the PLAY button. When your score is displayed, right-click the score and then click Print on the shortcut menu to print a hard copy.

6 Crossword Puzzle Challenge

Below Dreamweaver Project 9, click the Crossword Puzzle Challenge link. Read the instructions, and then enter your first and last name. Click the SUBMIT button. Work the crossword puzzle. When you are finished, click the Submit button. When the crossword puzzle is redisplayed, click the Print Puzzle button to print a hard copy.

7 Tips and Tricks

Below Dreamweaver Project 9, click the Tips and Tricks link. Click a topic that pertains to Project 9. Right-click the information and then click Print on the shortcut menu. Construct a brief example of what the information relates to in Dreamweaver to confirm that you understand how to use the tip or trick.

8 Newsgroups

Below Dreamweaver Project 9, click the Newsgroups link. Click a topic that pertains to Project 9. Print three comments.

9 Expanding Your Horizons

Below Dreamweaver Project 9, click the Expanding Your Horizons link. Click a topic that pertains to Project 9. Print the information. Construct a brief example of what the information relates to in Dreamweaver to confirm that you understand the contents of the article.

10 Search Sleuth

Below Dreamweaver Project 9, click the Search Sleuth link. To search for a term that pertains to this project, select a term below the Project 9 title and then use the Google search engine at google.com (or any major search engine) to display and print two Web pages that present information on the term.

Apply Your Knowledge

1 Creating a Splash Page for Andy's Lawn Service

Problem: Andy's Lawn Service would like to add a splash page to its Web site. The management prefers something attractive and interesting, but somewhat conservative. You decide to copy a data file that contains five layers and images and then add Flash text for the page title. Next, you add a Flash movie, a link to the index.htm page, and a background song. The splash page is shown in Figure 9-56. Appendix C contains instructions for uploading your local site to a remote server.

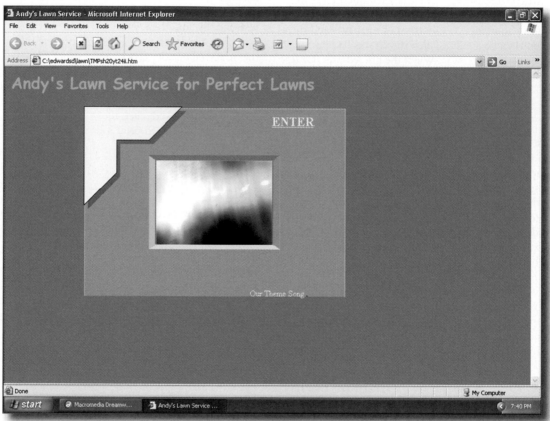

FIGURE 9-56

Instructions: See the inside back cover of this book for instructions for downloading the Data Disk, or see your instructor for information on accessing the files in this book.

1. Use the Windows My Computer option to copy the lawn_splash.htm file, images from the images folder, and the media folder from the DataFiles folder to your lawn folder.
2. Start Dreamweaver. If necessary, display the Property inspector, Standard toolbar, and panel groups. Select Lawn Service on the Files pop-up menu in the Files panel. Open the lawn_splash.htm file.
3. The lawn_splash.htm Web page contains five layers. Click to the right of the layer-code markers in the upper-left corner of the page.
4. Click Flash Text on the Insert bar Media pop-up menu. Change the font to Comic Sans MS, the color to #CCCC00, the rollover color to #CC9900, and the background color to #669966. Type Andy's Lawn Service for Perfect Lawns in the Text text box. Bold the text. Save the Flash text as media/lawn01.swf.

Apply Your Knowledge

5. Click the fourth layer-code marker from the left. Click in Layer 4 in the Document window. Type ENTER, create a link to the index.htm page, and then change the font color to #FFFFCE.

6. Click the fifth layer-code marker from the left. Scroll down and click in Layer 5 in the Document window. Type Our Theme Song as the entry, and change the font color to #FFFFCE, if necessary. Click the Media pop-up menu and then click Plugin. In the Select File dialog box, navigate to the media folder and then select the lawn.wav file. Change the plugin placeholder height to 2 and the width to 2. Click the Parameters button and then add the parameters listed in Table 9-7.

Table 9-7 Parameters for Lawn Service Web site	
PARAMETER	VALUE
Hidden	True
Autoplay	True
Loop	False

7. Click the third layer-code marker from the left. Click inside Layer 3 and then click the Flash command on the Media pop up menu. Navigate to the lawn\media folder. Click the lawns.swf file and then click OK.

8. In the Flash Property inspector, change W to 220 and H to 160. If necessary, click the Loop and Autoplay check boxes to select them. Click the Scale box arrow and then click Exact fit. Adjust the size of Layer 3 to fit the Flash movie.

9. Click the Save button on the Standard toolbar.

10. Press the F12 key to view the page in your browser. Click the index link and then click the browser Back button. A speaker or headphones are required to hear the audio.

11. Print a copy of the lawn_splash.htm page, if instructed to do so. Upload the page to the lawn Web site on a remote server, if instructed to do so. Close the browser. Quit Dreamweaver.

In the Lab

1 The CandleWix Web Site

Problem: Martha would like a splash page for the CandleWix Web site. She is receiving orders from all over the world and wants to emphasize that her Web site is now an international site. Martha wants to use the same background, but wants a two-row table containing Flash text at the top of the page. She has found a Flash movie that she would like to add to the site. She also wants to add a link to the index page. The splash page is shown in Figure 9-57. Appendix C contains instructions for uploading your local site to a remote server.

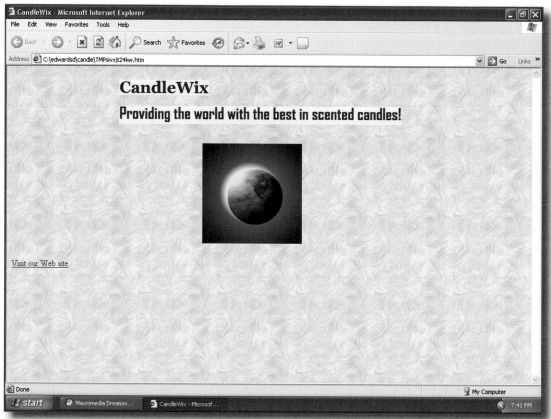

FIGURE 9-57

Instructions: Perform the following tasks:

1. Use the Windows My Computer option to copy the media folder from the DataFiles folder to your candle folder.
2. Start Dreamweaver. Select CandleWix on the Files pop-up menu in the Files panel. Open a new Document window. Save the page as candle_splash.htm and then title the page CandleWix. Apply the candlebg.gif image to the background.
3. If necessary, click the top of the page and then insert a two-row, one-column table with a width of 60 percent and cell padding of 10. Type Heading for CandleWix Splash page in the Summary text box. Center-align the table.
4. Click in the first cell (row) in the table and then click Flash Text on the Media pop-up menu of the Insert bar.

5. Add the following attributes to the Insert Flash Text dialog box — Font: Georgia (or a font of your choice); Size: 30; Bold; Color: #990000; Rollover color: #FF9966; Bg color: #FFFFCC. Type CandleWix in the Text text box and then save the Flash text as media/heading01.swf.

6. Click in the second cell (row) in the table and then click Flash Text on the Media pop-up menu.

7. Add the following attributes to the Insert Flash Text dialog box — Font: Agency FB (or a font of your choice); Size: 30; Bold; Color: #990000; Rollover color: #FF9966; Bg color: #FFFFCC. Type Providing the world with the best in scented candles! in the Text text box. Save the Flash text as media/heading02.swf.

8. Click to the right of the table (outside the table) and then press the ENTER key. Insert a layer, select the layer, and then add the following properties — Layer ID: world; L: 375px; T: 145px; W: 200px; and H: 115px. Click inside the layer.

9. Click the Flash button on the Media pop-up menu and then insert the candle.swf file located in the CandleWix media folder.

10. Click to the right of the layer code-marker, press ENTER seven times, and then type Visit our Web site as the entry. Select the text and create a link to the index.htm page.

11. Save the candle_splash.htm page and then press the F12 key to view the page in your browser. Note that settings on some computers may display the Flash movie in a different location from that shown in Figure 9-57. Move the mouse pointer over the text heading to view the Flash text animation. Check your link to verify that it works.

12. Print a copy of the Web page if instructed to do so. Upload the page to the candle Web site on a remote server if instructed to do so. Close the browser. Quit Dreamweaver.

2 Adding Video and Sound to the Credit Web Site

Problem: Monica is interested in identity theft and identity security. She recently read about a proposal requiring that a person's driver's license become part of a national database. She has mixed feelings about this suggestion and has located a video file detailing this proposal. She would like to create a dramatic splash page for her Web site and add this movie to the site. The splash page would contain a title, the movie, and a link to the credit index.htm page. The splash page is shown in Figure 9-58 on the next page. Appendix C contains instructions for uploading your local site to a remote server.

(continued)

Adding Video and Sound to the Credit Web Site *(continued)*

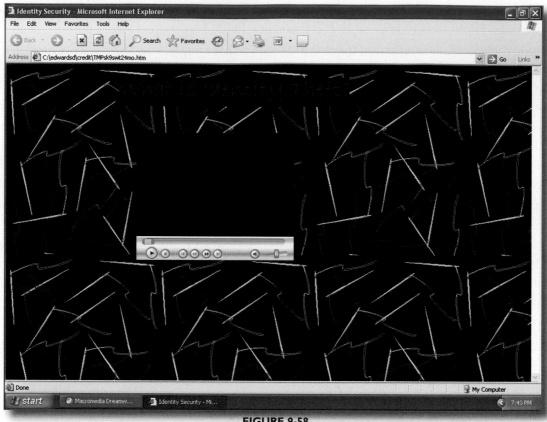

FIGURE 9-58

Instructions: Perform the following tasks:

1. Use the Windows My Computer option to copy both the bkg.gif image and the media folder from the DataFiles folder to your credit folder.

2. Start Dreamweaver. Select Credit Protection from the Files pop-up menu in the Files panel. Open a new Document window. Save the page as credit_splash.htm in the Credit Web site and then title the page Identity Security.

3. Insert and center a one-row, one-column table with a width of 60 percent at the top of the page.

4. Click in the table cell and then click Flash Text on the Media pop-up menu. Add the following attributes to the Insert Flash Text dialog box — Font: Bradley Hand ITC (or a font of your choice); Size: 45; Color: #FF3300; Rollover color: #CC00FF; and Bg color: #000000. Type What is Identity Theft? in the Text text box. Save the Flash text as media/heading1.swf.

5. Click to the right of the table (outside the table) and then press the ENTER key.

6. Insert a layer and then select the layer. Add the following properties — Layer ID: identity; L: 250px; T: 130px; W: 200px; and H: 115px. Click inside the layer.

7. Click ActiveX on the Media pop-up menu. Add the following properties in the ActiveX Property inspector — ActiveX name: security; W: 300; and H: 240. Click the ClassID box arrow and then click the CLSID number you entered earlier in this project.

8. Click the Embed check box and then click the Browse for File icon located to the right of the Src text box. Navigate to the credit media folder. Click the Files of type arrow and then click All Files. Select the ID security.wmv file from the media folder and then click the OK button.

9. Click the Parameters button and then add the parameters listed in Table 9-8.

10. Click outside the layer. Press the ENTER key several times or scroll down to move to the end of the document. Type Home Page and then change the text color to #0000FF and bold. Select the text and then create a link to the credit index.htm page.

11. Change the background color to #000000, and then apply the bkg.gif file as the background image. Click the OK button.

12. Save the document. Press the F12 key to view the page in your browser. Note that settings on some computers may display the movie in a different location from that shown in Figure 9-58. Click the Play button to view the movie. Print a copy of the Web page, if instructed to do so. Upload the page to the credit Web site on a remote server, if instructed to do so. Close the browser. Quit Dreamweaver.

Table 9-8 Parameters for Credit Web Site	
PARAMETER	VALUE
FileName	media/ID security.wmv
AutoStart	False
ShowControls	True
ShowDisplay	False
AutoRewind	True

3 Creating a Splash Page for the Lexington, NC Web Site

Problem: John wants to add some excitement to the Lexington, NC Web site by adding a splash page. You explain to John that a splash page can be simple but effective. You suggest adding some rollover text and a Flash movie. The page also will contain a link to the home page. The splash page is shown in Figure 9-59. Appendix C contains instructions for uploading your local site to a remote server.

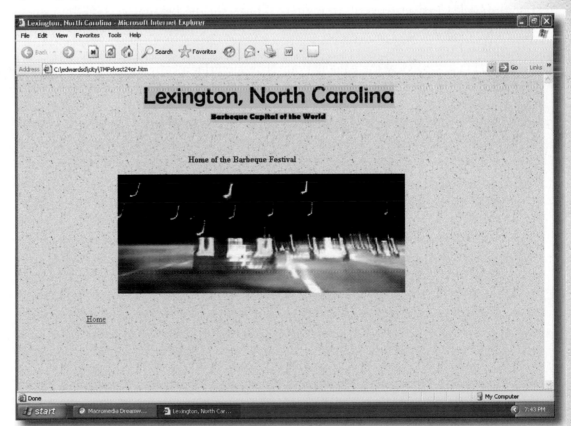

FIGURE 9-59

(continued)

In the Lab

Creating a Splash Page for the Lexington, NC Web Site *(continued)*

Instructions: Perform the following tasks:

1. Use the Windows My Computer option to copy both the city_splash.htm file and the media folder from the DataFiles folder to your city folder.
2. Start Dreamweaver. Select Lexington, NC from the Files pop-up menu in the Files panel. Open the city_splash.htm file.
3. Click in the first cell (row 1) in the table and then click Flash Text on the Media pop-up menu. Apply the following attributes — Font: Berlin Sans FB (or a font of your choice); Size: 45; Color: #000000; Rollover color: #990000; and Bg color: #FFCC99. Type Lexington, North Carolina in the Text text box. Save the Flash text as media/heading01.swf.
4. Click in the second cell (row 2) in the table and then click Flash Text on the Media pop-up menu. Apply the following attributes — Font: Berlin Sans FB, Bold; Size: 15; Color: #000000; Rollover color: #990000; and Bg color: #FFCC99. Type Barbeque Capital of the World in the Text text box. Save the Flash text as media/heading02.swf.
5. Select the layer and name it movie. Click in the layer. Type Home of the Barbeque Festival in bold text, set the color to #990000, center align the text, and then press the ENTER key.
6. Click Flash on the Media pop-up menu and then navigate to the media folder. Click the city.swf file and then click the OK button to insert the Flash movie into the layer. Save the Web page.
7. Use the Link Checker to verify the internal links for the Lexington, NC Web site, and update broken links as necessary. Save changes to pages containing corrected links. If necessary, navigate back to the city_splash.htm page.
8. Press the F12 key to view the page in your browser. Print a copy of the Web page, if instructed to do so. Upload the page to the city Web site on a remote server, if instructed to do so. Close the browser. Quit Dreamweaver.

Cases and Places

The difficulty of these case studies varies:
■ are the least difficult and ■■ are the most difficult. The last exercise is a group exercise.

1 ■ You would like to add some pizzazz to your sports Web site. You decide to add a splash page. Add a background image and a title to the page. Add some Flash text and then create a link to an audio file. Create a link to the home page. Save the page in your sports Web site. For a selection of images and backgrounds, visit the Dreamweaver 8 Media Web page (scsite.com/dw8/media) and then click Media below Project 9.

2 ■ Your hobby Web site is receiving more and more hits each day. You would like to add some interactivity to your site. You decide to do this by adding a splash page. First, add a background image to the page and then add an appropriate title. Next, insert Flash text and Flash buttons. Then insert a Flash movie. Create a link to your home page. Upload the new page to a remote site, if instructed to do so. For a selection of images and backgrounds, visit the Dreamweaver 8 Media Web page (scsite.com/dw8/media) and then click Media below Project 9.

3 ■■ Add a new page to your music hobby Web site and then add a background image to the page. Add relevant content and then add Flash text. Add a Flash movie and then embed an audio file. Create links to and from your home page. Upload the page to a remote site. For a selection of images and backgrounds, visit the Dreamweaver 8 Media Web page (scsite.com/dw8/media) and then click Media below Project 9.

4 ■■ Your campaign for political office is going well, and you want to enhance your campaign Web site by adding a splash page. Create a new Web page and then add an appropriate background image and title. Add Flash text and Flash buttons. Embed an audio file and then add a video file. Create a link to your index page. Upload the revised Web site to a remote server. For a selection of images and backgrounds, visit the Dreamweaver 8 Media Web page (scsite.com/dw8/ media) and then click Media below Project 9.

5 ■■ **Working Together** The student government Web site has become even more popular. You and your team would like to add a splash page. You would also like to add videos to the page that describe various locations available for the student trips. Each team member is responsible for locating an appropriate Flash movie. On the splash page, add one of the Flash movies, Flash text, and a link to an audio file. On the page that includes trip locations, add two or three Flash movies illustrating some of the activities available at the different sites. Create a link to the index page. Upload the new pages to a remote server. For a selection of images and backgrounds, visit the Dreamweaver 8 Media Web page (scsite.com/dw8/media) and then click Media below Project 9.

MACROMEDIA
Dreamweaver 8

Dreamweaver Web Photo Album

CASE PERSPECTIVE

The Colorado Parks Web site has been very successful thus far. Recently, David has received several e-mail messages complimenting the Web site. Many of the messages mention the photographs of the scenery and the other special features and landmarks included in the Web site. David shares the e-mails with Tracy and mentions that a Web page with just photos would be a nice addition to the site. He shows Tracy some Web sites that contain groups of thumbnail images. Clicking the image opens a new page with a larger picture of the thumbnail.

Tracy thinks that adding a photo page is an excellent idea which will not only showcase some of the parks' scenic images, but will add more interaction to the site. However, she has concerns that this type of page will require that each image be coded separately, which can be quite time consuming. Still, she will investigate and see what options she can find.

After some research, Tracy discovers that Dreamweaver has a special command that will create the thumbnails and the individual pages. She shares this information with David and points out that this feature also requires that Macromedia Fireworks be installed on the computer. David tells Tracy that they have Fireworks — it is part of the Dreamweaver 8 Studio. So it is settled. Everyone agrees that adding a photo page is a good idea, and you move forward with the creation of the Web photo album. All are eager to get started on this new addition to the Colorado Parks Web site.

Objectives

You will have mastered the material in this project when you can:

- Describe a Web Photo Album
- Understand and Plan a Web Photo Album
- Create a Web Photo Album
- View a Web Photo Album

Introduction

This Special Feature introduces Dreamweaver's Web Photo Album. Creating the photo album requires that Fireworks be installed on your computer.

Creating a photo album in Dreamweaver is very easy. Depending on the number and size of the images, the album is created in less than a minute. The Dreamweaver Web Photo Album is a special feature that works with Fireworks automatically to generate a set of thumbnails from selected images. If viewers want to see more detail or a larger image, they click the thumbnail.

Web Photo Album

In this Special Feature, you create a Web photo album showcasing one of Dreamweaver's unique commands — the Web Photo Album. To create a photo album requires two elements: (a) that Fireworks be installed on your computer, and (b) that all of the images for your photo album be stored in a single folder. You add these new pages (Figures 1a and 1b) to the Colorado Parks Web site and then create a link from the index page to the new page containing the thumbnails.

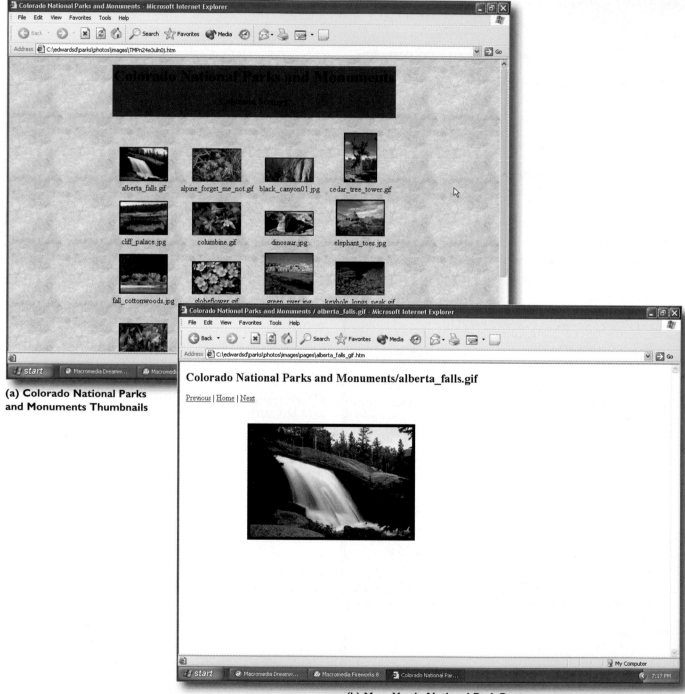

(a) Colorado National Parks and Monuments Thumbnails

(b) Mesa Verde National Park Page

FIGURE 1

Copying Data Files to the Local Web Site

Your Data Disk contains images for the Special Feature. These images are in a folder titled photos. You use the Windows My Computer option to copy the photos folder to your parks folder. See the inside back cover for instructions for downloading the Data Disk, or see your instructor for information about accessing the files required for this book.

The Data Files folder for this project is stored on Local Disk (C:). The location on your computer may be different. If necessary, verify with your instructor the location of the Data Files folder. The following steps illustrate how to copy the files to the parks local root folder.

To Copy Data Files to the Parks Folder

1 Click the Start button on the Windows taskbar and then click My Computer.

2 Double-click Local Disk (C:) and then navigate to the location of the data files for the Special Feature.

3 Double-click the DataFiles folder and then double-click the ProjSF folder.

4 Double-click the parks folder.

5 Right-click the photos folder to display the context menu.

6 Click the Copy command and then click the My Computer Back button the number of times necessary to navigate to the your name folder.

7 Double-click the your name folder and then double-click the parks folder.

8 Right-click anywhere in the open window to display the context menu, and then click Paste.

9 Close the My Computer window.

The photos folder is pasted into the Colorado Parks Web site.

It is not required that the folder containing the images be kept in the site folder. Generally, however, it is a good practice to keep everything with the site.

Additionally, the image filenames can have any of the following extensions: .gif, .jpg, .jpeg, .png, .psd, .tif, or .tiff. When the photo album is created, Fireworks converts these to the format which you specify in the Create Web Photo Album dialog box.

Starting Dreamweaver and Closing Open Panels

Each time you start Dreamweaver, it opens to the last site that was displayed when you closed the program. Therefore, it may be necessary for you to open the parks Web site. The Files pop-up menu in the Files panel lists sites you have defined. When you open the site, a list of pages and subfolders within the site is displayed. The next steps illustrate how to start Dreamweaver and open the Colorado Parks Web site.

To Start Dreamweaver and Open the Colorado Parks Web Site

1 Click the Start button on the Windows taskbar.

2 Point to All Programs on the Start menu, point to Macromedia on the All Programs submenu, and then click Macromedia Dreamweaver 8 on the Macromedia submenu.

3 Click the Files panel box arrow and click Colorado Parks on the Files pop-up menu. If necessary, click the plus sign to open the site folder.

Dreamweaver opens, and the Colorado Parks Web site hierarchy is displayed in the Files panel. The photos folder is part of the hierarchy (Figure 2).

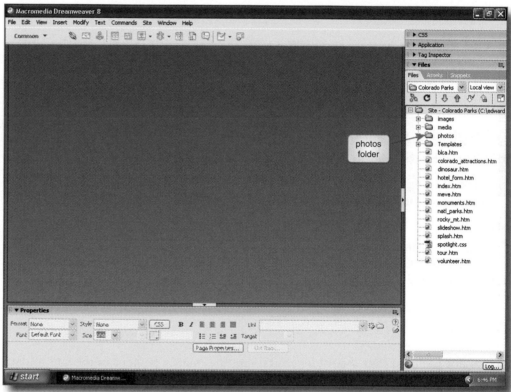

FIGURE 2

Creating the Web Photo Album

Your photos folder is copied to the parks Web site. In this instance, the extensions for the file names are either .gif or .jpg. When the photo album is created, Fireworks converts these to the format which you specify in the Create Web Photo Album dialog box.

Additionally, Fireworks also creates a Web page which will contain the thumbnails and links to the larger images. Each of the larger images is displayed in its own individual page.

When you are creating the album, you can select from five thumbnail sizes and whether to show or not show the file name, the number of columns, and the thumbnail and photo formats. Four options are available from the pop-up menus for the thumbnail and photo (larger-size images) formats. These are GIF webSnap 128, GIF webSnap 256, JPEG better quality, and JPEG smaller size. You also can set a Scale percentage. The default is 100 percent and creates large-size images that are the same size as the original images. When you select a Scale percentage, it is applied to all images. If your original images are different sizes, scaling them by the same percentage may cause some distortion. Generally, it is better to stay with the 100 percent scale option.

If your preference is to create only a thumbnail page, then you should deselect the Create navigation page for each photo check box. All of the above options are available through the Create Web Photo Album dialog box.

The next step requires you to open a new or existing Web page before creating the photo album. This can be any page, and it is not part of the album. If a page is not open, Dreamweaver displays an error message when you try to create the album. In this instance, you will open a blank page. After the page is open, you will begin the process of creating your photo album.

The following steps illustrate how to open a new page and then create the photo album.

To Open a Web Page and Create the Web Photo Album

1

• **Click File on the menu bar, click New, select Basic page from the New Document dialog box. Click the Create button.**

• **Click Commands on the menu bar and point to Create Web Photo Album.**

A new untitled page is created and the Create Web Photo Album command is selected (Figure 3).

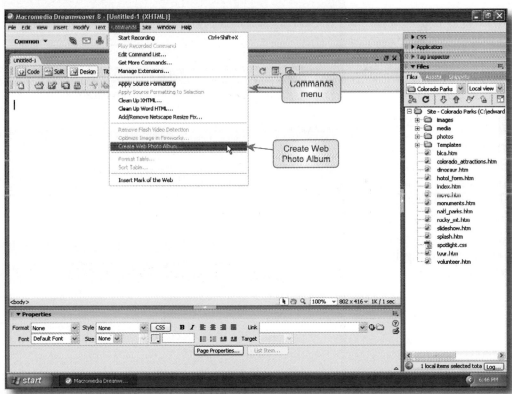

FIGURE 3

2

• **Click Create Web Photo Album.**

The Create Web Photo Album dialog box is displayed (Figure 4).

FIGURE 4

3

• **Click the Photo album title text box and type** Colorado National Parks and Monuments.

• **Press the TAB key and type** Colorado Scenery **in the Subheading info text box.**

The Photo album title and Subheading info is added to the dialog box (Figure 5).

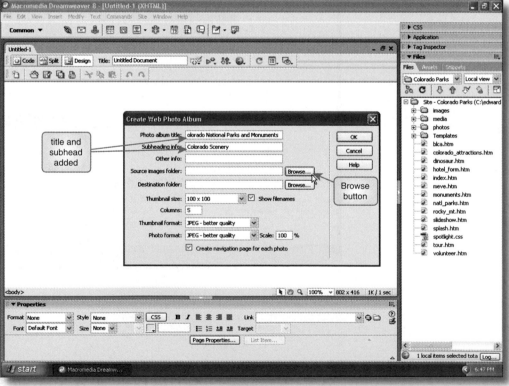

FIGURE 5

4

• **Click the Browse button to the right of the Source images folder text box and navigate to the photos folder.**

The Choose a folder dialog box is displayed (Figure 6).

FIGURE 6

5

• **Click the Select button.**

• **Click the Browse button to the right of the Destination folder text box and navigate to the photos folder.**

• **Click the Select button.**

The paths to the Source images and Destination folders are inserted into the text boxes (Figure 7).

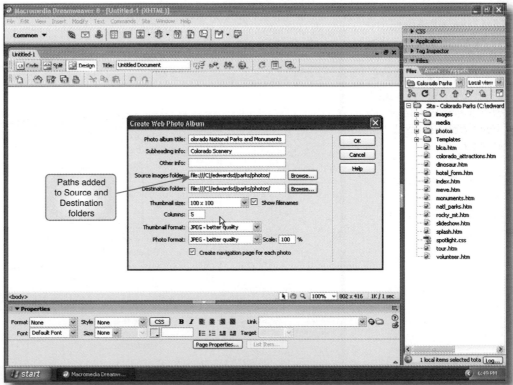

FIGURE 7

6

• **Click the Columns text box and type** 4.

The number of columns is changed to 4 (Figure 8).

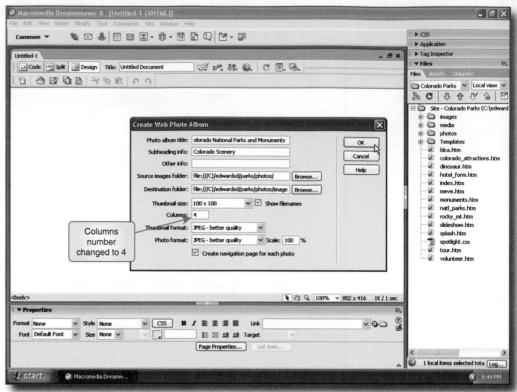

FIGURE 8

7

• **Click the OK button.**

Fireworks opens and prepares the thumbnails and other folders, and then displays a dialog box indicating that the album is created (Figure 9). The index.htm file is saved in the photos folder.

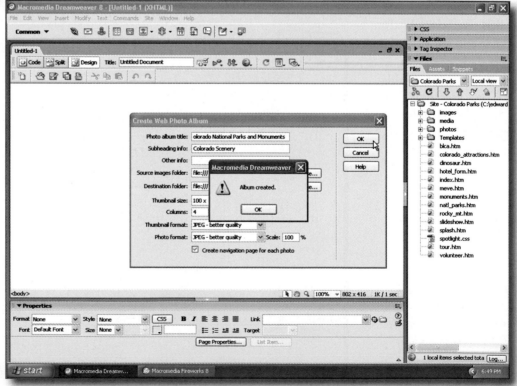

FIGURE 9

Dreamweaver Special Feature

8

• **Click the OK button.**

The Album is created and the page automatically is named index.htm (Figure 10).

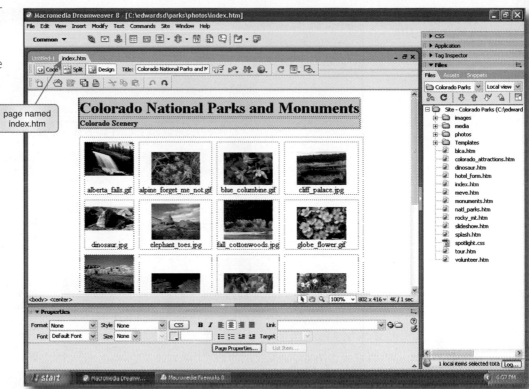

FIGURE 10

9

• **Click the Page Properties button in the Property inspector and then apply the bg.jpg image to the background.**

• **Select the table that contains the heading and type #993333 in the Bg color text box.**

• **Center the subtitle Colorado Scenery in the table row and change the heading format to Heading 3.**

• **Double-click the photos folder in the Files panel to display the subfolders and then double-click the images folder to display its contents.**

• **Save the file.**

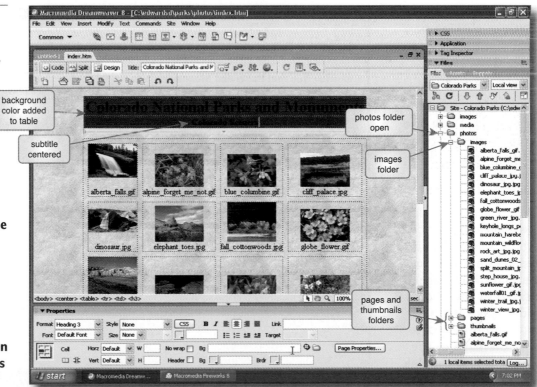

FIGURE 11

The background image is applied, the table background is changed, the subtitle is centered, and the file is saved. The photos folder now contains three additional folders—images, pages, and thumbnails (Figure 11).

10

• **Press F12 to view the page in your browser.**

The thumbnails are displayed in the browser (Figure 12).

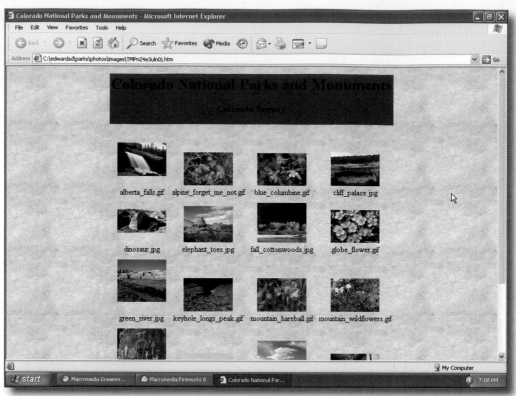

FIGURE 12

11

• **Click the first thumbnail (alberta_falls.gif).**

The Alberta_falls page is displayed (Figure 13).

• **Click the Next link to display the next image. Continue clicking Next until you have viewed all images.**

• **Close the browser.**

• **Open the index.htm page for the Web site. Scroll to the bottom of the page and click to the right of the Colorado Tour link.**

• **Insert a line break and then type** Photo Album. **Select the text and create a link to the index.htm page located in the photos folder. Save the page and then press F12 to view the page in the browser. Test the link and close the browser.**

• **Close Fireworks and then close Dreamweaver.**

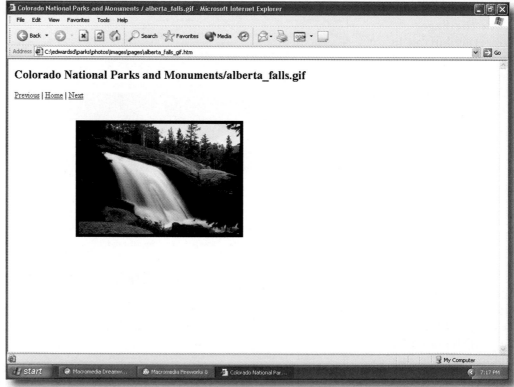

FIGURE 13

Special Feature Summary

This Special Feature introduced you to using Dreamweaver and Fireworks to create a Web photo album. You copied a folder containing images into your parks folder. You then used Dreamweaver's Create Web Photo Album command, along with Fireworks, to create the thumbnails and individual pages for the Web site.

What You Should Know

Having completed this project, you now should be able to perform the tasks below. The tasks are listed in the same order they were presented in the project. For a list of keyboard commands for topics introduced in this project, see the Quick Reference for Windows at the back of this book and refer to the Shortcut column.

1. Copy Data Files to the Parks Folder (DW 753)
2. Start Dreamweaver and Open the Colorado Parks Web Site (DW 754)
3. Open a Web Page and Create a Web Photo Album (DW 755)

1 Adding a Web Photo Album to the Andy's Lawn Service Web Site

Instructions: Start Dreamweaver. See the inside back cover of this book for instructions for downloading the Data Disk, or see your instructor for information on accessing the files in this book.

The proprietors of Andy's Lawn Service would like to add a Web photo album to their Web site that contains pictures of the lawn equipment they use. You start by downloading the data files and copying them to the Lawn Service Web site. Next, you will create the Web photo album. After inserting the Web photo album, you will create a link to the photo album on the Web site's home page. The new Web photo album page is shown in Figure 14. Software and hardware settings determine how a Web page is displayed in a browser. Your Web page may display differently than the one shown in Figure 14. Appendix C contains instructions for uploading your local site to a remote server.

FIGURE 14

1. If necessary, display the Property inspector, Standard toolbar, and panel groups. Select Lawn Service on the Files pop-up menu in the Files panel.
2. Use the Windows My Computer option to copy the album folder and its files from the DataFiles folder to your lawn folder.
3. Open the index.htm page. Click Commands on the menu bar, and then click Create Web Photo Album to display the Create Web Photo Album dialog box.
4. Type Andy's Lawn Service Equipment as the Photo album title, and then press the TAB key.
5. Type The Best Equipment for the Best Lawns as the Subheading info.
6. Click the Browse button next to the Source images folder text box. Double-click the album folder when the Choose a folder dialog box is displayed, and then double-click the mowers folder. Click the Select button.
7. Click the Browse button next to the Destination folder text box. Double-click the album folder when the Choose a folder dialog box is displayed, and then click the Select button.

Apply Your Knowledge

8. Replace the value in the Columns text box with the number 2, and then click the OK button in the Create Web Photo Album dialog box to create the Web Photo Album. When the Macromedia Dreamweaver dialog box is displayed, click the OK button.

9. Click Modify on the menu bar, and then click Page Properties to display the Page Properties dialog box. Click the Browse button next to the Background image text box. Double-click the images folder in the Select Image Source dialog box. Click lawnbg.jpg and then click the OK button. Click the OK button in the Page Properties dialog box to apply the background image.

10. Select the table that contains the heading, and then type #FFCC66 in the Bg color text box. Center the text Andy's Lawn Service Equipment in the table row and change the heading format to Heading 2. Center the text The Best Equipment for the Best Lawns. Click File on the menu bar, and then click Save to save the album/index.htm page.

11. Double-click index.htm in the Files panel to navigate back to the Andy's Lawn Service home page. Click at the end of the last item in the bulleted list and press the SHIFT+ENTER keys two times. Press the ENTER key. Type Equipment and create a link to the index.htm page in the album folder. Select _blank from the Target pop-up menu in the Property inspector. Click the Save button and then press the F12 key to view the Web page in your browser. Click the Equipment link to display the Web photo album. Close the browser windows to return to Dreamweaver.

12. Print a copy of the index.htm and album/index.htm pages, if instructed to do so. Upload the pages to the lawn Web folder on a remote server, if instructed to do so. Close the index.htm pages.

In the Lab

1 Adding a Web Photo Album to the CandleWix Web Site

Problem: Martha would like to add a page to the CandleWix Web site that shows a sampling of their candles. Due to time constraints, she asks you to create this new page as quickly as possible. You inform Martha about the Web Photo Album feature in Dreamweaver, and she agrees an online photo album containing pictures of her candles will be ideal. You immediately get started creating the album. The album Web page is shown in Figure 15. Appendix C contains instructions for uploading your local site to a remote server.

FIGURE 15

Instructions: Perform the following tasks:

1. Use the Windows My Computer option to copy the album folder and its files from the DataFiles folder to your candle folder.
2. Start Dreamweaver. If necessary, display the Property inspector, Standard toolbar, and panel groups. Select CandleWix on the Files pop-up menu in the Files panel.
3. Open the index.htm page. Click Commands on the menu bar, and then click Create Web Photo Album.
4. Type CandleWix Candles as the Photo album title, and then press the TAB key.
5. Type Satisfaction Always Guaranteed! as the Subheading info.
6. Click the Browse button next to the Source images folder text box. Double-click the album folder, and then double-click the candles folder. Click the Select button.
7. Click the Browse button next to the Destination folder text box. Double-click the album folder, and then click the Select button.
8. Replace the value in the Columns text box with the number 4, and then click the OK button. When the Macromedia Dreamweaver dialog box is displayed, click the OK button.
9. Apply the candlebg.gif background image. The candlebg.gif file is located in the candle/images folder.

In the Lab

10. Center the page heading and subheading, and apply the Heading 2 format to the heading. Change the heading and subheading font color to #990000, and then apply the candlebg.gif background image to the table containing the heading and subheading. Save the album/index.htm page.

11. Display the CandleWix home page. Click at the end of the sentence that begins, "Our candles make a perfect gift...", and press the SPACEBAR. Type See samples of our work. and create a link to the index.htm page in the album folder. Select _blank from the Target pop-up menu in the Property inspector. Click the Save button, and then press the F12 key to view the Web page in your browser. Click the See samples of our work link to display the Web photo album. Close the browser windows to return to Dreamweaver.

12. Print a copy of the index.htm and album/index.htm pages, if instructed to do so. Upload the pages to the candle folder on a remote server, if instructed to do so. Close the index.htm pages in Dreamweaver.

2 Creating a Web Photo Album for the Credit Protection Web Site

Problem: Due to the overwhelming success of the Credit Protection Web site, Monica would like to encourage other Web developers to reach out to more people by creating additional Web sites about credit protection. She asks you to create a page that contains each of the images used in the current Credit Protection Web site, in hopes that others will use the images to create similar sites. The new Web page is shown in Figure 16. Appendix C contains instructions for uploading your local site to a remote server.

FIGURE 16

In the Lab

Creating a Web Photo Album for the Credit Protection Web Site *(continued)*

Instructions: Perform the following tasks:

1. Use the Windows My Computer option to copy the album folder from the DataFiles folder to your credit folder.
2. Start Dreamweaver. If necessary, display the Property inspector, Standard toolbar, and panel groups. Select Credit Protection on the Files pop-up menu in the Files panel.
3. Open the index.htm page. Click Create Web Photo Album on the Commands menu.
4. Type `Credit Protection Web Site Resources` as the photo album title.
5. Type `Use these images to create your own Web site about credit protection!` as the Subheading info.
6. Click the Browse button next to the Source images folder text box. Double-click the images folder, and then click the Select button.
7. Click the Browse button next to the Destination folder text box. Double-click the album folder, and then click the Select button.
8. Click the OK button. When the Macromedia Dreamweaver dialog box is displayed, click the OK button.
9. Apply the #FFFFFF background color to the table containing the heading and subheading, and then center the heading and subheading. Save the album/index.htm page.
10. Display the Credit Protection home page. Create a link under the Spending Wisely link that reads, Create Your Own Credit Protection Web Site!. This link should open the index.htm page in the album folder, and the Target should be set to _blank. Click the Save button, and then press the F12 key to view the Web page in your browser. Click the new link to display the Web photo album. Close the browser windows to return to Dreamweaver.
11. Print a copy of the index.htm and album/index.htm pages, if instructed to do so. Upload the pages to the credit Web site on a remote server, if instructed to do so. Close the index.htm pages in Dreamweaver.

3 Creating a Web Photo Album for the Lexington, NC Web Site

Problem: John would like to add a page containing pictures of popular Lexington places to the Lexington Web site. You suggest to John that a Web photo album would be a good addition and would enhance the overall site. John likes your idea, and you are ready to get started. The new page is shown in Figure 17.

Instructions: Perform the following tasks:

1. Use the Windows My Computer option to copy the album folder and its contents from the DataFiles folder to your city folder.
2. Start Dreamweaver. If necessary, display the Property inspector, Standard toolbar, and panel groups. Select Lexington, NC on the Files pop-up menu in the Files panel.

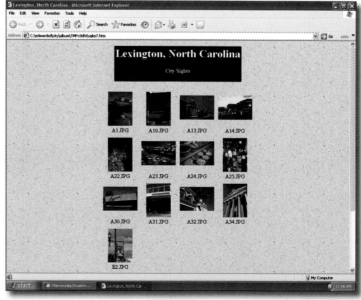

FIGURE 17

Apply Your Knowledge

3. Open the index.htm page. Click Create Web Photo Album on the Commands menu.

4. Type Lexington, North Carolina as the Photo album title, and City Sights as the Subheading info.

5. Click the Browse button next to the Source images folder text box. Double-click the album folder, and then double-click the places folder. Click the Select button.

6. Click the Browse button next to the Destination folder text box. Double-click the album folder, and then click the Select button.

7. Type 4 in the Columns text box, and then click the OK button. When the Macromedia Dreamweaver dialog box is displayed, click the OK button.

8. Apply the citybg.gif background image to the page. The citybg.gif background image is located in the city/images folder.

9. Center the page heading and subheading, and then change the heading and subheading font color to #FFFFFF. Change the background color of the table containing the heading and subheading to #660000. Save the album/index.htm page.

10. Open the Lexington, North Carolina home page. Click at the end of the City Tour link. Press the SPACEBAR, and then type | City Sights. Create a link from the City Sights text to the index.htm page in the album folder. Set the Target to _blank. Click the Save button, and then press the F12 key to view the Web page in your browser. Click the City Sights link to display the Web photo album. Close the browser windows to return to Dreamweaver.

11. Print a copy of the index.htm and album/index.htm pages, if instructed to do so. Upload the pages to the city Web site on a remote server, if instructed to do so.

12. Close Dreamweaver. If necessary, close Fireworks.

Appendix A

Dreamweaver Help

Dreamweaver Help

This appendix shows you how to use the many components of Dreamweaver Help. At any time while you are using Dreamweaver, you can interact with its Help system and display information on any Dreamweaver topic. It is a complete reference manual at your fingertips.

The Using Dreamweaver 8 Help system is viewed through your browser. The system contains comprehensive HTML-based information about all Dreamweaver features, including the following:

- A table of contents in which the information is organized by subject.
- An alphabetical index that points to important terms and links to related topics.
- A search tool that allows you to find any character string in all topic text.
- A Favorites folder to which you can add frequently accessed topics.

Other Help features include tutorial lessons, context-sensitive help, information on Dreamweaver extensions, help on using Cold Fusion, and 13 online reference manuals, including an HTML reference manual. For additional tutorials and online movies, you can access the Macromedia Dreamweaver Web site at http://www.macromedia. com/software/dreamweaver/productinfo/features/.

The Dreamweaver Help Menu

One of the more commonly used methods to access Dreamweaver's Help features is through the Help menu and function keys. Dreamweaver's Help menu provides an easy system to access the available Help options (Figure A-1 on the next page). Table A-1 on the next page summarizes the commands available through the Help menu.

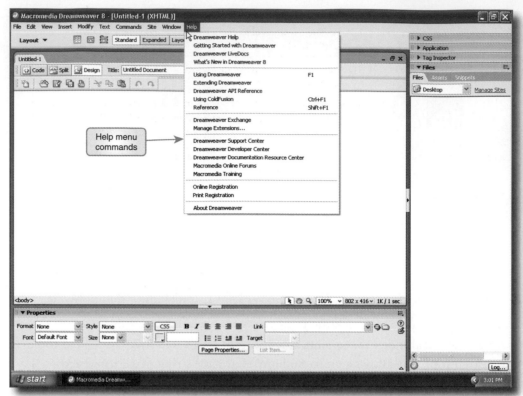

Help menu
commands

FIGURE A-1

Table A-1 Summary of Commands on the Help Menu

COMMAND ON HELP MENU	FUNCTION
Dreamweaver Help	This command accesses the Dreamweaver 8 Help window.
Getting Started with Dreamweaver	This command accesses the Dreamweaver 8 Help window and opens the Getting Started with Dreamweaver guide. The guide provides access to several links and tutorials. Each tutorial takes 30 to 45 minutes to complete.
Dreamweaver LiveDocs	This command accesses the Dreamweaver Help files online; these are the same files accessed through the Dreamweaver Help command.
What's New in Dreamweaver 8	This command is a direct link to the What's New in Dreamweaver 8 section located in the Dreamweaver Help files.
Using Dreamweaver	This command accesses the Dreamweaver Help files and opens the Using Dreamweaver window.
Extending Dreamweaver	The Extending Dreamweaver command opens the Extending Dreamweaver 8 Help files.
Dreamweaver API Reference	The Dreamweaver API Reference command opens the Dreamweaver API Reference Help files.
Using ColdFusion	The Using ColdFusion command displays the ColdFusion Documentation window. ColdFusion MX is a Web application server that lets you create applications that interact with databases.

Table A-1 Summary of Commands on the Help Menu (*continued*)

COMMAND ON HELP MENU	FUNCTION
Reference	The Reference command opens the Reference panel, which displays below the document windows. The Reference panel contains the complete text from several reference manuals, including references on HTML, Cascading Style Sheets, JavaScript, and other Web-related features.
Dreamweaver Exchange	This command links to the Macromedia Exchange Web site, where you can download for free and/or purchase a variety of Dreamweaver add-on features.
Manage Extensions	The Extensions command displays the Macromedia Extension Manager window where you can install, enable, and disable extensions. An extension is an add-on piece of software or a plug-in that enhances Dreamweaver's capabilities. Extensions provide the Dreamweaver developer with the capability to customize how Dreamweaver looks and works.
Dreamweaver Support Center and Dreamweaver Developer Center	The Dreamweaver Support Center and Dreamweaver Developer Center commands provide access to the online Macromedia Dreamweaver Support and Developer Centers Web sites. These Web sites offer search options and support developer assistance.
Dreamweaver Documentation Resource Center	This online site provides a documentation search option for an item in the documentation, the documentation Web site, or the Knowledge Base of Support and Developer content.
Macromedia Online Forums	The Macromedia Online Forums command provides access to the Macromedia Online Forums Web page. The forums provide a place for developers of all experience levels to share ideas and techniques.
Macromedia Training	This online site provides information and links related to training and certification.
Online Registration	This Web site provides access to product license transfer and online registration.
Print Registration	This Web site displays your registration information and provides a print option.
About Dreamweaver	The About Dreamweaver command opens a window that provides copyright information and the product license number.

Navigating the Dreamweaver 8 Help System

The Dreamweaver Help command accesses Dreamweaver's primary Help system and provides comprehensive information about all Dreamweaver features. Four options are available: Contents, Index, Search, and Favorites.

Using the Contents Sheet

The **Contents** sheet is useful for displaying Help when you know the general category of the topic in question, but not the specifics. Each topic in the Contents list is preceded by a book icon or question mark icon. A **book icon** indicates that subtopics are available. Clicking the book icon (or associated link) displays the list of subtopics below that particular book. A **question mark icon** means information on the topic will display if you click the icon or the associated linked text. The following example shows how to use the Contents sheet to obtain information on how to spell check a Web page.

To Obtain Help Using the Contents Sheet

1

• **Open Dreamweaver, if necessary.**

• **Click Help on the menu bar and then click Dreamweaver Help.**

• **Dreamweaver displays the Dreamweaver 8 Help window.**

• **If necessary, double-click the title bar to maximize the window and click the Contents tab.**

• **To display a better view of the text, you can adjust the width of the left pane by moving the mouse pointer over the border separating the two panes.**

• **When the mouse pointer changes to a double-headed arrow, drag to the right or left to adjust the width of the left pane.**

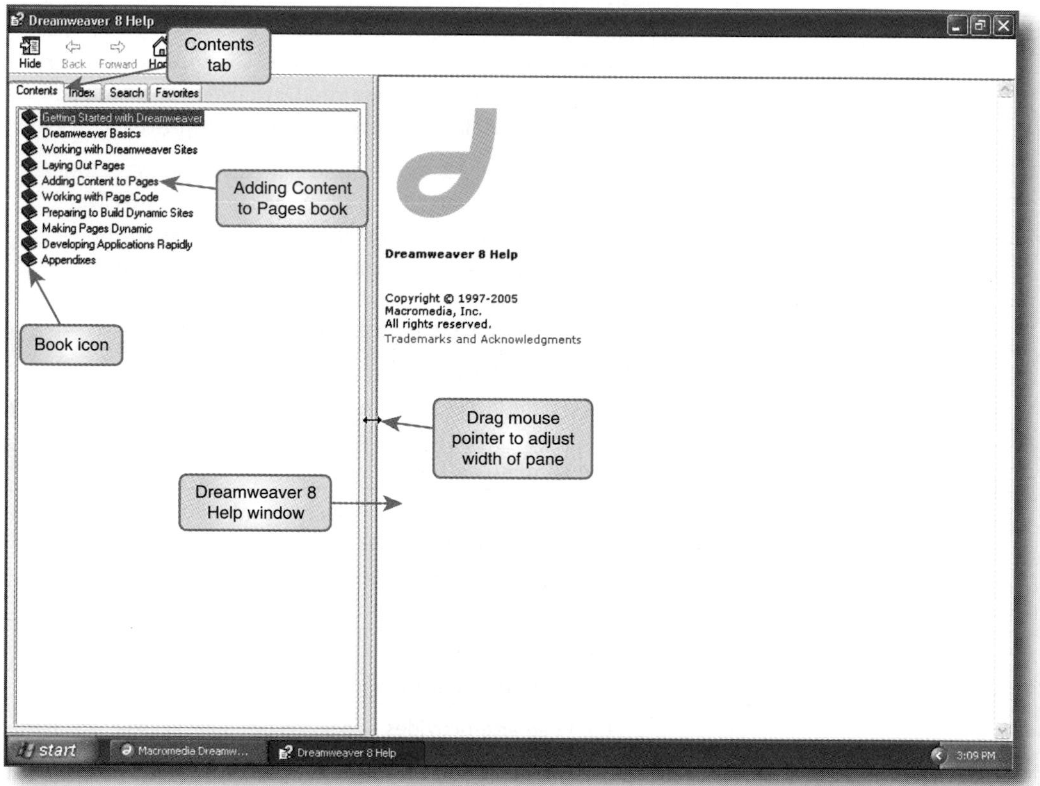

FIGURE A-2

The Dreamweaver 8 Help window is displayed (Figure A-2). Four options are available: Contents, Index, Search, and Favorites.

2

• **Click the Adding Content to Pages link.**

The Adding Content to Pages book is opened, and the help information is displayed in the right pane (Figure A-3). Additional books are displayed below the chosen topic. Links to these books also are displayed in the right pane.

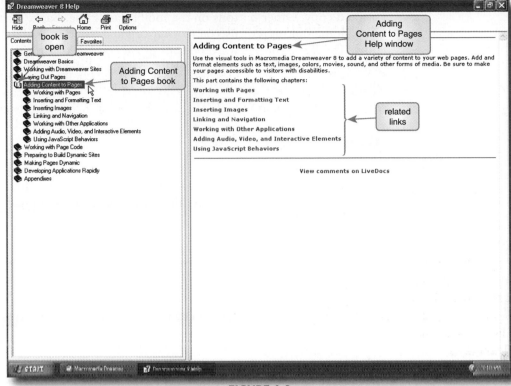

FIGURE A-3

3

• **Click the Inserting and Formatting Text book and then click the Checking spelling link.**

The information on the subtopic displays in the right pane (Figure A-4).

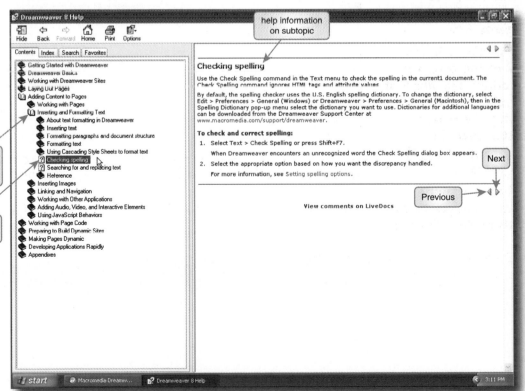

FIGURE A-4

Once the information on the subtopic displays, you can read it, you can click a link contained within the subtopic, or you can click the Print button on the toolbar to obtain a printed copy. Other buttons on the toolbar are Hide, Back, Forward, Home, and Options. The Home button returns you to your original location within the Dreamweaver Help window. The Back and Forward buttons move you back or forward to previously accessed screens. The Hide button hides the left pane, and the Options button displays a pop-up menu with all of the displayed buttons, plus Internet options. To view related topics, click the Previous or Next buttons in the displayed window.

Using the Index Sheet

The second sheet in the Using Dreamweaver window is the Index sheet. Use the Index sheet to display Help when you know the keyword or the first few letters of the keyword. The next steps show how to use the Index sheet to obtain help on cropping images.

To Use the Index Sheet

1

• **Click the Index tab.**

The Index sheet is displayed (Figure A-5). The insertion point is blinking in the Type in the keyword to find text box.

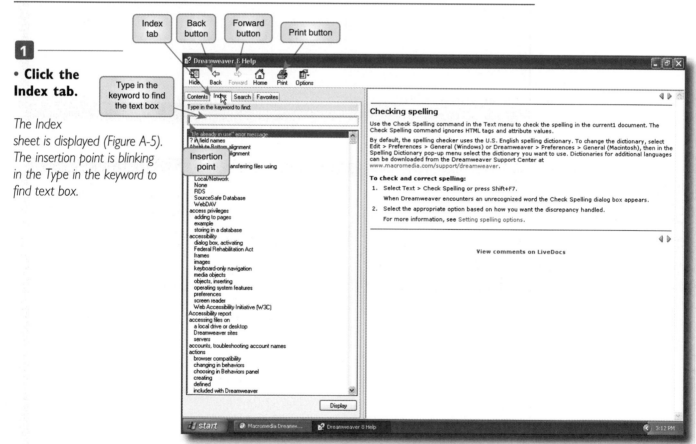

FIGURE A-5

2

• **Type** images **in the text box. Point to the cropping subtopic.**

As you type, Dreamweaver scrolls through the list of topics. The topic, images, and subtopics below the images topic are displayed in the left pane (Figure A-6).

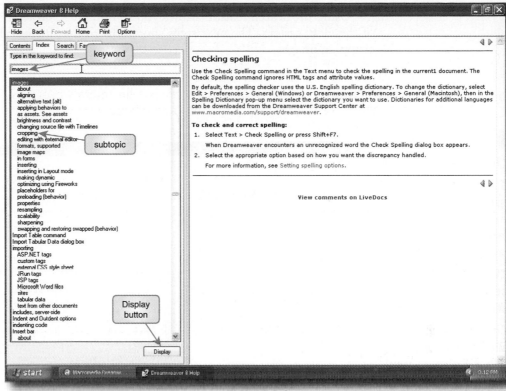

FIGURE A-6

3

• **Click the cropping subtopic and then click the Display button.**

Information about cropping an image displays in the right pane (Figure A-7).

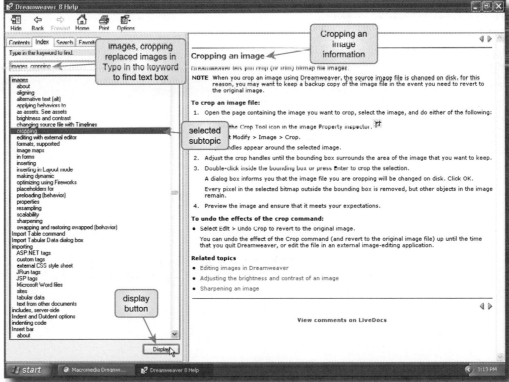

FIGURE A-7

Using the Search Sheet

Using the Search feature allows you to find any character string, anywhere in the text of the Help system. The next steps show how to use the Search sheet to obtain help about cropping images.

To Use the Search Sheet

1

• **Click the Search tab.**

• **Type** cropping **in the Type in the word(s) to search for text box.**

• **Click the List Topics button.**

• **Click Cropping an image in the Select Topic to display box.**

The Search sheet displays a list of eight topics containing references to cropping in the left pane (Figure A-8). All of these topics contain the word cropping somewhere within the document. The location of each Help topic and the rank (related to relevance) are included in Select topic

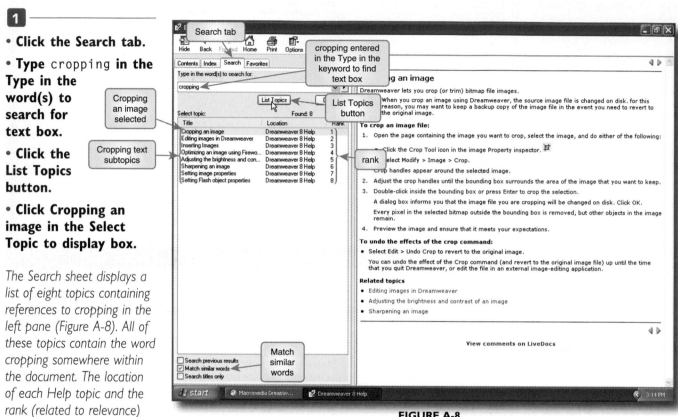

FIGURE A-8

list. The left pane is expanded to show the three columns. The Match similar words checkbox is selected at the bottom of the left pane. Selecting one of the other options (Search previous results or Search titles only) limits the search.

2

• Click the Display button.

The Help screen for Cropping an image displays in the right pane. All incidents of the word crop and cropping are highlighted in the document in the right pane (Figure A-9).

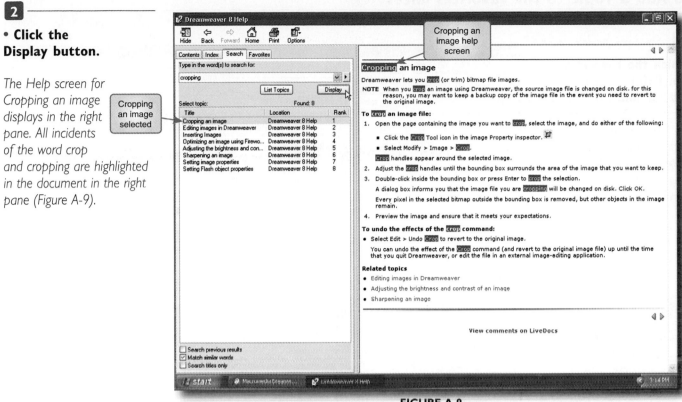

FIGURE A-9

Using the Favorites Sheet

If you find that you search or reference certain topics frequently, you can save these topics in the Favorites sheet. The following steps show how to add the information about the cropping an image topic to the Favorites sheet.

To Add a Topic to the Favorites Sheet

1

• **Click the Favorites tab. Point to the Add button.**

The Favorites sheet displays in the left pane. The information (Cropping an image) is displayed in the Current topic text box in the left pane. (Figure A-10).

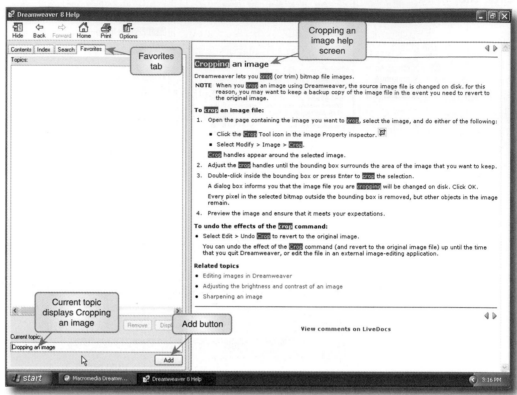

FIGURE A-10

2

• **Click the Add button.**

The Cropping an image topic is added to the Favorites sheet (Figure A-11).

3

• **Close the Dreamweaver 8 Help window and return to Dreamweaver.**

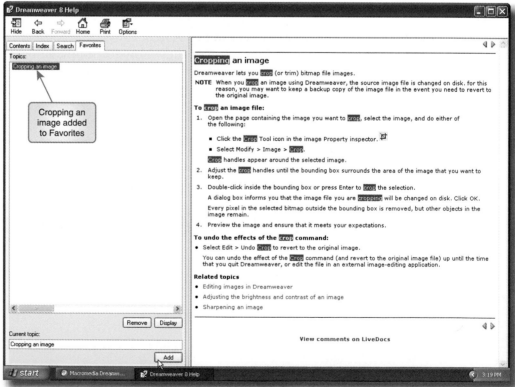

FIGURE A-11

Context-Sensitive Help

Using **context-sensitive help**, you can open a relevant Help topic in panels, inspectors, and most dialog boxes. To view these Help features, you click a Help button in a dialog box, choose Help on the Options pop-up menu in a panel group, or click the question mark icon in an inspector.

Using the Question Mark Icon to Display Help

Many of the panels and inspectors within Dreamweaver contain a question mark icon. Clicking this icon displays context-sensitive help. Assume for the following example that you want to know about tables. The following steps show how to use the question mark icon to view context-sensitive help through the Property inspector. In this example, the default Property inspector for text is displayed.

To Display Context-Sensitive Help on Text

1

• **Point to the question mark icon in the Property inspector (Figure A-12).**

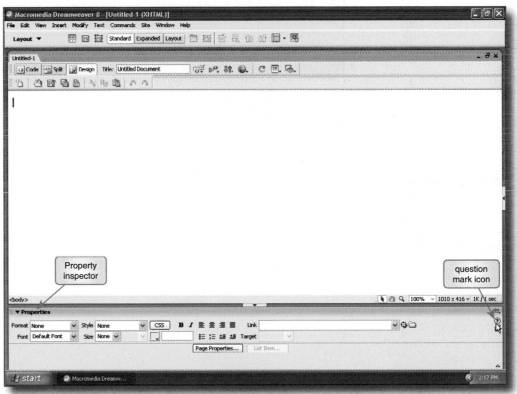

FIGURE A-12

• **Click the question mark icon.**

The Dreamweaver 8 Help window displays, and information pertaining to Setting text properties displays in the right pane (Figure A-13). The Favorites tab is selected in the left pane because this was the last tab previously selected.

3

• **Close the Dreamweaver 8 Help window and return to Dreamweaver.**

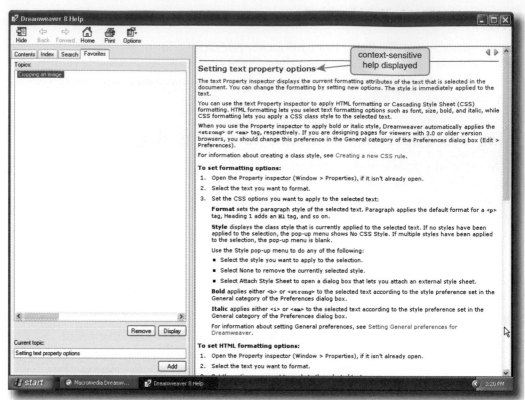

FIGURE A-13

Using the Options Menu to Display Help

Panels and dialog boxes also contain context-sensitive help. The following steps show how to display context-sensitive help for the Files panel. In this example, the Files panel is open and displayed within the Dreamweaver window.

Dreamweaver Appendix A

To Use the Options Menu to Display Context-Sensitive Help for the Files Panel

1

• **Click the Options button on the Files title bar and then point to Help on the Options pop-up menu.**

The Options pop-up menu is displayed (Figure A-14).

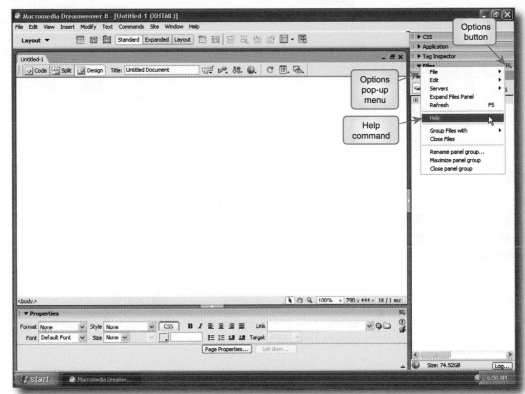

FIGURE A-14

2

• **Click the Help
command.**

*The Dreamweaver 8 Help
window is displayed, and
information pertaining to
using the Files panel is
displayed in the right pane
(Figure A-15). The Favorites
tab is selected in the left
pane because this was the
last tab previously selected.*

3

• **Close the
Dreamweaver 8 Help
window and return to
Dreamweaver.**

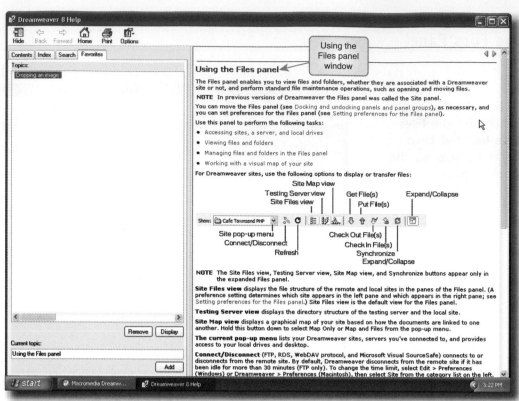

FIGURE A-15

Using the Reference Panel

The Reference panel is another valuable Dreamweaver resource. This panel provides
you with a quick reference tool for HTML tags, JavaScript objects, Cascading Style
Sheets, and other Dreamweaver features. The next example shows how to access the
Reference panel, review the various options, and select and display information on
the <body> tag.

To Use the Reference Panel

1

• **Click Window on the menu bar and then point to Reference (Figure A-16).**

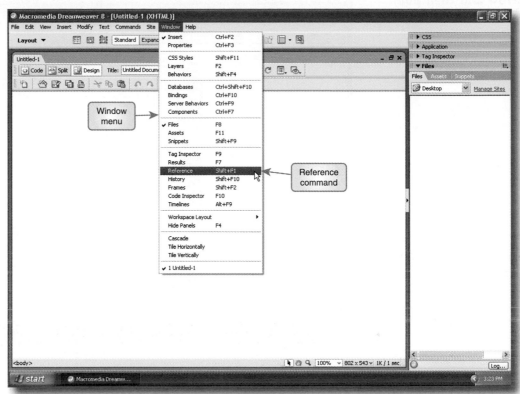

FIGURE A-16

2

• **Click Reference, and then, if necessary, click O'REILLY HTML Reference in the Book pop-up menu.**

The Reference panel in the Code panel group displays tag information (Figure A-17).

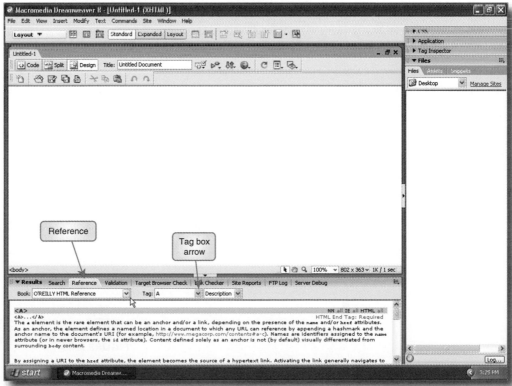

FIGURE A-17

3

• **Click the Tag box arrow and then point to BODY in the tag list.**

BODY is highlighted in the tag list (Figure A-18).

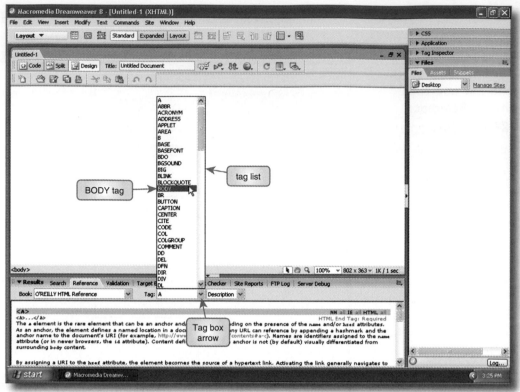

FIGURE A-18

4

• **Click BODY.**

Information on the <body> tag is displayed (Figure A-19).

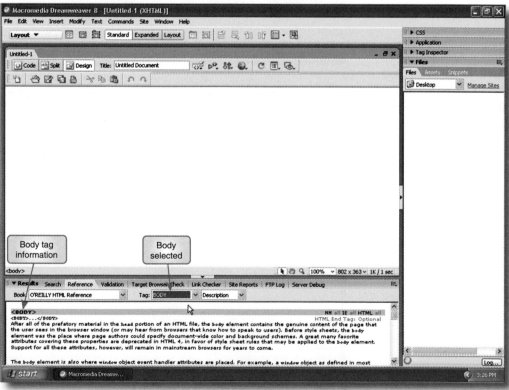

FIGURE A-19

5

• **Click the Book box arrow and review the list of available reference books.**

A list of 13 reference books displays (Figure A-20). These are complete books and can be accessed in the same way the HTML reference book was accessed.

6

• **Close Dreamweaver.**

• **If the Macromedia Dreamweaver dialog box to save changes is displayed, click the No button.**

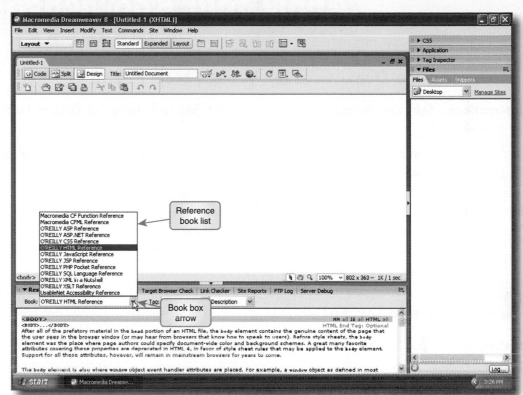

FIGURE A-20

Online Help Support

Dreamweaver also provides several support Web sites, including online forums and links to third-party online forums. Examples of these online forums and discussion groups are as follows:

- Dreamweaver — For Dreamweaver users developing Web sites.
- Dreamweaver Application Development — For Dreamweaver users creating dynamic Web sites.
- Dreamweaver Extensibility — For Dreamweaver users interested in extending the functionality of Dreamweaver.
- Dynamic HTML — This group discusses questions and issues regarding Dynamic HTML.
- General Information — This group discusses general information regarding Macromedia products that does not pertain to the other online forums.

For a selection of Help links, visit the Dreamweaver 8 Web page (scsite.com/dreamweaver8) and then click Appendix Help.

1 Viewing the Dreamweaver What's New Features

Instructions: Start Dreamweaver. Perform the following tasks using the Getting Started with Dreamweaver command.

1. Click Help on the menu bar and then click Getting Started with Dreamweaver to open the Dreamweaver 8 Help window.
2. Click Tutorial: Adding Content to Pages in the right pane and then click Locate your files.
3. Read the information in the right pane and then complete the tutorial.
4. Use a word-processing program to write a short overview of what you learned.
5. Print a copy and submit or e-mail your overview to your instructor.

2 Using the Index Sheet

Instructions: Start Dreamweaver. Perform the following tasks using the Index sheet in the Dreamweaver 8 Help system.

1. Press the F1 key to display the Dreamweaver 8 Help window.
2. Click the Index tab and then type links in the Type in the keyword to find text box.
3. Click checking in the subtopic list and then click the Display button. Read the information in the right pane.
4. Use a word-processing program to write a short overview of what you learned.
5. Print a copy and submit or e-mail your overview to your instructor.

3 Using Context-Sensitive Help

Instructions: Start Dreamweaver. Perform the following tasks using context-sensitive help in the Assets panel.

1. Click the Assets tab in the Files panel group. Verify that the Images icon is selected.
2. Click the Options button and then click Help on the Options pop-up menu.
3. Read the information in the right pane about the Assets panel.
4. Use your word-processing program to prepare a report on how to set up a favorite list of assets.
5. Print a copy and submit or e-mail your overview to your instructor.

Appendix B

 Dreamweaver and Accessibility

Dreamweaver and Accessibility

Tim Berners-Lee, World Wide Web Consortium (W3C) founder and inventor of the World Wide Web, indicates that the power of the Web is in its universality. He says that access by everyone, regardless of disability, is an essential aspect of the Web. In 1997, the W3C launched the **Web Accessibility Initiative** and made a commitment to lead the Web to its full potential. The initiative includes promoting a high degree of usability for people with disabilities. The United States government established a second initiative addressing accessibility and the Web through Section 508 of the Federal Rehabilitation Act.

Dreamweaver includes features that assist you in creating accessible content. Designing accessible content requires that you understand accessibility requirements and make subjective decisions as you create a Web site. Dreamweaver supports three accessibility options: screen readers, keyboard navigation, and operating system accessibility features.

Using Screen Readers with Dreamweaver

Screen readers assist the blind and vision-impaired by reading text that is displayed on the screen through a speaker or headphones. The screen reader starts at the top-left corner of the page and reads the page content. If the Web site developer uses accessibility tags or attributes during the creation of the Web site, the screen reader also recites this information and reads nontextual information such as button labels and image descriptions. Dreamweaver makes it easy to add text equivalents for graphical elements and to add HTML elements to tables and forms through the accessibility dialog boxes. Dreamweaver supports two screen readers: JAWS and Window Eyes.

Activating the Accessibility Dialog Boxes

To create accessible pages in Dreamweaver, you associate information, such as labels and descriptions, with your page objects. After you have created this association, the screen reader can recite the label and description information.

You create the association by activating and attaching the accessibility dialog boxes to objects on your page. These dialog boxes appear when you insert an object for which you have activated the corresponding Accessibility dialog box. You activate the Accessibility dialog boxes through the Preferences dialog box. You can activate Accessibility dialog boxes for form objects, frames, images, and media. Accessibility for tables is accomplished by adding Summary text to the Table dialog box and adding image Ids and Alt text through the Property inspector. The steps on the following pages use the Colorado Parks index page as an example to show how to display the Preferences dialog box and activate the Image Accessibility dialog box.

To Activate the Images Accessibility Dialog Box

1

• **Start Dreamweaver and, if necessary, open the Colorado Parks site.**

• **Double-click index.htm in the Files panel to open the index.htm page.**

• **Click Edit on the menu bar and then point to Preferences (Figure B-1).**

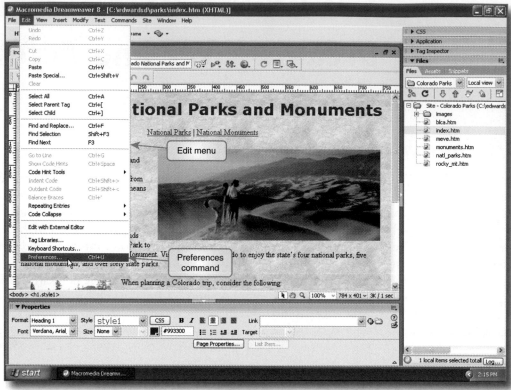

FIGURE B-1

2

• **Click Preferences.**

The Preferences dialog box is displayed (Figure B-2).

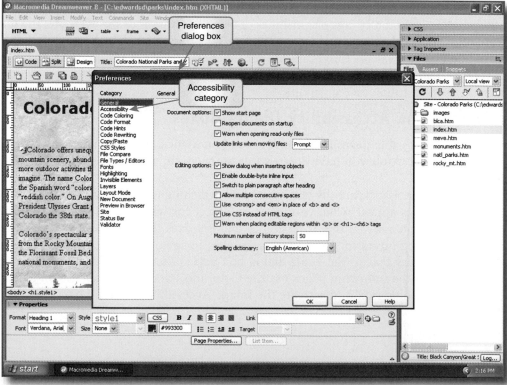

FIGURE B-2

3

• **Click Accessibility in the Category list, click the Images check box in the Accessibility area to select it, and then point to the OK button.**

The Accessibility category is highlighted, and the Images check box is selected (Figure B-3). The Accessibility area includes four different options for which you can activate Accessibility dialog boxes: Form objects, Frames, Media, and Images.

4

• **Click the OK button.**

The Preferences dialog box closes, and the Dreamweaver Document window is displayed. No change is apparent in the Document window, but the Image Tag Accessibility Attributes dialog box has been activated.

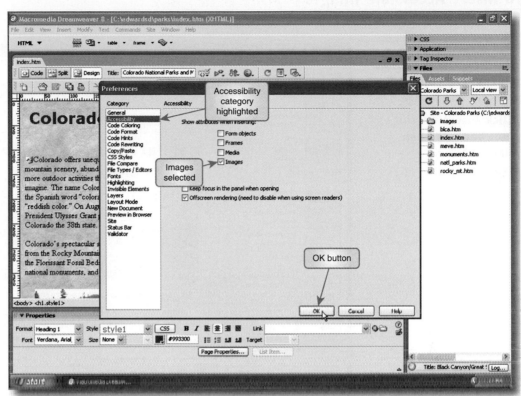

FIGURE B-3

Inserting Accessible Images

Selecting Images in the Accessibility category activates the Image Tag Accessibility Attributes dialog box. Thus, any time you insert an image into a Web page, this dialog box will display. This dialog box contains two text boxes: Alternate Text and Long Description. The screen reader reads the information you enter in both text boxes. You should limit your Alternate Text entry to about 50 characters. For longer descriptions, provide a link in the Long Description text box to a file that gives more information about the image. It is not required that you enter data into both text boxes. The steps on the next page show how to use the Image Tag Accessibility Attributes dialog box when inserting an image.

To Insert Accessible Images

1

• Position the insertion point where you wish to insert the image.

• Click Insert on the menu bar and then point to Image (Figure B-4).

FIGURE B-4

2

• Click Image. If necessary, open the images folder and then click a file name.

• Point to the OK button.

The Select Image Source dialog box is displayed (Figure B-5).

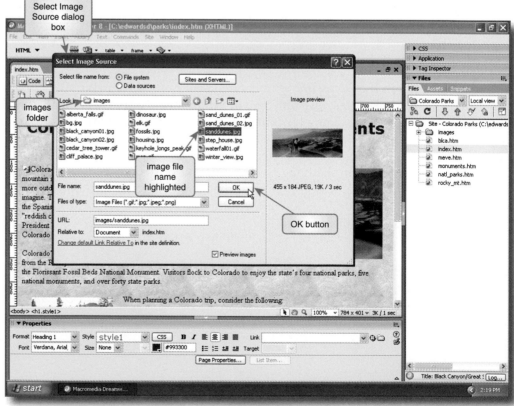

FIGURE B-5

3

• **Click the OK button.**

The Image Tag Accessibility Attributes dialog box is displayed. The insertion point is blinking in the Alternate text text box (Figure B-6). To display the Image Tag Accessibility Attributes dialog box, you must insert the image by using the Insert menu or by clicking the Image button on the Common tab of the Insert bar. Dragging an image from the Assets panel to the Document window does not activate the Image Tag Accessibility Attributes dialog box.

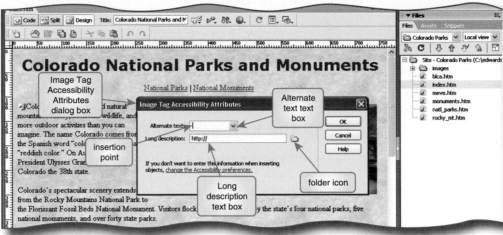

FIGURE B-6

4

• **Type a brief description of the image in the Alternate text text box.**

• **Click the folder icon to display the Select File dialog box. Locate and then click the description file name. Click the OK button in the Select File dialog box.**

• **Point to the OK button.**

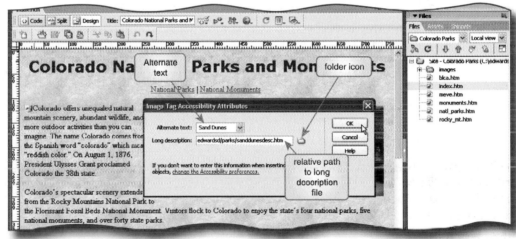

FIGURE B-7

The image description is displayed in the Alternate text text box, and the long description file location is displayed in the Long description text box (Figure B-7).

5

• **Click the OK button in the Image Tag Accessibility Attributes dialog box.**

No changes are displayed in the Document window. When the page is displayed in the browser, however, the screen reader recites the information you entered in the Image Tag Accessibility Attributes Alternate text text box. If you included a link to a file with additional information in the Long description text box, the screen reader accesses the file and recites the text contained within the file.

6

• **Close Dreamweaver. Do not save the changes to the Web page.**

Navigating Dreamweaver with the Keyboard

Keyboard navigation is a core aspect of accessibility. This feature also is of particular importance to users who have repetitive strain injuries (RSIs) or other disabilities, and to those users who would prefer to use the keyboard instead of a mouse. You can use the keyboard to navigate the following elements in Dreamweaver: floating panels, the Property inspector, dialog boxes, frames, and tables.

Using the Keyboard to Navigate Panels

When you are working in Dreamweaver, several panels may be open at one time. To move from panel to panel, press CTRL+ALT+TAB. A dotted outline around the panel title bar indicates that the panel is selected (Figure B-8). Press CTRL+ALT+SHIFT+TAB to move to the previous panel. If necessary, expand the selected panel by pressing the SPACEBAR. Pressing the SPACEBAR again collapses the panel. Use the arrow keys to scroll the panel choices. Press the SPACEBAR to make a selection.

FIGURE B-8

Using the Keyboard to Navigate the Property Inspector

The following steps use the Colorado Parks index page to show how to use the keyboard to navigate the Property inspector.

To Use the Keyboard to Navigate the Property Inspector

1

• **Start Dreamweaver and, if necessary, open the Colorado Parks site. Double-click index.htm in the Files pane to open the index.htm file. Hide the Property inspector. Open a Web page. Press CTRL+F3 to display the Property inspector and then press CTRL+ALT+TAB until the Property inspector is selected.**

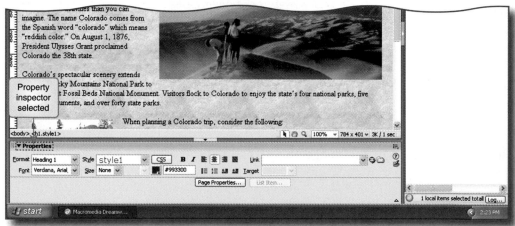

FIGURE B-9

The dotted black outline around the word Properties indicates that the focus is on the Property inspector (Figure B-9).

2

• Press the TAB key
three times to move to
the Format box.

*Heading 1 is selected in the
Format box (Figure B-10).*

FIGURE B-10

3

• Use the keyboard
DOWN ARROW key to
select Heading 3
and then press the
ENTER key.

*A dotted outline is displayed
around the Heading 3
selection (Figure B-11).
Heading 3 is applied to
the text.*

4

• Close Dreamweaver.
Do not save any of the
changes.

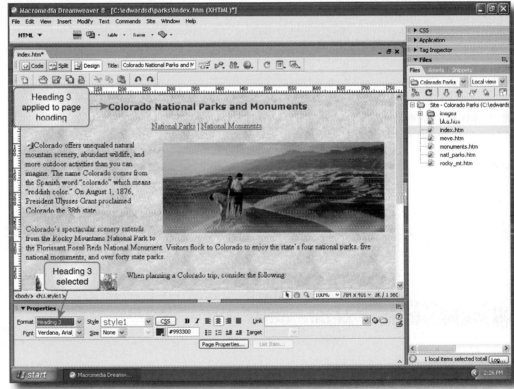

FIGURE B-11

Operating System Accessibility Features

The third method of accessibility support in Dreamweaver is through the Windows operating system's high contrast setting. **High contrast** changes the desktop color themes for individuals who have vision impairment. The color schemes make the screen easier to view by heightening screen contrast with alternative color combinations. Some of the schemes also change font sizes.

You activate this option through the Windows Control Panel. The high contrast setting affects Dreamweaver in two ways:

- The dialog boxes and panels use system color settings.
- Code view syntax color is turned off.

Design view, however, continues to use the background and text colors you set in the Page Properties dialog box. The pages you design, therefore, continue to render colors as they will display in a browser. The steps on the next page show how to turn on high contrast and how to change the current high contrast settings.

To Turn On High Contrast

1

• In Windows XP, click the Start button on the taskbar and then click Control Panel on the Start menu. If necessary, switch to Classic View. If necessary, click View on the menu bar and then click Icons. Double-click the Accessibility Options icon.

The Accessibility Options dialog box is displayed (Figure B-12).

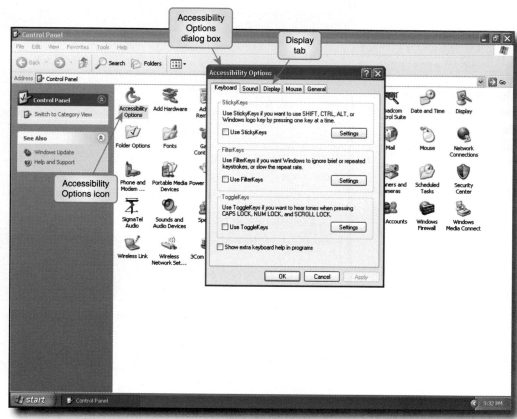

FIGURE B-12

2

• **Click the Display tab and then click the Use High Contrast check box.**

The Display sheet is displayed. A checkmark appears in the Use High Contrast check box (Figure B-13).

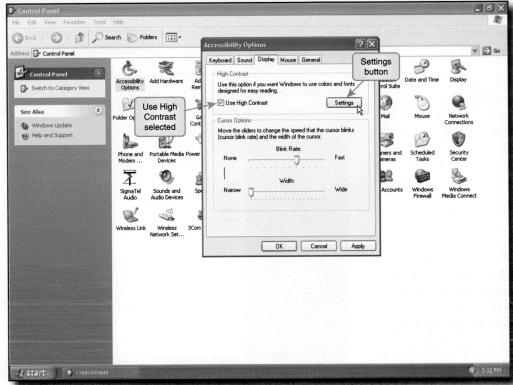

FIGURE B-13

3

• **Click the Settings button.**

The Settings for High Contrast dialog box is displayed (Figure B-14).

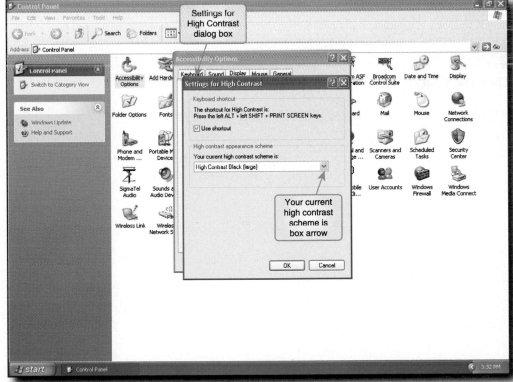

FIGURE B-14

4

• **Click the Your current high contrast scheme is box arrow.**

A list of available high contrast options is displayed (Figure B-15). High Contrast Black (large) is selected. The Web designer, however, would select the appropriate option to meet the needs of the project for which he or she is designing.

5

• **Click the Cancel button to close the Settings for High Contrast dialog box.**

• **Click the Cancel button to close the Accessibility Options dialog box.**

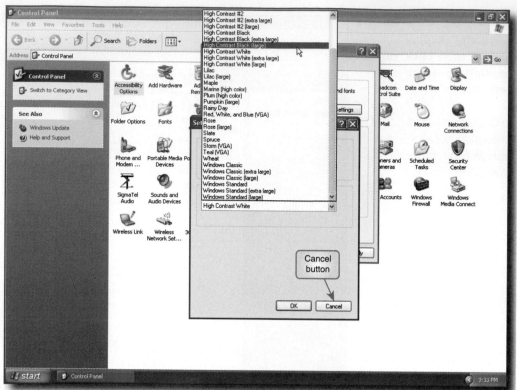

FIGURE B-15

The settings return to their original values. To retain these settings on your computer would require that you click the OK button.

6

• **Click the Control Panel Close button.**

The Control Panel closes, and the Windows XP desktop is displayed.

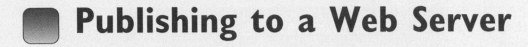

Appendix C

Publishing to a Web Server

Publishing to a Remote Site

With Dreamweaver, Web designers usually define a local site and then do the majority of their designing using the local site. You defined a local site in Project 1. In creating the projects in this book, you have added Web pages to the local site, which resides on your computer's hard disk, a network drive, USB drive, or possibly a Zip disk. To prepare a Web site and make it available for others to view requires that you publish your site by uploading it to a Web server for public access. A Web server is an Internet- or intranet-connected computer that delivers the Web pages to online visitors. Dreamweaver includes built-in support that enables you to connect and transfer your local site to a Web server. Publishing to a Web server requires that you have access to a Web server. Your instructor will provide you with the location, user name, and password information for the Web server on which you will publish your site.

After you establish access to a Web server, you will need a remote site folder. The remote folder will reside on the Web server and will contain your Web site files. Generally, the remote folder is defined by the Web server administrator or your instructor. The name of your local root folder in this example is your last name and first initial. Most likely, the name of your remote folder also will be your last name and first initial. You upload your local site to the remote folder on the Web server. The remote site connection information must be defined in Dreamweaver through the Site Definition Wizard. You display the Site Definition Wizard and then enter the remote site information. Dreamweaver provides five different protocols for connecting to a remote site. These methods are as follows:

- **FTP** (File Transfer Protocol): This protocol is used on the Internet for sending and receiving files. It is the most widely used method for uploading and downloading pages to and from a Web server.
- **Local/Network:** This option is used when the Web server is located on a local area network (LAN) or a company or school intranet. Files on LANs generally are available for internal viewing only.
- **SourceSafe Database, RDS (Remote Development Services), and WebDAV:** These three protocols are systems that permit users to edit and manage files collaboratively on remote Web servers.

You most likely will use the FTP option to upload your Web site to a remote server.

Defining a Remote Site

You define the remote site by changing some of the settings in the Site Definition dialog box. To allow you to create a remote site using FTP, your instructor will supply you with the following information:

- **FTP host:** the Web address for the remote host of your Web server.
- **Host directory:** the directory name and path on the server where your remote site will be located.
- **Login:** your user name.
- **Password:** the FTP password to authenticate and access your account.

Assume for the following example that you are defining a remote site for the Colorado Parks Web site.

To Define a Remote Site

1

• **If necessary, open Dreamweaver.**

• **Click Site on the menu bar and then click Manage Sites.**

• **Click Colorado Parks in the Manage Sites dialog box.**

The Manage Sites dialog box is displayed, and Colorado Parks is selected (Figure C-1).

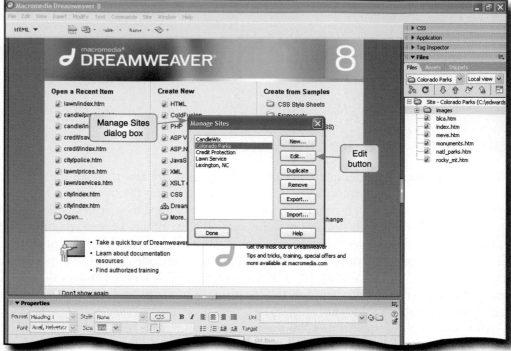

FIGURE C-1

2

• **Click the Edit button and then click the Advanced tab.**

The Site Definition dialog box is displayed, and Local Info is selected in the Category column (Figure C-2).

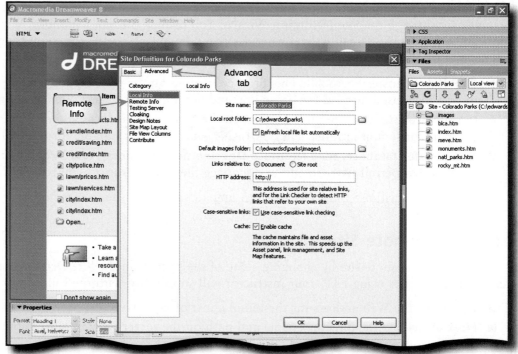

FIGURE C-2

3

• **Click the Remote Info category.**

• **Click the Access box arrow in the Remote Info pane and point to FTP.**

Remote Info is selected in the Category column, and FTP is selected in the pop-up menu. (Figure C-3).

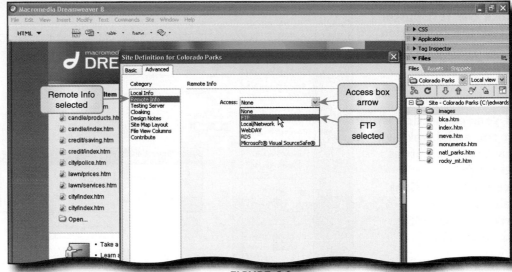

FIGURE C-3

4

• **Click FTP.**

• **Click each of the following boxes in the Site Definition dialog box, and fill in the information as provided by your instructor: FTP host, Host directory, Login, and Password.**

Information for one of the authors, Steven Freund, is displayed in Figure C-4. Your screen will contain the information provided by your instructor.

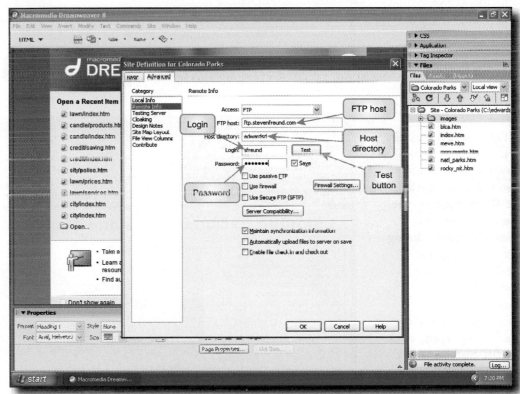

FIGURE C-4

5

• **Click the Test button to test the connection. If the Windows Security Alert dialog box displays, click the Unblock button.**

• **If your connection is not successful, review your text box entries and make any necessary corrections. If all entries are correct, check with your instructor.**

Dreamweaver tests the connection and responds with a Macromedia Dreamweaver dialog box (Figure C-5).

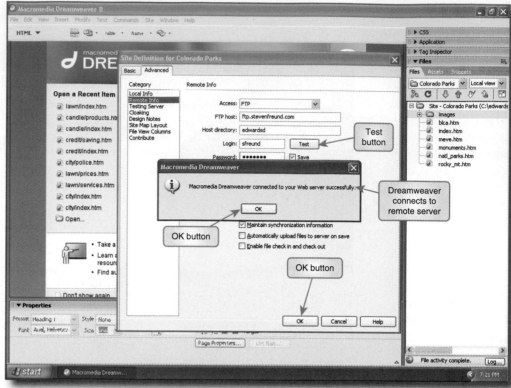

FIGURE C-5

6

• **Click the OK button in the Macromedia Dreamweaver dialog box and then click the OK button in the Site Definition for Colorado Parks dialog box to return to the Dreamweaver workspace. If a Macromedia Dreamweaver dialog box is displayed, click the OK button. Click the Done button to close the Manage Sites dialog box.**

• **If necessary, use the Files panel to open the Colorado Parks site and double-click the index.htm file to display the index.htm Web page.**

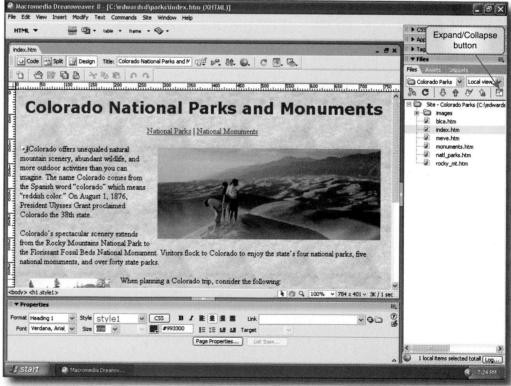

FIGURE C-6

The Colorado National Parks and Monuments page is displayed (Figure C-6).

Connecting to a Remote Site

Now that you have completed the remote site information and tested your connection, you can interact with the remote server. The remote site folder on the Web server for your Web site must be established before a connection can be made. This folder, called the **remote site root**, generally is created by the Web server administrator or your instructor. This book uses the last name and the first initial (edwardsd) for the name of the remote site folder. Naming conventions other than your last name and first initial may be used on the Web server to which you are connecting. Your instructor will supply you with this information. If all information is correct, connecting to the remote site is done easily through the Files panel. The following steps illustrate how to connect to the remote site and display your remote site folder.

To Connect to a Remote Site

1

• **Click the Files panel Expand/Collapse button.**

The Site panel expands to show both a right and left pane (Figure C-7). The right pane contains the local site. The left pane contains information for accessing your remote files by clicking the Connects to remote host button.

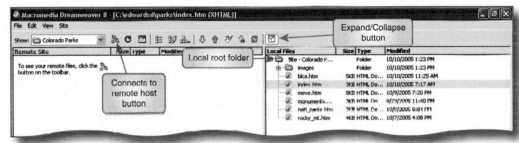

FIGURE C-7

2

• **Verify that the root folder is selected. Click the Connects to remote host button.**

The connection is made, and the parks root folder is displayed (Figure C-8). The Connects to remote host/Disconnects from remote host button is a toggle button; it changes to indicate that the connection has been made. The root folder on the remote site must be created by your instructor or Web server administrator before a connection can be made.

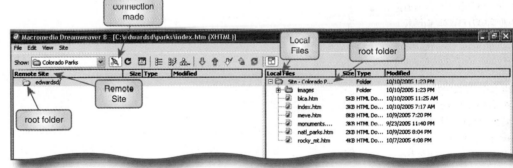

FIGURE C-8

Uploading Files to a Remote Server

Your next step will be to upload your files to the remote server. **Uploading** is the process of transferring your files from your computer to the remote server. **Downloading** is the process of transferring files from the remote server to your computer. Dreamweaver uses the term **put** for uploading and **get** for downloading.

To Upload Files to a Remote Server

1

• **Click the Put File(s) button. Point to the OK button.**

The Macromedia Dreamweaver dialog box is displayed to verify that you want to upload the entire site (Figure C-9).

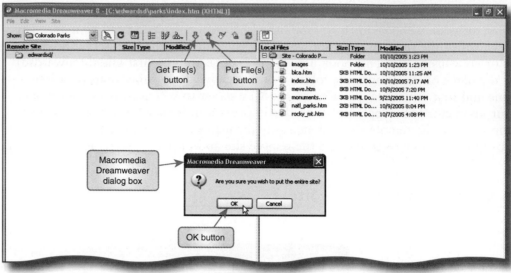

FIGURE C-9

2

• **Click the OK button.**

As the files begin to upload, a Status dialog box displays the progress information. The files are uploaded to the server (Figure C-10). The files may display in a different order from that on the local site. The display order on the server is determined by the settings on that computer.

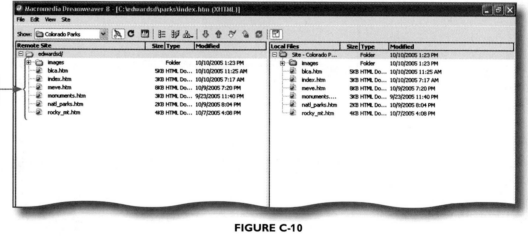

FIGURE C-10

3

• **Close Dreamweaver.**

Remote Site Maintenance and Site Synchronization

Now that your Web site is on a Web server, you will want to continue to maintain the site. When you are connected to the remote site, you can apply many of the same commands to a folder or file on the remote site as you do to a folder or file on the local site. You can create and delete folders; cut, copy, delete, duplicate, paste, and rename files; and so on. These commands are available through the context menu.

To mirror the local site on the remote site, Dreamweaver provides a synchronization feature. Synchronizing is the process of transferring files between the local and remote sites so both sites have an identical set of the most recent files. You can select to synchronize the entire Web site or select only specific files. You also can specify Direction. Within Direction, you have three options: upload the newer files from the local site to the remote site (put); download newer files from the remote site to the local site (get); or upload and download files to and from the remote and local sites. Once you specify a direction, Dreamweaver automatically synchronizes files. If the files are already in sync, Dreamweaver lets you know that no synchronization is necessary. To access the Synchronize command, you first connect to the remote server and then select Synchronize on the Site menu (Figure C-11).

To save the verification information to a local file, click the Save Log button at the completion of the synchronization process. Another feature within Dreamweaver allows you to verify which files are newer on the local site or the remote site. These options are available through the Files panel Edit menu by selecting Select Newer Local or Select Newer Remote.

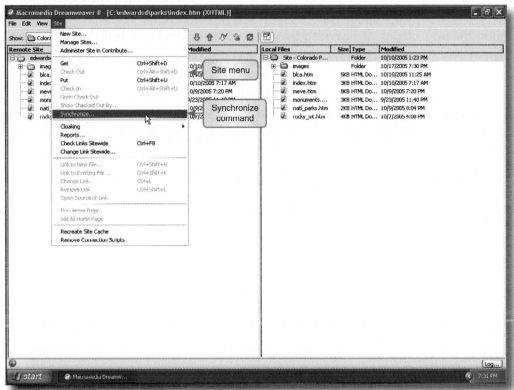

FIGURE C-11

Apply Your Knowledge

1 Defining and Uploading the Andy's Lawn Service Web Site to a Remote Server

Instructions: Perform the following steps to define and upload the Andy's Lawn Service Web site to a remote server.

1. If necessary, open Dreamweaver. Click Site on the menu bar, click Manage Sites, and then click Lawn Service. Click the Edit button. When the Site Definition dialog box is displayed, click the Advanced tab and then click Remote Info. Fill in the information as provided by your instructor, and then test the connection. Click the OK button to close the Site Definition dialog box, and then click the Done button to close the Manage Sites dialog box.

2. Click the Expand/Collapse button on the Files panel toolbar and then click the Connects to remote host button. Click the local file root folder and then click the Put File(s) button on the Site panel toolbar to upload your Web site. Click the OK button in response to the Are you sure you wish to put the entire site? dialog box. Review your files to verify that they were uploaded. The files on the remote server may be displayed in a different order from those on the local site.

3. Click the Disconnects from remote host button on the Files panel toolbar. Click the Expand/Collapse button on the Files panel toolbar to display the local site and the Document window.

4. Close Dreamweaver.

2 Defining and Uploading the CandleWix Web Site to a Remote Server

Instructions: Perform the following steps to define and upload the CandleWix Web site to a remote server.

1. If necessary, open Dreamweaver. Click Site on the menu bar, click Manage Sites, and then click CandleWix. Click the Edit button to display the Site Definition dialog box. Click the Advanced tab and then click Remote Info. Fill in the information as provided by your instructor, and then test the connection. Click the OK button to close the Site Definition dialog box, and then click the Done button to close the Manage Sites dialog box.

2. Click the Expand/Collapse button on the Files panel toolbar and then click the Connects to remote host button. Click the local file root folder and then click the Put File(s) button on the Files panel toolbar to upload your Web site. Click the OK button in response to the Are you sure you wish to put the entire site? dialog box. Review your files to verify that they were uploaded. The files on the remote server may display in a different order from those on the local site.

3. Click the Disconnects from remote host button. Click the Expand/Collapse button on the Files panel toolbar to display the local site and the Document window. Close Dreamweaver.

Apply Your Knowledge

3 Defining and Uploading the Credit Protection Web Site to a Remote Server

Instructions: Perform the following steps to define and upload the Credit Protection Web site to a remote server.

1. If necessary, open Dreamweaver. Click Site on the menu bar, click Manage Sites, and then click Credit Protection. Click the Edit button. Click the Advanced tab and then click Remote Info. Fill in the information as provided by your instructor, and then test the connection. Click the OK button to close the Site Definition dialog box, and then click the Done button to close the Manage Sites dialog box.
2. Click the Expand/Collapse button on the Files panel toolbar and then click the Connects to remote host button. Click the local file root folder and then click the Put File(s) button on the Files panel toolbar to upload your Web site. Click the OK button in response to the Are you sure you wish to put the entire site? dialog box. Upload your files to the remote site. Review your files to verify that they were uploaded. The files on the remote server may display in a different order from those on the local site.
3. Disconnect from the site. Click the Expand/Collapse button on the Files panel toolbar to display the local site and the Document window. Close Dreamweaver.

4 Defining and Uploading the Lexington, NC Web Site to a Remote Server

Instructions: Perform the following steps to define and upload the Lexington, NC Web site to a remote server.

1. If necessary, open Dreamweaver. Click Site on the menu bar, click Manage Sites, and then click Lexington, NC. Click the Edit button. Click the Advanced tab and then click Remote Info. Fill in the information as provided by your instructor, and then test the connection. Click the OK button to close the Site Definition dialog box, and then click the Done button to close the Manage Sites dialog box.
2. Connect to the remote site and then click the local file root folder. Upload your files to the remote site. Disconnect from the site. Click the Expand/Collapse button on the Files panel toolbar to display the local site and the Document window. Close Dreamweaver.

FILE MENU

Action	Shortcut
New document	Control+N
Open an HTML file	Control+O, or drag the file from the Explorer or Files panel to the Document window
Open in frame	Control+Shift+O
Close	Control+W
Close all	Control+Shift+W
Save	Control+S
Save as	Control+Shift+S
Exit/Quit	Control+Q or Alt+F4

EDIT MENU

Action	Shortcut
Undo	Control+Z or Alt+Backspace
Redo	Control+Y or Control+Shift+Z
Cut	Control+X or Shift+Delete
Copy	Control+C or Control+Insert
Paste	Control+V or Shift+Insert
Paste Special	Control+Shift+V
Clear	Delete
Select all	Control+A
Select parent tag	Control+[
Select child	Control+]
Find and replace	Control+F
Find next	F3
Show Code Hints	Control+Spacebar
Go to line	Control+G
Indent code	Control+Shift+>
Outdent code	Control+Shift+<
Balance braces	Control+'
Preferences	Control+U

PAGE VIEWS

To toggle the display of	Shortcut
Layout mode	Control+F6
Expanded Tables mode	F6
Live Data mode	Control+R
Live Data	Control+Shift+R
Switch between Design and Code views	Control+`
Head content	Control+Shift+H

To toggle the display of	Shortcut
Server debug	Control+Shift+G
Refresh Design view	F5
Switch to next document	Control+Tab
Switch to previous document	Control+Shift+Tab
Close window	Control+F4

VIEWING PAGE ELEMENTS

To toggle the display of	Shortcut
Visual aids	Control+Shift+I
Rulers	Control+Alt+R
Guides	Control+;
Lock guides	Control+Alt+;
Snap to guides	Control+Shift+;
Guides snap to elements	Control+Shift+/
Grid	Control+Alt+G
Snap to grid	Control+Alt+Shift+G
Page properties	Control+J

EDITING TEXT

Action	Shortcut
Create a new paragraph	Enter
Insert a line break ‹BR›	Shift+Enter
Insert a nonbreaking space	Control+Shift+ Spacebar
Move text or object to another place in the page	Drag selected item to new location
Copy text or object to another place in the page	Control-drag selected item to new location
Select a word	Double-click
Go to next word	Control+Right
Go to previous word	Control+Left
Go to previous paragraph	Control+Up
Go to next paragraph	Control+Down
Select until next word	Control+Shift+Right
Select from previous word	Control+Shift+Left
Select until next paragraph	Control+Shift+Down
Select from previous paragraph	Control+Shift+Up
Open and close the Property inspector	Control+F3
Check spelling	Shift+F7

FORMATTING TEXT

Action	Shortcut
Indent	Control+Alt+]
Outdent	Control+Alt+[
Format > None	Control+0 (zero)
Paragraph Format	Control+Shift+P
Apply Headings 1 through 6 to a paragraph	Control+1 through 6
Align > Left	Control+Alt+Shift+L
Align > Center	Control+Alt+Shift+C
Align > Right	Control+Alt+Shift+R
Align > Justify	Control+Alt+Shift+J
Make selected text bold	Control+B
Make selected text italic	Control+I

Note: Some text formatting shortcuts have no effect when working in the code editors.

FINDING AND REPLACING TEXT

Action	Shortcut
Find	Control+F
Find next/Find again	F3
Find selection	Shift+F3

CODE EDITING

Action	Shortcut
Switch to Design view	Control+`
Print code	Control+P
Validate markup	Shift+F6
Edit tag	Shift+F5
Open Quick Tag Editor	Control+T
Open Snippets panel	Shift+F9
Show code hints	Control+Spacebar
Insert tag	Control+E
Surround with #	Control+Shift+3
Select parent tag	Control+[
Balance braces	Control+'
Select all	Control+A
Bold	Control+B
Italic	Control+I
Copy	Control+C
Find and replace	Control+F
Find selection	Shift+F3
Find next	F3
Paste	Control+V
Paste Special	n/a
Cut	Control+X

Action	Shortcut
Redo	Control+Y
Undo	Control+Z
Delete word left	Control+Backspace
Delete word right	Control+Delete
Go to line	Control+G
Select line up	Shift+Up
Select line down	Shift+Down
Character select left	Shift+Left
Character select right	Shift+Right
Move to page up	Page Up
Move to page down	Page Down
Select to page up	Shift+Page Up
Select to page down	Shift+Page Down
Move word left	Control+Left
Move word right	Control+Right
Select word left	Control+Shift+Left
Select word right	Control+Shift+Right
Move to start of line	Home
Move to end of line	End
Select to start of line	Shift+Home
Select to end of line	Shift+End
Move to top of code	Control+Home
Move to end of code	Control+End
Select to top of code	Control+Shift+Home
Select to end of code	Control+Shift+End
Collapse selection	Control+Shift+C
Collapse outside selection	Control+Alt+C
Expand selection	Control+Shift+E
Collapse full tag	Control+Shift+J
Collapse outside full tag	Control+Alt+J
Expand All	Control+Alt+E

WORKING IN TABLES

Action	Shortcut
Select table (with insertion point inside the table)	Control+A (+A, +A)
Move to the next cell	Tab
Move to the previous cell	Shift+Tab
Insert a row (before current)	Control+M
Add a row at end of table	Tab in the last cell
Delete the current row	Control+Shift+M
Insert a column	Control+Shift+A

Action	Shortcut
Delete a column	Control+Shift+ - (hyphen)
Merge selected table cells	Control+Alt+M
Split table cell	Control+Alt+S
Increase column span	Control+Shift+]
Decrease column span	Control+Shift+[

Note: Some table shortcuts do not work in Layout view.

WORKING IN FRAMES

Action	Shortcut
Select a frame	Alt-click in frame
Select next frame or frameset	Alt+Right Arrow
Select previous frame or frameset	Alt+Left Arrow
Select parent frameset	Alt+Up Arrow
Select first child frame or frameset	Alt+Down Arrow
Add a new frame to frameset	Alt-drag frame border
Add a new frame to frameset using push method	Alt+Control-drag frame border

WORKING WITH TEMPLATES

Action	Shortcut
Create new editable region	Control+Alt+V

WORKING WITH LAYERS

Action	Shortcut
Select a layer	Control+Shift-click
Select and move layer	Shift+Control-drag
Add or remove layer from selection	Shift-click layer border
Move selected layer by pixels	Arrow keys
Move selected layer by snapping increment	Shift+arrow keys
Resize selected layer by pixels	Control+arrow keys
Resize selected layer by snapping increment	Control+Shift+arrow keys
Align layers left	Control+Shift+1
Align layers right	Control+Shift+3
Align layers top	Control+Shift+4
Align layers bottom	Control+Shift+6
Make same width	Control+Shift+7
Make same height	Control+Shift+9

WORKING WITH THE TIMELINE

Action	Shortcut
Display Timeline	Alt+F9
Add object to Timeline	Control+Alt+Shift+T

WORKING WITH IMAGES

Action	Shortcut
Change image source attribute	Double-click image
Edit image in external editor	Control-double-click image

ZOOMING

Action	Shortcut
Zoom in	Control+=
Zoom out	Control+-
Magnify 50%	Control+Alt+5
Magnify 100%	Control+Alt+1
Magnify 200%	Control+Alt+2
Magnify 300%	Control+Alt+3
Magnify 400%	Control+Alt+4
Magnify 800%	Control+Alt+8
Magnify 1600%	Control+Alt+6
Fit selection	Control+Alt+0
Fit all	Control+Shift+0
Fit width	Control+Shift+Alt+0
Switch to Zoom mode from Regular mode	Shift+Control+Alt+Z
Switch to Regular mode from Zoom mode	V+0
Switch to Hand mode from Regular mode	Shift+Control+Alt+H
Switch to Hand mode from Zoom mode	H+Spacebar

MANAGING HYPERLINKS

Action	Shortcut
Check links	Shift+F8
Create hyperlink (select text)	Control+L
Remove hyperlink	Control+Shift+L
Drag and drop to create a hyperlink from a document	Select the text, image, or object, then Shift-drag the selection to a file in the Files panel
Drag and drop to create a hyperlink using the Property inspector	Select the text, image, or object, then drag the point-to-file icon in Property inspector to a file in the Files panel
Open the linked-to document in Dreamweaver	Control-double-click link
Check links in the entire site	Control+F8

GETTING HELP

Action	Shortcut
Using Dreamweaver Help topics	F1
Using ColdFusion Help topics	Control+F1
Reference	Shift+F1

TARGETING AND PREVIEWING IN BROWSERS

Action	Shortcut
Preview in primary browser	F12
Preview in secondary browser	Shift+F12 or Control+F12

DEBUGGING IN BROWSERS

Action	Shortcut
Debug in primary browser	Alt+F12
Debug in secondary browser	Control+Alt+F12

SITE MANAGEMENT AND FTP

Action	Shortcut
Refresh	F5
Create new file	Control+Shift+N
Create new folder	Control+Alt+Shift+N
Delete file	Delete
Copy file	Control+C
Cut file	Control+X
Paste file	Control+V
Duplicate file	Control+D
Rename file	F2
Get selected files or folders from remote FTP site	Control+Shift+D or drag files from Remote to Local pane in Files panel
Put selected files or folders to remote FTP site	Control+Shift+U or drag files from Local to Remote pane in Files panel
Check out	Control+Alt+Shift+D
Check in	Control+Alt+Shift+U
View site map	Alt+F8
Cancel FTP	Escape

SITE MAP

Action	Shortcut
View site files	F8
View as root	Control+Shift+R
Link to existing file	Control+Shift+K
Change link	Control+L
Remove link	Control+Shift+L
Show/Hide link	Control+Shift+Y
Show page titles	Control+Shift+T

RECORDING COMMANDS

Action	Shortcut
Start recording	Control+Shift+X

PLAYING PLUGINS

Action	Shortcut
Play plugin	Control+Alt+P
Stop plugin	Control+Alt+X
Play all plugins	Control+Alt+Shift+P
Stop all plugins	Control+Alt+Shift+X

INSERTING OBJECTS

Action	Shortcut
Any object (image, Shockwave movie, and so on)	Drag file from the Explorer or Files panel to the Document window
Image	Control+Alt+I
Table	Control+Alt+T
Flash	Control+Alt+F
Shockwave	Control+Alt+D
Named anchor	Control+Alt+A

OPENING AND CLOSING PANELS

Action	Shortcut
Insert bar	Control+F2
Properties	Control+F3
CSS Styles	Shift+F11
Behaviors	Shift+F4
Tag Inspector	F9
Snippets	Shift+F9
Reference	Shift+F1
Databases	Control+Shift+F10
Bindings	Control+F10
Server Behaviors	Control+F9
Components	Control+F7
Files	F8
Assets	F11
Results	F7
Code inspector	F10
Frames	Shift+F2
History	Shift+F10
Layers	F2
Timeline	Alt+F9
Show/Hide panels	F4

Index